Environmental Ethics

Environmental Ethics

Second Edition

Edited by Michael Boylan

WILEY Blackwell

This edition first published 2014

Edition history: Prentice Hall (1e, 2001)

Wiley-Blackwell is an imprint of John Wiley & Sons, formed by the merger of Wiley's global Scientific, Technical and Medical business with Blackwell Publishing.

Registered Office
John Wiley & Sons Ltd, The Atrium, Southern Gate, Chichester, West Sussex, PO19 8SQ, UK

Editorial Offices
350 Main Street, Malden, MA 02148-5020, USA
9600 Garsington Road, Oxford, OX4 2DQ, UK
The Atrium, Southern Gate, Chichester, West Sussex, PO19 8SQ, UK

For details of our global editorial offices, for customer services, and for information about how to apply for permission to reuse the copyright material in this book please see our website at www.wiley.com/wiley-blackwell.

Library of Congress Cataloging-in-Publication Data

Environmental ethics / edited by Michael Boylan. – Second edition.
pages cm
Includes bibliographical references.
ISBN 978-1-118-49472-1 (pbk. : alk. paper) 1. Environmental ethics. I. Boylan, Michael, 1952–
GE42.B69E67 2015
179′.1–dc23

2013006627

A catalogue record for this book is available from the British Library.

Cover image: Five Arch Bridge, Virginia Water, Surrey © Martin Stavars, martinstavars.com
Cover design by www.simonlevy.co.uk

Set in 10.5/12.5pt Dante by SPi Publisher Services, Pondicherry, India
Printed in Singapore by Ho Printing Singapore Pte Ltd

1 2014

For Seán

Contents

Notes on Contributors

Wilfred Beckerman was Senior Economist in the Environment Department of the World Bank, where he helped to develop policy guidelines related to sustainable development and is now a professor at the School of Public Policy, University of Maryland, College Park.

Murray Bookchin (deceased) was co-founder and Director Emeritus of the Institute for Social Ecology.

Michael Boylan is Professor and Chair of Philosophy at Marymount University, Bethesda.

Randall Curren is Professor and Chair of Philosophy at the University of Rochester.

Herman E. Daly is an ecological economist and Professor at the School of Public Policy, University of Maryland, College Park.

Stephen M. Gardiner is Professor in the Department of Philosophy and holds the Ben Rabinowitz Endowed Professor in Human Dimensions of the Environment in the College of the Environment, both at the University of Washington, Seattle.

Alan Gewirth (deceased) was Edward Carson Waller Distinguished Service Professor of Philosophy at the University of Chicago.

Benjamin Hale is Assistant Professor of Philosophy and the Environmental Studies program, Center for Values and Social Policy, Center for Science and Technology Research, University of Colorado, Boulder.

Ruth Irwin is Senior Lecturer in Ethics, Centre for Business Interdisciplinary Studies, Auckland University of Technology, New Zealand.

Dale Jamieson is Director of Environmental Studies at New York University, where he is also Professor of Environmental Studies and Philosophy, and Affiliated Professor of Law.

Aldo Leopold (deceased) was Professor of Wildlife Management at the University of Wisconsin.

Carolyn Merchant is Professor in the Department of Environmental Science, Policy, and Management, University of California, Berkeley.

Seumas Miller is Professor of Philosophy at Charles Sturt University, Australia, and from 2000 to 2007 was the head of the Centre for Applied Philosophy and Public Ethics at the Australian National University.

Arne Naess (deceased) was for many years Head of the Philosophy Department, University of Oslo.

Bryan G. Norton is Professor of Philosophy at Georgia Tech University, Atlanta.

Onora O'Neill Baroness of Bengarve, crossbench member of the House of Lords and Professor of Philosophy at Cambridge University.

Tom Regan is Professor Emeritus of Philosophy at North Carolina State University, Raleigh.

Holmes Rolston III is Distinguished Professor of Philosophy at Colorado State University, Fort Collins.

Mark A. Seabright is Professor of Management, Division of Business and Economics, Western Oregon University, Monmouth.

Peter Singer is Ira W. DeCamp Professor of Bioethics, University Center of Human Values, Princeton University, and Laureate Professor at the University of Melbourne, Australia.

James P. Sterba is Professor of Philosophy at the University of Notre Dame.

Brian K. Steverson is the John L. Aram Professor of Business Ethics at Gonzaga University, Spokane, WA.

Paul W. Taylor is Professor Emeritus of Philosophy, Brooklyn College, City University of New York.

Wanda Teays is Professor and Chair of the Philosophy Department, Mount St. Mary's College, Los Angeles.

Janna Thompson is Professor of Philosophy at La Trobe University, Melbourne, Australia.

Karen J. Warren was formerly Professor of Philosophy, Macalester College, St. Paul, MN.

Mary Anne Warren (deceased) taught philosophy at San Francisco State University.

Preface to the Second Edition

Environmental Ethics is one of my three texts on applied ethics that is now being published by Wiley-Blackwell. The idea behind each of the books, in general, is to present some of the most pressing questions in applied ethics through a mixture of classic essays and some new essays commissioned precisely for these volumes. The result is a dialogue that I think readers will find enriching.

In addition to the essays, there is an ongoing pedagogical device on how to write an essay in applied ethics: using case response as the model. To this end, the major chapters of the book are followed by two sorts of cases: macro cases and micro cases. In macro cases, the student takes the roll of a supervisor and must solve a problem from that perspective. In the micro cases, the student becomes a line worker and confronts dilemmas from that vantage point. Some felicity at both perspectives can enable the student to better understand the complication of using ethical theories (set out in Chapter 1) to real-life problems.

Others using the book may choose instead to evaluate selected essays through a "pro" or "con" evaluation. This approach emphasizes close reading of an article and the application of ethical theory (set out in Chapter 1) to show why you believe the author is correct or incorrect in her or his assessment of the problem. In order to make this approach appealing to readers, some effort has been made to offer different approaches to contemporary questions in healthcare ethics.

What is new in this second edition:

- more than a third of the selections have been replaced (most with essays solicited especially for this volume);
- the book is introduced with a new discussion on "Ethical Decision-making" by the editor;
- an original chapter on "The Self in Context" provides a theoretical context for the succeeding essays;
- Chapter 3 has been re-arranged with new essays on aesthetics and eco-feminism;
- an entirely new Chapter 5 on "Pollution and Climate Change";
- a new section on "Sustainability".

It is my hope that this second edition will meet the needs of classroom instruction in a unique way, while recognizing that the practice of responsible environmental policy occurs within a diverse context that must be recognized in order to be effective. The world moves on, and the many practitioners whose purview overlaps with environmental ethics and public policy have to know when and how to adapt the principles of its theoretical core in order to meet these practical demands.

As is always the case in projects like this there are many to thank. I would first like to thank all the scholars who have written original essays expressly for this edition. Their fine work has added a unique character to the book. To the anonymous reviewers of this book, a thank you for your thoughtful comments. I would also like to thank Jeff Dean, my editor, for his support of the project, Lyn Flight, my copy-editor, and the whole Wiley-Blackwell team. I would also like to thank my research team at Marymount: Tanya Lanuzo and Lynn McLaughlin. Their expertise helped with my original essays that are in this volume. Finally, I would like to thank my family: Rebecca, Arianne, Seán, and Éamon. They continually help me to grow as a person.

Source Credits

The editor and publisher gratefully acknowledge the permission granted to reproduce the copyright material in this book:

Chapter 3

Aldo Leopold, "The Land Ethic," *A Sand County Almanac: and Sketches Here and There*, Oxford: Oxford University Press, 1949; pp. 41–48. Reprinted with the permission of Oxford University Press.

Arne Naess, "The Shallow and the Deep, Long-Range Ecology Movement," *Inquiry*, 16 (1983): 95–100. Reprinted with permission of Taylor & Francis Journals.

Carolyn Merchant, "Ecofeminism and Feminist Theory," in *Reweaving the World: The Emergence of Ecofeminism* (ed. Irene Diamond and Gloria Orenstein), Sierra Club Books, 1990; pp. 77–83. Reprinted with permission of the author.

Karen J. Warren, "The Power and Promise of Ecological Feminism," *Environmental Ethics*, 12 (1990): 125–126, 138–145. With kind permission from the author.

Janna Thompson, "Aesthetics and the Value of Nature," *Environmental Ethics*, 17 (3) (1995): 291–306. Reprinted with permission.

Chapter 4

Onora O'Neill, "Environmental Values, Anthropocentrism and Speciesism," *Environmental Values*, 6 (1997): 127–142. Reprinted with permission.

Holmes Rolston III, "Environmental Ethics: Values in and Duties to the Natural World," from F. Herbert Bormann and Stephen R. Kellert (eds.), *The Broken Circle: Ecology, Economics, and Ethics*, Yale University Press, 1991; pp. 228–247. Reprinted with permission of Yale University Press.

Paul Taylor, "Respect for Nature: A Theory of Environmental Ethics," from *Respect for Nature*, Princeton University Press, 1986; pp. 248–259. © 1986 Princeton University Press. Reprinted with permission.

James P. Sterba, "Reconciling Anthropocentric and Nonanthropocentric Environmental Ethics," *Environmental Values*, 3 (1994): 229–244. Reprinted with permission.

Brian K. Steverson, "On the Reconciliation of Anthropocentric and Nonanthropocentric Environmental Ethics," *Environmental Values*, 5 (1996): 349–361. Reprinted with permission.

James P. Sterba, "Reconciliation Reaffirmed: A Reply to Steverson," *Environmental Values*, 5 (1996): 363–368. Reprinted with permission.

Chapter 6

Peter Singer, "Animal Liberation," *New York Review of Books*, April 5, 1973 © Peter Singer, 1973. Reprinted with kind permission of the author.

Tom Regan, "The Radical Egalitarian Case for Animal Rights," from *In Defence of Animals* (ed. Peter Singer), Blackwell, 1985; pp 320–330. Reprinted with permission of John Wiley & Sons Ltd.

Mary Anne Warren, "A Critique of Regan's Animal Rights Theory," from *Between Species*, 2 (4) (1987): 331–333, see at: http://digitalcommons.calpoly.edu/bts. Reprinted with permission.

Dale Jamieson, "Against Zoos," in *In Defense of Animals: The Second Wave* (ed. Peter Singer), Blackwell, 2005; pp. 132–143. Reprinted with permission of John Wiley & Sons Ltd.

Chapter 7

Stephen Gardiner, "A Perfect Moral Storm: Climate Change, Intergenerational Ethics, and the Problem of Moral Corruption," *Environmental Values*, 15 (3) (August 2006): 397–413. Reprinted with permission.

Wilfred Beckerman, "'Sustainable Development': Is It a Useful Concept?" *Environmental Values*, 3 (1994): 191–209. Reprinted with permission.

Herman E. Daly, "On Wilfred Beckerman's Critique of Sustainable Development," *Environmental Values*, 4 (1995): 49–55. Reprinted with permission.

Part I

Theoretical Background

1

Ethical Reasoning

MICHAEL BOYLAN

What is the point of studying ethics? This is the critical question that will drive this chapter. Many people do not think about ethics as they make decisions in their day-to-day lives. They see problems and make decisions based upon practical criteria. Many see ethics as rather an affectation of personal taste. It is useful only when it can get you somewhere. Is this correct? Do we act ethically only when there is a *win–win* situation in which we can get what we want, and also appear to be an honorable, feeling, and caring person?

A Prudential Model of Decision-Making

In order to begin answering this question we must start by examining the way most of us make decisions. Everyone initiates the decision-making process with an established worldview. A worldview is a current personal consciousness that consists in one's understanding of the facts and about the values in the world. It is the most primitive term to describe our factual and normative conceptions. This worldview may be one that we have chosen or it may be one that we passively accepted as we grew up in a particular culture. Sometimes, this worldview is wildly inconsistent. Sometimes, this worldview has gaping holes so that no answer can be generated. Sometimes, it is geared only to perceived self-interest. And sometimes, it is fanciful and can never be put into practice. Failures in one's personal worldview model will lead to failures in decision-making.

One common worldview model in the Western world is that of celebrity fantasy. Under this worldview, being a celebrity is everything. Andy Warhol famously claimed that what Americans sought after most was 'fifteen minutes of fame'.[1] Under this worldview model we should strive to become a celebrity if only for a fleeting moment. What does it mean to be a celebrity? It is someone who is seen and recognized by a large number of people. Notice, that this definition does not stipulate that once recognized the object is given positive assent. That would be to take an additional step.

Environmental Ethics, Second Edition. Edited by Michael Boylan.

To be seen and recognized is enough. One can be a sinner or a saint—all the same. To be recognized is to be recognized. If this is the end, then it is probably easier to take the sinner route. In this way, the passion for celebrity is at heart contrary to ethics.

Another popular worldview model is one of practical competence. Under this model the practitioner strives to consider what is in his or her best interest and applies a practical cost–benefit analysis to various situations in order to ascertain whether action x or action y will maximize the greatest amount of pleasure for the agent (often described in terms of money). Thus, if you are Bernie Madoff (a well-known financial swindler) you might think about the risks and rewards of creating an illegal Ponzi scheme as opposed to creating a legitimate investment house that operates as other investment houses do. The risks of setting off on your own direction are that you might get caught and go to prison. The rewards are that you might make much more money than you would have done under the conventional investment house model. Since you think you are smarter than everyone else and will not get caught, the prudential model would say: "go for it!" Madoff did get caught, but who knows how many others do not? We cannot know because they *have not been caught*. But even if you are not caught, is that the best worldview approach? The prudential model says yes.

Possible Ethical Additions to the Prudential Model

Some people, including this author, think that the prudential model is lacking. Something else is necessary in order have a well-functioning worldview by which we can commit purposive action (here understood to be the primary requirement of fulfilled human nature). We first have to accept that the construction of our worldview is within our control. What I suggest is a set of practical guidelines for the construction of our worldview: "All people must develop a single comprehensive and internally coherent worldview that is good and that we strive to act out in our daily lives." I call this the personal worldview imperative. Now one's personal worldview is a very basic concept. One's personal worldview contains all that we hold good, true, and beautiful about existence in the world. There are four parts to the personal worldview imperative: completeness, coherence, connection to a theory of ethics, and practicality. Let us briefly say something about each.

First, *completeness*. Completeness is a formal term that refers to a theory being able to handle all cases put before it, and being able to determine an answer based upon the system's recommendations. In this case, I think that the notion of the good will provides completeness to everyone who develops one. There are two senses of the good will. The first is the rational good will. The rational good will means that each agent will develop an understanding about what reason requires of one as we go about our business in the world. In the various domains in which we engage this may require the development of different sorts of skills. In the case of ethics, it would require engaging in a rationally-based philosophical ethics and abiding by what reason demands.

Another sort of goodwill is the affective good will. We are more than just rational machines. We have an affective nature, too. Our feelings are important, but just as was the case with reason, some guidelines are in order. For ethics we begin with sympathy. Sympathy will be taken to be the emotional connection that one forms with other humans. This emotional connection must be one in which the parties are considered to be on a level basis. The sort of emotional connection I am talking about is open and between equals. It is not that of a superior "feeling sorry" for an inferior. It is my conjecture that those who engage in interactive human sympathy that is open and level will respond to another with care. Care is an action-guiding response that gives moral motivation to acting properly. Together sympathy, openness, and care constitute love.

When confronted with any novel situation one should utilize the two dimensions of the good will to generate a response. Because these two orientations act differently, it is possible that they may contradict each other. When this is the case, I would allot the tiebreaker to reason. Others, however, demur.[2] Each reader should take a moment to think about his or her own response to such an occurrence.

Second, *coherence*. People should have coherent worldviews. This also has two varieties: deductive and inductive. Deductive coherence speaks to our not having overt contradictions in our worldview. An example of an overt contradiction in one's worldview would be for Sasha to tell her friend Sharad that she has no prejudice against Muslims and yet in another context she tells anti-Muslim jokes. The coherence provision of the personal worldview imperative states that you should not change who you are and what you stand for depending upon the context in which you happen to be.

Inductive coherence is different. It is about adopting different life strategies that work against each other. In inductive logic this is called a sure loss contract. For example, if a person wanted to be a devoted husband and family man and yet also engaged in extramarital affairs, he would involve himself in inductive incoherence. The very traits that make him a good family man—loyalty, keeping your word, sincere interest in the well-being of others—would hurt one in being a philanderer, which requires selfish manipulation of others for one's own pleasure. The good family man will be a bad philanderer and vice versa. To try to do both well involves a sure loss contract. Such an individual will fail at both. This is what inductive incoherence means.

Third, *connection to a theory of being good, that is, ethics*. The personal worldview imperative enjoins that we consider and adopt an ethical theory. It does not give us direction, as such, as to which theory to choose except that the chosen theory must not violate any of the other three conditions (completeness, coherence, and practicability). What is demanded is that one connects to a theory of ethics and uses its action guiding force to control action.

Fourth, *practicability*. In this case there are two senses to the command. The first sense refers to the fact that we actually carry out what we say we will do. If we did otherwise, we would be hypocrites and also deductively incoherent. But, second, it is important that the demands of ethics and social/political philosophy be doable. One cannot command another to do the impossible! The way that I have chosen to describe this is the distinction between the utopian and the aspirational. The utopian is a command that may have logically valid arguments behind it, but are existentially unsound (meaning that some of the premises in the action-guiding argument are untrue by virtue of their being impractical). In a theory of global ethics, if we required that everyone in a rich country gave up three-quarters of their income so that they might support the legitimate plight of the poor, this would be a utopian vision. Philosophers are very attracted to utopian visions. However, unless philosophers want to be marginalized, we must situate our prescriptions in terms that can actually be used by policy makers. Beautiful visions that can never be should be transferred to artists and poets.

How to Construct Your Own Model

The first step in creating your own model for which you are responsible is to go through personal introspection concerning the four steps in the personal worldview imperative. The first two are types of global analyses in which an individual thinks about who he or she is right now in terms of consistency and completeness. These criteria are amenable to the prudential model. They are instrumental to making whatever worldview one chooses to be the most *effective* possible. This is a prudential standard of excellence. What constitutes the moral turn is the connection to a theory of the good: ethics.

Thus, the third step is to consider the principal moral theories and to make a choice as to which theory best represents your own considered position. To assist readers in this task, I provide a brief gloss of the major theories of ethics.

Theories of ethics

There are various ways to parse theories of ethics. I will parse theories of ethics according to what they see as the ontological status of their objects. There are two principal categories: (1) the realist theories that assert that theories of ethics speak to actual realities that exist;[3] and (2) the anti-realists who assert that theories of ethics are merely conventional and do not speak about ontological objects.

Realist theories

Utilitarianism. Utilitarianism is a theory that suggests that an action is morally right when that action produces more total utility for the group as a consequence than any other alternative. Sometimes this has been shortened to the slogan: "The greatest good for the greatest number." This emphasis upon calculating quantitatively the general population's projected consequential utility among competing alternatives appeals to many of the same principles that underlie democracy and capitalism (which is why this theory has always been very popular in the United States and other Western capitalistic democracies). Because the measurement device is natural (people's expected pleasures as outcomes of some decision or policy), it is a realist theory. The normative connection with aggregate happiness and the good is a factual claim. Advocates of utilitarianism point to the definite outcomes that it can produce by an external and transparent mechanism. Critics cite the fact that the interests of minorities may be overridden.

Deontology. Deontology is a moral theory that emphasizes one's duty to do a particular action, because the action itself is inherently right and not through any other sort of calculations, such as the consequences of the action. Because of this non-consequentialist bent, deontology is often contrasted with utilitarianism, which defines the right action in terms of its ability to bring about the greatest aggregate utility. In contradistinction to utilitarianism, deontology will recommend an action based upon principle. "Principle" is justified through an understanding of the structure of action, the nature of reason, and the operation of the will. Because its measures deal with the nature of human reason or the externalist measures of the possibility of human agency, the theory is realist. The result is a moral command to act that does not justify itself by calculating consequences. Advocates of deontology like the emphasis upon acting on principle or duty alone. One's duty is usually discovered via careful rational analysis of the nature of reason or human action. Critics cite the fact that there is too much emphasis upon reason and not enough on emotion and our social selves situated in the world.

Swing theories (may be realist or anti-realist)

Ethical intuitionism. Ethical intuitionism can be described as a theory of justification about the immediate grasping of self-evident ethical truths. Ethical intuitionism can operate on the level of general principles or on the level of daily decision making. In this latter mode many of us have experienced a form of ethical intuitionism through the teaching of timeless adages, such as "Look before you leap," and "Faint heart never won fair maiden." The truth of these sayings is justified through intuition. Many adages or maxims contradict each other (such as the two above), so that the ability to properly apply these maxims is also understood through intuition. When the source of the intuitions is either God or Truth itself as independently existing, then the theory is realist. The idea being that everyone who has a proper understanding of God or Truth will have the same revelation. When the source of the intuitions is the person herself living as a biological being in a social environment, then the theory is anti-realist because many different people will have various intuitions and none can take precedent over another.

Virtue ethics. Virtue ethics is also sometimes called agent-based or character ethics. It takes the viewpoint that in living your life you should try to cultivate excellence in all that you do and all that others do. These excellences or virtues are both moral and non-moral. Through conscious training, for example, an athlete can achieve excellence in a sport (non-moral example). In the same way, a person can achieve moral excellence as well. The way these habits are developed and the sort of community that nurtures them all come under the umbrella of virtue ethics. When the source of these community values is Truth or God, then the theory is realist. When the source is the random creation of a culture based upon geography or other accidental features, then the theory is anti-realist. Proponents of the theory cite the real effect that cultures have in influencing our behavior. We are social animals and this theory often ties itself with communitarianism, which affirms the positive interactive role that society plays in our lives. Detractors often point to the fact that virtue ethics does not give specific directives on particular actions. For example, a good action is said to be one that a person of character would make. To detractors, this sounds like begging the question.

Anti-realist theories

Ethical non-cognitivism. Ethical non-cognitivism is a theory that suggests that the descriptive analysis of language and culture tells us all we need to know about developing an appropriate attitude in ethical situations. Ethical propositions are neither true nor false, but can be analyzed via linguistic devices to tell us what action-guiding meanings are hidden there. We all live in particular and diverse societies. Discerning what each society commends and admonishes is a task for any person living in a society. We should all fit in and follow the social program as described via our language/society. Because these imperatives are relative to the values of the society or social group being queried, the maxims generated hold no natural truth-value and, as such, are anti-realist. Advocates of this theory point to its methodological similarity to deeply felt worldview inclinations of linguistics, sociology, and anthropology. If one is an admirer of these disciplines as seminal directions of thought, then ethical non-cognitivism looks pretty good. Detractors point to corrupt societies and that ethical non-cognitivism cannot criticize these from within (because the social milieu is accepted at face value).

Ethical contractarians. Ethical contractarians assert that freely made personal assent gives credence to ethical and social philosophical principles. These advocates point to the advantage of the participants being happy/contented with a given outcome. The assumption is that within a context of competing personal interests in a free and fair interchange of values those principles that are intersubjectively agreed upon are sufficient for creating a moral "ought." The "ought" comes from the contract and extends from two people to a social group. Others universalize this, by thought experiments, to anyone entering such contracts. Because the theory does not assert that the basis of the contract is a proposition that has natural existence as such, the theory is anti-realist. Proponents of the theory tout its connection to notions of personal autonomy that most people support. Detractors cite the fact that the theory rests upon the supposition that the keeping of contracts is a good thing; but why is this so? Does the theory pre-suppose a meta-moral theory validating the primacy of contracts? If not, then the question remains: "what about making a contract with another creates normative value?"

For the purposes of this text, we will assume these six theories to be exhaustive of philosophically based theories of ethics or morality.[4] In subsequent chapters, you should be prepared to apply these terms to situations and compare the sort of outcomes that different theories would promote.

The fourth step, in modifying one's personal worldview (now including ethics) is to go through an examination of what is possible (aspirational) as opposed to what is impos sible (utopian). This is another exercise in pragmatic reasoning that should be based on the agent's own abilities and their situation in society given her or his place in the scheme of things. Once this is determined, the agent is enjoined to discipline herself to actually bring about the desired change. If the challenge is great, then she should enlist the help of others: family, friends, community, and other support groups.

How Do Ethics Make a Difference in Decision-Making?

In order to get a handle on how the purely prudential worldview differs from the ethically enhanced worldview, let us consider two cases and evaluate the input of ethics. First, we will consider a general case in social/political ethics and then one from environmental ethics. The reader should note how the decision-making process differs when we add the ethical mode. In most cases in life the decisions we make have no ethical content. It does not matter ethically whether we have the chocolate or vanilla ice cream cone. It does not matter ethically if we buy orchestra seats for the ballet or the nose-bleed seats. It does not matter ethically if I wear a red or a blue tie today. The instances in which ethics are important are a small subset of all the decisions that we make. That is why many forgo thought about ethical decision making: it is important only in a minority of our total daily decisions. In fact, if we are insensitive to what *counts* as an ethical decision context, then we might believe that we are *never* confronted with a decision that has ethical consequences.

To get at these relations let us consider a couple of cases in which the ethical features are highly enhanced. Readers are encouraged to participate in creating reactions to these from the worldviews they now possess.

Case 1: Social/Political Ethics

The Trolley Problem

You are the engineer of the Bell Street Trolley. You are approaching Lexington Avenue Station (one of the major hub switching stations). The switchman on duty there says there is a problem. A school bus filled with 39 children has broken down on the right track (the main track). Normally, this would mean that he would switch you to the siding track, but on that track is a car containing four adults that has broken down. The switchman asks you to apply your brakes immediately. You try to do so, but you find that your brakes have failed, too. There is no way that you can stop your trolley train. You will ram either the school bus or the car killing either 39 children or four adults. You outrank the switchman. It is your call: what should you do?

Secondary nuance: what if the switchman were to tell you that from his vantage point on the overpass to the Lexington Avenue Station there is a rather obese homeless person who is staggering about. What if (says the switchman) he were to get out of his booth and push the homeless person over the bridge and onto the electric lines that are right below it? The result would be to stop all trains coming into and out of the Lexington Avenue Station. This would result in saving the lives of the occupants of the two vehicles. Of course, it would mean the death of the obese homeless person. The switchman wants your OK to push the homeless man over the bridge. What do you say?

Analysis

This case has two sorts of interpretation: before and after the nuance addition. In the first instance, one is faced with a simple question: should you kill four people or 39? The major moral theories give different answers to this question. First, there is the point of view of utilitarianism. It would suggest that killing four causes less pain than killing 39. Thus, one should tell the switchman to move you to the siding.

There is the fact that when the car was stuck on the siding, the driver probably viewed his risk as different from being stuck on the main line. Thus, by making that choice you are altering that expectation: versus the bus driver who has to know that he is in imminent danger of death. Rule utilitarians might think that moving away from normal procedures requires a positive alternative. Killing four people may not qualify as a positive alternative (because it involves breaking a rule about willful killing of innocents). Thus, the utilitarian option may be more complicated than first envisioned.

Rule utilitarianism would also find it problematic to throw the homeless person over the bridge for the same reason; though the act utilitarian (the variety outlined above) might view the situation as killing one versus four or 39. However, there is the reality that one is committing an act of murder to save others. This would be disallowed by the rule utilitarian. If the act utilitarian were to consider the long-term social consequences in sometimes allowing murder, he would agree with the rule utilitarian. However, without the long-term time frame, the act utilitarian would be committed to throwing the homeless person over the bridge.

The deontologist would be constrained by a negative duty not to kill. It would be equally wrong from a moral viewpoint to kill *anyone*. There is no *moral* reason to choose between the car and the bus. Both are impermissible. However, there is no avoidance alternative. You will kill a group of people unless the homeless person is thrown over the bridge. But throwing the homeless person over the bridge is murder. Murder is impermissible. Thus, the deontologist cannot allow the homeless person to be killed—even if it saved four or 39 lives. Because of this, the deontologist would use other normative factors, such as aesthetics, to choose whether to kill four or 39 (probably choosing to kill four on aesthetic grounds).

The virtue ethics person or the ethical intuitionist would equally reply that the engineer should act from the appropriate virtue, say justice, and do what a person with a just character would do. But this does not really answer the question. One could construct various scenarios about it being more just to run into the school bus rather than the car when the occupants of the car might be very important to society: generals, key political leaders, great physicists, etc. In the same way, the intuitionists will choose what moral maxim they wish to apply at that particular time and place. The end result will be a rather subjectivist decision-making process.

Finally, non-cognitivism and contractarianism are constrained to issues such as: "What does the legal manual for engineers tell them to do in situations like this?" If the manual is silent on this sort of situation, then the response is: what is the recommended action for situations *similar* to this in some relevant way? This is much like the decision-making process in the law where *stare decisis et non quieta movere* (support the decisions and do not disturb what is not changed). In other words, one must act based upon a cultural–legal framework that provides the only relevant context for critical decisions.

In any event, the reader can see that the way one reasons about the best outcome of a very difficult situation changes when one adds ethics to the decision-making machinery. I invite readers to go through several calculations on their own for class discussion. Pick one or more moral theory and set it out along with prudential calculations such that morality is the senior partner in the transaction. One may have to return to one's personal worldview (critically understood, as per above), and balance it with the practical considerations and their embeddedness to make this call.

Case 2: Environmental Ethics

You are the head of the McDowell County Commission in West Virginia. Your county has been hit hard by poverty over the past few decades due to the decrease in coal production. ABC Coal Company that still operates a large mine has applied for a permit to construct a large coal-generated power plant. The plant will mean 1000 jobs and the taxes it will generate will allow the county to revive many social services that have been lost in recent years. The sort of plant that will be built is a conventional 500 megawatt plant that will consume 1.4 million tons of coal a year (from ABC's own mine). The problem is a new clean air and water act passed by Congress that will come into effect in 14 months. The new law sets limits on soot, smog, acid rain, toxic air emissions, and metal trailing, including arsenic, mercury, chromium, and cadmium. The tree huggers contend that these metals cause cancer and that the resulting air pollution will cause respiratory ailments and lead to global warming. The new plant as designed will not meet the new Federal guidelines.

ABC wants the environmental impact study *fast tracked* with a board of sympathetic scientists. ABC has even provided you with a confidential list of these scientists. They will produce a report in three months that will allow the permit to be issued in six months and ground breaking in nine months. Any ongoing permit-approved projects have been grandfathered out of the new clean and water act. The plant could be operational in 18 months. Your next election is in 22 months. There is one county commissioner who is against the project. He says that jobs are important, but so is the health of the environment. Your own father died of black lung disease at the age of 59. You are sensitive to the concerns for clean air and water, but people need to live. How could you turn down ABC and look your poverty-torn constituents in the eyes?

Analysis

The prudential perspective from the head commissioner's vantage point has several elements. His or her job is in jeopardy if the power plant is not built. Being the head commissioner is crucial to this individual's worldview perspective. This slant of the prudential viewpoint would be to get the ball rolling as soon as possible. The clock is ticking in order to achieve the "grandfathered status." You must have a permit in hand and in the process of construction to get this. Thus, you should act immediately.

If we expand the prudential slightly there are more angles to consider. For one, the air quality in the county would become lower. This might hurt your slightly asthmatic daughter. It might also lower your own and your family's life expectancy. However, though your father died early, your grandfather (who did not work underground) lived to be 80! Black lung is a miner's hazard. Topside, the air is so much cleaner than down below (especially before they had the modern ventilation systems) that you are inclined to discount this risk as theoretical, but not practical. This would include your thoughts about other county residents.

If we look from the perspective of ethical non-cognitivism, we have to isolate the culture of coal mining in West Virginia. This is an arena of people with a strong sense of individualism. They want to be able have a decent job so that they can take care of their families. The current economy has eroded these possibilities while not replacing them with others. Under this shared community worldview the most important outcome is *jobs*. The new plant promises jobs. The new plant should be built.

Virtue ethics (here interpreted as anti-realist) would suggest that the key character trait *fortitude* is most important here. Generations of West Virginians have had to surmount incredible odds in order to put food on the table and raise their families. Men in the mines have had to endure great pain, and so have their spouses who have had to struggle with little in order to keep life moving forward. When faced with the downside of a little air pollution that (even if the science is right) will shorten life only by a few years, the historic character of the people in the region is strongly in favor of building the power plant. After all, the downside is minimal compared with life underground. You will not get black lung from the light pollution of the power plant.

Contractarianism would center on what sort of laws and societal social contracts exist. In individually oriented West Virginia the scale is slanted toward each person in the county. If you build the plant and the people sign up for the jobs, then is that not that an indication that the people want this outcome? If they were against it, they would just stay at home.

Ethical intuitionism might side with either position according to the sort of moral maxims brought forward, and how they are popularly received.

Utilitarianism would be forced to focus on the general happiness. But *whose* happiness? Will it be the happiness of the county? Will it be the happiness of the state? Will it be the happiness of the country? Will it be the happiness of the world? And once this is determined, then the subsequent question is what is the time frame? Are we talking about three years, 30 years, or 300 years? The answer to the utilitarian calculation may be different according to how one parses the population to be examined and how one understands the relevant time frame. Under most of these scenarios (given a time frame of at least 50 years and a scope that covers the wind dispersement of a majority of the pollutants and heavy metal contaminants), the risks will outweigh the benefits (even for the county involved). Therefore, utilitarianism will reject the building of the power plant.

Deontology (since Kant) has been very keen to think of duties in terms of thought experiments that create models that are universal in scope. In the current example, the operative question might be: "what if every county in America were to build a conventional coal-powered energy plant?" Could we do so without logical contradiction? Here we tread in uncharted territory. According to most scientists, if every county in the United States built such a power plant the amount of pollution (both air and heavy metals) would be so great that people would begin dying in high numbers causing high social and political unrest. High social and political unrest is called *anarchy*. Anarchy is the breakdown of government. There would be no cohesive society under this description. Therefore, the model is inconsistent. Inconsistent models are illogical. All illogical models are to be rejected. Therefore, deontology would create a prohibition against building the power plant.

Conclusion

This chapter began by asking the rhetorical question: "what is the point in studying ethics?" The examination of the question took us to various places. First, it took us to prudential decision making and the possible problems that many decision models face because of unreflective worldviews. Next, some suggestions were made to remedy this problem, including the personal worldview imperative. Finally, the chapter worked through two case studies in which difficult decisions were presented. In this context, the prudential models were supplemented with an overlay of some ethical theories that might offer a more coherent direction in decision making. The slant of this author was toward the realist ethical theories and the swing theories interpreted realistically. However, each side was presented in order that the reader might make up his or her own mind on how he or she intends to adopt the overlay of ethics into his or her worldview and decision-making model. This is an important, on-going task. I exhort each reader to take this quest seriously. It may just be the best investment in time that you have ever made!

Notes

1 Cited in *The Philosophy of Andy Warhol* (1975) New York: Harcourt, Brace, Jovanovich. At an art exhibition in Stockholm, Sweden he is reported to have said: "In the future everyone will be world-famous for fifteen minutes." Since that time, the quotation has morphed into several different formulations.

2 This is particularly true of some feminist ethicists. See Rosemarie Tong (2009) "A Feminist Personal Worldview Imperative," in *Morality and Justice: Reading Boylan's A Just Society* (ed. John-Stewart Gordon), Lanham, MD and Oxford: Lexington / Rowman & Littlefield; pp. 29–38.

3 Another popular distinction is *natural* versus *non-natural*. This is a sub-category of realism. For example, the philosopher G.E. Moore was a realist about the existence of "good," but he felt that "good" was an non-natural property. Thus, realists can be naturalists and non-naturalists. Anti-realists are neither natural nor unnatural: they do not think that the good (for example) actually exists at all: in or out of nature.

4 For the purposes of this book the words "ethics" and "morality" will be taken to be exact synonyms.

2

The Self in Context

A Grounding for Environmentalism

Michael Boylan

What are you? This is certainly a fundamental question that has been answered in various ways from *featherless biped*, to *rational animal*, to *caring creature*, among others. Each of these definitions seeks to characterize an individual human as a subsumable member of an intensional set: *H* (*homo sapiens*). Logically, this says, for example, that the defining formula of set *H* is that for any *x*, if *x* possesses *R* (rational animal), then *x* is a member of *H*.[1] Set membership in first-order logic is determined by possessing a defining property that confers set membership upon any individual possessing that property. Of course, the property will change as the intensionality of *H* changes.

This is certainly one way of understanding what a human is. It delivers some important information about picking out an individual in such a way that we can, with confidence, refer to him or her as "human." However, this is not the end of the story. There is more to being a human than just being either a rational, featherless biped, or caring creature. What is left out is an understanding of humans as relational beings. The logic of relational definitions is a bit more complicated than simple intensional definitions. It requires the construction of types via quantified predicates (second-order logic) to capture the complexity of relational identity. In order to get a hold of this in a non-technical fashion, let us take a big step and look at real people who are situated in the world. We will begin with a simple depiction of people as individuals *sui generis*, and then move to people within a social context. This will be the purpose of Part One.

Part One: The Individual Alone and the Individual in Community

We start with you. You are the reader of this essay. I can ask various questions of you. What is your favorite flavor of ice cream? Who is your favorite pop singer? Do you enjoy Reality TV? These questions are meant to individualize you, such that you become distinct from the many other individuals in your age group. These characteristics might be attitudes (such as evidenced by the prior questions).

Environmental Ethics, Second Edition. Edited by Michael Boylan.

Another way to individuate you might be to describe your physiogamy. Are you tall or short? Are you fat or slim? Do you have big feet? What is the topography of your nose? These sort of questions tell something about your physical characteristics. The physical characteristics are not as important as your attitudes, because if you met your doppelganger who looked just like you but had different attitudes, then most would choose the attitudes as being primary in establishing *who* you are. Thus, they are more important. However, if your body were to be changed by illness or accident, but your attitudes remained the same, then most would say that you remained essentially unchanged. This is because we think attitudes to be more indicative of self-identity than physical characteristics.

So, if you are most essentially a collection of attitudes, these attitudes of taste can be supplemented by those of personal understanding of the facts of the world: what is the boiling point of water at sea level? What is the tallest mountain in the world? What is the mass of the Antarctic ice caps? These sort of understandings are different than the first category of attitudes. In the first case, the source of verification is the agent's own personal tastes. No one else can say that one's personal tastes are incorrect, because they are subjectively based upon one's own perceptions and judgments made about them. In the second case, there is reference to intersubjective data that are amenable to measurement according to commonly held standards. Enter the community.

We all belong to many different communities. These range from the family, church, schools, vocational communities, volunteer groups, etc. Our identity in communities is relational depending upon our role within that community. For example, if one of my communities is being on a basketball team at the YMCA, then I might be the off-guard, first off the bench. This would be who I am within that community. It would involve certain social roles and responsibilities. Each of us is situated within communities to which we belong.

We also have stations within the community that confer conventional rights and duties that arise from that community.[2] For example, I may be the treasurer of my church. This gives me the right to collect funds from parishioners and the duty to enter the data into an accounting program, deposit the monies at the bank, and print and present checks to the rector for his signature.

The roles and stations that we occupy within communities both designate us and create an institutional place whereby we do our part to execute our individual and corporate responsibility.[3] Communities thus have bodies (institutions) that create and sanction various rules and their enforcement (formal and informal). We can think of this as the community being a collection of people, and the institution as being a sort of power-mapping machine that sorts us out and puts us into proper subsets according to properties that define our membership (relational role) and our functional place (relational station).

Given this rather informal characterization of communities, let us return to the perspective of the individual within the community. How should he or she act? This question can be answered in two ways: (a) the way I understand my own ability to act; and (b) the way I see this as important in a social context. I address (a) via an argument that claims that an examination of human agency requires that I recognize certain conditions that I and others share.[4]

I address (b) via the shared community worldview imperative: "Each agent must contribute to a common body of knowledge that supports the creation of a shared community worldview (that is itself complete, coherent, and good), through which social institutions and their resulting policies might flourish within the constraints of the essential core commonly held values (ethics, aesthetics, and religion)."[5] What this imperative means is that the individual in a community (whatever community it is) must take an active participatory stance (beyond his or her individual role and station responsibilities) to assess the mission of the community and to judge whether that mission and its goals are logically complete, coherent, and good, and how this mission is being carried out via its associated social institutions. If the community is logically complete, coherent, and good in how it identifies itself and how it seeks to act on that understanding (mission), then it is up to each and every individual in the community to take an active role in this process consonant with their critical personal worldview.[6] This means that all community members must become active participants in the community. How can this be achieved? At a minimal level, it involves each person's continual surveillance of the community in order to see how it is performing its mission (one critical ingredient for the common body of knowledge).[7] At the next level one should engage others in the community in dialogue about how the community is fulfilling its mission. (This dialogue critically examines the common body of knowledge.) Such social dialogue should also include ways that might be employed to revise the policies of the community and how they are being executed.[8] Finally, the third level is to actively lead proposals for change and renewal of the community according to the criteria of the Shared Community Worldview Imperative (SCWI). This can go as far as taking a leadership role in the community.

Everyone must participate at least on the lowest level. But it should not stop there. According to the SCWI, people should then also strive to participate at levels two and three according to their abilities. The SCWI is a foundational principle that is necessary for democratic institutions and moderately representative non-democratic institutions.[9]

I have argued that there are various sorts of community.[10] The most common sort is one in which a person can have personal contact with most of the community members. I call these communities *micro communities*. In micro communities (generally 500 people or less), one can envision a political process that works on the committee as a whole. There can be discourse and influence by all at this level. As the community grows larger we move to *macro communities*. Because of their size we cannot realistically make contact with all other members. Thus, we move toward indirect contact via representative government. In this case, all the duties of the SCWI still hold, but the participatory component is less direct because the unit is so large. Levels one and two are still possible, but level three is generally structured around elected leaders: sending letters, petitions, organizing protest events, etc.

Each of the aforementioned communities, micro and macro, are set within the context of nations. But I assert that there is also an extended sense of community that goes beyond the areas in which we actually live or where we can travel unimpeded (within the boundaries of a nation).[11] This sense of community is remote. Without the benefits of modern media, we might not be very aware of their plight. But because of the devices of communication that presently exist, information is available. This information can be input toward the creation of knowledge, which, in turn, will lead individuals to contemplate those without the basic goods of agency. This reflection should lead to the acceptance of duties to those far removed from our daily lives: cosmopolitanism:

> Each agent must educate himself as much as he is able about the peoples of the world—their access to the basic goods of agency, their essential commonly held cultural values, and their governmental and institutional structures—in order that he might individually and collectively accept the duties that ensue from those peoples' legitimate rights claims, and to act accordingly within what is aspirationally possible.[12]

Conceptually, the extended community worldview imperative is important because it says that we can have strong moral duties that extend to people we have not met or are ever likely to meet. Their verified existence and situation is enough to generate a known moral duty (subject to "ought implies can"). This sort of intellectual assessment and its consequent moral effects lies behind the moral assessment process of nature. We will begin this segment of our journey by agreeing that there are more than human communities in which we exist. The ecosystem is a natural community that can be dealt with in an analogous fashion.

Part Two: The Individual in the Natural Community

We begin this section by admitting that we all live somewhere, and that *somewhere* is naturally situated. Since we are emphasizing relational identity in this essay, our relation with nature is somewhat different than our relationship with other people in social communities. This is because nature "speaks" to us in ways we do not always understand. The reason for this is that nature does not properly *speak* at all. This is because nature is not sentient and only sentient beings execute speech acts. Nature "acts" according to the laws of material necessity, for the most part. The powerful tsunami that struck Japan in 2011 was the result of an earthquake that itself was the result of a sliding of tectonic plates in the Earth's crust. The exact science relating to this is still beyond accurate prediction. When the conditions are right, it just happens. At present, no one believes that the existence of humans on Earth has anything to do with whether or not earthquakes will occur. Their etiology is not related to humanity.

Other natural occurrences, such as *El niño* and *La niña* (atypical warm and cold ocean conditions that affect global weather), are thought to be caused (at least in part) by human activity.[13] Thus, these natural events (though they are still governed by material necessity) are the result of nature–human interaction. Indeed, nature surrounds us: en-viron (from Anglo-Saxon to surround or encircle). It can be an active relationship even at the basic level of inanimate objects, such as the geology of the earth, the physical mechanics of fresh and salt water in the hydro-cycle, the physical mechanics of ice, and the dynamic behavior of gasses. The way that we treat these natural inanimate entities makes a difference to those entities and to us who are surrounded by them, *environed* by them. There are two important standpoints that condition the way we think about this: (a) the standpoint of humans looking out; and (b) the standpoint of the inanimate objects themselves as internal, physical systems. These standpoints "view" human behavior differently. For example, for humans it may be beneficial to take off the top of a mountain to allow coal to be mined cheaply in order to create electricity that humans have come to depend upon. Thus, mountain-top removal might be seen to be good for humans, the anthropocentric perspective. However, it might be bad for the mountain. This is because the existing physical system is altered in ways that are mostly deleterious to that physical system (where deleterious means leading to the diminishment or destruction of the physical system). We will call this perspective the intrinsic natural standpoint (when nature refers to living organism it is called the biocentric standpoint). It will be the position of this essay that the relational interaction between physical systems and people requires consideration from both angles, with the tiebreaker going to the sustainable intrinsic natural standpoint. However, the *justification* for the intrinsic natural standpoint (and its analogue, the biocentric standpoint) is anthropocentric (because the argument is made among and between humans).

Other parts of the natural community include plants and animals. Together with the natural physical systems, they form an even more interactive local relationship that can be called an ecosystem.[14] The attention paid to the ecosystem can be called ecology. The etymology of ecology = *oikos* (household in ancient Greek) + *logos* (the account of or reason for), which is also similar to the entomology for economics = *oikos* + *nomos* (the laws governing). Thus, the *account of* is a relational term. This suggests that the definition of the household (the paradigm of a social institution within the micro family community) is essentially relational. We cannot talk about communities or their social institutions without language about contexts. And the resulting social rules that govern the communities and their social institutions are also steeped in contextual relations.

What I am suggesting here is that these contextual relations *include* nature: as land, as flora, and as fauna. At this point let us examine the micro community of humans in nature: the ecosystem. Within the ecosystem (just as in micro human communities) every entity—land, plants, and animals—interact with each other in either a benign relation or a predator–prey relation. Seen holistically in a state of equilibrium, the various systemic actors share a symbiotic relationship. This is the fundamental relational reality of the ecosystem. When one actor becomes predominant it is at the expense of another: this is a zero-sum game.

Given that within the ecosystem every actor is affected by every other actor, there is a sort of version of the prisoner's dilemma at work.[15] In the traditional prisoner's dilemma there is a tension between cooperation and self-interest. The best and the worst options go to the individualist who does not accept relational definition. The socially connected positions are in the middle. When various people play out the game statistically, they begin with a bias toward one particular sort of identity understanding: disconnected individual versus connected relational individual. This initial bias generally colors the interpretation.[16]

When we consider relational versus disconnected individuals regarding nature in the context of the ecosystem, there are analogous dynamics. The prison guard becomes the oppressive environment and crisis at hand (instead of being civil freedom becomes freedom from disease). As these dynamics might seem strange to some, consider the following grid:

1. Myself — The ecosystem near term.
2. Myself — The ecosystem long term.
3. Myself — Other humans in the ecosystem near term.
4. Myself — Other humans in the ecosystem long term.

Figure 2.1 Potential ecosystem change from a relational standpoint

So when we think about Figure 2.1, I believe that there are strong analogies between 1 and 3 and 2 and 4. The near term is easier to think about and to quantify. Thinking about the long term is, by necessity, fuzzy. This can lead to a stance that discounts future states.[17] What should be foundational throughout these calculations is the community worldview sensibility. We must accept that we live in a context. Despite all the narrative stories to the contrary, we are not lone individuals such as "cowboys living on a harsh environmental terrain" or a "lone explorer in the jungle who has to make it or perish." Rather, we are "individuals who live in context." We live in a human community and we live within a natural community. To deny our context is a factual error of description.

Some may say: "Okay, we live in a context, but the context is *noise*. It really does not matter. All that matters is my own maneuvering against stubborn obstacles toward the goal." This reasoning tries to maintain the narrative of an individual existing solo. A revised version of the prisoner's dilemma is to change the other prisoner into the ecosystem in which he lives:

Jason has been upset about his daughter, Angelique. Her asthma is getting worse and he and his physician are convinced that the cause is air pollution in his home city of Anywhere, USA. Jason does not know what to do. He feels like a prisoner where he lives. He could do nothing and try to save enough money to move to a different part of the country (though there is no guarantee that she would be healthier there). He could become active in the local chapter of an organization whose mission it is to force Anywhere to live up to the standards of the Clean Air Act. However, if he acts effectively the environment may get better (along with his daughter) or the environment may not respond (and his daughter Angelique might die). It is also possible that the environment, all by itself, will become clean via some strange new air currents that will sweep the pollution to another city and away from Anywhere. What should Jason do?

Figure 2.2 The environmental prisoner's dilemma

In this scenario, there is a considerably different landscape. Absent is the detached jailer and the all-powerful controlling entity. These roles are merged into another actor, the environment. But there is still the dynamic of a cooperative stance versus an individualistic approach. The cooperative individual will see the pollution problem in Anywhere, USA as a community concern. Sure, his daughter is affected, but then so are countless others as well. Many of these other sufferers may not have the option to move—jobs are hard to come by. Should Jason become politically active and attack the issue within that context? It is the slowest option. Will Angelique be strong enough to make it if the family stays in Anywhere? Or should Jason flee with his daughter to another city (the individual approach)? This is much quicker and, all things considered, would probably score higher in computer-simulated games. But this is no sure thing either. Besides, there is more to moving than just changing locations. If we were to complicate the game a bit with how moving affects childhood development—particularly among sick children (who may require more nurturing)—then the individual approach becomes more nuanced.

I think that the individualistic approach to this dilemma may be the most successful to the individual, depending upon the side conditions set forth, but it will also insure that the environment will continue to deteriorate from human pollution efforts. Unless, and until, we can group together in an effort that recognizes the ecosystem in a different way, the future of ecosystems and larger definable systemic units will be progressively hostile to life as we know it on the Earth—especially that represented by complex biological organisms.

These reflections lead us to the question: "how should we think about the ecosystem?" The ecosystem is not a person, and therefore does not have moral standing, as such.[18] So how should we think about the larger paradigm that this dilemma suggests? My suggestion is to think of the environment as part of our community identity. I will call this relation another sort of worldview imperative that has normative implications.

Eco-community worldview imperative

Each agent must educate herself about the proximate natural world in which she lives relating to her agency within this eco-system: (a) what her natural place in this order is vis-à-vis her personal agency; (b) how her natural place may have changed in recent history vis-à-vis her personal agency; (c) how her social community's activities have changed the constitution of the natural order and how this has affected community agency; (d) the short-term and long-term effects of those changes vis-à-vis agency; and (e) what needs to be done to maintain the natural order in the short and long term so that the ecosystem might remain vibrant.

Let us examine the various parts of this worldview imperative. First, there is a requirement for people to educate themselves as much as is practically possible about the proximate environment in which they live. This will require some attention to the three parts of the environment discussed above: the land, the plant life, and the animal life. In the age of the Internet, most people in countries that have widespread digital access can view reports by national and international agencies. In countries that do not have this access, then individual must themselves make continued personal surveys of the area in which he or she lives.

Second, is an admission that we live in a natural context that is interactive. All people should access how this context affects them personally and how they are actors that affect nature. It is a mutual relation.

Third, requires a sense of recent history. How has the natural context changed and who is responsible for that change? This is a factual search that will be more exact in richer countries (such as the G20 nations). But it will still be possible in the rest of the world, albeit at a more anecdotal, less precise level. Once we know what has happened and which parties are to blame, then the political community is in a position to call for change.

The fourth and last point, is to form an action plan for the short and long term with a sustainability sensibility in mind. Sustainability is a pivotal concept in environmental ethics. It gives recognition to the dynamic reality of natural systems. A natural system is a robust interactive collection of animate and inanimate objects geographically proximate. Though there are different ways to parse such collections, this essay will rely on a threefold classification: ecosystems, watersheds, and biomes (in ascending size).[19] In order for a natural system to be sustainable it must exhibit feedback loops that interact to protect the existence of the natural system. A natural system that is sustainable can thus adapt to changes to the inanimate and animate parts of the system. When a natural system fails to be able to adapt, its very existence is threatened. The eco-community worldview imperative seeks to involve people in the task of maintaining sustainability at the ecosystem level. It is the proximate level at which we live.

But what about watersheds and biomes that are remote to us? This is the subject of the next section.

Part Three: The Impact of the Eco-Community Imperative and the Extended Eco-Community Imperative

It is one thing to create ethical duties based upon our proximate community membership. Communities that touch us each day capture our attention. But larger and extended communities are important to recognize as well. The problem is that they are remote. The problem with remote is *out of sight, out of mind*.[20] Most of us respond more readily to problems that confront us head-on where we live. Thus, it may be the case that readers will sign onto the eco-community worldview imperative because it affects them personally. In this way, it is a manifestation of psychological egoism: people are out to advance only what they perceive to be their personal self-interest. I have argued in the past that basing communal public policy upon the self-interest of powerful people in the community is unjust.[21] Thus, I believe that social and political public policy should follow the argument: "The Moral Status of Basic Goods." This argument suggests that various goods of human agency are hierarchically ordered and that satisfying the most important for everyone first trumps the idiosyncratic preferences of the marketplace. This is because the marketplace should be viewed as a opportunity-neutral: accidental economic circumstances that exists at some particular time and place. The preferences of the marketplace can be understood much like the changing environments of evolutionary theory. If a variegated-patterned moth prevails in an unpolluted forest and the black-colored moth prevails in a polluted forest, this is considered to be a simple fact.[22] Neither moth coloring is *better*, as such. But in an environment with high evolutionary pressures, one is better in environment$_1$ and the other is better in environment$_2$ where "better" is functionally defined.

In an analogous way, the "preferences" of the market are also contextually linked. If a group of people having a particular trait—such as the ability to focus on one particular task—is an advantage in one social/economic environment, then they will flourish. However, in another environment (such as one that rewards multi-tasking) they might founder. Thus, in the same way that moth color does not assign moral merit, economic advantage is similarly restricted to functional criteria.

If this reasoning is correct, then success is at least somewhat accidental. One way to react to this is to say: "well that's the way it is: let it be—it is the way of evolution."[23] Those who take this approach will view remote ecosystems, watersheds, and biomes as, at most, a fact to stimulate intellectual speculation: "is not it interesting that the hundred square mile wetland in Thailand dried up and the flora, fauna, and the historic water table that sustained the wetland is no more." Curious that!

In order to avoid this sort of reaction, I believe that another sort of worldview imperative is called for.

Extended eco-community worldview imperative

Each agent must educate herself about the world's biomes: freshwater, saltwater, arid regions, forests, prairies and grassland, tundra, and Arctic regions. This education should be ongoing and should include how the relative stability and natural sustainability is faring at various points in time. This knowledge will entail a factual valuing that also leads to an aesthetic valuing. Since all people seek to protect what they value, this extended community membership will ground a duty to protect the global biomes according to what is aspirationally possible.

What this worldview imperative prescribes is first to educate oneself about the scientific *facts* of the world. This doxastic responsibility is primary. Far too often people create beliefs that are unsupported by hard data. This is irresponsible and immoral.[24] As the late US New York Senator Daniel Patrick Moynihan, is reputed to have said: "We are all entitled to our own opinions, but not our own facts." What this means is that each individual, according to his or her own abilities, should seek objective scientific facts about the global environment. This fact-searching should be in the context of what will be sustainable for the distant ecosystem, watershed, or biome. Such a project will involve some education in geography, as well as the physical and biological systems that exist globally.

Now some will say that I am asking too much of people.[25] But I do not think so. Remember, I couch my duty upon the caveat of what each person is capable of learning. Now, I must admit that I think that the Bell curve shifts more to the right than many other academics admit: meaning that I think that many more people have a higher intellectual capability than many of my colleagues do. I base my belief on nearly forty years of teaching at all levels in the educational hierarchy. What is often the case among those in lower socioeconomic groups is that they have internalized the low expectation levels that others have projected upon them. I say give them a challenge and they will respond to it if they believe they are capable and they feel a responsibility to do so.[26]

Statistically, I think it is correct that many do not fire themselves up to the task of surveying a variety of sources to ascertain the facts about the environment in which they live or the extended environment. As a result, many take their lead from politicians, who often have a self-interested motive in espousing opinions that do not coincide with highly accepted scientific findings, such as whether there is global warming (regardless of the cause). In a 2009 *Washington Post* poll it was found that 28 percent of the general public and 46 percent of Republicans doubted that there was global warming (regardless of the cause).[27] This is in contrast to virtually unanimous consensus by scientists, who compare composite and disparate biome readings by mechanical measuring devices that have been in place for a century. My only account for this is that many people skip ahead to the policy responses to certain factual states of affairs. If they do not like the policy response, then they will decry the facts as well. Such reactions are prohibited by the extended eco-community worldview imperative.

A second consequence of the extended eco-community worldview imperative is to transition from factual understanding to aesthetic valuing. It is my contention that this is a seamless process (see "Worldview and the Value-Duty Link" in this volume). To understand the operation of a complex natural system will result in a valuing of that system. To value a system is to undertake a duty to protect said system. Thus, the second part of the extended eco-community worldview imperative is to undergo this process. It all begins with education and it ends with an intellectual cum aesthetic appreciation that translates into a duty to protect.

At the end of day, the extended eco-community worldview imperative is a duty to protect all of the world's natural systems according to our resources.

Conclusion

This essay began with a simple question in first-order logic on how to define people. When the question only involves a single people (as representative stand-ins, i.e., quantified variables), then the answer is quite simple. However, if we invoke relations of any sort of sophistication, then we need some sort second-order logical analysis that involves quantified predicate relations. This leads us into an analysis of the relational nature of humans: first, as members of social communities and, then, as members of natural communities. Such speculation leads us to the "Environmental Prisoner's Dilemma," which requires the "Eco-community Worldview Imperative" and the "Extended Eco-community Worldview Imperative" for its solution.

The essay ends with an exploration of just how these eco-community imperatives would change the way individuals recognize their moral duties both to local and global locales, respectively. It is the contention of this essay that if sufficient numbers of people accept their eco-community duties, the world might transition to the gold standard of global environmental ethics: sustainability. The stakes are high. Time is short.

Notes

1 df H: $(\forall x)\,[Rx \rightarrow (Hx)]$.

2 I am thinking here of John Austin's (1885) analysis (as opposed to modern theories of sociology).

3 I am following Miller (2009) here with a few caveats from Boylan (2009).

4 I call this argument: "The Moral Status of Basic Goods" (essentials necessary for fundamental action):

1. before anything else, all people desire to act: assumption about human nature;
2. whatever all people desire before anything else is natural to that species: fact;
3. desiring to act is natural to *homo sapiens*: 1, 2;
4. people value what is natural to them: assertion;
5. what people value they wish to protect: assertion;

6. all people wish to protect their ability to act beyond all else: 1, 3, 4, 5;
7. the strongest interpersonal "oughts" are expressed via our highest value systems, i.e., religion, morality, and aesthetics: assertion;
8. all people must agree, upon pain of logical contradiction, that what is natural and desirable to them individually is natural and desirable to everyone collectively and individually: assertion;
9. everyone must seek personal protection for his or her own ability to act via religion, morality, and/or aesthetics: 6, 7;
10. everyone, upon pain of logical contradiction, must admit that all other humans will seek personal protection of their ability to act via religion, morality, and/or aesthetics: 8, 9;
11. all people must agree, upon pain of logical contradiction, that since the attribution of the basic goods of agency are predicated generally, that it is inconsistent to assert idiosyncratic preferences: fact;
12. goods that are claimed through generic predication apply equally to each agent and everyone has a stake in their protection: 10, 11;
13. rights and goods are correlative: assertion;
14. everyone has at least a moral right to the basic goods of agency and others in the society have a duty to provide those goods to all: 12, 13.

5 Boylan (2004a: ch. 6).

6 My take on a critical personal worldview is one that meets the criteria of the personal worldview imperative: "All people must develop a single comprehensive and internally coherent worldview that is good and that we strive to act out in our daily lives" (Boylan 2004a: ch. 2).

7 The common body of knowledge consists in socially recognized facts about the world and those values recognized by that community. Obviously, some communities can be mistaken about both facts and values. Many medieval towns believed the world was flat (error in fact). Many communities around the world have held human slavery to be permissible (error in value).

8 One way to think about this is via qualified epistemic claims as per Estlund (2008).

9 Boylan (2011: ch. 10).

10 Boylan (2011: ch. 2).

11 There are some countries that have internal passports and citizens are not permitted full freedom of travel. For these individuals, they should look to the extended community worldview imperative.

12 Boylan (2011: ch. 2).

13 See NOAA's web site on this: www.pmel.noaa.gov/tao/elnino/el-nino-story.html.

14 Miller (1991: A7) says an ecosystem is a: "community of organisms interacting with one another and with the chemical and physical factors making up their environment." My account above is close to this.

15 The prisoner's dilemma was developed by Merrill Flood and Melvin Dresher for the Rand Corporation in 1950. There are many variations on the prisoner's dilemma. The version to which I am referring comes from Steven Kuhn (1995).

16 This naturalistic version of the prisoner's dilemma is made in more detail by Martin A. Nowak (2006).

17 See Broome (1994).

18 Paul Taylor (2011) has a famous version of the biocentric argument.

19 My account of these collections follows: Smith (1992: G12), who defines watershed as an "entire region drained by a waterway that drains into a lake or reservoir; total area above a given point on a stream that contributes water to the flow at that point; the topographic dividing line from which surface streams flow in two different directions"; and Tootill (1980: 29), who defines biome as "major regional community of plants and animals with similar life forms and environmental conditions. It is the largest geographical biotic unit, and is named after the dominant type of life form, such as tropical rain forest, grassland, or coral reef."

20 This dynamic has been discussed by Peter Unger (1996: chs 1 and 2) in relation to human duties to other humans who live in remote communities.

21 Boylan (2004b, 2011).

22 This, of course, follows H. Kettlewell (1973).

23 Elliott Sober (1986) takes this approach.

24 See Julie Kirsch's take on this (2011).

25 Anita Allen (1999) made this sort of comment about the "Personal Worldview Imperative."

26 Examples of this in my own teaching are two nontraditional students who in middle age went to college from the trades (plumber and electrician) and they soared. Both went to graduate school. They were determined to stretch themselves and were surprised at what they could do. I am very proud of them both.

27 Eilperin (2009).

References

Allen, Anita (1999) "Confronting Moral Theories: Gewirth in Context," in *Gewirth* (ed. Michael Boylan), Lanham, MD: Rowman & Littlefield, pp. 91–96.

Austin, John (1885) *Lectures on Jurisprudence*, 5th edn (ed. Robert Campbell), London: John Murray.

Boylan, Michael (ed.) (2001) "Worldview and the Value-Duty Link," in *Environmental Ethics*, Upper Saddle River, NJ: Prentice-Hall.

Boylan, Michael (2004a) *A Just Society*, Lanham, MD: Rowman & Littlefield.

Boylan, Michael (2004b) "The Moral Imperative to Maintain Public Health," in *Public Health Policy and Ethics* (ed. Michael Boylan), Dordrecht: Kluwer/Springer, pp. xvii–xxxiv.

Boylan, Michael (2009) "Institutions, Actors, and Moral Accountability: *The Moral Foundations of Social Institutions: a Philosophical Study*," International Journal of Applied Philosophy, 23 (2), 335–346.

Boylan, Michael (2011) *Morality and Global Justice: Justifications and Applications*, Boulder, CO: Westview.

Broome, John (1994) "Discounting the Future," Philosophy and Public Affairs, 23 (2), 128–156.

Eilperin, Juliet (2009) "Fewer Americans Believe in Global Warming, Poll Shows," *Washington Post*, November, 25, available at: www.washingtonpost.com/wp-dyn/content/article/2009/11/24/AR2009112402989.html.

Estlund, David (2008) *Democratic Authority: A Philosophical Framework*, Cambridge: Cambridge University Press.

Kettlewell, H. (1973) *The Evolution of Melanism*, London: Oxford University Press.

Kirsch, Julie (2011) "When is Ignorance Morally Objectionable?" in *The Morality and Global Justice Reader* (ed. Michael Boylan), Boulder, CO: Westview, pp. 51–64.

Kuhn, Steven and Serge Moresi (1995) "Pure and Utilitarian Prisoner's Dilemmas," Economics and Philosophy, 11, 123–133.

Miller, G. Tyler Jr. (1991) *Environmental Science: Sustaining the Earth*, Belmont, CA: Wadsworth Publishing.

Miller, Seumas (2009) *The Moral Foundations of Social Institutions: a Philosophical Study*, Cambridge: Cambridge University Press.

NOAA, on El niño and La niña, see at: www.pmel.noaa.gov/tao/elnino/el-nino-story.html, accessed May 2011.

Nowak, Martin A. (2006) "Five Rules for the Evolution of Cooperation," Science, 314, 1560–1563.

Taylor, Paul W. (2011) *Respect for Nature: A Theory of Environmental Ethics: 25th Anniversary Edition*, Princeton, NJ: Princeton University Press.

Smith, Robert L. (1992) *Elements of Ecology*, 3rd edn, New York: Harper Collins.

Sober, Elliott (1986) "Philosophical Problems for Environmentalism," in *The Preservation of Species* (ed. B. G. Norton), Princeton, NJ: Princeton University Press, pp. 173–194.

Tootill, Elizabeth (ed.) (1980) *Dictionary of Biology*, Maidenhead: Berkshire Intercontinental Kook Productions.

Unger, Peter (1996) *Living High and Letting Die*, New York: Oxford University Press.

Evaluating a Case Study

Developing a Practical Ethical Viewpoint

Your goal in this book is to respond critically to case studies on various aspects of Environmental Ethics. To do this, you must be able to assess the ethical impact of some critical factor(s) in situations that pose ethical problems. One factor in assessing the case is the ethical impact of the project/policy/action. This chapter and Chapters 3 through 6 end with an "Evaluating a Case Study" section that focuses on a particular exercise. These sections include case studies to which you can apply the insight you gained from the readings and discussion in the chapter. Because the information presented in these "Evaluating a Case Study" sections is cumulative, you should be able to write a complete critical response to a case study by the end of Chapter 6.

Macro and Micro Cases

Beginning with this chapter, each chapter will end with cases for you to consider. The cases section is divided into two categories, macro and micro. Each type of case employs a different point of view.

Macro Case. The macro case takes the perspective of someone in an executive position of authority who supervises or directs an organizational unit. His or her decisions will affect many people and resonate in a larger sociological sphere.

Micro Case. The micro case examines the perspective of someone at the proximate level of professional practice. Obviously, this case applies to more people than does the macro case.

Case Development. This book suggests one way to develop critical evaluations of ethical cases. In the "Evaluating a Case Study" sections, you will be asked to apply a specific skill to the cases presented. At the end of Chapter 6, you will be able to write an essay concerning the application of an ethical perspective to a specific problem.

Please note that although the cases presented here have fictional venues, they are based on composites of actual practice.

These end-of-chapter evaluations seek to bridge the gap between Normative Ethics and Applied Ethics. Skill in using Applied Ethics is very important, for this is where the practical decision making occurs. My approach in these essays is to allow you to employ techniques that you have been taught elsewhere in addition to those found in this text. Depending on your background in science or the public policy field, you can write a critical response to a case study that demonstrates your professional acumen along with your sensitivity to the ethical dimensions found in the situation you are examining. Classes that have few students with environmentally oriented backgrounds (such as in biology, ecology, and environmental policy) will deemphasize the fundamental details of science and concentrate instead on a less technical response.

Environmentalists often concentrate on the practices they so detest that they lose their ability to discern the rational grounds for their beliefs, a difficulty experienced in all professions.[1] But this is wrong. The "Evaluating a Case Study" sections will help you analyze both ethical and practical situations. The approach will invoke a technique that rates a proposal as having three levels of complexity: surface, medium, and deep. The level of interaction allows you to see at a glance how the competing areas of interest and ethical value conflict.

The five "Evaluating a Case Study" sections are intended to sequentially lead you to develop the abilities to write a critical response to a case study: (a) Developing a Practical Ethical Viewpoint, (b) Finding the Conflicts, (c) Assessing Embedded Levels, (d) Applying Ethical Issues, and (e) Structuring the Essay.

At the end of Chapters 3 through 6, you will be presented case studies to which you can apply your newfound skills. By the end of the term, you should be able to create an ethical impact statement of some sophistication.

Let us begin first by choosing an ethical theory and proceed to develop a practical viewpoint. Few people bother to choose an ethical theory; most pick up a few moral maxims that they apply when the occasion seems appropriate. The manner of this acquisition is often environment dependent, that is, having to do with their upbringing, friends, and the community(ies) in which they live. As such, their maxims reflect those other viewpoints.

The Personal Worldview Imperative enjoins us to develop a single comprehensive and internally coherent worldview that is good and that we will strive to act out in our lives (see Chapter 1). One component of this world-view is an ethical theory. Thus, each us must *develop* an ethical theory. This does not mean that we must all start from scratch. Those before us have done much good work. But we must personally choose an ethical theory and assume ownership for it as being the most correct theory in existence. It is not enough merely to accept someone else's theory without any active work on our part. We must go through the process of personal introspection and evaluation to determine what we think is best and to be open to ways we can improve the theory (in concept or in practice).

This process of making an ethical theory our own can take years. This course is only a few months. Does this pose a problem? Not really when you consider that part of the process of making an ethical theory our own involves provisional acceptance and testing of various moral maxims. Obviously, this testing has a limit. We should not test whether it is morally permissible to murder by going out and murdering various people. The testing I am advocating is a way to examine various moral commands and evaluate whether their application is consonant with other worldview values we hold. The process will perhaps go back and forth in a progressive dialectic until we have accepted or rejected the commands.

To begin this process of testing, we must identify the most prominent ethical theories and their tenets. Many books survey and evaluate the major ethical theories. In this series of textbooks, *Basic Ethics in Action*, I have written one such survey entitled, *Basic Ethics*. I would suggest that you refer either to that book or to another like it to obtain enough information to enable you to begin the process of choosing an ethical theory.

For the purposes of this book, I have highlighted four major theories: Utilitarianism, Deontology, Ethical Intuitionism, and Virtue Ethics. To begin the process, I recommend that you choose a single theory from these four (or from among others your instructor may offer) as your critical tool as you prepare for class. How do I know which viewpoint to choose? This is a difficult question. It concerns the justification of the various ethical theories.

Many criteria can be used to justify an ethical theory. One criterion is Naturalism. Each theory presupposes a naturalistic or nonnaturalistic epistemological standpoint. Naturalism is complicated; for our purposes, let us describe it as a view that holds that no entities or events are in principle beyond the domain of scientific explanation. Cognitive claims are valid only if they are based on accepted scientific modes.

Ethical Naturalism states that moral judgments are also merely a subclass of facts about the natural world that can be studied scientifically. From this study, we can determine moral correctness as a corollary of certain facts that can be scientifically investigated (e.g., how much pleasure various alternatives will produce for the group). Thus, utilitarians believe that moral judgments *are* judgments about which alternative will be most beneficial to some group's survival.

A utilitarian might point to the scientific study of nature and say that the instinct to seek pleasure is evidenced in all species. Furthermore, an evolutionary advantage seems to exist for those species that act for the benefit of the group against those that do not act in this way.

Many sociobiologists make this sort of claim. The main imperative of evolutionary theory is that a person's own genes be passed on to another generation. If passing on a person's own genes is impossible, the next best thing is to pass on the genes of the individual's relatives. Thus, seemingly altruistic behavior (such as a bird that stays behind in dangerous situations so that the group might survive) is really selfish because helping the group *is* helping the bird to pass on its genes (or those of its relatives).

Sociobiology, of course, is not universally accepted, nor is it necessary for a utilitarian to be a sociobiologist. However, this example does illustrate a type of justification that the utilitarian might make. He could move from the concept of group happiness in animals and extrapolate to humans. The supporting data are scientific; therefore, the theory is naturalistic.

Deontologists may or may not be naturalists. Since Deontology involves a duty-based ethics, the key question to be asked concerns how we know whether a binding duty exists to do such and such. Are all moral "oughts" derivable from factual, scientifically ascertainable "is" statements? If they are, then the deontologist is a naturalist. If they are not, then the deontologist is not a naturalist.

In his book *Reason and Morality*, Alan Gewirth claims to derive ought from is. There is no reference to knowledge claims that are not compatible with the scientific inquiry of natural objects. This would make Gewirth a naturalist. Kant and Donagan are somewhat different. Each refers to supernatural entities that are not scientifically supported. Kant spends considerable effort trying to define these boundaries in the "Transcendental Dialectic" section of his book *The Critique of Pure Reason*. This aside, neither Kant nor Donagan considered that a problem about integrating the factual and the normative existed.

If you are inclined to view reality as an extension of evolutionary biology or to believe that group advantage immediately entails a moral ought, then you are leaning toward Utilitarianism. If you think that people should act from pure duty alone without reference to anything except the rightness of the action, then Deontology is probably your preference.

The is-ought problem was sharpened by intuitionist G.E. Moore,[2] who rejected Ethical Naturalism because he believed it contained a fallacy (which he dubbed *the naturalistic fallacy)*. This fallacy claims that it is false to define goodness in terms of any natural property. This is so because good is not definable and because good is not subject to scientific examination. This is true because the factual realm is separate from the normative ought realm. The chasm between the two cannot be crossed.

Good for Moore is a unique, unanalyzable, non-natural property (as opposed, for example, to yellow which is a natural property). Clearly, scientific methods are of no use. Science can tell us things about yellow but can tell us nothing about the meaning of good. Other intuitionists also hold that we understand important moral terms and/

or moral maxims by cognitive means that are not scientific. Generally, these are immediate and cannot be justified in factual "is" language.

Intuitionism is therefore a non-naturalistic theory. Still, it has some remote connections to Naturalism. For example, one can point to the *plausibility* of accepting certain common moral maxims—such as a prohibition against murder—by reference to other societies. (In other words, since all societies prohibit murder, the prohibition against murder must be immediately apparent to all.) However, plausibility is not the same thing as exhaustive scientific demonstration. Justification in Intuitionism lies in its alleged unarguable truth that can be grasped in principle immediately by all.

If you are having trouble adopting any of the other theories and believe that acceptance or rejection of an ethical theory comes down to some sort of brute immediate acceptance, then you will probably want to accept Intuitionism as your ethical theory.

Finally, we turn to Virtue Ethics. This theory seems at first to be naturalistic. Aristotle lends credence to this when he talks about relying on the common opinions of people about what is considered to be a virtue. The common opinions could be gathered and reviewed much as a sociologist or anthropologist might do, and this "scientific" method would yield definitive results. Aristotle believed that some common agreement existed about a core set of virtues.

Justification, therefore, was not an issue for Aristotle. If we accept a worldview such as Aristotle presents, then we would all agree that everyone considers courage (for example) to be a virtue. The confirming data can be gathered and scientifically studied; ergo, it is naturalistic. The proof depends on the community that values these traits. This emphasis on community makes Virtue Ethics a favorite theory among those who call themselves *communitarians*. The communitarian begins with the group and its institutions and depends on individual members to submit to the authority of the group (or to change the group in ways it accepts).

How does Communitarianism affect today's pluralistic society? Some might argue that consensus about the virtues no longer exists nor does a single community to which we all belong. If there is no consensus as Aristotle envisioned, then what constitutes a virtue may collapse into a form of Intuitionism. For example, I think that X is a virtue. You think Y is a virtue. X and Y are mutually exclusive traits. You and I come from different communities/societies; therefore, we cannot come to an agreement. All each of us can say is I am right and you are wrong. Personal insight (Intuitionism) is all we have to justify our practices (to ourselves and to others).

If you believe that courage, wisdom, self-control, piety, and so forth are virtues in every society, then perhaps you will choose Virtue Ethics as your model.

To help you choose an ethical theory, try this exercise. Examine one or more of the following moral situations and (a) interpret what is right and wrong according to each of the four theories, (b) then give an argument that might be proposed according to each theory, and (c) state your own assessment of the strengths of each theory.

Situation One

You are the constable of a small, remote, rural town in Northern Ireland. The town is divided into the Catholics (20 percent minority) and the Protestants (80 percent majority). All Catholics live in one section of town on a peninsula jutting into the river just east of the main part of town.

One morning a young Protestant girl is found raped and murdered next to the town green. According to general consensus, a Catholic must have committed the crime. The Protestants form a citizens committee that demands the following of the constable: "We believe you to be a Catholic sympathizer, and we don't think you will press fast enough to bring this killer to justice. We know a Catholic committed the crime. We've sealed off the Catholic section of town; no one can go in or out. If you don't hand over the criminal by sundown, we will torch the entire Catholic section of town, killing all 1,000 people. Don't try to call for help. We've already disabled all communications."

You made every effort to find out who did it, but you made no progress. You could not find out. At one hour before sundown, you don't know what to do. Your deputy says, "Why don't we just pick a random Catholic and tell them he did it? At least we'd be saving 999 lives."

"But then I'd be responsible for killing an innocent man!" you reply.

"Better one innocent die and 999 be saved. After all, there's no way the two of us can stop the mob. You have to give them a scapegoat," the deputy responds.

Describe how each ethical theory might approach this situation. Which one is most consonant to your own worldview, and why?

Situation Two

You are on the executive committee of the XYZ organization of health care professionals. Each year the committee gives an award to one of its members who displays high moral character in his or her work. This year you are among the four judges for the award. There is some disagreement among the judges, however, about what constitutes a good person. The judges, besides yourself, are Ms. Smith, Mrs. Taylor, and Mr. Jones. The candidates for the award are Mr. Big and Mrs. Little.

Ms. Smith says that the award should go to Mr. Big because he saved a man from drowning. However, Mr. Jones demurred, saying that Mr. Big's motives are suspect because the man he saved was in the midst of a very big financial deal with Mr. Big. If the man had been allowed to drown, Mr. Big would have lost a lot of money. Ms. Smith said motives are not important but that the goodness of the act counts and the man who was saved runs a big business in town. Many people besides Mr. Big would have been hurt if he had not saved the man.

Mr. Jones said the award should go to Mrs. Little because she performed a kind act of charity in chairing the town's United Way Campaign this last year. Surely such an act could not be said to benefit Mrs. Little in any way (unlike Mr. Big).

Mrs. Taylor says that she is somewhat unsure about either Mr. Big or Mrs. Little because both of them have been recommended on the basis of a single good act. Mrs. Taylor believed that it would be better to choose a candidate who has shown over time to have performed many good actions and to be of good character. "After all," she said, "a single swallow does not make a spring." Mr. Jones and Ms. Smith scratched their heads at this remark and turned to you. Who is right?

Describe how each ethical theory might approach this situation. Which one is most consonant to your own worldview, and why?

Choosing an ethical theory is only the first step in developing a practical ethical viewpoint. A link between the normative theory and application of the theory is needed. In Chapter 1, I outlined my basic position concerning a personal worldview and how it might be utilized when applying an ethical theory. In the last section of Chapter 1, I outlined a principle of fair competition that I believe can be used to apply the general theory chosen to the moral decision at hand.

The point is that one important aspect of developing a practical ethical viewpoint is to challenge ourselves to think about and provisionally accept certain tenets necessary to effectively apply ethical principles to practice. These concepts should allow individuals to connect normative theories to the real-life problems that confront them.

Before addressing ethical cases, try first to provisionally accept one moral theory. Then try to determine what connecting principles or concepts are necessary to translate theory to practice. Concentrate your efforts on these connections. They will be very useful to you as you address what you see as the important issues residing in each case.

Notes

1 For a fuller discussion of this, see *Basic Ethics*, Chapter 7.

2 I cannot stress too much the impossibility of completely pigeonholing philosophers. In some important ways, Moore was an intuitionist because "good" had to be accepted as an unanalyzable, unnatural fact. Toward the end of *Principia Ethica*, however, he sounds much like an agathistic utilitarian, one who wishes to maximize the group's good. This mixture of labels among philosophers shows only that labels are limited in what they can do.

Ross and Rawls have deontological and intuitionistic aspects to their theories. Therefore, one label alone cannot adequately capture the spirit of their philosophy. In an introductory text, such as this one, labels are used to simplify—but hopefully not obfuscate—the dynamics present in these thinkers.

3

Worldview Arguments for Environmentalism

General Overview: Worldview arguments for environmentalism give more specification of the contextual nature of environmentalism. In the first subsection there are three essays that discuss one's relational identity with the land (land ethic); holistically with nature broadly understood (deep ecology); and with linking relational considerations with land to that of ethical–social considerations among humans (social ecology).

In the next subsection the range of social ecology finds focus in linking one's relationship with nature to the particular social problems involved in gender discrimination and oppression (eco-feminism).

Finally, in the last subsection, aesthetics is brought forward as a way to restructure a connection with another fundamental normative worldview source. Aesthetic value is brought forward as a way to specify a key contextual relationship with nature.

A. The Land Ethic and Deep Ecology

Overview: This subsection begins with Aldo Leopold (1887–1948). He wrote, among other things, the famous essay, "The Land Ethic." In it, Leopold argues that our relationship with the land is an ethical one in which we understand ourselves as being a part of a biotic community that includes the land. "Right" and "wrong" are to be understood through the well-being of the community as a whole. Under this understanding a person could justify farming, hunting, or other use of natural resources as long as the integrity, stability, and beauty of the particular natural community has been maintained. Such an outlook has been called *ethical holism* because ethical judgments about projects involving nature are made from this perspective. Pivotal to this understanding is the notion of a land pyramid in which one distinguishes the importance of the pyramid's lower layers: the soil and the primary producers. Leopold speaks of these in terms of an energy circuit. If lower levels are not nurtured, then those at the top are in jeopardy. Thus, a duty arises to the land and those primary

Environmental Ethics, Second Edition. Edited by Michael Boylan.

producers at the bottom of the pyramid. This duty is prudential in nature. Leopold creates a backdrop for many of the selections in this chapter.

The next author is Arne Naess (1912–2009). He was one of the founders of deep ecology. Deep ecology seeks to move the locus of value away from the individual to some other unit. One is reminded (by analogy) of Hegel's assertion (in the *Phenomenology of Spirit*) that the family is the basic unit, and of the communitarians who assert that some particular (robustly defined) community is the basic unit of human value. Utilitarians also tend to identify human communities as primitive units—though their "community" is rather changeable (since group calculations of happiness are subject to revision and alteration). In these cases, the individual's desires and plans can be overridden by those of the group.

The deep ecologists go one step further and identify the biosphere as the basic unit. Thus, not only an individual's desires, but also the self-interested desires of all the human community *can be overridden*. Naess' contrast of the shallow and the deep leads to a redefinition of the self along the lines of the Hindu concept of *atman*, or true self.[1] Through a plan of conscious simplicity of life ("simple in means and rich in ends"), Naess proposes a profound and fundamental shift in the way we situate ourselves vis-à-vis the natural environment. In his essay, Naess contrasts the viewpoint of mainstream anthropocentric environmentalists (shallow ecology) with the position he is advocating (deep ecology). To this end, he calls for seven principles: (1) rejection of man-in-environment image in favor of the relational, total-field image; (2) biosphere egalitarianism, in principle; (3) principles of diversity and symbiosis; (4) anti-class posture; (5) fight against pollution and resource depletion; (6) complexity, not complication; and (7) local autonomy and decentralization. In this way, Naess redefines individual rights and responsibilities.

Murray Bookchin (1921–2006) was a social ecologist. Social ecologists differ from deep ecologists because social ecologists do not think that deep ecologists give enough emphasis to the roles that capitalism and government play in nature's destruction. The deep ecologists' reply is that such an emphasis on human institutions makes social ecology anthropocentric rather than biocentric (as deep ecologists advocate). Bookchin's worldview has elements of Marxism and deep ecology that are united to a more general purpose: using the worldview created by these values to reform society from top to bottom. This view has been characterized as "social/political anarchism" and "libertarian social ecology." Unlike most Marxists, Bookchin does not believe in economic determinism or in the dictatorship of the proletariat. The aspect of Marx that Bookchin most admires is the analysis of social domination. We can easily see how accepting the tenets of deep ecology (especially the redefinition of self) can lead to a more cooperative social organization. This is really at the heart of Bookchin's approach.

B. Eco-Feminism and Social Justice

Overview: Eco-feminism is a term coined by Françoise d'Eaubonne (1920–2005). The concept is that a connection exists between the aspects of domination that humans exert on the biosphere and the male-dominated social system that exerts domination over women. The various aspects of this logic of domination are central to eco-feminism.

Carolyn Merchant's classic essay shows how mainstream feminist theory might profit from adopting the eco-feminist model. Behind this model are assumptions that are not too dissimilar to Bookchin's previous essay, except that the focus is on the domination of women in the context of domination, in general. Merchant is interested in putting these connections into a comparative context with: (a) liberal feminism; (b) Marxist feminism; (c) radical feminism; and (d) socialist feminism. The ultimate end of this analysis is to create a synergy of interests, tactics, and intended results.

Karen J. Warren seeks to portray eco-feminism as an essential element in any environmental ethical theory. She identifies eight points of feminism that center on the pluralism and contextualism that are missing in the current social climate. A key feature that should be noted is that Warren does not believe that any objective social–ethical theory can ever be proposed. The question then becomes: which biased theory is better? After proposing the feminist position, she emends each of the eight points with eco-feminism objectives to show how similar these two worldviews are, and that they should therefore be accepted as a package.

Wanda Teays sets out a concrete instance where she sees domination gone haywire. It has to do with the patenting of seeds. The 1980 Supreme Court decision in *Diamond* v. *Chakrabarty* was groundbreaking by affirming that living things could be patented. From the human-modified bacterium at the center of that case to plants, animals, and human embryos, there has been a rush to patent genetically engineered organisms. The significance of this on our lives—and our environment—is still unfolding. I will examine aspects of the Court's reasoning in this case and the later *Monsanto* v. *Homan McFarling* and *Monsanto* v. *Geertson Seed Farm*. The shift from the word "seed" to "intellectual property" has moved the discussion to a more abstract and legalistic level, putting farmers at a disadvantage. The dissenting opinions raise key concerns that deserve further thought. Aristotle's Virtue Ethics and Feminist Ethics give us some tools for examining the patenting of living organisms—and the commercialization of life forms that has followed in its wake.

C. Aesthetics

Overview: I have often listed aesthetics as a principal source of worldview normative value.[2] It is therefore natural to examine how this independent value strain affects one's commitment to environmentalism.

Shifting to aesthetics, in the first essay Janna Thompson begins her essay with the assertion that nature is beautiful. This is a simple but powerful statement. G.E. Moore viewed beauty (whether it was found in art or in nature) to be an intrinsic good. The ethical imperative, according to Moore, is to increase the total amount of good in the world. If all people have a duty to be ethical, then (by the same reasoning), all people have a duty to promote and protect beauty (whether it be art or nature). By diminishing nature, a person diminishes the total amount of good in the world and thus violates Moore's dictum.[3]

Thompson's argument also depends on whether beauty (in art or in nature) is intrinsically or instrumentally good. Much of this essay addresses this issue and seeks to create a standard that makes the aesthetic standard plausible.

In the next essay of the section, Michael Boylan examines a rather different approach, which broaches on solving the so-called "is-ought" problem. The process is set out in a seventeen-step argument that begins with a person regarding some artifact or natural object and how the very process of factual assessment also involves a personal valuation. This is part of the human psyche. If the act of valuing is positive, then an ongoing interaction with the artifact or natural object is engaged, ending with an obligation to protect and defend the object against threats to its existence. Since one cannot merely give lip service to an obligation to protect and defend (because of the fourth stage of the personal worldview imperative), this argument provides both a personal, practical incentive for protective environmental action, and a community approach as well. Together, these contend that there is a worldview-based aesthetic approach to command environmental nurturing and protection.

Notes

1 Arne Naess (1985) "Identification as a Source of Deep Ecological Attitudes," in *Deep Ecology* (ed. Michael Tobias), San Diego, CA: Avant Books; pp. 256–270.
2 See Michael Boylan (2004) *A Just Society*, Lanham, MD: Rowman & Littlefield, ch. 4; cf. Michael Boylan (2011) *Morality and Global Justice: Justifications and Applications*, Boulder, CO: Westview; pp. 24–25.
3 Moore's position can be described as a sort of utilitarianism: agathistic utilitarianism (maximizing the amount of good rather than the traditional definition of maximizing pleasure or happiness).

A. The Land Ethic and Deep Ecology

The Land Ethic

ALDO LEOPOLD

When god-like Odysseus returned from the wars in Troy, he hanged all on one rope a dozen slave-girls of his household whom he suspected of misbehavior during his absence.

Aldo Leopold, "The Land Ethic," *A Sand County Almanac: and Sketches Here and There*, Oxford: Oxford University Press, 1949; pp. 41–48. Reprinted with the permission of Oxford University Press.

This hanging involved no question of propriety. The girls were property. The disposal of property was then, as now, a matter of expediency, not of right and wrong.

Concepts of right and wrong were not lacking from Odysseus' Greece: witness the fidelity of his wife through the long years before at last his blackprowed galleys clove the wine-dark seas for home. The ethical structure of that day covered wives, but had not yet been extended to human chattels. During the three thousand years which have since elapsed, ethical criteria have been extended to many fields of conduct, with corresponding shrinkages in those judged by expediency only.

The Ethical Sequence

This extension of ethics, so far studied only by philosophers, is actually a process in ecological evolution. Its sequences may be described in ecological as well as in philosophical terms. An ethic, ecologically, is a limitation on freedom of action in the struggle for existence. An ethic, philosophically, is a differentiation of social from anti-social conduct. These are two definitions of one thing. The thing has its origin in the tendency of interdependent individuals or groups to evolve modes of co-operation. The ecologist calls these symbioses. Politics and economics are advanced symbioses in which the original free-for-all competition has been replaced, in part, by co-operative mechanisms with an ethical content.

The complexity of co-operative mechanisms has increased with population density, and with the efficiency of tools. It was simpler, for example, to define the anti-social uses of sticks and stones in the days of the mastodons than of bullets and billboards in the age of motors.

The first ethics dealt with the relation between individuals; the Mosaic Decalogue is an example. Later accretions dealt with the relation between the individual and society. The Golden Rule tries to integrate the individual to society; democracy to integrate social organization to the individual.

There is as yet no ethic dealing with man's relation to land and to the animals and plants which grow upon it. Land, like Odysseus' slave-girls, is still property. The land-relation is still strictly economic, entailing privileges but not obligations.

The extension of ethics to this third element in human environment is, if I read the evidence correctly, an evolutionary possibility and an ecological necessity. It is the third step in a sequence. The first two have already been taken. Individual thinkers since the days of Ezekiel and Isaiah have asserted that the despoliation of land is not only inexpedient but wrong. Society, however, has not yet affirmed their belief. I regard the present conservation movement as the embryo of such an affirmation.

An ethic may be regarded as a mode of guidance for meeting ecological situations so new or intricate, or involving such deferred reactions, that the path of social expediency is not discernible to the average individual. Animal instincts are modes of guidance for the individual in meeting such situations. Ethics are possibly a kind of community instinct in-the-making.

The Community Concept

All ethics so far evolved rest upon a single premise: that the individual is a member of a community of interdependent parts. His instincts prompt him to compete for his place in the community, but his ethics prompt him also to co-operate (perhaps in order that there may be a place to compete for).

The land ethic simply enlarges the boundaries of the community to include soils, waters, plants, and animals, or collectively: the land.

This sounds simple: do we not already sing our love for and obligation to the land of the free and the home of the brave? Yes, but just what and whom do we love? Certainly not the soil, which we are sending helter-skelter down-river. Certainly not the waters, which we assume have no function except to turn turbines, float barges, and carry off sewage. Certainly not the plants, of which we exterminate whole communities without batting an eye. Certainly not the animals, of which we have already extirpated many of the largest and most beautiful species. A land ethic of course cannot prevent the alteration, management, and use of these 'resources,' but it does affirm their right to continued existence, and, at least in spots, their continued existence in a natural state.

In short, a land ethic changes the role of *Homo sapiens* from conqueror of the land-community to plain member and citizen of it. It implies respect for his fellow-members, and also respect for the community as such.

The Land Pyramid

An ethic to supplement and guide the economic relation to land presupposes the existence of some mental image of land as a biotic mechanism. We can be ethical only in relation to something we can see, feel, understand, love, or otherwise have faith in.

The image commonly employed in conservation education is "the balance of nature." For reasons too lengthy to detail here, this figure of speech fails to describe accurately what little we know about the land mechanism. A much truer image is the one employed in ecology: the biotic pyramid. I shall first sketch the pyramid as a symbol of land, and later develop some of its implications in terms of land-use.

Plants absorb energy from the sun. This energy flows through a circuit called the biota, which may be represented by a pyramid consisting of layers. The bottom layer is the soil. A plant layer rests on the soil, an insect layer on the plants, a bird and rodent layer on the insects, and so on up through various animal groups to the apex layer, which consists of the larger carnivores.

The species of a layer are alike not in where they came from, or in what they look like, but rather in what they eat. Each successive layer depends on those below it for food and often for other services, and each in turn furnishes food and services to those above. Proceeding upward, each successive layer decreases in numerical abundance. Thus, for every carnivore there are hundreds of his prey, thousands of their prey, millions of insects, uncountable plants. The pyramidal form of the system reflects this numerical progression from apex to base. Man shares an intermediate layer with the bears, raccoons, and squirrels which eat both meat and vegetables.

The lines of dependency for food and other services are called food chains. Thus soil-oak-deer-Indian is a chain that has now been largely converted to soil-corn-cow-farmer. Each species, including ourselves, is a link in many chains. The deer eats a hundred plants other than oak, and the cow a hundred plants other than corn. Both, then, are links in a hundred chains. The pyramid is a tangle of chains so complex as to seem disorderly, yet the stability of the system proves it to be a highly organized structure. Its functioning depends on the co-operation and competition of its diverse parts.

In the beginning, the pyramid of life was low and squat; the food chains short and simple. Evolution has added layer after layer, link after link. Man is one of thousands of accretions to the height and complexity of the pyramid. Science has given us many doubts, but it has given us at least one certainty: the trend of evolution is to elaborate and diversify the biota.

Land, then, is not merely soil; it is a fountain of energy flowing through a circuit of soils, plants, and animals. Food chains are the living channels which conduct energy upward; death and decay return it to the soil. The circuit is not closed; some energy is dissipated in decay, some is added by absorption from the air, some is stored in soils, peats, and long-lived forests; but it is a sustained circuit, like a slowly augmented revolving fund of life. There is always a net loss by downhill wash, but this is normally small and offset by the decay of rocks. It is deposited in the ocean and, in the course of geological time, raised to form new lands and new pyramids.

The velocity and character of the upward flow of energy depend on the complex structure of the plant and animal community, much as the upward flow of sap in a tree depends on its complex cellular organization. Without this complexity, normal circulation would presumably not occur. Structure means the characteristic numbers, as well as the characteristic kinds and functions, of the component species. This interdependence between the complex structure of the land and its smooth functioning as an energy unit is one of its basic attributes.

When a change occurs in one part of the circuit, many other parts must adjust themselves to it. Change does not necessarily obstruct or divert the flow of energy; evolution is a long series of self-induced changes, the net result of which has been to elaborate the flow mechanism and to lengthen the circuit. Evolutionary changes, however, are usually slow and local. Man's invention of tools has enabled him to make changes of unprecedented violence, rapidity, and scope.

One change is in the composition of floras and faunas. The larger predators are lopped off the apex of the pyramid; food chains, for the first time in history, become shorter rather than longer. Domesticated species from other lands are substituted for wild ones, and wild ones are moved to new habitats. In this world-wide pooling of faunas and floras, some species get out of bounds as pests and diseases, others are extinguished. Such effects are seldom intended or foreseen: they represent unpredicted and often untraceable readjustments in the structure. Agricultural science is largely a race between the emergence of new pests and the emergence of new techniques for their control.

Another change touches the flow of energy through plants and animals and its return to the soil. Fertility is the ability of soil to receive, store, and release energy. Agriculture, by overdrafts on the soil, or by too radical a substitution of domestic for native species in the superstructure, may derange the channels of flow or deplete storage. Soils depleted of their storage or of the organic matter which anchors it, wash away faster than they form. This is erosion.

Waters, like soil, are part of the energy circuit. Industry, by polluting waters or obstructing them with dams, may exclude the plants and animals necessary to keep energy in circulation.

Transportation brings about another basic change: the plants or animals grown in one region are now consumed and returned to the soil in another. Transportation taps the energy stored in rocks, and in the air, and uses it elsewhere; thus we fertilize the garden with nitrogen gleaned by the guano birds from the fishes of seas on the other side of the Equator. Thus the formerly localized and self-contained circuits are pooled on a world-wide scale.

The process of altering the pyramid for human occupation releases stored energy, and this often gives rise, during the pioneering period, to a deceptive exuberance of plant and animal life, both wild and tame. These releases of biotic capital tend to becloud or postpone the penalties of violence.

This thumbnail sketch of land as an energy circuit conveys three basic ideas:

1. That land is not merely soil.
2. That the native plants and animals kept the energy circuit open; others may or may not.
3. That man-made changes are of a different order than evolutionary changes, and have effects more comprehensive than is intended or foreseen.

These ideas, collectively, raise two basic issues: Can the land adjust itself to the new order? Can the desired alterations be accomplished with less violence?

Biotas seem to differ in their capacity to sustain violent conversion. Western Europe, for example, carries a far different pyramid than Caesar found there. Some large animals are lost; swampy forests have become meadows or plowland; many new plants and animals are introduced, some of which escape as pests; the remaining natives are greatly changed in distribution and abundance. Yet the soil is still there and, with the help of imported nutrients, still fertile; the waters flow normally; the new structure seems to function and to persist. There is no visible stoppage or derangement of the circuit.

Western Europe, then, has a resistant biota. Its inner processes are tough, elastic, resistant to strain. No matter how violent the alterations, the pyramid, so far, has developed some new *modus vivendi* which preserves its habitability for man, and for most of the other natives.

Japan seems to present another instance of radical conversion without disorganization.

Most other civilized regions, and some as yet barely touched by civilization, display various stages of disorganization, varying from initial symptoms to advanced wastage. In Asia Minor and North Africa diagnosis is confused by climatic changes, which may have been either the cause or the effect of advanced wastage. In the United States the degree of disorganization varies locally; it is worst in the South-west, the Ozarks, and parts of the South, and least in New England and the North-west. Better land-uses may still arrest it in the less advanced regions. In parts of Mexico, South America,

South Africa, and Australia a violent and accelerating wastage is in progress, but I cannot assess the prospects.

This almost world-wide display of disorganization in the land seems to be similar to disease in an animal, except that it never culminates in complete disorganization or death. The land recovers, but at some reduced level of complexity, and with a reduced carrying capacity for people, plants, and animals. Many biotas currently regarded as "lands of opportunity" are in fact already subsisting on exploitative agriculture, i.e., they have already exceeded their sustained carrying capacity. Most of South America is over populated in this sense.

In arid regions we attempt to offset the process of wastage by reclamation, but it is only too evident that the prospective longevity of reclamation projects is often short. In our own West, the best of them may not last a century.

The combined evidence of history and ecology seems to support one general deduction: the less violent the man-made changes, the greater the probability of successful readjustment in the pyramid. Violence, in turn, varies with human population density; a dense population requires a more violent conversion. In this respect, North America has a better chance for permanence than Europe, if she can contrive to limit her density.

This deduction runs counter to our current philosophy, which assumes that because a small increase in density enriched human life, that an indefinite increase will enrich it indefinitely. Ecology knows of no density relationship that holds for indefinitely wide limits. All gains from density are subject to a law of diminishing returns.

Whatever may be the equation for men and land, it is improbable that we as yet know all its terms. Recent discoveries in mineral and vitamin nutrition reveal unsuspected dependencies in the up-circuit: incredibly minute quantities of certain substances determine the value of soils to plants, of plants to animals. What of the down-circuit? What of the vanishing species, the preservation of which we now regard as an esthetic luxury? They helped build the soil; in what unsuspected ways may they be essential to its maintenance? Professor Weaver proposes that we use prairie flowers to reflocculate the wasting soils of the dust bowl: who knows for what purpose cranes and condors, otters and grizzlies may some day be used?

The Outlook

It is inconceivable to me that an ethical relation to land can exist without love, respect, and admiration for land, and a high regard for its value. By value, I of course mean something far broader than mere economic value; I mean value in the philosophical sense.

Perhaps the most serious obstacle impeding the evolution of a land ethic is the fact that our educational and economic system is headed away from, rather than toward, an intense consciousness of land. Your true modern is separated from the land by many middlemen, and by innumerable physical gadgets. He has no vital relation to it; to him it is the space between cities on which crops grow. Turn him loose for a day on the land, and if the spot does not happen to be a golf links or a "scenic" area, he is bored stiff. If crops could be raised by hydroponics instead of farming, it would suit him very well. Synthetic substitutes for wood, leather, wool, and other natural land products suit him better than the originals. In short, land is something he has "outgrown."

Almost equally serious as an obstacle to a land ethic is the attitude of the farmer for whom the land is still an adversary, or a taskmaster that keeps him in slavery. Theoretically, the mechanization of farming ought to cut the farmer's chains, but whether it really does is debatable.

One of the requisites for an ecological comprehension of land is an understanding of ecology, and this is by no means co-extensive with "education"; in fact, much higher education seems deliberately to avoid ecological concepts. An understanding of ecology does not necessarily originate in courses bearing ecological labels; it is quite as likely to be labeled geography, botany, agronomy, history, or economics. This is as it should be, but whatever the label, ecological training is scarce.

The case for a land ethic would appear hopeless but for the minority which is in obvious revolt against these "modern" trends.

The "key-log" which must be moved to release the evolutionary process for an ethic is simply this: quit thinking about decent land-use as solely an economic problem. Examine each question in terms of what is ethically and esthetically right, as well as what is economically expedient. A thing is right when it tends to preserve the integrity, stability, and beauty of the biotic community. It is wrong when it tends otherwise.

It of course goes without saying that economic feasibility limits the tether of what can or cannot be done for land. It always has and it always will. The fallacy the economic determinists have tied around our collective neck, and which we now need to cast off, is the belief that economics determines *all* land-use. This is simply not true. An innumerable host of actions and attitudes, comprising perhaps the bulk of all land relations, is determined by the land-users' tastes and predilections, rather than by his purse. The bulk of all land relations hinges on investments of time, forethought, skill, and faith rather than on investments of cash. As a land-user thinketh, so is he.

I have purposely presented the land ethic as a product of social evolution because nothing so important as an ethic is ever "written." Only the most superficial student of history supposes that Moses "wrote" the Decalogue; it evolved in the minds of a thinking community, and Moses wrote a tentative summary of it for a "seminar." I say tentative because evolution never stops.

The evolution of a land ethic is an intellectual as well as emotional process. Conservation is paved with good intentions which prove to be futile, or even dangerous, because they are devoid of critical understanding either of the land, or of economic land-use. I think it is a truism that as the ethical frontier advances from the individual to the community, its intellectual content increases.

The mechanism of operation is the same for any ethic: social approbation for right actions: social disapproval for wrong actions.

By and large, our present problem is one of attitudes and implements. We are remodeling the Alhambra with a steam-shovel, and we are proud of our yardage. We shall hardly relinquish the shovel which after all has many good points, but we are in need of gentler and more objective criteria for its successful use.

The Shallow and the Deep, Long-Range Ecology Movement

A Summary

ARNE NAESS

Ecologically responsible policies are concerned only in part with pollution and resource depletion. There are deeper concerns which touch upon principles of diversity, complexity, autonomy, decentralization, symbiosis, egalitarianism, and classlessness.

The emergence of ecologists from their former relative obscurity marks a turning-point in our scientific communities. But their message is twisted and misused. A shallow, but presently rather powerful movement, and a deep, but less influential movement, compete for our attention. I shall make an effort to characterize the two.

1. The Shallow Ecology Movement

Fight against pollution and resource depletion. Central objective: the health and affluence of people in the developed countries.

2. The Deep Ecology Movement

(1) Rejection of the man-in-environment image in favour of the relational, total-field image. Organisms as knots in the biospherical net or field of intrinsic relations. An intrinsic relation between two things *A* and *B* is such that the relation belongs to the definitions or basic constitutions of *A* and *B*, so that without the relation, *A* and *B* are no longer the same things. The total-field model dissolves not only the man-in-environment concept, but every compact thing-in-milieu concept—except when talking at a superficial or preliminary level of communication.

(2) Biospherical egalitarianism, in principle. The 'in principle' clause is inserted because any realistic praxis necessitates some killing, exploitation, and suppression. The ecological field-worker acquires a deep-seated respect, or even veneration, for ways and forms of life. He reaches an understanding from within, a kind of understanding that others reserve for fellow men and for a narrow section of ways and

Arne Naess, "The Shallow and the Deep, Long-Range Ecology Movement," *Inquiry*, 16 (1983): 95–100. Reprinted with permission of Taylor & Francis Journals.

forms of life. To the ecological field-worker, *the equal right to live and blossom* is an intuitively clear and obvious value axiom. Its restriction to humans is an anthropocentrism with detrimental effects upon the life quality of humans themselves. This quality depends in part upon the deep pleasure and satisfaction we receive from close partnership with other forms of life. The attempt to ignore our dependence and to establish a master–slave role has contributed to the alienation of man from himself.

Ecological egalitarianism implies the reinterpretation of the future-research variable, 'level of crowding', so that *general* mammalian crowding and loss of life-equality is taken seriously, not only human crowding. (Research on the high requirements of free space of certain mammals has, incidentally, suggested that theorists of human urbanism have largely underestimated human life-space requirements. Behavioural crowding symptoms [neuroses, aggressiveness, loss of traditions ...] are largely the same among mammals.)

(3) Principles of diversity and of symbiosis. Diversity enhances the potentialities of survival, the chances of new modes of life, the richness of forms. And the so-called struggle of life, and survival of the fittest, should be interpreted in the sense of ability to coexist and cooperate in complex relationships, rather than ability to kill, exploit, and suppress. 'Live and let live' is a more powerful ecological principle than 'Either you or me'.

The latter tends to reduce the multiplicity of kinds of forms of life, and also to create destruction within the communities of the same species. Ecologically inspired attitudes therefore favour diversity of human ways of life, of cultures, of occupations, of economies. They support the fight against economic and cultural, as much as military, invasion and domination, and they are opposed to the annihilation of seals and whales as much as to that of human tribes or cultures.

(4) Anti-class posture. Diversity of human ways of life is in part due to (intended or unintended) exploitation and suppression on the part of certain groups. The exploiter lives differently from the exploited, but both are adversely affected in their potentialities of self-realization. The principle of diversity does not cover differences due merely to certain attitudes or behaviours forcibly blocked or restrained. The principles of ecological egalitarianism and of symbiosis support the same anti-class posture. The ecological attitude favours the extension of all three principles to any group conflicts, including those of today between developing and developed nations. The three principles also favour extreme caution towards any over-all plans for the future, except those consistent with wide and widening classless diversity.

(5) Fight against pollution and resource depletion. In this fight ecologists have found powerful supporters, but sometimes to the detriment of their total stand. This happens when attention is focused on pollution and resource depletion rather than on the other points, or when projects are implemented which reduce pollution but increase evils of the other kinds. Thus, if prices of life necessities increase because of the installation of anti-pollution devices, class differences increase too. An ethics of responsibility implies that ecologists do not serve the shallow, but the deep ecological movement. That is, not only point (5), but all seven points must be considered together.

Ecologists are irreplaceable informants in any society, whatever their political colour. If well organized, they have the power to reject jobs in which they submit themselves to institutions or to planners with limited ecological perspectives. As it is now, ecologists sometimes serve masters who deliberately ignore the wider perspectives.

(6) Complexity, not complication. The theory of ecosystems contains an important distinction between what is complicated without any Gestalt or unifying principles—we may think of finding our way through a chaotic city—and what is complex. A multiplicity of more or less lawful, interacting factors may operate together to form a unity, a system. We make a shoe or use a map or integrate a variety of activities into a workaday pattern. Organisms, ways of life, and interactions in the biosphere in general, exhibit complexity of such an astoundingly high level as to colour the general outlook of ecologists. Such complexity makes thinking in terms of vast systems inevitable. It also makes for a keen, steady perception of the profound *human ignorance* of biospherical relationships and therefore of the effect of disburbances.

Applied to humans, the complexity-not-complication principle favours division of labour, *not fragmentation of labour*. It favours integrated actions in which the whole person is active, not mere reactions. It favours complex economies, an integrated variety of means of living. (Combinations of industrial and agricultural activity, of intellectual and manual work, of specialized and non-specialized occupations, of urban and non-urban activity, of work in city and recreation in nature with recreation in city and work in nature …)

It favours soft technique and 'soft future-research', less prognosis, more clarification of possibilities. More sensitivity towards continuity and live traditions, and—most importantly—towards our state of ignorance.

The implementation of ecologically responsible policies requires in this century an exponential growth of technical skill and invention—but in new directions, directions which today are not consistently and liberally supported by the research policy organs of our nation-states.

(7) Local autonomy and decentralization. The vulnerability of a form of life is roughly proportional to the weight of influences from afar, from outside the local region in which that form has obtained an ecological equilibrium. This lends support to our efforts to strengthen local self-government and material and mental self-sufficiency. But these efforts presuppose an impetus towards decentralization. Pollution problems, including those of thermal pollution and recirculation of materials, also lead us in this direction, because increased local autonomy, if we are able to keep other factors constant, reduces energy consumption. (Compare an approximately self-sufficient locality with one requiring the importation of foodstuff, materials for house construction, fuel and skilled labour from other continents. The former may use only five per cent of the energy used by the latter.) Local autonomy is strengthened by a reduction in the number of links in the hierarchical chains of decision (For example a chain consisting of local board, municipal council, highest sub-national decision-maker, a state-wide institution in a state federation, a federal national government institution, a coalition of nations, and of institutions, e.g. E.E.C. top levels, and a global institution, can be reduced to one made up of local board, nation-wide institution, and global institution.) Even if a decision follows majority rules at each step, many local interests may be dropped along the line, if it is too long.

Summing up, then, it should, first of all, be borne in mind that the norms and tendencies of the Deep Ecology movement are not derived from ecology by logic or induction. Ecological knowledge and the lifestyle of the ecological field-worker have *suggested, inspired, and fortified* the perspectives of the Deep Ecology movement. Many of the formulations in the above seven-point survey are rather vague generalizations, only tenable if made more precise in certain directions. But all over the world the inspiration from ecology has shown remarkable convergencies. The survey does not pretend to be more than one of the possible condensed codifications of these convergencies.

Secondly, it should be fully appreciated that the significant tenets of the Deep Ecology movement are clearly and forcefully *normative*. They express a value priority system only in part based on results (or lack of results, cf. point [6]) of scientific research. Today, ecologists try to influence policy-making bodies largely through threats, through predictions concerning pollutants and resource depletion, knowing that policy-makers accept at least certain minimum *norms* concerning health and just distribution. But it is clear that there is a vast number of people in all countries, and even a considerable number of people in power, who accept as valid the wider norms and values characteristic of the Deep Ecology movement. There are political potentials in this movement which should not be overlooked and which have little to do with pollution and resource depletion. In plotting possible futures, the norms should be freely used and elaborated.

Thirdly, in so far as ecology movements deserve our attention, they are *ecophilosophical* rather then ecological. Ecology is a *limited* science which makes *use* of scientific methods. Philosophy is the most general forum of debate on fundamentals, descriptive as well as prescriptive, and political philosophy is one of its subsections. By an *ecosophy* I mean a philosophy of ecological harmony or equilibrium. A philosophy as a kind of *sofia* wisdom, is openly normative, it contains *both* norms, rules, postulates, value priority announcements *and* hypotheses concerning the state of affairs in our universe. Wisdom is policy wisdom, prescription, not only scientific description and prediction.

The details of an ecosophy will show many variations due to significant differences concerning not only 'facts' of pollution, resources, population, etc., but also value priorities. Today, however, the seven points listed provide one unified framework for ecosophical systems.

In general system theory, systems are mostly conceived in terms of causally or functionally interacting or interrelated items. An ecosophy, however, is more like a system of the kind constructed by Aristotle or Spinoza. It is expressed verbally as a set of sentences with a variety of functions, descriptive and prescriptive. The basic relation is that between subsets of premisses and subsets of conclusions, that is, the relation of derivability. The relevant notions of derivability may be classed according to rigour, with logical and mathematical deductions topping the list, but also according to how much is implicitly taken for granted. An exposition of an ecosophy must necessarily be only moderately precise considering the vast scope of relevant ecological and normative (social, political, ethical) material. At the moment, ecosophy might profitably use models of systems, rough approximations of global systematizations. It is the global character, not preciseness in detail, which distinguishes an ecosophy. It articulates and integrates the efforts of an ideal ecological team, a team comprising not only scientists from an extreme variety of disciplines, but also students of politics and active policy-makers.

Under the name of *ecologism*, various deviations from the deep movement have been championed—primarily with a one-sided stress on pollution and resource depletion, but also with a neglect of the great differences between under- and over-developed countries in favour of a vague global approach. The global approach is essential, but regional differences must largely determine policies in the coming years.

Selected Literature

Commoner, B., *The Closing Circle: Nature, Man, and Technology*, Alfred A. Knopf, New York 1971.

Ehrlich, P. R. and A. H., *Population, Resources, Environment: Issues in Human Ecology*, 2nd ed., W. H. Freeman & Co., San Francisco 1972.

Ellul, J., *The Technological Society*, English ed., Alfred A. Knopf, New York 1964.

Glacken, C. J., *Traces on the Rhodian Shore. Nature and Culture in Western Thought*, University of California Press, Berkeley 1967.

Kato, H., 'The Effects of Crowding', Quality of Life Conference, Oberhausen, April 1972.

McHarg, Ian L., *Design with Nature*, 1969. Paperback 1971, Doubleday & Co., New York.

Meynaud, J., *Technocracy*, English ed., Free Press of Glencoe, Chicago 1969.

Mishan, E. J., *Technology and Growth: The Price We Pay*, Frederick A. Praeger, New York 1970.

Odum, E. P., *Fundamentals of Ecology*, 3rd ed., W. E. Saunders Co., Philadelphia 1971.

Shepard, Paul, *Man in the Landscape*, A. A. Knopf, New York.

What Is Social Ecology?

Murray Bookchin

We are clearly beleaguered by an ecological crisis of monumental proportions—a crisis that visibly stems from the ruthless exploitation and pollution of the planet. We rightly attribute the social sources of this crisis to a competitive marketplace spirit that reduces the entire world of life, including humanity, to merchandisable objects, to mere commodities with price tags that are to be sold for profit and economic expansion. The ideology of this spirit is expressed in the notorious marketplace maxim: "Grow or die!"—a maxim that identifies limitless growth with "progress" and the "mastery of nature" with "civilization." The results of this tide of exploitation and pollution have been grim enough to yield serious forecasts of complete planetary breakdown, a degree of devastation of soil, forests, waterways, and atmosphere that has no precedent in the history of our species.

An original essay from the 1st edition of this volume.

In this respect, our market-oriented society is unique in contrast with other societies in that it places no limits on growth and egotism. The antisocial principles that "rugged individualism" is the primary motive for social improvement and competition the engine for social progress stand sharply at odds with all past eras that valued selflessness as the authentic trait of human nobility and cooperation as the authentic evidence of social virtue, however much these prized attributes were honored in the breach. Our marketplace society has, in effect, made the worst features of earlier times into its more honored values and exhibited a degree of brutality in the global wars of this century that makes the cruelties of history seem mild by comparison.

In our discussions of modern ecological and social crises, we tend to ignore a more underlying mentality of domination that humans have used for centuries to justify the domination of each other and, by extension, of nature. I refer to an image of the natural world that sees nature itself as "blind," "mute," "cruel," "competitive," and "stingy," a seemingly demonic "realm of necessity" that opposes "man's" striving for freedom and self-realization. Here, "man" seems to confront a hostile "otherness" against which he must oppose his own powers of toil and guile. History is thus presented to us as a Promethean drama in which "man" heroically defies and willfully asserts himself against a brutally hostile and unyielding natural world. Progress is seen as the extrication of humanity from the muck of a mindless, unthinking, and brutish domain or what Jean Paul Sartre so contemptuously called the "slime of history," into the presumably clear light of reason and civilization.

This image of a demonic and hostile nature goes back to the Greek world and even earlier, to the Gilgamesh Epic of Sumerian society. But it reached its high point during the past two centuries, particularly in the Victorian Age, and persists in our thinking today. Ironically, the idea of a "blind," "mute," "cruel," "competitive," and "stingy" nature forms the basis for the very social sciences and humanities that profess to provide us with a civilized alternative to nature's "brutishness" and "law of claw and fang." Even as these disciplines stress the "unbridgeable gulf" between nature and society in the classical tradition of a dualism between the physical and the mental, economics literally defines itself as the study of "scarce resources" (read: "stingy nature") and "unlimited needs," essentially rearing itself on the interconnection between nature and humanity. By the same token, sociology sees itself as the analysis of "man's" ascent from "animality." Psychology, in turn, particularly in its Freudian form, is focused on the control of humanity's unruly "internal nature" through rationality and the imperatives imposed on it by "civilization"—with the hidden agenda of sublimating human powers in the project of controlling "external nature."

Many class theories of social development, particularly Marxian socialism, have been rooted in the belief that the "domination of man by man" emerges from the need to "dominate nature," presumably with the result that once nature is subjugated, humanity will be cleansed of the "slime of history" and enter into a new era of freedom. However ambiguous these self-definitions of our major social and humanistic disciplines may be, they are still embedded in nature and humanity's relationships with the natural world, even as they try to sharply divide the two and impart complete autonomy to cultural development and social evolution.

Taken as a whole, it is difficult to convey the enormous amount of mischief this simplistic image of nature has done to our ways of thinking, not to speak of the ideological rationale it has provided for human domination. More so than any single notion in the history of religion and philosophy, the image of a "blind," "mute," "cruel," "competitive," and "stingy" nature has opened a wide, often unbridgeable chasm between the social world and the natural world, and in its more exotic ramifications, between mind and body, subject and object, reason and physicality, technology and "raw materials," indeed, the whole gamut of dualisms that have fragmented not only the world of nature and society but the human psyche and its biological matrix.

From Plato's view of the body as a mere burden encasing an ethereal soul, to René Descartes' harsh split between the God-given rational and the purely mechanistic physical, we are the heirs of a historic dualism: between, firstly, a misconceived nature as the opponent of every human endeavor, whose "domination" must be lifted from the shoulders of humanity (even if human beings themselves are reduced to mere instruments of production to be ruthlessly exploited with a view toward their eventual liberation), and, secondly, a domineering humanity whose goal is to "subjugate" the natural world, including human nature itself. Nature, in effect, emerges as an affliction that must be removed from the human condition by the technology and methods of domination that paradoxically justify human domination of humans in the name of "human freedom."

This all-encompassing image of an intractable nature that must be tamed by a rational humanity has given us domineering notions of reason, science, and technology—a fragmentation of humanity into hierarchies, classes, state institutions, gender, and ethnic divisions. It has fostered nationalistic hatreds, imperialistic adventures, and a global philosophy of rule that identifies order with dominance and submission. In slowly corroding every familial, economic, aesthetic, ideological, and cultural tie that provided a sense of place and meaning for the individual in a vital human community, this antinaturalistic mentality has filled the awesome vacuum created by an utterly nihilistic and antisocial development with massive urban entities that are neither cities nor villages, with ubiquitous bureaucracies that impersonally manipulate the lives of faceless masses of atomized human beings, with giant corporate enterprises that spill beyond the boundaries of the world's richest nations to conglomerate on a global scale and determine the material life of the most remote hamlets on the planet, and finally, with highly centralized State institutions and military forces of unbridled power that threaten not only the freedom of the individual but the survival of the species.

The split that clerics and philosophers projected centuries ago in their visions of a soulless nature and a denatured soul has been realized in the form of a disastrous fragmentation of humanity and nature, indeed, in our time, of the human psyche itself. A direct line or logic of events flows almost unrelentingly from a warped image of the natural world to the warped contours of the social world, threatening to bury society in a "slime of history" that is not of nature's making but of man's—specifically, the early hierarchies from which economic classes emerged; the systems of domination, initially of woman by man, that have yielded highly rationalized systems of exploitation; and the vast armies of warriors, priests, monarchs, and bureaucrats who emerged from the simple status groups of tribal society to become the institutionalized tyrants of a market society.

That this authentic jungle of "claw and fang" we call the "free market" is an extension of human competition into nature—an ideological, self-serving fiction that parades under such labels as social Darwinism and sociobiology—hardly requires emphasis any longer. Lions are turned into "Kings of the Beasts" only by human kings, be they imperial monarchs or corporate ones; ants belong to the "lowly" in nature only by virtue of ideologies spawned in temples, palaces, manors, and, in our own time, by subservient apologists of the powers that be. The reality, as we shall see, is different, but a nature conceived as "hierarchical," not to speak of the other "brutish" and very bourgeois traits imputed to it, merely reflects a human condition in which dominance and submission are ends in themselves, which has brought the very existence of our biosphere into question.

Survival of the Fittest.

Far from being the mere "object" of culture (technology, science, and reason), nature is always with us: whether as the parody of our self-image, as the cornerstone of the very disciplines which deny it a place in our social and self-formation, even in the protracted infancy of our young which renders the mind open to cultural development and creates those extended parental and sibling ties from which an organized society emerged.

And nature is always with us as the conscience of the transgressions we have visited on the planet—and the terrifying revenge that awaits us for our violation of the ecological integrity of the planet.

What distinguishes social ecology is that it negates the harsh image we have traditionally created of the natural world and its evolution. And it does so not by dissolving the social into the natural, like sociobiology, or by imparting mystical properties to nature that place it beyond the reach of human comprehension and rational insight. Indeed, as we shall see, social ecology places the human mind, like humanity itself, within a natural context and explores it in terms of its own natural history, as well as its cultural history, so that the sharp cleavages between thought and nature, subject and object, mind and body, and the social and natural are overcome, and the traditional dualisms of Western culture are *transcended* by an evolutionary interpretation of consciousness with its rich wealth of gradations over the course of natural history.

Social ecology "radicalizes" nature, or more precisely, our understanding of natural phenomena, by questioning the prevailing marketplace image of nature from an ecological standpoint: nature as a constellation of communities that are neither "blind" nor "mute," "cruel" nor "competitive," "stingy" nor "necessitarian" but, freed of all anthropocentric moral trappings, a *participatory* realm of interactive life forms whose most outstanding attributes are fecundity, creativity, and directiveness, marked by complementarity that renders the natural world the *grounding* for an ethics of freedom rather than domination.

Seen from an ecological standpoint, life-forms are related in an ecosystem not by the "rivalries" and "competitive" attributes imputed to them by Darwinian orthodoxy, but by the mutualistic attributes emphasized by a growing number of contemporary ecologists—an image pioneered by Peter Kropotkin. Indeed, social ecology challenges the very premises of "fitness" that enter into the Darwinian drama of evolutionary development with its fixation on "survival" rather than differentiation and fecundity. As William Trager has emphasized in his insightful work on symbiosis:

> The conflict in nature between different kinds of organisms has been popularly expressed in phrases like the "struggle for existence" and the "survival of the fittest." Yet few people realized that mutual cooperation between organisms—symbiosis—is just as important, and that the "fittest" may be the one that helps another to survive.[1]

It is tempting to go beyond this pithy and highly illuminating judgment to explore an ecological notion of natural evolution based on the development of *ecosystems*, not merely individual species. This is a concept of evolution as the dialectical development of ever-variegated, complex, and increasingly fecund *contexts* of plant-animal communities as distinguished from the traditional notion of biological evolution based on the atomistic development of single life-forms, a characteristically entrepreneurial concept of the isolated "individual," be it animal, plant, or bourgeois—a creature which fends for itself and either "survives" or "perishes" in a marketplace "jungle." As ecosystems become more complex and open a greater variety of evolutionary pathways, due to their own richness of diversity and increasingly flexible forms of organic life, it is not only the environment that "chooses" what "species" are "fit" to survive but species themselves, in mutualistic complexes as well as singly, that introduce a dim element of "choice"—by no means "intersubjective" or "willfull" in the *human* meaning of these terms.

Concomitantly, these ensembles of species alter the environment of which they are part and exercise an increasingly *active* role in their own evolution. Life, in this *ecological* conception of evolution, ceases to be the passive *tabula rasa* on which eternal forces which we loosely call "the environment" inscribe the destiny of "a species," an atomistic term that is meaningless outside the context of an ecosystem within which a life-form is truly definable with respect to other species.[2]

Life is active, interactive, procreative, relational, and contextual. It is not a passive lump of "stuff," a form of metabolic "matter" that awaits the action of "forces" external to it and is mechanically "shaped" by them. Ever striving and always producing new life-forms, there is a sense in which life is self-directive in its own evolutionary development, not passively reactive to an in-organic or organic world that impinges upon it from outside and "determines" its destiny in isolation from the ecosystems which it constitutes and of which it is a part.

And this much is clear in social ecology: our studies of "food webs" (a not quite satisfactory term for describing the interactivity that occurs in an ecosystem or, more properly, an ecological *community*) demonstrate that the complexity of biotic interrelationships, their diversity and intricacy, is a crucial factor in assessing an ecosystem's stability. In contrast to biotically complex temperate zones, relatively simple desert and arctic ecosystems are very fragile and break down easily with the loss or numerical decline of only a few species. The thrust of biotic evolution over great eras of organic evolution has been toward the increasing diversification of species and their interlocking into highly complex, basically mutualistic relationships, without which the widespread colonization of the planet by life would have been impossible.

Unity in diversity (a concept deeply rooted in the Western philosophical tradition) is not only the determinant of an ecosystem's stability; it is the source of an ecosystem's fecundity, of its innovativeness, of its evolutionary potential to create newer, still more complex life-forms and biotic interrelationships, even in the most inhospitable areas of the planet. Ecologists have not sufficiently stressed the fact that a multiplicity of life-forms and organic interrelationships in a biotic community opens new evolutionary pathways of development, a greater variety of evolutionary interactions, variations, and degrees of flexibility in the capacity to evolve, and is hence crucial not only in the community's stability but also in its innovativeness in the natural history of life.

The ecological principle of unity in diversity grades into a richly mediated social principle, hence my use of the term *social* ecology.[3] Society, in turn, attains its "truth," its self-actualization, in the form of richly articulated, mutualistic networks of people based on community, roundedness of personality, diversity of stimuli and activities, an increasing wealth of experience, and a variety of tasks. Is this grading of ecosystem diversity into social diversity, based on humanly scaled, decentralized communities, merely analogic reasoning?

My answer would be that it is not a superficial analogy but a deep-seated continuity between nature and society that social ecology recovers from traditional nature philosophy without its archaic dross of cosmic hierarchies, mystical absolutes, and cycles. In the case of social ecology, it is not in the *particulars* of differentiation that plant-animal communities are ecologically united with human communities; rather, it is the *logic* of differentiation that makes it possible to relate the mediations of nature and society into a living continuum.

What makes unity in diversity in nature more than a suggestive ecological metaphor for unity in diversity in society is the underlying fact of wholeness. By wholeness I do not mean any finality of closure in a development, any "totality" that leads to a terminal "reconciliation" of all "Being" in a complete identity of subject and object or a reality in which no further development is possible or meaningful. Rather, I mean varying degrees of the actualization of potentialities, the organic unfolding of the wealth of particularities that are latent in the as-yet-undeveloped potentiality. This potentiality can be a newly planted seed, a newly born infant, a newly formed community, a newly emerging society—yet, given their radically different specificity, they are all united by a processual reality, a shared "metabolism" of development, a unified catalysis of growth as distinguished from mere "change" that provides us with the most insightful way of *understanding* them we can possibly achieve. Wholeness is literally the unity that finally gives order to the particularity of each of these phenomena; it is what has emerged from the process, what integrates the particularities into a unified form, what renders the unity an operable reality and a "being" in the literal sense of the term—an order as the actualized *unity* of its diversity from the flowing and emergent process that yields its self-realization, the fixing of its directiveness into a clearly contoured form, and the creation in a dim sense of a "self" that is identifiable with respect to the "others" with which it interacts. Wholeness is the *relative* completion of a phenomenon's potentiality, the fulfillment of latent possibility as such, all its concrete manifestations aside, to become more than the realm of *mere* possibility and attain the "truth" or fulfilled reality of possibility. To think this way—in terms of potentiality, process, mediation, and wholeness—is to reach into the most underlying nature of things, just as to know the biography of a human being and the history of a society is to know them in their authentic reality and depth.

The natural world is no less encompassed by this processual dialectic and developmental ecology than the social, although in ways that do not involve will, degrees of choice, values, ethical goals, and the like. Life itself, as distinguished from the nonliving, however, emerges from the inorganic latent with all the potentialities and particularities it has immanently produced from the logic of its own nascent forms of self-organization. Obviously, so does society as distinguished from biology, humanity as distinguished from animality, and individuality as distinguished from humanity in the generic sense of the word. But these distinctions are not absolutes. They are the unique and closely interrelated phases of a shared continuum, of a process that is united precisely by its own differentiations just as the phases through which an embryo develops are both distinct from and incorporated into its complete gestation and its organic specificity.

This continuum is not simply a philosophical construct. It is an earthy anthropological fact which lives with us daily as surely as it explains the emergence of humanity out of mere animality. Individual socialization is the highly nuanced "biography" of that development in everyday life and in everyone as surely as the anthropological socialization of our species is part of its history. I refer to the biological basis of all human socialization: the protracted infancy of the human child that renders its cultural development possible, in contrast to the rapid growth of nonhuman animals, a rate of growth that quickly forecloses their ability to form a culture and develop sibling affinities of a lasting nature; the instinctual maternal drives that extend feelings of care, sharing, intimate consociation, and finally love and a sense of responsibility for one's own kin into the institutional forms we call "society"; and the sexual division of labor, age-ranking, and kin-relationships which, however culturally conditioned and even mythic in some cases, formed and still inform so much of social institutionalization today. These formative elements of society rest on biological facts and, placed in the contextual analysis I have argued for, require ecological analysis.

In emphasizing the nature-society continuum with all its gradations and "mediations," I do not wish to leave the impression that the known ways and forms in which society emerged from nature and still embodies the natural world in a shared process of cumulative growth follow a logic that is "inexorable" or "preordained" by a telos that mystically guides the unfolding by a supranatural and suprasocial process. Potentiality is not necessity; the logic of a process is not a form of inexorable "law"; the truth of a development is what is *implicit* in any unfolding and defined by the extent to which it achieves stability, variety, fecundity, and enlarges the "realm of freedom," however dimly freedom is conceived.

No specific "stage" of a process necessarily yields a still later one or is "presupposed" by it—but certain obvious conditions, however varied, blurred, or even idiosyncratic, form the determining ground for still other conditions that can be expected to emerge. Freedom and, ultimately, a degree of subjectivity that make choice and will possible along rational lines may be desiderata that the natural world renders possible and in a "self"-directive way plays an active role in achieving. But in no sense are these desiderata predetermined certainties that must unfold, nor is any such unfolding spared the very real possibility that it will become entirely regressive or remain unfulfilled and incomplete. That the *potentiality* for freedom and consciousness exists in nature and society; that nature and society are not merely "passive" in a development toward freedom and consciousness, a passivity that would make the very notion of potentiality mystical just as the notion of "necessity" would make it meaningless by definition; that natural and social history bear existential witness to the potentiality and processes that form subjectivity and bring consciousness more visibly on the horizon in the very natural history of mind—all constitute *no guarantee* that these latent desiderata are certainties or lend themselves to systematic elucidation and teleological explanations in any traditional philosophical sense.

Our survey of organic and social experience may stir us to interpret a development we know to have occurred as reason to presuppose that potentiality, wholeness, and *graded* evolution are realities after all, no less real than our own existence and personal histories, but presuppositions they remain. Indeed, no outlook in philosophy can ever exist that is free of presuppositions, any more than speculation can exist that is free of some stimulus by the objective world. The only truth about "first philosophy," from Greek times onward, is that what is "first" in any philosophical outlook are the presuppositions it adopts, the background of unformulated experience from which these presuppositions emerge, and the intuition of a coherence that must be validated by reality as well as speculative reason.

One of the most provocative of the graded continuities between nature and society is the nonhierarchical relationships that exist in an ecosystem, and the extent to which they provide a grounding for a nonhierarchical society.[4] It is meaningless to speak of hierarchy in an ecosystem and in the succession of ecosystems which, in contrast to a monadic species-oriented development, form the true story of natural evolution. There is no "king of the beasts" and no "lowly serf"—presumably, the lion and the ant—in *ecosystem* relationships. Such terms, including words like "cruel nature," "fallen nature," "domineering nature," and even "mutualistic nature" (I prefer to use the word "complementary" here) are projections of our own social relationships into the natural world. Ants are as important as lions and eagles in ecosystems; indeed, their recycling of organic materials gives them a considerable "eminence" in the maintenance of the stability and integrity of an area.

As to accounts of "dominance-submission" relationships between *individuals* such as "alpha" and "beta" males, utterly asymmetrical relationships tend to be grouped under words like "hierarchy" that are more analogic, often more metaphoric, than real. It becomes absurd, I think, to say that the "dominance" of a "queen bee," who in no way knows that she is a "queen" and whose sole function in a beehive is reproductive, is in any way equatable with an "alpha" male baboon, whose "status" tends to suffer grave diminution when the baboon troop moves from the plains to the forest. By the same token, it is absurd to equate "patriarchal harems" among red deer with "matriarchal" elephant herds, which simply expel bulls when they reach puberty and in no sense "dominate" them. One could go through a whole range of asymmetrical relationships to show that, even among our closest primate relatives, which include the utterly "pacific" orangutans as well as the seemingly "aggressive" chimpanzees, words like "dominance" and "submission" mean very different relationships depending upon the species one singles out and the circumstances under which they live.

I cannot emphasize too strongly that hierarchy in society is an *institutional* phenomenon, not a biological one. It is a product of organized, carefully crafted power relationships, not a product of the "morality of the gene," to use E.O. Wilson's particularly obtuse phrase in his *Sociobiology*. Only institutions, formed by long periods of human history and sustained by well-organized bureaucracies and military forces, could have placed absolute rule in the hands of mental defects like Nicholas II of Russia and Louis XVI of France. We can find nothing even remotely comparable to such institutionalized systems of command and obedience in other species, much less in ecosystems. It verges on the absurd to draw fast-and-loose comparisons between the "division of labor" (another anthropocentric phrase when placed in an ecological context) in a beehive, whose main function is reproducing bees, not making honey for breakfast tables, and human society, with its highly contrived State forms and organized bureaucracies.

What renders social ecology so important in comparing ecosystems to societies is that it decisively challenges the very function of hierarchy as a way of *ordering* reality, of dealing with differentiation and variation—with "otherness" as such. Social ecology ruptures the association of order with hierarchy. It poses the question of whether we can experience the "other," not hierarchically on a "scale of one to ten" with a continual emphasis on "inferior" and "superior," but ecologically, as variety that enhances the unity of phenomena, enriches wholeness, and more closely resembles a food-web than a pyramid. That hierarchy exists today as an even more fundamental problem than social classes, that domination exists today as an even more fundamental problem than economic exploitation, can be attested to by every conscious feminist, who can justly claim that long before man began to exploit man through the formation of social classes, he began to dominate woman in patriarchal and hierarchical relationships.

We would do well to remember that the abolition of classes, exploitation, and even the State is no guarantee whatever that people will cease to be ranked hierarchically and dominated according to age, gender, race, physical qualities, and often quite frivolous and irrational categories, unless liberation focuses as much on hierarchy and domination as it does on classes and exploitation. This is the point where socialism, in my view, must extend itself into a broader libertarian tradition that reaches back into the tribal or band-type communities ancestral to what we so smugly call "civilization," a tradition, indeed an abiding human impulse, that has surged to the surface of society in every revolutionary period, only to be brutally contained by those purely societal forms called "hierarchies."

Social ecology raises all of these issues in a fundamentally new light, and establishes entirely new ways of resolving them. I have tried to show that nature is always present in the human condition, and in the very ideological constructions that deny its presence in societal relationships. The *notion* of dominating nature literally *defines* all our social disciplines, including socialism and psychoanalysis. It is the apologia *par excellence* for the domination of human by human. Until that apologia is removed from our sensibilities in the rearing of the young, the first step in socialization as such, and replaced by an ecological sensibility that sees "otherness" in terms of complementarity rather than rivalry, we will never achieve human emancipation. Nature lives in us ontogenetically as different layers of experience which analytic logic often conceals from us: in the sensitivity of our cells, the remarkable autonomy of our organ systems, our so-called layered brain which experiences the world in different ways and attests to different worlds, which analytic logic, left to its own imperialistic claims, tends to close to us—indeed, in the *natural history* of the nervous system and mind, which bypasses the chasm between mind and body, or subjectivity and objectivity, with an organic continuum in which body grades into mind and objectivity into subjectivity. Herein lies the most compelling refutation of the traditional dualism in religion, philosophy, and sensibility that gave ideological credence to the myth of a "domineering" nature, borne by the suffering and brutalization of a socially dominated humanity.

Moreover, this natural history of the nervous system and mind is a cumulative one, not merely a successive one—a history whose past lies in our everyday present. It is not for nothing that one of America's greatest physiologists, Walter B. Cannon, titled his great work on homeostasis *The Widsom of the Body*. Running through our entire experiential apparatus and organizing experience for us are not only the categories of Kant's first *Critique* and Hegel's *Logic*, but also the *natural history of sensibility* as it exists in us hormonally, from our undifferentiated nerve networks to the hemispheres of our brains. We metabolize with nature in production in such a way that the materials with which we work and the tools we use to work on them enter reciprocally into the technological imagination we form and the social matrix in which our technologies exist. Nor can we ever permit ourselves to forget, all our overriding ideologies of class, economic interest, and the like notwithstanding, that we socialize with each other not only as producers and property owners, but also as children and parents, young and old, female and male, with our bodies as well as our minds, and according to graded and varied impulses that are as archaic as they are fairly recent in the natural evolution of sensibility.

Hence, to become conscious of this vast ensemble of natural history as it enters into our very beings, to see its place in the graded development of our social history, to recognize that we must develop new sensibilities, technologies, institutions, and forms of experiencing that give expression to this wealth of our inner development and the complexity of our biosocial apparatus is to go along with a deeper grain of evolution and dialectic than is afforded to us by the "epistemological" and "linguistic" turns of recent philosophy.[5] On this score, just as I would argue that science *is* the history of science, not merely its latest "stage," and technology *is* the history of technology, not merely its latest designs, so reason *is* the history of reason, not merely its present analytic and communicative dimensions. Social history includes natural history as a graded dialectic that is united not only in a continuum by a shared logic of differentiation and complementarity; it includes natural history in the socialization process itself, in the natural as well as the social history of experience, in the imperatives of a harmonized relationship between humanity and nature that presuppose new ecotechnologies and ecocommunities, and in the desiderata opened by a decentralized society based on the values of complementarity and community.

The ideas I have advanced so far take their point of departure from a radically different image of nature than the prevailing one, in which philosophical dualism, economics, sociology, psychology, and socialism have their roots. As a social ecologist, I see nature as essentially creative, directive, mutualistic, fecund, and marked by complementarity, not "mute," "blind," "cruel," "stingy," or "oppressive." This shift in focus from a marketplace to an ecological image of nature obliges me to challenge the time-honored notion that the domination of human by human is necessary in order to "dominate nature." In emphasizing how meaningless this rationale for hierarchy and domination is, I conclude—with considerable historical justification, which our own era amply illuminates with its deployment of technology primarily for purposes of social control—that the idea of dominating nature stems from human domination, initially in hierarchical forms as feminists so clearly understand, and later in class and statist forms.

Accordingly, my ecological image of nature leads me to drastically redefine my conception of economics, sociology, psychology, and socialism, which, ironically, advance a shared dualistic gospel of a radical separation of society from nature even as they rest on a militant imperative to "subdue" nature, be it as "scarce resources," the realm of "animality," "internal nature," or "external nature." Hence, I have tried to re-vision history not only as an account of power over human beings that by far outweighs any attempt to gain power over things, but also as power ramified into centralized states and urban environments, a technology, science, and rationality of social control, and a message of "liberation" that conceals the most awesome features of domination, notably, the traditional capitalist orthodoxies of our day.

At the juncture where nature is conceived either as a ruthless, competitive marketplace or a creative, fecund biotic community, two radically divergent pathways of thought and sensibility emerge, following contrasting directions and conceptions of the human future. One ends in a totalitarian and antinaturalistic terminus for society: centralized, statist, technocratic, corporate, and sweepingly repressive. The other ends in a libertarian and ecological beginning for society: decentralized, stateless, artistic, collective, and sweepingly emancipatory. These are not tendentious words. It is by no means certain that western humanity, currently swept up in a counterrevolution of authoritarian values and adaptive impulses, would regard a libertarian vision as less pejorative than a totalitarian one. Whether or not my own words seem tendentious, the full logic of my view should be seen: the view we hold of the natural world profoundly shapes the image we develop of the social worlds, even as we assert the "supremacy" and "autonomy" of culture over nature.

In what sense does social ecology view nature as a grounding for an ethics of freedom? If the story of natural evolution is not understandable in Locke's atomistic account of a particular species' evolution, if that story is basically an account of ecosystem evolution toward ever more complex and flexible evolutionary pathways, then natural history itself cannot be seen simply as "necessitarian," "governed" by "inexorable laws" and imperatives. Every organism is in some sense "willful," insofar as it seeks to preserve itself, to maintain its identity, to resist a kind of biological entropy that threatens its integrity and complexity. However dimly, every organism transforms the essential attributes of self-maintenance that earn it the status of a distinct form of life into a capacity to *choose* alternatives that favor its survival and well-being—not merely to react to stimuli as a purely physico-chemical ensemble.

This dim, germinal freedom is heightened by the growing wealth of ecological complexity that confronts evolving life in synchronicity with evolving ecosystems. The elaboration of possibilities that comes with the elaboration of diversity and the growing multitude of alternatives confronting species development opens newer and *more fecund pathways* for organic development. Life is not passive in the face of these possibilities for its evolution. It drives toward them actively in a shared process of mutual stimulation between organisms and their environment (including the living and non-living environment they create) as surely as it also actively creates and colonizes the niches that cradle a vast diversity of life-forms in our richly elaborated biosphere. This image of active, indeed striving, life requires no Hegelian "Spirit" or Heraklitean *Logos* to explain it. Activity and striving are presupposed in our very definition of metabolism. In fact, metabolic activity is coextensive with the notion of activity as such and imparts an identity, indeed, a rudimentary "self," to every organism. Diversity and complexity, indeed, the notion of evolution as a diversifying history, superadd the dimension of variegated alternatives and pathways to the simple fact of choice—and, with choice, the rudimentary fact of *freedom*. For freedom, in its most germinal form, is also a function of diversity and complexity, of a "realm of necessity" that is diminished by a growing and expanding multitude of alternatives, of a widening horizon of evolutionary possibilities, which life in its ever-richer forms both creates and in its own way "pursues," until consciousness, the gift of nature as well as society to humanity, renders this pursuit willful, self-reflexive, and consciously creative.

Here, in this ecological concept of natural evolution, lies a hidden message of freedom based on the "inwardness of life," to use Hans Jonas's excellent expression, and the ever greater diversification produced by natural evolution. Ecology is united with society in new terms that reveal moral tension in natural history, just as Marx's simplistic image of the "savage" who "wrestles with nature" reveals a moral tension in social history.

We must beware of being prejudiced by our own fear of prejudice. Organismic philosophies can surely yield totalitarian, hierarchical, and eco-fascistic results. We have good reason to be concerned over so-called nature philosophies that give us the notion of *Blut und Boden* and "dialectical materialism," which provide the ideological justification for the horrors of Nazism and Stalinism. We have good reason to be concerned over a mysticism that yields social quietism at best and the aggressive activism of reborn Christianity and certain Asian gurus at worst. We have even better reason to be concerned over the eco-fascism of Garrett Hardin's "lifeboat ethic" with its emphasis on scarce resources and the so-called tragedy of the commons, an ethic which services genocidal theories of imperialism and a global disregard for human misery. So, too, sociobiology, which roots all the savage features of "civilization" in our genetic constitution. Social ecology offers the coordinates for an entirely different pathway in exploring our relationship to the natural world—one that accepts neither genetic and scientistic theories of "natural necessity" at one extreme, nor a romantic and mystical zealotry that reduces the rich variety of reality and evolution to a cosmic "oneness" and energetics at the other extreme. For in both cases, it is not only our vision of the world and the unity of nature and society that suffers, but the "natural history" of freedom and the basis for an objective ethics of liberation as well.

We cannot avoid the use of conventional reason, present-day modes of science, and modern technology. They, too, have their place in the future of humanity and humanity's metabolism with the natural world. But we can establish new *contexts* in which these modes of rationality, science, and technology have their proper place—an *ecological* context that does not deny other, more qualitative modes of knowing and producing which are participatory and emancipatory. We can also foster a new sensibility toward otherness that, *in a nonhierarchical society*, is based on complementarity rather than rivalry, and new communities that, scaled to human dimensions, are tailored to the ecosystem in which they are located and open a new, decentralized, self-managed public realm for new forms of selfhood as well as directly democratic forms of social management.

Notes

1 William Trager, *Symbiosis*, New York: Van Nostrand Reinhold Co., 1970; vii.

2 The traditional emphasis on an "active" environment that determines the "survival" of a passive species, altered in a cosmic game of chance by random mutations, is perhaps another reason why the term "environmentalism," as distinguished from social ecology, is a very unsatisfactory expression these days.

3 My use of the word "social" cannot be emphasized too strongly. Words like "human," "deep," and "cultural," while very valuable as general terms, do not explicitly pinpoint the extent to which our image of nature is formed by the kind of society in which we live and by the abiding natural basis of all social life. The evolution of society out of nature and the ongoing interaction between the two tend to be lost in words that do not tell us enough about the vital association between nature and society and about the importance of defining such disciplines as economics, psychology, and sociology in natural as well as social terms. Recent uses of "social ecology" to advance a rather superficial account of social life in fairly conventional ecological terms are particularly deplorable. Books like *Habits of the Heart* which glibly pick up the term serve to coopt a powerful expression for rather banal ends and tend to compromise efforts to deepen our understanding of nature and society as interactive rather than opposed domains.

4 Claims of hierarchy as a ubiquitous natural fact cannot be ignored by still further widening the chasm between nature and society—or "natural necessity" and "cultural freedom" as it is more elegantly worded. Justifying social hierarchy in terms of natural hierarchy is one of the most persistent assaults on an egalitarian social future that religion and philosophy have made over the ages. It has surfaced recently in sociobiology and reinforced the antinaturalistic stance that permeates so many liberatory ideologies in the modern era. To say that culture is precisely the "emancipation of man from nature" is to revert to Sartre's "slime of history" notion of the natural world that not only separates society from nature but mind from body and subjectivity from objectivity.

5 Our disastrously one-sided and rationalized "civilization" has boxed this wealth of inner development and complexity away, relegating it to preindustrial lifeways that basically shaped our evolution up to a century or two ago. From a sensory viewpoint, we live atrophied, indeed, starved lives compared to hunters and food cultivators, whose capacity to experience reality, even in a largely cultural sense, by far overshadows our own. The twentieth century alone bears witness to an appalling dulling of our "sixth senses" as well as to our folk creativity and craft creativity. We have never experienced so little so loudly, so brashly, so trivially, so thinly, so neurotically. For a comparison of the "world of experience we have lost" (to reword Peter Laslett's title), read the excellent personal accounts of so-called Bushmen, or San people, the Ituri Forest pygmies, and the works of Paul Radin on food-gatherers and hunters—not simply as records of their lifeways but of their epistemologies.

B. Eco-Feminism and Social Justice

Ecofeminism and Feminist Theory

CAROLYN MERCHANT

The term *ecofeminisme* was coined by the French writer Françoise d'Eaubonne in 1974 to represent women's potential for bringing about an ecological revolution to ensure human survival on the planet.[1] Such an ecological revolution would entail new gender relations between women and men and between humans and nature. Liberal, radical, and socialist feminism have all been concerned with improving the human/nature relationship, and each has contributed to an ecofeminist perspective in different ways.[2] Liberal feminism is consistent with the objectives of reform environmentalism to alter human relations with nature through the passage of new laws and regulations. Radical ecofeminism analyzes environmental problems from within its critique of patriarchy and offers alternatives that could liberate both women and nature. Socialist ecofeminism grounds its analysis in capitalist patriarchy and would totally restructure, through a socialist revolution, the domination of women and nature inherent in the market economy's use of both as resources. While radical feminism has delved more deeply into the woman/nature connection, I believe that socialist feminism has the potential for a more thorough critique of the domination issue.

Liberal feminism characterized the history of feminism from its beginnings in the seventeenth century until the 1960s. Its roots are liberalism, the political theory that incorporates the scientific analysis that nature is composed of atoms moved by external forces with a theory of human nature that views humans as individual rational agents who maximize their own self-interest and capitalism as the optimal economic structure for human progress. Historically, liberal feminists have argued that women do not differ from men as rational agents and that exclusion from educational and economic opportunities have prevented them from realizing their own potential for creativity in all spheres of human life.[3]

For liberal feminists (as for liberalism generally), environmental problems result from the overly rapid development of natural resources and the failure to regulate environmental pollutants. Better science, conservation, and laws are the proper approaches to resolving resource problems. Given equal educational opportunities to become scientists, natural resource managers, regulators, lawyers, and legislators,

Carolyn Merchant, "Ecofeminism and Feminist Theory," in *Reweaving the World: The Emergence of Ecofeminism* (ed. Irene Diamond and Gloria Orenstein), Sierra Club Books, 1990; pp. 77–83. Reprinted with permission of the author.

women like men can contribute to the improvement of the environment, the conservation of natural resources, and the higher quality of human life. Women, therefore, can transcend the social stigma of their biology and join men in the cultural project of environmental conservation.

Radical feminism developed in the late 1960s and 1970s with the second wave of feminism. The radical form of ecofeminism is a response to the perception that women and nature have been mutually associated and devalued in Western culture and that both can be elevated and liberated through direct political action. In prehistory an emerging patriarchal culture dethroned the mother Goddesses and replaced them with male gods to whom the female deities became subservient.[4] The scientific revolution of the seventeenth century further degraded nature by replacing Renaissance organicism and a nurturing earth with the metaphor of a machine to be controlled and repaired from the outside. The Earth is to be dominated by male-developed and -controlled technology, science, and industry.

Radical feminism instead celebrates the relationship between women and nature through the revival of ancient rituals centered on Goddess worship, the moon, animals, and the female reproductive system. A vision in which nature is held in esteem as mother and Goddess is a source of inspiration and empowerment for many ecofeminists. Spirituality is seen as a source of both personal and social change. Goddess worship and rituals centered around the lunar and female menstrual cycles, lectures, concerts, art exhibitions, street and theater productions, and direct political action (web weaving in anti-nuclear protests) are all examples of the re-visioning of nature and women as powerful forces. Radical ecofeminist philosophy embraces intuition, an ethic of caring, and weblike human/nature relationships.

For radical feminists, human nature is grounded in human biology. Humans are biologically sexed and socially gendered. Sex/gender relations give men and women different power bases. Hence the personal is political. Radical feminists object to the dominant society's perception that women are limited by being closer to nature because of their ability to bear children. The dominant view is that menstruation, pregnancy, nursing, and nurturing of infants and young children should tie women to the home, decreasing their mobility and inhibiting their ability to remain in the work force. Radical feminists argue that the perception that women are totally oriented toward biological reproduction degrades them by association with a nature that is itself devalued in Western culture. Women's biology and nature should instead be celebrated as sources of female power.

Turning the perceived connection between women and biological reproduction upside down becomes the source of women's empowerment and ecological activism. Women argue that male-designed and -produced technologies neglect the effects of nuclear radiation, pesticides, hazardous wastes, and household chemicals on women's reproductive organs and on the ecosystem. They argue that radioactivity from nuclear wastes, power plants, and bombs is a potential cause of birth defects, cancers, and the elimination of life on Earth.[5] They expose hazardous waste sites near schools and homes as permeating soil and drinking water and contributing to miscarriage, birth defects, and leukemia. They object to pesticides and herbicides being sprayed on crops and forests as potentially affecting children and the childbearing women living near them. Women frequently spearhead local actions against spraying and power plant siting and organize others to demand toxic cleanups. When coupled with an environmental ethic that values rather than degrades nature, such actions have the potential both for raising women's consciousness of their own oppression and for the liberation of nature from the polluting effects of industrialization. For example, many lower-middle-class women who became politicized through protests over toxic chemical wastes at Love Canal in New York simultaneously became feminists when their activism spilled over into their home lives.[6]

Yet in emphasizing the female, body, and nature components of the dualities male/female, mind/body, and culture/nature, radical ecofeminism runs the risk of perpetuating the very hierarchies it seeks to overthrow. Critics point to the problem of women's own reinforcement of their identification with a nature that Western culture degrades.[7] If "female is to male as nature is to culture," as anthropologist Sherry Ortner argues,[8] then women's hopes for liberation are set back by association with nature. Any analysis that makes women's essence and qualities special ties them to a biological destiny that thwarts the possibility of liberation. A politics grounded in women's culture, experience, and values can be seen as reactionary.

To date, socialist feminists have had little to say about the problem of the domination of nature. To them, the source of male domination of women is the complex of social patterns called capitalist patriarchy, in which men bear the responsibility for labor in the marketplace and women for labor in the home. Yet the potential exists for a socialist ecofeminism that would push for an ecological, economic, and social revolution that would simultaneously liberate women, working-class people, and nature.

For socialist ecofeminism, environmental problems are rooted in the rise of capitalist patriarchy and the ideology that the Earth and nature can be exploited for human progress through technology. Historically, the rise of capitalism eroded the subsistence-based farm and city workshop in which production was oriented toward use values and men and women were economic partners. The result was a capitalist economy dominated by men and a domestic sphere in which women's labor in the home was unpaid and subordinate to men's labor in the marketplace. Both women and nature are exploited by men as part of the progressive liberation of humans from the constraints imposed by nature. The consequence is the alienation of women and men from each other and both from nature.

Socialist feminism incorporates many of the insights of radical feminism, but views both nature and human nature as historically and socially constructed. Human nature is seen as the product of historically changing interactions between humans and nature, men and women, classes, and races. Any meaningful analysis must be grounded in an understanding of power not only in the personal but also in the political sphere. Like radical feminism, socialist feminism is critical of mechanistic science's treatment of nature as passive and of its male-dominated power structures. Similarly, it deplores the lack of a gender analysis in history and the omission of any treatment of women's reproductive and nurturing roles. But rather than grounding its analysis in biological reproduction alone, it also incorporates social reproduction. Biological reproduction includes the reproduction of the species and the reproduction of daily life through food, clothing, and shelter; social reproduction includes socialization and the legal/political reproduction of the social order.[9]

Table 3.1 Feminism and the environment

	Nature	Human Nature	Feminist Critique of Environmentalism	Image of a Feminist Environmentalism
Liberal Feminism	Atoms Mind/body dualism Domination of nature	Rational agents Individualism Maximization of self-interest	"Man and his environment" leaves out women	Women participate in natural resources and environmental sciences
Marxist Feminism	Transformation of nature by science and technology for human use Domination of nature as a means to human freedom Nature is material basis of life: food, clothing, shelter, energy	Creation of human nature through mode of production, praxis Historically specific—not fixed Species nature of humans	Critique of capitalist control of resources and accumulation of goods and profits	Socialist/communist society will use resources for good of all men and women Resources will be controlled by workers Environmental pollution will be minimal since no surpluses will be produced Environmental research by men and women
Radical Feminism	Nature is spiritual and personal Conventional science and technology problematic because of their emphasis on domination	Biology is basic Humans are sexually reproducing bodies Sexed by biology/Gendered by society	Unaware of interconnectedness of male domination of nature and women Male environmentalism retains hierarchies Insufficient attention to environmental threats to women's reproduction (chemicals, nuclear war)	Woman/nature both valued and celebrated Reproductive freedom Against pornographic depictions of both women and nature Radical ecofeminism
Socialist Feminism	Nature is material basis of life: food, clothing, shelter, energy Nature is socially and historically constructed Transformation of nature by production	Human nature created through biology and praxis (sex, race, class, age) Historically specific and socially constructed	Leaves out nature as active and responsive Leaves out women's role in reproduction and reproduction as a category Systems approach is mechanistic not dialectical	Both nature and human production are active Centrality of biological and social reproduction Multileveled structural analysis Dialectical (not mechanical) systems Socialist ecofeminism

Like Marxist feminists, socialist feminists see nonhuman nature as the material basis of human life, supplying the necessities of food, clothing, shelter, and energy. Materialism, not spiritualism, is the driving force of social change. Nature is transformed by human science and technology for use by all humans for survival. Socialist feminism views change as dynamic, interactive, and dialectical, rather than as mechanistic, linear, and incremental. Nonhuman nature is dynamic and alive. As a historical actor, nature interacts with human beings through mutual ecological relations. Socialist feminist environmental theory gives both reproduction and production central places. A socialist feminist environmental ethic involves developing sustainable, non-dominating relations with nature and supplying all peoples with a high quality of life.

In politics, socialist feminists participate in many of the same environmental actions as radical feminists. The goals, however, are to direct change toward some form of an egalitarian socialist state, in addition to resocializing men and women into nonsexist, nonracist, nonviolent, anti-imperialist forms of life. Socialist ecofeminism deals explicitly with environmental issues that affect working-class women, Third World women, and women of color. Examples include support for the women's *Chipco* (tree-hugging) movement in India that protects fuel resources from lumber interests, for the women's Green Belt movement in Kenya that has planted more than 2 million trees in 10 years, and for Native American women and children exposed to radioactivity from uranium mining.[10]

Although the ultimate goals of liberal, radical, and socialist feminists may differ as to whether capitalism, women's culture, or socialism should be the ultimate objective of political action, shorter-term objectives overlap. In this sense there is perhaps more unity than diversity in women's common goal of restoring the natural environment and quality of life for people and other living and nonliving inhabitants of the planet.

Notes

1 Françoise d'Eaubonne, "Feminism or Death," in Elaine Marks and Isabelle de Courtivron (eds.), *New French Feminisms: An Anthology* (Amherst: University of Massachusetts Press, 1980).

2 See Karen Warren, "Feminism and Ecology: Making Connections," *Environmental Ethics* 9 (no. 1: 1981): 3–20.

3 See Alison M. Jaggar, *Feminist Politics and Human Nature* (Totowa, NJ: Rowman and Allanheld, 1983).

4 Merlin Stone, *When God Was a Woman* (New York: Harcourt Brace Jovanovich, 1976.)

5 See Dorothy Nelkin, "Nuclear Power as a Feminist Issue," *Environment* 23 (no. 1: 1981): 14–20, 38–39.

6 Carolyn Merchant, "Earthcare: Women and the Environmental Movement," *Environment* 22 (June 1970): 7–13, 38–40.

7 Donna Haraway, "A Manifesto for Cyborgs," *Socialist Review* 15 (no. 80: 1985): 65–107.

8 Sherry Ortner, "Is Female to Male as Nature Is to Culture?" in Michelle Rosaldo and Louise Lamphere (eds.), *Woman, Culture, and Society* (Stanford, CA: Stanford University Press, 1974); pp. 67–87.

9 Carolyn Merchant, "The Theoretical Structure of Ecological Revolutions," *Environmental Review* 11 (no. 4: Winter 1987): 265–74.

10 See Jeanne Henn, "Female Farmers—The Doubly Ignored," *Development Forum* 14 (nos. 7 and 8: 1986); and Gillian Goslinga, "Kenya's Women of the Trees," *Development Forum* 14 (no. 8: 1986): 15.

The Power and the Promise of Ecological Feminism

Karen J. Warren

Introduction

Ecological feminism (ecofeminism) has begun to receive a fair amount of attention lately as an alternative feminism and environmental ethic.[1] Since Françoise d'Eaubonne introduced the term *ecofeminisme* in 1974 to bring attention to women's potential for bringing about an ecological revolution,[2] the term has been used in a variety of ways. As I use the term in this essay, ecological feminism is the position that there are important connections—historical, experiential, symbolic, theoretical—between the domination of women and the domination of nature, an understanding of which is crucial to both feminism and environmental ethics. Here I discuss the nature of a feminist ethic and the ways in which ecofeminism provides a feminist and environmental ethic. I conclude that any feminist theory *and* any environmental ethic which fails to take seriously the twin and interconnected dominations of women and nature is at best incomplete and at worst simply inadequate. ...

Ecofeminism as a Feminist and Environmental Ethic

A feminist ethic involves a twofold commitment to critique male bias in ethics wherever it occurs, and to develop ethics which are not male-biased. Sometimes this involves articulation of values (e.g., values of care, appropriate trust, kinship, friendship) often lost or underplayed in mainstream ethics.[3] Sometimes it involves engaging in theory building by pioneering in new directions or by revamping old theories in gender sensitive ways. What makes the critiques of old theories or conceptualizations of new ones "feminist" is that they emerge out of sex-gender analyses and reflect whatever those analyses reveal about gendered experience and gendered social reality.

As I conceive feminist ethics in the pre-feminist present, it rejects attempts to conceive of ethical theory in terms of necessary and sufficient conditions, because it assumes that there is no essence (in the sense of some transhistorical, universal, absolute abstraction) of feminist ethics. While attempts to formulate joint necessary and sufficient conditions of a feminist ethic are unfruitful, nonetheless, there are some necessary conditions, what I prefer to call "boundary conditions" of a feminist ethic.

Karen J. Warren, "The Power and Promise of Ecological Feminism," *Environmental Ethics*, 12 (1990): 125–126, 138–145. With kind permission from the author.

These boundary conditions clarify some of the minimal conditions of a feminist ethic without suggesting that feminist ethics has some ahistorical essence. They are like the boundaries of a quilt or collage. They delimit the territory of the piece without dictating what the interior, the design, the actual pattern of the piece looks like. Because the actual design of the quilt emerges from the multiplicity of voices of women in a cross-cultural context, the design will change over time. It is not something static.

What are some of the boundary conditions of a feminist ethic? First, nothing can become part of a feminist ethic—can be part of the quilt—that promotes sexism, racism, classism, or any other "isms" of social domination. Of course, people may disagree about what counts as a sexist act, racist attitude, classist behavior. What counts as sexism, racism, or classism may vary cross-culturally. Still, because a feminist ethic aims at eliminating sexism and sexist bias, and sexism is intimately connected in conceptualization and in practice to racism, classism, and naturism, a feminist ethic must be anti-sexist, anti-racist, anti-classist, anti-naturist and opposed to any "ism" which presupposes or advances a logic of domination.

Second, a feminist ethic is a *contextualist* ethic. A contextualist ethic is one which sees ethical discourse and practice as emerging from the voices of people located in different historical circumstances. A contextualist ethic is properly viewed as a *collage* or *mosaic*, a *tapestry* of voices that emerges out of felt experiences. Like any collage or mosaic, the point is not to have *one picture* based on a unity of voices, but a *pattern* which emerges out of the very different voices of people located in different circumstances. When a contextualist ethic is *feminist*, it gives central place to the voices of women.

Third, since a feminist ethic gives central significance to the diversity of women's voices, a feminist ethic must be structurally pluralistic rather than unitary or reductionistic. It rejects the assumption that there is "one voice" in terms of which ethical values, beliefs, attitudes, and conduct can be assessed.

Fourth, a feminist ethic reconceives ethical theory as theory in process which will change over time. Like all theory, a feminist ethic is based on some generalizations.[4] Nevertheless, the generalizations associated with it are themselves a pattern of voices within which the different voices emerging out of concrete and alternative descriptions of ethical situations have meaning. The coherence of a feminist theory so conceived is given within a historical and conceptual context, i.e., within a set of historical, socioeconomic circumstances (including circumstances of race, class, age, and affectional orientation) and within a set of basic beliefs, values, attitudes, and assumptions about the world.

Fifth, because a feminist ethic is contextualist, structurally pluralistic, and "in-process," one way to evaluate the claims of a feminist ethic is in terms of their *inclusiveness*: those claims (voices, patterns of voices) are morally and epistemologically favored (preferred, better, less partial, less biased) which are more inclusive of the felt experiences and perspectives of oppressed persons. The condition of inclusiveness requires and ensures that the diverse voices of women (as oppressed persons) will be given legitimacy in ethical theory building. It thereby helps to minimize empirical bias, e.g., bias rising from faulty or false generalizations based on stereotyping, too small a sample size, or a skewed sample. It does so by ensuring that any generalizations which are made about ethics and ethical decision making include—indeed cohere with—the patterned voices of women.[5]

Sixth, a feminist ethic makes no attempt to provide an "objective" point of view, since it assumes that in contemporary culture there really is no such point of view. As such, it does not claim to be "unbiased" in the sense of "value-neutral" or "objective." However, it does assume that whatever bias it has as an ethic centralizing the voices of oppressed persons is a *better bias*—"better" because it is more inclusive and therefore less partial—than those which exclude those voices.[6]

Seventh, a feminist ethic provides a central place for values typically unnoticed, underplayed, or misrepresented in traditional ethics, e.g., values of care, love, friendship, and appropriate trust.[7] Again, it need not do this at the exclusion of considerations of rights, rules, or utility. There may be many contexts in which talk of rights or of utility is useful or appropriate. For instance, in contracts or property relationships, talk of rights may be useful and appropriate. In deciding what is cost-effective or advantageous to the most people, talk of utility may be useful and appropriate. In a feminist *quo* contextualist ethic, whether or not such talk is useful or appropriate depends on the context; *other values* (e.g., values of care, trust, friendship) are *not* viewed as reducible to or captured solely in terms of such talk.[8]

Eighth, a feminist ethic also involves a reconception of what it is to be human and what it is for humans to engage in ethical decision making, since it rejects as either meaningless or currently untenable any gender-free or gender-neutral description of humans, ethics, and ethical decision-making. It thereby rejects what Alison Jaggar calls "abstract individualism," i.e., the position that it is possible to identify a human essence or human nature that exists independently of any particular historical context.[9] Humans and human moral conduct are properly understood essentially (and not merely accidentally) in terms of networks or webs of historical and concrete relationships.

All the props are now in place for seeing how ecofeminism provides the framework for a distinctively feminist and environmental ethic. It is a feminism that critiques male bias wherever it occurs in ethics (including environmental ethics) and aims at providing an ethic (including an environmental ethic) which is not male biased—and it does so in a way that satisfies the preliminary boundary conditions of a feminist ethic.

First, ecofeminism is quintessentially anti-naturist. Its anti-naturism consists in the rejection of any way of thinking about or acting toward nonhuman nature that reflects a logic, values, or attitude of domination. Its anti-naturist, anti-sexist, anti-racist, anti-classist (and so forth, for all other "isms" of social domination) stance forms the outer boundary of the quilt: nothing gets on the quilt which is naturist, sexist, racist, classist, and so forth.

Second, ecofeminism is a contextualist ethic. It involves a shift *from* a conception of ethics as primarily a matter of rights, rules, or principles predetermined and applied in specific cases to entities viewed as competitors in the contest of moral standing, *to* a conception of ethics as growing out of what Jim Cheney calls "defining relationships," i.e., relationships conceived in some sense as defining who one is.[10] As a contextualist ethic, it is not that rights, or rules, or principles are *not* relevant or important. Clearly they are in certain contexts and for certain purposes.[11] It is just that what *makes* them relevant or important is that those to whom they apply are entities *in relationship with* others.

Ecofeminism also involves an ethical shift *from* granting moral consideration to nonhumans *exclusively* on the grounds of some similarity they share with humans (e.g., rationality, interests, moral agency, sentiency, right-holder status) *to* "a highly contextual account to see clearly what a human being is and what the nonhuman world might be, morally speaking, *for* human beings."[12] For an ecofeminist, *how* a moral agent is in relationship to another becomes of central significance, not simply *that* a moral agent is a moral agent or is bound by rights, duties, virtue, or utility to act in a certain way.

Third, ecofeminism is structurally pluralistic in that it presupposes and maintains difference—difference among humans as well as between humans and at least some elements of nonhuman nature. Thus, while ecofeminism denies the "nature/culture" split, it affirms that humans are both members of an ecological community (in some respects) and different from it (in other respects). Ecofeminism's attention to relationships and community is not, therefore, an erasure of difference but a respectful acknowledgment of it.

Fourth, ecofeminism reconceives theory as theory in process. It focuses on patterns of meaning which emerge, for instance, from the storytelling and first-person narratives of women (and others) who deplore the twin dominations of women and nature. The use of narrative is one way to ensure that the content of the ethic—the pattern of the quilt—may/will change over time, as the historical and material realities of women's lives change and as more is learned about women–nature connections and the destruction of the non-human world.[13]

Fifth, ecofeminism is inclusivist. It emerges from the voices of women who experience the harmful domination of nature and the way that domination is tied to their domination as women. It emerges from listening to the voices of indigenous peoples such as Native Americans who have been dislocated from their land and have witnessed the attendant undermining of such values as appropriate reciprocity, sharing, and kinship that characterize traditional Indian culture. It emerges from listening to the voices of those who, like Nathan Hare, critique traditional approaches to environmental ethics as white and bourgeois, and as failing to address issues of "black ecology" and the "ecology" of the inner city and urban spaces.[14] It also emerges out of the voices of Chipko women who see the destruction of "earth, soil, and water" as intimately connected with their own inability to survive economically.[15] With its emphasis on inclusivity and difference, ecofeminism provides a framework for recognizing that what counts as ecology and what counts as appropriate conduct toward both human and nonhuman environments is largely a matter of context.

Sixth, as a feminism, ecofeminism makes no attempt to provide an "objective" point of view. It is a social ecology. It recognizes the twin dominations of women and nature as social problems rooted both in very concrete, historical, socioeconomic circumstances and in oppressive patriarchal conceptual frameworks which maintain and sanction these circumstances.

Seventh, ecofeminism makes a central place for values of care, love, friendship, trust, and appropriate reciprocity—values that presuppose that our relationships to others are central to our understanding of who we are.[16] It thereby gives voice to the sensitivity that in climbing a mountain, one is doing something in relationship with an "other," an "other" whom one can come to care about and treat respectfully.

Lastly, an ecofeminist ethic involves a reconception of what it means to be human, and in what human ethical behavior consists. Ecofeminism denies abstract individualism. Humans are who we are in large part by virtue of the historical and social contexts and the relationships we are in, including our relationships with nonhuman nature. Relationships are not something extrinsic to who we are, not an "add on" feature of human nature; they play an essential role in shaping what it is to be human. Relationships of humans to the nonhuman environment are, in part, constitutive of what it is to be a human.

By making visible the interconnections among the dominations of women and nature, ecofeminism shows that both are feminist issues and that explicit acknowledgment of both is vital to any responsible environmental ethic. Feminism *must* embrace ecological feminism if it is to end the domination of women because the domination of women is tied conceptually and historically to the domination of nature.

A responsible environmental ethic also must embrace feminism. Otherwise, even the seemingly most revolutionary, liberational, and holistic ecological ethic will fail to take seriously the interconnected dominations of nature and women that are so much a part of the historical legacy and conceptual framework that sanctions the exploitation of nonhuman nature. Failure to make visible these interconnected, twin dominations results in an inaccurate account of how it is that nature has been and continues to be dominated and exploited and produces an environmental ethic that lacks the depth necessary to be truly *inclusive* of the realities of persons who at least in dominant Western culture have been intimately tied with that exploitation, viz., women. Whatever else can be said in favor of such holistic ethics, a failure to make visible ecofeminist insights into the common denominators of the twin oppressions of women and nature is to perpetuate, rather than overcome, the source of that oppression.

This last point deserves further attention. It may be objected that as long as the end result is "the same"—the development of an environmental ethic which does not emerge out of or reinforce an oppressive conceptual frame-work—it does not matter whether that ethic (or the ethic endorsed in getting there) is feminist or not. Hence, it simply is *not* the case that any adequate environmental ethic must be feminist. My argument, in contrast, has been that it *does* matter, and for three important reasons. First, there is the scholarly issue of accurately representing historical reality, and that, ecofeminists claim, requires acknowledging the historical feminization of nature and naturalization of women as part of the exploitation of nature. Second, I have shown that the conceptual connections between the domination of women and the domination of nature are located in an oppressive and, at least in Western societies, patriarchal conceptual framework characterized by a logic of domination. Thus, I have shown that failure to notice the nature of this connection leaves at best an incomplete, inaccurate, and partial account of what is required of a conceptually adequate environmental ethic. An ethic which *does* not acknowledge this is simply *not* the same as one that does, whatever else the similarities between them. Third, the claim that, in contemporary culture, one can have an adequate environmental ethic which is *not* feminist assumes that, in contemporary culture, the label *feminist* does not add anything crucial to the nature or description of environmental ethics. I have shown that at least in contemporary culture this is false, for the word *feminist* currently helps to clarify just *how* the domination of nature is conceptually linked to patriarchy and, hence, how the liberation of nature is conceptually linked to the termination of patriarchy. Thus, because it has critical bite in contemporary culture, it serves as an important reminder that in contemporary sex-gendered, raced, classed, and naturist culture, an unlabeled position functions as a privileged and "unmarked" position. That is, without the addition of the word *feminist*, one presents environmental ethics as if it has no bias, including male-gender bias, which is just what ecofeminists deny: failure to notice the connections between the twin oppressions of women and nature *is* male-gender bias.

One of the goals of feminism is the eradication of all oppressive sex-gender (and related race, class, age, affectional preference) categories and the creation of a world in which *difference does not breed domination*—say, the world of 4001. If in 4001 an "adequate environmental ethic" is a "feminist environmental ethic," the word *feminist* may then be redundant and unnecessary. However, this is *not* 4001, and in terms of the current historical and conceptual reality the dominations of nature and of women are intimately connected. Failure to notice or make visible that connection in 1990 perpetuates the mistaken (and privileged) view that "environmental ethics" is *not* a feminist issue, and that *feminist* adds nothing to environmental ethics. ...[17]

Notes

1 Explicit ecological feminist literature includes works from a variety of scholarly perspectives and sources. Some of these works are Leonie Caldecott and Stephanie Leland, eds., *Reclaim the Earth: Women Speak Out for Life on Earth (London*: *The* Women's Press, 1983); Jim Cheney, "Eco-Feminism and Deep Ecology," *Environmental Ethics* 9 (1987): 115–45; André Collard with Joyce Contrucci, *Rape of the Wild: Man's Violence against Animals and the Earth* (Bloomington: Indiana University Press, 1988); Katherine Davies, "Historical Associations: Women and the Natural World," *Women & Environments* 9, no. 2 (Spring 1987): 4–6; Sharon Doubiago, "Deeper than Deep Ecology: Men Must Become Feminists," in *The New Catalyst Quarterly*, no. 10 (Winter 1987/88): 10–11; Brian Easlea, *Science and Sexual Oppression: Patriarchy's Confrontation with Women and Nature* (London: Weidenfeld & Nicholson, 1981); Elizabeth Dodson Gray, *Green Paradise Lost* (Wellesley, Mass.: Roundtable Press, 1979); Susan Griffin, *Women and Nature: The Roaring Inside Her* (San Francisco: Harper and Row, 1978); Joan L. Griscom, "On Healing the Nature/History Split in Feminist Thought," in *Heresies #13*: *Feminism and Ecology* 4, no. 1 (1981): 4–9; Ynestra King, "The Ecology of Feminism and the Feminism of Ecology," in *Healing Our Wounds: The Power of Ecological Feminism*, ed. Judith Plant (Boston: New Society Publishers, 1989); pp. 18–28; "The Ecofeminist Imperative," in *Reclaim the Earth*, ed. Caldecott and Leland (London: The Women's Press, 1983); pp. 12–16. "Feminism and the Revolt of Nature," in *Heresies #13: Feminism and Ecology* 4, no. 1 (1981): 12–16, and "What is Ecofeminism?" *The Nation*, 12 December 1987; Marti Kheel, "Animal Liberation Is A Feminist Issue," *The New Catalyst Quarterly*, no. 10 (Winter 1987–88): 8–9; Carolyn Merchant, *The Death of Nature: Women, Ecology and the Scientific Revolution* (San Francisco, Harper and Row, 1980); Patrick Murphy, ed., "Feminism, Ecology, and the Future of the Humanities," special issue of *Studies in the Humanities* 15, no. 2 (December 1988); Abby Peterson and Carolyn Merchant, "Peace with the Earth: Women and the Environmental Movement in Sweden," *Women's Studies International Forum* 9, no. 5–6 (1986): 465–79; Judith Plant, "Searching for Common Ground: Ecofeminism and Bioregionalism," in *The New Catalyst Quarterly*, no. 10 (Winter 1987/88): 6–7; Judith Plant, ed., *Healing Our Wounds; The Power of Ecological Feminism* (Boston: New Society Publishers, 1989); Val Plumwood, "Ecofeminism: An Overview and Discussion of Positions and Arguments," *Australasian Journal of Philosophy*,

Supplement to vol. 64 (June 1986): 120–37; Rosemary Radford Ruether, *New Woman/New Earth: Sexist Ideologies & Human Liberation* (New York: Seabury Press, 1975); Kirkpatrick Sale, "Ecofeminism—A New Perspective," *The Nation*, 26 September 1987): 302–05; Ariel Kay Salleh, "Deeper than Deep Ecology: The Eco-Feminist Connection," *Environmental Ethics* 6 (1984): 339–45, and "Epistemology and the Metaphors of Production: An Eco-Feminist Reading of Critical Theory," in *Studies in the Humanities* 15 (1988): 130–39; Vandana Shiva, *Staying Alive: Women, Ecology and Development* (London: Zed Books, 1988); Charlene Spretnak, "Ecofeminism: Our Roots and Flowering," *The Elmswood Newsletter*, Winter Solstice 1988; Karen J. Warren, "Feminism and Ecology: Making Connections," Environmental Ethics 9 (1987): 3–21; "Toward an Ecofeminist Ethic," *Studies in the Humanities* 15 (1988): 140–56; Miriam Wyman, "Explorations of Ecofeminism," *Women & Environments* (Spring 1987): 6–7; Iris Young, "'Feminism and Ecology' and 'Women and Life on Earth: Eco-Feminism in the 80's'," *Environmental Ethics* 5 (1983): 173–80; Michael Zimmerman, "Feminism, Deep Ecology, and Environmental Ethics," Environmental Ethics 9 (1987): 21–44.

2 Francoise d'Eaubonne, *Le Feminisme ou la Mort* (Paris: Pierre Horay, 1974); pp. 213–52.

3 This account of a feminist ethic draws on my paper "Toward an Ecofeminist Ethic."

4 Marilyn Frye makes this point in her illuminating paper, "The Possibility of Feminist Theory," read at the American Philosophical Association Central Division Meetings in Chicago, 29 April–1 May 1986. My discussion of feminist theory is inspired largely by that paper and by Kathryn Addelson's paper "Moral Revolution," in *Women and Values: Reading in Recent Feminist Philosophy*, ed. Marilyn Pearsall (Belmont, Calif.: Wadsworth Publishing Co., 1986); pp. 291–309.

5 Notice that the standard of inclusiveness does not exclude the voices of men. It is just that those voices must cohere with the voices of women.

6 For a more in-depth discussion of the notions of impartiality and bias, see my paper, "Critical Thinking and Feminism," *Informal Logic* 10, no. 1 (Winter 1988): 31–44.

7 The burgeoning literature on these values is noteworthy. See, e.g., Carol Gilligan, *In a Different Voice: Psychological Theories and Women's Development* (Cambridge: Harvard University Press, 1982); *Mapping the Moral Domain: A Contribution of Women's Thinking to Psychological Theory and Education*, ed. Carol Gilligan, Janie Victoria Ward, and Jill McLean Taylor, with Betty Bardige (Cambridge: Harvard University Press, 1988); Nel Noddings, *Caring: A Feminine Approach to Ethics and Moral Education* (Berkely: University of California Press, 1984); Maria Lugones and Elizabeth V. Spelman, "Have We Got a Theory for You! Feminist Theory, Cultural Imperialism, and the Women's Voice," *Women's Studies International Forum* 6 (1983): 573–81; Maria Lugones, "Playfulness"; Annette C. Baier, "What Do Women Want In A Moral Theory?" Nous 19 (1985); 53–63.

8 Jim Cheney would claim that our fundamental relationships to one another as moral agents are not as moral agents to rights holders, and that whatever rights a person properly may be said to have are relationally defined rights, not rights possessed by atomistic individuals conceived as Robinson Crusoes who do not exist essentially in relation to others. On this view, even rights talk itself is properly conceived as growing out of a relational ethic, not vice versa.

9 Alison Jaggar, *Feminist Politics and Human Nature* (Totowa, N.J.: Rowman and Allan-held, 1980); pp. 42–44.

10 Henry West has pointed out that the expression "defining relations" is ambiguous. According to West, "the 'defining' as Cheney uses it is an adjective, not a principle—it is not that ethics defines relationships: it is that ethics grows out of conceiving of the relationships that one is in as defining what the individual is."

11 For example, in relationships involving contracts or promises, those relationships might be correctly described as that of moral agent to rights holders. In relationships involving mere property, those relationships might be correctly described as that of moral agent to objects having only instrumental value, "relationships of instrumentality." In comments on an earlier draft of this paper, West suggested that possessive individualism, for instance, might be recast in such a way that an individual is defined by his or her property relationships.

12 Cheney, "Eco-Feminism and Deep Ecology," p. 144.

13 One might object that such permission for change opens the door for environmental exploitation. This is not the case. An ecofeminist ethic is anti-naturist. Hence, the unjust domination and exploitation of nature is a "boundary condition" of the ethic; no such actions are sanctioned or justified on ecofeminist grounds. What it *does* leave open is some leeway

about what counts as domination and exploitation. This, I think, is a strength of the ethic, not a weakness, since it acknowledges that *that* issue cannot be resolved in any practical way in the abstract, independent of a historical and social context.

14 Nathan Hare, "Black Ecology," in *Environmental Ethics*, ed. K. S. Shrader-Frechette (Pacific Grove, Calif.: Boxwood Press, 1981); pp. 229–36.

15 For an ecofeminist discussion of the Chipko movement, see my "Toward an Ecofeminist Ethic," and Shiva's *Staying Alive*.

16 See Cheney, "Eco-Feminism and Deep Ecology," p. 122.

17 I offer the same sort of reply to critics of ecofeminism such as Warwick Fox who suggest that for the sort of ecofeminism I defend, the word *feminist* does not add anything significant to environmental ethics and, consequently, that an ecofeminist like myself might as well call herself a deep ecologist. He asks: "Why doesn't she just call it [i.e., Warren's vision of a transformative feminism] deep ecology? Why specifically attach the label *feminist* to it...?" (Warwick Fox, "The Deep Ecology-Ecofeminism Debate and Its Parallels," Environmental Ethics 11, no. 1 [1989]: 14, n. 22). Whatever the important similarities between deep ecology and ecofeminism (or, specifically, my version of ecofeminism)—and, indeed, there are many—it is precisely my point here that the word *feminist* does add something significant to the conception of environmental ethics, and that any environmental ethic including deep ecology) that fails to make explicit the different kinds of interconnections among the domination of nature and the domination of women will be, from a feminist (and ecofeminist) perspective such as mine, inadequate.

Patently Wrong

The Commercialization of Life Forms

Wanda Teays

Janice Armstrong, a Monsanto [corporation] spokeswoman, said the company invested hundreds of millions of dollars to develop the seed [Roundup Ready]. "We need to protect our intellectual property so that we can continue to develop the next wave of products," she said.

Adam Liptak, *The New York Times*

The practice of caring for the earth has traditionally fallen upon farmers. In the past the vast majority of people were directly or indirectly involved in agriculture; but in the past few centuries farms have been transformed into agribusinesses, becoming a branch of the ever-growing industrial-technological economy.

Norman Wirzba, *The Christian Century*

It used to be that there were farmers, seeds, and dirt. The three formed a triad that endured for centuries, with the resulting crops feeding the world. In time "farmers" were not just Mom-and-Pop operations, with the parents and some collection of children doing the bulk of the work required to sustain the family's livelihood. They became agents of agribusiness overseeing operations on a global scale.

The dirt that provided the fertile soil was no longer that which nature supplied at this place or the next. It was replaced by a mix of soil, chemicals, and additives—a result of the efforts of chemists and others who perfected the formulae out of which the seeds would sprout and mature, preferably strong, vital, and pest-free. With that, the very soul of agriculture changed in ways that defied turning back the clock. And the seeds; what of them? They used to be *one* thing we could count on. Not any more.

Taking a historical perspective John Seabrook (2007) observed that:

> From the beginning, farmers must have realized that by saving a certain portion of the seeds from the previous year's crop they could insure themselves of a future harvest. (In Jarmo, Iraq, archeologists have found seed deposits that date from 6750 B.C.) Seed saving was one of the most important acts that a farming community performed ... When the community moved, it took its seeds along, too.

That relationship between the farmer, the community, and its bank of seeds underwent a radical transformation in just over 30 years. No longer the property of the farmer who grew the plants or the society that shared the means for survival, seeds became something that one person or one corporation could control and exert ownership rights with little, if any, regard for the human cost. That cost extends past the level of the individual farmer or local businessman, past the level of the community's survival in harsh times, to the level of the diverse species of plants and animals worldwide.

Plant and animal diversity is crucial for climate–atmospheric change or other unexpected challenges to the food supply. Stephen Smith, a research fellow at Pioneer Hi-Bred, one of the world's largest seed companies, said: "How humans use diversity in farming determines our food, our health, and our economic well-being, and that in turn determines our political security" (Seabrook 2007).

Seeds became something that could be patented, that could be considered someone else's *intellectual* property. We cannot reconstruct the past, but we can step back and give the situation our attention. We might then be able to see what further steps are necessary to minimize the chances of a global catastrophe. The commercialization of forms of life has taken us down a path shrouded in fog and driven by greed. We need to see more clearly before proceeding.

In this essay, I will try to shed light on the problems and offer some suggestions for moving forward. That the Monsanto Company is at the center of the storm is both intentional (on their part, as they have patented various genetically modified seeds) and accidental (if they had not, someone else would sooner or later). That does not mean that there are not concerns about the adversarial ways in which they have dealt with farmers. In this respect, both Virtue Ethics and Feminist Ethics are useful in assessing the ethical dilemmas we face and trying to arrive at a resolution.

Let us start with a few background details to set the context. It is vital that we see how we became entangled in the use of words, that we look at the major concerns, examine the reasoning, and see what can be achieved. At the level of the Court of Appeals and the Supreme Court, the dissenting statements have both expressed opinions and raised concerns with which Aristotle and the Feminist Ethicists would agree.

Setting the Stage: Patenting Micro-Organisms

The US Supreme Court case of *Diamond* v. *Chakrabarty* (1980) set the stage for the patenting of living organisms and the commercialization of life. The decision has had long-reaching effects—far beyond the "oil-eating" bacteria that Ananda Mohan Chakrabarty modified. The Court held that "live, *human-made* micro-organisms" (emphsis added) could be patented. Indeed, "Anything under the sun that is made by man can be patented," the Court stated (s. III). Journalist Marie-Monique Robin (2008) reports that: "based on U.S. precedents, the European Patent Office in Munich granted patents on microorganisms in 1982, on plants in 1985, on animals in 1988, and on human embryos in 2000." As far as the United States goes: "The U.S. Patent and Trademark Office grants more than seventy thousand patents a year, about 20 percent of which involving living organisms," according to a 2008 report (Robin 2008).

The *Diamond* decision rested on the view that Chakrabarty's bacterium could be considered a "manufacture" or "composition of matter" within the statute. In order for that to happen, the two concepts had to be stretched. What counts as a "manufacture" or a "composition of matter" had to be expanded if a living thing could be so categorized. Certainly, there was no historical precedent for doing so. Without a prior example to point to, either a new law would have to be enacted or the current law would have to be reinterpreted.

The latter route was evidently deemed preferable, in spite of the linguistic challenges for accomplishing that objective. Congress did this by giving patent laws a wider scope, as they called it. Moreover, previous legislation was said to *support* the broader use of the terms. As the Court stated: "Broad general language is not necessarily ambiguous when congressional objectives require broad terms" (*Diamond*, s. IV(b)).

Previous legislation might be said to "support" a particular interpretation in the negative. That is, in the absence of an apparent contradiction or a specific prohibition *against* the policy in question, stretching the law is then thought permissible. The failure to explicitly disallow a course of action ("X") is taken as a green light for X being a legitimate option.

The Court's reasoning also rests on an unwarranted assumption. In referring to Chakrabarty's bacterium, the justices in *Diamond* used descriptions that lacked the neutrality we might expect of the Supreme Court. The first reference is to an "invention of a *human-made*, genetically-engineered bacterium capable of breaking down crude oil." The second is to a "live, *human-made* micro-organism" (*Diamond*, s. I). This seems to be begging the question. Let us see how.

The reasoning of the Court is this: Chakrabarty's claim "is not to a hitherto unknown natural phenomenon." In contrast to "laws of nature, physical phenomena, and abstract ideas," products "of human ingenuity" that are "nonnaturally occurring manufacture or composition of matter" can be patented (s. III). To further clarify, the "mark of human ingenuity can be found in having a distinct name, character [and] use," according to the ruling.

The Court asserts that the meaning of the terms is crucial, which is clearly true. They draw from a much earlier definition, the 1793 Patent Act. Authored by Thomas Jefferson, it defined statutory subject matter as "any new and useful art, machine, manufacture, or composition of matter, or any new or useful improvement [thereof]." In addition, the ruling holds that: "The Act embodied Jefferson's philosophy that 'ingenuity should receive a liberal encouragement'" (s. III).

As far as the Court is concerned, this seals the deal, even though neither the Patent Act nor Thomas Jefferson mentions nature or living things as a member of the class of "art, machine, manufacture or composition of matter," whether improved upon or not. In addition, it is not readily apparent that Jefferson's concept of "ingenuity" included altering life forms and claiming them as one's own private (= sovereign) property.

The fact that the 1793 Patent Act says "any" was seen to imply an application so broad as to include virtually anything that was not a law of nature, an abstract idea, etc. So anything "made by man" that is a machine or manufacture might qualify for a patent (s. III). Greenpeace spokesman Christoph Then, expressed the concern that: "To get a patent, it is no longer necessary to present a real invention, often all you need is a simple discovery ... [such as] a therapeutic use for a plant ... The deciding factor is that the description be done in a laboratory" (Robin 2008).

The inference on the part of Congress and the Supreme Court in *Diamond* was to opt for the broadest interpretation of the 1793 Patent Act that could be drawn. As we saw, this was done by redefining the terms. They did not take into account that during the time between 1793 (Jefferson's Patent Act) and 1980 (the *Diamond* court ruling) there were no living organisms that had received a patent, regardless of the amount of "ingenuity" that was demonstrated.

Chakrabarty produced "new bacteria" markedly different from that found in nature, and one "having the potential for significant utility" (s. III). Presumably it is the latter achievement that was the catalyst for the patent, given the commercial potential. No one doubts the usefulness of an oil-eating organism, given the spills and other potential ecological disasters that need to be addressed in a timely fashion. Nevertheless, the Court may not have foreseen how such a liberal interpretation of the language would have such powerful consequences. Many patent applications that followed staked out ownership of life forms, thanks to *Diamond*.

The Court's bottom line was that, Chakrabarty's discovery "is not nature's handiwork, but his own; accordingly it is patentable subject matter under 101" (s. III). So we have the subject of the dispute (the micro-organism) described as both an "invention" and "human-made." In other words, we have an *invented* micro-organism that is, at the same time, *human-made*. The fact that the raw material is a living thing and thus something found in nature and *not* human-made, is de-emphasized. And yet that is one of the central issues.

The implication is that anyone capable of genetically, or otherwise, modifying a life form for a set of objectives (e.g., to develop drought-resistant plants or PERV-resistant pigs, etc.) would likely be able to patent the resulting organism. At the time of *Diamond*, the focus was on bacteria (plants), and the more far-reaching and unsettling ethical issues attached to modifying animals was not on the table.

It is no minor matter to allow patents for bacteria that are not considered "nature's handiwork." The Court saw the Plant Patent Act 1930 as setting the foundation. Passed by Congress, the Plant Patent Act considered that "the work of the plant breeder 'in aid of nature' was patentable invention" (s. IV(a)). In other words, Congress viewed such aids to nature as *inventions*. This is an interesting claim, one that turns on a degree of ambiguity. What are the boundaries for the plant breeder to claim that an "invention" has taken place? Evidently no member of Congress excluded living things from the list. That was a striking omission.

Without a line drawn in the sand, bacteria and any number of other living things could potentially be patented, as long as the required minimum "aid to nature" had been met. According to the justices in *Diamond*, the distinction that mattered was between products of nature (living or not) and human-made inventions—*not* between living and inorganic things (s. IV). This makes some sense, though the bifurcation may be part of the problem. It reduces the options to products of nature *or* human-made inventions.

The question is what falls into the category of "human-made inventions." If a human uses a "product of nature" and modifies, transforms, or builds upon the natural thing, is that sufficient to be considered a patentable "human-made *invention*"? How minor need the alterations be to make the grade? And if the Court defines Chakrabarty's modified bacterium as "human-made," it can hardly be a "product of nature." Thus, it would fall into the classification of an "invention."

Once there, the decision in Chakrabarty's favor falls into place. The commercial fallout from the decision is significant. And once the description of the bacterium as a "human-made invention" versus a "product of nature" is allowed to stick, the cows are out of the barn. There is no easy way to get them back—the only option is to try to set down some qualifications, limits, or controls.

Meanwhile, patenting bacterium seems minor in comparison with what followed. Within 30 years, the distinction drawn in *Diamond* moved to a level of abstraction that painted over the discrepancies around the use of language we saw in that case. With the Supreme Court decision in *Monsanto* v. *Geertson Seed Farms*, the focus moved away from "human-made inventions," which seemed positively primitive next to "intellectual property." That became the new battleground.

And, as the rules of the game changed with the new use of language, the question of who controls what comes to the surface. For some commentators (e.g., Vandana Shiva), the key questions are: Can life be made? Can life be owned? Who controls living organisms? We might also add: And what happens when the commercialization of one organism has a deleterious effect on others? Are there any boundaries whatsoever?

Seeds as Intellectual Property

"It doesn't look right for them to have a patent on something that you can grow yourself," observed Homan McFarling, Mississippi farmer of 5000 acres of land (Liptak 2003). On the one hand, McFarling admits that he did buy and plant 1000 bags of saved seeds that had been genetically altered. As McFarling noted: "Every farmer that ever farmed has saved some of his seed to plant again." He did not seem to realize that things were different in the era of patented life forms.

The seeds, ironically named "Roundup Ready," drew more to him than McFarling's worst nightmare. Monsanto struck with the vengeance of a jilted lover—those seeds that were saved from the previous year's efforts were not just any old seed. They were *patented* seeds. Indeed, corporate spokesperson Janice Armstrong, showed her hand by saying: "We need to protect our intellectual property so that we can continue to develop the next wave of products" (Liptak 2003).

Come again on Armstrong's claim: "We need to protect our intellectual property." She did not say: "We need to protect our seeds from being misused or misappropriated." Her focus was on what those seeds represented. They were not seeds—not primarily anyway. They were *intellectual property* and, like most property, they had an owner that had a controlling interest in its use. And given that Monsanto's soybean seeds account for at least two-thirds of the US soybean harvest, as Adam Liptak reports in *The New York Times*, then that use is a lucrative proposition.

We need to understand what is being asserted here. Monsanto's argument was persuasive enough to bring a ruling that McFarling owed them US$780,000. A similar case, *Monsanto Co.* v *David* (2008) arrived at a similar result, affirming a significant damages award owed to Monsanto. Both rest on the concept of "intellectual property." The fact that seeds or any life forms could be categorized as intellectual property raises important issues.

Intellectual property law professor William Fisher, III (1997), points out that the term "intellectual property" has a much broader scope than patents. He indicates that it: "encompasses several, partially overlapping doctrines." Fisher sets them out as follows:

- *copyright law* protects "original forms of expression" (e.g., *Magic Mountain*, "Star Wars");
- *patent law* protects inventions (e.g., windsurfers, chemical processes, genetically engineered mice);
- *trademark law* protects words and symbols that identify goods and services (e.g., "McDonalds," the distinctive shape of a Ferrari Testarosa);
- *trade-secret law* protects information that a company has tried but failed to conceal from competitors (e.g., secret formulas for soft drinks, confidential marketing strategies); and
- *"right of publicity"* protects celebrities' interests in their images and identities.

"The history of each of these doctrines (like the histories of most areas of the law)," notes Fisher, "is involuted and idiosyncratic, but one overall trend is common to all: expansion. With rare exceptions, the set of entitlements created by each of the doctrines has grown steadily and dramatically from the eighteenth century to the present" (1997). We might then consider the term a bundle of concepts, only one of which is focused on patents.

The question is what advantage did Monsanto acquire in referring to *intellectual property* rights instead of the rights granted under the patent? Why call seeds "intellectual property"? It seems unlikely that the average person thinks about seeds in this way. The average farmer would presumably be even less inclined to speak of seeds as intellectual property, given that his or her connection to crops is almost certainly stronger than that of the typical consumer. This would be the case even if they *did* think of the seeds as Monsanto's property. Replacing the word "seeds" with "intellectual property" for the purpose of asserting one's controlling interest elevates the dispute to a more abstract and legalistic level. It may also be strategically advantageous not to actually call a seed a "seed."

In a fight over *my* seeds versus *your* seeds, it may be hard to see where the battle lines should be drawn. It is one thing when we each have our bags of seed to compare. But in a conflict over my seeds versus your intellectual property, are we talking about the same thing? The idea that my barn or field contains any of your intellectual property is hard to wrap our minds around.

As far as Monsanto is concerned, the planting of saved seed is "piracy" (Liptak 2003). Opponents contend that the problem is not piracy; it is *biopiracy* (White Earth Land Recovery Project n.d.). They rest this accusation on the global scope of Monsanto's operation, as well as the commercialization of natural processes and resources. In arguing that any unauthorized use of their seeds is piracy, Monsanto is pitting ownership interests in the fruits (so to speak) of scientific advancements against community-based, agrarian life styles. The latter relies far more on the model of handshakes and collaboration than that of the patented product with a strict enforcement policy to keep consumers in line. As we will see in Circuit Judge Clevenger's dissenting opinion in *Diamond* v. *Chakrabarty*, this very policy is heavy-handed and alienating.

One thing that is different with biotechnology is that farmers are expected to give up their traditional rights, such as seed saving, argues Colorado farmer David Dechant (2002). From the company's perspective, Monsanto would effectively lose control of their rights if farmers were allowed to replant the seed, regardless of the historical precedent. But that was then, this is now. And the "now" we are looking at is not of the *mi casa es su casa* variety. It is a fiercely competitive, high stakes game, and one with corporate interests and their considerable legal and financial resources to deal with those who do not abide by the rules. The question is whether those rules are fair.

This is a concern raised by then President Clinton's Secretary of Agriculture, Dan Glickman. "Contracts with farmers need to be fair and not result in a system that reduces farmers to mere serfs on the land or create an atmosphere of mistrust among farmers or between farmers and companies," he declared as far back as 1999 (Robin 2008).

Company representative Karen Armstrong, acknowledges that Monsanto must walk a fine line. "'These people are our customers,'" she said, "'and we do value them. But we also have to protect our intellectual property rights" (Liptak 2003). This translated into a rather unbending relationship with the farmers, with "seed police" trying to catch farmers who are suspected of seed "piracy." As Charles Niebylski pointed out in his case brief for *Diamond*, shopping for Roundup Ready soybean seeds was not simply a trek to the local farm supply store:

> To obtain Monsanto's soybean seeds, farmers had to purchase the seeds from an authorized Monsanto dealer and had to sign a "Technology Agreement," promising not to replant seeds from the first generation of soybean crops and not to sell seeds that were produced by the first generation crop to others. Monsanto collected a license fee of $6.50 per fifty-pound bag of seed and the dealer charged $19 to $22 per bag of seed. (Niebylski 2007)

Monsanto was successful in its case against farmer Homan McFarling. McFarling had signed a standard contract when he bought the seed. He said he did not read the contract at the time. The fact that the majority of people downloading software updates without a careful examination of the contract that they "agree" to shows how trusting or naïve is the general public.

McFarling said he had no idea that he was doing anything unlawful until Monsanto contacted him with a US$135 000 settlement offer. He had paid about US$24 000 for 1000 bags of seed, including the license/technology fee (Liptak 2003). The contract, Monsanto's "Technology Agreement," said buyers could use the seed only for a single season and could not save any seed produced from this crop for replanting. The upshot is that McFarling violated the contract in saving any seeds for future use. Both the Appeals Court and the Supreme Court sided with Monsanto, citing the terms of the patent.

Not all agree. Circuit Judge Clevenger of the US Court of Appeals stated in his (2002) dissenting opinion that the contract put McFarling at a great disadvantage. "No one perusing the Technology Agreement can doubt that its terms are decidedly one-sided in Monsanto's favor," he stated. He cited two reasons in support of McFarling: "The terms printed on the reverse of the technology agreement are not subject to negotiation and Monsanto's billions of dollars in assets far exceed McFarling's alleged net worth of $75,000" (*Monsanto*, Court of Appeals).

To get a better sense of the severity of this situation, consider this scenario: we city dwellers love to garden and cannot wait to get some flower seeds to plant for spring. You hear there are some new ones called Stampede flower seeds that have the pesticides right in them. Fantastic! Trotting off to the local nursery, you discover that they no longer sell flower seeds—just plants. You are referred to an "authorized dealer" of flower seeds and off you go. You then discover the Stampede seeds require a contract. Yes, a contract, and one with penalties should you trade or sell some of their seeds to your neighbor or set some aside for next year's garden. As for the penalty—US$10 worth of the flower seeds used or reused in a way that violates the contract would result in a fine of US$1200!

The stern warning in the contract clues us in that we may need to consult a lawyer before buying the flower seeds. "That's outrageous," you say, opting to get seeds from your aunt in Kentucky, and to order the rest from an organic seed store you have heard about. Happy with your decision, in just a few weeks, you have planted your garden. But you did not count on seeds blowing over the fence from your neighbor's garden they planted with Stampede seeds. And now your garden is contaminated. Or maybe your neighbor was mad that you cut their loquat tree hanging over your side of the fence—and she threw Stampede seeds into *your* garden, knowing that they would mix with your seeds. In either case, Stampede is coming after you!

Come on, now, really. Whenever we watch a DVD, we first see that FBI warning to remind us of the multi-thousand dollar fine that we could face if we do not obey the warning. Surely, DVD piracy and seed piracy are analogous. But they are not, if for no other reason than that DVDs do not rely on living organisms. In contrast, genetically modified seeds are fully dependent upon "nature's handiwork."

Stiff penalties for ripping off an artist's creation is not the same sort of thing as using genetically enhanced seeds. Artists, musicians, and authors start from scratch, whereas the scientist here does not. Those Roundup Ready or Stampede seeds are not human-made; they are human-*modified* seeds. The transformation from a regular seed (soybean, alfalfa, flower, etc.) would not be possible if there had not been seeds in the first place. Without the base seed there could be no genetically altered seed to plant, replant, or sell to the next guy.

Corporations like Monsanto using terms like "intellectual property" instead of "seed" suggest a comparison with artistic works. This comparison falls short. Also, when you buy a book, DVD, or CD, you can read or play them over and over again, and sell them at yard sells or the like. But not so genetically modified seeds. The restrictions are on a different level altogether.

These "technology agreements" are considered "contracts of adhesion," noted Judge Clevenger. These are contracts between two unequal parties (here the corporation with its patented seeds and the farmer-customers) in which one party has all the bargaining power and uses it to his or her advantage. Judge Clevenger summarized the situation as follows:

> Monsanto's own state of Missouri has defined an adhesive contract as "one in which the parties have unequal standing in terms of bargaining power (usually a large corporation versus an individual)" and often involve take-it-or-leave-it provisions in printed form contracts.

With all the power on the one side, any willingness to negotiate seems less likely. This is the situation farmers found themselves in. Judge Clevenger made it clear that the contract that farmers must sign when purchasing the Roundup Ready soybeans is stacked in Monsanto's favor. He argued that:

> No one perusing the Technology Agreement can doubt that its terms are decidedly one-sided in Monsanto's favor. A farmer signing the 1998 Technology Agreement did not merely agree to submit to the jurisdiction of the Eastern District of Missouri and to refrain from saving and replanting seed. Sale of Roundup Ready seed to the farmer was made on the condition that the farmer shall not use on that crop the glyphosate herbicides of any of Monsanto's competitors.
>
> The farmer further agreed that Monsanto's damages for saving and replanting seed shall include, in addition to Monsanto's other remedies, liquidated damages based on 120 times the applicable Technology Fee. The farmer further agreed to bear the costs of Monsanto's suit against him by paying all of Monsanto's legal fees and costs. By the terms of the Technology Agreement, all that the farmer received in exchange for these promises was the "opportunity" to purchase and plant Roundup Ready seed and the "opportunity" to participate in Monsanto's crop insurance programs.

Judge Clevenger seems incredulous about the specifics of the "Technology Agreement." "Someone versed in the specialized decisions collected in law books might have understood it," he pointed out, "'but we may presume that few feed stores stock the *Federal Reporter* on their shelves."

The thinking of Justice Stevens of the US Supreme Court is similar to that of Judge Clevenger in questioning the direction the courts have taken with respect to Monsanto's patented seeds. In his dissent in the Supreme Court 2010 decision of *Monsanto* v. *Geertson Seed Farms*, Justice Stevens raised concerns about farmers' fields being contaminated by genetically modified seeds. In particular, Monsanto's Roundup Ready alfalfa (RRA) seeds that get into fields because of weather conditions, spillage in transport, inadequately cleaned machinery, etc. could harm the non-RRA seeds and destroy their crop.

Justice Stevens thought it troubling that we may be making law without paying attention to the critical questions. This is especially the case when "the environmental threat is novel" and someone is "conducting a new type of activity with completely unknown effects on the environment" (p. 12). Expressing concern about "environmental injury," he notes that, "if it were to spread through open land the environmental and economic consequences could be devastating" (p. 15). This is not an idle matter.

Moreover, once gene transfer has occurred, it would be "difficult—if not impossible—to reverse the harm," Justice Stevens asserts (p. 16). This view is echoed by molecular biologist John Fagan. He warns of unexpected, harmful side-effects that cannot be reversed and, consequently, will affect future generations. "The side effects caused by genetic manipulations are not just long-term," he argues. "They are permanent" (Fagan 2011).

The Ethical Perspective

Some see individual farmers battling Monsanto as analogous to David and Goliath—except that these Davids have had their butts kicked. Whether they failed to read the fine details of the technology agreement or even had one to sign, whether their crops were contaminated by the wind blowing neighboring seed into their fields, or whether corporate investigators caught them in some transgression, the errant farmers crossed the line and paid the price. How many have to be put through the wringer before we see that Monsanto (or other multinationals patenting plants or animals) may have the law on their side, but it is a heartless win. A pyrrhic victory only goes so far.

Farmer David Dechant recommends that: "Something first should be done about the terms under which competitive pressures force farmers to eventually adopt it. Otherwise, there are going to be thousands more farmers who find themselves in a legal battle with an infinitely more powerful opponent" (2002).

If you need a herd of investigators and a team of lawyers to ensure compliance, something is wrong. Breeding an atmosphere of fear and loathing is not what any self-respecting business wants or needs. And no matter how often you call a seed "intellectual property," it still looks like a seed and blows about from one field to the next, just like other seeds. Furthermore, the long history of humanity's relationship with life forms cannot be eradicated by any number of court decisions. Something is out of whack. Action is needed to break the reprisals and high-mindedness of corporations, on the one hand, and the bitterness and/or resignation of farmers, on the other.

This is the point at which Virtue Ethics and Feminist Ethics can offer some guidance. feminist ethicists have decried the emphasis on rights- and rule-based thinking, arguing that the exclusion of relationships from the equation is fundamentally misguided. This realignment of values suggests that we need to find a balance that is sorely missing.

Aristotle's Virtue Ethics offers a good start. Aristotle divides virtues into two categories: moral virtues and intellectual virtues. His moral virtues include such traits as courage, self-control, generosity, compassion, and modesty. All of these virtues are the result of finding the mean between two extremes. Basically, we ought not to have a deficiency of virtue (e.g., cowardice) and ought not to have an excess of virtue (e.g., recklessness), but aim for the mean (e.g., courage). He thinks we ought to use this approach as a model for most of our ethical decisions and actions. Achieving a life of virtue and meaning—developing the moral character to find fulfillment—will then be within reach.

This advice ("aim for the mean, not the extreme") is in line with Judge Clevenger's observations about the imbalance in Monsanto's contract—leaving farmers few options and little recourse. The one-sidedness of the "Technology Agreement" Monsanto presented to soybean farmers was, as Judge Clevenger implied, simply not fair dealing. The very fact that the "damages" (= penalty) for saving and replanting the seed (thus not abiding by the terms of the sale) included not only other "remedies" and Monsanto's legal fees, but 120 times "the applicable Technology fee," shows that the terms contract are unfair. The Federal Circuit ruled that a District Court finding that McFarling infringed Monsanto's patent was justified and affirmed a jury award of US$375,000 against McFarling.

Aristotle would look askance at the damages fee structure and see deficiencies in three moral virtues. First, he would likely say a corporation appears shameless, petty, and callous in threatening or actually slapping farmers with such a large penalty for patent violations. These are deficiencies of modesty, nobility, and even-temperedness, respectively. Contracts of adhesion, as Judge Clevenger pointed out, are overly harsh—perhaps merciless—tools for a business to use with its customers. Moreover, they inject tension, anxiety, fear, and distrust into the relationship.

A feminist ethicist would voice concern over this, given their emphasis on a care-based value system that gives relationships much more importance than do either deontological (duty-based) ethicists or teleological (goal-based) ethicists. Ethicist Mary Anne Warren puts it this way: "The ethic of care requires that proximate strangers be met with a caring attitude. This does not preclude vigorous self-defense when needed ... Nor are we obliged to impoverish ourselves and our families for the sake of strangers" (1997: 140).

Feminist ethicists would say that Justice Stevens is right on the money in stating that the Court did not give sufficient attention to the critical issues. In addition, the Court failed to bring into their assessment of the case both a concern for the environment and greater interest as to long-term consequences of the genetically modified seeds that received patent protections.

As Justice Stevens wrote in his dissent, the environmental threat is novel: unknown, unpredictable, and possibly permanent. He also indicated that there could be environmental injury from the genetically modified seeds that is devastating and could affect generations to come. These are the words of someone who *cares* deeply about future populations and about the environment.

Justice Stevens' expression of concern resonates with Feminist Ethics' commitment to integrating relationships into our moral reasoning. We are not alone: we are among others like and unlike ourselves. We live on and off the land and must care for it in order for us all to survive. We have to work together to be caretakers of the earth. "We have good reasons to hold that earth, air, water, biological species, and natural ecosystem have more than instrumental value," Warren says. "Human beings may be more included to protect these vulnerable elements of the natural world if they accept moral obligations towards them" (1997: 167).

We need to rethink our approach to patenting life forms and declaring them "intellectual property." Philosopher-lawyer David Koepsell observes that: "Most ordinary people do not seem viscerally to accept the fact that products of nature ... could be declared to be private property. Moreover, no other analogous legal entity enjoys this status" (2009: 26). He points out that "currently and without adequate reason DNA is being treated like software, steam engines, manmade chemical compounds, and other more likely candidates for patent. It is not too late to consider where there is a strong theoretical basis for this" (p. 27). No, it is not too late. But that does not mean there is any time to waste.

References

Aristotle, *Nicomachean Ethics*, available at: www.classics.mit.edu/Aristotle/nicomachaen.html.

Dechant, David (2002) "Monsanto vs Homan McFarling: Judge Clevenger Understands," *CropChoice*, December 5, 2002, available at: www.biotech-info.net/monsanto_v_homan.html.

Diamond v. *Chakrabarty*, 447 US 303 (1980).

Fagan, John (2011) quoted in "Farmers' Woes," *Say No to GMOS*, 2011, available at: www.saynotogmos.org/farmers2.htm.

Fisher, III, William (1997) "The Growth of Intellectual Property: A History of the Ownership of Ideas in the United States," available at: http://cyber.law.harvard.edu/property99/history.html.

Koepsell, David (2009) *Who Owns You?* Malden, MA: Wiley-Blackwell.

Liptak, Adam (2003) "Saving Seeds Subjects Farmers to Suits Over Patent," *The New York Times*, November 2.

Monsanto v. *David*, 2007-1104, (Fed. Cir.) February 5, 2008, available at: www.ll.georgetown.edu/federal/judicial/fed/opinions/07opinions/07-1104.pdf.

Monsanto Company et al. v. *Geertson Seed Farms et al.*, US Supreme Court, 561 US, No. 09-475, June 21, 2010, available at: www.supremecourt.gov/opinions/09pdf/09-475.pdf.

Monsanto Company v. *Homan McFarling*, Case Brief authored by, Charles Niebylski, Nos. 05-1570, 05-1598, May 24, 2007, available at: www.nathlaw.com/news/publications/05-1570_1598.pdf.

Monsanto Co. v. *McFarling*, No. 01-1390 (Fed. Cir.) August 23, 2002. Dissenting Opinion (Circuit Judge Clevenger), available at: http://openjurist.org/302/f3d/1291/monsanto-company-v-mcfarling.

Robin, Marie-Monique (2008) *The World According to Monsanto*, New York: New Press.

Seabrook, John (2007) "Sowing for Apocalypse," *The New Yorker*, August 27.

Warren, Mary Anne (1997) *Moral Status*, New York: Oxford University Press.

White Earth Land Recovery Project(n.d.) "Patents and Biopiracy," available at: http://nativeharvest.com/node/249.

Wirzba, Norman (1999) "Caring and Working: An Agrarian Perspective," *The Christian Century*, September 22–29, 1999, available at: www.emmitsburg.net/archive_list/articles/thoughtful/jcfs/caring_working.htm.

C. Aesthetics

Aesthetics and the Value of Nature

JANNA THOMPSON

Like many environmental philosophers, I find the idea that the beauty of wildernesses makes them valuable in their own right and gives us a moral duty to preserve and protect them to be attractive. However, this appeal to aesthetic value encounters a number of serious problems. I argue that these problems can best be met and overcome by recognizing that the appreciation of natural environments and the appreciation of great works of arts are activities more similar than many people have supposed.

I

Nature is beautiful. Few people would doubt that this claim, and the aesthetic value of an environment is something that often figures as a consideration in environmental planning and development. In this context, the beauty of a forest or river is treated alongside "recreational use" as an instrumental value: beauty is understood to be whatever happens to delight people. Because individuals are pleased by different things and fashions in taste are subject to change, an appeal to beauty thus seems to make a weak case for preservation. However, philosophers and environmentalists have sometimes argued that beauty is not a mere instrumental value and not merely a matter of personal taste, and that when properly appreciated, the existence of natural beauty is a good reason for its preservation. G.E. Moore regarded beauty, whether in nature or art, as an intrinsic good, something worthy of respect for its own sake, and therefore something we have an ethical duty to promote.[1] Eugene Hargrove develops this view into an argument for the preservation of nature: "Since the loss of both natural and artistic beauty represents a loss in the total good in the world, it is our duty to try to preserve both kinds of beauty as best we can."[2]

Like Moore, Hargrove is saying that a thing of beauty has a value in its own right. Aesthetic value cannot be reduced to the capacity to give us pleasure or feelings of awe and wonder. Their way of understanding beauty or, more generally, aesthetic value seems to answer much better to the desire of preservationists and deep ecologists to

---

Janna Thompson, "Aesthetics and the Value of Nature," *Environmental Ethics*, 17 (3) (1995): 291–306. Reprinted with permission.

find noninstrumental ways of valuing nature.[3] Moreover, aesthetic worth is something that people can come to identify with and appreciate, and thus it seems that the appeal to the beauty of nature can provide a more satisfactory and defensible ground for preservation than do appeals to an inherent value that is independent of the human point of view. I have argued elsewhere that a conception of value in nature that transcends human concerns leaves it unclear what in nature is to be regarded as valuable in its own right, and thus does not provide us with the basis for a practical ethic.[4] For those who have similar concerns, Hargrove's attempt to derive an ethical position from the aesthetic value of nature seems like a promising direction to take: justice can be done to the deep ecological intuition that nature is intrinsically valuable and at the same time we can obtain, it seems, a well-grounded understanding of what our duties are. The critical issues are whether and how this promise can be fulfilled.

II

Most people can be persuaded that art has a value that is not merely instrumental. We do think that great works of art are worthy of respect, that we ought to make an effort to appreciate them (and that those who do not are Philistines), and that anyone who tries to destroy or damage them deserves moral condemnation. Because nature too is beautiful, it seems reasonable to insist that the same attitudes and prohibitions should be extended to natural things.

However, the success of this argument clearly depends upon our being able to establish that aesthetic value, whether in art or in nature, is intrinsic, noninstrumental, value. It also depends crucially on the objectivity of our value claims. The link that Moore and Hargrove want to make between aesthetic judgment and ethical obligation fails unless there are objective grounds—grounds that rational, sensitive people can accept—for thinking that something has value. If beauty in nature or in art is merely in the eyes of the beholder, then no general moral obligation arises out of aesthetic judgments, except the weaker obligation to preserve, if possible, what some individuals happen to value. A judgment of value that is merely personal and subjective gives us no way of arguing that everyone ought to learn to appreciate something, or at least to regard it as worthy of preservation.[5]

To insist that value judgments must be objective in this sense does not require us to suppose that beauty and other aesthetic values are real properties of objects. Nor do we have to suppose that the value of works of art or nature is independent of human perceivers. Claims to aesthetic objectivity clearly raise ontological questions about the nature of value. However, it is not necessary to settle metaphysical questions about beauty in order to defend the idea that our aesthetic judgments are, or can be, objective. We can and do give reasons for our aesthetic judgments. Critics are expected to provide a justification for why they think a work of art ought to be valued, and through appreciating what critics say and by training our perceptions and our responses, we can also learn to value it. The fact that this is so makes it possible to believe that aesthetic judgments can be objective even though there is a considerable amount of disagreement about what should be valued and why. The assumption that judgments about works of art can be objective is closely tied to the claim that art is intrinsically valuable.

Making proper aesthetic judgments requires that people learn how to appreciate and enjoy an object for its own sake. They learn that they must accommodate their perceptions and reactions to the object and not expect immediate gratification. It is undeniable that great works of art do often give us enjoyment, but their value cannot be reduced to the production of pleasure, for our ability to enjoy them properly is predicated on developing a respect for the object as something valuable for what it is.

I will assume that these considerations provide a good, if not indisputable, case for thinking that some works of art ought to be respected by everyone, and that from this respect follows a moral obligation to protect and preserve them. The question remains whether an analogous case can be made for the preservation of natural beauty. There are two closely related reasons for doubt. The first lies behind a commonly held opinion that ethical appraisal is reserved for objects designed and produced by human beings. "Only *artifacts* which have been fashioned with the *intention* of being, at least, in part, objects of aesthetic judgment can be objects of aesthetic judgment," declares Mannison.[6] Is this refusal to regard aesthetic responses to nature as real judgments a mere prejudice? Callicott clearly thinks so, and deplores the equation of aesthetics with art criticism as "one more symptom of the cramped anthropocentrism and narcissism of our culture."[7] However, what I think motivates Mannison's declaration (at least in part) is a doubt about the objectivity of our aesthetic responses to nature. The intentions of artists, whether they are fulfilled and how, is an obvious focus for the criticism and justification of value claims in art. There is no such reference point for making judgments about objects that do not have human creators. To defend an environmental aesthetics which has ethical implications it is necessary to find an alternative ground for making and justifying *judgments* about aesthetic value in nature.

The second worry about the objectivity of aesthetic responses to nature is closely related. There is a disturbing variety in our ideas about what is beautiful in nature. Some people prefer the beauty of park lands, gardens, and other landscapes that have been shaped, civilized, and cultivated by human beings. John Passmore believes that gardens convert nature into "something at once more agreeable and more intelligible than a wilderness." "From wilderness," he says, "[we] are always in some measure alienated."[8] Others prefer the grand scenic wonders of nature: the roaring cataracts, the precipitous peaks, and the awesome abysses that have for the last two centuries been the objects of what Raymond Williams calls "conspicuous aesthetic consumption." On the other hand, such environmentalist ethicists as Callicott insist that we can and should learn to appreciate environments which at first sight seem ugly and hostile: for example, a mosquito-infested swamp.

The mere fact that people have different opinions about what is especially beautiful in nature does not mean that aesthetic judgments about nature are not objective—anymore than a variety of contrary opinion undermines the idea that art criticism can be objective. It does mean that we have to consider what reasons people can give for their preferences. Are there any good aesthetic reasons for judging some features of nature to be more aesthetically worthy than others? Does the wilderness lover have tastes that are superior to the lover of formal gardens, or for that matter, of city skylines? What is at stake is not merely particular views about what is beautiful. Those who, like Mannison, deny that our responses to nature count as aesthetic judgments are also doubting that our preferences are anything more than our personal likes and dislikes. To satisfy the objectivity requirement an environmental aesthetics must not only provide a general strategy for justifying value claims; it should also be able to make and justify, however tentatively, comparative evaluations of natural beauty. Let us consider how Hargrove, Callicott, and other advocates of an environmental aesthetic have met this challenge.

III

Most advocates of environmental aesthetics agree that the appreciation of beauty in nature requires a different approach and a different basis for judgment from that required for the appreciation of art. Callicott objects to the inclination of people in our culture to judge nature according to the standards of landscape art. A land aesthetic, he says, requires the development of a sensibility that is able to enjoy being in a natural environment with its sounds, scents, and feel—and not just looking at it.[9] It also requires a sensibility able to appreciate natural objects and environments that are not conventionally pretty or culturally valued. This kind of appreciation can be developed, he thinks, through a knowledge of ecological relationships and the natural history of an environment and the creatures in it:

> Our appreciation of the crane grows with the slow unraveling of earthly history. His tribe, we now know, stems out of the remote Eocene. The other members of the fauna in which he originated are long since entombed within the hills. When we hear his call, we hear no mere bird. He is the symbol of our untamable past, of that incredible sweep of millennia which underlines the daily affairs of birds and men.[10]

Because everything in nature has a natural history stretching back through millennia, Callicott seems to be suggesting that virtually any environment or creature can, or should, be an object of aesthetic appreciation. Allen Carlson develops this idea into what he calls "positive aesthetics." We make judgments about the value of works of art or objects of nature, he says, by reference to categories or standards. In the case of art the categories are provided by art criticism and art history. But, like Callicott, he insists that these standards are not appropriate to nature. Natural objects, whether environmental systems or species of plants or animals, should be appreciated for what they are: something we can discover by learning about their natural history and life cycle. The important difference between art and nature is, thus, that the categories we apply to nature essentially depend upon what exists. They have to be created to fit. The aesthetics of nature, Carlson says, is a positive aesthetics. "All virgin nature is essentially aesthetically good. The appropriate or correct aesthetic appreciation of the natural world is basically positive, and negative aesthetic judgments have little or no place."[11]

For Hargrove, the creativity of nature is the foundation for a positive aesthetics. Both nature and art exhibit creativity, he says, but need to be evaluated in different ways. Artistic creations are judged according to the standards of a tradition or the goals of an artist. But what nature brings forth is not designed in accordance with standards or goals. "Nature's existence precedes its essence, and therefore nature is its own standard of goodness and beauty, making ugliness impossible as a product of nature's own creative activity."[12] This means, he says, that it is even more important to preserve wild nature than it is to preserve objects of art, for natural beauty does not preexist in anyone's imagination. "It must exist physically in order to exist in any sense at all."[13] We not only have a moral duty to protect nature, but this duty takes precedence over our duty to protect works of art.

Positive aesthetics deals with the problem of finding an objective basis for judgments about natural beauty by pointing out that our appreciation of nature grows and deepens with knowledgeable experience of it. Scientific knowledge, particularly knowledge about the natural history of a particular environment or creature, plays a role analogous to the role of art history and art criticism. It makes proper appreciation possible and at the same time provides a basis for judgments about aesthetic worth. Positive aesthetics is also able to provide an answer to the question: "What in nature is beautiful?" All of wild nature is beautiful and thus deserves our appreciation and protection. The more wild, the better. Hargrove argues that those who force nature to serve their purposes, whether this purpose is aesthetic or economic, are not improving on nature. By constraining nature's creative freedom, they are detracting from the aesthetic value of nature. "The beauty of nature arises out of self-creation, which requires freedom from nonnatural influence."[14] Passmore's cultivated gardens, according to these standards, are less rather than more beautiful than wilderness.

The idea that all of nature, above all, wild nature, should be judged to be beautiful is extremely appealing, and not one that I want to dispute. What concerns me is not the positivity of positive aesthetics, but the question of whether its advocates have supplied us with an adequate basis for objective aesthetic judgments and discriminations. There are reasons for doubting this point.

IV

Cultivated nature can also be beautiful. To dispute Passmore's preference for informal gardens over wilderness, we must examine critically the claim that nature untouched by human activities is more aesthetically valuable than nature affected or shaped by human beings. One obvious difficulty for Carlson and Hargrove's positive aesthetics is defining what counts as wild nature. Most areas of the world that are regarded as wilderness areas are either the home of traditional cultures, or they were at some time, and the activities of these people, over thousands of years, have had an effect on the ecology (as in Australia where Aborigines have for centuries encouraged certain species of plants and animals by regularly burning off large areas of bush). If wild nature means areas that have never been affected by human beings, there is practically no wild nature in the world outside of Antarctica. I suspect that advocates of positive aesthetics would be happy to regard as wild nature areas that are or were inhabited by traditional cultures—and so they should. It would be difficult to regard Australian wilderness as less beautiful because generations of Aborigines made parts of it into a kind of park land.

Why not say the same of the environments affected by more recent settlement? Agriculture has sometimes produced landscapes that most people do find beautiful. On the other hand, some human activities have devastated the environment. But, whether an environment has been altered a lot or a little by human hands, it is not clear why this fact should make a difference to our view of it, as far as positive aesthetics is concerned. The creative power of nature is as manifest in its response to human interventions as it is in its response to contingencies that are completely natural. The worst of human interference is no more drastic than changes created by natural forces: volcanoes, hurricanes, continental drift. To all these changes nature adjusts in its creative, and sometimes unexpected, way. Some of the results may be bad for us—but this circumstance is no concern of nature's, and represents no diminution of its creative powers.

What I am suggesting is that if the free creativity of nature is the reason for finding wilderness beautiful, then we have no less of a reason for valuing environments affected by human beings and finding them beautiful. For one thing, because human beings too are part of nature, in an obvious way whatever we do can be regarded as a manifestation of the creativity of nature. Even granted the human–nature distinction, it is not clear why we can't regard the way in which nature responds to our interferences as another manifestation of its creativity, and therefore a proper object of respect and positive evaluation. Indeed, it is not clear why we should value environments affected by human beings less than environments that are free of such interference.

The problem that this extension of positive aesthetics poses is that if, according to its criteria for judgment, every manifestation of nature's creativity turns out to be of value, and if there is no way of justifying a preference for one manifestation over another, then positive aesthetics lacks what is required for objective aesthetic judgment. It gives us no way of making a case for valuing wilderness more than cultivated nature—not even a case for preferring a pristine environment to a trash dump overgrown with weeds. However, if positive aesthetics is not discriminating in its assignment of values, then it will not be able give us a reason for thinking that we have an ethical duty to preserve wilderness, or indeed anything else in nature.

Although my criticism of positive aesthetics is directed most obviously against Hargrove's insistence that the creativity of nature is what gives it value, the same point can be made against other attempts to provide reasons for valuing wild nature. Carlson points out that many people admire wild nature because it is both complex and orderly: systems and organisms are diverse and related in complex ways, and at the same time create a unity.[15] Let us allow that this claim is a reason for finding natural systems and processes aesthetically pleasing. But these are not qualities that distinguish wilderness areas from those systems that are not so natural. A system with introduced animals and plants can be complex and orderly; so can an area used for agriculture or even a lot full of weeds or a flower bed or a compost heap. It is true that a wilderness may contain more diversity than land used for agriculture, but this agricultural land is likely to have other qualities that we can value aesthetically: e.g., a pleasing color or design.

Can an appeal to natural history or ecology give us a reason why we should appreciate some environments more than others? A wilderness does have a different history, a different ecology, from a domesticated environment. The problem is to justify the idea that one history or ecology makes something more aesthetically valuable than another. A rural neighborhood, a city, a trash dump, or a garden all have a history, a complex relationship between parts, that we can come to appreciate.[16] It is not clear why a history of human interference should require us to value an environment less.

Understanding how a land has been shaped by the deeds of past and present people can increase our appreciation of it just as understanding the natural history of the crane can heighten our aesthetic experience of it.

The problem is that science cannot provide us with the foundation that positive aesthetics needs for making objective evaluations. As far as evolutionary history is concerned, there is no reason for preferring one development of our evolutionary heritage over another. Species come and go, and human interference is simply contributing in its own way to the pageant of life and death on Earth. A knowledge of evolutionary history with its millions of years of contingencies and catastrophes might even encourage the view that the results of devastation and destruction are no less natural or aesthetically pleasing than the harmonious, untampered-with environments that environmentalists generally prefer.

My aim, however, is not to question the aesthetic tastes of those who advocate a positive aesthetics. I am arguing that these tastes have not been adequately justified. This problem is a serious one for those who want to draw ethical conclusions from aesthetic judgments, for the idea that things of beauty ought to be respected and protected depends on being able to make objective judgments about what is beautiful, and being able to do so in turn requires that we can make a case for saying that some things are distinguishable from others because of their particular beauty or aesthetic worth. Hargrove himself makes this point and adds that the problem can be solved by "accepting the view that there are degrees of beauty, that some objects are more beautiful than others, and that more beautiful objects ought to be given priority for preservation over less beautiful ones."[17] What I have argued is that neither he nor other advocates of positive aesthetics have as yet given us adequate resources for making such discriminations.

My criticisms might be taken to give ammunition to those who want to drive a wedge between art and nature: to those who say that only human products can have real aesthetic value. There are, however, some good reasons for rejecting this position. The first is the remarkable similarity between the way in which people learn to appreciate art, especially art that is difficult to appreciate, and the way in which they learn to appreciate and value natural environments that at first seem to them ugly or uninteresting. The first European settlers in Australia described the landscape as hostile, perverse, and depressing. There was little in this new world that answered to their pre-existing aesthetic categories. It took them some time to learn how to discover beauty in their new environment and to develop appropriate ways of perceiving and representing it. Their success depended upon the idea that there is something of value about the Australian bush worth the effort of discovery.[18] The idea that an aesthetic response to nature is merely a matter of personal taste does not do justice to the motivations that made this development possible. We need some account of why their efforts to appreciate the beauty of the bush were justified and worthwhile.

The second reason for rejecting the idea that art, but not nature, can be objectively evaluated is that the evaluation of art can also be a problematic exercise. The advocates of positive aesthetics tend to assume that criteria for evaluating human creations lie ready to hand. Carlson believes that art, unlike nature, can be measured according to preexisting aesthetic categories, and Hargrove's idea that artistic objects preexist in the imagination suggests that art (unlike nature) can be evaluated in terms of how well the actual product measures up to what the artist imagined. Both too readily accept the idea that the intentional nature of artistic products makes their evaluation different from the evaluation of natural objects, and given the problems with finding a foundation for natural value, the insistence on this difference can easily lead to scepticism about judgments of beauty in nature.

However, art, particularly the art we judge to be superior, is continually overstepping or rejecting the categories of criticism and the assumptions of a culture, or applying techniques or ideas in ways that no one anticipated. Artists can find that they have produced something different from, and sometimes better than, what they had intended. Creativity in art doesn't seem to be different in kind from the creativity of nature, and therefore the question of why we should value artistic objects, and why we should value them discriminately, is sometimes as urgent for art as it is for nature. For this reason, it seems to me that the best way of developing an environmental aesthetic is to try to apply to natural objects and environments some of the same kinds of reasoning that people use to discriminate great works of art from those which are merely pleasing or interesting.[19] Not all of the ways that we judge art are relevant to nature. Judgments that make essential reference to artists' intentions are clearly irrelevant. But not all judgments about art do or can depend upon reference to artists' intentions, and therefore the fact that natural things are not human products is not a reason for thinking that many of the same judgments we make about art cannot also be applied to nature.

The environmental aesthetic that I am advocating can be regarded as a way of developing a positive aesthetics. It is, at least, not incompatible with the projects of Carlson, Callicott, and Hargrove. However, it can, as I show, lead to somewhat different conclusions about what is beautiful.

V

The only way of demonstrating that something can be done is, sometimes, to do it. The ability to make good judgments about art is demonstrated in the practice of making and justifying judgments about particular works of art. So too our ability to make aesthetic judgments about nature is demonstrated by the way we make and justify judgments about particular environments or objects. Otherwise, my attempt to show that aesthetic judgment can be applied to nature will be incomplete, and in its details contentious. My aim is not to persuade everyone to agree with my particular judgments, but merely to show that we can be discriminating in our aesthetic appreciation of nature and justified in our discriminations. I proceed by making some fairly obvious comparisons between works of art that are regarded as superior and some natural environments.

Some art is great because it provides an inexhaustible feast for the senses, the intellect, and the imagination. Chartres Cathedral is an obviously impressive and inspiring monument. ("Its spires, like beacons, draw the traveller on, promising him comfort and sanctuary."[20]) Walking through it or around it, the observer continually discovers new aspects and arresting perspectives: the buttresses fanning out from its sides, the great spaces of the nave, the more intimate spaces of the chapels. Every detail, however small, is a delight and a source of new connections and interpretations: the "drunkeness of colour" in the stained glass windows, the fluid curves and lines in the stone carvings, and all of these details are a greater source of enjoyment because of their contribution to the whole.[21]

Some natural environments are equally magnificent and rich. The Grand Canyon of North America and the Olgas in Central Australia are two obvious examples. What makes them worth a pilgrimage, and the effort required to look at them closely, to wander around and through them, to spend time in their midst, is much the same thing that motivates people to make a pilgrimage to Chartres Cathedral or the Sistine Chapel. They are undeniably magnificent sights and there is no end to what we can discover there. Every perspective, every change in the weather or the position of the sun, is a new and unexpected revelation of line and color. As in the case of Chartres, the smallest details are beautiful in themselves: the swirls and knobs in the rock formed by erosion, the plants sheltering beneath overhangs, water finding its way down through the crevices in the rock. Geological and biological information contributes to the appreciation of these details and so does learning something about the meaning of the environment for early inhabitants. However, it is, above all, the experience of being in the midst of something so magnificent, overwhelming, and endlessly fascinating that persuades us that these natural environments are of great aesthetic worth.

The Olgas and the Grand Canyon are of greater aesthetic value than, say, a bluff on the Mississippi River, just as Chartres Cathedral is of more value than any cathedral in Minneapolis or Melbourne. This judgment does not mean that the river bluff is not beautiful in its own way. From a scientific point of view, it might be more interesting than the Olgas or the Grand Canyon. The fact remains that as far as aesthetic richness and grandeur is concerned, the latter are of greater worth.

To be great, works of art don't necessarily have to be obviously beautiful or immediately impressive. Some works of art are great because they portray something in a strikingly original way or because they present us with a new way of perceiving. They make the ordinary extraordinary, the mundane into something charged with meaning; they put together elements in a different way or present us with experiences that we have never had before. Van Gogh paintings or the music of Stravinsky are examples of art that pose this kind of challenge. They disturb and challenge our old habits of perception and imagination, and those who take the trouble to meet this challenge can feel that their organs of sensation have been altered, enhanced, and made more responsive and discriminating. The world becomes more vibrant and life a greater joy.

To take an example that I am familiar with, the eucalypt forests of south-eastern Australia present people with the same kind of challenge and the same kind of reward. There is nothing else like the color, light, and scents of a forest of mountain ash (*eucalyptus regnans*) or the hazy blue of a eucalypt-covered mountainside. European settlers found these environments to be a new world for the senses, and for those who learn to respond to it, an ordinary experience such as walking through a forest, catching the whiff of eucalypt on a warm breeze, or hearing a bell bird, sharpens the senses and lifts the spirit.

From this point of view, a forest of mountain ash is more beautiful than a boulevard of oaks or plane trees in the same way that a landscape painting by the Australian artists Arthur Streeton or Tom Roberts is better than the same scenes painted by an amateur artist.[22] The planted oaks and plane trees may be fine trees and the landscape that they are part of is agreeable; the amateur artist may also produce something that is pleasing to the eye. But it is Streeton and Roberts, and not the amateur artists, whose works are capable of changing our way of seeing, and it is the eucalypt forest, not the row of planted trees, that challenges and enhances our ability to use our senses.

Sometimes works of art are regarded as great not simply because they are beautiful, but also because of their cultural significance or connection with the past. By learning to appreciate, say, the works of early Renaissance painters or fine examples of Romanesque architecture, we are also learning to appreciate a tradition, a way of perceiving, and the preoccupations and problems of those who belonged to that tradition. Our response to art is also a response to these things—a way of connecting ourselves and our culture to the past; sometimes a way of appreciating the expression of people in cultures that are very different from our own. Through this experience we get a better sense of who we are and our relationship to our history and to other histories.

Nature also connects us with the past. Near Melbourne in southern Australia is a small grassland along the banks of the Merri Creek which seems, at first glance, an unremarkable piece of scenery. You have to go there and spend some time, look at how the colors change from season to season, hear the wind rustling the blades of grass, before you can fully appreciate its subtle beauty. But it is its cultural significance, as well as its beauty, that makes it of great aesthetic worth. It is one of the last remaining patches of the native grassland that once stretched over the basalt plain from Melbourne to South Australia. The Koori people hunted and gathered food on these grasslands and the wood for their shields was carved out of its ancient red gums. When the first European settlers arrived they looked out over "open plains as far as the eye can see westward."[23] A small field of kangaroo grass is a reminder of how things were, of the fact that this part of Victoria had a habitat that was unique. By learning how to appreciate its beauty and its connection to the past, we connect ourselves to the place we live, its peculiarities, its history, and its unique beauty.

From an aesthetic point of view, the Merri Creek grassland is more worthy of our appreciation than a city park. The park with its lush domesticated grass and beds of roses is pleasing to the eye. The subtle beauty of the grassland is not only more challenging, but the connection of this particular place with the past gives our experience a resonance and depth that we cannot obtain from the park. I am not saying that the grassland is of special significance simply because it has a past. All nature has a past—a history that stretches back into geological time. The grassland is special because it has a past that is or can be significant to the people who experience it, a past that connects them to their history and their land as the Koori knew it and as the first White settlers found it.

Works of art are sometimes of great value because they tacitly criticize a tradition or a way of life, and because they pose a challenge to the way we live or think. They force us to put our lives and our values in perspective, to recognize the existence of alternatives or the possibility of a happiness or simplicity that we have never experienced. Gaughin's paintings sometimes have that power, as do some of the novels of Dostoevksy.

Wild nature, above all, puts things in perspective. We live in a human world surrounded by human-made products, and however beautiful or terrible, predictable or unpredictable, these products are, they belong to us and reflect us back to ourselves.

Wild nature is an environment that is not of our making; it is indifferent to our interests and cuts us down to size. Thoreau said that "we need to witness our own limits transgressed, and some life pasturing freely where we never wander."[24] The Australian poet Judith Wright sees wilderness as a necessary refuge from the human environment:

> The thought of "the calm, the leaf and the voice of the forest" is itself a refuge from stress, a wilderness at the back of the strained mind. When we finally know that the last forest has gone, that there is nowhere to go but along the runways of our steel and concrete anthills, that the last link with our past has snapped, then perhaps we may snap too. We will have no refuge left at all.[25]

Nature has aesthetic value, from this point of view, to the extent that it exists as a refuge, or at least as a counterweight to the human-made world. Some parts of nature do this better or more completely than others. The informal garden praised by Passmore is restful to the eye and the spirit, a nice place to go to relieve city stress, but it is still a human-made distraction; it is calculated to please, and thus it is not so capable as wilderness of posing a challenge or providing an alternative to civilization or to our self-conception.

This discussion suggests that the preference of advocates of positive aesthetics for undomesticated nature can in many cases be justified. Wilderness areas are likely to be more of an inexhaustible feast for the senses than parks or other settings shaped by human beings. The experience of wild nature is more likely to enhance our ability to use our senses than experiences of more tame environments, especially in Australia and the Americas, where people of European or Asian origin are still trying to come to terms with a new land and learning to find a way of appreciating it for what it is. For the same reason, land untouched by modern cultures is more likely to have a history and genesis of significance for us. By responding to it and appreciating its history, we are connecting ourselves with the land that was used by the native inhabitants and invested by them with meaning; we are connecting ourselves with the past of our own culture, with the land as it was first seen by the new settlers. Above all, wilderness is a continuing reminder of a nature outside of human control, a refuge from the preoccupations and priorities of the human world.

However, it does not follow that people who prefer gardens to wilderness are always mistaken. Considered aesthetic judgment could reach the conclusion that a particular garden is of great aesthetic worth and is more valuable in this respect than some wilderness areas. The approach to environmental aesthetics that I am advocating does not allow us to assume that (relatively) wild nature is always preferable to more domesticated environments, that a wilderness will always be worth more than a garden. Nor can we assume that all wilderness areas are equal in their aesthetic value (and indeed advocates of positive aesthetics are also not committed to this idea). Some will turn out to have more worth than others and will for that reason demand from us a greater duty of care. This does not mean that only those wilderness areas that are judged to be of great aesthetic worth should be preserved. There are lots of reasons for preserving wilderness, and there may be other grounds besides aesthetic ones for thinking that some aspects of nature have intrinsic value.

However, the aesthetic approach to the evaluation of nature does provide us with a way of arguing for the protection and preservation of some natural objects and environments. The comparisons and evaluations I have made do not provide a systematic or complete account of the reasons that we might give for valuing works of art or parts of nature. The creativity of both means that an a priori list of criteria of judgment is impossible. However, they do demonstrate that we can make aesthetic judgments about nature in the same way that we do about art. We can make and justify objective claims about the relative merits of natural things; we can give reasons for saying that some things in nature are of very great aesthetic worth. Discrimination is clearly compatible with the idea that all of nature is beautiful in some way or another. However, the fact that we can discriminate and justify our discriminations before others means that we can effectively argue that some parts of nature have a worth that demands respect. This respect brings with it ethical obligations. Everyone (whether they make the effort to appreciate this worth or not) has a duty to protect and preserve natural beauty that is at least as demanding as the duty to preserve great works of art.

The argument that connects aesthetic worth to ethical obligation can thus be shown to be valid in the case of nature, as in the case of art. This is the conclusion that advocates of positive aesthetics aimed to reach. My somewhat different approach can be regarded as a way of overcoming the principle difficulties that lie in the path of this argument. It shows that we can have objective grounds for regarding natural beauty as intrinsically valuable. This intrinsic value is not a nonanthropocentric value. An aesthetics of nature must appeal to what human beings, situated as they are, can find significant, enhancing, a joy for the senses, or a spur to the imagination and intellect, and the ethical obligations that follow from this appreciation are thus tied to human ways of perceiving and judging. Nevertheless, an environmental aesthetics requires of human perceivers that they learn how to value natural things for what they are. Like Hargrove, I favor this way of defending the idea that there are intrinsic values in nature. My version of environmental aesthetics shows, I hope, how the aesthetic approach can also serve as a useful starting point for a practical environmental ethics: not only by providing the discriminations that ethical judgment requires, but also by promoting a love and respect for nature.

Notes

1 G.E. Moore, *Principia Ethica* (Cambridge: Cambridge University Press, 1965); pp. 83–85.

2 Eugene C. Hargrove, *Foundations of Environmental Ethics* (Englewood Cliffs, N.J.: Prentice Hall); p. 192.

3 Beauty and aesthetic value are not the same thing. It is not difficult to think of artworks that have aesthetic value but are not beautiful. Nevertheless, as Hargrove remarks, other aesthetic evaluations that used to be applied to nature, such as "the sublime," have become incorporated into modern notions of natural beauty. I therefore make no attempt in this essay to discuss the relation between beauty and aesthetic value.

4 Janna Thompson, "A Refutation of Environmental Ethics," *Environmental Ethics* 12 (1990): 147–60.

5 Robert Elliot, in "Intrinsic Value, Environmental Obligation and Naturalness," *The Monist* 75 (1992): 138–60, argues that a subjective account of what is an intrinsic value is adequate for the purposes of aesthetics and environmentalism. For the above reasons, I doubt whether this claim is so. However, Elliot's and my accounts of intrinsic value may not be as far apart

as they first seem, for he believes that the attribution of intrinsic value depends upon the existence of relevant properties or relations, and allows that the nature and relevance of the properties can serve as reasons for accepting and rejecting value claims.

6 Don Mannison, "A Prolegomenon to a Human Chauvinist Aesthetics," in D. Mannison, M. McRobbie, and R. Routley, eds., *Environmental Philosophy*, Monograph Series 2 (Canberra: Australia: Research School of Social Science, 1980); p. 212.
7 J. Baird Callicott, "The Land Aesthetic," *Environmental Review* 7 (1983): 346.
8 John Passmore, *Man's Responsibility for Nature: Ecological Problems and Western Tradition* (London: Duckworth, 1974); p. 37.
9 Callicott, "The Land Aesthetic," p. 350.
10 Ibid., p. 348. He is quoting from Aldo Leopold, *Sand County Almanac: With Essays on Conservation from Round River* (New York: Ballantine, 1970), pp. 102–03.
11 Allen Carlson, "Nature and Positive Aesthetics," *Environmental Ethics* 6 (1984): 5.
12 Hargrove, *Foundations of Environmental Ethics*, p. 184.
13 Ibid., p. 193.
14 Ibid.
15 Carlson, "Nature and Positive Aesthetics," p. 24.
16 Paul Ziff makes the point that "anything that can be viewed is a fit object for aesthetic attention. Garbage strewn about is apt to be as delicately variegated in hue and value as the subtlest Monet. Discarded beer cans create striking cubistic patterns" ("Anything Viewed," *Anti-Aesthetics: An Appreciation of the Cow with the Subtile Nose* [Dordrecht, Boston, London: D. Reidel, 1984]; pp. 137–38).
17 Hargrove, *Foundations of Environmental Ethics*, p. 179.
18 Brian Elliot, *The Landscape of Australian Poetry* (Melbourne, Cambridge, Sydney: F.W. Chesire, 1967), and contributors to P. R. Eaden and F. H. Mares, eds., *Mapped But Not Known* (South Australia: Wakefield Press, 1986), discuss this aesthetic history. Hargrove, *Foundation of Environmental Ethics*, chap. 3, relates a similar development of North American sensibilities.
19 Mary McCloskey made this suggestion to me.
20 Robert Branner, *Chartres Cathedral* (New York: W. W. Norton & Co., 1969); p. 69.
21 See Henry Adams, "Mont Saint Michel and Chartres," *Works* (New York: Library of America, 1983); pp. 467–68.
22 Arthur Streeton and Tom Roberts were artists of the Heidelberg School who managed to evoke the light and color of the Australian bush in a way that remains inspiring.
23 According to the words of John Batman, the founder of the first Victorian colony.
24 Henry David Thoreau, *Walden* (Princeton: Princeton University Press, 1971); p. 318.
25 Judith Wright, "A Refuge in the Mind," *Victorian National Parks Association Newsletter*, 1989: 29.

Worldview and the Value-Duty Link to Environmental Ethics

MICHAEL BOYLAN

This essay seeks to enunciate a practical link to applied Environmental Ethics through the Personal Worldview Imperative, the Shared Community Worldview Imperative, the value-duty relationship, and several other associated principles. It is the position of this essay that when created through one's personal worldview, the value-duty relationship

An original essay from the 1st edition of this volume.

will engender environmental duties on the agent and that these duties require the agent to enter into the dictates of the Shared Community Worldview Imperative. This process necessarily includes (through a series of intermediary steps) the duty to become involved in a political process that will seek to defend the environment.

This essay begins by presenting some key terms and distinctions. It proceeds to apply both through the Personal Worldview and the Shared Community Worldview.

I. Key Terms and Distinctions

To begin, let us consider several principles that I hold to be crucial when discussing questions of value.

A. First is the *Personal Worldview Imperative*: All people must develop a single comprehensive and internally coherent worldview that is good and that we strive to act out in our daily lives.[1] There are at least two divisions of the Personal Worldview Imperative; the first is a theoretical one that commands the agent to undergo a thorough self-examination of her values. This entails exposing what she believes in and organizing this inventory into some comprehensive and coherent whole. An underlying assumption of this theoretical stage is that the agent sees her own values in the context of her vision of the world.

The second stage is a practical one that commands the agent to act according to her basic values. This means that if she believes that killing animals is immoral, then she should not eat animals killed for human consumption or wear their skins.[2] It does no good for an individual to hold a belief but not practice it.

Both stages—reasoned beliefs and actions that follow from them[3]—are necessary for the ethical life.

B. This is not the end of the story, however. In the next stage, each agent (after he has created his personal worldview) must also engage other agents with whom he lives in his community[4] in creating a shared community worldview. This is dictated by the *Shared Community Worldview Imperative*: Each agent must strive to create a common body of knowledge that supports the creation of a shared community worldview (that is complete, coherent, and good) through which social institutions and their resulting policies might flourish within the constraints of the essential core commonly held values (ethics, aesthetics, and religion). There are several key elements to this imperative. First is the exhortation to create a common body of knowledge (discussed later).[5] This is an essential element so that positive group discussion can proceed. Second is a dialectical process of discussion among members of a single community and between members of various single communities that are united in another, larger heterogeneous community. This discussion should seek to form an understanding about the community's mission within the context of the common body of knowledge and the core values commonly held by members of the community. These values will include ethical maxims, aesthetic values, and religious values. Of course, there will be disagreements, but a process is enjoined that will create a shared worldview that is complete, coherent, and good.[6]

Third is that the result of this dialectical creation of a shared community worldview is to employ it in the creation (or revision of) social institutions that are responsible for setting policy within the community or social unit. It should be clear that this tenet seems highly inclined toward democracy; it is. However, it is not restricted to this. Even in totalitarian states, the influence of the shared community worldview is significant. One can, for example, point to the differences among communist states in Eastern Europe, the Soviet Union, China, North Korea, and Cuba during the 1960s to the 1980s. All were communist, yet major differences can be found in the way the totalitarian regimes operated in each instance because, even without the vote, the shared community worldview casts a strong influence on the operation of society's institutions and their resultant policies.

Finally, note that the actions of those institutions must always be framed within the core values of the people who make up the society. When the society veers too far in its implementation of the social worldview from the personal worldviews of its members, a realignment must occur. In responsive democracies, this takes the form of defeating incumbents in the next election. In totalitarian regimes, change also occurs but generally through coup d'état or armed revolution.

C. The next principle to consider is the *common body of knowledge*, a set of factual and normative principles about which there is general agreement among a community or between communities of people. This includes (but is not limited to) agreement on what constitutes objective facts and how to measure them. It also includes (but is not limited to) what values will be recognized as valid in the realms of ethics, aesthetics, and religion.[7]

At first glance, many would hold that the creation of the common body of knowledge is a very simple thing. In our contentious world, however, these points are not to be taken for granted. By engaging the issue head on, there is a much greater chance for meaningful dialogue among those involved in serious disputation.

The import of these distinctions in private and public morality is clear. The Personal Worldview Imperative is a command that each of us examine our own lives and strive to create coherence, completeness, and goodness among the myriad of value maxims that we hold. In the social sphere, the Shared Community Worldview Imperative demands that we seek to do the same with others. In this way, a set of concentric spheres of influence is created that should also include the even broader context of the environment. Figure 3.1 illustrates the way most people view relationships among themselves, their communities, and their environment. The large arrow representing the personal worldview is meant to depict the high stake that each human places on her own view of reality (both facts and values).

The middle-size arrow represents the lesser stake that most people invest in the community. Finally, the smallest arrow seeks to illustrate the rather small role that most attribute to the environment.

Although Figure 3.1 may be factually true (though some will dispute this), this is not the way it *should* be. By investing so little worldview attention to the natural environment, many people are able to give it corresponding little value and respect.

From a biological point of view, however, even this minimalist position contains some strong duties.[8] None of us lives in some sort of hermetically sealed bubble with all we need inside. We are social animals; we live with other humans; we also live in community with all of nature. We cannot confine this concern to the immediate

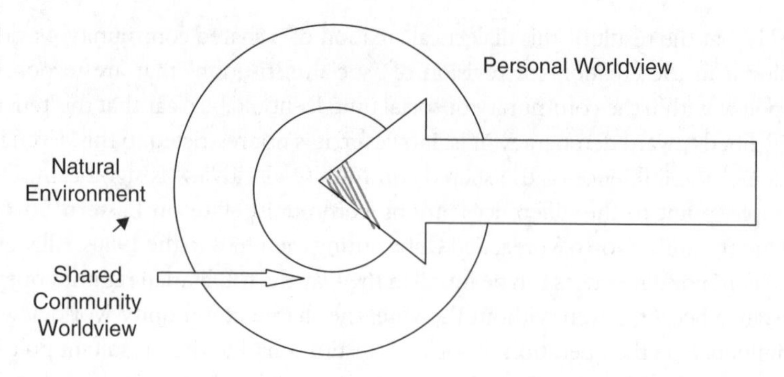

Figure 3.1 Relationships between personal worldview, shared community worldview, and the natural environment

environments in which we live but must extend this to the entire world (and perhaps, by extension, the solar system, the galaxy, and beyond). Within our own world, warm waters off of Peru called El Niño affect the weather and the well-being of ecosystems from eastern Asia to North America to Europe. It may be a stretch to say that a butterfly suddenly falling from the sky in Brazil affects a farmer in Canada (as some of the purveyors of popular chaos theory have said), but it is a meteorological commonplace that regional weather and global weather are intricately connected.[9] The weather is an important component of the well-being of the ecosphere (the combined ecosystems of the world). Therefore, at the very least, everyone must acknowledge that people do not act in isolation. Almost every action that we commit has personal, social, and ecological consequences.

D. A fourth principle that must be enunciated is the *Principle of Human Survival*, which says that humans may be obliged in their struggle for survival to kill animals and plants and to alter the natural landscape. In this way, humans are acting just as other animals do in their own quest for survival. It is also assumed that humans are justified in continuing in these practices past the point of basic primitive survival to some level of moderate, comfortable living.

The intent of the Principle of Human Survival is to highlight the fact that the natural world is not some pristine, static system but a robust, ever-changing arena of competition in which animals kill other animals, forests are destroyed by fires caused by lightning, and earthquakes violently alter the landscape. Humans are one component of this mix and are entitled to follow the same rules that other species follow. However, what makes humans unique is that they can reflect on what they do in such a way that they may refrain from certain actions for which they are naturally inclined because these actions conflict with other core values.

The reason for the abuse of this principle lies in these words: It is further assumed that humans are justified to continue in these practices past the point of basic, primitive survival to some level of moderate, comfortable living. These standards are somewhat plastic. What is comfortable to one person might be a studio apartment for two families but to another might be a house of 6,000 square feet on many acres of ground.

Clearly, the wide range of reference in the words "moderate" and "comfortable" is a problem. The worldviews of various people differ widely on what is an acceptable moderate use of resources. For example, I remember as a boy going to a friend's house for dinner and being shocked when my friend (who could not eat all of his dinner) simply took his plate to the garbage can and scraped it all away. In my Depression-era parents' house, we cut our food one bite at a time so that if we could not finish the food, we could save it for another meal or a leftover casserole. Throwing out food was *not* a part of our shared community worldview. If we had chicken or beef for dinner, the bones were collected for use in future soup dishes. In short, wasting food was absolutely forbidden. Both of my parents knew the experience of going to bed hungry. Thus, throwing away food, or wasting anything, was forbidden. I like to call this the *frugality ethic*. Behind this ethic is the basic economic problem: Humans have unlimited desires, but there are limited resources.

It is difficult to draw a precise line that demarcates moderate usage. Often economic necessity makes conservationists of us all. From anecdotal evidence from my friends who have lived in less-developed countries, it seems to me that in these countries many uses are made for everything. You eat the chicken or the contents of the can of beans. You use the carcass and the feathers of the dead animal for other practical uses. You also use the can for something, too. Nothing is wasted.

Thus, although the Principle of Human Survival is open to debate because of the rather amorphous term *moderate*, it does signify that extravagance and waste in our dealings with the natural world are wrong.

I suggest that readers think of the Principle of Human Survival in the way that we think of the doctrine of proportional retaliation in self-defense. When someone attacks you, you are permitted to respond in proportion to the attack. Thus, if a person is attacking your big toe (by stepping on it), your response would be different than if he were attacking your life. The exact line is plastic, but there is some general direction. In the same way, we can elucidate some community sense of what is an appropriate or moderate level of consumption—so long as the community in this case is sufficiently broad.

This is not a pure comparison because there are more objective touchstones in the self-defense case than in the moderate usage case, but some general directions can be seen.

E. The last principle that I would like to discuss in this section of the essay is the value-duty relationship. In some ways (for the purposes of my argument in this essay), this is the most important principle of all. I contend that when agent X values P (where P is an artifact, a natural object, an agent, or a human institution[10]), X assumes a corresponding duty to protect and defend P subject to the constraints of the Principle of Human Survival and the "ought implies can" doctrine.[11]

The import of the Value-Duty Doctrine is to assert that in the act of valuing, a person proceeds through various steps (refer to Figure 3.2).

Thus, according to this argument, when an individual perceives anything, she undergoes a process whereby she values it (positively or negatively) according to the standards of her personal worldview. If she values it to be good, then she has a duty to protect and defend it. The extent of this duty is proportional to the gradation of positive value that she assigns to it.

1. X apprehends P (where X is an agent and P is an artifact, a natural object, and agent, or a human institution—among other things/processes/activities)—fact.
2. All apprehensions involve the internal value filter of the personal worldview—fact.
3. The act of valuation assesses a negative, neutral, or positive value according to a gradated scale that begins with disapproval, moves by steps to neutrality, and finally moves by steps of approbation to total approval—assertion.
4. When X apprehends P, X engages in a process of valuation according to the standards set by her personal worldview—1–3.
5. The act of positively valuing anything means that X is giving some gradated approval to P—assertion.
6. Giving approval to P means that X thinks P exists and that P is good—assertion.
7. When X encounters a P that is good, an interaction with P occurs—assertion.
8. The act of valuing P creates an ongoing interaction between X and that which X judges to be good (P)—5–7.
9. Ongoing interactions wiht what is judged to be good constitute striving to act out what is good in individual lives—assertion.
10. The Personal Worldview Imperative commands all people to develop a single comprehensive and internally coherent worldview that is good and that individuals strive to act out in their daily lives—f act.
11. The Personal Worldview Imperative commands that when X values P, X creates an ongoing interaction with P in X's daily life—8–10.
12. X cannot have an ongoing interaction with a P that is destroyed or no longer exists—fact.
13. When X is commanded to maintain an ongoing interaction with P, then X must maintain P's existence (as much as it is in X's power to do so.)—assertion.
14. Maintaining the existence of P (as much as it is in X's power) is to protect and defend P—fact.
15. The Personal Worldview Imperative commands individuals to protect and defend what they value—11–14.
16. When X is commanded to do Y, then X has a duty to do Y—fact.

---

17. When X apprehends P and judges it to be good (i.e., positively values P), then X incurs a duty to protect and defend P—4, 8, 11, 15, 16.

Figure 3.2 Value-duty relationship

II. Application through Personal and Shared Community Worldview

We now have the principles necessary to outline a theory of environmental duty via the worldview.

A. Application through personal worldview

In presenting the Personal Worldview Imperative, it has been my custom to highlight three areas of value: ethics, aesthetics, and religion. In keeping with this organization, I will examine each in order to determine which value areas (and their resultant duties) might arise.

The realm of ethical values

Of course, a number of ways can be used to ground ethical value.[12] However, most traditional theories are grounded in aspects of *rationality*, which is often understood as the ability to demonstrate rudimentary skills in inductive and deductive logic. This, in turn, is operationally understood through an organism using language to communicate in ways that demonstrate these skills. Although there may be some debate at the fringes regarding some species of monkey, it is generally agreed that only humans are rational in just this way. If rationality alone is the ground for moral rights and duties, clearly there are only *moral* rights and duties to other humans.[13] If this position is correct, there are no moral duties to animals, plants, or the landscape, as such. One might construct a theory of duties to future generations or other such anthropocentric justifications that are really duties to people that include the environment as a part of that duty.

Another strategy along this line is a Virtue Ethics approach in which one of the virtues involves a certain disposition by humans to the environment. Bill Shaw makes one such argument in his essay, "A Virtue Ethics Approach to Aldo Leopold's Land Ethic."[14] Virtue Ethics is often used in conjunction with Communitariansim in traditional ethical theory. In this way, Shaw seeks to extend the usage to the natural community described by Leopold. Shaw seeks to examine the worldview change necessary to seriously consider adapting Virtue Ethics to Leopold's natural community. If such a view could be effected, then virtues such as respect or ecological sensitivity, prudence, and practical judgment might be adopted.

The problem, of course, is that Virtue Ethics requires some general agreement within the community about what constitutes a virtue. If a substantial shift in personal worldview among large numbers of people is a requirement, then it is certainly possible that the practical adoption of said virtue will never occur.

Even if one cannot go all the way to the worldview shift that Shaw is suggesting, it is still within the purview of most traditional lists of human virtue to adopt frugality as a desirable trait. By frugality, I mean an attitude of taking only what one needs, using it fully, not being wasteful. (Refer to the frugality ethic mentioned earlier.) For example, a frugal person does not take more food than he needs, does not build more housing space than he needs, does not buy more things than he needs. He, in turn, eats the food he has taken, uses the living space he has built, and utilizes the things he has until they are no longer functional. If large numbers of people exhibited such a virtue, then society would be less consumption driven and, by extension, exert less harmful pressure on the environment.

I believe that such a notion of frugality was a generally accepted virtue in the Depression era. As mentioned earlier, children of Depression era parents (like myself) were schooled in the virtue of the frugality ethic. Thus, a considerable number of people might already value measured and moderate use of our natural resources.

The only trouble with the virtue of frugality is that since 1980, conspicuous consumption appears to be more the norm than frugality. Instead of gas-efficient automobiles, the most popular models are sports utility vehicles that have low gas mileage and require a large amount of energy to produce. Suburbs are ringed with gigantic "trophy" houses of 6000 to 7000 feet that serve as domiciles for two or three people!

Thus, although I certainly argue in favor of considering frugality to be a virtue, I think that it may be becoming a minority position.

The alternative to these anthropocentric theories is a biocentric theory that sets the criteria for moral respect to be (among other things) (a) sentience, (b) active existence within a vital, powerful ecological system, or even (c) mere existence. The trouble with these accounts from my perspective is that they fail to provide a convincing reciprocal account that I believe is essential for any theory of ethics. For example, if I should refrain from killing the lion, should the lion refrain from killing me? Of course not because lions do not exhibit freedom (that comes from rationality alone). Lions act on a principle of survival. Humans also act on a principle of survival (as per the Principle of Human Survival). However, humans are free to use discretion (in situations of non-subsistence) about *what* they kill and *when*. This is different from other animals, plants, and the landscape.

Reciprocity requires that what is a duty to one agent is also a duty to another equal agent. One-sided (paternalistic) duties apply only to unequal entities (such as a parent to a child), but even these may not be strict moral duties.[15] And of course, the entire environmental ethics debate is about how humans should respect nature. If ethics presupposes free will and reciprocity of agency and if only humans exhibit this type of free will, then the best a bio-centric theory can hope for is one-sided paternalistic quasi-moral duties. It seems to me that we get more justifiable environmental protection from anthropocentric moral theories than from biocentric ones.

The realm of aesthetic values

In many ways, I believe the realm of aesthetic values to be the most promising strategy from the personal worldview perspective. Aesthetic values regarding nature may be understood in two ways: (a) artistic appreciation and (b) scientific appreciation.

In artistic appreciation, we point to the fact that nature is beautiful. Unlike ordinary artifacts in galleries and museums, this beauty is from an inscrutable maker. Still, the presence of a majestic landscape is powerful:

> Five years have passed: five summers with the length
> Of five long winters and again I hear
> These waters, rolling from their mountain-springs
> With a soft inland murmur. Once again
> Do I behold these steep and lofty cliffs,
> That on a wild secluded scene impress
> Thoughts of a more deep seclusion: and connect
> The landscape with the quiet of the sky.
>
> William Wordsworth,
> *Lines Composed a Few Miles above Tintern Abbey*

Wordsworth and the other Lake Country poets exhibit an aesthetic appreciation that borders on worship. It is an odd individual, indeed, who would look at a parking lot or a mass of concrete and steel (such as midtown Manhattan) and exhort such lofty sensibilities—unless she were making an artistic judgment about architecture. But even then, considering the process of human city building and development, most would assert that the works of nature far outshine those of humankind.

According to the value-duty relationship, if a person values nature as beautiful, he is also saying that it is good and should be protected and defended.[16] The act of valuing incurs the duty of protecting/defending.

This works well for most who *do* view nature as beautiful and valuable. However, it ignores some who view it not as beautiful but as a market basket of raw resources just ripe for human development (exploitation). These individuals have no intrinsic aesthetic experience of nature but view only their own accomplishments as beautiful. They view a shopping center that sits on what once was a an aviary as a great feat of human engineering and know-how. For these individuals (I believe them to be a minority), no duty will arise from the aesthetic valuing of nature because they do not aesthetically value it.

In the mode of *scientific appreciation*, I believe there is also a large audience. The basic principle behind this mode is that when a person appreciates something intellectually, she automatically acquires a value for that thing as being beautiful. Many field biologists, for example, cite their love of the beauty of nature,[17] and by this they mean that the more they *understand* about the species/ecosystem they are observing, the more it enhances their appreciation/valuing of it.[18]

For this reason, I believe that most who understand or seek to understand something of the science of nature also value it aesthetically in this second mode. In this second mode, a person's rational appreciation of the intricate balance of natural systems creates within the subject an emotional response that I call *aesthetic*. The word *aesthetic* comes from the Greek meaning sensory perception. According to the *Oxford English Dictionary*, after 1830, a sentimental attachment also was associated with the word (although at first this was rather controversial). The point in this context is that a person's sensory experience could occasion an emotional response such as Wordsworth's rapture upon seeing the ruins of Tintern Abbey in southeastern Wales. We often attribute emotion to sense impressions that strike us forcefully.

In classical Greek, *aisthesis* and *noesis* were complementary concepts: When a person *sensed*, he was operating in a different mode than when he *thought*. But in the late eighteenth century when standards of artistic taste began being discussed using the word *aesthetics*, the gap between these two traditional antagonists narrowed. An individual could ratiocinate about what she sensed. A dialectical relationship between the two became a given in the developing canons of nineteenth century criticism that led to Impressionism and Expressionism.

I am suggesting that we think seriously about this dialectical relationship—only this time, let us start it from *noesis*. Beginning with a scientific study of nature, the practitioner gains a heightened aesthetic appreciation of the phenomenon that is accompanied by sentiment. This valuing also incurs a duty to defend and protect based on the value-duty relationship.

I believe that we often begin with *noesis* and subsequently acquire *aisthesis*. Let's call this acquisition of aesthetic value mode two. (Mode one occurs when we begin with *aisthesis* and move to *noesis*.) I base my conjecture about how common mode two aesthetic acquisition is upon the large number of public television programs on nature to indicate the general interest in its operation. Viewers of these programs, too, will incur an aesthetic valuing that arises from their original rational quest. This aesthetic valuing creates a duty based on the value-duty relationship.

Taken together (mode 1 and mode 2), the aesthetic valuing of nature creates a duty to protect and defend it among a significant majority of people but not everyone (as mentioned).

The realm of religious values

Religious duties are important; 80 percent of the world's population affirm belief in a monotheistic religion. The world's two largest religions, Christianity and Islam, accept the Jewish book of *Genesis* that asserts that God created the world from nothing. When God was finished, God declared it was good.[19] From this account alone, we have an assertion that all of nature is good (i.e., is to be valued). According to the value-duty relationship, this means that those who believe in *Genesis* should strive to protect and defend the environment out of a religious duty born of a religiously oriented valuing.

Most other religions ascribe to creation accounts that also would, on the same principle, incur duties to nature. In addition to this, other duties may also arise through the work of theologians who interpret the holy scriptures of the various religions. For example, in the *Mishnah* and the *Talmud*, a concept of *bal tashit* ("do not destroy") evolved.[20] This dictum argues against wanton destruction and conspicuous consumption (similar to the frugality ethic described earlier). In this way, a religious duty is formed to protect the environment from wanton destruction and to prevent people from being overly driven by consumption.

Between these two modes (the holy scriptures themselves in their creation accounts and the commentators on those scriptures), a large portion of the world's population (in principle)[21] incurs a duty to protect and defend the environment.

In the end, the duties incurred by the Personal Worldview Perspective greatly enhance the environment. Although duties can be formulated from all three principal domains of worldview value (ethics, aesthetics, and religion), I believe that the realm of aesthetics is the most promising to reach the greatest number.[22]

B. Application through shared community worldview

Another source of duty to protect the environment comes from the shared community worldview. I will focus my comments in this section on examining the community's core values, questions of justice, and strategies and tactics for environmental protection.

Core community values

Core community values are the most prominent values that a group espouses as a part of its identity. They represent essential elements of that group's perceived mission or purpose. They include ethical, aesthetic, and religious values.

Core community values are developed in different ways. One way is from a discussion in the community about what is valuable in life. If we think of communities as social organizations that begin with the family and expand outward to include the city, county, state, nation, and the world,[23] then these discussions occur at these levels as well. Obviously, as we increase in levels of generality, the amount of personal interaction with the new level of community decreases. Thus, the sense that a dialectical interaction exists between individual and community best occurs at the family, neighborhood, and local town levels (including their various institutions such as schools and churches, synagogues, and mosques).

Another source of core community values might be through passively reading, listening, or viewing others discuss these issues. This might occur by attending a meeting and listening as a member of the audience or by reading, listening to, or viewing the popular media: newspapers, magazines, radio, and television.

Obviously, the potential also exists for propaganda and influence shaping (sometimes called *spinning*) from these sources as well. Thus, although they are a necessity of the modern age, they must be viewed with critical skepticism as well.

To better appreciate the dynamics of this process, let us turn to a concrete example. In Sleepy Hollow, a small town near Anywhere, USA, ABC Corporation has applied for a zoning variance to build one of its Floormart stores. Floormart has built its superstores around the country and undercut local merchants in cost, thus driving many of those merchants out of business. When people complain, Floormart replies, "We didn't drive the local merchants out of business; you [the people] did. You bought from us and stopped buying from them. It's the American way."

Your county planning board is holding a hearing to discuss the zoning proposal. At the meeting, advocates of both sides make their arguments. The proponents of Floormart proclaim that they can bring progress to Sleepy Hollow. "We can deliver you more goods and at a cheaper price than you've ever seen before. This will be the shot in the arm that this area has been waiting for!"

The opponents of Floormart say, "Floormart stores have driven local merchants out of business all around the country. At first, they will tell you that they can bring economic development to an area, but then they will offer such low wages that they will have to import workers who are willing to be exploited. And you know those six acres of woodlands at the edge of Johnson's farm? If they get this variance, it will all be asphalt and buildings. This project must be voted down, or we will lose everything that we cherish in Sleepy Hollow."

The proponents of the development appeal to the core prudential value of more money through more local development and cheaper costs for goods needed for day-to-day life. The opponents of development appeal to core values, as well (viz., looking after community jobs and not altering life as it is in Sleepy Hollow), both sociologically and ecoaesthetically.

Both sides appeal to issues that are meant to resonate within the community as represented at that meeting. Through an honest discussion that includes aspects of central worldview tenets, the debate will be engaged. This leads to the question of how worldview values are changed, which is a complicated process.[24] A shortened version is that there is an interaction between the proposal and a person's worldview. If the proposal creates a significant dissonance, the person will reject it. However, if sufficient similarity is found via the common body of knowledge, then change is possible. More on this in the strategies and tactics section.

Questions of justice

Justice is always in the province of shared community values. By *justice* (in this context), I am referring to distributive justice that is inherently an issue of allocation. There are, of course, many allocation principles. (I generally highlight the following list: to each equally (egalitarianism), to each according to his needs (socialism), to each according to his work or production (capitalism), to each according to his rank or station (aristocratism), and to each according to his ability to snatch it for himself (*kraterism*).) Connected to the principle of justice that is chosen is the question concerning the parties among whom the distribution is said to take place.

This is also a question about which communities to involve. Some candidates are (a) my family alone, (b) the local community at hand, (c) the county, (d) the state, (e) the country, (f) the world, (g) future generations in all of the preceding groups (i.e., my grandchildren, the grandchildren of each of the other categories in the same order).[25]

If a person were considering only her family, then the problem would concern it only. There are certainly microlevel problems about who gets to eat the tomatoes in the family garden. But the more pressing social issues occur when the community grows considerably larger. Many try to draw an artificial line that excludes considerations of all communities after items (e), (f), or (g). They do this based on some notion of national sovereignty. However, I believe this to be a mistake. The reason for this is that if natural resources are said to "belong" to humans at all, they belong only on the caveat that they are collectively owned. No person can say that he can properly own any natural thing himself (if ownership entails the ability to dispose of x as the owner pleases).[26] This is so because (a) natural resources are not discrete but interdependent and (b) the authority-granting ownership is a social institution that is thus ruled by principles of justice (a distribution principle that ought to consider all possible agents—now and in the future).

On the first point, natural resources are not discrete but interdependent. A person cannot utilize a natural resource as she pleases because what she does will affect the natural resources of the ecosystem, contiguous ecosystems, and even remote ecosystems. Thus, since the effects of resource utilization are communal, the obligations of stewardship/ownership are also communal.

Second, on the issue of justice, if we hold to the principle that I have enunciated elsewhere that, all things being equal, we must always begin with egalitarianism,[27] then considering all of these groups, we must modify absolute dominion over our property in favor of a limited use doctrine that considers all of the various stakeholders, both present and future.

Certainly, when we consider the fact that strong private property ownership is a given in most societies in the world, this is a radical proposition. I am arguing here (on the basis of egalitarian justice allocation of natural resources to all the peoples of the earth now and in the future) that individuals' ownership of anything in nature is conditional upon the conditions of this allocation.

If an individual is allocating natural resources, there is a difference between renewable and nonrenewable resources. The allocation of renewable resources is guided by the principle of sustainable development.[28] Humankind must "mother" its resources so that they continue to flourish under natural conditions. This means maintaining the integrity of wild species that have not been genetically engineered and are not endangered by such. The reasoning for this is that the mechanisms of nature are assumed to be more subtle and complex that we imagine and that creating an overly artificial breeding population will ultimately narrow the range of evolutionary fitness for that species. And since it is not just (under egalitarianism) to permit one person/company/country to "hog" nature's resources (i.e., claim an unequal share) and given the interdependence of resources argued for earlier, it is totally unacceptable for anyone or any community to deplete renewable resources. Thus, I am arguing that when allocating renewable resources, we must strictly adhere to sustainable development (including protection of wild species).

The argument for the permissibility of using nonrenewable resources is rather more difficult. If future generations stretch indefinitely in the future, then the utilization of nonrenewable resources automatically involves shortchanging someone else down the line. The obvious consequence of this is that utilization of nonrenewable resources is wrong because it violates the rights of future generations to utilize them. This right is supported by egalitarianism.

However, many of these nonrenewable resources are crucial for our survival. Practical arguments based upon human survival may refer to the "ought-implies-can" standard. I suggest that we should utilize only nonrenewable resources that can be recycled for continuous usage. This would cover metals but would say nothing about nonrecyclable minerals and petroleum. My response is that society must find alternatives to these so that we do not deplete the world of them.

Strategies and tactics for environmental preservation

The final section of this essay briefly suggests directions for the future given the principles already enunciated.

First, I would say that the primary task is to formulate a dialogue within various communities about the shared worldview. This dialogue should proceed along the lines dictated by the Shared Community Worldview Imperative: Constructive dialogue must be engaged in communities at all levels about a common way to discuss environmental issues. The result of this dialogue must be a set of agreed-upon ethical maxims that address the relationship between humans and nature. These maxims need to recognize that nature is valuable. This value can be agreed to from ethical, aesthetic, and religious sources. Once nature's value is asserted, because of the value-duty relationship, the members of the community must admit to a duty to protect and defend nature that includes supporting sustainable development (along with protection for wild species) and a long-term commitment to use only nonrenewable resources that can be recycled.

Second, if the community in which we live is deaf to these appeals for dialogue, then we must resort to the time-proven practical devices of engaging in various high-profile antics that will shake up public consciousness so that we might begin anew with our discussion. (The limitation on these high-profile antics is that they do not create more harm than they are meant to alleviate—Greenpeace and People for the Ethical Treatment of Animals have been adept at making public statements that have shocked but not resulted in more harm than what they are protesting).

Because the value-duty relationship, the Personal Worldview Imperative, and the Shared Community Worldview Imperative dictate that each of us become practically, not just intellectually, involved in these issues, the result is that each of us must take some action. We cannot make an intellectual commitment only because intellectual acceptance of these imperatives dictates personal action.

Such is the task before us all. Real duties toward the environment have been enunciated via the Personal Worldview Imperative and the Shared Community Worldview Imperative; they enjoin action. We cannot fail to become involved or to heed our duty. The stakes are simply too high.

Notes

1 The argument for the Personal Worldview Imperative is given in the Introduction to *Basic Ethics* (Upper Saddle River, NJ: Prentice Hall, 2000).

2 A possible exception to this might be those who might eat the flesh or wear the skins of animals that die from some other cause. In this case, the person does not kill the animal but only uses what is already dead. However, this seems a very far-fetched idea. In this context we are reminded of Theophrastus, student of Aristotle, who preferred eating only the fruit that had already fallen.

3 This position does not intend to exclude emotions within the context of reason. This is so because a person's worldview is representative of her entire person. Thus, there is some affinity between my depiction of the Personal Worldview Imperative and some versions of feminist ethics. For a further discussion of this, see *Basic Ethics*, chap. 5.

4 By community, I mean (in ascending order) the family, the neighbors in his geographical region—some natural unit of a mile or so, his city, township, county, state, country, and the world itself. All are in communities that we cannot ignore. I believe that we should begin in the order I have listed because that order allows the most interaction of individuals in the political process.

5 I discuss the common body of knowledge in greater detail as it pertains to logical argument in *The Process of Argument* (Englewood Cliffs, NJ: Prentice Hall, 1988); chap. 1.

6 I discuss an example of how this shared community worldview might arise in my essay, "Affirmative Action: Strategies for the Future," *Journal of Social Philosophy* (in press).

7 This is not to suggest that I am arguing for a sharp distinction between analytic and synthetic truths; I agree with Quine's insistence that analytic and synthetic truths do not easily segregate. See "Two Dogmas of Empiricism," *From a Logical Point of View* (Cambridge, MA: Harvard University Press, 1953); however, the structure of deontic truths and other propositions do form a natural classification.

8 It is not the purpose of this essay to argue that *only* the minimalist position ought to be adopted but that this position is so basic that all rational agents must accept its authority. Adoption of such a strategy can lead to a wider range of assent (cf., common body of knowledge).

9 One accessible overview of these relations can be found in Marcel Leroux, *Dynamic Analysis of Weather and Climate: Atmospheric Circulation, Perturbations, Climatic Evolution* (New York: John Wiley, 1998); especially part III.

10 This list is meant to be suggestive, not exhaustive of the entities that might fall under this principle.

11 The "ought implies can doctrine" is generally attributed to Kant (though there is some dispute about this). It is a straightforward doctrine that says that no one can command you to do what is impossible for you to do. However, this becomes rather slippery when we analyze what "impossible" means. Often, this transforms to inconvenient, and thus guts the force of the doctrine.

12 I provide a critical survey of many of the most prominent ethical theories in my book *Basic Ethics*.

13 Of course, some would like to add emotion—rationally tethered emotion—and caring to this scheme. Others would add a faith-based religious element to the mixture. I have indicated a willingness elsewhere to accept these additions as overlays to traditional theories.

14 William Shaw, "A Virtue Ethics Approach to Aldo Leopold's Land Ethic" *Environmental Ethics* 19.1 (1997): 53–68.

15 For a discussion of unequal entities and their relationship to moral duties, see Deryck Beyleveld and Shaun Pattinson, "Precautionary Reason as a Link to Moral Action," *Medical Ethics*, ed. Michael Boylan (Upper Saddle River, NJ: Prentice Hall, 2000).

16 One form of this argument is made by Janna Thompson, "Aesthetics and the Value of Nature" *Environmental Ethics* 17.3 (1995): 291–306.

17 There are many examples of this from Konrad Lorenz in *King Solomon's Ring* (New York: Plume, 1997) to E.O. Wilson in *The Diversity of Life* (New York: W.W. Norton, 1993). My point is that these scientists begin as observers but in the process begin to acquire an

appreciation for the phenomenon that carries with it a valuing of this phenomenon. I call this valuing aesthetics in the mode of scientific appreciation.

18 Some will say that "aesthetic" and "rational" appreciation are separate and rather unmixed. I counter to say that the two are intricately intertwined so that one reinforces the other. In this way, I support the position that Horace makes in the "Art of Poetry" in Q Horati Flacci, *Opera*, ed. E.C. Wickham, revised by H.W. Garrod (Oxford: Clarendon Press, 1975). Horace believes that poetry stimulates both rational and aesthetic responses but first must be beautiful to allow the other mode (reason) to function in conjunction with the former. Thus, art must both please and instruct, but it cannot instruct if it does not first please.

19 *Genesis*, 1:31.

20 For a discussion of this in more detail, see: Eilon Schwartz, "*Bal Tashit*: A Jewish Environmental Precept," in Chapter 3 of the first edition of this book.

21 I say "in principle" because there are many commands that organized religion(s) professes that are never realized. They seem to exist more in the realm of a utopian vision of things the way they *should* be but not the way they are. It has been my experience that many good people perform many noble actions because of their belief in organized religion. However, the numbers who respond in this way are nowhere near the 80 percent figure quoted earlier. This means that there are far more in organized religion who are willing to "talk the talk" but not willing to "walk the walk."

22 This does not mean that I would dismiss ethics or religion. Indeed, they are valuable. The more people who can be garnered to defend and protect the environment, the better. It is just that the nature of the aesthetic impulse (given the value-duty relationship) is a compelling principle that is amenable to the creation of a common body of knowledge among many different peoples.

23 I have obviously used the sociopolitical structure of the United States. This is easily adapted to countries that have a different political organization.

24 I outline this process in some detail in *Basic Ethics*, chap. 8.

25 Some would say that this last category is rather peculiar since there are no *actual* members of the future generation. Since these people do not exist, how can anyone owe them a duty? This is true, but barring a cataclysm, there will be future generations. These individuals are connected to present peoples through the normal process of sexual reproduction. Such a relationship has long been held to carry normative force (cf. the Jewish doctrine of responsibility unto the third generation).

26 Of course, if different definitions of ownership are given that are conditional on proper use, then I have no problem with private ownership. But many have traditionally taken the strong sense of ownership to justify all sorts of deleterious environmental action.

27 "Affirmative Action," *Business Ethics*, ed. Michael Boylan (Upper Saddle River, NJ: Prentice Hall, 2001").

28 One prominent critic of sustainable development as an independent concept apart from mere welfare maximization is Wilfred Beckerman, "'Sustainable Development': Is It a Useful Concept?" *Environmental Values* 3 (1994): 191–209.

Evaluating a Case Study

Finding the Conflicts

After establishing an ethical point of view (including a segue to application), we are ready to approach cases. The first stage in handling cases effectively is to analyze the situation according to normal practice and potential ethical issues. Obviously, sometimes ethical issues are involved in what one will do, and at other times they are not. It is your job to determine when ethical issues are involved. Let us consider specific cases.

Case 1

You work in the Human Resource Development department of a company that has an annual awards picnic in June. One of the traditional practices is the release of thousands of balloons sending the company's name and mission to the four corners of the earth. You have heard, however, that such balloon launchings are biologically hazardous to wildlife. Although it makes a striking motivational situation, you believe that the company should reconsider this tradition.

What ethical issues are involved in this case? List them and connect them to a major ethical theory.

Case 2

You work for Genie Biomedical Research whose mission is to create new techniques for gene therapy. The method for this experimentation is to work with monkeys (since their biological constitution is close to that of humans). Many of the procedures result in a monkey's painful death. If the mission of the company is successful, many inherited human disorders can be successfully treated, sparing humans the pain and disorientation of loss due to congenital conditions. Still, you wonder about the monkeys. Do the intended consequences of the research justify the experimental practices on monkeys?

Does this case involve any ethical issues? If so, what are they? What theories support your opinion?

An an aid for working through these two exercises, consider the following checklist for detecting ethical issues.

Checklist for Detecting Issues Concerning Professional Practice

Directions. Read your case carefully. Determine what (if any) relevant points of professional practice are at stake, and then decide which individual's perspective you will develop in your comments. Determine whether there are any clear violations of professional practice. Identify these violations and the various risks a person assumes when engaging in such behavior. Then consider whether the professional practice itself is immoral. Finally, if the practice is wrong, explain why it is and what major ethical theory judges it to be wrong. What arguments would a proponent of such a theory make?

Next follow the checklist for detecting ethical issues.

Checklist for Detecting Ethical Issues

Directions. Read your case carefully. Determine your ethical viewpoint (see "Developing a Practical Ethical Viewpoint," p. 25). Decide which individual's perspective you will develop in your comments. Create one or more detection questions that will identify ethical issues. These detection questions will follow from your own ethical perspective. For example, from my practical ethical perspective, I have chosen the following two detection questions to bring moral issues to my attention. These questions follow from a deontological viewpoint.

1. *Is any party being exploited solely for the advantage of another?* (Exploitation can include instances of lying, injuring, deliberately falsifying, creating an unequal competitive environment, and so forth.)
2. *Is every effort being made to assist and affirm the human dignity of all parties involved?* (Affirming human dignity can include instances of encouraging the fulfillment of legal and human rights as well as taking personal responsibility for results that are consonant with these principles. Thus, you cannot hide behind nonfunctioning rules.)

By asking these questions within the context of the case, I am able better to understand the moral dimensions that exist with other professional concerns.

A few other comments may be useful concerning my detection questions. Question 1 concerns "prohibitions" (i.e., actions that you must refrain from doing). Question 2 concerns "obligations" (i.e., actions that you are required to do). Anything that is not an ethical obligation or a prohibition is a "permission" (i.e., an action that you may do if you choose). Thus, if the case you present does not invoke a prohibition or an obligation, then you may act solely according to the dictates of your professional practice (such as those dictated as a governmental official or as an environmental scientist). It is often useful to group your detection questions as prohibitions and obligations, which emphasizes different types of moral duty.

Try creating detection questions and apply them to the earlier two cases. What do they reveal about the moral issues involved in the cases? How do different detection questions emphasize different moral issues? How different are these perspectives? How similar are they?

Once you have completed this preliminary ethical assessment, you can return to the ethical theory you have adopted and determine *how* and *why* the prohibitions and obligations are applicable to this theory.

Read the following macro and micro cases and follow the steps outlined:

A. Identify the professional practice issues at stake.
B. Identify your practical ethical viewpoint including any linking principles.
C. Determine which character's perspective you will adopt.
D. Identify two or more detection questions that define obligation and prohibition within the ethical theory you have chosen.
E. Apply the detection questions to the cases to bring attention to the ethical issues.

F. Discuss the interrelationships between the dictates of the ethical issues and those of the professional practice. How might they work together? How might they be opposed?

Macro and Micro Cases[1]

Macro Case 1. The Chicago Housing Authority is planning to tear down several high-rise public housing projects and build single-family townhouses and duplexes to rent and sell to the public. The purpose of this endeavor is to create mixed communities, meaning that people of various income levels would be living together. You are the head of a natural ecology organization dedicated to making such community development as environmentally friendly as possible. The proposal that makes the most ecological sense has the least density of new housing. It would provide for more green urban park space (meaning retrieving land for natural usages including planting trees and reviving habitants long since destroyed). Also in favor of this proposal is the appeal the housing will have for middle- and upper-middle-income families. It will seem to bring the suburbs into the city. Everything seems directed to this proposal except that it could negatively impact the poor people who currently live in the housing projects. First, the planned spaces are not sufficient to house all of the poor who currently live in the projects. (At present, vague plans have been suggested, but the reality is that people who cannot rent or purchase the new housing must move somewhere else. There will be no room for them here.) Does this constitute an ethical problem? Second, the new properties may be so attractive that pressure will be brought to build even more luxurious dwellings with the result that the new community will gradually be transformed from mixed housing to homogeneous rich housing. Does this constitute an ethical problem?

As head of an environmental organization, your duty is to support the most environmental friendly program. Analyze this problem from the points of view of a deep ecologist and a social ecologist. Use the format of a position paper that your organization will submit to Janet Smiley, the head of the Chicago Housing Authority.

Macro Case 2. Analyze Macro Case 1 from an ecofeminist point of view. Then make a recommendation using a worldview listed in the section "Aesthetics" to base your recommendation to Ms. Smiley.

Macro Case 3. As head of the AFL-CIO's auto contract negotiation team, you are working on the latest round of contracts with the major auto companies. Keeping to your historical pattern, you have chosen one company with which to create a model contract on which your negotiations with other companies will be based. You have entered negotiations with Company X in this regard and are presently addressing the issue of outsourcing parts. Traditionally, the union has been against outsourcing because of the potential loss of US jobs to foreign markets. However, Company X has offered an interesting proposal that would peg US jobs at a permanent level (*permanent* means for the life of the contract) in return for the right to outsource parts. This proposal would be a step forward from past negotiations because you have never been given a pegged level of employment before. From the point of view of your union members, this is a great deal. However, the plants in the countries that will supply these parts operate on standards you do not think are ethical. They pay very low wages to their workers for very long hours, and they have no environmental regulations by which they must abide. The question is whether to accept a deal that is great for your workers but bad for foreign workers and the environment in that country? You must respond to Company X's proposal in forty-eight hours. Write your response, making clear your ethical position and any linking principles.

Macro Case 4. You are head of the World Maritime Commission's Department of Ecology. You are considering the case against one of the premier luxury cruise ship companies in the world, ABC Cruise Lines. The complaint is that ABC is in gross violation of the commission's waste disposal regulations and has egregiously polluted Prince William Sound in Alaska for the past twenty years. The company has admitted lax management but denies any systematic plan for pollution. However, the facts show that ABC has polluted four times as much as the next worst offender, which also faces charges. A tentative fine of $100 million has been assessed against ABC, which ABC says it cannot possibly pay, because it will lead to bankruptcy. If the cruise line goes bankrupt, 12 000 people will lose their jobs. ABC proposes that it be allowed to continue and that 5 percent of its net profits be diverted to an environmental fund for the next ten years. Critics say that this is merely a "slap on the wrist" that will do nothing to address the real problems. Environmental pollution is not a small matter. However, there is the issue of those who will be put out of work.

Write a recommendation for the other committee members to consider. Make clear the ethical position on which you base your recommendations.

Micro Case 1. You are a college senior about to enter the real world, and you have had several job offers. You have narrowed the list down to two; a nonprofit organization concerned with gender and social issues and a job on Wall Street as a stockbroker. As a stockbroker you will work long hours helping customers make money and perhaps growing rich yourself in the process. The former offer is for $30 000 a year, and the latter is for $50 000 a year (with the promise for lots more). There is nothing wrong about accepting either job. Both companies seem to be concerned about meeting their goals in a responsible way. However, a question that one of your philosophy professors put forth makes you wonder: What does it mean to simplify your life along the lines of Deep Ecology? Is this an important consideration for forming a world-view plan? What of the tenets of Social Ecology or Ecofeminism? What difference does it make? Write a diary entry that considers this choice, adding relevant details as necessary.

Micro Case 2. You are at the mall shopping for several pairs of new pants. One company, We Are Green, has attractive clothes that cost considerably more than the clothes in other stores. For example, a pair of pants that sells for $25 at another store costs $40 in the Green line. However, Green has an independent auditing company verify that all its clothes meet a core list of requirements for environmentally sensitive criteria. You believe that both lines of clothes are equally stylish, but you have only $50 to spend, so you can buy two pairs of pants from the other company or one pair of pants from Green. You like to support Green causes when you can, but you really need two pairs of pants. You become somewhat angry that the Green pants cost so much more. Perhaps these pants represent a luxury that you cannot afford. You decide to go to the coffee shop next door to think about it. You take out a pen and list arguments on your napkin. What should you do? Discuss the practical and ethical considerations to justify your decision.

Micro Case 3. You commute to work each day from your apartment in the suburbs to your job in one of the major metropolitan areas of the country (not New York), which has public transportation. You have considered using public transportation instead of driving a single occupancy vehicle to work. However, there is something empowering about knowing that your car is in the garage and that you can leave any time—just in case you have to (although you never have done so in the past three years). Often in the summer, the local Council of Governments issues a "code red" day, declaring that the pollution levels are at an unhealthy state; these days are becoming more and more frequent. In your locality, public transportation is half-price on these days. Should you change to public transit even though the commute would be forty-five minutes longer? Should you accept the loss of individual freedom that parking your wheels at home entails? Analyze the ethical components of this problem as well as their depth of embeddedness. Then choose one ethical viewpoint and use it to solve the problem.

Micro Case 4. An ounce of normal perfume based on flower sources requires 3 000 petals. You have recently heard about Aphrodisiac #18, a very potent perfume that not only requires 20 000 petals per ounce but also includes glands from 100 000 insects that are supposed to emit pheromones that will attract the opposite sex. You have sampled the "scratch and smell" ads and are convinced that this perfume is for you, but you also believe that this is a very wasteful product. On the other hand, the company that makes the product grows all the flowers on company lands, replanting them at regular intervals. It also breeds the insects for their glands. This is a "farmed" product, not an intrusion of natural, wild species. How is this any different from eating corn that has been bred to taste? Is there an ethical issue here? What would you say to those who say there is and those who say there is not?

Note

1 For more on macro and micro cases, see the overview on p. 26.

4

Anthropocentric versus Biocentric Justifications

General Overview: This chapter addresses one of the most important foundational distinctions in environmental ethics: anthropocentric versus biocentric justifications. The anthropocentric argument bases moral value on nature's utility to humans. It sees nature as an entity or a tool (albeit an important one) that humans utilize for their advantage and welfare. Under this scenario, a person's obligations are strictly prudential. A person does not want to spoil the thing he depends upon for life. The future generation argument is simply an extension of this. A person does not want to spoil what his children or grandchildren depend upon for life. (There is something wrong about bringing people into the world and then denying them what they need for their continued existence.)

The biocentric argument asserts a sort of egalitarianism between species: each species is necessary for the ecosystem; therefore, each has an equal claim to continue to exist in a relatively unfettered manner. To support such a position, a person must attribute intrinsic value to the ecosystem as a whole. Obviously, various persons might view this in terms of a turf battle. (In all turf battles, however, the dictum "power rules" generally carries the day. Humans have the most power. QED.)

Can a middle ground be found? If common strategies for action are identical, then what is the importance of the reason? This is an important question.

A. Anthropocentric Justifications

Overview: There are many forms of anthropocentric justification for environmental ethics. One of the most prominent is the duty to future generations. Alan Gewirth (1912–2004) sets out this argument from the viewpoint of his theory of human rights and duties. In his theory, human rights require a sense of mutuality. One factor that complicates mutuality in the case of future generations is that it is hard to define a generation since the term is rather imprecise. There is no clear point of demarcation

Environmental Ethics, Second Edition. Edited by Michael Boylan.

of a new generation. This problem of identifying what a generation is (much less a future generation) leads to the second point: future generations do not exist, so to say that they have rights or duties is rather a stretch (keeping in mind the requirement for mutuality). Does this mean we do nothing? No. Gewirth suggests a transgenerational position that distinguishes two bases for positing duties to future generations. The first is humanistic because its first concern is the interests of human beings and their moral rights (both present and future). The second is naturalistic because it posits nature as having an intrinsic claim. These two positions are examined and some suggestions are made about how each applies.

Onora O'Neill takes the position that all types of moral reasoning are anthropocentric because moral demands are made on agents. However, deep ecologists claim that if the source of obligation to the natural world rests ultimately in human agents, then there is little protection for the environment. Their claim is that the environment possesses a locus of real value. Various approaches to this end include the realist utilitarian and rights-based arguments. The problem with these revolves around defending a metaphysical position that is questionable (viz., moral realism). Instead, O'Neill wishes to argue for an anthropocentrically based approach that reaches many of the same goals to which biocentric realists aspire without the metaphysical baggage.

B. Biocentric Justifications

Overview: In the first essay, Holmes Rolston III argues for a biocentric justification for environmental ethics. He rejects the basis for much of the traditional ethics that is based on human reason. Quoting Jeremy Bentham, Rolston asks: "The question is not, Can they reason? Nor Can they talk? But Can they suffer?"[1] Preventing and alleviating pain and ensuring a healthy, natural diet are two ways in which humans can show their respect for all animal life. However, this respect does not stop with animals. Although plants and other living things cannot feel pain, they are part of an ecosystem that is really an intricate whole. Within this whole are various species of plants and animals that are alternately predators and prey; together they are all important, and their relationships should be preserved. This means that species and ecosystems must be valued intrinsically because they carry a strength (Latin: *valeo* = root for value).[2] One ought to value what works well and demonstrates strength. Thus, we should respect the environment because of the intrinsic value that is demonstrated by its strength.

Paul W. Taylor's essay calls for a worldview that respects nature. He believes that the proper worldview will shape many of the smaller issues. One of the key elements of this worldview is a commitment to the biocentric outlook. In this outlook, we recognize what the entire biotic community has done for this world: it has allowed us (humans) to come into existence. Such a service to us ought to engender various duties or rules: (a) the Rule of Nonmaleficence; (b) the Rule of Noninterference; (c) the Rule of Fidelity; and (d) the Rule of Restitutive Justice. Taylor's essay consists of an amplification of these duties.

C. Searching the Middle

Overview: In many ways, it might seem that the chasm between anthropocentrists and biocentrists cannot be bridged. Each creates a starting point in a different place. This section seeks to highlight one attempt to reconcile what seems to be an irreconcilable conflict.

In his essay, James P. Sterba creates a series of principles that rank goods of agency. This is similar to Gewirth's categories of goods (basic, nonsubtractive, and additive).[3] For example, Sterba sets out Principles of Human Defense and Preservation that allow the killing or harming of plants or animals for the sake of a basic good. However, on the other hand, if the good to be had is not essential, but additive and superfluous, then such a right is not justified (the Principle of Human Disproportionality). The intent of this approach is to create the foundation that supports principles on which both sides could agree. If Sterba is correct in this, and if we accept something similar to Leibnitz's principle of identity,[4] and if both the anthropocentric and biocentric approaches (under a certain interpretation) imply a common conclusion, then a middle ground has been achieved.

Brian K. Steverson would demur. He finds Sterba to be an anthropocentrist who believes that human needs trump those of the animal/biotic kingdoms. If we are to consider only the environment (in an even-handed way), then we will come to different conclusions. Specifically, Steverson criticizes Sterba's appeal to reciprocal altruism to justify the human preference permitted by the Principle of Human Preservation. He also claims that although it is reasonable from a nonanthropocentric position to select the Principle of Human Preservation, one could just as well select a principle of nonhuman preservation from that perspective.

In his reply, Sterba contends that Steverson is partially correct. Not all moral obligations can be given a reciprocal altruism foundation. But if only some can, then we have established a realistic possibility. This is not insignificant.

Second, Sterba defends a moral epistemological position (that implies a deontic standpoint) of the agent in question. How could an agent, for example, desire that his own basic goods not be fulfilled (even if it means killing another animal)? Certainly, lions and other animals are not saddled with such angst.

The answer to this debate requires the reader to choose a worldview perspective and then decide how everything else should fit into it.

Notes

1 Bentham, J. (1789) *Introduction to the Principles of Morals and Legislation*, New York: Hafner, p. 34.

2 The sense in Latin is that to be strong and effective implies worth. It is a functional theory of value that fits in well when describing ecosystems.

3 I discuss these in their practical ethical effects in *Basic Ethics*, Upper Saddle River, NJ: Prentice Hall, 2000; chs 4 and 6.

4 In a rough-and-ready fashion this says that if x has properties F, and if y has properties G, and if $F = G$, then $x = y$. Such an exact formulation in the case above is not strictly applicable, but the intent is clear.

A. Anthropocentric Justifications

Human Rights and Future Generations

ALAN GEWIRTH

Human rights are rights that every human being has simply by virtue of being human. Does this apply to future generations of human beings as well as to present ones? Let us recognize, to begin with, that it is artificial and potentially misleading to talk of specific "generations" of humans. Humans do not come neatly packaged into discrete collections labeled "generations"; they exist as a continuum which is constantly being added to and subtracted from. When we talk of "generations," we often intend to distinguish temporally demarcated groups of humans by reference to some portentous set of events or circumstances that have some special importance in human history; thus we may talk of "the generation of the Great Depression," the "Vietnam Generation," and so forth. But when we talk of "future generations," such a demarcation is usually not intended. We usually mean groups of humans who will be living when all of "us" are presumably dead.

Nevertheless, insofar as the temporal demarcation involves relations of possible dependence, and especially of rights, among human beings, it carries moral significance, for then the well-being of a later group may be affected by the actions or inactions of earlier groups. So, to repeat the question, do future generations of humans, thus understood, have any human rights? The answer depends on the kinds of policies that ought to be followed in the present insofar as they may impinge on humans of the future.

One difficulty with an affirmative answer to this question bears on the requirement of mutuality. Human rights are universalistically mutual, in that they are rights of all humans against all humans: every human is both the subject or right-holder and the respondent or duty-bearer, so that there is a mutual sharing of the benefits of rights and the burdens of duties among all humans. On another construal, it is only governments that are the respondents or duty-bearers of human rights, since it is usually only they that have the power both to violate human rights and to implement them. Still, in

An original essay from the 1st edition of this volume.

principle, governments here act as the representatives of their citizens, so that it is still the latter that ultimately bear the burdens of being the respondents of human rights.

Future generations, however, cannot be properly construed as owing duties to the present generation, since they are in no position to implement the present generation's human rights. So the mutuality required for human rights seems lacking in their case.

We can solve this problem by taking a future-oriented, transgenerational view. Generation B, which exists later than Generation A, does not owe duties to Generation A because B cannot influence or implement A's rights. But B can implement the rights of the following generations C, D, and so forth, so that in this more complex way, mutuality is preserved: A owes duties to B, which in turn owes duties to C, and so forth. So, correlatively, B has rights against A, and C against B, and so forth. In addition, of course, there is required mutuality within each generation.

What is the nature of these rights? Broadly speaking, human rights can be divided into two kinds, negative and positive. Negative rights entail duties to refrain from interfering with the right-holder's having the objects of his rights: thus the right to life entails at least the duty to refrain from killing. Positive rights entail duties to help the right-holder to have the objects of her rights: thus the right to food entails, in certain circumstances, the duty to provide food, and so forth.

Future generations have both kinds of rights. Thus, for example, the present generation has the duty to refrain from so polluting the environment that the next generation will have dirty air, poisonous food, and so forth. This may well require sacrifices by the present generation; it has the duty to refrain from enriching itself in ways that will bring drastic harm to the future generations. This includes the duty to avoid saddling future generations with heavy debts incurred because the present generation will not tax itself to pay for its consumption of goods. Population growth incorporates another phase of these negative duties. While coercion should not be used in this sphere, other phases of these negative duties may well require political enactments that help to forestall nuclear disasters and prevent free marketeers, among others, from pursuing profits in ways that endanger future generations. In a still more directly political way, the present generation in a constitutional democracy has the duty to preserve its liberal institutions by refraining from corrupting or weakening those institutions. It also has the positive obligation to promote social justice in a way that benefits future generations as well as one's own, and to encourage economic development and political democracy in ways that will benefit future generations.

Serious problems of intergenerational justice arise when the positive rights of future generations are at stake. An emphatic example involves the kinds of steps taken by the government in one generation to provide benefits for a future generation. Stalin's drive to build a collectivist society by policies that led to the starvation of millions of "kulaks" was a drastic instance of violating the present generation's rights with the avowed aim of enabling a future generation to thrive. This point indicates the severe limits that must be set to the positive rights of future generations. They should indeed be helped to improve their well-being, but not at a price that violates the present generation's human rights. It is important to note that a similar conclusion applies when the envisaged benefits to the future generation are even admirable. The Egyptian pyramids and the Parthenon are wondrous creations; but their having been built with slave labor was a violation of human rights. This point may be criticized on the ground that the ancients had no idea of human rights and so cannot be condemned for what they did not know. But that some of the ancients did have this idea is suggested by the fact that their eminent philosophers saw the need to defend the institution of slavery. Moreover, the subsequent generations had no right that these monuments be built at such expense for their benefit.

It may be contended that criticism of the implementation of future generations' positive rights leads to a slippery slope: whenever one tries to improve the conditions of the next generation, this involves lowering the opportunities or benefits of the present generation. But this need not be so: it is not a zero-sum situation. In improving the chances or benefits of the next generation, one may also improve those of the present one. The right to education is an example; there are many others.

The whole idea that future generations have human rights may be criticized in the following way. In the argument for human rights, the agent or protagonist claims for himself rights to freedom and well-being as the necessary conditions of his agency, and he does so on the ground of his being a prospective purposive agent, so that he logically must accept that every prospective purposive agent has these rights. But the sense of "prospective" here is primarily individual: each agent regards himself as "prospecting" or looking ahead to fulfill his future purposes, beyond his actual present agency. This prospectiveness, however, does not apply to humans who are members of future generations; it is not to them as "prospective" future agents that the argument refers.

This objection overlooks the fact that future agents are still agents who will have the same agency needs as present agents, so that the argument also applies to them. A right is an individual's interest that ought to be protected for his own sake and controlled by him. Since future agents will have such interests, they have rights.

As was noted earlier, a main sphere of the application of human rights of future generations is environmental ethics. There is an important distinction, however, between two types of environmental ethics. One type is humanist: its basic concern is for the interests of human beings, and it regards the natural environment as providing means for the fulfillment of those interests. Since human rights are grounded in these human interests, the humanist type of environmental ethics is also focused on human rights. The natural environment is to be treated in a way that serves to fulfill human needs of well-being. On this view, then, the environment is the object of human rights, what they are rights to, while the subject of the rights, the right-holder, is humankind. The correlative duties incumbent on humans, including governments, are that the natural environment be treated in ways that fulfill human needs. The environment has no value independent of such humanist fulfillment. Future generations of humans have rights to be benefited by appropriate use of the natural environment.

This view sets both drastic limits and expansive opportunities for the human treatment of the natural environment. That environment must not be despoiled in ways that adversely affect the prospects of future generations as well as of the present one. But at the same time, within these limits, humans have the right to exploit natural resources in ways that contribute immeasurably to human well-being.

The alternative type of environmental ethics is naturalistic. It regards the natural environment as having value in itself, independent of any contributions it may make to fulfilling human needs. The environment is the subject of environmental rights, and humans are the respondents who have the correlative duty to preserve and enhance the environment.

The basis of the independent value attributed to the natural environment varies with different theories; it may be aesthetic, religious, organismic, or other. But central to many of these theories is the idea that the natural environment has a value, a grandeur, a nobility of structure and scope that makes it a fitting object of respect and indeed reverence. It is not to be used as a mere means to human ends; it is an end in itself that requires the utmost consideration and allegiance.

On the naturalist view, two aspects of the concept of rights can be fittingly applied to defend the idea of environmental rights as rights of the environment. One aspect is the point that rights are interests that ought to be protected. On the naturalist view, the environment has interests that are not primarily psychological but rather teleological: natural entities, especially biological ones, have patterns of inherent development that move normally to fruition (acorns become oak trees, and so forth). These entities can be approximately construed as having interests in such fruition, including their not being destroyed or mutilated. The other aspect is that of control. Although the environment usually cannot of itself control how humans will deal with it, both governmental and nongovernmental agencies can be appointed to represent its interests and thereby exercise appropriate control.

It is not always easy to distinguish between the humanist and the naturalist types of environmental ethics. Consider an analogy. The theoretical structure of physical science, amid its many complexities, is an enormously impressive system of ideas that has a profound intellectual beauty of so exalted a kind that knowledge of it is sometimes likened to a mystical experience. The system is constructed by human beings, but it has a significance and value that go beyond the uses made of it by human beings. At least since Aristotle such a system has been regarded as a good in itself, and devotion to its work as the highest human good.

It would be a misconception, then, to hold, with some pragmatists, that such a scientific system has value only insofar as it can be made to serve practical human needs. It does indeed involve obligations to future generations, but this is only to transmit and increase such knowledge, not to convert it into an engineering or other technological tool, let alone to subject it to obscurantist distortions. Nevertheless, it is sometimes held that the scientific system can be positively related to human needs: the basic need to know, to satisfy curiosity, to fulfill the profound desire to understand the world.

In a parallel way, it may be contended that the natural environment, entirely apart from its supplying food and other practical necessities for human beings, fulfills the human need to appreciate and to marvel at the majestic structure of the natural world. Human rights may also be invoked here because humans have a right to develop such appreciation. There is a correlative obligation to future generations to refrain from damaging the natural environment so that it can continue to be such an object of reverence.

The respect owed to the natural environment has certain implications for the rights of animals and other living beings. Entirely apart from the obligation to refrain from inflicting gratuitous pain on animals, there remains the question of the extent to which animals and even plants should be used to fulfill the imperative needs of human beings for food and clothing. Here the rights of present and future generations of human beings may come into conflict with the rights of animals. The basic argument for human rights shows why, in cases of such conflict, human rights must take precedence.

This consideration also bears on the question of whether the natural environment and its various parts have moral rights. For the naturalist, the intrinsic value of the environment provides sufficient justification for answering this question in the affirmative. It must be recognized, however, that even if we have duties toward animals, plants, and other parts of the environment, this does not prove that they have rights. The duties may derive not from the intrinsic worth of the environmental entities; it may not be for their own sake that we have duties toward them. The duties may derive instead from the complex ways in which, according to the humanist view, these entities sub-serve complex human needs. In this as in other cases, duties may not be correlative with rights.

Environmental Values, Anthropocentrism and Speciesism

Onora O'Neill

Most of us agree that we should value the environment, or at least some bits of the environment; fewer of us agree why we should do so. Leaving aside answers that appeal to sheer prudence or mere preference and looking at some of the array of answers offered under the heading of 'environmental ethics' leaves a great deal obscure.

One reason for valuing the environment might be that it is the locus of distinctive 'environmental values', which we can discover, recognise and then respect and preserve in appropriate ways—or, of course, and more worryingly, fail to respect and preserve. This conception of environmental values as real features of the natural world is often invoked on behalf of views that are broadly speaking vaguely realist and (at least) *biocentric*, or (more commonly) emphatically *ecocentric*, and supposedly reject *anthropocentric* positions. Advocates of realist forms of ecocentric ethics assert that intrinsic ecological values are objectively there in the natural world, whether or not there are any human beings who will recognise these values, and whether or not human beings who recognise the values act to preserve or respect them. Ecological realism can seem both thorough and objective. The values, whatever they may be, are part of the furniture of the universe and make their claims regardless of whether there is any audience, let alone an attentive audience, for the claims.

By contrast, living by an anthropocentric ethics is taken to put the environment, and above all the natural environment, at risk. If anthropocentric ethics derives its views of how we may act on the natural world from features of human life, it can supposedly accord the natural world little respect or protection. Such fears make it easy to understand the appeal of

Onora O'Neill, "Environmental Values, Anthropocentrism and Speciesism," *Environmental Values*, 6 (1997): 127–142. Reprinted with permission.

a realist and ecocentric ethic, which ostensibly puts real values, among them real environmental values, first, so is able both to underpin appeals for animal rights or liberation, and to support the wider ethical claims of various sorts of 'deep' or radical ecology.

The main drawback of appeals to real environmental values is that the ambitious claim that the environment, or nature, is the locus of distinctive, real values is so hard to establish. Yet unless we can show that there are indeed real environmental values, appealing to them will not provide *any* sort of reason for respecting or protecting the environment.[1] What makes it hard to establish these real values is the *realism* rather than the *ecocentrism*, a metaphysical difficulty that cannot be overcome by the merits of the cause which real environmental values are supposed to support. Appeals to a position which, if true, would have strong implications will establish nothing at all if the truth of the position cannot be shown. If no realist account of value, environmental or other, can be established, we have very strong reasons not to rely on one.

I cannot show that moral realism, and with it the view that there are real values located in the natural world, is false. What I shall try to show is that a plausible anthropocentric approach may provide a very great proportion of what many people hope to find in a realist and ecocentric approach, without making the same exacting metaphysical demands.

1. Anthropocentrism, Speciesism and Results: Utilitarianism

If realist approaches to environmental ethics cannot be sustained, non-realist approaches may be more convincing. Yet the long-standing worry about non-realist approaches is that they are all anthropocentric,[2] in that they take human life (rather than some independent moral reality) as the starting point of ethical reasoning. Anthropocentric positions in ethics vary greatly. They include many forms of consequentialism (such as utilitarianism) as well as positions that take action rather than results as central (such as forms of contractualism, or action-based positions that take rights and obligations as the basic ethical categories).

A common criticism of anthropocentrist positions in ethics is that they all incorporate what has come to be called *speciesism*. The term *speciesism*, which was coined by analogue with terms such as *racism* or *chauvinism*, is usually used as a label for *unjustified* preference for the human species. The problem with any form of speciesism, critics complain, is that it accords humans moral standing, but unjustifiably accords animals of other species no, or only lesser, standing. On some views speciesism is also unjustifiable in its denial of moral standing to other aspects of the environment, ranging from plants and rivers to abstract entities such as species, habitats and ecosystems, bio-diversity and the ozone layer. Speciesism, as defined, is self-evidently to be condemned, since it builds on something that cannot be justified.

Unfortunately the term *speciesism* is also often used (derogatorily) for *any* preference for the human species, regardless of whether the preference is justified or not. This dual usage makes it easy to beg questions. In order to avoid begging questions I shall use the term *speciesism* strictly for *unjustified* views about the moral standing of certain species, and leave the question whether any preferences can be justified open for discussion. However, I shall use the terms *anti-speciesist* and *speciesist* descriptively to refer to those who do and do not accord non-human animals (full) moral standing. Speciesists in this merely descriptive sense would be guilty of speciesism only if the preference they accord humans cannot be justified.

The view that anthropocentric positions in ethics are invariably committed to speciesism, so unjustifiably blind to the claims of non-humans, is, I believe, unconvincing. Anthropocentrism views ethics as created by or dependent on human action; speciesism builds a preference for human beings into substantive ethical views. Many anthropocentric positions have benign implications for environmental issues, and specifically for the lives of non-human animals.

To show this it might seem reasonable to turn first to that supposedly *least* speciesist of anthropocentric positions, utilitarianism. Utilitarianism is anthropocentric in the straightforward and indispensable sense that it takes it that ethical argument is addressed to human agents, and that only humans can take up (or flout) utilitarian prescriptions.[3] However, Utilitarians claim to repudiate (human) speciesism because they offer reasons for according moral standing to all sentient animals. As Bentham put it, the way to determine moral standing is to ask not 'Can they *reason?* or can they *talk?* but can they *suffer?*'[4] By taking sentience rather than ability to reason as the criterion of moral standing, utilitarians can show the ethical importance of animal welfare; some of them even aim or claim to justify a conception of animal liberation.[5]

Still, it is worth remembering that utilitarianism needs only a little twist to reach conclusions which anti-speciesists do not welcome. John Stuart Mill agreed with Bentham that happiness was the measure of value, but thought that it came in various kinds, and that the higher kinds were restricted to humans. He concluded that it was better to be a human being dissatisfied than a pig satisfied.[6] Utilitarian reasoning about required trade-offs between different types of pleasure may demand that human happiness (of the higher sort) be pursued at the cost of large amounts of porcine misery. The readiness with which utilitarian thinking can return to prescriptions which favour humans is not unimportant: in a world in which xenotransplantation from pigs to humans may be possible, Millian and Benthamite forms of utilitarianism will perhaps reach quite different conclusions about permissible action.

Even if this difficulty were set aside, there are other reasons why Utilitarian thinking cannot provide a comprehensive environmental ethics. Utilitarianism relies on a subjective conception of value which allows it to take account of non-human pleasure and pain, but equally prevents it from valuing either particular non-sentient beings or dispersed and abstract features of the environment: anything that is not sentient cannot suffer or enjoy, so is denied moral standing. Oak trees, bacteria and Mount Everest, species and habitats, ecosystems and bio-diversity, the ozone layer and CO_2 levels are not sentient organisms, so utilitarians will conclude that they can have at most derivative value. They may value bacteria and habitats as constituting or providing the means of life for individual sentient animals; they may value bio-diversity as increasing the likelihood of future survival or pleasure for sentient animals: but they will not value these aspects of the environment except as means to pleasure or happiness in the lives of sentient beings.

A second, equally central feature of utilitarianism also suggests that, far from being the most environmentally benign of anthropocentric positions, it is inevitably highly selective in its concern for the environment. Utilitarian thinking, like other forms of consequentialism, insists that trading-off results is not merely permitted but required.

Maximising happiness or welfare or pleasure can be achieved only by trading-off some outcomes to achieve others. There is no way in which to pursue the greatest happiness of the greatest number without pursuing happiness that will be enjoyed in some lives at the expense of suffering that is to be borne in other lives. Some of the outcomes that yield a lot of happiness (or welfare, or pleasure) in some lives—for example, economic growth and exclusive patterns of consumption—have high environmental costs which are not, or not fully, registered as suffering experienced in any sentient lives. Equally environmental damage that affects no sentient beings (e.g. destruction of arctic or desert wilderness with no or little destruction of sentient life) will not count as a cost or harm. More generally, maximising approaches that rely on a subjective measure of value will not merely *permit* but *require* pleasurable environmental damage whose costs escape their calculus.[7]

These worries might perhaps be assuaged to a limited degree by working out how environmental gain or damage could be more fully or better represented in utilitarian and cognate calculations.[8] But better representation of environmental gain or damage in utilitarian and kindred reasoning is still only representation of their effects on sentient lives: a subjective measure of value is still assumed. There is no guarantee that such measures of value will register all environmental gain or damage, and no guarantee that widely shared or trivial short-term pleasures that damage the environment will not outweigh the pains caused by that damage. The destruction of wilderness or environmentally sensitive areas will be a matter for concern only insofar as it is not outweighed by the pleasure of destroying them; the suffering caused by destruction of fragile habitats with few but rare sentient inhabitants might be outweighed, for example, by the pleasures of tourism or gold-mining.

Utilitarianism and environmentalism are therefore inevitably uneasy allies, not simply because some versions of utilitarianism reinstate conclusions anti-speciesists would not welcome, but mainly because of the larger implications of an ethical position which treats a system of trade-offs among expected pleasure and suffering for the sentient as ethical bed-rock.

2. Anthropocentrism and Action: Rights and Obligations

Some anthropocentric ethical positions may appear less hospitable to speciesism than utilitarianism is, in that they may be better structured to take account of a wider range of environmental concerns. For example, ethical reasoning that focuses on *action* rather than on *results* is quite evidently anthropocentric, since (as far as we know) only humans have full capacities for agency, and only they can heed (or flout) ethical prescriptions and recommendations. Yet such agent-centred reasoning may, I shall argue, offer a promising way of looking at environmental issues, and may even be less open than is utilitarian reasoning to the conclusions anti-speciesists dislike.

Most act-oriented ethical reasoning looks at required action, at rights and at obligations, rather than at preferred outcomes. It does not assume that there is any fundamental metric of value, objective or subjective; it does not identify required action by its contribution to results weighed in terms of that metric; it does not recommend or require that value be maximised by trading-off less valuable for more valuable results. Act-centred ethics, in its many forms, seeks to establish certain principles of obligation, or certain rights, which are to constrain not only individual action but institutions and practices. It accepts institutions or practices that permit or require systems of trading-off for certain domains of life, such as commercial life. However, there is no general reason why act-centred ethics should endorse institutions and practices that permit, let alone require, trading-off or maximising to regulate all domains of life, and no reason why the trade-offs which they permit should be conducted in terms of utilitarian conceptions of value (a monetary metric could often be appropriate). The best known forms of act-centred ethics, which treat rights or obligations as the fundamental ethical categories, limit the domains of life in which trading-off is even permitted, and since they provide no general measure of value, objective or subjective, don't provide a framework for introducing it into all domains of life.

Yet act-centred ethics is often seen as hostile to the environment, because its explicit anthropocentrist starting point is thought to entail an ineradicable preference for the human species. This criticism is often directed specifically at forms of act-oriented ethical reasoning which treat *rights* as central. Several criticisms are recurrent. First, although not all rights need be human rights, rights for other animals can be fitted in only with a bit of pushing and shoving.[9] Second, some supposedly central human rights (such as certain property rights)—and perhaps some animal rights (such as rights to habitat)—can have high environmental costs.[10] Third, rights-based thought appears every bit as blind as utilitarianism to concern for non-sentient particulars and abstract or dispersed features of the natural world.

However, these criticisms pale in the face of more general, structural problems in rights-based thought. The great advantage of rights-based ethics is that it is so beautifully adapted to making claims; its great disadvantage is that these claims can be made with flourish and bravado while leaving it wholly obscure who, if anyone, has a duty or obligation to meet them. Yet if nobody has obligations that correspond to a supposed right, then, however loudly it is claimed or proclaimed, the right amounts to nothing. Proclaiming rights is all too easy; taking them seriously is another matter, and they are not taken seriously unless the corollary obligations are identified and taken seriously. Although the rhetoric of rights has become the most widely used way of talking about justice in the last fifty years, it is the discourse of obligations that addresses the practical question *who ought to do what for whom?*[11] The anthropocentrism of rights discourse is, as it were, the wrong way up: it begins from the thought that humans are claimants rather than from the thought that they are agents. By doing so it can disable rather than foster practical thinking.

The profound structural difficulties of the discourse of rights can be obscured because many discussions of rights veer unselfconsciously between claims about *fundamental, natural* or *moral* rights and claims about *institutional* or *positive* rights. Identifying the obligations which are the counterparts to institutionalised or positive rights is unproblematic: here the move back to practical discourse is easily achieved. However, appeals to institutional and positive rights are not justifications of those rights: institutional and positive rights are the objects rather than the sources of ethical criticism and justification. In some societies some humans have had the positive rights of slavemasters, in others bears who kill or maim other animals have had positive rights to a trial. Neither fact establishes *anything* about the justice or the ethical acceptability of slavery or about the capacities of bears to act wrongly or unjustly, or their rights to due process. To establish what is right or wrong, just or unjust, rights-based reasoning would have to appeal to *fundamental, moral* or *natural* rights—yet these are the very rights whose counterpart obligations can so easily be overlooked, with the consequence that they are merely proclaimed and not taken seriously, and that a rhetorical rather than a practical approach to ethics is adopted.

These are ample reasons for act-oriented ethical reasoning to take obligations rather than rights as basic. A switch of perspective from recipience to action, from rights to obligations, carries no theoretical costs and may yield considerable gain: a focus on obligations will incorporate everything that can be covered by a focus on rights (since any genuine right must be matched by a converse obligation)[12] and can also incorporate any other less tightly specified obligations, which lack counterpart rights. (These obligations, traditionally termed *imperfect obligations*, may be the basis of certain virtues.[13]) By contrast, if rights are treated as basic, obligations without rights may simply be lost from sight.

Moreover, this switch of focus from rights to obligations is productive for environmental ethics, and for clarifying the differences between anthropocentrism and speciesism. The main advantage of taking obligations as basic is a simple gain in clarity about anthropocentrism. Even if some rights are not human rights, all obligations will be human obligations. Or, putting the matter more carefully, obligations can be held and discharged only where capacities for action and for reasoning reach a certain degree of complexity, and we have no knowledge of such capacities except among human beings and in the institutions created and staffed by human beings. Even among human beings these capacities are not universal. So in thinking about obligations, anthropocentrism about the locus of obligations is indispensable rather than inappropriate: without it obligations are not taken seriously. Since we cannot take rights seriously unless we take obligations seriously, anthropocentrism *about obligations* will be needed if we are to think seriously about any rights, including animal rights. This anthropocentrism about the locus of obligations accepts that all obligation-bearers are humans, more or less 'in the maturity of their faculties', but leaves open whether any right-holders are non-human, or lack 'mature' faculties.

In taking obligations seriously we have also to take an accurate view of the claims of entities which may end up on the receiving end of action, and it is here that issues about speciesism arise. Some of those on the receiving end will be individual human beings; others will be individual members of other species (sentient or non-sentient); yet others will be non-living features of the world (such as glaciers or volcanoes) or abstract and dispersed features of the world (such as species or bio-diversity, such as genetic traits or the ozone layer).

Noting the variety of beings who may be on the receiving end of action does not establish which of them have rights of which sorts. Some obligations to individuals, whether human or non-human, may have counterpart rights, which those individuals could claim or waive, or which could be claimed or waived on their behalves; other obligations may lack counterpart rights. Even where there are counterpart rights, they may not be vested in all the beings on the receiving end of required action. For example, there may be obligations to preserve bio-diversity or endangered species or genetic traits, and it is conceivable that we owe such action to certain others, but it barely makes sense to speak of these aspects or features of the natural world as having rights.

Individual sentient animals, whether human or not, and other locatable features of the world, have a certain unity and certain capacities for independent activity and response, which enable us at least to make sense of ascribing rights to them. It is far less plausible to ascribe rights to particulars which lack all capacities to act, let alone to abstract or dispersed aspects of the natural world that lack unity as well as capacities for independent activity or response. Obligations may be directed to entities of any type, but the coherence of attributing rights to inanimate or to abstract or dispersed features of the natural world is questionable. So a second advantage of an obligation-based over a rights-based approach to environmental ethics is that it readily allows for obligations that are directed towards wide ranges of features of the natural world, to some of which a rights-based approach will be blind.

None of this is to deny that certain obligations may have counterpart rights. Yet even when they do there is advantage in treating obligations as the basic ethical notion. Once obligations have been established, a central task of those on whom they fall may be to work out where they must be directed and whether those who are on the receiving end of action, or others, have rights to their performance, in short to determine whether there are any right-holders. A second task may be to collaborate in the construction of institutions and the fostering of practices which make a reality of meeting obligations and of respecting any counterpart rights. These tasks may prove obscure and burdensome, but in beginning with obligations we at least see them as the tasks of identifiable agents, whether individual or collective. The discourse of obligations, *because rather than despite of its evident anthropocentrism*, has the practical merit that it addresses agents rather than claimants.

3. Environmental Obligations: Rejecting Injury

These are the substantial advantages in taking obligations rather than rights as the basic category of act-oriented ethics. However, in acknowledging these advantages we do not yet know *which* obligations human agents and the agencies they construct hold, nor *which* (if any) of these obligations have counterpart rights, or *who* the holders of these rights may be. The advantages are, so to speak, *structural*: they allow one to approach ethical questions, including those of environmental ethics, in full recognition of the unavoidable core of anthropocentrism, namely that obligations must be held by humans (often working in and through institutions), and without assuming either that there are real values embedded in the environment or that there is some generally valid subjective metric of value. If these structural advantages are to be of practical use the next step must be to provide some account, if inevitably a sketchy and incomplete account, of at least some obligations which could be environmentally important.

A first move in trying to identify environmentally significant obligations might be to ask which sorts of fundamental, as opposed to positive and institutional, obligations *could* be taken seriously. Like rights, obligations may be divided into *fundamental (moral, natural)* obligations, and *positive* or *institutional* obligations which presuppose certain institutions and practices. Many of the obligations which we discuss on a daily basis are positive or institutional obligations. Their basis and their justification is tied to that of certain institutions, practices and roles; if the institutions, practices or roles lack justification, so may their derivative or component norms and obligations. If institutions, practices and roles, and with them their derivative norms and obligations, are to be justified, the justification will have to go deeper and appeal to *fundamental* (*moral*, *natural*), or (we may wish to say) to *human* obligations, which are not so tied.

One feature of fundamental, human obligations which obligations of role or status lack, is that their principles must be *universal* obligations, in the sense that they could be accepted and adopted (not necessarily discharged) by all agents. Whereas institutional and positive obligations are always *special* obligations, held in virtue of *special* relationships or roles, or entered into by *specific* transactions (promises, contracts), a *fundamental human obligation* cannot presuppose the legitimacy of differentiations on which special obligations build, hence must be adoptable by all agents if by any.

These considerations provide a basis for identifying the underlying principles for many obligations. If fundamental, human obligations must be universal obligations, then their principles must be adoptable by all. Many principles of action can readily be adopted by each and by all: anybody and everybody can make it a principle not to commit perjury, to cultivate a good reputation or to refrain from lying (how far each individual succeeds in translating these principles into action is quite a different matter and will depend on many contingent circumstances). Other principles of action that can be adopted by some, even by many, cannot be thought of as universally adoptable. Consider, for example, a principle of injuring others: if we try to imagine a world of agents all of whom adopt this principle we are bound to fail because (since a hypothesis of universal failure is unreasonable) at least some people will succeed in injuring others, thereby rendering at least some others their victims, thereby preventing those others from acting, and in particular from acting on a principle of injuring. A principle of injuring cannot coherently be thought of as a principle all can adopt: to use an old technical term, it is not *universalisable*.

Many universalisable principles are entirely optional: their rejection is equally universalisable. For example, both the principle of fasting by day and the principle of eating by day are universalisable; either could be a principle for all, and the rejection of either could be a principle for all; neither day-time fasting nor day-time eating is a matter of obligation. By contrast, other universalisable principles are required because their rejection is not universalisable. For example, if principles of injuring, or of deceiving, or of doing violence are non-universalisable, their rejection must be a matter of obligation.

This line of thought establishes a good deal less than some people might hope. For example, by showing that there is an obligation to reject the principle of injury we do not establish any fundamental human obligation not to injure, but only a fundamental human obligation to reject injury, i.e. an obligation not to make injury a basic principle of lives and institutions. Those who adopt a principle of non-injury must prefer non-injury to injury in each and every context; they must be pacifists; they must not retaliate to injury against self and others, however catastrophic their restraint. By contrast, those who reject a principle of injury will indeed seek to limit injury, but may find that in certain cases this requires selective injury. Examples might be self-defence and the defence of innocent others, which in turn point to the construction of institutions which coerce, hence injure, in limited ways, where this will secure some overall limitation of injury. Rejecting injury is roughly a matter of refraining from *systematic* or *gratuitous* injury (either of these would count against any claim to have rejected the principle of injury), rather than a matter of blanket and undiscriminating commitment to non-injury.

Since injury takes many different forms, some direct and others indirect, a fundamental obligation to reject injury, hence not to injure gratuitously or systematically, will have numerous and powerful implications. *Rejecting direct injury* to others may require complex legal and political institutions that secure ranges of rights of the person and of political rights, as well as a social and economic order that secures at least a certain range of economic and social rights. *Rejecting indirect injury* is mainly a matter of limiting injury that arises from damage either to the social fabric or to natural and man-made environments. For present purposes, it is the rejection of injurious ways of damaging natural and man-made environments that is of central concern.

It is commonly supposed that speciesism follows from anthropocentric ethical reasoning that works along these lines. An argument that agents should not arrogantly assume that they may adopt principles which are unavailable for other agents seemingly will take no account of those who are not agents. Yet this form of anthropocentrism also has powerful anti-speciesist implications, and will establish considerable constraints on ways in which agents may use their environment.

Of course, an obligation-based ethic will not prescribe unlimited care for the environment. A commitment to reject injury does not require agents to refrain from all change to or intervention in the natural world. Since all living creatures interact with the natural world in ways that change it, it is incoherent to suppose that those of them who are agents should have obligations to refrain from all action that changes or damages any part of their environment. However, if the rejection of systematic or gratuitous injury to other agents is a fundamental obligation, then it will also be obligatory not to damage or degrade the underlying powers of renewal and regeneration of the natural world. The basic thought here is that it is wrong to destroy or damage the underlying reproductive and regenerative powers of the natural world because such damage may inflict systematic or gratuitous injury (which often cannot be foreseen with much accuracy or any detail) on some or on many agents. This argument is of course anthropocentric; but it is likely to have numerous anti-speciesist corollaries.

By this standard it might not be wrong to irrigate a desert or to bring land under plough—unless, for example, the cost of so doing is the permanent destruction of habitats, of species and of bio-diversity, which might lead to systematic or gratuitous injury to agents (and inevitably harms many other sentients). It might not be wrong to use an industrial process—unless, for example, that process would damage conditions of life, such as the ozone layer or the CO_2 level, in ways that will injure agents, (and inevitably harm many other sentients). In acting in disregard of such considerations we at the very least risk injuring agents gratuitously and at worst actually injure them systematically. Because these features form the shared environment of human and non-human life, arguments derived from the requirement of not making injury to humans basic to our lives are likely to have numerous anti-speciesist implications, even if they do not support a comprehensive anti-speciesism.

Moreover, these obligations point to a wide range of further and more specific obligations, and to ranges of institutional and positive obligations by means of which fundamental obligations may be discharged at a given time and place. These positive and institutional obligations might range from obligations to preserve or establish agricultural practices which do not irreversibly damage the bio-diversity of the natural world, to obligations to reject energy and transport policies which irreversibly damage the ozone layer or the CO_2 level, to obligations to work towards economic and social institutions and practices which are robust in the face of low-growth or no-growth economic policies. As is evident from these examples, a great merit of taking an obligation-based approach to environmental issues is that it is not blind to the importance of abstract and dispersed features of the environment.

Moreover, these ways of thinking about environmental obligations do not return us to patterns of cost-benefit analysis and maximising ways of thought. They simply spell out some constraints on what may be done in a given time and place, with its actual resources and population, if agents are not to act on the environment in ways that will or may injure systematically or gratuitously. The constraints that must be met by those who seek not to injure either systematically or gratuitously set complex tasks, which must be met in constructing and maintaining institutions and practices, as well as in individual decisions and action.

4. What about the Animals?

Still, this type of anthropocentrism will be only incompletely anti-speciesist; it will also have speciesist implications. As has often been noted, arguments that establish reasons to protect species, bio-diversity and habitats do not always provide reasons for protecting individual organisms, or for protecting individual sentient organisms. The advantage of a framework that takes account of action that affects abstract and dispersed features of the natural world has to be weighed against the seeming disadvantage of lacking comprehensive reasons for valuing individual non-human animals, or for thinking that they have fundamental rights.

The traditional move of anti-speciesists is to try to show that any failure to accord all sentient animals full moral standing, and so as having the same rights as humans, would amount to speciesism, so be unjustifiable. This is usually done by pointing to analogies between human and other animals that minimise the differences between them, so as to establish that non-human animals too have moral standing. If the appeal to analogy is to be plausible it has to be quite subtle, since it is not meant to leave us with the view (for example) that humans have no more obligations than non-human animals, and that a person torturing a cat is on a par with a cat torturing a bird. It is meant to be an appeal that leaves the indispensable anthropocentrism of ethical reasoning intact, while wholly derailing speciesist views by showing that any preferences for the human species that are implied are indeed unjustified. Humans are to be shown to resemble non-humans, who should therefore have the same rights—but not the same obligations.

Indeed, if the appeal to analogy is to be plausible, it will have to support even more differentiated conclusions. For anti-speciesists do not in fact seek to establish that non-human animals have *all* the rights of humans. They do not, for example, worry about animals lacking political or cultural rights. The rights that matter to anti-speciesists are mainly rights against certain sorts of ill treatment. It is not clear how very *general* arguments for the unimportance of the differences between human and non-human animals can be used to establish a very *selective* parity of rights and obligations.

Perhaps one could look for a more selective argument from analogy by emphasising that the boundary between (human) agents and (non-human) nonagents is pretty fuzzy. Although we do not hold non-human animals morally responsible in the ways in which we try to hold one another responsible, we do think of them as acting, and apply a wide range of evaluative vocabulary to them. We take a considerably different view of violent and destructive behaviour by non-human animals and of their peaceful behaviour; we take a considerably similar view of pain and distress in non-humans and humans. Perhaps then there is nothing implausible in the thought that quite specific obligations, for example not to do bodily injury, might hold between humans and great apes, or between humans and certain animals with whom they work and live. Where the boundary of such thoughts lie, and whether they could be used to put into question all the forms of cruelty to animals that anti-speciesists condemn is a harder question. As with all arguments from analogy, much will depend on the specificity and completeness of the comparisons.

Let us suppose that obligation-based thinking can be stretched only a certain distance towards the anti-speciesist goal, in that it offers no convincing arguments for a wholly general prohibition on, say, limiting animals' liberties or reducing their habitat, although it may offer quite good specific arguments against certain cruelties, or against cruelties to certain non-human animals. Would that be the end of the story?

There would be no reason for it to be the end of the story *either* if there are indirect arguments deriving from human obligations for extending animals wider protection, *or* if people choose to establish positive obligations to do so. For example, it might be that basic obligations to protect species and bio-diversity will carry with them many derivative reasons to protect or benefit individual non-human animals. Or it might be that the ideals of certain cultures will provide reason to accord (some) non-human animals (some) further protections or concern. An anthropocentric starting point does not entail speciesism, and need not have relentlessly speciesist conclusions.

Still, many friends of non-human animals will think that this is simply not enough, because it will not establish fundamental rights for all individual non-human animals. (Utilitarians can hardly complain at this selectivity, since their own conclusions are highly selective for differing reasons.) Yet, as soon as one considers the project of showing that all animals should have the same fundamental rights as humans it becomes evident that many of the rights that would be part and parcel of an obligation to reject injury to other humans are irrelevant for non-human animals. For example, rights to free speech or to a fair trial have no place in the lives of non-human animals. More generally, very many personal, political, economic, social, and cultural rights appear to have no useful place in the lives of non-human animals. Only a few personal rights such as a right not to be tormented, or a right not to be killed without reason, and possibly some analogues of (more controversial) economic or social rights, such as a right to an adequate habitat or to food, could even make sense for non-human animals; that they make sense does not, of course, show that any of them is a fundamental right.

Perhaps in the end we should ask whether all animal rights need be fundamental or moral rights, or whether all or many of them should be understood as the positive and institutional rights of a particular social order. For an obligation-based approach does not stand in the way of constructing institutional or positive rights for individual non-human animals, or for the individual non-human animals of certain species, even if it does not establish that all non-human animals have fundamental rights. (This thought might be congenial to some friends of non-human animals because it would allow us to think differently of animal killing by (say) subsistence farmers and pastoralists and by affluent societies, for whom vegetarian diets may be more feasible.) These are further reasons for thinking that an anthropocentric starting point clearly need lead to relentlessly speciesist conclusions.

No doubt this limited conclusion about animal rights will seem inadequate or disappointing to some. I take a more optimistic view. I set it against five considerable advantages of an obligation-based approach to ethical reasoning about the environment. The first advantage is that with this approach we do not attempt the Sysiphean metaphysical labours of showing that there are real environmental values embedded in the natural world. The second is that we do not have to approach environmental issues in terms of a subjective metric of value and the system of trade-offs which are implied in subordinating action to that conception of value, with all the risks for the environment and for individual non-human (and human!) animals that this can imply, even where 'environmentally sensitive' ways of costing results are used. The third is that we approach environmental issues in a sufficiently broad way to be able to take serious account of abstract and dispersed aspects of the environment. The fourth is that we do not lead with the confused anthropocentrism of a rhetoric of rights, so do not leave it perennially vague just who is obliged to do what for whom (even a comprehensive anti-speciesism will not be particularly attractive if its status is largely rhetorical). The fifth is that an obligation-based approach allows that individuals and groups may advocate and follow more comprehensively anti-speciesist ways of life than its basic arguments can establish.

To this I would like to add one consolation for those who are still sad at the thought that animal rights might be no more than positive and institutional rights, and that arguments for their importance could not demonstrate that sentient animals had complete moral standing. It is that this is where we would hope that all the best rights would end up, and that a derivative place in a process of justification need not entail a derivative place in our lives. It means only that good arguments for the construction of positive rights for non-human animals may not shadow arguments for constructing accounts of positive rights among (human) agents. There are plenty of other arguments that could be offered for constructing positive rights for certain non-human animals: some might derive from the positive obligations and rights of humans, others might be internal to ways of life, or invoke certain ideals or virtues. If we call to mind the systematic problems of realist, utilitarian and rights-based reasoning in addressing environmental issues, we may find merit in obligation-based reasoning, and welcome its various eco-friendly implications, even if they do not sustain the unrestricted conclusions anti-speciesists would most welcome.

Notes

This essay arises from a presentation in the Allied Domecq public lecture series organised by Dr J. Smith for the Cambridge University Committee for Interdisciplinary Environmental Studies in the Lent term, 1996. I am grateful to him and to a lively audience, as well as to Dr T. Hayward, for searching comments.

1 Without the realism, appeals to environmental values are reifications which explain nothing. Just as we fail to explain why opium has its well known properties by citing its dormitive virtues, so we fail to show why we should value the environment if we merely invoke but do not establish environmental values.

2 The term anthropocentrism, rather than the more obvious humanism, has become conventional for ethical views that take human life as the starting point of ethical reasoning. The older term humanism is inappropriate for this purpose, since is taken to refer specifically to a set of claims about the human rather than divine basis of ethical relations.

3 I am grateful to Tim Hayward, who refereed this essay, for sending me a copy of his paper 'Anthropocentrism: A Misunderstood Problem', *Environmental Values* 6(1), in which he sharpens distinctions between anthropocentric and speciesist claims. I have found his thinking constructive and suggestive, and have drawn on it at several points.

4 Bentham, 1967, ch. 17, p. 412 n. The position has its limits for environmental ethics: it puts the entire non-sentient world at the disposal of sentient beings.

5 The term liberation seems adrift in utilitarian waters: what is there in utilitarian right conduct to animals which would not be covered by the term animal welfare?

6 'It is better to be a human being dissatisfied than a pig satisfied', Mill, 1962, p. 260.

7 Unless, of course, non-utilitarian considerations are introduced. Cf. Goodin, 1992, who introduces the non-subjective value of organic wholes into a broadly utilitarian account of environmental ethics in order to explain what is wrong about the destruction of wilderness that nobody is enjoying.

8 David Pearce *et al.*, 1989, 1991, 1993, and 1995.

9 The pushing and shoving is usually accomplished by stressing the analogies between some non-human animals and some humans, while minimising the disanalogies between other non-human animals and other humans. Cf. Singer, 1976; Clark, 1977; Regan, 1983; Regan and Singer, 1989; more recently Singer and Cavalieri, 1993.

10 Cf. Aiken, 1992.

11 For more extensive argument on these points see O'Neill, 1996. ch. 5.

12 The sole and for these purposes unimportant exceptions are so-called 'mere liberties' or 'unprotected rights', such as rights to pick up a coin from the pavement where there is no obligation on others to desist from picking it up if they can do so first.

13 See O'Neill, 1996, ch. 7 for discussion of imperfect duties and virtues.

References

Aiken, William 1992. 'Human Rights in an Ecological Era', *Environmental Values* 1: 189–203.

Bentham, Jeremy 1967. *Introduction to the Principles of Morals and of Legislation*, in *A Fragment on Government and Introduction to the Principles of Morals and of Legislation*, ed. Wilfrid Harrison. Oxford: Blackwell.

Clark, Stephen 1977. *The Moral Status of Animals*. Oxford: Oxford University Press. *Environmental Values*, 1994, vol. 3, no. 4, special issue on Values and Preferences in Environmental Economics.

Goodin, Robert 1992. *Green Politics*. Oxford: Polity Press.

Hayward, Tim 1997. 'Anthropocentrism: A Misunderstood Problem', *Environmental Values* 6: 49–63.

O'Neill, Onora 1996. *Towards Justice and Virtue: A constructive account of practical reasoning*. Cambridge: Cambridge University Press.

Pearce, David, *et al.*, 1989. *Blueprint for a Green Economy*. London: Earthscan.

Pearce, David, *et al.*, 1991. *Blueprint 2: Greening the World Economy*. London: Earthscan.

Pearce, David, *et al.*, 1993. *Blueprint 3: Measuring Sustainable Development*. London: Earthscan.

Pearce, David, *et al.*, 1995. *Blueprint 4: Capturing Global Environmental Values*. London: Earthscan.

Regan, Thomas 1983. *The Case for Animal Rights*. Berkeley: University of California Press.

Regan, Thomas and Singer, Peter 1989. *Animal Rights and Human Obligations*. 2nd edn. Englewood Cliffs, NJ: Prentice Hall.

Singer, Peter 1976. *Animal Liberation*. London: Jonathan Cape.

Singer, Peter and Cavalieri, Paola 1993. *The Great Ape Project*. London: Fourth Estate.

B. Biocentric Justifications

Environmental Ethics

Values in and Duties to the Natural World

HOLMES ROLSTON III

Environmental ethics stretches classical ethics to the breaking point. All ethics seeks an appropriate respect for life. But we do not need just a humanistic ethic applied to the environment as we have needed one for business, law, medicine, technology, international development, or nuclear disarmament. Respect for life does demand an ethic concerned about human welfare, an ethic like the others and now applied to the environment. But environmental ethics in a deeper sense stands on a frontier, as radically theoretical as it is applied. It alone asks whether there can be nonhuman objects of duty.

Neither theory nor practice elsewhere needs values outside of human subjects, but environmental ethics must be more biologically objective—nonanthropocentric. It challenges the separation of science and ethics, trying to reform a science that finds nature value-free and an ethics that assumes that only humans count morally. Environmental ethics seeks to escape relativism in ethics, to discover a way past culturally based ethics. However much our worldviews, ethics included, are embedded in our cultural heritages, and thereby theory-laden and value-laden, all of us know that a natural world exists apart from human cultures. Humans interact with nature. Environmental ethics is the only ethics that breaks out of culture. It has to evaluate nature, both wild nature and the nature that mixes with culture, and to judge duty thereby. After accepting environmental ethics, you will no longer be the humanist you once were.

Environmental ethics requires risk. It explores poorly charted terrain, where one can easily get lost. One must hazard the kind of insight that first looks like foolishness. Some people approach environmental ethics with a smile—expecting chicken liberation and rights for rocks, misplaced concern for chipmunks and daisies. Elsewhere, they think, ethicists deal with sober concerns: medical ethics, business ethics, justice in public affairs, questions of life and death and of peace and war. But the questions here are no less serious: The degradation of the environment poses as great a threat to life as nuclear war, and a more probable tragedy.

Holmes Rolston III, "Environmental Ethics: Values in and Duties to the Natural World," from F. Herbert Bormann and Stephen R. Kellert (eds.), *The Broken Circle: Ecology, Economics, and Ethics*, Yale University Press, 1991; pp. 228–247. Reprinted with permission of Yale University Press.

Higher Animals

Logically and psychologically, the best and easiest breakthrough past the traditional boundaries of interhuman ethics is made when confronting higher animals. Animals defend their lives; they have a good of their own and suffer pains and pleasures like ourselves. Human moral concern should at least cross over into the domain of animal experience. This boundary crossing is also dangerous because if made only psychologically and not biologically, the would-be environmental ethicist may be too disoriented to travel further. The promised environmental ethics will degenerate into a mammalian ethics. We certainly need an ethic for animals, but that is only one level of concern in a comprehensive environmental ethics.

One might expect classical ethics to have sifted well an ethics for animals. Our ancestors did not think about endangered species, ecosystems, acid rain, or the ozone layer, but they lived in closer association with wild and domestic animals than we do. Hunters track wounded deer; ranchers who let their horses starve are prosecuted. Still, until recently, the scientific, humanistic centuries since the so-called Enlightenment have not been sensitive ones for animals, owing to the Cartesian legacy. Animals were mindless, living matter; biology has been mechanistic. Even psychology, rather than defending animal experience, has been behaviorist. Philosophy has protested little, concerned instead with locating values in human experiences at the same time that it disspirited and devalued nature. Across several centuries of hard science and humanistic ethics there has been little compassion for animals.

The progress of science itself smeared the human–nonhuman boundary line. Animal anatomy, biochemistry, cognition, perception, experience, behavior, and evolutionary history are kin to our own. Animals have no immortal souls, but then persons may not either, or beings with souls may not be the only kind that count morally. Ethical progress further smeared the boundary. Sensual pleasures are a good thing; ethics should be egalitarian, nonarbitrary, nondiscriminatory. There are ample scientific grounds that animals enjoy pleasures and suffer pains; and ethically there are no grounds to value these sensations in humans and not in animals. So there has been a vigorous reassessment of human duties to sentient life. The world cheered in the fall of 1988 when humans rescued two whales from winter ice.

"Respect their right to life": A sign in Rocky Mountain National Park enjoins humans not to harass bighorn sheep. "The question is not, Can they reason, nor Can they talk? but, Can they suffer?" wrote Jeremy Bentham, insisting that animal welfare counts too.[1] The Park Service sign and Bentham's question increase sensitivity by extending rights and hedonist goods to animals. The gain is a vital breakthrough past humans, and the first lesson in environmental ethics has been learned. But the risk is a moral extension that expands rights as far as mammals and not much further, a psychologically based ethic that counts only felt experience. We respect life in our nonhuman but near-human animal cousins, a semianthropic and still quite subjective ethics. Justice remains a concern for just-us subjects. There has, in fact, not been much of a theoretical breakthrough, no paradigm shift.

Lacking that, we are left with anomaly and conceptual strain. When we try to use culturally extended rights and psychologically based utilities to protect the flora or even the insentient fauna, to protect endangered species or ecosystems, we can only stammer. Indeed, we get lost trying to protect bighorns, because, in the wild, cougars are not respecting the rights or utilities of the sheep they slay, and, in culture, humans slay sheep and eat them regularly, while humans have every right not to be eaten by either humans or cougars. There are no rights in the wild, and nature is indifferent to the welfare of particular animals. A bison fell through the ice into a river in Yellowstone Park; the environmental ethic there, letting nature take its course, forbade would-be rescuers from either saving or killing the suffering animal to put it out of its misery. A drowning human would have been saved at once. Perhaps it was a mistake to save those whales.

The ethics by extension now seems too nondiscriminating; we are unable to separate an ethics for humans from an ethics for wildlife. To treat wild animals with compassion learned in culture does not appreciate their wildness. Man, said Socrates, is the political animal; humans maximally are what they are in culture, where the natural selection pressures (impressively productive in ecosystems) are relaxed without detriment to the species *Homo sapiens*, and indeed with great benefit to its member persons. Wild animals cannot enter culture; they do not have that capacity. They cannot acquire language at sufficient levels to take part in culture; they cannot make their clothing or build fires, much less read books or receive an education. Animals can, by human adoption, receive some of the protections of culture, which happens when we domesticate them, but neither pets nor food animals enter the culture that shelters them.

Worse, such cultural protection can work to their detriment; their wildness is made over into a human artifact as food or pet animal. A cow does not have the integrity of a deer, or a poodle that of a wolf. Culture is a good thing for humans but often a bad thing for animals. Their biology and ecology—neither justice nor charity, nor rights nor welfare—provide the benchmark for an ethics.

Culture does make a relevant ethical difference, and environmental ethics has different criteria from interhuman ethics. Can they talk? and, Can they reason?—indicating cultural capacities—are relevant questions; not just, Can they suffer? *Equality* is a positive word in ethics, *discriminatory* a pejorative one. On the other hand, simplistic reduction is a failing in the philosophy of science and epistemology; to be "discriminating" is desirable in logic and value theory. Something about treating humans as equals with bighorns and cougars seems to "reduce" humans to merely animal levels of value, a "no more than" counterpart in ethics of the "nothing but" fallacy often met in science. Humans are "nothing but" naked apes. Something about treating sheep and cougars as the equals of humans seems to elevate them unnaturally and not to value them for what they are. There is something insufficiently discriminating in such judgments; they are species-blind in a bad sense, blind to the real differences between species, valuational differences that do count morally. To the contrary, a discriminating ethicist will insist on preserving the differing richness of valuational complexity, wherever found. Compassionate respect for life in its suffering is only part of the analysis.

Two tests of discrimination are pains and diet. It might be thought that pain is a bad thing, whether in nature or culture. Perhaps when dealing with humans in culture, additional levels of value and utility must be protected by conferring rights that do not exist in the wild, but meanwhile we should at least minimize animal suffering. That is indeed a worthy imperative in culture where animals are removed from nature and bred, but it may be misguided where animals remain in ecosystems. When the bighorn sheep of Yellowstone caught pinkeye, they were blinded, injured, and starving as a result, and three hundred of them, more than half the herd, perished. Wildlife veterinarians wanted to treat the disease, as they would have in any domestic herd, and as they did with Colorado bighorns infected with an introduced lungworm, but the Yellowstone ethicists left the animals to suffer, seemingly not respecting their life.

Had those ethicists no mercy? They knew rather that, although intrinsic pain is a bad thing whether in humans or in sheep, pain in ecosystems is instrumental pain, through which the sheep are naturally selected for a more satisfactory adaptive fit. Pain in a medically skilled culture is pointless, once the alarm to health is sounded, but pain operates functionally in bighorns in their niche, even after it becomes no longer in the interests of the pained individual. To have interfered in the interests of the blinded sheep would have weakened the species. Even the question, Can they suffer? is not as simple as Bentham thought. What we ought to do depends on what is. The *is* of nature differs significantly from the *is* of culture, even when similar suffering is present in both.

At this point some ethicists will insist that at least in culture we can minimize animal pain, and that will constrain our diet. There is predation in nature; humans evolved as omnivores. But humans, the only moral animals, should refuse to participate in the meat-eating phase of their ecology, just as they refuse to play the game merely by the rules of natural selection. Humans do not look to the behavior of wild animals as an ethical guide in other matters (marriage, truth telling, promise keeping, justice, charity). Why should they justify their dietary habits by watching what animals do?

But the difference is that these other matters are affairs of culture; these are person-to-person events, not events at all in spontaneous nature. By contrast, eating is omnipresent in wild nature; humans eat because they are in nature, not because they are in culture. Eating animals is not an event between persons but a human-to-animal event; and the rules for this act come from the ecosystems in which humans evolved and have no duty to remake. Humans, then, can model their dietary habits from their ecosystems, though they cannot and should not so model their interpersonal justice or charity. When eating, they ought to minimize animal suffering, but they have no duty to revise trophic pyramids whether in nature or culture. The boundary between animals and humans has not been rubbed out after all; only what was a boundary line has been smeared into a boundary zone. We have discovered that animals count morally, though we have not yet solved the challenge of how to count them.

Animals enjoy psychological lives, subjective experiences, the satisfaction of felt interests—intrinsic values that count morally when humans encounter them. But the pains, pleasures, interests, and welfare of individual animals are only one of the considerations in a more complex environmental ethics that cannot be reached by conferring rights on them or by a hedonist calculus, however far extended. We have to travel further into a more biologically based ethics.

Organisms

If we are to respect all life, we have still another boundary to cross, from zoology to botany, from sentient to insentient life. In Yosemite National Park for almost a century humans entertained themselves by driving through a tunnel cut in a giant sequoia. Two decades ago the Wawona tree, weakened by the cut, blew down in a storm. People said, "Cut us another drive-through sequoia." The Yosemite environmental ethic, deepening over the years, answered, "No. You ought not to mutilate majestic sequoias for amusement. Respect their life." Indeed, some ethicists count the value of redwoods so highly that they will spike redwoods, lest they be cut. In the Rawah Wilderness in alpine Colorado, old signs read, "Please leave the flowers for others to enjoy." When the signs rotted out, new signs urged a less humanist ethic: "Let the flowers live!"

But trees and flowers cannot care, so why should we? We are not considering animals that are close kin, nor can they suffer or experience anything. Plants are not valuers with preferences that can be satisfied or frustrated. It seems odd to assert that plants need our sympathy, odd to ask that we should consider their point of view. They have no subjective life, only objective life.

Perhaps the questions are wrong, because they are coming out of the old paradigm. We are at a critical divide. That is why I earlier warned that environmental ethicists who seek only to extend a humanistic ethic to mammalian cousins will get lost. Seeing no moral landmarks, those ethicists may turn back to more familiar terrain. Afraid of the naturalistic fallacy, they will say that people should enjoy letting flowers live or that it is silly to cut drive-through sequoias, that it is aesthetically more excellent for humans to appreciate both for what they are. But these ethically conservative reasons really do not understand what biological conservation is in the deepest sense.

It takes ethical courage to go on, to move past a hedonistic, humanistic logic to a bio-logic. Pains, pleasures, and psychological experience will no further be useful categories, but—lest some think that from here on I as a philosopher become illogical and lose all ethical sense—let us orient ourselves by extending logical, propositional, cognitive, and normative categories into biology. Nothing matters to a tree, but much is vital to it.

An organism is a spontaneous, self-maintaining system, sustaining and reproducing itself, executing its program, making a way through the world, checking against performance by means of responsive capacities with which to measure success. It can reckon with vicissitudes, opportunities, and adversities that the world presents. Something more than physical causes, even when less than sentience, is operating within every organism. There is information superintending the causes; without it, the organism would collapse into a sand heap. This information is a modern equivalent of what Aristotle called formal and final causes; it gives the organism a telos, or end, a kind of (nonfelt) goal. Organisms have ends, although not always ends in view.

All this cargo is carried by the DNA, essentially a linguistic molecule. By a serial reading of the DNA, a polypeptide chain is synthesized, such that its sequential structure determines the bioform into which it will fold. Ever lengthening chains are organized into genes, as ever-longer sentences are organized into paragraphs and chapters. Diverse proteins, lipids, carbohydrates, enzymes—all the life structures—are written into the genetic library. The DNA is thus a logical set, not less than a biological set, and is informed as well as formed. Organisms use a sort of symbolic logic, using these molecular shapes as symbols of life. The novel resourcefulness lies in the epistemic content conserved, developed, and thrown forward to make biological resources out of the physicochemical sources. This executive steering core is cybernetic—partly a special kind of cause-and-effect system and partly something more. It is partly a historical information system discovering and evaluating ends so as to map and make a way through the world, and partly a system of significances attached to operations, pursuits, and resources. In this sense, the genome is a set of conservation molecules.

The genetic set is really a propositional set—to choose a provocative term—recalling that the Latin *propositum* is an assertion, a set task, a theme, a plan, a proposal, a project, as well as a cognitive statement. From this, it is also a motivational set, unlike human books, because these life motifs are set to drive the movement from genotypic potential to phenotypic expression. Given a chance, these molecules seek organic self-expression. They thus proclaim a lifeway; and with this an organism, unlike an inert rock, claims the environment as source and sink, from which to abstract energy and materials and into which to excrete them. It takes advantage of its environment. Life thus arises out of earthen sources (as do rocks), but life (unlike rocks) turns back on its sources to make resources out of them. An acorn becomes an oak; the oak stands on its own.

So far we have only description. We begin to pass to value when we recognize that the genetic set is a normative set; it distinguishes between what is and what ought to be. This does not mean that the organism is a moral system, for there are no moral agents in nature; but the organism is an axiological, evaluative system. So the oak grows, reproduces, repairs its wounds, and resists death. The physical state that the organism seeks, idealized in its programmatic form, is a valued state. Value is present in this achievement. *Vital* seems a better word here than *biological*. We are dealing not simply with another individual defending its solitary life but with an individual having situated fitness in an ecosystem. Still, we want to affirm that the living individual, taken as a point-experience in the web of interconnected life, is per se an intrinsic value.

A life is defended for what it is in itself, without necessary further contributory reference, although, given the structure of all ecosystems, such lives necessarily do have further contributory reference. The organism has something it is conserving, something for which it is standing: its life. Though organisms must fit into their niche, they have their own standards. They promote their own realization, at the same time that they track an environment. They have a technique, a know-how. Every organism has a good of its kind; it defends its own kind as a good kind. In that sense, as soon as one knows what a giant sequoia tree is, one knows the biological identity that is sought and conserved.

There seems no reason why such own-standing normative organisms are not morally significant. A moral agent deciding his or her behavior ought to take account of the consequences for other evaluative systems. Within the community of moral agents, one has not merely to ask whether *x* is a normative system but also, because the norms are at personal option, to judge the norm. But within the biotic community, organisms are amoral normative systems, and there are no cases in which an organism seeks a good of its own that is morally reprehensible. The distinction between having a good of its kind and being a good kind vanishes, so far as any faulting of the organism is concerned. To this extent, everything with a good of its kind is a good kind and thereby has intrinsic value.

One might say that an organism is a bad organism if, during the course of pressing its normative expression, it upsets the ecosystem or causes widespread disease. Remember, though, that an organism cannot be a good kind without situated environmental fitness. By natural selection the kind of goods to which it is genetically programmed must mesh with its ecosystemic role. In spite of the ecosystem as a perpetual contest of goods in dialectic and exchange, it is difficult to say that any organism is a bad kind in this instrumental sense either. The misfits are extinct, or soon will be. In spontaneous nature any species that preys upon, parasitizes, competes with, or crowds another will be a bad kind from the narrow perspective of its victim or competitor.

But if we enlarge that perspective, we typically have difficulty in saying that any species is a bad kind overall in the ecosystem. An "enemy" may even be good for the "victimized" species, though harmful to individual members of it, as when predation keeps the deer herd healthy. Beyond this, the "bad kinds" typically play useful roles in population control, in symbiotic relationships, or in providing opportunities for other species. The *Chlamydia* microbe is a bad kind from the perspective of the bighorns, but when one thing dies, something else lives. After the pinkeye outbreak among the bighorns, the golden eagle population in Yellowstone flourished, preying on the bighorn carcasses. For the eagles, *Chlamydia* is a good kind instrumentally.

Some biologist-philosophers will say that even though an organism evolves to have a situated environmental fitness, not all such situations are good arrangements; some can be clumsy or bad. True, the vicissitudes of historical evolution do sometimes result in ecological webs that are suboptimal solutions, within the biologically limited possibilities and powers of interacting organisms. Still, such systems have been selected over millennia for functional stability, and at least the burden of proof is on a human evaluator to say why any natural kind is a bad kind and ought not to call forth admiring respect. Something may be a good kind intrinsically but a bad kind instrumentally in the system; such cases will be anomalous however, with selection pressures against them. These assertions about good kinds do not say that things are perfect kinds or that there can be no better ones, only that natural kinds are good kinds until proven otherwise.

In fact, what is almost invariably meant by a bad kind is an organism that is instrumentally bad when judged from the viewpoint of human interests, often with the further complication that human interests have disrupted natural systems. *Bad* as so used is an anthropocentric word; there is nothing at all biological or ecological about it, and so it has no force in evaluating objective nature, however much humanistic force it may sometimes have.

A vital ethic respects all life, not just animal pains and pleasures, much less just human preferences. The old signs in the Rawah Wilderness—"Please leave the flowers for others to enjoy"—were application signs using an old, ethically conservative, humanistic ethic. The new ones invite a change of reference frame—a wilder ethic that is more logical because it is more biological, a radical ethic that goes down to the roots of life, that really is conservative because it understands biological conservation at depths. What the injunction "Let the flowers live!" means is this: "Daisies, marsh marigolds, geraniums, and larkspurs are evaluative systems that conserve goods of their kind and, in the absence of evidence to the contrary, are good kinds. There are trails here by which you may enjoy these flowers. Is there any reason why your human interests should not also conserve these good kinds?" A drive-through sequoia causes no suffering; it is not cruel. But it is callous and insensitive to the wonder of life.

Species

Sensitivity to the wonder of life, however, can sometimes make an environmental ethicist seem callous. On San Clemente Island, the US Fish and Wildlife Service and the Natural Resource Office of the US Navy planned to shoot two thousand feral goats to save three endangered plant species (*Malacothamnus clementinus, Castilleja grisea*, and *Delphinium kinkiense*), of which the surviving individuals numbered only a few dozen. After a protest, some goats were trapped and relocated. But trapping all of them was impossible, and many thousands were killed. In this instance, the survival of plant species was counted more than the lives of individual mammals; a few plants counted more than many thousands of goats.

Those who wish to restore rare species of big cats to the wild have asked about killing genetically inbred, inferior cats presently held in zoos, in order to make space available for the cats needed to reconstruct and maintain a population that is genetically more likely to survive upon release. All the Siberian tigers in zoos in North America are descendants of seven animals; if these tigers were replaced by others nearer to the wild type and with more genetic variability, the species might be saved in the wild. When we move to the level of species, sometimes we decide to kill individuals for the good of their kind.

Or we might now refuse to let nature take its course. The Yellowstone ethicists let the bison drown, in spite of its suffering; they let the blinded bighorns die. But in the spring of 1984 a sow grizzly and her three cubs walked across the ice of Yellowstone Lake to Frank Island, two miles from shore. They stayed several days to feast on two elk carcasses, and the ice bridge melted. Soon afterward, they were starving on an island too small to support them. This time the Yellowstone ethicists promptly rescued the grizzlies and released them on the mainland, in order to protect an endangered species. They were not rescuing individual bears so much as saving the species.

Coloradans have declined to build the Two Forks Dam to supply urban Denver with water. Building the dam would require destroying a canyon and altering the Platte River flow, with many negative environmental consequences, including further endangering the whooping crane and endangering a butterfly, the Pawnee montane skipper. Elsewhere in the state, water development threatens several fish species, including the humpback chub, which requires the turbulent spring runoff stopped by dams. Environmental ethics doubts whether the good of humans who wish more water for development, both for industry and for bluegrass lawns, warrants endangering species of cranes, butterflies, and fish.

A species exists; a species ought to exist. An environmental ethics must make these assertions and move from biology to ethics with care. Species exist only instantiated in individuals, yet they are as real as individual plants or animals. The assertion that there are specific forms of life historically maintained in their environments over time seems as certain as anything else we believe about the empirical world. At times biologists revise the theories and taxa with which they map these forms, but species are not so much like lines of latitude and longitude as like mountains and rivers, phenomena objectively there to be mapped. The edges of these natural kinds will sometimes be fuzzy, to some extent discretionary. One species will slide into another over evolutionary time. But it does not follow from the fact that speciation is sometimes in progress that species are merely made up and not found as evolutionary lines with identity in time as well as space.

A consideration of species is revealing and challenging because it offers a biologically based counterexample to the focus on individuals—typically sentient and usually persons—so characteristic in classical ethics. In an evolutionary ecosystem, it is not mere individuality that counts; the species is also significant because it is a dynamic life-form maintained over time. The individual represents (re-presents) a species in each new generation. It is a token of a type, and the type is more important than the token.

A species lacks moral agency, reflective self-awareness, sentience, or organic individuality. The older, conservative ethic will be tempted to say that specific-level processes cannot count morally. Duties must attach to singular lives, most evidently those with a self, or some analogue to self. In an individual organism, the organs report to a center; the good of a whole is defended. The members of a species report to no center. A species has no self. It is not a bounded singular. There is no analogue to the nervous hookups or circulatory flows that characterize the organism.

But singularity, centeredness, selfhood, and individuality are not the only processes to which duty attaches. A more radically conservative ethic knows that having a biological identity reasserted genetically over time is as true of the species as of the individual. Identity need not attach solely to the centered organism; it can persist as a discrete pattern over time. From this way of thinking, it follows that the life the individual has is something passing through the individual as much as something it intrinsically possesses. The individual is subordinate to the species, not the other way around. The genetic set, in which is coded the telos, is as evidently the property of the species as of the individual through which it passes. A consideration of species strains any ethic fixed on individual organisms, much less on sentience or persons. But the result can be biologically sounder, though it revises what was formerly thought logically permissible or ethically binding. When ethics is informed by this kind of biology, it is appropriate to attach duty dynamically to the specific form of life.

The species line is the vital living system, the whole, of which individual organisms are the essential parts. The species too has its integrity, its individuality, its right to life (if we must use the rhetoric of rights); and it is more important to protect this vitality than to protect individual integrity. The right to life, biologically speaking, is an adaptive fit that is right for life, that survives over millennia. This idea generates at least a presumption that species in a niche are good right where they are, and therefore that it is right for humans to let them be, to let them evolve.

Processes of value that we earlier found in an organic individual reappear at the specific level: defending a particular form of life, pursuing a pathway through the world, resisting death (extinction), regenerating, maintaining a normative identity over time, expressing creative resilience by discovering survival skills. It is as logical to say that the individual is the species' way of propagating itself as to say that the embryo or egg is the individual's way of propagating itself. The dignity resides in the dynamic form; the individual inherits this form, exemplifies it, and passes it on. If, at the specific level, these processes are just as evident, or even more so, what prevents duties from arising at that level? The appropriate survival unit is the appropriate level of moral concern.

A shutdown of the life stream is the most destructive event possible. The wrong that humans are doing, or allowing to happen through carelessness, is stopping the historical vitality of life, the flow of natural kinds. Every extinction is an incremental decay in this stopping of life, no small thing. Every extinction is a kind of superkilling. It kills forms (species) beyond individuals. It kills essences beyond existences, the soul as well as the body. It kills collectively, not just distributively. It kills birth as well as death. Afterward nothing of that kind either lives or dies.

Ought species *x* to exist? is a distributive increment in the collective question, ought life on Earth to exist? Life on Earth cannot exist without its individuals, but a lost individual is always reproducible; a lost species is never reproducible. The answer to the species question is not always the same as the answer to the collective question, but because life on Earth is an aggregate of many species, the two are sufficiently related that the burden of proof lies with those who wish deliberately to extinguish a species and simultaneously to care for life on Earth.

One form of life has never endangered so many others. Never before has this level of question—superkilling by a superkiller—been deliberately faced. Humans have more understanding than ever of the natural world they inhabit and of the speciating processes, more predictive power to foresee the intended and unintended results of their actions, and more power to reverse the undesirable consequences. The duties that such power and vision generate no longer attach simply to individuals or persons but are emerging duties to specific forms of life. What is ethically callous is the maelstrom of killing and insensitivity to forms of life and the sources producing them. What is required is principled responsibility to the biospheric Earth.

Human activities seem misfit in the system. Although humans are maximizing their own species interests, and in this respect behaving as does each of the other species, they do not have any adaptive fitness. They are not really fitting into the evolutionary processes of ongoing biological conservation and elaboration. Their cultures are not really dynamically stable in their ecosystems. Such behavior is therefore not right. Yet humanistic ethical systems limp when they try to prescribe right conduct here. They seem misfits in the roles most recently demanded of them.

If, in this world of uncertain moral convictions, it makes any sense to assert that one ought not to kill individuals without justification, it makes more sense to assert that one ought not to superkill the species without superjustification. Several billion years' worth of creative toil, several million species of teeming life, have been handed over to the care of this late-coming species in which mind has flowered and morals have emerged. Ought not this sole moral species do something less self-interested than count all the produce of an evolutionary ecosystem as nothing but human resources? Such an attitude hardly seems biologically informed, much less ethically adequate. It is too provincial for intelligent humanity. Life on Earth is a many-splendored thing; extinction dims its luster. An ethics of respect for life is urgent at the level of species.

Ecosystems

A species is what it is where it is. No environmental ethics has found its way on Earth until it finds an ethic for the biotic communities in which all destinies are entwined. "A thing is right," urged Aldo Leopold, "when it tends to preserve the integrity, stability, and beauty of the biotic community. It is wrong when it tends otherwise."[2] Again, we have two parts to the ethic: first, that ecosystems exist, both in the wild and in support of culture; second, that ecosystems ought to exist, both for what they are in themselves and as modified by culture. Again, we must move with care from the biological assertions to the ethical assertions.

Giant forest fires raged over Yellowstone National Park in the summer of 1988, consuming nearly a million acres despite the efforts of a thousand fire fighters. By far the largest ever known in the park, the fires seemed a disaster. But the Yellowstone land ethic enjoined: "Let nature take its course; let it burn." So the fires were not fought at first, but in midsummer, national authorities overrode that policy and ordered the fires put out. Even then, weeks later, fires continued to burn, partly because they were too big to control but partly too because Yellowstone personnel did not really want the fires put out. Despite the evident destruction of trees, shrubs, and wildlife, they believe that fires are a good thing—even when the elk and bison leave the park in search of food and are shot by hunters. Fires reset succession, release nutrients, recycle materials, and renew the biotic community. (Nearby, in the Teton wilderness, a storm blew down fifteen thousand acres of trees, and some people proposed that the area be declassified from wilderness to allow commercial salvage of the timber. But a similar environmental ethic said, "No, let it rot.")

Aspen are important in the Yellowstone ecosystem. Although some aspen stands are climax and self-renewing, many are seral and give way to conifers. Aspen groves support many birds and much wildlife, especially beavers, whose activities maintain the riparian zones. Aspen are rejuvenated after fires, and the Yellowstone land ethic wants the aspen for their critical role in the biotic community. Elk browse the young aspen stems. To a degree this is a good thing, because it provides the elk with critical nitrogen, but in excess it is a bad thing. The elk have no predators, because the wolves are gone, and as a result the elk overpopulate. Excess elk also destroy the willows, and that destruction in turn destroys the beavers. So, in addition to letting fires burn, rejuvenating the aspen might require park managers to cull hundreds of elk—all for the sake of a healthy ecosystem.

The Yellowstone ethic wishes to restore wolves to the greater Yellowstone ecosystem. At the level of species, this change is desired because of what the wolf is in itself, but it is also desired because the greater Yellowstone ecosystem does not have its full integrity, stability, and beauty without this majestic animal at the top of the trophic pyramid. Restoring the wolf as a top predator would mean suffering and death for many elk, but that would be a good thing for the aspen and willows, the beavers, and the riparian habitat and would have mixed benefits for the bighorns and mule deer (the overpopulating elk consume their food, but the sheep and deer would also be consumed by the wolves). Restoration of wolves would be done over the protests of ranchers who worry about wolves eating their cattle; many of them also believe that the wolf is a bloodthirsty killer, a bad kind. Nevertheless, the Yellowstone ethic demands wolves, as it does fires, in appropriate respect for life in its ecosystem.

Letting nature take its ecosystemic course is why the Yellowstone ethic forbade rescuing the drowning bison but required rescuing the sow grizzly and her cubs, the latter case to insure that the big predators remain. After the bison drowned, coyotes, foxes, magpies, and ravens fed on the carcass. Later, even a grizzly bear fed on it. All this is a good thing because the system cycles on. On that account, rescuing the whales trapped in the winter ice seems less of a good thing, when we note that rescuers had to drive away polar bears that attempted to eat the dying whales.

Classical, humanistic ethics finds ecosystems to be unfamiliar territory. It is difficult to get the biology right and, superimposed on the biology, to get the ethics right. Fortunately, it is often evident that human welfare depends on ecosystemic support, and in this sense all our legislation about clean air, clean water, soil conservation, national and state forest policies, pollution controls, renewable resources, and so forth is concerned about ecosystem-level processes. Furthermore, humans find much of value in preserving wild ecosystems, and our wilderness and park system is impressive.

Still, a comprehensive environmental ethics needs the best, naturalistic reasons, as well as the good, humanistic ones, for respecting ecosystems. Ecosystems generate and support life, keep selection pressures high, enrich situated fitness, and allow congruent kinds to evolve in their places with sufficient containment. The ecologist finds that ecosystems are objectively satisfactory communities in the sense that organismic needs are sufficiently met for species to survive and flourish, and the critical ethicist finds (in a subjective judgment matching the objective process) that such ecosystems are satisfactory communities to which to attach duty. Our concern must be for the fundamental unit of survival.

An ecosystem, the conservative ethicist will say, is too low a level of organization to be respected intrinsically. Ecosystems can seem little more than random, statistical processes. A forest can seem a loose collection of externally related parts, the collection of fauna and flora a jumble, hardly a community. The plants and animals within an ecosystem have needs, but their interplay can seem simply a matter of distribution and abundance, birth rates and death rates, population densities, parasitism and predation, dispersion, checks and balances, and stochastic process. Much is not organic at all (rain, groundwater, rocks, soil particles, air), and some organic material is dead and decaying debris (fallen trees, scat, humus). These things have no organized needs. There is only catch-as-catch-can scrimmage for nutrients and energy, not really enough of an integrated process to call the whole a community.

Unlike higher animals, ecosystems have no experiences; they do not and cannot care. Unlike plants, an ecosystem has no organized center, no genome. It does not defend itself against injury or death. Unlike a species, there is no ongoing telos, no biological identity reinstantiated over time. The organismic parts are more complex than the community whole. More troublesome still, an ecosystem can seem a jungle where the fittest survive, a place of contest and conflict, beside which the organism is a model of cooperation. In animals the heart, liver, muscles, and brain are tightly integrated, as are the leaves, cambium, and roots in plants. But the so-called ecosystem community is pushing and shoving between rivals, each aggrandizing itself, or else seems to be all indifference and haphazard juxtaposition—nothing to call forth our admiration.

Environmental ethics must break through the boundary posted by disoriented ontological conservatives, who hold that only organisms are real, actually existing as entities, whereas ecosystems are nominal—just interacting individuals. Oak trees are real, but forests are nothing but collections of trees. But any level is real if it shapes behavior on the level below it. Thus the cell is real because that pattern shapes the behavior of amino acids; the organism, because that pattern coordinates the behavior of hearts and lungs. The biotic community is real because the niche shapes the morphology of the oak trees within it. Being real at the level of community requires only an organization that shapes the behavior of its members.

The challenge is to find a clear model of community and to discover an ethics for it: better biology for better ethics. Even before the rise of ecology, biologists began to conclude that the combative survival of the fittest distorts the truth. The more perceptive model is coaction in adapted fit. Predator and prey, parasite and host, grazer and grazed, are contending forces in dynamic process in which the well-being of each is bound up with the other—coordinated as much as heart and liver are coordinated organically. The ecosystem supplies the coordinates through which each organism moves, outside which the species cannot really be located.

The community connections are looser than the organism's internal interconnections but are not less significant. Admiring organic unity in organisms and stumbling over environmental looseness is like valuing mountains and despising valleys. The matrix that the organism requires to survive is the open, pluralistic ecological system. Internal complexity—heart, liver, muscles, brain—arises as a way of dealing with a complex, tricky environment. The skin-out processes are not just the support; they are the subtle source of the skin-in processes. In the complete picture, the outside is as vital as the inside. Had there been either simplicity or lockstep concentrated unity in the environment, no organismic unity could have evolved. Nor would it remain. There would be less elegance in life.

To look at one level for what is appropriate at another makes a mistake in categories. One should not look for a single center or program in ecosystems, much less for subjective experiences. Instead, one should look for a matrix, for interconnections between centers (individual plants and animals, dynamic lines of speciation), for creative stimulus and open-ended potential. Everything will be connected to many other things, sometimes by obligate associations but more often by partial and pliable dependencies, and, among other things, there will be no significant interactions. There will be functions in a communal sense: shunts and crisscrossing pathways, cybernetic subsystems and feedback loops. An order arises spontaneously and systematically when many self-concerned units jostle and seek to fulfill their own programs, each doing its own thing and forced into informed interaction.

An ecosystem is a productive, projective system. Organisms defend only their selves, with individuals defending their continuing survival and with species increasing the numbers of kinds. But the evolutionary ecosystem spins a bigger story, limiting each kind, locking it into the welfare of others, promoting new arrivals, increasing kinds and the integration of kinds. Species increase their kind, but ecosystems increase kinds, superposing the latter increase onto the former. Ecosystems are selective systems, as surely as organisms are selective systems. The natural selection comes out of the system and is imposed on the individual. The individual is programmed to make more of its kind, but more is going on systemically than that; the system is making more kinds.

Communal processes—the competition between organisms, statistically probable interactions, plant and animal successions, speciation over historical time—generate an ever-richer community. Hence the evolutionary toil, elaborating and diversifying the biota, that once began with no species and results today in five million species, increasing over time the quality of lives in the upper rungs of the trophic pyramids. One-celled organisms evolved into many-celled, highly integrated organisms. Photosynthesis evolved and came to support locomotion—swimming, walking, running, flight. Stimulus–response mechanisms became complex instinctive acts. Warm-blooded animals followed cold-blooded ones. Complex nervous systems, conditioned behavior, and learning emerged. Sentience appeared—sight, hearing, smell, taste, pleasure, pain. Brains coupled with hands. Consciousness and self-consciousness arose. Culture was superposed on nature.

These developments do not take place in all ecosystems or at every level. Microbes, plants, and lower animals remain, good of their kinds and, serving continuing roles, good for other kinds. The understories remain occupied. As a result, the quantity of life and its diverse qualities continue—from protozoans to primates to people. There is a push-up, lock-up ratchet effect that conserves the upstrokes and the outreaches. The later we go in time, the more accelerated are the forms at the top of the trophic pyramids, the more elaborated are the multiple trophic pyramids of Earth. There are upward arrows over evolutionary time.

The system is a game with loaded dice, but the loading is a pro-life tendency, not mere stochastic process. Though there is no Nature in the singular, the system has a nature, a loading that pluralizes, putting natures into diverse kinds: $nature_1$, $nature_2$, $nature_3$ … $nature_n$. It does so using random elements (in both organisms and communities), but this is a secret of its fertility, producing steadily intensified interdependencies and options. An ecosystem has no head, but it heads toward species diversification, support, and richness. Though not a superorganism, it is a kind of vital field.

Instrumental value uses something as a means to an end; intrinsic value is worthwhile in itself. No warbler eats insects to become food for a falcon; the warbler defends it own life as an end in itself and makes more warblers as it can. A life is defended intrinsically, without further contributory reference. But neither of these traditional terms is satisfactory at the level of the ecosystem. Though it has value *in* itself, the system does not have any value *for* itself. Though it is a value producer, it is not a value owner. We are no longer confronting instrumental value, as though the system were of value instrumentally as a fountain of life. Nor is the question one of intrinsic value, as though the system defended some unified form of life for itself. We have reached something for which we need a third term: systemic value. Duties arise in encounters with the system that projects and protects these member components in biotic community.

Ethical conservatives, in the humanistic sense, will say that ecosystems are of value only because they contribute to human experiences. But that mistakes the last chapter for the whole story, one fruit for the whole plant. Humans count enough to have the right to flourish in ecosystems, but not so much that they have the right to degrade or shut down ecosystems, not at least without a burden of proof that there is an overriding cultural gain. Those who have traveled partway into environmental ethics will say that ecosystems are of value because they contribute to animal experiences or to organismic life. But the really conservative, radical view sees that the stability, integrity, and beauty of biotic communities are what are most fundamentally to be conserved. In a comprehensive ethics of respect for life, we ought to set ethics at the level of ecosystems alongside classical, humanistic ethics.

Value Theory

In practice the ultimate challenge of environmental ethics is the conservation of life on Earth. In principle the ultimate challenge is a value theory profound enough to support that ethics. In nature there is negentropic construction in dialectic with entropic teardown, a process for which we hardly yet have an adequate scientific theory, much less a valuational theory. Yet this is nature's most striking feature, one that ultimately must be valued and of value. In one sense, nature is indifferent to mountains, rivers, fauna, flora, forests, and grasslands. But in another sense, nature has bent toward making and remaking these projects, millions of kinds, for several billion years.

These performances are worth noticing, are remarkable and memorable—and not just because of their tendencies to produce something else; certainly not merely because of their tendency to produce this noticing in certain recent subjects, our human selves. These events are loci of value as products of systemic nature in its formative processes. The splendors of Earth do not simply lie in their roles as human resources, supports of culture, or stimulators of experience. The most plausible account will find some programmatic evolution toward value, and not because it ignores Darwin but because it heeds his principle of natural selection and deploys it into a selection exploring new niches and elaborating kinds, even a selection upslope toward higher values, at least along some trends within some ecosystems. How do we humans come to be charged up with values, if there was and is nothing in nature charging us up so? A systematic environmental ethics does not wish to believe in the special creation of values or in their dumbfounding epigenesis. Let them evolve. Let nature carry value.

The notion that nature is a value carrier is ambiguous. Much depends on a thing's being more or less structurally congenial for the carriage. We value a thing and discover that we are under the sway of its valence, inducing our behavior. It has among its strengths (Latin: *valeo*, "be strong") this capacity to carry value. This potential cannot always be of the empty sort that a glass has for carrying water. It is often pregnant fullness. Some of the values that nature carries are up to us, our assignment. But fundamentally there are powers in nature that move to us and through us.

No value exists without an evaluator. So runs a well-entrenched dogma. Humans clearly evaluate their world; sentient animals may also. But plants cannot evaluate their environment; they have no options and make no choices. A fortiori, species and ecosystems, Earth and Nature, cannot be bona fide evaluators. One can always hang on to the assertion that value, like a tickle or remorse, must be felt to be there. Its *esse* is *percipi*. To be, it must be perceived. Nonsensed value is nonsense. There are no thoughts without a thinker, no percepts without a perceiver, no deeds without a doer, no targets without an aimer.

Such resolute subjectivists cannot be defeated by argument, although they can be driven toward analyticity. That theirs is a retreat to definition is difficult to expose, because they seem to cling so closely to inner experience. They are reporting, on this hand, how values always excite us. They are giving, on that hand, a stipulative definition. That is how they choose to use the word *value*.

If value arrives only with consciousness, experiences in which humans find value have to be dealt with as appearances of various sorts. The value has to be relocated in the valuing subject's creativity as a person meets a valueless world, or even a valuable one—one able to be valued but one that before the human bringing of valuableness contains only possibility and not any actual value. Value can only be extrinsic to nature, never intrinsic to it.

But the valuing subject in an otherwise valueless world is an insufficient premise for the experienced conclusions of those who respect all life. Conversion to a biological view seems truer to world experience and more logically compelling. Something from a world beyond the human mind, beyond human experience, is received into our mind, our experience, and the value of that something does not always arise with our evaluation of it. Here the order of knowing reverses, and also enhances, the order of being. This too is a perspective but is ecologically better-informed. Science has been steadily showing how the consequents (life, mind) are built on their precedents (energy, matter), however much they overleap them. Life and mind appear where they did not before exist, and with them levels of value emerge that did not before exist. But that gives no reason to say that all value is an irreducible emergent at the human (or upper-animal) level. A comprehensive environmental ethics reallocates value across the whole continuum. Value increases in the emergent climax but is continuously present in the composing precedents. The system is value-able, able to produce value. Human evaluators are among its products.

Some value depends on subjectivity, yet all value is generated within the geosystemic and ecosystemic pyramid. Systemically, value fades from subjective to objective value but also fans out from the individual to its role and matrix. Things do not have their separate natures merely in and for themselves, but they face outward and co-fit into broader natures. Value-in-itself is smeared out to become value-in-togetherness. Value seeps out into the system, and we lose our capacity to identify the individual as the sole locus of value.

Intrinsic value, the value of an individual for what it is in itself, becomes problematic in a holistic web. True, the system produces such values more and more with its evolution of individuality and freedom. Yet to decouple this value from the biotic, communal system is to make value too internal and elementary; this decoupling forgets relatedness and externality. Every intrinsic value has leading and trailing *and's*. Such value is coupled with value from which it comes and toward which it moves. Adapted fitness makes individualistic value too system-independent. Intrinsic value is a part in a whole and is not to be fragmented by valuing it in isolation.

Everything is good in a role, in a whole, although we can speak of objective intrinsic goodness wherever a point-event—a trillium, for example—defends a good (its life) in itself. We can speak of subjective intrinsic goodness when such an event registers as a point-experience, at which point humans pronounce both their experience and what it is to be good without need to enlarge their focus. Neither the trilliums nor the human judges of it require for their respective valuings any further contributory reference.

When eaten by foragers or in death resorbed into humus, the trillium has its value destroyed, transformed into instrumentality. The system is a value transformer where form and being, process and reality, fact and value, are inseparably joined. Intrinsic and instrumental values shuttle back and forth, parts-in-wholes and wholes-in-parts, local details of value embedded in global structures, gems in their settings, and their setting-situation a corporation where value cannot stand alone. Every good is in community.

In environmental ethics one's beliefs about nature, which are based upon but exceed science, have everything to do with beliefs about duty. The way the world is informs the way it ought to be. We always shape our values in significant measure in accord with our notion of the kind of universe that we live in, and this process drives our sense of duty. Our model of reality implies a model of conduct. Differing models sometimes imply similar conduct, but often they do not. A model in which nature has no value apart from human preferences will imply different conduct from one in which nature projects fundamental values, some objective and others that further require human subjectivity superimposed on objective nature.

This evaluation is not scientific description; hence it is not ecology per se but meta-ecology. No amount of research can verify that, environmentally, the right is the optimum biotic community. Yet ecological description generates this valuing of nature, endorsing the systemic rightness. The transition from *is* to *good* and thence to *ought* occurs here; we leave science to enter the domain of evaluation, from which an ethics follows.

What is ethically puzzling and exciting is that an *ought* is not so much derived from an *is* as discovered simultaneously with it. As we progress from descriptions of fauna and flora, of cycles and pyramids, of autotrophs coordinated with heterotrophs, of stability and dynamism, on to intricacy, planetary opulence and interdependence, unity and harmony with oppositions in counterpoint and synthesis, organisms evolved within and satisfactorily fitting their communities, and we arrive at length at beauty and goodness, we find that it is difficult to say where the natural facts leave off and where the natural values appear. For some people at least, the sharper *is–ought* dichotomy is gone; the values seem to be there as soon as the facts are fully in, and both values and facts seem to be alike properties of the system.

There is something overspecialized about an ethic, held by the dominant class of *Homo sapiens*, that regards the welfare of only one of several million species as an object and beneficiary of duty. If the remedy requires a paradigm change about the sorts of things to which duty can attach, so much the worse for those humanistic ethics no longer functioning in, or suited to, their changing environment. The anthropocentrism associated with them was fiction anyway. There is something Newtonian, not yet Einsteinian, besides something morally naive, about living in a reference frame in which one species takes itself as absolute and values everything else relative to its utility. If true to its specific epithet, which means wise, ought not *Homo sapiens* value this host of life as something that lays on us a claim to care for life in its own right?

Only the human species contains moral agents, but perhaps conscience on such an Earth ought not to be used to exempt every other form of life from consideration, with the resulting paradox that the sole moral species acts only in its collective self-interest toward all the rest. Is not the ultimate philosophical task the discovery of a whole great ethic that knows the human place under the sun?

Notes

1 J. Bentham, *Introduction to the Principles of Morals and Legislation* (1789; New York: Hafner, 1948); 311.

2 A. Leopold, *A Sand County Almanac, and Sketches Here and There* (New York: Oxford University Press, 1949); 224–225.

Respect for Nature
A Theory of Environmental Ethics

PAUL W. TAYLOR

Having and Expressing the Attitude of Respect for Nature

The central tenet of the theory of environmental ethics that I am defending is that actions are right and character traits are morally good in virtue of their expressing or embodying a certain ultimate moral attitude, which I call respect for nature. When moral agents adopt the attitude, they thereby subscribe to a set of standards of character and rules of conduct as their own ethical principles. Having the attitude entails being morally committed to fulfilling the standards and complying with the rules. When moral agents then act in accordance with the rules and when they develop character traits that meet the standards, their conduct and character express (give concrete embodiment to) the attitude. Thus ethical action and goodness of character naturally flow from the attitude, and the attitude is made manifest in how one acts and in what sort of person one is.

The Biocentric Outlook and the Attitude of Respect for Nature

The attitude we think it appropriate to take toward living things depends on how we conceive of them and of our relationship to them. What moral significance the natural world has for us depends on the way we look at the whole system of nature and our role in it. With regard to the attitude of respect for nature, the belief-system that renders it intelligible and on which it depends for its justifiability is the biocentric outlook. This outlook underlies and supports the attitude of respect for nature in the following sense. Unless we grasp what it means to accept that belief-system and so view the natural order from its perspective, we cannot see the point of taking the attitude of respect. But once we do grasp it and shape our world outlook in accordance with it, we immediately understand how and why a person would adopt that attitude as the only appropriate one to have toward nature. Thus the biocentric outlook provides the explanatory and justificatory background that makes sense of and gives point to a person's taking the attitude.

The beliefs that form the core of the biocentric outlook are four in number:

1. The belief that humans are members of the Earth's Community of Life in the same sense and on the same terms in which other living things are members of that Community.

Paul Taylor, "Respect for Nature: A Theory of Environmental Ethics," from *Respect for Nature*, Princeton University Press, 1986; pp. 248–259.

2. The belief that the human species, along with all other species, are integral elements in a system of interdependence such that the survival of each living thing, as well as its chances of faring well or poorly, is determined not only by the physical conditions of its environment but also by its relations to other living things.
3. The belief that all organisms are teleological centers of life in the sense that each is a unique individual pursuing its own good in its own way.
4. The belief that humans are not inherently superior to other living things.

To accept all four of these beliefs is to have a coherent outlook on the natural world and the place of humans in it. It is to take a certain perspective on human life and to conceive of the relation between human and other forms of life in a certain way. Given this world view, the attitude of respect is then seen to be the only suitable, fitting, or appropriate moral attitude to take toward the natural world and its living inhabitants.

The Basic Rules of Conduct

... I shall now set out and examine four rules of duty in the domain of environmental ethics. This is not supposed to provide an exhaustive account of every valid duty of the ethics of respect for nature. It is doubtful whether a complete specification of duties is possible in this realm. But however that may be, the duties to be listed here are intended to cover only the more important ones that typically arise in everyday life.... [I]n all situations not explicitly or clearly covered by these rules we should rely on the attitude of respect for nature and the biocentric outlook that together underlie the system as a whole and give it point. Right actions are always actions that express the attitude of respect, whether they are covered by the four rules or not. They must also be actions which we can approve of in the light of the various components of the biocentric outlook.

The four rules will be named (1) the Rule of Nonmaleficence, (2) the Rule of Noninterference, (3) the Rule of Fidelity, and (4) the Rule of Restitutive Justice.

1. *The Rule of Nonmaleficence.* This is the duty not to do harm to any entity in the natural environment that has a good of its own. It includes the duty not to kill an organism and not to destroy a species-population or biotic community, as well as the duty to refrain from any action that would be seriously detrimental to the good of an organism, species-population, or life community. Perhaps the most fundamental wrong in the ethics of respect for nature is to harm something that does not harm us.

The concept of nonmaleficence is here understood to cover only non-performances or intentional abstentions. The rule defines a negative duty, requiring that moral agents refrain from certain kinds of actions. It does not require the doing of any actions, such as those that *prevent* harm from coming to an entity or those that help to *alleviate* its suffering. Actions of these sorts more properly fall under the heading of benefiting an entity by protecting or promoting its good. (They will be discussed in connection with the Rule of Restitutive Justice.)

The Rule of Nonmaleficence prohibits harmful and destructive acts done by moral agents. It does not apply to the behavior of a nonhuman animal or the activity of a plant that might bring harm to another living thing or cause its death. Suppose, for example, that a Rough-legged Hawk pounces on a field mouse, killing it. Nothing morally wrong has occurred. Although the hawk's behavior can be thought of as something it does intentionally, it is not the action of a moral agent. Thus it does not fall within the range of the Rule of Nonmaleficence. The hawk does not violate any duty because it *has* no duties. Consider, next, a vine which over the years gradually covers a tree and finally kills it. The activity of the vine, which involves goal-oriented movements but not, of course, intentional actions, is not a moral wrongdoing. The vine's killing the tree has no moral properties at all, since it is not the conduct of a moral agent.

Let us now, by way of contrast, consider the following case. A Peregrine Falcon has been taken from the wild by a falconer, who then trains it to hunt, seize, and kill wild birds under his direction. Here there occurs human conduct aimed at controlling and manipulating an organism for the enjoyment of a sport that involves harm to other wild organisms. A wrong is being done but not by the falcon, even though it is the falcon which does the actual killing and even though the birds it kills are its natural prey. The wrong that is done to those birds is a wrong done by the falconer. It is not the action of the Peregrine that breaks the rule of duty but the actions of the one who originally captured it, trained it, and who now uses it for his own amusement. These actions, it might be added, are also violations of the Rule of Noninterference, since the falcon was removed from its wild state. Let us now turn our attention to this second rule of duty.

2. *The Rule of Noninterference*. Under this rule fall two sorts of negative duties, one requiring us to refrain from placing restrictions on the freedom of individual organisms, the other requiring a general "hands off" policy with regard to whole ecosystems and biotic communities, as well as to individual organisms.

Concerning the first sort of duty, the idea of the freedom of individual organisms[,] … freedom is absence of constraint, [and] a constraint is any condition that prevents or hinders the normal activity and healthy development of an animal or plant. A being is free in this sense when any of four types of constraints that could weaken, impair, or destroy its ability to adapt successfully to its environment are absent from its existence and circumstances. To be free is to be free *from* these constraints and to be free *to* pursue the realization of one's good according to the laws of one's nature. The four types of constraints, with some examples of each, are:

1. Positive external constraints (cages; traps).
2. Negative external constraints (no water or food available).
3. Positive internal constraints (diseases; ingested poison or absorbed toxic chemicals).
4. Negative internal constraints (weaknesses and incapacities due to injured organs or tissues).

We humans can restrict the freedom of animals and plants by either directly imposing some of these constraints upon them or by producing changes in their environments which then act as constraints upon them. Either way, if we do these things knowingly we are guilty of violating the Rule of Noninterference.

The second kind of duty that comes under this rule is the duty to let wild creatures live out their lives in freedom. Here freedom means not the absence of constraints but simply being allowed to carry on one's existence in a wild state. With regard to individual organisms, this duty requires us to refrain from capturing them and removing them from their natural habitats, *no matter how well we might then treat them*. We have violated the duty of noninterference even if we "save" them by taking them out of a natural danger or by restoring their health after they have become ill in the wild. (The duty is not violated, however, if we do such things with the intention of returning the creature to the wild as soon as possible, and we fully carry out this intention.) When we take young trees or wildflowers from a natural ecosystem, for example, and transplant them in landscaped grounds, we break the Rule of Noninterference *whether or not we then take good care of them and so enable them to live longer, healthier lives than they would have enjoyed in the wild*. We have done a wrong by not letting them live out their lives in freedom. In all situations like these we intrude into the domain of the natural world and terminate an organism's existence as a wild creature. It does not matter that our treatment of them may improve their strength, promote their growth, and increase their chances for a long, healthy life. By destroying their status as wild animals or plants, our interference in their lives amounts to an absolute negation of their natural freedom. Thus, however "benign" our actions may seem, we are doing what the Rule of Noninterference forbids us to do.

Of still deeper significance, perhaps, is the duty of noninterference as it applies to the freedom of whole species-populations and communities of life. The prohibition against interfering with these entities means that we must not try to manipulate, control, modify, or "manage" natural ecosystems or otherwise intervene in their normal functioning. For any given species-population, freedom is the absence of human intervention of any kind in the natural lawlike processes by which the population preserves itself from generation to generation. Freedom for a whole biotic community is the absence of human intervention in the natural lawlike processes by which all its constituent species-populations undergo changing ecological relationships with one another over time. The duty not to interfere is the duty to respect the freedom of biologically and ecologically organized groups of wild organisms by refraining from those sorts of intervention. Again, this duty holds even if such intervention is motivated by a desire to "help" a species-population survive or a desire to "correct natural imbalances" in a biotic community. (Attempts to save endangered species which have almost been exterminated by past *human* intrusions into nature, and attempts to restore ecological stability and balance to an ecosystem that has been damaged by past *human* activity are cases that fall under the Rule of Restitutive Justice and may be ethically right. These cases will be considered in connection with that rule.)

The duty of noninterference, like that of nonmaleficence, is a purely negative duty. It does not require us to perform any actions regarding either individual organisms or groups of organisms. We are only required to respect their wild freedom by letting them alone. In this way we allow them, as it were, to fulfill their own destinies. Of course some of them will lose out in their struggle with natural competitors and others will suffer harm from natural causes. But as far as our proper role as moral agents is concerned, we must keep "hands off." By strictly adhering to the Rule of Noninterference, our conduct manifests a profound regard for the integrity of the system of nature. Even when a whole ecosystem has been seriously disturbed by a natural disaster (earthquake, lightning-caused fire, volcanic eruption, flood, prolonged drought, or the like) we are duty-bound not to intervene to try to repair the damage. After all, throughout the long history of life on our planet natural disasters ("disasters," that is, from the standpoint of some particular organism or group of organisms) have always taken their toll in the death of many creatures. Indeed, the very process of natural selection continually leads to the extinction of whole species. After such disasters a gradual readjustment always takes place so that a new set of relations among species-populations emerges. To abstain from intervening in this order of things is a way of expressing our attitude of respect for nature, for we thereby give due recognition to the process of evolutionary change that has been the "story" of life on Earth since its very beginnings.

This general policy of nonintervention is a matter of disinterested principle. We may want to help certain species-populations because we like them or because they are beneficial to us. But the Rule of Noninterference requires that we put aside our personal likes and our human interests with reference to how we treat them. Our respect for nature means that we acknowledge the sufficiency of the natural world to sustain its own proper order throughout the whole domain of life. This is diametrically opposed to the human-centered view of nature as a vast piece of property which we can use as we see fit.

In one sense to have the attitude of respect toward natural ecosystems, toward wild living things, and toward the whole process of evolution is to believe that nothing goes wrong in nature. Even the destruction of an entire biotic community or the extinction of a species is not evidence that something is amiss. If the causes for such events arose within the system of nature itself, nothing improper has happened. In particular, the fact that organisms suffer and die does not itself call for corrective action on the part of humans *when humans have had nothing to do with the cause of that suffering and death.* Suffering and death are integral aspects of the order of nature. So if it is ever the case in our contemporary world that the imminent extinction of a whole species is due to entirely natural causes, we should not try to stop the natural sequence of events from taking place in order to save the species. That sequence of events is governed by the operation of laws that have made the biotic Community of our planet what it is. To respect that Community is to respect the laws that gave rise to it.

In addition to this respect for the sufficiency and integrity of the natural order, a second ethical principle is implicit in the Rule of Noninterference. This is the principle of species-impartiality, which serves as a counterweight to the dispositions of people to favor certain species over others and to want to intervene in behalf of their favorites. These dispositions show themselves in a number of ways. First, consider the reactions of many people to predator–prey relations among wildlife. Watching the wild dogs of the African plains bring down the Wildebeest and begin devouring its underparts while it is still alive, they feel sympathy for the prey and antipathy for the predator. There is a tendency to make moral judgments, to think of the dogs as vicious and cruel, and to consider the Wildebeest an innocent victim. Or take the situation in which a snake is about to kill a baby bird in its nest. The snake is perceived as wicked and the nestling is seen as not deserving such a fate. Even plant life is looked at in this biased way. People get disturbed by a great tree being "strangled" by a vine. And when it comes to instances of bacteria-caused diseases, almost everyone has a tendency to be on the side of the organism which has the disease rather than viewing the situation from the standpoint of the living bacteria inside the organism. If we accept the biocentric outlook and have genuine respect for nature, however, we remain strictly neutral between predator and prey, parasite and host, the disease-causing and the diseased. To take sides in such struggles, to think of them in moral terms as cases of the maltreatment of innocent victims by evil animals and nasty plants, is to abandon the attitude of respect for all wild living things. It is to count the good of some as having greater value than that of others. This is inconsistent with the fundamental presupposition of the attitude of respect: that all living things in the natural world have the same inherent worth....

3. *The Rule of Fidelity*. This rule applies only to human conduct in relation to individual animals that are in a wild state and are capable of being deceived or betrayed by moral agents. The duties imposed by the Rule of Fidelity, though of restricted range, are so frequently violated by so many people that this rule needs separate study as one of the basic principles of the ethics of respect for nature.

Under this rule fall the duties not to break a trust that a wild animal places in us (as shown by its behavior), not to deceive or mislead any animal capable of being deceived or misled, to uphold an animal's expectations, which it has formed on the basis of one's past actions with it, and to be true to one's intentions as made known to an animal when it has come to rely on one. Although we cannot make mutual agreements with wild animals, we can act in such a manner as to call forth their trust in us. The basic moral requirement imposed by the Rule of Fidelity is that we remain faithful to that trust.

The clearest and commonest examples of transgressions of the rule occur in hunting, trapping, and fishing. Indeed, the breaking of a trust is a key to good (that is, successful) hunting, trapping, and fishing. Deception with intent to harm is of the essence. Therefore, unless there is a weighty moral reason for engaging in these activities, they must be condemned by the ethics of respect for nature. The weighty moral reason in question must itself be grounded on disinterested principle, since the action remains wrong in itself in virtue of its constituting a violation of a valid moral rule. Like all such violations, it can be justified only by appeal to a higher, more stringent duty whose priority over the duty of fidelity is established by a morally valid priority principle.

When a man goes hunting for bear or deer he will walk through a woodland as quietly and unobtrusively as possible. If he is a duck hunter he will hide in a blind, set out decoys, use imitative calls. In either case the purpose, of course, is to get within shooting range of the mammal or bird. Much of the hunter's conduct is designed to deceive the wild creature. As an animal is approaching, the hunter remains quiet, then raises his rifle to take careful aim. Here is a clear situation in which, first, a wild animal acts as if there were no danger; second, the hunter by stealth is deliberately misleading the animal to expect no danger; and third, the hunter is doing this for the immediate purpose of killing the animal. The total performance is one of entrapment and betrayal. The animal is manipulated to be trusting and unsuspicious. It is deliberately kept unaware of something in its environment which is, from the standpoint of its good, of great importance to it. The entire pattern of the hunter's behavior is aimed at taking advantage of an animal's trust. Sometimes an animal is taken advantage of in situations where it may be aware of some danger but instinctively goes to the aid of an injured companion. The hunter uses his knowledge of this to betray the animal. Thus when the hunting of shorebirds used to be legally permitted, a hunter would injure a single bird and leave it out to attract hundreds of its fellows, which would fly in and gather around it. This way the hunter could easily "harvest" vast numbers of shorebirds. Even to this day a similar kind of trickery is used to deceive birds. Crow hunters play recordings of a crow's distress calls out in the field. The recording attracts crows, who are then easy targets to shoot. This aspect of hunting, it should be repeated, is not some peripheral aberration. Much of the excitement and enjoyment of hunting as a sport is the challenge to one's skills in getting animals to be trusting and unsuspecting. The cleverer the deception, the better the skill of the hunter....

It is not a question here of whether the animal being hunted, trapped, or fished has a *right* to expect not to be deceived. The animal is being deceived in order to bring advantage to the deceiver and this itself is the sign that the deceiver considers the animal as either having no inherent worth or as having a lower degree of inherent worth than the deceiver himself. Either way of looking at it is incompatible with the attitude of respect for nature....

Besides breaking the Rule of Fidelity, hunting, trapping, and fishing also, of course, involve gross violations of the Rules of Nonmaleficence and Noninterference. It may be the case that in circumstances where the only means for obtaining food or clothing essential to human survival is by hunting, trapping, or fishing, these actions are morally permissible. The ethical principles that justify them could stem from a system of human ethics based on respect for persons plus a priority principle that makes the duty to provide for human survival outweigh those duties of nonmaleficence, noninterference, and fidelity that are owed to nonhumans. But when hunting and fishing are done for sport or recreation, they cannot be justified on the same grounds.

There are cases of deceiving and breaking faith with an animal, however, which can be justified *within* the system of environmental ethics. These cases occur when deception and betrayal must (reluctantly) be done as a necessary step in a wider action of furthering an animal's good, this wider action being the fulfillment of a duty of restitutive justice. If breaking faith is a temporary measure absolutely needed to alleviate great suffering or to prevent serious harm coming to an animal, such an act may be required as an instance of restitutive justice. Putting aside for the moment a consideration of the idea of restitutive justice as it applies to environmental ethics, it may be helpful to look at some examples.

Suppose a grizzly bear has wandered into an area close to human habitation. In order to prevent harm coming not only to people but also to the bear (when people demand that it be killed), the bear may be deceived so that it can be shot with harmless tranquilizer darts and then, while it is unconscious, removed to a remote wilderness area. Another example would be the live-trapping of a sick or injured animal so that it can be brought to an animal hospital, treated, and then returned to the wild when it is fully recovered. Still another kind of case occurs when a few birds of an endangered species are captured in order to have them raise young in captivity. The young would then be released in natural habitat areas in an effort to prevent the species from becoming extinct.

These human encroachments upon the wild state of mammals and birds violate both the rule of Noninterference and the Rule of Fidelity. But the whole treatment of these creatures is consistent with the attitude of respect for them. They are not being taken advantage of but rather are being given the opportunity to maintain their existence as wild living things....

... Hunters and fishermen often argue that they show true respect for nature because they advocate (and pay for) the preservation of natural areas which benefit wild species-populations and life communities. And it is quite true that the setting aside of many "wildlife refuges," both public and private, has resulted from their efforts. Wild animals and plants have benefited from this. What is being overlooked in this argument is the difference between doing something to benefit oneself which happens also to benefit others, and doing something with the purpose of benefiting others as one's ultimate end of action. Hunters and fishermen want only those areas of the natural environment protected that will provide for them a constant supply of fish, birds, and mammals as game. Indeed, sportsmen will often urge the killing of nongame animals that prey on "their" (the sportsmen's) animals. In Alaska, for example, hunters have persuaded state officials to "manage" wolves—the method used is to shoot them from helicopters—so as to ensure that a large population of moose is available for hunting. The argument that hunters and fishermen are true conservationists of wildlife will stand up only when we sharply distinguish conservation (saving in the present for future consumption) from preservation (protecting from both present and future consumption). And if the ultimate purpose of conservation programs is future exploitation of wildlife for the enjoyment of outdoor sports and recreation, such conservation activities are not consistent with respect for nature, whatever may be the benefits incidentally brought to some wild creatures. Actions that bring about good consequences for wildlife do not express the attitude of respect unless those actions are motivated in a certain way. It must be the case that the actions are done with the intention of promoting or protecting the good of wild creatures as an end in itself and for the sake of those creatures themselves. Such motivation is precisely what is absent from the conversation activities of sportsmen.

4. *The Rule of Restitutive Justice*. In its most general terms this rule imposes the duty to restore the balance of justice between a moral agent and a moral subject when the subject has been wronged by the agent. Common to all instances in which a duty of restitutive justice arises, an agent has broken a valid moral rule and by doing so has upset the balance of justice between himself or herself and a moral subject. To hold oneself accountable for having done such an act is to acknowledge a special duty one has taken upon oneself by that wrongdoing. This special duty is the duty of restitutive justice. It requires that one make amends to the moral subject by some form of compensation or reparation. This is the way one restores the balance of justice that had held between oneself and the subject before a rule of duty was transgressed.

The set of rules that makes up a valid system of ethics defines the true moral relations that hold between agents and subjects. When every agent carries out the duties owed to each subject and each subject accordingly receives its proper treatment, no one is wronged or unjustly dealt with. As soon as a rule is willfully violated, the balance of justice is tilted against the agent and in favor of the subject; that is, the agent now has a special burden to bear and the victim is entitled to a special benefit, since the doing of the wrong act gave an undeserved benefit to the agent and placed an unfair burden on the subject. In order to bring the tilted scale of justice back into balance, the agent must make reparation or pay some form of compensation to the subject.

The three rules of duty so far discussed in this section can be understood as defining a moral relationship of justice between humans and wild living things in the Earth's natural ecosystems. This relationship is maintained as long as humans do not harm wild creatures, destroy their habitats, or degrade their environments; as long as humans do not interfere with an animal's or plant's freedom or with the overall workings of ecological interdependence; and as long as humans do not betray a wild animal's trust to take advantage of it. Since these are all ways in which humans can express in their conduct the attitude of respect for nature, they are at the same time ways in which each living thing is given due recognition as an entity possessing inherent worth. The principles of species-impartiality and of equal consideration are adhered to, so that every moral subject is treated as an end in itself, never as a means only.

Now, if moral agents violate any of the three rules, they do an injustice to something in the natural world. The act destroys the balance of justice between humanity and nature, and a special duty is incurred by the agents involved. This is the duty laid down by the fourth rule of environmental ethics, the Rule of Restitutive Justice.

What specific requirements make up the duty in particular cases? Although the detailed facts of each situation of an agent's wrongdoing would have to be known to make a final judgment about what sorts of restitutive acts are called for, we can nevertheless formulate some middle-range principles of justice that generally apply. These principles are to be understood as specifying requirements of restitution for transgressions of *any* of the three rules. In all cases the restitutive measures will take the form of promoting or protecting in one way or another the good of living things in natural ecosystems.

In working out these middle-range principles it will be convenient to distinguish cases according to what type of moral subject has been wronged. We have three possibilities. An action that broke the Rule of Nonmaleficence, of Noninterference, or of Fidelity might have wronged an individual organism, a species-population as a whole, or an entire community. Violations of the Rules in all cases are ultimately wrongs done to individuals, since we can do harm to a population or community only by harming the individual organisms in it (thereby lowering the median level of well-being for the population or community as a whole). The first possibility, however, focuses on the harmed individuals taken separately.

If the organisms have been harmed but have not been killed, then the principle of restitutive justice requires that the agent make reparation by returning those organisms to a condition in which they can pursue their good as well as they did before the injustice was done to them. If this cannot wholly be accomplished, then the agent must further the good of the organisms in some other way, perhaps by making their physical environment more favorable to their continued well-being. Suppose, on the other hand, that an organism has been killed. Then the principle of restitutive justice states that the agent owes some form of compensation to the species-population and/or the life community of which the organism was a member. This would be a natural extension of respect from the individual to its genetic relatives and ecological associates. The compensation would consist in promoting or protecting the good of the species-population or life community in question.

Consider as a second possibility that a whole species-population has been wrongly treated by a violation of either nonmaleficence or noninterference. A typical situation would be one where most of the animals of a "target" species have been killed by excessive hunting, fishing, or trapping in a limited area. As a way of making some effort to right the wrongs that have been committed, it would seem appropriate that the agents at fault be required to ensure that permanent protection be given to all the remaining numbers of the population. Perhaps the agents could contribute to a special fund for the acquisition of land and themselves take on the responsibility of patrolling the area to prevent further human intrusion.

Finally, let us consider those circumstances where an entire biotic community has been destroyed by humans. We have two sorts of cases here, both requiring some form of restitution. The first sort of case occurs when the destructive actions are not only wrong in themselves because they violate duties of nonmaleficence and noninterference but are wrong, all things considered. They are not justified by a rule of *either* environmental ethics *or* of human ethics. The second sort of case is one in which the actions are required by a valid rule of human ethics though they are contrary to valid rules of environmental ethics. Even when greater moral weight is given to the rule of human ethics, so that the actions are justified, all things considered, they still call for some form of restitution on grounds of justice to all beings having inherent worth. This idea holds also within the domain of human ethics.

A duty of restitutive justice (as a corollary of the Rule of Reciprocity) arises whenever one of the other valid rules of human ethics is broken. Even if the action was required by a more stringent duty, a human person has been unjustly treated and therefore some compensation is due her or him. That the action was morally justified, all things considered, does not license our overlooking the fact that someone has been wronged. Hence the propriety of demanding restitution. So in our present concerns, even if the destruction of a biotic community is entailed by a duty of human ethics that overrides the rules of environmental ethics, an act of restitutive justice is called for in recognition of the inherent worth of what has been destroyed.

There are many instances in which human practices bring about the total obliteration of biotic communities in natural ecosystems. Whether or not these practices are justified by valid rules of human ethics, they all come under the Rule of Restitutive Justice. A northern conifer woodland is cut down to build a vacation resort on the shore of a lake. A housing development is constructed in what had been a pristine wilderness area of cactus desert. A marina and yacht club replace a tidal wetland which had served as a feeding and breeding ground for multitudes of mollusks, crustacea, insects, birds, fish, reptiles, and mammals. A meadow full of wildflowers, both common and rare, is bulldozed over for a shopping mall. Strip mining takes away one side of a mountain. A prairie is replaced by a wheat farm. In every one of these situations and in countless others of the same kind, wholesale destruction of entire natural ecosystems takes place. Unrestrained violence is done to whole communities of plants and animals. Communities that may have been in existence for tens of thousands of years are completely wiped out in a few weeks or a few days, in some cases in a few hours. What form of restitution can then be made that will restore the balance of justice between humanity and nature? No reparation for damages can possibly be given to the community itself, which exists no more. As is true of a single organism that has been killed, the impossibility of repairing the damage does not get rid of the requirement to make some kind of compensation for having destroyed something of inherent worth.

If restitutive justice is to be done in instances of the foregoing kind, what actions are called for and to whom are they due? Two possibilities suggest themselves here. One is that compensation should be made to another biotic community which occupies *an ecosystem of the same type* as the one destroyed. If it is a northern conifer woodland, then the organizations or individuals who were responsible for its destruction owe it to the life community of another conifer woodland to help it in some way to further or maintain its well-being. Perhaps a partially damaged area of woodland could be restored to ecological health (removing trash that had been put there, cleaning up a polluted stream flowing through the area, stopping any further contamination by acid rain or other atmospheric pollution, and so on).

The other possible recipient of compensation would be any wild region of nature that is being threatened by human exploitation or consumption. Compensatory action would be taken in behalf of a biotic community somewhere on Earth that might be damaged or destroyed unless special efforts are made to protect it. Acquiring the land and giving it legal status as a nature preserve would be suitable measures.

These suggested middle-range principles are all derived from the one broad Rule of Restitutive Justice: that any agent which has caused an evil to some natural entity that is a proper moral subject owes a duty to bring about a countervailing good, either to the moral subject in question or to some other moral subject. The perpetrating of a harm calls for the producing of a benefit. The greater the harm, the larger the benefit needed to fulfill the moral obligation.

It is worth adding here that all of us who live in modern industrialized societies owe a duty of restitutive justice to the natural world and its wild inhabitants. We have all benefited in countless ways from large-scale technology and advanced modes of economic production. As consumers we not only accept the benefits of industrialization willingly, but spend much of our lives trying to increase those benefits for ourselves and those we love. We are part of a civilization that can only exist by controlling nature and using its resources. Even those who go out to a natural area to enjoy "the wilderness experience" are recipients of the benefits of advanced technology. (What marvels of modern chemistry went into the creation of plastics and synthetic fabrics in their backpacks, tents, sleeping bags, and food containers!) None of us can evade the responsibility that comes with our high standard of living; we all take advantage of the amenities of civilized life in pursuing our individual values and interests. Since it is modern commerce, industry, and technology that make these amenities possible, each of us is a consumer and user of what the natural world can yield for us. Our well-being is constantly being furthered at the expense of the good of the Earth's nonhuman inhabitants. Thus we all should share in the cost of preserving and restoring some areas of wild nature for the sake of the plant and animal communities that live there. Only then can we claim to have genuine respect for nature.

C. Searching the Middle

Reconciling Anthropocentric and Nonanthropocentric Environmental Ethics

JAMES P. STERBA

A central debate, if not the most central debate, in contemporary environmental ethics is between those who defend an anthropocentric ethics and those who defend a nonanthropocentric ethics. This debate pits deep ecologists like George Sessions against reform or shallow ecologists like John Pass-more.[1] It divides biocentric egalitarians like Paul Taylor from social ecologists like Murray Bookchin.[2] In this paper I propose to go some way toward resolving this debate by showing that when the most morally defensible versions of each of these perspectives are laid out, they do not lead to different practical requirements. In this way I hope to show how it is possible for defenders of anthropocentric and nonanthropocentric environmental ethics, despite their theoretical disagreement concerning whether humans are superior to members of other species, to agree on a common set of principles for achieving environmental justice.[3]

Nonanthropocentric Environmental Ethics

Consider first the nonanthropocentric perspective. In support of this perspective it can be argued that we have no nonquestion-begging grounds for regarding the members of any living species as superior to the members of any other. It allows that the members of species differ in a myriad of ways, but argues that these differences do not provide grounds for thinking that the members of any one species are superior to the members of any other. In particular, it denies that the differences between species provides grounds for thinking that humans are superior to the members of other species. Of course, the nonanthropocentric perspective recognises that humans have distinctive traits which the members of other species lack, like rationality and moral agency. It just points out that the members of nonhuman species also have distinctive traits that humans lack, like the homing ability of pigeons, the speed of the cheetah, and the ruminative ability of sheep and cattle.

Nor will it do to claim that the distinctive traits that humans have are more valuable than the distinctive traits that members of other species possess because there is no

James P. Sterba, "Reconciling Anthropocentric and Nonanthropocentric Environmental Ethics," *Environmental Values*, 3 (1994): 229–244. Reprinted with permission.

nonquestion-begging standpoint from which to justify that claim. From a human standpoint, rationality and moral agency are more valuable than any of the distinctive traits found in nonhuman species, since, as humans, we would not be better off if we were to trade in those traits for the distinctive traits found in nonhuman species. Yet the same holds true of nonhuman species. Pigeons, cheetahs, sheep and cattle would not be better off if they were to trade in their distinctive traits for the distinctive traits of other species.[4]

Of course, the members of some species might be better off if they could retain the distinctive traits of their species while acquiring one or another of the distinctive traits possessed by some other species. For example, we humans might be better off if we could retain our distinctive traits while acquiring the ruminative ability of sheep and cattle.[5] But many of the distinctive traits of species cannot be even imaginatively added to the members of other species without substantially altering the original species. For example, in order for the cheetah to acquire the distinctive traits possessed by humans, presumably it would have to be so transformed that its paws became something like hands to accommodate its humanlike mental capabilities, thereby losing its distinctive speed, and ceasing to be a cheetah. So possessing distinctively human traits would not be good for the cheetah. And with the possible exception of our nearest evolutionary relatives, the same holds true for the members of other species: they would not be better off having distinctively human traits. Only in fairy tales and in the world of Disney can the members of non-human species enjoy a full array of distinctively human traits. So there would appear to be no nonquestion-begging perspective from which to judge that distinctively human traits are more valuable than the distinctive traits possessed by other species. Judged from a nonquestion-begging perspective, we would seemingly have to regard the members of all species as equals.[6]

Nevertheless, regarding the members of all species as equals still allows for human preference in the same way that regarding all humans as equals still allows for self-preference. First of all, human preference can be justified on grounds of defence. Thus, we have

A Principle of Human Defence: Actions that defend oneself and other human beings against harmful aggression are permissible even when they necessitate killing or harming animals or plants.[7]

This Principle of Human Defence allows us to defend ourselves and other human beings from harmful aggression first against our persons and the persons of other humans beings that we are committed to or happen to care about and second against our justifiably held property and the justifiably held property of other humans beings that we are committed to or happen to care about. This principle is strictly analogous to the principle of self-defence that applies in human ethics[8] and permits actions in defence of oneself or other human beings against harmful human aggression.[9] In the case of human aggression, however, it will sometimes be possible to effectively defend oneself and other human beings by first suffering the aggression and then securing adequate compensation later. Since in the case of nonhuman aggression, this is unlikely to obtain, more harmful preventive actions such as killing a rabid dog or swatting a mosquito will be justified.

Second, human preference can also be justified on grounds of preservation. Accordingly, we have

A Principle of Human Preservation: Actions that are necessary for meeting one's basic needs or the basic needs of other human beings are permissible even when they require aggressing against the basic needs of animals and plants.

Now needs, in general, if not satisfied, lead to lacks or deficiencies with respect to various standards. The basic needs of humans, if not satisfied, lead to lacks or deficiencies with respect to a standard of a decent life. The basic needs of animals and plants, if not satisfied, lead to lacks or deficiencies with respect to a standard of a healthy life. The means necessary for meeting the basic need of humans can vary widely from society to society. By contrast, the means necessary for meeting the basic need of particular species of animals and plants tend to be invariant.[10]

In human ethics, there is no principle that is strictly analogous to this Principle of Human Preservation. There is a principle of self-preservation in human ethics that permits actions that are necessary for meeting one's own basic needs or the basic needs of other people, even if this requires *failing to meet* (through an act of omission) the basic needs of still other people. For example, we can use our resources to feed ourselves and our family, even if this necessitates failing to meet the basic needs of people in Third World countries. But, in general, we don't have a principle that allows us to *aggress against* (through an act of commission) the basic needs of some people in order to meet our own basic needs or the basic needs of other people to whom we are committed or happen to care about. Actually, the closest we come to permitting aggressing against the basic needs of other people in order to meet our own basic needs or the basic needs of people to whom we are committed or happen to care about is our acceptance of the outcome of life and death struggles in lifeboat cases, where no one has an antecedent right to the available resources. For example, if you had to fight off others in order to secure the last place in a lifeboat for yourself or for a member of your family, we might say that you justifiably aggressed against the basic needs of those whom you fought to meet your own basic needs or the basic needs of the member of your family.[11]

Nevertheless, our survival requires a principle of preservation that permits aggressing against the basic needs of at least some other living things whenever this is necessary to meet our own basic needs or the basic needs of other human beings. Here there are two possibilities. The first is a principle of preservation that allows us to aggress against the basic needs of both humans and nonhumans whenever it would serve our own basic needs or the basic needs of other human beings. The second is the principle, given above, that allows us to aggress against the basic needs of only nonhumans whenever it would serve our own basic needs or the basic needs of other human beings. The first principle does not express any general preference for the members of the human species, and thus it permits even cannibalism provided that it serves to meet our own basic needs or the basic needs of other human beings. In contrast, the second principle does express a degree of preference for the members of the human species in cases where their basic needs are at stake. Happily, this degree of preference for our own species is still compatible with the equality of all species because favouring the members of one's own species to this extent is characteristic of the members of all species with which we interact and is thereby legitimated. The reason it is legitimated is that we would be required to sacrifice the basic needs of members of the human species only if the members of other species were making similar sacrifices for the sake of members of the human species.[12] In addition, if we were to prefer consistently the basic needs of the members of other species whenever those needs conflicted with our own (or even if we do so half the time), given the characteristic behaviour of the members of other species, we would soon be facing extinction, and, fortunately, we have no reason to think that we are morally required to bring about our own extinction. For these reasons, the degree of preference for our own species found in the above Principle of Human Preservation is justified, even if we were to adopt a nonanthropocentric perspective.[13]

Nevertheless, preference for humans can go beyond bounds, and the bounds that are compatible with a nonanthropocentric perspective are expressed by the following:

A Principle of Disproportionality: Actions that meet nonbasic or luxury needs of humans are prohibited when they aggress against the basic needs of animals and plants.

This principle is strictly analogous to the principle in human ethics mentioned previously that prohibits meeting some people's nonbasic or luxury needs by aggressing against the basic needs of other people.[14]

Without a doubt, the adoption of such a principle with respect to non-human nature would significantly change the way we live our lives. Such a principle is required, however, if there is to be any substance to the claim that the members of all species are equal. We can no more consistently claim that the members of all species are equal and yet aggress against the basic needs of some animals or plants whenever this serves our own nonbasic or luxury needs than we can consistently claim that all humans are equal and aggress against the basic needs of some other human beings whenever this serves our nonbasic or luxury needs.[15] Consequently, if species equality is to mean anything, it must be the case that the basic needs of the members of nonhuman species are protected against aggressive actions which only serve to meet the nonbasic needs of humans, as required by the Principle of Disproportionality.[16]

So while a nonanthropocentric perspective allows for a degree of preference for the members of the human species, it also significantly limits that preference.[17]

It might be objected here that I have not yet taken into account the conflict within a nonanthropocentric ethics between holists and individualists. According to holists, the good of a species or the good of an ecosystem or the good of the whole biotic community can trump the good of individual living things.[18] According to individualists, the good of each individual living thing must be respected.[19]

Now one might think that holists would require that we abandon my Principle of Human Preservation. Yet consider. Assuming that people's basic needs are at stake, how could it be morally objectionable for them to try to meet those needs, even if this were to harm other species, whole ecosystems, or even, to some degree, the whole biotic community?[20] Of course, we can *ask* people in such conflict cases not to meet their basic needs in order to prevent harm to other species, ecosystems or the whole biotic community. But if people's basic needs are at stake, we can not reasonably demand that they make such a sacrifice. We could demand, of course, that people do all that they reasonably can to keep such conflicts from arising in the first place, for, just as in human ethics, many severe conflicts of interest can be avoided simply by doing what is morally required early on.[21] Nevertheless, when people's basic needs are at stake, the individualist perspective seems incontrovertible. We cannot reasonably require people to be saints.

At the same time, when people's basic needs are not at stake, we would be justified in acting on holistic grounds to prevent serious harm to a species, an ecosystem, or the whole biotic community. Obviously, it will be difficult to know when our interventions will have this effect, but when we can be reasonably sure that they will, such interventions (e.g. culling elk herds in wolf-free ranges or preserving the habitat of endangered species) would be morally permissible, and maybe even morally required.[22] This shows that it is possible to agree with individualists when the basic needs of human beings are at stake, and to agree with holists when they are not.

Yet this combination of individualism and holism appears to conflict with the equality of species by imposing greater sacrifices on the members of nonhuman species than it does on the members of the human species. Fortunately, appearances are deceiving here. Although the proposed resolution only justifies imposing holism when people's basic needs are not at stake, it does not justify imposing individualism at all. Rather it would simply permit individualism when people's basic needs *are* at stake. Of course, we could impose holism under all conditions. But given that this would, in effect, involve going to war against people who are simply striving to meet their own basic needs in the only way they can, as permitted by the Principle of Human Preservation, intervention is such cases would not be justified.

Nevertheless, this combination of individualism and holism may leave animal liberationists wondering about the further implications of this resolution for the treatment of animals. Obviously, a good deal of work has already been done on this topic. Initially, philosophers thought that humanism could be extended to include animal liberation and eventually environmental concern.[23] Then Baird Callicott argued that animal liberation and environmental concern were as opposed to each other as they were to humanism.[24] The resulting conflict Callicott called 'a triangular affair'. Agreeing with Callicott, Mark Sagoff contended that any attempt to link together animal liberation and environmental concern would lead to 'a bad marriage and a quick divorce'.[25] Yet more recently, philosophers such as Mary Ann Warren have tended to play down the opposition between animal liberation and environmental concern, and even Callicott now thinks he can bring the two back together again.[26] There are good reasons for thinking that such a reconciliation is possible.

Right off, it would be good for the environment if people generally, especially people in the First World, adopted a more vegetarian diet of the sort that animal liberationists are recommending. This is because a good portion of livestock production today consumes grains that could be more effectively used for direct human consumption. For example, 90% of the protein, 99% of the carbohydrate, and 100% of the fibre value of grain is wasted by cycling it through livestock, and currently 64% of the US grain crop is fed to livestock.[27] So by adopting a more vegetarian diet, people generally, and especially people in the First World, could significantly reduce the amount of farmland that has to be keep in production to feed the human population. This, in turn, could have beneficial effects on the whole biotic community by eliminating the amount of soil erosion and environmental pollutants that result from raising livestock. For example, it has been estimated that 85% of US topsoil lost from cropland, pasture, range land and forest land is directly associated with raising livestock.[28] So in addition to preventing animal suffering, there are these additional reasons to favour a more vegetarian diet.

But even though a more vegetarian diet seems in order, it is not clear that the interests of farm animals would be well served if all of us became complete vegetarians.

Sagoff assumes that in a completely vegetarian human world people would continue to feed farm animals as before.[29] But it is not clear that we would have any obligation to do so. Moreover, in a completely vegetarian human world, we would probably need about half of the grain we now feed livestock to meet people's nutritional needs, particularly in Second and Third World countries. There simply would not be enough grain to go around. And then there would be the need to conserve cropland for future generations. So in a completely vegetarian human world, it seems likely that the population of farm animals would be decimated, relegating many of the farm animals that remain to zoos. On this account, it would seem to be more in the interest of farm animals generally that they be maintained under healthy conditions, and then killed relatively painlessly and eaten, rather than that they not be maintained at all.[30] So a completely vegetarian human world would not seem to serve the interest of farm animals.[31]

Nor, it seems, would it be in the interest of wild species who no longer have their natural predators not to be hunted by humans. Of course, where possible, it may be preferable to reintroduce natural predators. But this may not always be possible because of the proximity of farm animals and human populations, and then if action is not taken to control the populations of wild species, disaster could result for the species and their environments. For example, deer, rabbits, squirrels, quails and ducks reproduce rapidly, and in the absence of predators can quickly exceed the carrying capacity of their environments. So it is in the interest of certain wild species and their environments that humans intervene periodically to maintain a balance. Of course, there will be many natural environments where it is in the interest of the environment and the wild animals that inhabit it to be simply left alone. But here too animal liberation and environmental concern would not be in conflict. For these reasons, animal liberationists would have little reason to object to the proposed combination of individualism and holism within a nonanthropocentric environmental ethics.

Anthropocentric Environmental Ethics

But suppose we were to reject the central argument of the nonanthropocentric perspective and deny that the members of all species are equal. We might claim, for example, that humans are superior because they, through culture, 'realize a greater range of values' than members of nonhuman species or we might claim that humans are superior in virtue of their 'unprecedented capacity to create ethical systems that impart worth to other life-forms'.[32] Or we might offer some other grounds for human superiority.[33] Suppose, then, we adopt this anthropocentric perspective. What follows?

First of all, we will still need a principle of human defence. However, there is no need to adopt a different principle of human defence from the principle favoured by a nonanthropocentric perspective. Whether we judge humans to be equal or superior to the members of other species, we will still want a principle that allows us to defend ourselves and other human beings from harmful aggression, even when this necessitates killing or harming animals or plants.

Second, we will also need a principle of human preservation. But here too there is no need to adopt a different principle from the principle of human preservation favoured by a nonanthropocentric perspective. Whether we judge humans to be equal or superior to the members of other species, we will still want a principle that permits actions that are necessary for meeting our own basic needs or the basic needs of other human beings, even when this requires aggressing against the basic needs of animals and plants.

The crucial question is whether we will need a different principle of disproportionality. If we judged humans to be superior to the members of other species, will we still have grounds for protecting the basic needs of animals and plants against aggressive action to meet the nonbasic or luxury needs of humans?

Here it is important to distinguish between two degrees of preference that we noted earlier. First, we could prefer the basic needs of animals and plants over the nonbasic or luxury needs of humans when to do otherwise would involve *aggressing against* (by an act of commission) the basic needs of animals and plants. Second, we could prefer the basic needs of animals and plants over the nonbasic or luxury needs of humans when to do otherwise would involve simply *failing to meet* (by an act of omission) the basic needs of animals and plants.

Now in human ethics when the basic needs of some people are in conflict with the nonbasic or luxury needs of others, the distinction between failing to meet and aggressing against basic needs seems to have little moral force. In such conflict cases, both ways of not meeting basic needs are objectionable.[34]

But in environmental ethics, whether we adopt an anthropocentric or a nonanthropocentric perspective, we would seem to have grounds for morally distinguishing between the two cases, favouring the basic needs of animals and plants when to do otherwise would involve *aggressing against* those needs in order to meet our own nonbasic or luxury needs, but not when it would involve simply *failing to meet* those needs in order to meet our own nonbasic or luxury needs. This degree of preference for the members of the human species would be compatible with the equality of species insofar as members of non-human species similarly fail to meet the basic needs of members of the human species where there is a conflict of interest.[35]

Even so, this theoretical distinction would have little practical force since most of the ways that we have of preferring our own nonbasic needs over the basic needs of animals and plants actually involve aggressing against their basic needs to meet our own nonbasic or luxury needs rather than simply failing to meet their basic needs.[36]

Yet even if most of the ways that we have of preferring our own nonbasic or luxury needs does involve aggressing against the basic needs of animals and plants, wouldn't human superiority provide grounds for making such sacrifices? Or put another way, shouldn't human superiority have more theoretical and practical significance than I am allowing? Not, I claim, if we are looking for the most morally defensible position to take.

For consider: The claim that humans are superior to the members of other species, if it can be justified at all, is something like the claim that a person came in first in a race where others came in second, third, fourth, and so on. It would not imply that the members of other species are without intrinsic value. In fact, it would imply just the opposite—that the members of other species are also intrinsically valuable, although not as intrinsically valuable as humans, just as the claim that a person came in first in a race implies that the persons who came in second, third, fourth, and so on are also meritorious, although not as meritorious as the person who came in first.

This line of argument draws further support once we consider the fact that many animals and plants are superior to humans in one respect or another, e.g., the sense of smell of the wolf or the acuity of sight of the eagle or the photosynthetic power of plants. So any claim of human superiority must allow for the recognition of excellences in nonhuman species, even for some excellences that are superior to their corresponding human excellences. In fact, it demands that recognition.

Moreover, if the claim of human superiority is to have any moral force, it must rest on nonquestion-begging grounds. Accordingly, we must be able to give a nonquestion-begging response to the nonanthropocentric argument for the equality of species. Yet for any such argument to be successful, it would have to recognise the intrinsic value of the members of nonhuman species. Even if it could be established that human beings have greater intrinsic value, we would still have to recognise that nonhuman nature has intrinsic value as well. So the relevant question is: How are we going to recognise the presumably lesser intrinsic value of nonhuman nature?

Now if human needs, even nonbasic or luxury ones, are always preferred to even the basic needs of the members of nonhuman species, we would not be giving any recognition to the intrinsic value of nonhuman nature. But what if we allowed the nonbasic or luxury needs of humans to trump the basic needs of nonhuman nature half the time, and half the time we allowed the basic needs of nonhuman nature to trump the nonbasic or luxury needs of humans. Would that be enough? Certainly, it would be a significant advance over what we are presently doing. For what we are presently doing is meeting the basic needs of nonhuman nature, at best, only when it serves our own needs or the needs of those we are committed to or happen to care about, and that does not recognise the intrinsic value of nonhuman nature at all. A fifty-fifty arrangement would be an advance indeed. But it would not be enough.

The reason why it would not be enough is that the claim that humans are superior to nonhuman nature no more supports the practice of aggressing against the basic needs of nonhuman nature to satisfy our own nonbasic or luxury needs than the claim that a person came in first in a race would support the practice of aggressing against the basic needs of those who came in second, third, fourth, and so on to satisfy the nonbasic or luxury needs of the person who came in first. A higher degree of merit does not translate into a right of domination, and to claim a right to aggress against the basic needs of nonhuman nature in order to meet our own nonbasic or luxury needs is clearly to claim a right of domination. All that our superiority as humans would justify is not meeting the basic needs of nonhuman nature when this conflicts with our nonbasic or luxury needs. What it does not justify is aggressing against the basic needs of nonhuman nature when this conflicts with our non-basic or luxury needs.

Now it might be objected that my argument so far presupposes an objective theory of value which regards things as valuable because of the qualities they actually have rather than a subjective theory of value which regards things as valuable simply because humans happen to value them. However, I contend that when both these theories are defensibly formulated, they will lead to the same practical requirements.

For consider. Suppose we begin with a subjective theory of value that regards things as valuable simply because humans value them. Of course, some things would be valued by humans instrumentally, others intrinsically, but, according to this theory, all things would have the value they have, if they have any value at all, simply because they are valued by humans either instrumentally or intrinsically.

One problem facing such a theory is why should we think that humans alone determine the value that things have? For example, why not say that things are valuable because the members of other species value them? Why not say that grass is valuable because zebras value it, and that zebras are valuable because lions value them, and so on? Or why not say, assuming God exists, that things are valuable because God values them?

Nor would it do simply to claim that we authoritatively determine what is valuable for ourselves, that nonhuman species authoritatively determine what is valuable for themselves, and that God authoritatively determines what is valuable for the Godhead. For what others value should at least be relevant data when authoritatively determining what is valuable for ourselves.

Another problem for a subjective theory of value is that we probably would not want to say that just anything we happen to value determines what is valuable for ourselves. For surely we would want to say that at least some of the things that people value, especially people who are evil or deficient in certain ways, are not really valuable, even for them. Merely thinking that something is valuable doesn't make it so.

Suppose then we modified this subjective theory of value to deal with these problems. Let the theory claim that what is truly valuable for people is what they would value if they had all the relevant information (including, where it is relevant, the knowledge of what others would value) and reasoned correctly.[37] Of course, there will be many occasions where we are unsure that ideal conditions have been realised, unsure, that is, that we have all the relevant information and have reasoned correctly. And even when we are sure that ideal conditions have been realised, we may not always be willing to act upon what we come to value due to weakness of will.

Nevertheless, when a subjective theory of value is formulated in this way, it will have the same practical requirements as an objective theory of value that is also defensibly formulated. For an objective theory of value holds that what is valuable is determined by the qualities things actually have. But in order for the qualities things actually have to determine our values, they must be accessible to us, at least under ideal conditions, that is, they must be the sort of qualities that we would value if we had all the relevant information and reasoned correctly.[38] But this is just what is valuable according to our modified subjective theory of value. So once a subjective theory of value and an objective theory of value are defensibly formulated in the manner I propose, they will lead us to value the same things.[39]

Now it is important to note here that with respect to some of the things we value intrinsically, such as animals and plants, our valuing them depends simply on our ability to discover the value that they actually have based on their qualities, whereas for other things that we value intrinsically, such as our aesthetic experiences and the objects that provided us with those experiences, the value that these things have depends significantly on the way we are constituted. So that if we were constituted differently, what we value aesthetically would be different as well. Of course, the same holds true for some of the things that we morally value. For example, we morally value not killing human beings because of the way we are constituted. Constituted as we are, killing is usually bad for any human that we would kill. But suppose that we were constituted differently such that killing human beings was immensely pleasurable for those humans that we killed, following which they immediately sprang back to life asking us to kill them again.[40] If human beings were constituted in this way, we would no longer morally value not killing. In fact, constituted in this new way, I think we would come to morally value *killing* and the relevant rule for us might be 'Kill human beings as often as you can.' But while such aesthetic and moral values are clearly dependent on the way we are constituted, they still are not anthropocentric in the sense that they imply human superiority. Such values can be recognised from both an anthropocentric and a nonanthropocentric perspective.

It might be objected, however, that while the intrinsic values of an environmental ethics need not be anthropocentric in the sense that they imply human superiority, these values must be anthropocentric in the sense that humans would reasonably come to hold them. This seems correct. However, appealing to this sense of anthropocentric, Eugene Hargrove has argued that not all living things would turn out to be intrinsically valuable as a non-anthropocentric environmental ethics maintains.[41] Hargrove cites as hypothetical examples of living things that would not turn out to be intrinsically valuable the creatures in the films *Alien* and *Aliens*. What is distinctive about these creatures in *Alien* and *Aliens* is that they require the deaths of many other living creatures, whomever they happen upon, to reproduce and survive as a species. Newly hatched, these creatures emerge from their eggs and immediately enter host organisms, which they keep alive and feed upon while they develop. When the creatures are fully developed, they explode out of the chest of their host organisms, killing their hosts with some fanfare. Hargrove suggests that if such creatures existed, we would not intrinsically value them because it would not be reasonable for us to do so.[42]

Following Paul Taylor, Hargrove assumes that to intrinsically value a creature is to recognise a negative duty not to destroy or harm that creature and a positive duty to protect it from being destroyed or harmed by others. Since Hargrove thinks that we would be loath to recognise any such duties with respect to such alien creatures, we would not consider them to be intrinsically valuable.

Surely it seems clear that we would seek to kill such alien creatures by whatever means are available to us, but why should that preclude our recognising them as having intrinsic value any more than our seeking to kill any person who is engaged in lethal aggression against us would preclude our recognising that person as having intrinsic value? To recognise something as having intrinsic value does not preclude destroying it to preserve other things that also have intrinsic value when there is good reason to do so. Furthermore, recognising a prima facie negative duty not to destroy or harm something and a prima facie positive duty to protect it from being destroyed or harmed by others is perfectly consistent with recognising an all-things-considered duty to destroy that thing when it is engaged in lethal aggression against us. Actually, all we are doing here is simply applying our Principle of Human Defence, and, as I have argued earlier, there is no reason to think that the application of this principle would preclude our recognising the intrinsic value of every living being.

In sum, I have argued that whether we endorse an anthropocentric or a nonanthropocentric environmental ethics, we should favour a Principle of Human Defence, a Principle of Human Preservation, and a Principle of Disproportionality as I have interpreted them. In the past, failure to recognise the importance of a Principle of Human Defence and a Principle of Human Preservation has led philosophers to overestimate the amount of sacrifice required of humans.[43] By contrast, failure to recognise the importance of a Principle of Disproportionality has led philosophers to underestimate the amount of sacrifice required of humans.[44] I claim that taken together these three principles strike the right balance between concerns of human welfare and the welfare of nonhuman nature.

Of course, the practical implications of these three principles would include proposals for conserving existing resources, particularly nonrenewable resources, proposals for converting to renewable resources, proposals for redistributing resources to meet basic needs of both humans and nonhumans, and proposals for population control, all implemented principally by educational changes and by changes in the tax and incentive structures of our society. In the longer work from which this essay is drawn, I go on to discuss these practical proposals in more detail. In this paper, what I have sought to do is provide the nonanthropocentric and anthropocentric grounding for such proposals in a common set of conflict resolution principles that are required for achieving environmental justice.

Notes

Earlier versions of this essay were presented at the University of Notre Dame, Carleton University, Gonzaga University, Shawnee State University, the University of Washington, the Second World Congress on Violence and Human Co-existence held in Montreal and the Tenth International Social Philosophy Conference held in Helsinki. I would like to thank William Aiken, Robin Attfield, Kendall D'Andrade, Baird Callicott, Richard DeGeorge, Michael DePaul, Wendy Donner, Jay Drydyk, David Duquette, Haim Gordon, Eugene Hargrove, Harlan Miller, Maria Maimonova, Ronald Moore, Brian Norton, Phillip Quinn, Tom Regan, Kenneth Sayre, David Solomon, Brian Steverson, Paul Taylor, Aviezer Tucker, Alvin Plantinga, John Wagner and Laura Westra for their helpful comments.

1 See Passmore 1974 and Devall and Sessions 1985.

2 See Taylor 1986 and Bookchin 1991. It is also possible to view Passmore as pitted against Taylor and Bookchin as pitted against Sessions, but however one casts the debate, those who defend an anthropocentric ethics are still opposed to those who defend a nonanthropocentric ethics.

3 My reconciliation project contrasts with Bryan Norton's (Norton 1991). While Norton's reconciliation project seeks to achieve a reconciliation at the level of practical policies, mine seeks a reconciliation at the level of general principles as well. While Norton's reconciliation project tends to exclude deep ecologists, like George Sessions, and biocentric egalitarians, like Paul Taylor, from the class of environmentalists that he is seeking to reconcile, my reconciliation project explicitly includes them.

4 See Taylor 1986, pp. 129–135 and Routley and Routley 1979.

5 Assuming God exists, humans might also be better off if they could retain their distinctive traits while acquiring one or another of God's qualities, but consideration of this possibility would take us too far afield. Nonhuman animals might also be better off it they could retain their distinctive traits and acquire one or another of the distinctive traits possessed by other non-human animals.

6 I am assuming here that either we treat humans as superior overall to other living things or we treat them as equal overall to other living things. Accordingly, if there is no self-evident or nonquestion-begging grounds for claiming that humans are superior overall to other living things, then, I claim that we should treat humans as equal overall to all other living things.

7 For the purposes of this essay, I will follow the convention of excluding humans from the class denoted by 'animals'.

8 By human ethics I simply mean those forms of ethics that assume without argument that only human beings count morally.

9 Of course, one might contend that no principle of human defence applied in human ethics because either 'nonviolent pacifism' or 'nonlethal pacifism' is the most morally defensible view. However, I have argued elsewhere (Sterba 1992) that this is not the case, and that still other forms of pacifism more compatible with just war theory are also more morally defensible than either of these forms of pacifism.

10 For further discussion of basic needs, see Sterba 1988, pp. 45–50.
11 It is important to recognise here that we also have a strong obligation to prevent lifeboat cases from arising in the first place.
12 Notice that this is not an argument that since the members of other species aren't sacrificing for us, we don't have to sacrifice for them, but rather an argument that since the members of other species are not sacrificing for us, we don't have to sacrifice our basic needs for them. An analogous principle holds in human ethics.
13 The Principle of Human Preservation also imposes a limit on when we can defend nonhuman living beings from human aggression.
14 This principle is clearly acceptable to welfare liberals, socialists, and even libertarians. For arguments to that effect, see Sterba 1988. See also the special issue of the *Journal of Social Philosophy* (Vol. XXII No. 3) devoted to my book, including my 'Nine Commentators: A Brief Response'.
15 Of course, libertarians have claimed that we can recognise that people have equal basic rights while failing to meet, but not aggressing against, the basic needs of other human beings. However, I have argued at length that this claim is mistaken. See the references in the previous note.
16 It should be pointed out that although the Principle of Disproportionality prohibits aggressing against the basic needs of animals and plants to serve the nonbasic needs of humans, the Principle of Human Defence permits defending oneself and other human beings against harmful aggression of animals and plants even when this only serves the nonbasic needs of humans.
17 It might be objected here that this argument is still speciesist in that it permits humans to aggress against nonhuman nature whenever it is necessary for meeting our own basic needs or the basic needs of humans we happen to care about. But this objection surely loses some of its force once it is recognised that it is also permissible for us to aggress against the nonbasic needs of humans whenever it is necessary for meeting our own basic needs or the basic needs of humans we happen to care about.
18 Aldo Leopold's view is usually interpreted as holistic in this sense. Leopold wrote 'A thing is right when it tends to preserve the integrity, stability and beauty of the biotic community. It is wrong when it tends otherwise.' See Leopold 1949.
19 For a defender of this view, see Taylor 1986.
20 I am assuming that in these cases of conflict the good of *other* human beings is not at issue. Otherwise, as we have already noted, other considerations will apply.
21 For example, it is now quite clear that our war with Iraq could have been avoided if early on we had refused to support the military buildup of Saddam Hussein.
22 Where it most likely would be morally required is where our negligent actions have caused the environmental problem in the first place.
23 Peter Singer's *Animal Liberation* (1975) inspired this view.
24 Callicott 1980.
25 Sagoff 1984.
26 Warren 1983; Callicott 1989, Chapter 3.
27 *Realities for the 90's*, p. 4.
28 Ibid., p. 5.
29 Sagoff 1984, pp. 301–305.
30 I think there is an analogous story to tell here about 'domesticated' plants.
31 Of course, if we permitted farmland and grazing land to return to its natural state, certain wild animals will surely benefit as a result, but why should we be required to favour the interests of these wild animals over the interests of farm animals, especially when favouring the latter serves our own interests as well? For further discussion, see Gruzalski 1983.
32 Rolston 1988, pp. 66–68; Bookchin 1991, p. xxxvi.
33 See the discussion of possible grounds of human superiority in Taylor, pp. 135–152 and in Norton 1987, 135–150.
34 This is clearly true for welfare liberals and socialists, and it can even be shown to be true for libertarians because most failings to meet the basic needs of others really turn out to be acts of aggressing against the basic needs of others. See note 14.
35 This is not an argument that any degree of preference for humans is acceptable, if the members of other species express the same degree of concern for their own members, but rather that this degree of preference for humans (failing to meet the basic needs of the members of other species in order to meet human needs) is acceptable if the members of other species express the same degree of concern for their own members.
36 The same holds true in human ethics where most of the ways that we have of preferring our own nonbasic needs over other humans actually involve

aggressing against those needs to meet our own nonbasic or luxury needs rather than simply failing to meet them. See note 34

37 I am assuming here that part of what is required for reasoning correctly is that the reasoning be done in a nonquestion-begging way.

38 I'm assuming that objective value theorists would want to incorporate a condition of accessibility into their accounts. It is difficult for me to conceive what would be the point of a value theory for humans without such a condition.

39 Subjective and objective theories of value have tended to highlight different features of a defensible theory of value. A subjective theory of value stresses that what is valuable for us must be accessible to us. An objective theory stresses that what is valuable for us depends not just on us but on the qualities of things in the world.

40 One might object here that if humans immediately came back to life, they would not have been 'killed'. Possibly, but what if they came back to life five minutes later or ten minutes later or fifteen minutes later ... In my judgment, a more telling objection is that creatures who came back to life in this way would no longer be humans. But irrespective of whether they are humans, given their constitution, they would favour the new moral rule about killing. And this is my point—that moral rules depend on one's constitution. Of course, nothing hangs on accepting this example. For my purposes, it suffices to recognise that our aesthetic judgments depend on the the way we are constituted.

41 Hargrove 1992, p. 147ff.

42 Ibid., p. 151

43 For example, Baird Callicott (1980) had defended Edward Abbey's assertion that he would sooner shoot a man than a snake.

44 For example, Eugene Hargrove argues that from a traditional wildlife perspective, the lives of individual specimens of quite plentiful nonhuman species count for almost nothing at all. See Chapter 4 of Hargrove 1989.

References

Bookchin, Murray 1991. *The Ecology of Freedom*. Montreal, Black Rose Books.

Callicott, J. Baird 1980. 'Animal Liberation: A Triangular Affair', *Environmental Ethics* 2: 311–328.

Callicott, J. Baird 1989. *In Defense of the Land Ethic*. Albany, SUNY Press.

Devall, Bill and Sessions, George (eds) 1985. *Deep Ecology: Living as if Nature Mattered*. Salt Lake City, Gibbs M. Smith.

Gruzalski, Bart 1983. 'The Case against Raising and Killing Animals for Food'. In H. Miller and W. Williams, *Ethics and Animals*, pp. 251–256. Clifton, Humana Press.

Hargrove, Eugene 1989. *Foundations of Environmental Ethics*. Englewood Cliffs, N.J., Prentice Hall.

Hargrove, Eugene 1992. 'Weak Anthropocentric Intrinsic Value'. In *After Earth Day*, edited by Max Oelschlaeger. Denton, Texas, University of North Texas Press.

Leopold, Aldo 1949. *A Sand County Almanac*, New York: Oxford University Press.

Norton, Bryan 1987. *Why Preserve Natural Variety?* Princeton, Princeton University Press.

Norton, Bryan 1991. *Toward Unity Among Environmentalists*. Oxford, Oxford University Press.

Passmore, John 1974. *Man's Responsibility for Nature*. London, Duckworth. *Realities for the 90's*. Santa Cruz, 1991.

Rolston, Holmes 1988. *Environmental Ethics*. Philadelphia, Temple University Press.

Routley, R. and Routley, V. 1979. 'Against the Inevitability of Human Chauvinism'. In *Ethics and Problems of the 21st Century* edited by K.E. Goodpaster and K.M. Sayre. Notre Dame, Notre Dame University Press.

Sagoff, Mark 1984. 'Animal Liberation and Environmental Ethics: Bad Marriage, Quick Divorce', *Osgood Hall Law Journal* 297–307.

Singer, Peter 1975. *Animal Liberation*. New York: New York Review.

Sterba, James 1988. *How To Make People Just*. Totowa, N.J., Rowman and Littlefield.

Sterba, James 1992. 'Reconciling Pacifists and Just War Theorists', *Social Theory and Practice* 18: 21–38.

Taylor, Paul 1987. *Respect for Nature*. Princeton, Princeton University Press.

Warren, Mary Ann 1983. 'The Rights of the Nonhuman World'. In *Environmental Philosophy*, edited by Robert Elliot and Arran Gare; pp. 109–134. London, Open University Press.

On the Reconciliation of Anthropocentric and Nonanthropocentric Environmental Ethics

Brian K. Steverson

James Sterba's recent essay in this journal, 'Reconciling Anthropocentric and Nonanthropocentric Environmental Ethics', represents the latest attempt to circumvent the decades old debate in environmental philosophy between the anthropocentrists and nonanthropocentrists, and to show that the axiological disagreement which has characterised the debate becomes moot as one proceeds to construct general normative principles and then to translate those principles into specific policy.[1] Sterba works to show that as regards principles of environmental justice, in their most morally defensible forms, both the anthropocentrist and nonanthropocentrist positions would ultimately concur on which such principles are acceptable. I have elsewhere argued that at least one such attempt to establish a convergence of anthropocentric and nonanthropocentric perspectives at the level of policy formation fails, and will here argue that Sterba's attempt at reconciling the two camps fails as well.[2] Though my critique of Sterba's argument is, of course, insufficient to show that no such reconciliation is possible, I think that it will provide grounds for recognising that such a unification project faces great difficulties, and that despite the growing weariness with the anthropocentric–nonanthropocentric debate, the foundational axiological division represented by the debate will remain a crucial point of contention for some time to come.

Sterba's approach is to interpret the nonanthropocentric–anthropocentric debate as a debate about the equality of species. Traditionally understood, the anthropocentrist is taken to believe that there exists a morally relevant inequality between humans and other species, while the nonanthropocentrist denies the existence of such an inequality. Sterba's project is to show that, despite their differences regarding species equality, both positions would allow for the exact same range of preferential satisfaction of human needs over those of members of nonhuman species. His general tack is this. He argues that even though the nonanthropocentrist is committed to species egalitarianism, that commitment does not preclude the possibility that preferential treatment of humans is morally justified in certain cases.[3] From the other direction, he argues that despite the fact that the anthropocentrist holds to the belief in interspecific inegalitarianism, this general inequality does not license all forms of preferential treatment, since to do so would in effect translate the initial inequality into a right to domination, a move which Sterba argues is indefensible. The upshot is that when the most reasonable versions of both axiological positions are considered, agreement is reached as to which general principles of preferential treatment are acceptable. My argument is that

Brian K. Steverson, "On the Reconciliation of Anthropocentric and Nonanthropocentric Environmental Ethics," *Environmental Values*, 5 (1996): 349–361. Reprinted with permission.

Sterba overestimates the necessity of agreement between the two camps at this juncture. I will argue that the nonanthropocentrist has available good reasons for thinking that the kind of human preference embodied in the three principles Sterba defends is too broad, and that the anthropocentrist has good reasons for thinking that the restrictions on human preference found in those principles are too strict.

Sterba begins his reconciliation project with the nonanthropocentrist position. For Sterba, the important question to be addressed is whether such a commitment to species egalitarianism eliminates the possibility of justifiably preferring humans over nonhumans in situations of conflict. A first, and easy answer, is that in cases of self-defence, humans are justified in preferring their own lives or well-being over that of nonhumans when the latter pose a threat to humans. The principle runs this way:

A Principle of Human Defence: Actions that defend oneself and other human beings against harmful aggression are permissible even when they necessitate killing or harming animals and plants.

As Sterba notes, this principle is perfectly analogous to the accepted principle of self-defence found in human ethics. Though nonanthropocentrists might demand that the domain of the set of actions counting as 'harmful aggression' be rather limited, they would obviously be committed to this principle.

A second type of justified preference occurs in cases where human preservation is at stake, though not due to the aggression of nonhumans. Sterba has in mind cases where the satisfaction of basic human needs requires the dissatisfaction of nonhuman basic needs, and sets out the following principle to cover such situations:

A Principle of Human Preservation: Actions that are necessary for meeting one's basic needs or the basic needs of other human beings are permissible even when they require aggressing against the basic needs of animals and plants.

Unlike the Principle of Human Defence, no such strictly analogous principle exists in human ethics. Sterba states that there is a principle which allows for the committing of acts which are necessary to satisfy basic needs even when doing so results in a failure to meet the basic needs of others, but that, in general, no such principle pertaining to aggressing against the basic needs of others exists. Nevertheless, Sterba takes the Principle of Human Preservation to be a requirement if the human species is to survive.

'Happily', as Sterba describes it, the kind of human preference found in the Principle of Human Preservation is consistent with the nonanthropocentric commitment to species equality. Sterba's argument for why it is consistent rests on an appeal to the notion of 'reciprocity'. According to him, we would only be obligated to sacrifice our own basic needs for the sake of nonhumans' basic needs if they were doing the same, or were willing to do the same. In the absence of such reciprocal treatment on their part, we are not so obligated.

What is one to make of such an argument? Surely, there are types of obligations which exist only in the context of reciprocity (e.g. contractual obligations). However, ethical contractarians to the contrary, many would argue that not all obligations are grounded on the presence of reciprocity on the part of the party to which the obligations are owed (e.g. parents' obligations to their children). Why should we believe that a potential obligation to avoid aggressing against the basic needs of nonhumans should be such a reciprocity-based obligation? It seems as if Sterba has something like a naturalistic argument working here. The absence of interspecific sacrificial behaviour in nature eliminates the moral necessity of humans acting in that fashion, since such sacrificial behaviour has an 'unnatural' character.[4] It is unnatural because, if pursued consistently, it would result in extinction. Sterba writes,

> ... if we were to prefer consistently the basic needs of members of other species whenever those needs conflicted with our own (or even if we do so half the time), given the characteristic behaviour of the members of other species, we would soon be facing extinction, and, fortunately, we have no reason to think that we are morally required to bring about our own extinction.

Assuming that Sterba is right to hold that there exists no reasonable justification for the view that humans have a moral obligation to bring about the extinction of the species (a safe assumption, no doubt), then it is permissible for humans to act so as to prevent their extinction, and the Principle of Human Preservation seems quite justified. Note, however, that all this line of reasoning, in itself, establishes is the *permissibility* of humans acting so as to prevent their own extinction. It does not establish the presence of an *obligation* on the part of humans to act so as to prevent their own extinction. Though an argument in support of such a view may be available (the beginnings of such an argument will be discussed later in connection with anthropocentrism and Sterba's Principle of Disproportionality), Sterba does not make such a claim. In the absence of such an obligation, acting so as to lead to our extinction remains, *prima facie*, permissible. An immediate implication of this possibility is that nonanthropocentrists, committed to species equality as they are, may consistently prefer the satisfaction of nonhuman basic needs over those of humans even if, following through with Sterba's logic, doing so entails the extinction of the human species.

Theoretically, Sterba's argument establishes very little regarding the nonanthropocentrists commitment to the Principle of Human Preservation since its complement, the Principle of Nonhuman Preservation, is an equally valid option. Any preference in the context of competing basic needs is permissible given the nonanthropocentrists' initial commitment to species equality. If some species must suffer, the equality of species plays no role in selecting which species will suffer; a coin toss would suffice. Consequently, though it is true that the nonanthropocentrist could justifiably accept the permissibility of sacrificing nonhuman basic needs for those of humans, they are not required to. Since sacrificing human basic needs for those of nonhuman species is equally permissible, the nonanthropocentrist could opt for that approach as a rule, or they could simply make alternating choices between the competing basic needs of humans and nonhumans. What is absent are reasons for believing that the nonanthropocentrist *ought* to prefer the Principle of Human Preservation on a consistent basis. To settle the dilemma consistently in favour of humans requires some independent argument to show that our obligation to prevent our own extinction is stronger than our obligation to prevent the extinction of other species. It is not apparent how a nonanthropocentrist, as defined by Sterba, could come up with such an argument, since no matter which argument is produced, it will involve some claim about the superior value of humans. So, though nonanthropocentrists *can* accept the Principle of Human

Preservation, it is not clear that they *must*, or even should prefer it. The impact on Sterba's reconciliation project is this. The most that can be said for the nonanthropocentrist is that the Principle of Human Preservation is an acceptable principle, though not in any way more acceptable than the Principle of Nonhuman Preservation. As will be shown later in this essay, the anthropocentrist position, as Sterba presents it, embodies a strong presumption in favour of the Principle of Human Preservation, though it may fall short of making commitment to that principle absolutely obligatory. If such a difference in strength of commitment exists between the two perspectives, one can seriously question the extent to which reconciliation has been achieved.

The third principle of justice to which Sterba argues both nonanthropocentrists and anthropocentrists would be committed is this:

A Principle of Disproportionality: Actions that meet nonbasic or luxury needs of humans are prohibited when they aggress against the basic needs of animals and plants.

Note that this principle makes a stronger claim than the first two in that it declares a particular kind of action to be *prohibited*, and not simply *permissible*. The importance of this will surface when the principle is considered from the anthropocentric perspective. That the nonanthropocentrist would be committed to such a principle is uncontroversial since, as Sterba notes, if the claim of species equality is to have any substance, one cannot accept the view that the satisfaction of any human need takes precedent over the satisfaction of nonhuman basic needs. Minimally, species equality requires a distinction between basic and nonbasic needs, and a weighting of the former over the latter; hence, the Principle of Disproportionality.

Both the Principle of Human Preservation and the Principle of Disproportionality trade upon the distinction between basic and nonbasic needs, at least as regards human needs. Making out such a distinction with precision is no easy task, and to demand that Sterba's argument include a precise explication of the distinction is misplaced, inasmuch as the generality of the principles of environmental justice he is concerned with require only a rough conceptual demarcation between basic and nonbasic needs. In fact, Sterba provides a working distinction when he addresses the moral importance of need satisfaction.

> Now needs, in general, if not satisfied, lead to lacks or deficiencies with respect to various standards. The basic needs of humans, if not satisfied, lead to lacks or deficiencies with respect to a standard of decent life. The basic needs of animals and plants, if not satisfied, lead to lacks or deficiencies with respect to a standard of healthy life. The means necessary for meeting the basic need of humans can vary widely from society to society. By contrast, the means necessary for meeting the basic need of particular species of animals and plants tend to be invariant.[5]

Since, for Sterba, the basic needs of humans are those connected with the maintenance of a 'decent life', it follows that nonbasic needs will be those not so connected. Likewise, nonhuman basic needs are those necessary for the maintenance of a 'healthy life', while nonhuman nonbasic needs (if there are any) will be those lacking such necessity.

Though this is not the place to critically assess Sterba's portrayal of the basic–nonbasic distinction, one comment pertinent to my critique is in order. In line with my earlier comment that in the context of agreeing to the Principle of Human Defence the nonanthropocentrist would undoubtedly opt for a narrow definition of 'harmful aggression', it is clear that as regards both the Principle of Human Preservation and the Principle of Disproportionality, the nonanthropocentrist would opt for an equally restrictive designation of which human needs count as basic, so as to guard against the potential for an overexpansion of the range of human aggression against nonhumans justified by the Principle of Human Preservation, as well as to guard against an undue shrinkage of the range of human aggression against nonhumans prohibited by the Principle of Disproportionality. Consequently, it is reasonable to presume that the nonanthropocentrist, at least, would require that both the Principle of Human Preservation and the Principle of Disproportionality be stated with greater precision than Sterba's current versions contain. It is interesting to note that Sterba employs different standards for qualifying basic needs. For humans, the standard is that of a *decent* life, whereas for nonhumans the standard is *healthy* life. Nonanthropocentrists might have reason to question such a 'double standard' in the light of their commitment to species equality, and wonder why the standard of *healthy* life is not sufficient for both human and nonhuman basic needs.

As regards nonanthropocentrism and Sterba's principles of justice, then, two general comments can be made. Though the nonanthropocentrist could accept the Principle of Human Preservation, they could just as easily accept the Principle of Nonhuman Preservation. The question is, which would the nonanthropocentrist most likely be committed to in practice? It is quite reasonable to presume that more often than not, the nonanthropocentrist would side with nonhuman species for various kinds of independent reasons, and that such a consistent preference for the basic needs of nonhumans over those of humans does not violate their commitment to species equality. As such, it is more reasonable to presume that the nonanthropocentrist would reject the Principle of Human Preservation, rather than accept it. As for the Principle of Disproportionality, Sterba is correct to believe that the nonanthropocentrist would be committed to it, but he fails to take into account that the version of that principle which the nonanthropocentrist would be committed to must be one which narrowly defines which human needs fall into the class of basic needs. Anticipating my treatment of the anthropocentric position, if the principle were expanded to include designations of basic and nonbasic needs, one would quickly discover that the nonanthropocentric version and the anthropocentric version have striking dissimilarities.

In addressing the anthropocentric side of his reconciliation project, Sterba's first step is to define what he takes to be its most defensible version. As a position on the equality of species, anthropocentrism is, of course, in-egalitarian: humans possesses a superior value to that of nonhuman species. Nonetheless, Sterba's position is that this superiority in value cannot imply a total absence of intrinsic value on the part of members of nonhuman species. He gives two arguments for his view. The first is an analogy.

> The claim that humans are superior to the members of other species, if it can be justified at all, is something like the claim that a person came in first in a race where others came in second, third, fourth, and so on. It would not imply that the members of other species are without intrinsic value. In fact it would imply just the opposite—that the members of

other species are also intrinsically valuable, although not as intrinsically valuable as humans, just as the claim that a person came in first in a race implies that the persons who came in second, third, fourth, and so on are also meritorious, although not as meritorious as the person who came in first.[6]

His second argument is based on the requirement that in order to have 'moral force' the anthropocentric claim of human superiority must be based on nonquestion-begging grounds. That is, whatever traits are selected as the basis for granting humans value superiority, one must be able to explain why those traits are sufficient to ground such superiority. For Sterba, no such nonquestion-begging explanation is forthcoming since nonhuman species possess their own distinctive traits which are as equally valuable to them as our distinctive traits are to us. His conclusion is that, '[j]udged from a nonquestion-begging perspective, we would seemingly have to regard the members of all species as equal'.[7]

Both arguments are, of course, open to possible criticism. One could question the adequacy of the race analogy as a model for the 'most morally defensible' version of anthropocentrism, and one could also propose reasons for thinking that simply possessing distinctive traits which are 'good for oneself' is an insufficient ground for attributions of intrinsic value. In this context, I will not pursue either line of discussion, but, instead, grant Sterba the claim that the most morally defensible version of anthropocentrism is one which, though it affords value superiority to humans, must grant some intrinsic value to members of nonhuman species. One quick comment, however, about this version of anthropocentrism. Recently, in the context of showing that environmental ethics rests on a mistaken requirement for an axiological theory capable of according differential intrinsic value to nature, Tom Regan has (persuasively, I think) argued that, depending on which kind of object one has in mind when ascribing intrinsic value, the concept of intrinsic value is either a categorical one, or one for which there exists no nonarbitrary standard of comparison by which to hierarchically rank intrinsically valuable things.[8] If Regan is correct, then, since it is characterised by a commitment to a theory of differential intrinsic value, Sterba's 'most morally defensible version of anthropocentrism' may itself embody an axiological mistake. But, I will leave that for another discussion.

The question, then, is whether the anthropocentrist, as described by Sterba, would be committed to the same principles of environmental justice as the nonanthropocentrist. As Sterba notes, the anthropocentrist would, of course, be committed to the Principle of Human Defence, and, not surprisingly given the superior value which their position attaches to being human, the anthropocentrist would find the Principle of Human Preservation quite acceptable. However, the latter claim misrepresents the nature of the anthropocentrist's commitment to the Principle of Human Preservation. Unlike the situation regarding nonanthropocentrism, the anthropocentrist does not have a choice between equally acceptable alternatives (the Principle of Human Preservation and the Principle of Nonhuman Preservation). If, as Sterba argues, a consistent preference for either the basic needs of humans or those of nonhumans would result in the extinction of the other, the anthropocentrist's commitment to the value superiority of humans clearly creates a strong presumption in favour of the Principle of Human Preservation The extent to which the anthropocentrist could opt for the Principle of Nonhuman Preservation is dependent upon the weight attached to the value difference between humans and nonhumans. The greater the gap between the degree of intrinsic value afforded nonhuman and that assigned to humans, the less likely it is that the anthropocentrist would find the Principle of Nonhuman Preservation acceptable. As such, to say that both positions would find the Principle of Human Preservation *acceptable* is, as it turns out, not very significant since the nonanthropocentrist has an equally acceptable alternative, while the anthropocentrist is committed to the Principle of Human Preservation, at least regarding consistent preferences.

For Sterba, the critical question is whether the anthropocentrist would be committed to the previously stated Principle of Disproportionality, to some different version of it, or to no such principle whatsoever. As Sterba recognises, at first glance it might appear that, given the assumption that humans are of greater value than nonhumans, the Principle of Disproportionality would be antithetical to the anthropocentric position. A characteristic criticism of Western society by environmental philosophers has been that it embodies a form of anthropocentrism which has historically licensed uninhibited exploitation of nature. If only humans are of intrinsic value, than human exploitation of nonhumans is restricted only by the potential for direct or indirect harm to fellow humans. In the absence of that, nonhuman nature can be used for any purpose. But, as Sterba holds, there exists no nonquestion-begging argument in support of this radical form of anthropocentrism, so that the most defensible version of anthropocentrism is one which attributes intrinsic value to the members of nonhuman species, albeit, lesser intrinsic value than that of members of the human species. Given this, exploitation of non-human species in order to satisfy human needs requires justification. Such exploitation, when necessary to satisfy the basic needs of humans, is allowable due to the Principle of Human Preservation. The remaining question to be addressed, as Sterba notes, is whether the value superiority of humans justifies the exploitation of nonhumans in order to satisfy nonbasic human needs.

Sterba finds it important to distinguish between *aggressing against* the basic needs of members of nonhuman species and *failing to meet* those needs. In his opinion, this distinction does not carry any moral weight in the context of interhuman ethics where both aggressing against and failing to meet the basic needs of fellow humans in order to satisfy one's own nonbasic needs are deemed immoral. In the context of interspecific ethics, however, Sterba believes the distinction to be ethically important. His position is that, at least theoretically, there are legitimate grounds for favouring human nonbasic needs over the basic needs of nonhuman species when to do so involves only failing to meet their basic needs, but that no such grounds exist for justifying aggressing against the basic needs of members of nonhuman species in order to satisfy the nonbasic needs of humans. What legitimates the former? In Sterba's opinion, the fact that nonhuman species fail to meet the basic needs of humans when there is a conflict with their own needs (basic and nonbasic I presume) entails that humans are under no such obligation themselves. This is simply the reciprocity argument again. Since nonhumans fail to sacrifice their own needs in order to avoid failing to meet the needs of humans, we do not act wrongly when we do the same. We have already seen the weakness of this argument in regards to the Principle of Human Preservation, and it fares no better here. The fact that members of nonhuman species, who are not moral agents, consistently prefer their own needs over those of humans or members of other species in general, does not entail that humans, who are moral agents, are free from any obligation to avoid failing to meet the basic needs of nonhumans in order to satisfy their own nonbasic needs.

Sterba recognises that most of the conflicts between human nonbasic needs and the basic needs of nonhuman species involves aggressing against the latter. Consequently, even if the theoretical distinction between 'aggressing against' and 'failing to meet' were to have ethical importance in the context of interspecific relations, it would have little if any practical significance. The question, then, to be addressed is whether there exist justifiable reasons for favouring human nonbasic needs over nonhuman basic needs when doing so requires aggressing against the latter. In other words, can the anthropocentrist reasonably reject the necessity of the Principle of Disproportionality? Sterba's position is that they cannot. They cannot because, given the version of anthropocentrism Sterba is working with, to allow that the needs of the members of nonhuman species can be aggressed against in order to satisfy any human needs, which would be the result of a denial of the Principle of Disproportionality combined with an acceptance of the Principle of Human Preservation, is, in effect, to deny that members of nonhuman species have any intrinsic value, a denial the anthropocentrist cannot make. Consequently, in order to respect the intrinsic value of members of nonhuman species, a line must be drawn. For Sterba, the Principle of Disproportionality represents that line.

Is it the case that the Principle of Disproportionality represents the absolute minimum which the anthropocentrist can consistently accept? Or, can the anthropocentrist consistently subscribe to a less restrictive principle which would allow for some human preference of their own nonbasic needs over the basic needs of members of nonhuman species? In Sterba's argument, there are two inequalities at work: humans are of greater intrinsic value than non-humans, and the satisfaction of basic needs is of greater value than the satisfaction of nonbasic needs. All else being equal, one is justified in opting for the satisfaction of basic needs over that of nonbasic needs, and the satisfaction of human needs over nonhuman needs. The key to Sterba's argument is that the latter preference is insufficient to trump the former. But, is it? As Sterba recognises, the failure to satisfy any need results in a lack or deficiency. These lacks or deficiencies can be of various kinds (e.g. poor health, lack of psychological development, etc.), but they nonetheless represent a worsening of the being's condition in some shape or form. Even though, considered in themselves, the failure to satisfy basic needs may result in a greater, even much greater, harm than the failure to satisfy nonbasic needs, the failure to satisfy nonbasic needs can be construed as a harm. What the Principle of Disproportionality represents is a preference for avoiding the harms attendant upon the failure to satisfy the basic needs of lesser intrinsically valuable entities over the harm resulting from a failure to satisfy the nonbasic needs of beings of greater intrinsic value. The question is, what grounds are there for this preference?

Reading between the lines, Sterba's reasoning seems to be this. Differences in the intrinsic value of beings has no effect on the magnitude of the harm produced by the failure to satisfy basic needs as opposed to the magnitude of harm produced by the failure to satisfy nonbasic needs. The former is categorically larger and morally more important than the latter; hence, the categorical prohibition found in the Principle of Disproportionality. However plausible this reasoning might be, it simply is not the case that the anthropocentrist must be committed to it. The anthropocentrist could offer plausible arguments for holding the view that in certain kinds of cases it is worse to avoid aggressing against the basic needs of members of nonhuman species in order to satisfy nonbasic human needs than it is to satisfy the latter. Consider the utilitarian perspective. If humans are presumed to be of greater intrinsic value, then the enhancement of their condition, even if such enhancement is, in itself relatively small, might be of sufficient value as to outweigh the harm caused a being of much less intrinsic value, especially in cases where the benefits to the more intrinsically valuable entities are distributed over a larger number while the harm to the lesser intrinsically valuable entities is restricted to a small number of them. The general question is this: Should one always opt for a state of affairs in which one seeks to maximise the satisfaction of the basic needs of all intrinsically valuable entities, at the expense of the satisfaction of other needs of the more intrinsically valuable beings? Or, is it possible that an arrangement in which a portion of the basic needs of the lesser intrinsically valuable entities is not met in order to meet some non-basic needs of more intrinsically valuable beings could produce a greater overall maximisation of intrinsic value? Put another way, are there any *a priori* reasons for believing that a world filled with a larger number of intrinsically valuable entities, the more intrinsically valuable of which are 'dissatisfied' in a number of ways, is of greater overall value than a world filled with a smaller number of intrinsically valuable entities, but one in which the more intrinsically valuable entities are more satisfied, have fewer lacks and deficiencies? There does not appear to be, and Mill's position on the relative value of a dissatisfied human life and the life of a satisfied pig could be offered up as a philosophical defence of the view that the alternate situation is morally preferable.

Sterba's version of anthropocentrism itself provides plausible grounds for denying the categorical prohibition present in the Principle of Disproportionality. If humans are deemed to be more intrinsically valuable, more 'meritorious', than nonhumans, that must be because they possess certain morally relevant traits, such as the capacity for rational, autonomous behaviour, self-consciousness, and a sense of psychophysical identity over time, which non-humans either do not possess or possess to a much lesser degree. If the possession of interests is a function of the presence of capacities like these, and one attaches moral significance to the possession of interests, then one could argue that taxonomic differences create differences in the kinds of interests at stake, and that sufficiently large differences in those interests has moral importance. So, one could reasonably argue that the interests of humans should be afforded greater moral weight than those of nonhuman species, how much greater weight depending on the phylogenetic differences present. Such a moral difference could easily be taken to outweigh any theoretical difference between basic and nonbasic needs, and in this way justify aggressing against the basic needs of members of some nonhuman species in order to satisfy the nonbasic needs of humans and perhaps other species. This recognition of morally relevant differences in the interests that can be ascribed to members of different species has, ironically, been recognised even by advocates of animal liberation/rights such as Peter Singer and Tom Regan.

What these considerations show is that the anthropocentrists have at their disposal the philosophical means by which to reject the categorical prohibition present in Sterba's Principle of Disproportionality in favour of a less restrictive principle which allows for, in certain well-defined cases, aggressing against the basic needs of members of nonhuman species in order to satisfy human nonbasic needs. As Sterba himself notes, 'To recognise something as having intrinsic value does not preclude destroying it to preserve other things that also have intrinsic value when there is good reason to do so.' If we substitute 'make better off' for 'preserve', and allow that the maximisation of the welfare of the most intrinsically valuable entities is a good reason, or that the inherent moral superiority of the interests of more intrinsically valuable beings demands our attention, then it does not appear that the anthropocentrist, upon pains of inconsistency, is committed to the Principle of Disproportionality. What we are left with is the reverse of the situation regarding the Principle of Human Preservation. There the anthropocentrist is strongly committed to the principle of justice under consideration, while the nonanthropocentrist is not. Here, the nonanthropocentrist is strongly committed to the principle, while the anthropocentrist is at best weakly committed to it. Again, if reconciliation is achieved, it is not very significant.

As mentioned at the outset, reconciliation projects such as those of Sterba and Norton are fuelled by the belief that when one moves beyond abstract, axiological debates about the value status of nonhuman nature relative to that of humans, one will discover that such debates have little or no effect on the formation of general principles by which to shape environmental policy. It would be quite nice, and quite philosophically convenient, if this were true. If it were true, then environmental ethicists could turn their attention to the admittedly more pressing issues of policy formation and environmental management, and, with great hope, reach some consensus as to how to proceed. However, the hope that foundational axiological differences might 'disappear' at the level of policy formation, or even at the level of general principles to guide policy formation, seems to me to be just that, a *hope*. The kind of theoretical 'reconciliation' or 'convergence' argued for by Sterba is too easily purchased. All it requires is an underestimation of the seriousness with which the nonanthropocentrist may hold to the belief in species equality, and a corresponding underestimation of the self-interested latitude which the notion of differential intrinsic value affords the anthropocentrist. Though for practical reasons, the differentially motivated environmental groups, organisations, and movements which now crowd the scene may have to make concessions to one another in order to achieve a politically effective level of cooperative activity, that is far from amounting to either a philosophical or operational 'reconciliation'.

Notes

I would like to thank James Sterba, the journal referees, and the Editor for their helpful comments.

1 Sterba 1994. Norton 1991 is the most developed effort at showing that as regards substantive policy issues, the axiological debate between nonanthropocentrists and anthropocentrists becomes quite insignificant.
2 Steverson 1995.
3 On this point, Sterba is entering the debate regarding speciesism which dates back to the mid-1970s. Sterba's position, a view very similar to what James Rachels has labelled 'mild speciesism', has been criticised by Rachels and others. For example, see Rachels 1990. Rachels' point is to show that even mild speciesism is unacceptable from the standpoint of interspecific equality. If Rachels' assessment is correct, then Sterba is mistaken in the first place to believe that the nonanthropocentrist can accept a principle which shows preference for human interests. My approach will be to allow Sterba his view

that preference for human interests is permissible, even for the nonanthropocentrist, but then to show that the claim of permissibility is too weak to support an effort of *reconciliation* of nonanthropocentrism and anthropocentrism.

4 As far back as 1979, Peter Singer, in the context of responding to objections to his argument for 'animal liberation', critically discussed the inadequacies of a naturalistic–contractarian approach such as this. See Singer 1979, pp. 68–71.

5 Sterba 1994, p. 231.

6 Ibid., p. 237.

7 Ibid., p. 230.

8 See Regan 1992.

References

Norton, Bryan 1991b. *Toward Unity Among Environmentalists*. New York: Oxford University Press.

Rachels, James 1990. *Created From Animals: The Moral Implications of Darwinism*. New York: Oxford University Press.

Regan, Tom 1992a. 'Does Environmental Ethics Rest on a Mistake?' *The Monist* 75: 161–183.

Singer, Peter 1979a. *Practical Ethics*. Cambridge: Cambridge University Press.

Sterba, James P. 1994a. 'Reconciling Anthropocentric and Nonanthropocentric Environmental Ethics'. *Environmental Values* 3: 229–244.

Steverson, Brian K. 1995. 'Contextualism and Norton's Convergence Hypothesis', *Environmental Ethics* 17: 135–150.

Reconciliation Reaffirmed

A Reply to Steverson

JAMES P. STERBA

In 'On the Reconciliation of Anthropocentric and Nonanthropocentric Environmental Ethics,' Brian Steverson raises a number of important objections to my attempt to show that when a nonanthropocentric perspective and an anthropocentric perspective are each given its most morally defensible interpretation, they both support the following principles of environmental justice:

A Principle of Human Defence: Actions that defend oneself and other human beings against harmful aggression are permissible even when they necessitate killing or harming animals or plants.

A Principle of Human Preservation: Actions that are necessary for meeting one's basic needs or the basic needs of other human beings are permissible even when they require aggressing against the basic needs of animals and plants.

James P. Sterba, "Reconciliation Reaffirmed: A Reply to Steverson," *Environmental Values*, 5 (1996): 363–368. Reprinted with permission.

A Principle of Human Disproportionality: Actions that meet nonbasic or luxury needs of humans are prohibited when they aggress against the basic needs of animals and plants. (Steverson, 1996)

Against my attempt to show that a nonanthropocentric perspective requires these principles, Steverson

i. criticises my appeal to reciprocal altruism to justify the human preference permitted by the Principle of Human Preservation; and
ii. claims that while it is reasonable from a nonanthropocentric perspective to select the Principle of Human Preservation, one could just as well select a Principle of Nonhuman Preservation from that perspective.

Against my attempt to show that an anthropocentric perspective requires these principles, Steverson

i. questions whether intrinsic value can comes in degrees as required to support the Principle of Disproportionality from an anthropocentric perspective;
ii. questions whether we are always prohibited from satisfying our nonbasic needs by aggressing against the basic needs of nonhuman nature as required by the Principle of Disproportionality, even assuming that nonhuman nature has intrinsic value. (Sterba, 1994, 1995)

These are very serious objections to my reconciliationist argument that go right to the heart of the matter. Unless there are adequate replies to these objections, there would be no point to pursuing my reconciliationist project further. So let me consider each of these objections in turn.

With respect to my appeal to reciprocal altruism to justify preferential treatment for humans, that is, my claim that the degree of human preference sanctioned by the Principle of Human Preservation is justified by the degree of reciprocal altruism that humans can reasonably expect from other humans, Steverson contends that it would be a mistake to ground all of our moral obligations in such reciprocity.[1]

Actually, I agree with Steverson here. I agree, that is, that not *all* of our moral obligations can be given a foundation in reciprocal altruism. What I have argued, however, is only that some of our obligations can be so grounded in the reciprocal altruism that we can reasonably expect of other humans, and Steverson offers no objection to this more limited appeal to reciprocal altruism.

With respect to my claim that it is reasonable to select the Principle of Human Preservation from a nonanthropocentric perspective, Steverson contends that it is equally reasonable from that perspective to select a Principle of Nonhuman Preservation, which maintains that actions that are necessary for meeting the basic needs of nonhumans are permissible even when they require aggressing against the basic needs of humans.

Here I doubt that Steverson is interpreting 'permissible' in the same sense or applying the notion in the same way in both of these principles. This is because as I interpret the Principle of Human Preservation, when it maintains that it is permissible to meet one's own basic needs or the basic needs of other humans even when this requires aggressing against the basic needs of animals and plants, it implies that other humans should not interfere with that aggression. Let us call this strong permissibility. Now, if we similarly interpret 'permissible' in the Principle of Nonhuman Preservation, it would imply that other humans should not interfere with any aggression that is directed against humans for the preservation of nonhumans, *even when that aggression happens to be directed against themselves*. Surely, this would be a very demanding requirement to impose on humans even from a nonanthropocentric perspective, and I doubt that Steverson wants to endorse it.

Alternatively, Steverson may want to interpret 'permissible' in the same way in both principles, but in such a way that it imposes almost no practical requirements on anyone. According to this interpretation, let us call it weak permissibility, its being permissible to meet one's own basic needs or the basic needs of other human beings by aggressing against the basic needs of nonhumans would be consistent with its being permissible for other humans to resist that aggression. And the same would hold true for the Principle of Nonhuman Preservation. Thus, its being permissible to meet the basic needs of nonhumans by aggressing against the basic needs of humans would be consistent with its being permissible for other humans to resist that aggression. On this interpretation of the two principles, since nothing is morally required or prohibited by them, what gets done obviously depends on the comparative power relations of the contending parties. Nevertheless, the problem with this interpretation is that it is certainly odd to think that morality imposes no prohibitions or requirements at all in such an area of severe conflicts of interest, given that it is in just such areas that we would expect morality to provide some sort of a resolution.

Another possibility is that Steverson may want to interpret 'permissible' as strong permissibility in both principles, but then limit the scope of application of the Principle of Nonhuman Preservation so that it would be permissible for humans to aggress against their own basic needs (i.e., sacrifice them) in order to meet the basic needs of nonhumans, but not permissible for humans to aggress against the basic needs of other humans for that purpose. Yet while this limitation on the scope of the Principle of Nonhuman Preservation seems defensible from a nonanthropocentric perspective, it also seems defensible from an anthropocentric perspective, which, of course, is just what Steverson wanted to deny. Thus, it would seem that the only defensible interpretations of the Principle of Human Preservation and the Principle of Nonhuman Preservation turn out to support rather than oppose my reconciliationist argument.

In objecting to my claim that intrinsic value can come in degrees, Steverson cites Tom Regan as having shown that such a claim makes a category mistake, like claiming that two persons can be half-married to each other (Regan, 1992a). Yet whether or not a category mistake is involved here depends on the particular notion of intrinsic value that one is using. In this context, there are at least two notions of intrinsic value that need to be distinguished. According to one notion of intrinsic value, which we can call agent-centred intrinsic value, to say that *X has intrinsic value* is to say that *X is good as an end for some agent Y* as opposed to saying that *X has instrumental value*, which is to say that *X is good as a means for some agent Y*. Now, according to this notion, intrinsic value does not come in degrees; one can't have more or less of it.[2] But there is another notion of intrinsic value, which we can call recipient-centred intrinsic value, according to which to say that *X has intrinsic value* is to say that *the good of X ought to constrain the way that others use X in pursuing their own interests*. Now it seems to me that recipient-centred intrinsic value, unlike recipient-centred intrinsic value, does allow for the possibility of different degrees of intrinsic value, provided that we can show that the good of some Xs should constrain others more than the good of other Xs. In fact, however, this is just what I have argued—that there *are* good reasons why the good of humans should constrain other humans more than the good of nonhumans. Specifically, they are the reasons of reciprocal altruism and what constitutes permissible defence and preservation as captured by the Principle of Human Defence and the Principle of Human Preservation. These reasons require a degree of preference for humans over nonhumans when the relevant needs of humans are at stake. Assuming, then, that it is possible to show in this way that humans are legitimately constrained more for the good of humans than by the good of nonhumans, it is possible to claim that humans have a greater degree of intrinsic value than nonhumans.[3]

Steverson further argues that those who accept an anthropocentric perspective would still have plausible grounds for rejecting the constraint of the Principle of Disproportionality, even assuming that nonhumans have intrinsic value, although less intrinsic value than humans. Specifically, Steverson denies that humans are always prohibited from satisfying their nonbasic needs by aggressing against the basic needs of nonhumans, despite the intrinsic value of nonhumans. But the only reason that Steverson offers for rejecting this prohibition is that the satisfaction of *many* nonbasic needs of humans may turn out in some utilitarian calculation to outweigh the frustration of a *few* basic needs of nonhumans.[4] Yet when this sort of reasoning is applied to humans, many utilitarians have been reluctant to embrace it (Hare, 1981). This is because it would seem to justify such practices as the sacrifice of the lives of Roman gladiators for the sake of the pleasures of the large crowds who witnessed those gladiator contests. Instead of defending the morality of such gladiator contests, utilitarians have been inclined to favour alternative social practices that preserve the lives of the few while still securing comparable pleasures for the many. It is also understandable why utilitarians have been reluctant to allow such trade-offs of the few for the many. The idea that a person's basic needs can be aggressed against to meet nonbasic needs of others seems opposed to the fundamental respect that we think is reasonably due to each and every person. So while utilitarians admit the theoretical possibility of such trade-offs, they tend to argue that, practically speaking, such trade-offs are unattainable, and so, even from a utilitarian perspective, the principles that we need to appeal to in order to carry on our affairs should not take such trade-offs into account (Hare, 1981).

Moreover, in considering such trade-offs with respect to our human/nonhuman cases, it is difficult to see how the numbers could turn out to be the way that they must turn out in order to be justified—with the satisfaction of nonbasic needs of *many* humans weighed against aggression against the basic needs of only a *few* nonhumans. Usually the numbers seem to be the other way round, with aggression against the basic needs of many nonhumans weighed against the satisfaction of the nonbasic needs of only a few humans. Nevertheless, just as in the analogous case involving only humans, we may not be able to theoretically rule out the possibility of trade-offs involving aggression against the basic needs of a few nonhumans for the sake of the satisfaction of the nonbasic needs of many humans. Nevertheless, even from a utilitarian perspective, we can rule them out practically speaking, excluding them, as I have done, from the principles of environmental justice.

In formulating these answers to Brian Steverson's objections to my reconciliationist argument, I have been led to develop my argument further than I had previously done. Specifically, I have clarified the requirements for others that follow from the actions that are permitted by the Principle of Human Defence and the Principle of Human

Preservation. I have also clarified the notion of intrinsic value that I am endorsing and the grounds on which my claim of greater intrinsic value for humans rests. So I obviously owe Steverson a debt of gratitude for eliciting these clarifications. My hope is that now that I have put the argument, with his help, in its present improved form, he and others will find the argument worthy of further development.

Notes

1 For support here, Steverson cites Singer (1979a, 1979b: 68–71). Singer, however, is arguing against an attempt to base *all* of our moral obligations on reciprocity.

2 Under this interpretation, however, it is possible for something to have both intrinsic value and instrumental value, to be both an end and a means.

3 Given this notion of intrinsic value, I don't see how there is any category mistake in affirming degrees of intrinsic value. In 'Does Environmental Ethics Rest on a Mistake?' Tom Regan argues that the various notions of intrinsic value that do not allow for degrees of intrinsic value do not serve the goals of an environmental ethics very well. I think that he may be right about this, which may be a good reason in favour of my proposed notion of intrinsic value which does allow for degrees of intrinsic value.

4 Steverson also thinks that John Stuart Mill's claim in *Utilitarianism* that it is better to be Socrates dissatisfied than a pig satisfied also somehow supports a preference for nonbasic needs of humans over basic needs of nonhumans. But it isn't clear just how Mill's claim could provide this support. Mill makes his claim in the context of setting out his test of higher and lower pleasures:

> Of two pleasures, if there be one to which all or almost all who have experience of both give a decided preference … that is the more desirable pleasure.

Yet has any human ever really experienced what it is like being a pig? Mill considers cases in which humans actually do prefer lower to high pleasures and claims that the reason why they do so is because they have 'become incapable of the other.' But isn't that just what pigs are—animals that are incapable of our so-called higher pleasures. In order then to interpret Mill's claim so that his test of higher and lower pleasures applies to it, we must interpret it as claiming that it is better for people who are capable of both higher and lower pleasures to experience the higher pleasures (the Socrates-like pleasures) even if that leaves them somewhat discontent than it is for them to experience only lower pleasures (the pig-like pleasures) even if that leaves them perfectly content.

Unfortunately, the trade-offs that we are considering in the context of an environmental ethics are quite different. They are between at least two different entities, not one entity that is capable of being in one of two ways. In fact, aggressing against the basic needs of nonhumans to satisfy the nonbasic needs of humans will frequently involve killing off nonhumans to satisfy the non-basic needs of humans. So we don't have a common entity that is capable of existing in one of two ways as we do in Mill's case. Accordingly, Mill's claim about the preferability of higher to lower pleasures cannot be used to support the satisfaction of nonbasic needs of humans by aggressing against basic needs of nonhumans.

References

Hare, R.M. 1981 *Moral Thinking*. Oxford: Oxford University Press.

Regan, Tom. 1992b 'Does Environmental Ethics Rest on a Mistake?' *The Monist* 75: 161–183.

Singer, Peter. 1979b *Practical Ethics*. Cambridge: Cambridge University Press.

Sterba, James P. 1994 'Reconciling Anthropocentric and Nonanthropocentric Environmental Ethics', *Environmental Values* 3: 229–244.

Sterba, James P. 1995 'From Biocentric Individualism to Biocentric Pluralism', *Environmental Ethics* 17: 191–208.

Steverson, Brian. 1996 'On the Reconciliation of Anthropocentric and Nonanthropocentric Environmental Ethics', *Environmental Values* 5: 349–361.

Evaluating a Case Study

Assessing Embedded Levels

The goal in this series of exercises is for you to be able to write an essay that critically evaluates an environmental problem involving ethical issues. Your essay should include an examination of professional practice as well as the ethical dimensions. In Chapter 3, we discussed how to bring the ethical dimensions to the fore through the use of detection questions. These were put side by side the principles of professional practice.

In this chapter, we compare these two types of issues. This comparison can be accomplished in multiple ways; the one offered here invokes a technique that rates professional practice as having three levels of complexity: surface, medium, and deep. The level of interaction allows you to see at a glance how professional practice issues, cost issues, and ethical issues conflict.

You need a model of some type to evaluate the professional practice issues, cost considerations, and ethical issues that may conflict. When ethical issues and practical issues conflict, you do not *automatically* choose either. Some ethical problems can be solved easily and do not require forgoing the dictates of the professional practice. At other times, an ethical problem must be solved in such a way that professional practices or cost considerations must be overridden.

You need a methodology for comparison. The *embedded concept model* is one such methodology. I illustrate how this works with several examples that employ a chart to clarify the ways the concepts conflict. You may also want to use this technology if you have access to one of the popular computer spreadsheet programs, but the use of a spreadsheet is not necessary. A more conventional approach is to discuss these differences. The spreadsheet is no substitute for solid narrative description, but at the very least it simplifies and makes visual the model I propose.

Case 1

You are the environmental impact officer of a mining company that mines copper in Montana. The most efficient way to operate your mine is via strip mining, by which a portion of the earth (in this case an entire mountain) is removed to expose the ore-bearing earth underneath to cyanide and various other toxic chemicals that are captured within a clay-capped reservoir and treated according to Environmental Protection Agency guidelines. Your company is in legal compliance with all existing laws on the treatment of such waste, but your have learned that although it is in compliance, it is leaching toxic chemicals into the earth, which could infect the region's water table. To change this process is somewhat expensive but well within the company's ability. It involves creating a stronger more effective cap or seal to the leach pond. This probably will solve the problem, but it goes beyond what is required by law. Do you have a duty to do more than the law requires?

Let us examine this situation via professional practice issues, ethical issues, and cost issues. All three of these areas are important in forming an ethical decision.

Professional Practice Issues

1. A professional is required only to follow the law and the guidelines of its professional association. The mining company has obeyed all relevant regulations. However, the mining association has said repeatedly that it intends to be a friend to the environment. Critics say that this is hypocrisy, but you intend to take such statements seriously.
2. Going beyond the law and the association's guidelines could be perceived as raising the standard that other mining companies would be required to follow. Meeting this additional standard could require the use of funds that had not been budgeted.

Ethical Issues

1. When a company receives clearance to begin a mining operation, it must submit an environmental impact statement that promises to maintain the environment essentially as it was—as much as possible. Thus, the company is involved in keeping and maintaining a promise.
2. *Informed* consent is necessary for autonomous decision making.

Cost Issues

1. Creating a better leach pond seal for the waste products is possible but will cut into profits.
2. If profits fall, some people might lose their jobs.

In this simple case, the ethical guidelines override those of the cost or professional issues. That means the ethical guidelines are "easier" to solve. When a great disparity exists between the embeddedness of one alternative as opposed to the other, that direction should drive the decision. One should implement the other side as it is possible. This is not to suggest that either the professional or cost issues are unimportant. Rather, this analysis is useful to determine which are the most embedded.

Thus, in this case, the mining company's embedded status quo arguments are less embedded than implementing the use of the improved seal on its leach pond; therefore, the company should improve the leach pond seal because (a) the professional issues are not deeply embedded, (b) the ethical issues are deeply embedded, and (c) the cost issues are not deeply embedded (and one issue cuts both ways, that is, may actually be an advantage).

Table 4.1 Analysis of the illustration practices at XYZ Mining

	Surface	Medium	Deep
Professional Practice Issues			
A professional is required to follow only the law and the professional association's guidelines		x	
The company may be accused of raising the standard	x		
Ethical Issues			
One's promise to leave the land as it was			x
Only a truly *informed* consent satisfies the conditions of autonomy (as well as the contract with the state)			x
Cost Issues			
New guidelines may affect future profits	x		
Additional costs may be incurred in implementing a new leach pond seal	x		

Case 2

This case is not so simple. You are a regional director at the World Health Organization. One of your duties is to supervise the distribution of birth control devices to women in less-developed countries. The product of choice has been the intrauterine device (IUD) that has proved to be effective and inexpensive. The problem is that in the United States, several hundred users of the IUD have contracted pelvic inflammatory infections that have been linked to use of the IUD. These infections can cause sterility and death. As regional director, you must decide whether to continue to supply IUDs to women in less-developed countries.

There is also the ABC Corporation, a large multinational company that has a considerable inventory of IUDs that it cannot sell in the United States. The company would rather not write off its entire inventory and has consequently made a very attractive offer to sell the World Health Organization all of its existing inventory and to assist in distributing the product regionally.

As regional director, you must decide whether to accept ABC's offer to supply IUDs for the World Health Organization's program for women in less-developed countries.

Professional Practice Issues

1. As a professional in the public health field, your responsibility is to choose public policy that maximizes the health and minimizes the health risks in the general population.
2. Sexual activity without birth control in less-developed countries will lead to an increasing population that, in turn, will lead to severe poverty and mass starvation.
3. Mass starvation kills millions; pelvic inflammatory infections kill hundreds. Thus, it is better to save the many (in the spirit of the profession's mission).

Ethical Issues

1. Each person's life is precious.
2. The end of saving more lives does not justify the means of sacrificing others.

Cost Issues

1. ABC Corporation is willing to give the World Health Organization a substantial price break on its existing inventory of IUDs. This price break will allow the World Health Organization to serve more women of child-bearing age than its original strategic plan had projected. ABC's offer to assist in regional distribution will save the World Health Organization additional money.
2. White knights are not lining up at your door to help you fulfill the mission of this program.

This case differs from Case 1 because the professional, ethical, and cost guidelines are equally embedded. In this case, the dictates of the ethical imperative must be followed because it is more deeply embedded in a person's worldview than is the imperative of professional practice or cost issues. The components of ethics enter the worldview generically as a feature of a person's humanity.[1] The imperatives of professionalism enter the worldview as one of many modes of personal fulfillment; the imperatives of cost enter the worldview as modes of day-to-day practical consumption.

Although many people may create pessimistic scenarios (such as state of nature) to the contrary, a decision such as this case will not cause your death or that of a family member. It may cause you to be discharged, drastically affecting your lifestyle. In the United States (at the writing of this book), making such a decision almost never causes an individual to face starvation.[2]

My experience has been that businesspeople are very prone to hyperbole when they describe the consequences of an ethical decision that entails the loss of money and worldly goods. This overstatement culture has the effect of blocking people from taking the right action because they fear exaggerated consequences.[3]

As with scientific theories, the dictates of a universally binding imperative founded on generic structures trump those of a particular person's individual interests. More details on this appear in the "Evaluating a Case Study" section in Chapter 5.

In this essay, the main concern is the ability to assess the levels of embeddedness. Some common mistakes that my students have made in performing this assessment follow:

1. *Not giving the imperatives of professional practice their due.* Remember that whether you assess embeddedness via a spreadsheet or through discursive paragraphs, you are working from your original analysis of the problem. A failure to uncover all the important facets will be reflected in your depiction of embeddedness. You will notice gaps in the reasoning and will feel that something is missing. If this happens, go back over the issues lists. Rewrite the case in your own words; expand or recast the case in some way. By doing this, you become the author and are forced to recognize key elements in the case as presented.

Table 4.2 Analysis of population control in the less-developed countries

	Surface	Medium	Deep
Professional Practice Issues			
Public health mission to preserve the health of as many as possible			x
Sexual activity without birth control leads to mass starvation			x
The end justifies the means			x
Ethical Issues			
Human life is precious			x
The end does not justify the means			x
Cost Issues			
ABC's inventory can be used to serve many women			x
The World Health Organization needs help from someone or it may be unable to continue this program			x

2. *Seeing everything at the same level of embeddedness*. You need to view embeddedness as a way to describe the degree to which an issue is essential to the case. A less essential issue should be given less consideration. To better understand the essential structure of a professional practice, prepare short justifications of your choice of that element as an issue in the case. As you prepare your justifications, think about each element in its relation to the whole. If that relation could not be different without seriously altering the whole, then it is essential. If you can find substitutes that would work just as well, the relation is incidental.

3. *Listing too many professional, cost, and ethical issues*. This is the flip side to step 1. You have given too much detail that is not essential to the case at hand, or you are listing one issue in a number of different ways. In either event, preparing an essential description of your elements (as in step 2) can help you shorten your issue list to only those required for your evaluation.

Good solid work avoiding these mistakes will enable you to create a more satisfactory result in the argumentative stage, in which you may finally apply your ethical theory to your annotated embeddedness charts.

Macro and Micro Cases

Macro Case 1. As the secretary of the interior, you are about to draft legislation to send to Congress outlining principles of land use in the nation's national park system. The first issue you are considering is access to the parks by vacationing citizens. The most popular parks in the system are well over capacity. Cars move in gridlock along two-lane roads to famous landmarks (such as Old Faithful). Your staff has prepared two solutions to this problem. Jack Development suggested the first solution; he says that the nation's parks are for its citizens to enjoy, but they aren't enjoying them by being stuck in long traffic jams. The answer is to build six-lane roads through the park connected by two-lane roads that will lead tourists to outlying areas. The cost of the project will be supported by increased user fees. "People will be willing to pay more if you give them their money's worth," says Jack.

Cindy Conservation takes a contrary position; she says that Jack's plan will ruin the natural beauty of the parks and harm wildlife tremendously. What Cindy proposes is to limit entry to the parks through several embarkation points. These points would lie just outside the park and consist of parking lots that have a set number of spaces. Cindy would like to set the figure at 75 percent of current levels. From these points of entry, buses powered by natural gas and electricity would ferry people to existing lodges and campgrounds. People could also bicycle into the park if they register first. Hiking would also be permitted with proper registration. The point of this limitation is to offer nature more protection by keeping private automobiles out of our nation's parks. "The parks are being destroyed. We must reverse this trend," says Cindy.

You must craft either Cindy's or Jack's position. To do this, write a scene in which Cindy and Jack argue their respective points of view before you. Be sure that each uses practical, professional, and ethical arguments (with linking principles). Then write a summary of the position you will take and why.

Macro Case 2. You are the secretary of the interior, and the second half of the report you are sending to Congress concerns mining and oil rights for private companies on government land. Presently, these companies pay royalties, but they are nowhere near their market value. Thus, the government is (in effect) subsidizing them. Three groups are trying to lobby you concerning your policy recommendation. The first is an environmental group that exhorts you to stop all mining on federal lands. The second says that mining of reusable minerals (such as copper and gold) should be permitted, but that mining nonreusable minerals and petroleum should cease. This group also wants the royalties raised to market rates. A third group suggests that you leave things as they are because the economy is relatively good and the country cannot afford the human displacement that radical policies might cause.

Write arguments for all three positions, identifying the relevant issues concerning economic impact, professional issues, and ethical issues. After you have done this, write the position you will take to Congress. Be sure to adequately support your position.

Micro Case 1. You are visiting Lemar, your best friend, and Latasha, his wife. Lemar is reading the newspaper, and you are playing chess with Latasha. Suddenly, Lemar exclaims, "Hey, they're going to build a new power plant right here in Hudson County!"

"Oh yeah?" says Latasha. "Where?"

"Just off Route 123 near Backlick Road. On the old Miller Farm, I reckon."

"That's pretty close."

"Yeah. Close is right. Not more than a few miles away."

"What kind of plant are they going to build? Nuclear?"

"No—coal. Lots of cheap coal on the market right now. Going to change things around here, that's for sure." Each of them sighs as if to say, oh well, what can you do?

Then you say, "Is that all there is to it? Just shrug it off with a sigh?"

"What do you want?" asks Lemar. "People need their electricity."

You are taken aback. You want to mention something about values and principles, but you are not sure what to say. Are any ethical principles involved? Does it matter that the old Miller Farm is one of the most beautiful vistas in the valley? Does it matter that the plant will alter everyone's life with more noise, smoke, commotion, and outsiders coming in? What is important here?

Using the principles you have studied, discuss the ethical issues in this situation. Then identify any relevant ethical theory and associated cogent linking principles. With these data, create a response to Lemar and Latasha.

Micro Case 2. Your name is Carmelita. You live near San Francisco, and your town has a voluntary recycling law. The law says people should separate bottles and cans into a blue container and put newspapers into a yellow container (these are free). Yard waste is put into a can with a yard sticker (yearly cost is $25). All other garbage is put into a can with a general sticker (yearly cost $50). The problem is that your husband, Juan, likes to throw his refuse (no matter what it is) into the general garbage pile because he doesn't like to take the time to walk to the end of the kitchen and open the pantry door to find the recycling bins. You have confronted him about this several times, but he says that he can do what he wants because the law is voluntary and he pays the freight for general garbage when he could save money by using the free recycling bins—"It's my business if I want to pay, right?"

You think Juan is wrong and you want to appeal to his mother (the only person he will listen to). Make the argument in terms that will identify the ethical issues involved and connect a moral theory to the situation at hand via linking principles. Outline how you will approach Juan's mother with a few responses in case she disagrees.

Notes

1 For a further discussion of the mechanics, see Chapter 1 of *Basic Ethics*.

2 Of course the dead hero problem comes in here. Would one prefer to be a live coward (here understood to mean a moral coward) or a dead hero (here understood to mean someone who has suffered for his or her beliefs). This is not an easy question and lies at the heart of all discussions of Environmental Ethics.

3 It is not the worst thing in the world to have to step back and live on less. It has been my personal experience that the essential elements of personal happiness have no price tag. Truly supported caring relationships cannot be taken away from you no matter what hard times befall you (except through some unrelated event—such as disease or accident).

Part II

Applied Environmental Problems

5

Pollution and Climate Change

General Overview: In Part II of this volume we will explore various ways that environmental ethics becomes a topic of interest in a concrete, applied way. This means that we will explore various moral problems. It is important for readers to engage these problems with some theoretical standpoint (found in Part I of this book). Without a theoretical perspective by which to defend your solutions to the problems raised, you will fall prey to the anti-realist ethical intuition position in which people *feel* one way or the other based upon some personal immediate grasping. Since these are private, by definition, public dialogue is impossible. This leads away from democratic public decision making and toward oligarchs who will act under the imperative of power.

In this section, two of the most discussed sorts of practical problems are addressed: (1) air and water pollution; and (2) climate change. These two categories are related. But in the United States at the writing of this volume the two principal political parties (Republicans and Democrats) are divided about what the nature of the problem is and how the country (and by extension the world) should respond. Because of these divisions, I predict lively discussions on these topics along these lines.

A. Air and Water Pollution

Overview: Since the beginning of the Industrial Revolution in the nineteenth century, the relationship between factories and transportation and pollution has been generally accepted. This is not a new phenomenon. One question concerns the ability of the environment to accept and "process" this pollution so that the effects that they exhibit are only short-lived. From around 1820 until the 1960s, it was generally thought that nature could simply "absorb" pollutants and all would be fine. But then critical science has kicked in. In the last fifty years, the various scenarios (based upon scientific studies) have been doomsday tales. The only question is *how soon* and *to what degree*.

Environmental Ethics, Second Edition. Edited by Michael Boylan.

In the first essay, I argue that there is a basic human right to clean water and sanitation. The present state of the world is not even close to providing this human right. Various considerations of the origins of the current problem are examined in the context of public health. Then some modest suggestions for beginning the process of positive change are recommended.

In the second essay, Benjamin Hale begins with a little story about swimming pools. If Dodgson owns a swimming pool and Duckworth dumps a 5-gallon bucket of ammonia into Dodgson's swimming pool, many would rightly charge Duckworth with polluting Dodgson's pool. Depending on the facts of the case, many would further charge that, in polluting Dodgson's pool, Duckworth has wronged Dodgson. That is, Duckworth's pollution of Dodgson's pool is wrong. This sentiment stems, presumably, from the simple fact that ammonia is damaging to pools and pool water, and that by dumping the bucket of ammonia in the pool, Duckworth has thereby injured Dodgson.

The rest of the essay engages in ways to think about pollution and what follows from this. Hale begins with examining the "harms" view, the "trespass" view, and the "vice" view, but then moves on to set out a variety of ways to conceptualize pollution and who is to pay for cleaning it up. This conceptual journey is essential because once we have found a way to think about a problem, then we are a long way toward forming a policy to solve it.

Mark Seabright begins his essay by mentioning that in the discourse on environmental policy it is often the case that moral language is used to help support one's case. Because of this fact, Seabright's essay explores what motivates moral claims about environmental issues. In particular, he uses the context of contingent valuation studies to examine several psychological explanations for moral motivations, including moral identity and moral intensity, protected or sacred values, and moral heuristics. Seabright considers the implications of each of these explanations for biases in contingent valuation and, more broadly, for the role of moral concerns in environmental decisions.

B. Climate Change

Overview: The most serious outcome to result from polluting the earth's environment is that it may cause permanent climate change that will be detrimental to life on earth. If we have (as Gewirth and O'Neill argued earlier) duties to future generations, and if we are rendering the planet less habitable for *homo sapiens*, then we are failing in our moral duty. The overwhelming majority of climatologists believe that we are doing just that. But there are others in the polis who demur. They discount scientific studies as biased and part of a group-think clique that they assert presently controls the community of scientists. Such cliques have occurred in the past. But if it is true that the Earth's climate is changing in a dangerous way, then what are we to do about it?

In the first essay, Ruth Irwin argues that part of the typical doomsday scenario posits two factors: climate change and a continually rising population (that mutually intensify each other). But instead of viewing climate change and peak population as a calamity, Irwin proposes that together they constitute conditions for renewal. For example, in the developed countries of the world there is already a decline in birth rates. Because climate change brings into sharp focus what elements of industrialism are sustainable and what elements put us at risk, we have a unique opportunity to revise the model under which we are living to one that is neither utopian nor dystopian. This new paradigm will probably involve a story in which technology saves technology as we simultaneously undergo significant cultural changes.

In his essay, Seumas Miller makes use of several concepts, which he set out in more detail in his 2010 book, *The Moral Foundations of Social Institutions: A Philosophical Study*. In this instance, he addresses the issue of collective moral responsibility for climate change. In the first section, he outlines his account of joint action, including joint epistemic action, as a necessary preliminary to elaborating his account of collective moral responsibility in the second section. In the third and final section, he applies this account of collective moral responsibility to the matter of human-induced, harmful climate change.

A. Air and Water Pollution

Blue Water

MICHAEL BOYLAN

What is blue water? Blue water is clean, potable water. It is free from parasites and chemical additives that are toxic to most life on earth. In short, blue water is necessary for life. However, paradoxically, this essential ingredient is beginning to be in short supply. At the same time, the population of the world is increasing. The WHO (2000) estimates that each person in northern climates needs 2–3 liters of water a day. This increases to 6–10 liters in hot equatorial climates. This creates a complex problem as one of the essential components of survival becomes more scarce. Lack of blue water puts up to 3.5 billion people annually at risk of disease (Ahmed 2002).[1] Every 8 seconds a child dies from drinking unclean water (Children's Water Fund 2004). With an increasing population, pollution, global business investment, and geopolitics the issue of scarcity is critical (Global Water Futures 2005; Boberg 2006).

This essay will introduce the reader to the problem of water, first as a human right and, second, within the context of public health. Turning to solutions, the third goal is to suggest a classification of the arena of action and finally to what might be done within that arena so that some progress might be made that will satisfy public health concerns within the context of human rights.

Water and Human Rights

It is the position of this essay that public health policy (whether it be national or international) should be based upon moral principles rather than on mere perceived expediency (Boylan 2004b, 2011). This accepted, what is the status of the moral right to water? Most of us would admit that water is very important—given that it is a biological necessity for life on a very regular basis. But how should we understand this? In order to obtain clarity on the issue, we must return to the foundation of all ethical rights and duties. Now, of course, these are justified in various ways according to the normative theory that is put forth by the proponent.[2] This author puts forth a rights-based theory that is justified by the natural human inclination toward purposive action (Boylan 2004a: chs 1–2). Those goods most necessary for purposive action are those goods to which all potential agents have the strongest claim (i.e., they are most embedded regarding the foundations of the possibility of action). The claims are derived via biological, philosophical, psychological, and anthropological analyses of *homo sapiens*, as such. It is not a claim of Jamal or Juanita as individuals, but is a species-level attribution.

I have tried to sort out these sorts of claims hierarchically as follows:

Table 5.1 The Table of Embeddedness[3]

Basic goods

Level One: *Most Deeply Embedded*[4] (that which is absolutely necessary for human action): food and water/sanitation, clothing, shelter, protection from unwarranted bodily harm (including basic health care).

Level Two: *Deeply Embedded* (that which is necessary for effective basic action within any given society):

- literacy in the language of the country;
- basic mathematical skills;
- other fundamental skills necessary to be an effective agent in that country, e.g., in the United States some computer literacy is necessary,
- some familiarity with the culture and history of the country in which one lives;
- the assurance that those you interact with are not lying to promote their own interests;
- the assurance that those you interact with will recognize your human dignity (as per above) and not exploit you as a means only;
- basic human rights such as those listed in the US Bill of Rights and the United Nations Universal Declaration of Human Rights.

Secondary goods

Level One: *Life Enhancing* (medium to high–medium embeddedness):

- basic societal respect;
- equal opportunity to compete for the prudential goods of society;
- ability to pursue a life plan according to the personal worldview imperative;
- ability to participate equally as an agent in the shared community worldview imperative.

Level Two: *Useful* (medium to low–medium embeddedness):

- ability to utilize one's real and portable property in the manner one chooses;

Table 5.1 (Continued)

- ability to gain from and exploit the consequences of one's labor regardless of starting point;
- ability to pursue goods that are generally owned by most citizens, e.g., in the United States today a telephone, television, and automobile would fit into this class.

Level Three: *Luxurious* (low embeddedness):

- ability to pursue goods that are pleasant, even though they are far removed from action and from the expectations of most citizens within a given country, e.g., in the United States today a European vacation would fit into this class;
- ability to exert one's will so that one might extract a disproportionate share of society's resources for one's own use.

If readers would accept the Table of Embeddedness (or something like it) as the grounds for species' rights claims, then all individuals within the species would also possess these claims on the basis of logical subsumption. If rights and duties are correlative, then all others have a duty to provide the claimant his or her rights claims (subject only to the caveat of "ought implies can"). In *A Just Society* (Boylan 2004a), I concentrate upon duties within a society, but there is no reason to stop there. In *Morality and Global Justice*, I extend this to all people on Earth through an extended community worldview imperative:

> Each agent must educate himself as much as he is able about the peoples of the world—their access to the basic goods of agency, their essential commonly held cultural values, and their governmental and institutional structures—in order that he might individually and collectively accept the duties that ensue from those peoples' legitimate rights claims, and to act accordingly within what is aspirationally possible. (Boylan 2011)

In this way the rights claims based upon the Table of Embeddedness are extended to every person on Earth *against* every person on Earth: we are all in this together. Since water is named as a first-level basic good, and since this is the strongest right claim (because it is most highly embedded to the possibility of human action), then the claim right to water is as strong as any other claim right, and the duty to provide all with potable water is also the highest.

Various other rights claims that get in the way of providing water to all are weaker on the Table of Embeddedness. For example, political liberties (often sought via war and embargos) are a level two basic good.[5] Visions of social castes, such as aristocratic or oligarchic orderings, are level one secondary goods. Economic development falls either at level two secondary or level three secondary goods (depending upon net profitability and proximity to essential action). All of these pretenders (and others) are less embedded than the claim for clean water. Thus, in a conflict, the right to clean water wins every time.

The argument becomes even stronger when one realizes that water when adulterated can also turn into a source of unwarranted bodily harm. Thus, in two respects the right to potable water is very strong indeed. In order to appreciate this in greater detail, let's turn to the basic areas where water becomes a crucial agent in maintaining public health.[6]

Water and Public Health

There are four generally accepted categories of water as a contributing agent to human disease (Gleick 2004: 7–9; Whiteford and Whiteford 2005: 9–10). These are:

1. *Water-borne diseases*. These diseases occur directly as an individual drinks contaminated water. The principal cause of this contamination is human waste. Untreated waste gives rise to protozoan, bacterial, and viral diseases. These most commonly attack the human intestines. Specific water-borne diseases include cholera, typhoid, hepatitis, ameobiasis, giardiasis, *Taenia solium* taeniasis, ascariasis, hookworm, trichuriasis, and strongyloidiasis. These often attack groups of people causing local epidemics that are often deadly.
2. *Water-washed diseases*. These diseases occur when there is not enough water for proper hygiene or cooking sanitation. People cannot rid themselves of contaminants with which they might come in contact and as a result become ill with diseases such as trachoma, typhus, and diarrheal diseases.
3. *Water-based diseases*. These diseases come from hosts that live in water during part or all of their life cycles. When people bathe, swim, or wash their clothing, the contaminated water may come into contact with their skin. Diseases such as schistosomiasis, dracunculiasis, lung flukes (caused by carrier snails) affect as many as 200 million people in seventy countries (WHO 2000). Elimination of such "black water" would solve this source of disease.
4. *Water-related insect vectors*. These diseases include those spread by insects, such as mosquitoes, that breed in water. These insects infect humans with malaria, onchocerciasis (river blindness), West Nile fevers, yellow fever, and dengue fever.

One should also add to this list the sanitation infrastructure. In most of the world, this infrastructure is lacking or incomplete (WHO 2000; Babbitt and Reilly 2005). With almost 60% of the world's population at risk of death because from one or more of these four categories (and their causal connections with poor sanitation), we are not very far along the road toward reaching the United Nations' Millennium Development Goal 7, target 10 to "halve by 2015 the proportion of people without sustainable access to safe drinking water" (UNDP 2003).

Ever since the classic case of Dr John Snow in the mid-nineteenth century in London, who discovered that a common source (the Broad Street pump) was the cause of a cholera outbreak, public health officials have been keen on using the powerful tool of water control for short-term disease control and sanitation/pollution efforts for long-term solutions (Johnson 2006; Hempel 2007).

In Dr Snow's London, the solution was rather straightforward. There was only one country involved and a limited number of polluting sources. In the case of modern water contamination, it can be more complicated (Barah 1996; Börkey 2006; Stevens 2006). There are many players and interests at stake. This makes crafting a solution more complicated. In order to make suggestions on what might be done, it is necessary to examine the various stakeholders and power brokers to set the stage for our drama.

A Description of the Action Arena

There are various actors in our action arena. Those that this section will examine are: nature, humankind's basic activities, international organizations and treaties, global corporations, and intranational dynamics.

Nature. Genuine water availability is a function of the hydrological cycle. The cycle works this way: the sun's heat evaporates water into the atmosphere. The heat of the sun, the dryness of the prevailing air, and the wind *control the speed* of this process. The heated liquid becomes gas. This gas rises in the atmosphere, becomes colder, and as a result condenses into precipitation. The water returns to terrestrial land striking the soil, streams and lakes, and man-made coverings. The water also returns to marine (ocean) locales. Marine water is returned by evaporation, while terrestrial water is also returned by flora in the form of transpiration.

The total amount of water on earth is fixed. It is continually changing from solid to liquid to gas. It is a self-renewing cycle. A sense of where water is located can be set out per Figure 5.1.

Figure 5.1 illustrates how most water on the planet is marine saltwater (not proximately useful for domestic activities of life). For human needs, the most important of these water reservoirs is surface terrestrial water in lakes and rivers, and underground terrestrial water. These are the primary, proximate sources of potable water. The large geographic regions that support these rivers, lakes, and underground terrestrial water are called water basins (Boberg 2005). For example, there is a single water basin supporting Lake Superior that extends across the states of Minnesota and Wisconsin and into Ontario, Canada. This is important. The geography of the land creates the conditions that make rainwater and melted snow move in particular directions. This geography does not recognize artificial man-made boundaries such as nations and intranational divisions. Because of their size, water-basin management can be rather difficult (Fischendler and Freitelson 2005).

Smaller divisions within water basins are called watersheds. Watersheds are topographical units that are more amenable to local control. Because of their more limited scope there has been more success in creating and executing water management programs within watersheds.

The strategy for water management of watersheds is to focus upon the particular ecosystem that supports it. Since an ecosystem is naturally self-sustaining and interactive, it provides a good model for adaptation and management. By beginning with the natural sustainable dynamic, we have a pattern or goal to try to re-create or approximate. Water basins are more difficult because they are affected by many different ecosystems and may cut across more than one biome. This means that many different strategies must be undertaken (according to the circumstances) and that the interaction between these may result in counterproductive outcomes.

Terrestrial atmosphere: 4.5
Marine atmosphere: 1.1
Ice and snow: 43 500
Biomas: 2.0
Surface terrestrial water: 350
Rivers: 35.0
Underground terrestrial water: 15 300
Marine: 1 400 000
Terrestrial precipitation: 107.0
Terrestrial evaporation and transpiration: 71.0
Marine precipitation: 398.0
Marine evaporation: 434.0
Volumes in 10^{15} kg (10^3 km^3)
Fluxes in 10^{15} kg yr^{-1} (10^3 km^3 yr^{-1})
(Source: National Resources Canada).

Figure 5.1 Where water is on earth

It is important to emphasize that we should not be overly anthropocentric about water management. It is not only humans that need water. There are three other natural classes that depend upon water to maintain their identity. The first of these is the land itself. The structural integrity of hills, topsoil, and even mountains over time can be altered by too much or too little water. If one considers the problem from a land ethics point of view, then water management is important to maintain the land as it is (Leopold 1949). Many in the United States have not considered the needs of the land itself. Strip mining and poor agricultural practices have often had the effect of altering the character of the land—and the character of the land is a crucial element in the creation of ecosystems and biomes.

Sometimes the land can be a source of pollution. This often occurs due to extreme weather conditions in which large areas of land mix with water and block out sunlight and possibly affect the oxygen content of water. However, this is a sporadic rather than a regular occurrence.

Second is the flora. Plants need water, minerals, and sunlight to survive. Minerals are a function of the land's character. Water availability is determined by the water basin and watershed dynamics. Sunlight is sensitive to the atmospheric medium that separates plants from sunlight entering the earth's exosphere. Without adequate water, plants will die. When plants die they affect the land because they cease to fix minerals into the soil as well as to maintain topsoil. Again, the entire ecosystem or biome can significantly alter.

Third is the fauna. Animals need clean water to stay alive and complete their life cycle. Animals provide nourishment to plants through their excretions and the decomposition of their bodies. They also participate in helping to pollinate plants and to promote vigorous growth by their eating habits.

Both flora and fauna can contribute to water contamination. In the first case, dead trees (for example) can become habitats for bacteria that are harmful to other ecosystem members. In the second case, animal defecation and animal carcasses both provide more virulent host opportunities for parasites and bacteria to thrive. These events can work to the detriment of other animals that drink from the stream or pond.

It is most often the case that the question of water is viewed from the anthropocentric viewpoint, but it is important to see the biocentric position, as well.

Humankind. Of course, humans (like other animals) require clean water to stay alive and complete their life cycles. Humans drink water and use it to wash themselves and to clean food preparation items and apparel (domestic usages). In addition, because humans are tool-making creatures and bent on habitat alteration, humans require water for many of their life activities. In fact, unlike other animals, humans use water most to support these activities. Worldwide humans use water for the following classes of action: agriculture, 70%; industry, 20%; and domestic (daily life of drinking, cooking, bathing, washing dishes, etc.), 10%. This works out differently according to the region of the world involved.

What Table 5.2 tells us is that most of the water that humans use is not directly concerned with the activities of day-to-day living (domestic uses). Other animals only consume water for domestic purposes, and those purposes are limited to drinking and

Table 5.2 How water is used around the world

	Agricultural (%)	Domestic (%)	Industry (%)
Europe	40	15	45
North America	50	10	40
Australia/Oceania	60	28	12
South America	62	25	13
Africa	80	15	5
Asia	70	10	20

Source: Boberg (2005).

sometimes to bathing. Because 90% of fresh water usage worldwide is involved in agriculture (most often for the purpose of irrigation) and industry, this may provide an area of hope for the future, *if* better and more efficient practices are developed. At present, both agriculture and industry are great sources of pollution. In agriculture, fertilizers mix with the water. In most cases this means mixing human and animal fecal matter into water that will runoff into either ground water (affecting the watershed) or into local streams and lakes. This mixture of water and fecal matter creates a breeding ground for parasites, bacteria, and viruses that will constitute a threat to the health of humans and animals.

When farmers use chemical fertilizers the situation is not much better. Chemical fertilizers can also affect the ecosystems of rivers, lakes, and marine bodies of water. These chemicals act as poison and can have the effect of killing large numbers of animals, as well as affecting human health by raising the risk of cancer and other diseases.

Industrial wastes are much like the chemical runoff from farms, except the by-products are often more toxic. Some extreme cases, such as Love Canal, can cause epidemic illness that is often fatal (Reed 2002). Thus the activities of humans constitute a real threat to clean water. This exponentially exceeds the impact of the land or fauna or flora upon the supply of clean water.

Social/political entities. Since humans deleteriously affect water so much, it is useful to identify certain combinations of humans and their behaviors as key actors in the tragedy of water contamination. These entities are the social and political constructs of human culture. Beginning with the largest, they include international organizations (such as the United Nations, and its various operational bodies such as the World Health Organization, and the policies and treaties that flow from these). Other international bodies, such as the World Bank, can also play pivotal roles in the financing of public health initiatives that might not otherwise occur.

Second, there are international companies whose business ventures within a country often play a pivotal role in the consequent water pollution. As was noted in Table 5.2, this ensuing industrial impact can be significant in total water usage. And baring governmental restraints (corporations are often loath to lower their bottom line by making investments that have no direct shareholder value, such as voluntary pollution controls), there is no realistic change in sight.

Third, are the international relations between countries. Since water basins are often situated over extended geographic regions that overlap to two or more countries, what happens in one place can have an immediate effect in another. This requires cooperation. But what if relations between the countries are strained? The result, sad to say, is often close to the worst possible outcome.

Lastly, is the role of intracountry, local government. Local populations see water as an asset to their own communities. Their interests may be different from other localities. This is similar to the problem between countries, with the exception that within one nation it is often easier to find some sort of peaceful, political resolution of the problem.

Thus, the stage is set with the players and their props. Now we must view the agents of crisis that bring our drama to a climax.

Key Obstacles to Progress

The plot thickens in our drama as we set out some of the underlying conflicts between our leading characters. This essay will highlight two classes of conflict: humankind versus nature and social/political conflicts.

Humankind versus nature. The preeminent conflict concerning water between humans and nature, as such, revolves around agriculture. As we saw in Table 5.2, agriculture uses up to 80% of a region's water resources. This is more the case in poorer countries than in rich ones. The poorer countries are those with the fewest indigenous resources to address the problem. Because of the fertilizer problem (mentioned earlier), there is a continual problem with finding clean water due to water-borne and water-based factors. But there are also nature issues in the artificial re-creation of water basins. This is often accomplished by the construction of large dams. Dams are often created for water management. The principal aims are controlled irrigation and electricity. But the construction of dams comes at a price. By interrupting the natural flow of water, ecosystems, along with the animals and plants they support, are greatly disrupted.

Those living on the streams that have been diverted will likely suffer from water-washed factors. The new body of reservoir water may (unless proper sanitation measures are observed) be subject to water-borne disease and new habitats for water-related insect vectors. Thus, dams can be the instruments of disease (Johnson, 2005; Manderson and Huang 2005). Dams also exemplify water allocation changes with winners and losers.

In short, the law of unintended consequences is so prevalent with large water-management projects that it is essential that as much caution as possible be used. This is often called the principle of precautionary reason.

Humans can live with nature (even sloppily) without much incident, as long as the human population does not become too large. Just like any other animal species, when one exceeds its sustainability ratio, given a particular ecosystem in a particular time, then problems occur. In nature, starvation and disease step in to cull the numbers. In the case of humans, this is an unethical solution when we have the power to stop it (*contra* Malthus 1798). This is because each human has a claim right to level one basic goods.

However, often we move in this direction indirectly when we create opaque contexts. In an opaque context, two synonymous entities are not linked due to the mode of expression.[7] Thus, if I am correct about this, people do not interrupt the water cycle because they want to cause disease and death. Rather, they do so because they have some other, immediate prudential aim in mind. The fact that the aim will *also* cause disease and death is not seen (because of the context).

This may *explain* why people act to disrupt the cycle when their own personal needs are at stake, but it does not *justify it*. Dams and other alterations of the natural flow of waters to other regions (such as in the United States from the Colorado River to California for irrigation; Glenn *et al.* 1996; Rowell *et al.* 2005) are examples of altering the hydrological cycle. As per above, when we interfere with natural systems, we do so at our peril. We may be involved in artificially raising expectations in the region receiving the water, and at the same time harming the source of that water by removing the mass of liquid from its geographically situated hydrological cycle location. Thus, the most important point about the human–nature conflict is the potential long-term damage that interruption and degradation of this cycle can cause.

Social/political conflicts. The next area to consider concerns interhuman constructions. First, there is economic development. There are at least two dynamics at play here: industry, as such, and the effects of globalization. As we saw in the last section, industry uses up to 45% of a region's water. Aside from the problems mentioned earlier about untreated runoff from industry, there is the further problem of the commercialization of water (Mulreany *et al.* 2006; Payen 2006). Privatization of water management in various poorer countries around the world has had the affect of limiting domestic access to poorer people within the society (Guillet 2005; Whiteford and Cortez 2005). This is because the goal of private companies (without public oversight) (Boylan 2008) is profit. The social goals of equal access to clean water among all segments of society is not in step with the private goal of returning shareholder value. The most common way access is restricted is by price. This creates a shortage of water among the poor and an increase in water-washed disease. The poor often turn to untreated water and are then subject to water-borne disease as well.

Even in the G-8 wealthy countries, the commercialization of drinking water occurs. An example of this is bottled water, sales of which have been increasing by 10% per year (Gleick 2004). Bottled water represents a possible move toward making this the option of choice for human consumption. But in 2003 bottled water cost as much as US$1000 per m^3 in California, while municipal water in the same locale is US$1 per m³. This is an example of a paradigm of transferring attractive potable water to a high-cost delivery system, where the quality of the water is not significantly better than the municipal water (Gleick 2004). One could imagine a possible scenario in which bottled water acquires 80% + market share and local governments decide to be less diligent in maintaining the quality of municipal water for drinking (thinking that most people *buy* their drinking water via bottled water). With an 80% + market share this is probably a true assumption. But what about the other 20%? These would be the people who could not afford to pay the prices for bottled water. They would then be subject to water-washed and water-borne diseases. It is not too great a stretch to imagine a future scenario not too much different from this. The commercialization of water, even in affluent countries, can pose potential risks.

Further, the overlay of globalization intensifies some of these problems and adds new ones. For example, the scarcity problem in Equator created a water-borne cholera outbreak that was focused in poor areas (Whiteford 2005). Also, globalization has led to deregulation through treaties designed to nurture economic growth, for example, NAFTA and FTAA. But some of the regulations that have been scrapped protected water and the environment. Sometimes, a water payment system is set in place in which water pollution levels can be bought and sold in an effort to lower macro contamination. But often the effect is to transfer water protection away from the poor and dispossessed to the affluent centers of industrial wealth (Hong 2000).

This essay has taken the position that water is a level one basic good of agency. Thus, there is no justification that it be treated as a level two or level three secondary good subject to barter and commercialization. The nature of basic goods is that they are commonly claimed and cooperatively delivered. Systems of capitalistic distribution that aim at efficiency at the expense of equity should not be the default distribution mechanisms of basic goods of agency (Boylan 2004a).

The second deals with the dynamics of social discrimination. For purposes of brevity let us confine ourselves to gender and economic differences. In much of the developing world (as mentioned above) poor areas are often severely short-changed in being provided with potable water and proper sanitation. Since it is often the case that the preponderance of those most affected in these situations are women and children (Ferguson 2005), unequal access to clean water and adequate sanitation ends up as de facto gender discrimination. This is especially compounded in sub-Saharan Africa, where there is an epidemic of HIV/AIDS. Poor women are statistically more at risk in this region and thus their immune systems are compromised. This puts the female and juvenile population at even greater peril in the face of contaminated water. People with compromised immune systems are more likely to contract serious diseases that they otherwise might have been able to fight off. Thus, the availability of clean water further underscores the sorry plight of poor women and children in developing countries.

The social and political causes continue to haunt subsistence societies with a markedly higher differential impact upon marginalized peoples. This is hardly an appropriate response to delivering a good to which all humans have a basic claim right. The plot has reached its crisis.

A Few Modest Proposals

The clean water debate in developing countries has largely been driven by the World Bank, which has sought to instigate competitive, market-based solutions to problems that I argue above are really cooperative domains requiring competent government oversight. The current system is disintegrating quickly. Some restorative action is desperately needed. Here are a few modest proposals that this author feels will begin the process of recovery.

Conceptual.

1. Public health principles should be guided by morality (e.g., valid claim rights).
2. There should be a general acceptance that clean water and sanitation is a level one basic good. Since all basic goods constitute claim rights that entail correlative duties, the entire world must accept its duty to provide all people on the planet with clean water and sanitation. This is a strong moral ought.
3. There should be a general acceptance that the interests of the poor, women, and children, etc. are included in No. 2.
4. There should be a general acceptance that natural environmental systems be respected. The principle of precautionary reason should always be applied when tampering with any ecosystem, biome, watershed, or water basin.
5. All interruptions in the natural order should be required to meet the burden of proof that the intervention will create a sustainable outcome. This thesis should be subjected to public and scientific scrutiny before proceeding.
6. Economic development should not be mixed up with executing moral duty. If option A will give more economic development at the expense of the poor, and if option B will give less economic development but recognize the societal duty to provide clean water and sanitation to all, then B should trump A.[8]

Concrete.

1. International organizations, such as the World Bank, should not try to mix evangelical capitalism in their development grants to subsistent societies.
2. Competition and commercialization of water as a resource should be avoided until all citizens within a society have access to clean water and sanitation.
3. An international body with stature, such as the United Nations, the WHO, the IMF, or the World Bank, should monitor all new water projects with respect to the principle of precautionary reason and environmental sustainability (above).
4. The wealthy nations of the world should devote substantial resources (progressively: according to their ability to pay) toward the capitalization of substantial sanitation and water purification projects at both the national and local levels in subsistent societies (monitored as per No. 3).
5. Wealthy societies should look within their own countries in order to avoid compromising the availability of water for domestic use (including the monitoring of agricultural and industrial pollution).

6. A binding system of arbitration should be established to adjudicate international disputes concerning pollution and water shed / water basin management as well as verifiable alterations in the hydrological cycle within a region.

Conclusion

This essay has argued that every person on earth has a very strong claim right to clean water. The sad reality is that a large portion of the world lacks potable water and proper sanitation. This fact creates a nest of public health problems—mostly due to the ensuing infectious diseases and parasites via the modes of water-borne and water-based situations. Lack of water (water-washed) and water-related insect vectors are also sources of morbidity and mortality. Too often those who are *not* subject to these public health challenges have met these states of affairs with a shrug of the shoulders. This reaction is unacceptable. The solutions that have been tried over the past twenty years have not really been effective. This is because they have been aimed at the affluent segments of society. The situation of those billions who constitute the poor are not improved by capitalist-inspired market solutions. Level one basic goods require concerned, competent governmental oversight for the sake of society. We are about to begin the final act of our drama. Let us do everything we can to avoid our drama becoming a human tragedy.

Notes

1 It should be noted that here and elsewhere the availability of clean water is also linked to the issue of sanitation.
2 I discuss some of these fundamental justifications in Boylan (2009).
3 Boylan (2004a: ch. 3).
4 "Embedded" means proximity to the fundamental goods that allow the possibility of purposive action.
5 Some would disagree here, as per Düwell (2009) who rank liberty alongside food, water, clothing, etc.
6 Boylan (2004a: Pt Two), makes the case that because the justification is at the species level, individual rights claims naturally can be attributed to all subsets within the species: countries, regions, ethnic groups, etc.
7 For example, "'Tully was a Roman' is trochaic while 'Cicero was a Roman' is not trochaic," even though Tully is a synonym of Cicero. Synonyms should render an equal context, unless there is another variable at hand: here the scansion of the lead word. When the context of expression makes synonymous relationships unclear, then there is an opaque context (Quine 1960: 142–146).
8 In Boylan (2004a: ch. 8) there are some further nuances to this.

References

Ahmed, A.K. (2002) "Serious Environmental and Public Health Impacts of Water-related Diseases and Lack of Sanitation on Adults and Children: A Brief Summary," available at: www.cec.org/files/pdf/POLLUTANTS/karim_ahmed.pdf, accessed January 15, 2007.

Babbitt, Harriet C. and William K. Reilly (2005) "A Silent Tsunami: The Urgent Need for Clean Water and Sanitation," Washington, DC: Aspen Institute.

Barah, B.C. (1996) *Traditional Water Harvesting Systems in India*, New Delhi: John Wiley Eastern.

Boberg, Jill (2005) *Liquid Assets: How Demographic Changes and Water Management Policies Affect Freshwater Resources*, Santa Monica, CA: Rand Corporation.

Boberg, Jill (2006) "One World, One Well: How Populations can Grow on a Finite Water Supply," *Rand Review*, 30(1): 12–15.

Börkey, Peter (2006) "Safe Water: A Quality Conundrum," *Organization for Economic Cooperation and Development Observer*, 254: 16–18.

Boylan, Michael (2004a) *A Just Society*, Lanham, MD: Rowman & Littlefield.

Boylan, Michael (2004b) "The Moral Imperative to Maintain Public Health," in *Public Health Policy and Ethics* (ed. Michael Boylan), Dordrecht: Kluwer/Springer; pp. xvii–xxxiv.

Boylan, Michael (2008) "Medical Pharmaceuticals and Distributive Justice," *Cambridge Quarterly of Healthcare Ethics*, 17 (1): 32–46.

Boylan, Michael (2009) *Basic Ethics*, 2nd edn, Upper Saddle River, NJ: Prentice Hall.

Boylan, Michael (2011) *Morality and Global Justice: Justifications and Applications*, Boulder, CO: Westview.

Children's Water Fund (2004) "Did You Know: Facts," available at: www.childrenswaterfund.org, accessed May 26, 2004.

Düwell, Marcus (2009) "On the Possibility of a Hierarchy of Moral Goods," in *Morality and Justice: Reading Boylan's A Just Society* (ed. John-Stewart Gordon), Lanham, MD: Lexington; pp. 71–80.

Ferguson, Anne (2005) "Water Reform, Gender, and HIV/AIDS," in *Globalization, Water, and Health: Resource Management in Times of Scarcity* (eds L. Whiteford and S. Whiteford), Oxford: James Currey; pp. 45–66.

Fischendler, Itay and Eran Feitelson (2005) "The Formation and Viability of a Non-basin Water Management: The US–Canada Case," *Geoforum*, 36 (6): 792–804.

Gleick, Peter H. (2004) *The World's Water 2004–2005: The Biennial Report on Freshwater Resources*, Washington, DC and London: Covelo and Island Press.

Glenn, Edward P., Christopher Lee, and Richard Felger (1996) *Conservation Biology*, 10: 1175–1186.

Global Water Futures (2005) "Addressing Our Global Water Future," Center for Strategic and International Studies, Sandia National Laboratories, September 30.

Guillet, David (2005) "Water Management Reforms, Farmer-managed Irrigation Systems, and Food Security: The Spanish Experience," in *Globalization, Water, and Health: Resource Management in Times of Scarcity* (eds L. Whiteford and S. Whiteford), Oxford: James Currey; pp. 185–208.

Hempel, Sandra (2007) *The Strange Case of the Broad Street Pump*, Berkeley, CA: University of California Press.

Hong, Evelyne (2000) "Globalization and the Impact on Health: A Third World Perspective," paper presented at the Peoples' Health Assembly, Savar, Bangladesh.

Johnson, Barbara Rose (2005) "The Commodification of Water and the Human Dimensions of Manufactured Scarcity," in *Globalization, Water, and Health: Resource Management in Times of Scarcity* (eds L. Whiteford and S. Whiteford), Oxford: James Currey; pp. 133–152.

Johnson, Steven (2006) *The Ghost Map*, New York: Riverhead Books.

Leopold, Aldo (1949) *A Sand Country Alamac: and Sketches Here and There*, Oxford: Oxford University Press.

Malthus, Thomas (1798) *An Essay on the Principles of Population*, London: J. Johnson.

Manderson, Lenore and Yixin Huang (2005) "Water, Vectorborne Disease, and Gender: Schistosomiasis in Rural China," in *Globalization, Water, and Health: Resource Management in Times of Scarcity* (eds L. Whiteford and S. Whiteford), Oxford: James Currey; pp. 67–84.

Mulreany, John P., Sule Calikoglu, Sonia Ruiz, and Jason W. Sapsin (2006) "Water Privatization and Public Health," *Pan American Public Health*, 19 (1): 23–32.

National Resources Canada (2005) "Weathering the Changes: Climate Change in Ontario," *Climate Change in Canada: Our Water*, available at: http://adaptation.nrcan.gc.ca/posters/articles/on_05_en.asp?Region=on&language=en.

Payen, Gérard (2005) "Water Business," *Organization for Economic Cooperation and Development Observer*, 254: 24–25.

Quine, Willard Van Orman (1960). *Word and Object*. Cambridge, MA: MIT Press.

Reed, Jennifer Bond (2002) *Love Canal*, New York: Chelsea House.

Rowell, Kirsten, Karl Flessa, and David Dettmen (2005) "The Importance of Colorado River Flow to Nursery Habitats of the Gulf Corvina," *Canadian Journal of Fisheries and Aquatic Sciences*, 62 (12): 2874–2885.

Stevens, Barrie (2006) "Assessing the Risks," *Organization for Economic Cooperation and Development Observer*, 254: 26–27.

United Nations Development Programme (UNDP), Development Goals, available at: http://www.undp.org/mdg and http://www.worldbank.org/data, accessed January 15, 2007.

Whiteford, Linda (2005) "Casualties in the Globalization of Water," in *Globalization, Water, and Health: Resource Management in Times of Scarcity* (eds L. Whiteford and S. Whiteford), Oxford: James Currey; pp. 24–44.
Whiteford, Linda and Scott Whiteford (eds) (2005) *Globalization, Water, and Health: Resource Management in Times of Scarcity*, Oxford: James Currey.
Whiteford, Scott and Alfonso Cortez-Lara (2005) "Good to the Last Drop: The Political Ecology of Water and Health on the Border," in *Globalization, Water, and Health: Resource Management in Times of Scarcity* (eds L. Whiteford and S. Whiteford), Oxford: James Currey; pp. 231–254.
World Health Organization (WHO) (2000) "Global Water Supply and Sanitation Assessment 2000 Report," available at: www.who.int/entity/water_sanitation_health/monitoring/globalassess/en, accessed January 15, 2007.

Polluting and Unpolluting

Benjamin Hale

If Dodgson owns a swimming pool and Duckworth dumps a 5-gallon bucket of ammonia into Dodgson's swimming pool, many would rightly charge Duckworth with polluting Dodgson's pool. Depending on the facts of the case, many would further charge that, in polluting Dodgson's pool, Duckworth has wronged Dodgson. That is, Duckworth's pollution of Dodgson's pool is wrong. This sentiment stems, presumably, from the simple fact that ammonia is damaging to pools and pool water, and that by dumping the bucket of ammonia in the pool, Duckworth has thereby injured Dodgson.

The degree of wrongness of Duckworth's action may well be mitigated by external factors, of course. Duckworth's pollution of Dodgson's pool may be a case of malicious vandalism, or it may easily have been an accident. Depending on the facts, Dodgson may have more reason to forgive Duckworth in one case than in another. This much seems clear enough. It is also possible that Dodgson may have asked Duckworth to put the ammonia in the water, perhaps if Dodgson were a pool manager and Duckworth his assistant, or if Dodgson were filming a movie and Duckworth were in place to create a toxic fog on the surface of the pool. So it is not clear, from the mere fact that Duckworth has dumped ammonia in Dodgson's pool, and therefore polluted the pool with ammonia, that he has therefore wronged Dodgson. Most readers will likely accept these explanations as well.

Nevertheless, many people think that pollution is wrong, and that everything else being equal, dumping ammonia in a person's pool is wrong. Many people further believe that what makes pollution wrong, or what makes dumping ammonia wrong, is that it is harmful. The question for this essay relates to the wrong of pollution, or by extension, the wrong of environmental damage. Does the wrong of pollution consist fundamentally in the harm-causing effects of sullying some environment? Or is there something more?

On one hand, the problem with polluting seems obvious: polluting degrades the environment, in this case, the pool, but in many other cases the natural environment. Closer examination, however, reveals several possible answers.

At least three alternatives present themselves:

- *the harms view*: that pollution devalues the environment, either intrinsically or extrinsically;
- *the trespass view*: that pollution disrespects and / or trespasses on the rights of others;
- *the vice view*: that polluting is not the sort of thing that a person of upstanding or virtuous moral character would do.

I will argue against the harms view here, with an eye toward articulating a somewhat more robust defense of the trespass view. I believe the harms view to be the dominant position, and thus in need of critical assessment. The view is woefully insufficient to capture environmental wrongdoing, I want to claim, and a more satisfying view can be had by appealing to the idea of trespass. I will suggest specifically that the wrong of pollution consists in the unjustifiability of the polluting act. In many circumstances, unjustifiability will track either the degradation of value or, more closely, disrespect and trespass on rights, thus contributing to the confusion. The position I advocate nevertheless falls within the purview of the rights tradition. For reasons of space, I will outline the virtue view only briefly in the following section. I will not address it at length.

I. Harm, Vice, and Trespass

For many people the wrong of pollution is self-evident. Take any natural and pristine environment, introduce a deleterious additive, and this additive, by virtue of the harm that it does to this natural and pristine environment, is rightly considered a pollutant. Call this the "harms view" of pollution.

Roughly speaking, the harms view proposes that the wrong of pollution consists in the harm or damage caused by the pollution. Pollution is wrong because it damages the environment. The case of Duckworth and Dodgson above is paradigmatic in this respect, though this case is crafted around two actors, one of whom has clearly established property rights. The pollution introduces a substance that damages (or diminishes the utility of) water. So, water with high dioxin levels, say, is said to be polluted by virtue of the damage done to the water, whereas water that otherwise may carry pathogens, but that has been "treated" with chlorine (an otherwise toxic chemical) is said not to be polluted. By contrast, water with ostensibly healthy levels of fluoride is generally not thought to be polluted—except by fictional conspiracy theorists like US Air Force Brigadier General, Jack D. Ripper[1]—as fluoride is an additive conferring health benefits, but not "fixing" the water per se. In other words, it is the *utility* of the water, and the purpose to which the water is being put, that will establish whether the additive is harmful or beneficial. At its base, this is a deeply consequentialist position, mostly utilitarian in origin, locating the wrong of the polluting action fundamentally in the bad consequences brought about from the action.

The harms view works well to describe the wrong of almost any form of pollution: air pollution (as air is damaged through the addition of deleterious substances); soil contamination (as soil loses its capacity to support life); litter (as aesthetic properties of the landscape become degraded); noise pollution (as the aural environment becomes congested); light pollution; thermal pollution; visual pollution; polluting one's body, and so on.

The cheap undergraduate trick of turning to the dictionary reveals that, etymologically speaking, the term "pollution" as related specifically to the environment can only be traced back to 1828, when it was used for the first recorded time, ostensibly metaphorically, to mean "contamination of the environment." The term more historically conjures "defilement" or "desecration of that which is sacred," and dates as far back as 1390, when it was used to mean, bizarrely, "ejaculation of semen without sexual intercourse."[2] To my great embarrassment, this meaning still lingers in other non-English languages. As an American student living and studying post-Soviet Russia, I once remarked innocently to a Muscovite friend about the pollution outside the city. He found my pidgin Russian hilarious in the extreme. Needless to say, it turns out that the term 'поллуция' (pronounced *pollutsia*) does not mean what it sounds like it means, but instead refers to male nocturnal emissions. So much for dabbling in international environmental issues.

I raise this etymological point only to suggest that the harms view, intuitive though it seems to modern English speakers, is in fact relatively new. The more archaic use of the term carries not the harms view, but instead the vice view: that pollution is a blemish, or a mar, on a person's character. The vice of defilement is not aptly our focus here, though certainly some contemporary environmental ethicists have sought to characterize pollution as the sort of thing that a person of strong moral character would not do (Van Wensveen 1999).

Though it stems from ancient views on moral character, the vice view predominates to this day throughout the environmental discourse. It is reflected in a variety of anti-pollution advertisements that characterize the early environmental movement. The famous "Crying Indian" advertisement of the 1970s, in which a Native American lands his canoe on a trash strewn riverbank and sheds a tear for the loss of natural beauty, offers an instance of this. The voiceover in the ad says it all: "Some people have a deep abiding respect for the natural beauty that was once this country. Some people don't. People start pollution. People can stop it." Or, memorably from roughly the same era, the Woodsy Owl commercials admonishing children never to be a dirty bird, with the catchy bi-slogan: "Give a hoot; don't pollute."

In any event, it is the harms view that is our target here, as it is reflected throughout environmental legislation, including the National Environmental Policy Act (NEPA), the Clean Air Act (CAA), the Clean Water Act (CWA), Superfund (CERCLA), the Pollution Prevention Act 1990 (PPA),[3] among many other federal and state laws. Each of these laws specifies the degree and extent to which a polluter is responsible for damage resulting from his or her actions. NEPA, for instance, is in place "to promote efforts which will prevent or eliminate damage to the environment ..."[4] Through this charge, NEPA aims at "pollution prevention."[5] The CAA specifically seeks out "harmful pollution." Each of the other acts, similarly, aim to prevent pollution damage to the environment.

In our opening case, it is easy to find great fault with Duckworth's actions. Many would like to believe that what Duckworth has done wrong is that he has harmed Dodgson. He has cost Dodgson money—money that he otherwise might have spent on a new yacht or a new car. He has also, conceivably, put Dodgson at risk of chlorine gas inhalation—ammonia and chlorine combine to form chlorine gas—or he has damaged the filters in Dodgson's pool, or he has shortened the lifespan of the paint on the pool walls.[6] Of course, for our purposes, the pool need not be a pool at all. It can be a pond, or a lake, or quadrant of air, or any unowned anything. As long as that unowned anything can be sullied, it is pollutable. What, ultimately, is wrong with what Duckworth has done to Dodgson?

Plainly, harm is not the only factor that goes into a determination of wrongdoing. There are other factors as well, including a consideration of the reasons why damages subtract value or utility, or also why a person may be polluting in the first place. Most people will accept the influence of extraneous factors like motive and bad luck, just as they may have accepted Duckworth's excuses for unintentionally or accidentally poisoning Dodgson's pool. We tend to treat these as "mitigating factors," but I think that ignoring these factors can lead to big problems, some of which I will explain in the next section.

II. Bootstrapping: Or, Why This Matters

The above discussion may smack of hair-splitting triviality, but how we conceive of the wrong of pollution has far-reaching practical implications. It impacts how we address pollution. If, for instance, we view the problem of pollution as fundamentally a problem of harm, then we may be inclined to approach pollution in a distinctively economic fashion: as a "negative externality." That is, we may claim that the harms caused by pollution are unaccounted for negative costs, external to a producer's and a consumer's expense figuration.

Assuming such about pollution then invites a prescription. One simple way of dealing with pollution, if it is aptly understood as a harm, is to alter the incentives of the polluter: perhaps with a Pigouvian tax, with the threat of regulation, or with a cap-and-trade regime. These approaches are put into place in order to "internalize the externality" by forcing the polluting producer to account for overlooked costs. A tax, for instance, may shift the purchase price of the product, thereby reducing demand and shifting supply, in which case a more optimum outcome can be achieved. Similarly, regulation may shift the production cost of a product, or ensure that the externality is produced only to an acceptable degree, once again ensuring a more optimal outcome.

Naturally there are cases in which the harms from pollution are too grave to countenance: say, a pollutant is found to cause mesothelioma. If this is the case, then a different prescription for the harms problem arises. Instead of taxing, regulating, or capping the pollutant, we may place strict side-constraints on the behavior of the producer: restricting pollution altogether, thereby forcing the producer to develop new technologies that rely on substitute resources, to choose an alternate supply path, or to develop new industries entirely. This is essentially the history of asbestos. As its carcinogenicity became more evident, the harms from asbestos were deemed to be too extreme, and industries reliant upon it were forced to adjust. Some fell away and alternative industries emerged in their place. In fact, a whole new market for asbestos clean-up was created.

Taxes and side-constraints are two exceptionally common, albeit politically controversial, responses to pollution. The underlying idea is the same: to shore up—or bootstrap—the inefficiencies or failures in the market by introducing top-down fixatives that force the market to right itself.

It is important to note, however, that these top-down prescriptions are objectionable to many. The famous economist Ronald Coase, for instance, claimed that in some instances they can be inefficient. He proposed that we should assign property rights to producers and polluters in order to more optimally internalize external costs. Assigning property rights, he reasoned, would allow producers to achieve equilibrium between one another without bearing the inefficient bureaucratic costs associated with collective action problems (Coase 1960). Coase's solution argues for the expansion, not the constriction, of property rights, insisting that a more optimal outcome can be achieved by way of putting control in the hands of those with a vested interest. Of course, the extent of this efficiency is an empirical matter, and Coase was speaking only theoretically. Even still, his position represents the core reasoning of a view that frowns upon top-down responses to negative externalities.

The "Coase Theorem" demonstrates this important position by appealing to the case of a railroad operator and several farmers to make his case. Imagine, Coase proposed, the locomotive to get from one destination to another. Lining the railroad, however, are several farms that are periodically set aflame by the passing coal engine.

Among other things, what Coase demonstrated was that the market would be a pretty efficient method for arriving at a resolution between the parties. Where the standard view has been to hold one or the other party *liable* for causing damage to the other party—suggesting, for instance, that the railroad operator is responsible for causing damages to the farmer, and therefore, further, that due to this liability the railroad must pay the farmers for damages to their crops.

But the Coasian solution to the pollution problem calls attention to another often overlooked feature of pollution. That is, pollution is not neatly characterized as a straight harm–benefit problem. Whether an additive is rightly considered deleterious will depend on who is doing the accounting. A farmer keeping his hay near a railroad may consider the sparks emitted from a passing railcar to be a negative externality, a pollutant. But in the same arrangement, the railroad operator considers not the sparks, but the hay, to be the negative externality. Coase's observation is vital here: damages are reciprocal. What is a negative externality to the farmer is a positive externality to the locomotive operator, and vice versa. As a consequence, the liability and resolution is not clearly established simply by the damaging arrangement.

Coase, too, was operating on the presupposition that the wrong of pollution consists in the harms of pollution, though his unique observation was that the harm itself is relative to the baseline arrangement.

From the standpoint of moral wrongdoing (as opposed to mere economic efficiency), theorists have tended to presume the harms view and then bootstrap from there. Henry Shue, for instance, has stipulated a distinction between necessary emissions and luxury emissions (Shue 1993) in an attempt to accept the harms view, but also to call attention to the varieties of activities that give rise to pollution. His point is important, and it is tied up in the justice discussion: some emissions are easier (more acceptable) to reduce than others. Shue does not elaborate much on how one might distinguish between a luxury and a subsistence emission, but at least one handy metric may be to cut the distinction according to elasticity of demand.

Price elasticity of demand is a measurement of how much the demand for a good changes in the face of marginal increases or decreases in price. Goods that are very elastic, like yachts and high-definition televisions (HDTVs), demonstrate a precipitous drop off as they get more expensive. These "luxury goods" stand in sharp contrast, economically speaking, to goods that are less elastic, like pasta, rice, and potatoes. If the price of these goods were suddenly to skyrocket, assuming that there were no other backstop resources, consumers would continue to purchase them and make adjustments to their budgets elsewhere.[7]

Emissions that have a low elasticity of demand can thereby be said to be subsistence emissions, where those with higher elasticity of demand fall into the luxury category. For instance, fossil-fuel emissions from daily trips to the grocery store may be considerably less elastic than fossil-fuel emissions from heating one's house, which can be offset by other technologies. Or, conversely, fossil-fuel emissions from daily trips to the grocery store may be more elastic than the use of wood for a cookstove. Many factors can go into the determination of whether a good is a luxury or a necessity / subsistence good.

On the other end of the spectrum, William Baxter points out that some pollution is necessary for us to do the sort of things that we want to do, even if it is sometimes harmful (Baxter 1974). Need dinner? You will have to cook it, which will take energy, and will involve some sort of degradation of the environment. Need shelter? You will have to build it, which will take space, and involve some degradation of the environment. He cartoons the pollution challenge a bit when he asks whether we should privilege people or penguins, and he was much maligned by many in the environmental community for his stance. But the point is an important one, inasmuch as it points to a wide failing of the harms view. The harms view cannot easily accommodate prevalent intuitions that many of us have about pollution.

The strategy that I shall take in this essay is to move in the direction of undoing or correcting a wrong. If my thesis is correct, then I should be able to show rather handily that the simple harms view of pollution is too narrow. I borrow this strategy in part from the environmental ethicist Robert Elliot, who wrote in 1982 an article called "Faking Nature," which he later expanded to become a book (Elliot 1982, 1997), that destroying a valuable artwork and replacing it with a passable fake invariably leaves an ineffable remainder: the intrinsic value of the artwork. Elliot's objective is to argue on behalf of the intrinsic value of nature. The "causal genesis of forests, rivers, lakes and so on is important to establishing their value" (Elliot 1997: 85). Elliot uses the case of artworks to illustrate his point. Just as Elliot does, I will give cases of nonenvironmental harm and trespass in hopes of priming your intuitions to see that there is quite a bit more to pollution than environmental harm.

There is one final consequence of the harms view: that it comes ready-made with a prescription for violations: fix the harm. It is my contention that pollution is a sort of disrespect that can be adequately characterized only by looking at the entirety of the act. What I want to defend here, essentially, is a conception of pollution as a form of trespass, rather than as characterizable in terms of harms.

III. Polluter Pays Principle: Or, Undoing the Damage

The Polluter Pays Principle (PPP) is principle of environmental law and ethics that requires parties responsible for polluting the natural environment also to pay to clean up the natural environment. It is a reasonable principle, all things considered, inasmuch as damage to the environment is precisely the sort of thing that appears to be the core concern of pollution.

The PPP is supported by a range of legal entities, including the United Nations (UN), the European Community (EC), the United States in many of the aforementioned laws, and the Organization for Economic Cooperation and Development (OECD). In the Rio Declaration on Environment and Development, it is codified as Principle 16: "National authorities should endeavour to promote the internalization of environmental costs and the use of economic instruments, taking into account the approach that the polluter should, in principle, bear the cost of pollution, with due regard to the public interest and without distorting international trade and investment."[8] The Comprehensive Environmental Response, Compensation, and Liability Act 1980 (CERCLA), which goes by the more portentous heading of "Superfund," authorizes the US Federal government to clean up spills that place the environment or public health in danger. Though Superfund is thought by many people—indeed, as the nickname implies—to be a fund established by the US Government to clean up spills, more than 75% of the funding for the cleanup actually comes from the polluters themselves.[9] Thus, the polluter pays. The US Corporate Average Fuel Economy (CAFE) standards impose a fine on those who sell cars below a set fuel economy standard, essentially requiring them to pay for polluting.

Polluter pays is essentially a guiding presupposition of "corrective justice," which proposes that in order to rectify a wrong, the injurer must repair what injury he or she is responsible for. Corrective justice stands in sharp contrast to "retributive justice," which proposes not only that the injurer must pay damages for harm done, but that the injurer must also pay an extra penalty and/or must be made to suffer, over-and-above the corrective cost, for wrongdoing.

Let us take this first by examining a simple case of damage or harm. As I mentioned, Robert Elliot has an instructive set of thought experiments in which he encourages readers to wonder what is lost when a work of art is first destroyed and then restored with a passable fake. We should here invoke a variation on Elliot's examples to illustrate further. Suppose:

> *Malicious Vandal*: You have very expensive, original John Tenniel woodcut print hanging in your hall. A notorious art vandal breaks into your house and cuts the print to pieces, irrevocably destroying it.

Malicious Vandal is a case in which there are at least two sorts of wronging going on. For one, the vandal has damaged a valuable artwork, causing harm either extrinsically or intrinsically. Second, the vandal has broken into your house, trespassing on your person. This scenario is akin to the pollution scenario, and the problem with the PPP can here be made clear. Simply replacing the woodcut, or paying for damages, does not undo the wrong.

Suppose the following comparison case:

Clever Vandal: You have a very expensive, original Tenniel woodcut print hanging as before. A clever vandal—a detractor of important illustration art—deeply desires to destroy this original Tenniel. He breaks into your house and does so. To cover his tracks, and to avoid penalty, he replaces your Tenniel print with cheap but perfect fake; a replica so good that not even the best expert can tell the difference between the two prints. By assumption the print is so good that it would sell at market for the same price as the original. You are none the wiser.

It seems to me that despite the fact that you are not harmed in any way by the Clever Vandal's act, you have still been wronged. This is akin to Elliot's classic "faking nature" case, and it would appear that what is wrong here is that the intrinsically valuable artwork, the Tenniel, is destroyed. Something inimitable has been lost. Elliot would have us observe that in light of this loss we can understand intrinsic value. But notice:

Impulsive Vandal: Again you have the expensive Tenniel. An impulsive vandal sneaks into your house while you are away. So incensed that you have a Tenniel print on your wall, he proceeds to destroy it. Immediately feeling release after destroying your artwork, he grows worried about the legal implications of his impulsive act. To make amends, he digs deep into his bank account, and though it pains him to do so, purchases another identical woodcut to hang on your wall. He does so before you return home. You are neither better nor worse off. You simply have a different original and expensive Tenniel.

This is a classic case of trespass, and the wrong here consists solely in the breaking and entering, as well as in the destruction of the art. The two are, essentially, the same act. The destruction of the art is a violation of your will, a wronging of you, and it is very much this wronging of you that qualifies the act as wrong. Had you invited the vandal into your home and asked him to destroy your artwork, the circumstances would be different indeed. So, too, if you had invited him into your home, thereby removing considerations about trespass into your home, and he had impulsively destroyed your art, or accidentally destroyed your art. We should reject such vandalism as a violation, despite the fact that you may never learn of the home invasion. Now consider this case:

Benevolent Vandal: As a long-time aficionado of children's literature, you have a cheap replica of a famous Tenniel print hanging on your wall. Suppose that a notorious vandal and detractor of cheap *kitsch* breaks into your house and destroys this print on your wall. Ugh! Gross. He cannot stand such garbage! Courteously, he replaces the replica with an original and authentic Tenniel print.

You may think this quite nice of the Benevolent Vandal. He has have given you a precious artwork. But there is still the minor matter of the breaking and entering, as well as the kitschy fake that had previously adorned your wall. Without any information about you, or about your commitment to that kitschy fake, it seems to me that the benevolent vandal has still wronged you in some way, even though, in retrospect, his actions may have benefited you in perhaps such a way that you are grateful to the vandal. I want to hold that there is still an important violation of your person, and that you would be correct to criticize the vandal for doing as he has. This, at least, is what I shall claim about pollution. But let us examine a bit more closely.

IV. A Mad Tea Party: Or, the Hatter's Riddle

In an earlier work, my colleague William P. Grundy and I introduced several cases in which we argued that environmental remediation technologies point to an often overlooked aspect of environmental damage: that respect for others is also in play (Hale and Grundy 2009). Those cases were the following, modified here slightly to suit the above example:

Poison: The Mad Hatter develops a poison that has the potential to kill Alice, but for which he has the antidote. Once the antidote is administered, Alice will suffer no ill effects.

Suppose the Hatter puts this poison in Alice's tea while they are chatting, fully intending to administer the antidote immediately once Alice has ingested the tea. Grundy's and my intuitions on this case are straightforward and strong: the Hatter will be wronging Alice by adding the poison to her tea, even though Alice will not be harmed by the poison.

You may have your doubts. Perhaps you think that the problem here is that the Hatter has put Alice at *risk*. Grundy and I anticipate such objections and offer other examples to address such concerns. I will not pain you by going through them all, but consider instead:

Inert additive: Before putting the poison in Alice's tea, the Mad Hatter mixes the poison with the antidote, thus making the poison an inert additive.

Even with this knowledge, it would appear that the Mad Hatter is wronging Alice by adding an inert additive to her tea. We eventually urge readers to consider the possibility that even adding a substance so inert and harmless to Alice's tea as water without her consent, is on its face, a kind of wronging of Alice.

To see the conflict here, it may help to parallel this case with Benevolent Vandal:

Health potion: The Hatter has discovered an additive that will add years to a person's life. He and Alice are having tea.

Where in the Vandal cases there was a clear two-step violation—first an incidence of trespass and then an incident of vandalism or harm—the two-step process has been collapsed in the Mad Tea Party cases. It appears at first that the problem lies clearly with the harm or risk to Alice, but removing the harm or risk suggests that even here there is a sort of trespass. Grundy and I claim that the wrong of pollution lies in the trespass, or the disrespect, of Alice's will. Plainly, there are circumstances that would make the Hatter's actions permissible: if, for instance, he acquires here consent first, or if, through a bizarre twist, the Hatter finds Alice unresponsive but understands that, had she her druthers, she would have willed herself into health. In these cases, the unauthorized addition of a health potion can be understood not as a breach of respect, but as a considered and respectful action. The critical consideration is not whether Alice is benefited, but whether the Hatter has taken the full suite of facts about Alice, including her interests, her desires, and her autonomy, into account.

This is all very abstract, I confess, but the upshot of my argument will begin to take on a more plausible ring if we consider a real case. In the next section, I would like to drill deeper.

V. The Caterpillar: Or, the Real Problem with Second-Hand Smoke

Cigarette smoke is "classified as a 'known human carcinogen' by the US Environmental Protection Agency (EPA), the US National Toxicology Program, and the International Agency for Research on Cancer (IARC), a branch of the World Health Organization."[10] It is responsible for an estimated 443000 deaths per year in the United States alone, which accounts for almost one-fifth of US mortality.[11] Among other complications, it is the leading cause of lung cancer and lung disease in the United States, and it more than doubles the risk of coronary heart disease and stroke.

Perhaps more shockingly, *second-hand* smoke[12] is associated with an estimated 46000 deaths from heart disease of non-smokers living with smokers, 3400 lung cancer deaths in non-smoking adults, between 50000 and 300000 lung infections in children, and even up to 750000 middle ear infections in children. The numbers are staggering, and they have moved many municipalities and private businesses to prohibit indoor smoking, much enraging the smoking community. There has been a fair bit written about political, legislative, and legal battles to regulate cigarette smoke (see, e.g. Pertschuk 2001; Derthick 2005). For our purposes, however, it will be important simply to assess the nature of the arguments that can be lodged against smoking.

For instance, someone may argue that the problem with first-hand smoke inhalation is, essentially, that it is harmful to one's health. If smoking is bad for you, then insofar as you ought not to harm yourself, you ought not to smoke. As with many anti-pollution arguments, this argument functions along harms lines. It can also easily translate over to second-hand smoke. If smoking is bad for others, then insofar as you ought not to cause harm to others, you ought not to smoke. Again, this argument functions along harms lines.

But notice the gaping hole here. First-hand harms arguments depend entirely on the harms, and gain their force either by persuading the smoker that he or she should not harm him or herself, or insisting that such harms are so grave (and arguably cigarette smoking so addictive) that the smoker is not in a position to reason for him or herself about his or her own welfare. Second-hand arguments against smoking are nowhere near this clean. They insist not simply that harm is done, but that the harm is *unauthorized*. The unauthorized aspect, not the harm, is doing the work.

The practical and political danger here is that the harms discussion overshadows the trespass discussion, instigating an extraordinary battle over the science, instead of the morality, of smoking. To wit: to make both claims requires substantial data and information on the effects of smoke. The wrong of second-hand smoke is contingent on the fact of, and the extent to which, the harm to others is significant. In emphasizing the harm and downplaying the trespass on others, the question of wrongdoing shifts from a question about what is good and right, to an empirical matter regarding the degree and likelihood of damages. It is easy, once this shift has occurred, to take advantage of the lacking empirical information.

Historically, this is precisely how the discussion unfolded: opponents of regulation and restriction claimed for years that there was no demonstrable negative outcome from second-hand smoke. Research money and policy energy was redirected to making a very strong scientific case against second-hand smoke. Cigarette manufacturers objected vociferously to the science. Meanwhile, they waged another argument on rights grounds, not on harms grounds. They claimed that smoking is essentially a victimless crime, a choice that any free individual could voluntarily make. In a freedom-respecting world, went the line of reasoning, every citizen ought to be empowered to take risks with his or her own life. The decision to smoke, therefore, was a personal decision.

The same was also said of second-hand smoke: we take the goods with the bads. We do not have to associate with chain-smokers, but because we prefer their company, we enter their smoky environment—their home or a bar, say—and accept that this is the price of being around them. Or, more generally, that this is the price of living in a free society.

Lying just under the surface of this discussion, as I have said, was a presumption about the nature of the harm, about the extent to which the harm is permissible. What I am saying here, is not that harm does not matter. Clearly, the degree and extent of harm matters quite a bit. Most people do not give much thought to benevolent vandals, or polluters who dump water in the street. Rather, I am saying that the undue emphasis on harms, to the exclusion of trespass considerations, plays a core role in the permissibility of polluting actions. Many people would not give a second thought to sitting in front of a campfire, or having a bonfire on the beach, even though such activities produce a fair bit of second-hand smoke. Many more people would happily spend their holidays roasting chestnuts by the fire, or warming their toes by the woodstove after a long day skiing; and most certainly would not wag a disapproving finger at a family in the Congo who *rely* on carbon-burning stoves to cook their dinner, or fires to heat their homes.

The problem with the harms view can thus be articulated. What makes the emission of a pollutant wrong is not necessarily whether its presence causes harm, but whether it opens the possibility of causing this harm in an unauthorized or unwarranted way, or whether it trespasses on the lives of others. That is the true problem with passive, second-hand smoke, not merely that it does, in some cases, cause cancer, or cause ear infections, or cause irritation to innocent bystanders. The problem, in other words, is that second-hand intrusion cannot easily be justified for a non-necessity practice like smoking. It is not, after all, as though the second-hand smoke emanates from cookstoves or campfires, which surely also have deleterious effects of the health of innocent bystanders. Still, ardent environmentalists may be reticent to adopt the trespass view for fear that it is too anthropocentric. I think this is not necessarily true.

VI. The Cheshire Cat: Non-Human Animals and Non-Rational Nature

One ostensible strength of the harms view is that it elides any deeply embedded anthropocentrism that the trespass view may engender. Trespass seems limited to entities that can be trespassed upon, which is more or less limited to rights holders. Without an account clearly spelling out the rights of non-human animals, the trespassed upon are mostly humans. This would appear to be a strike against the trespass view. I want to argue here that this need not necessarily be so; that, essentially, what makes the account I am arguing for unique is that it is cast in terms of duties and not in terms of rights. What I want to suggest, namely, is that the wrongs associated with pollution stem from a failure of the duty of justification, where this duty is understood fundamentally in terms of what can be justified.

First, note that non-rational nature is not a problem for the harms view. Many environmental strategies deploy the harms view in the service of environmental protection. By finding the wrongs of pollution to be associated with harms from that pollution, they keep the question of rights off the table:

Stray cat: The Dormouse poisons a bowl of milk and leaves it out for a cat, killing the cat.

Most assume that this case of poisoning is wrong. It is wrong because the cat, or the cat's owners, have been harmed in some important way. Naturally, poisoning a cat is bad for the cat, just as it would be bad for Alice. But I actually think that the same can be said of trespass. Poisoning the milk trespasses upon the cat, and it does so because in most circumstances, poisoning a cat cannot be easily justified. Put slightly differently. If I poison a cat, I must have a good reason:

Prank: Suppose that Tweedledum sets out to fool Tweedledee and thus make a production of dumping the poison in the stray cat's milk, even though there is a readily available antidote. Dum will fool Dee into believing that he has harmed the cat, though he will immediately cure the cat of all illness as soon as Dee falls for the prank.

I think it is wrong to add the poison to the milk bowl and then to give the cat the antidote, even if the cat will be none the wiser, even if the cat will not be harmed in any way, and even if it will make for great giggles between Tweedledum and Tweedledee. It is wrong, I believe, because Tweedledum will not be acting respectfully of the cat; he will be failing in his responsibility to justify his action.

Compare this with:

> *Cat nurse*: The March Hare offers the cat a bowl of milk, and in doing so adds health potion to the cat's milk.

The Hare is permitted to add medicines and health potions into the cat's milk in a way that the Mad Hatter is not permitted to add medicines or health potions to Alice's tea. The Hare does not wrong the cat by adding medication to its milk, because the act of giving the cat milk, which he does out of good will for the cat, essentially authorizes him to benefit the cat by giving it a health potion.

Cats are the sort of creatures that cannot make complex decisions about their long-term health and welfare, so human proxies—pet owners and the like—are left to make decisions for them. People are not of this sort, and so the Mad Hatter's generous, but surreptitious, Mickey-slipping is objectionable. Naturally, there are defeaters of this position. If a person or rational agent—a pet owner or a vet, say—has recognized jurisdiction over the cat, this person or agent may need to offer consent or authorization.

I am of the mind that wrongdoing consists in the justifiability or unjustifability of an action. To gain access to the justifiability of adding a health potion to the cat, or more widely, a pesticide to the brush—in order to prevent the spread of plague or malaria, say—requires boots-on-the-ground pragmatic consideration of all factors associated with the justifiability of that act. Harms and benefits matter, as I have said, but what will matter as well is whether such trespass could be agreed by all affected parties (Habermas 1991; Hale and Grundy 2009; Hale and Dilling 2010; Hale 2011). Our strategy of unpolluting reveals the strong undercurrent of moral trespass in these stances, but it falls short for revealing the complications with a simplistic trespass perspective.

Conclusion

Return finally to Duckworth and Dodgson's pool. What Duckworth is doing by dumping ammonia in Dodgson's pool is trespassing on Dodgson's morally established jurisdiction: his rights. If Duckworth adds ammonia and then immediately neutralizes the ammonia, he will still be trespassing on Dodgson's jurisdiction, much like Clever Vandal. If Duckworth is making a product and accidentally spills ammonia in Duckworth's pool, he will certainly be required, among other things, to clean up his mess, but he will nevertheless be trespassing on Duckworth's jurisdiction. Whether Duckworth forgives him for the accident, it is plain enough to see, will depend not entirely on the damage done, but on the reason that Dodgson can give for having caused the problem in the first place.

It is interesting to note that on the harms view a pond of water equivalent in volume to Dodgson's pool, but absent in chlorine does not form the same toxic chloramines that may lead us to evaluate Duckworth's ammonia dumping harshly. In other words, Duckworth's addition of ammonia to a swimming pool is made that much worse by the fact that Dodgson has added chlorine to the pool; and though both Dodgson and Duckworth have engaged in roughly the same act—one the addition of chlorine, the other the addition of ammonia—it is the act of adding ammonia and not the act of adding chlorine that we evaluate as contaminating the pool.

The nature of Duckworth's wrongdoing is contingent largely on the reasons that Duckworth has for doing what he did. Far from hair-splitting, these reasons lie at the heart of moral action. They alone explain the difference between necessity and luxury emissions. They alone are crowded out by attempts to internalize the externalities. They alone are absorbed into the Coasian argument for the efficient assignment, administration, and enforcement of property rights.

What I have been trying to suggest is that environmental wrong of pollution amounts to a unique sort of trespass. This is a trespass on the rights of other citizens, a disrespect of others, but it is more fundamentally the failure of the agent to adequately to justify his or her actions, to fulfill the requirement that actions be justified.

I have made my case first by exploring three rough categories of positions related to pollution: the harms view, the trespass view, and the virtue view. I proposed that the harms view holds the presumptive crown in this triumvirate, and that this dominance is reflected throughout environmental law. In section II, I discussed the potential implications of the harms view, hoping to show how widespread it is. In section III, I discussed the PPP and suggested that it is self-undermining. In section IV, I introduced the case of Alice and the Hatter to help to crystallize the trespass view. In section V, I discussed the practical implications of the trespass position. And in section VI, I attempted to address the objection that the trespass view is overly anthropocentric.

In a big, shared environment, we often do not have discrete property boundaries like those that enable Dodgson to claim that he has been trespassed upon. As a consequence, the moral idea of trespass faces into the dominance of concern over harms. But theorists like Ronald Coase (1960), J.J. Thomson (1980, 1992), Joel Feinberg (1990), and Mark Sagoff (2004), among others, remind us that much more than harms are already in play. The circumstances in which the addition of ammonia to a swimming pool, and the conditions under which such an act might be deemed wrong, are contingent in large part on the full suite of reasons that best explains, and either does or does not, justify the action. To deny this is to reduce the question of wrongdoing from pollution to simplified caricature; and more distressingly, to de-fang the bit of the environmentalist's claim against the polluter.

Notes

1 See, if you have not seen already, Stanley Kubrick's cult classic film, *Dr Strangelove or: How I Learned to Stop Worrying and Love the Bomb*.(Kubrick 1964).

2 "pollution, n," *Oxford English Dictionary*, 3rd edn, September 2006; online version June 2011, available at: http://www.oed.com/view/Entry/146992, accessed July 27, 2011. An entry for

this word was first included in the *New English Dictionary*, 1907.

3 See at: http://www.epa.gov/p2/pubs/p2policy/act1990.htm.

4 42 USC § 4321.

5 See at: http://ceq.hss.doe.gov/nepa/regs/poll/ppguidnc.htm.

6 Please note: this reaction is extremely volatile and dangerous. Do not, under any circumstances, try to create this chemical reaction. Doing so could result in serious injury or death.

7 For instance, at the time of this writing, a decent 48-in HDTV sells for about US$1000. Some are more expensive, some less expensive, but roughly speaking, this is what they sell for. Suppose that there is a sale on these televisions, say offering them for US$100 each. One assumes naturally that such a sale would result in a rush of buyers for the televisions. At a low price, demand is very high for the televisions. Suppose, instead, that there is a sudden scarcity in these televisions, raising the price to US$10 000 for a television. One would assume naturally that such a price would yield a significant drop in demand. At a high price, demand is quite a bit lower. This is the price elasticity of demand. Whether a good is more or less elastic is an empirical matter. It is also, however, a question of luxury.

8 See at: http://en.wikisource.org/wiki/Administrative_Instruction_ST/AI/189.

9 See at: http://www.epa.gov/superfund/community/today/pdfs/whopays.pdf, accessed August 3, 2011.

10 See at: http://www.cancer.org/cancer/cancer-causes/tobaccocancer/secondhand-smoke.

11 See at: http://www.cdc.gov/tobacco/data_statistics/fact_sheets/health_effects/effects_cig_smoking.

12 According to the American Cancer Society: "Secondhand smoke is also known as environmental tobacco smoke (ETS) or passive smoke. It is a mixture of 2 forms of smoke that come from burning tobacco: sidestream smoke (smoke that comes from the end of a lighted cigarette, pipe, or cigar) and mainstream smoke (smoke that is exhaled by a smoker). Even though we think of these as the same, they aren't. The sidestream smoke has higher concentrations of cancer-causing agents (carcinogens) than the mainstream smoke. And, it contains smaller particles than mainstream smoke, which make their way into the body's cells more easily" (2011).

References

American Cancer Society (2011) (cited August 3, 2011), available at: http://www.cancer.org/cancer/cancer-causes/tobaccocancer/secondhand-smoke.

Baxter, William F. (1974) *People or Penguins: The Case for Optimal Pollution*, New York: Columbia University Press.

Coase, Ronald (1960) "The Problem of Social Cost," *Journal of Law and Economics*, 3: 1–44.

Derthick, Martha (2005) *Up In Smoke: From Legislation to Litigation in Tobacco Politics*, Washington DC: CQ Press.

Elliot, Robert (1982) "Faking Nature," *Inquiry* 25: 81–93.

Elliot, Robert (1997). *Faking Nature*, London: Routledge.

Feinberg, Joel (1990) *Harmless Wrongdoing*, New York: Oxford University Press.

Habermas, Jürgen (1991) "Discourse Ethics," in *Moral Consciousness and Communicative Action*, Cambridge, MA: MIT Press.

Hale, Benjamin (2011) "Getting the Bad Out: Remediation Technologies and Respect for Others," in *The Environment: Topics in Contemporary Philosophy*, vol. 9 (eds J.K. Cambell, M. O'Rourke, and M. Slater), Cambridge, MA: MIT Press.

Hale, Benjamin, and Lisa Dilling (2010) "Geoengineering, Ocean Fertilization, and the Problem of Permissible Pollution," *Science, Technology, and Human Values, Online first, August* 3, 2010.

Hale, Benjamin and William Grundy (2009) "Remediation and Respect: Do Remediation Technologies Alter Our Responsibilities?" *Environmental Values* 18 (4): 397–415.

Pertschuk, Michael (2001) *Smoke in Their Eyes: Lessons in Movement Leadership from the Tobacco Wars*, Nashville, TN: Vanderbilt University Press.

Sagoff, Mark (2004) "The Philosophical Common Sense of Pollution," in *Price, Principle, and the Environment*, New York: Cambridge University Press.

Shue, Henry (1993) "Subsistence Emissions and Luxury Emissions," *Law and Policy* 15 (1): 39–59.
Thomson, Judith Jarvis (1980) "Rights and Compensation," *Nous* 14 (1): 3–15.
Thomson, Judith Jarvis (1992) *The Realm of Rights*, Cambridge, MA: Harvard University Press.
Van Wensveen, Louke (1999) *Dirty Virtues: The Emergence of Ecological Virtue Ethics*, Amherst, NY: Humanity Books.

Moral Valuation of Environmental Goods

Mark A. Seabright

A notable aspect of discourse about environmental goods and services is that moral claims often enter into the discussion, in contrast to a focus on ecological, social/political, or economic concerns. For example, a number of leaders have argued that there is a moral imperative to address climate change above and beyond its political or economic ramifications (Gore 2006; Kerim 2007; Tutu 2007). Moreover, moral claims about environmental issues are often difficult to integrate with other perspectives. In the context of climate change, for example, Felder (2007) has noted that: "much, but not all, of the climate debate is ships passing in the night. Some argue that the basis for our policy response is the moral imperative, regardless of the costs or its cost-effectiveness, whereas others believe that one must consider costs, either implicitly or explicitly, when fashioning policies."

As a first step in exploring the role of moral concerns in environmental decisions, this essay examines the fundamental question of what motivates a moral stance on environmental issues. I use the context of contingent valuation (CV) studies to examine this topic because of its explicit focus on the economic valuation of environmental goods and services; moral considerations in this context stand in sharp contrast to monetary trade-offs. My approach to the topic draws on the behavioral ethics literature. In particular, I examine several psychological explanations for moral motivations in CV studies, including moral identity (Aquino and Reed 2002) and moral intensity (Jones 1991), protected or sacred values (Baron and Spranca 1997; Tetlock 2003), and moral heuristics (Sunstein 2005). I consider the implications of each of these explanations for biases in contingent valuation and, more broadly, for the role of moral concerns in environmental decisions.

Contingent valuation is a useful method for estimating the value of natural capital. The method presents respondents with a hypothetical scenario about environmental goods or services, and then asks them to state their willingness to pay (WTP) for, or willingness to accept (WTA), a change in the resource being investigated. For example, Stevens *et al.* (1991: Study 1) presented subjects with a hypothetical scenario involving the need to set up a private trust fund to protect Atlantic salmon from extinction, and asked them if they would be willing to contribute a specific amount to this fund. Contingent valuation studies typically include a clear description of the environmental good, the form of payment (e.g., tax increases or trust fund), and the response format for WTP (e.g., open-ended versus yes/no to specific dollar amounts), as well as attitudinal and behavioral questions about the good in question and background demographic information (Kotchen and Reiling 2000; Pearce and Barbier 2000: 66–69). Although the method has its critics and its share of methodological concerns (Pearce and Barbier 2000: 66–69), the number of CV studies has increased considerably over the last fifteen years or so (Adamowicz 2004).

Several CV studies have shown that subjects are often motivated by moral considerations in valuing natural capital. Stevens *et al.* (1991), for example, found that 79% of the respondents in a CV survey about salmon restoration agreed that: "All species of wildlife have a right to exist independently of any benefit or harm to people" (p. 396). They also found that subjects assigned approximately 48% of their total WTP for bald eagle, coyote, and salmon preservation to the intrinsic category "because animals have a right to exist" (p. 396). Using a verbal protocol methodology in which subjects are asked to "think aloud" as they make WTP bids, Schkade and Payne (1994) indicated that 23% of subjects gave a symbolic reason for their bid that "suggested a desire to signal their concern for larger or more inclusive issues, such as preserving the environment or leaving the planet for their progeny" (p. 100), and 17% explicitly framed their WTP decision in terms of a contribution to a charitable cause. Chilton and Hutchinson (2003) used a similar methodology and also found that many subjects explained their WTP decisions in terms of a charitable contribution to an important cause, rather than focusing on the receipt of a personal good. Bulte *et al.* (2005) found that subjects exhibited an "outrage effect" (Kahneman *et al.* 1993); they provided higher WTP bids to protect seal populations from threats due to human causes than those due to natural causes. Spash (2006) reported that 37% of the subjects in his CV study of wetland and bird preservation assigned rights to birds, and most of these subjects indicated that they would uphold these rights even if it significantly reduced their standard of living. This and other studies (e.g., Kotchen and Reiling 2000; Hansla *et al.* 2008) have shown a relationship between WTP and ethical values such as rights and an altruistic concern for others or for the biosphere.

Several studies examining WTP for public goods, and not following the full CV protocol, have also pointed to the importance of moral considerations in valuing the environment. Kahneman and Knetsch (1992) provided evidence that ratings of moral satisfaction are correlated with WTP for public goods. They suggested that this offers an explanation for the "embedding effect"—wherein WTP is insensitive to the level or amount of the good that is purchased (e.g., WTP for fish preservation in a small area of Ontario approximating WTP for preservation in all Ontario lakes)—because the scope of the cause should not have much affect on the amount of moral satisfaction that results from a WTP bid. Building on this work, Kahneman *et al.* (1993) proposed that WTP for public goods reflects a "*contribution model*, treating the protection of the environment as a good cause that needs supporting" (p. 311, added emphasis), rather than an economic model of purchasing behavior. Consistent with this psychological explanation of WTP, they found that WTP for public goods was higher when the harm was due to human causes rather than to natural causes (i.e., the so-called outrage effect); they also found strong correlations between various attitudinal measures, such as the importance of the threat, and WTP. Guagnano *et al.* (1994) provided additional support for a contribution model of WTP for public goods. They found that a model of altruistic behavior (awareness of negative effect on others and felt personal responsibility for improving the situation) generally predicted WTP, beyond any effects for ability to pay (income).

It is important to note that moral motivations are not necessarily inconsistent with the (expected) utility assumptions of WTP valuation (Pearce and Barbier 2000: 8). For example, a consequentialist ethical orientation—i.e., one that focus on outcomes, such as utilitarianism's concern for the "greatest good for the greatest number"—adopts a decision rule that has much in common with neoclassical utility theory (Spash 2006). However, some types or features of moral positions can pose a problem for the validity of CV studies, and it is for this reason that this topic has received considerable attention in the environmental economics literature. Two concerns about moral motivations stand out in the literature.

One concern is that a WTP bid motivated by a moral position produces its own "warm glow of giving," and that this psychic reward represents a benefit unrelated to the environmental good itself (Kahneman and Knetsch 1992; Chilton and Hutchinson 2003; Cooper *et al.* 2004). As noted above, this may account for the anomalous effect known as embedding, wherein WTP is insensitive to the level or amount of the good that is purchased, because "the moral satisfaction associated with contributions to an inclusive cause extends with little loss to any significant subset of that cause" (Kahneman and Knetsch 1992: 64). The more general concern, though, is that any moral satisfaction derived from a WTP contribution changes the "good" that is being valued, and the "indirect private benefit" (Cooper *et al.* 2004: 71) from moral satisfaction affects respondents' WTP in a way that is difficult to tease apart from the value of the environmental good itself. Subjects are responding to a different set of goods and benefits than those constituting the focus of the study.

The other main concern is that some types of moral motivations may limit or preclude the calculation of trade-offs between income and environmental goods. The economic rationale of CV studies is that respondents make such trade-offs, but an ethical concern for the rights of other people or of other species may constitute a moral obligation, taking precedence over personal costs and benefits. One type of moral motivation that may undermine income–environment trade-offs is altruism. Research on moral motivations in CV studies has indicated that, in addition to self-interest, respondents have altruistic concerns for other people, or for other species, or the biospheric conditions that support them (Stern 2000; Spash 2006; Hansla *et al.* 2008). To the extent that altruistic motives place the welfare of the other over self-interest, they can inform choice in a way that is divorced from trade-offs involving personal welfare (Edwards 1986; Stevens *et al.* 1991). Another type of moral motivation that poses a problem for trade-offs is deontological reasoning. Deontology determines whether an action is ethical based on whether it upholds basic duties or principles, such as human or animal rights, rather than by evaluating its consequences as in utilitarianism and other consequentialist theories. Deontological conclusions imply moral obligations that are not subject to trade-off.

Both altruistic and deontological motives can lead to a decision rule that does not involve trade-offs with personal welfare. One such rule that has received a lot of attention in the CV literature is lexicographic ordering. A lexicographic rule arranges items in a clear order by applying a particular rule to each pair of items to determine which ranks above the other (e.g., words in a dictionary based on the alphabet); no two items can be of equal rank. A person with a strong moral stance may establish preferences based on an ethical rule, without the joint consideration of, or trade-offs with, personal welfare (Edwards 1986; Stevens *et al.* 1991). For example, a person who is committed to animal rights may establish preferences based on the protection of these rights, with more protection always being valued over less protection, irrespective of other factors such as personal welfare (Edwards 1986).

For both of these reasons—the "warm glow" of contributions and altruistic or deontological positions—moral motivations may bias WTP responses. These biases could include protest responses (refusals to bid) or high bids. Stevens *et al.* (1991) found that 25% of subjects protested the bid vehicle for ethical reasons, "claiming that wildlife values should not be measured in dollar terms" (p. 397). More recent studies have found that moral motivations tend to inflate WTP responses rather than result in protest responses (Kotchen and Reiling 2000; Cooper *et al.* 2004; Spash 2006).

The following sections explore why subjects have moral reactions to contingent valuation scenarios, even though they are explicitly framed in terms of monetary trade-offs. I do not assume that there is only one reason for, or one type of, moral consideration in CV studies. Instead, I will examine several psychological explanations for moral motivations in CV studies, including moral identity (Aquino and Reed 2002) and moral intensity (Jones 1991), protected or sacred values (Baron and Spranca 1997; Tetlock 2003), and moral heuristics (Sunstein 2005). I will also consider the implications of each of these explanations for biases in WTP bids and, more broadly, for the role of moral concerns in environmental decisions.

Moral Identity and Moral Intensity

A natural starting point is to consider why CV scenarios generate *moral* reactions, as opposed to ecological, social, economic, or any other type of response. I adopt a simple framework that suggests that moral reactions are a function of both individual differences and contextual factors. More specifically, drawing on behavioral ethics research, I suggest that moral identity (Aquino and Reed 2002) captures an important individual difference, and that moral intensity (Jones 1991) identifies central contextual factors that affect moral reactions.

Moral identity is defined as "a self-conception organized around a set of moral traits" (Aquino and Reed 2002: 1424). As such, moral identity can vary in content; justice may figure prominently in one person's moral identity, whereas human rights may be central to another person's. Moral identity can also vary in self-importance. Moral traits that are important to a person's self-conception are likely to be invoked in various types of situation.

One implication of this concept for CV studies is that the stronger the self-importance of a respondent's moral identity, the more likely he or she is to have moral reactions to the presenting scenario. The self-importance of moral identity predicts the strength of respondents' moral reactions. Another implication is that the specific traits that are central to a respondent's moral identity (e.g., fairness versus rights) are likely to shape the type of moral sentiments that are activated by the scenario. The traits that comprise moral identity predict the type of moral reaction.

The concept of moral intensity stipulates that moral reasoning depends upon the type of issue that is considered (Jones 1991). As Jones (1991) has noted, minor theft of workplace supplies is not likely to be thought about in the same way, or to the same degree, as the introduction of an unsafe product to the marketplace. Moral intensity, defined as "the extent of issue-related moral imperative in a situation" (Jones 1991: 372), consists of six components: magnitude of consequences (net harm); social consensus (social agreement about morality of act); probability of effect (likelihood that the act will occur and that it will result in the predicted outcomes); temporal immediacy (length of time until the consequences occur); proximity (physical or psychosocial closeness to the victims); and concentration of effect (the degree to which the magnitude of the consequences are focused on a relatively small number of people). Research has shown that the components that have the biggest affect on ethical reasoning are magnitude of consequences, social consensus, probability of effect, and temporal immediacy (McMahon and Harvey 2007; Tsalikis *et al.* 2008).

Applied to CV studies, this concept suggests that the stronger the moral intensity of the issues presented in a hypothetical scenario, the more likely it is to generate strong moral reactions. Scenarios with a salient threat of species extinction (Stevens *et al.* 1991), for example, are more likely to lead to moral concern than scenarios involving support for green electricity (Hansla *et al.* 2008). Moreover, the four critical dimensions of moral intensity (magnitude of consequences, social consensus, probability of effect, and temporal immediacy) offer a useful way to measure, or manipulate, moral intensity. Bennett's and Blaney's (2002) CV study of moral intensity provides an example of this approach. They manipulated the social consensus information that subjects received about the morality of different methods for slaughtering pigs and found that social consensus had a positive effect on moral intensity and on the size of WTP bids.

Both concepts possess implications for how moral motivations may bias WTP bids. Moral identity may affect psychic rewards from WTP bids. Aquino and Reed (2002: Study 5) found that stronger the self-importance of moral identity, the greater is a person's intrinsic satisfaction from behaving in a way that is consistent with their moral traits. This suggests that both self-importance and the type of traits that are activated by a CV scenario may affect whether respondents experience a "warm glow" from their WTP contribution. Although less clear, moral identity may also affect reliance on income–environment trade-offs. Moral traits that are outcome-oriented (e.g., fairness) may be more open to trade-offs with personal welfare than those that focus on the actions themselves or the rules associated with them (e.g., compassion). As discussed earlier, consequentialist positions are more amenable to trade-offs than deontological positions. Moral intensity, in contrast, is likely to exert a moderating effect on psychic rewards and trade-offs, rather than having a direct effect. I would predict that the greater the moral intensity of a CV scenario, the greater the effect of moral identity on psychic rewards and the calculation of income–environment trade-offs.

Both concepts also possess implications for understanding the broader role of moral motivations in environmental decisions. The concept of moral identity asserts the standing of moral concerns relative to social/political, economic, or other stakes. It indicates that "self-interest" in environmental issues extends beyond social/political or economic stakes to include moral positions (see DesJardins 2011, for a similar point about virtue ethics). Such positions reflect who we are and, in this sense, have equal footing with other interests. The challenge, however, is that moral positions may conflict with other interests, requiring self-awareness and self-regulation to resolve the conflict. The broader significance of the concept of moral intensity is that some types of environmental issues—that is, ones high in magnitude of consequences, social consensus, probability of effect, and temporal immediacy—are more likely to generate moral reactions than others. As mentioned above, this can help to explain why the threat of species extinction (Stevens *et al.* 1991), for example, is more likely to lead to moral concern than the use of green electricity (Hansla *et al.* 2008). It can also help to explain why environmental issues can generate inconsistent moral responses. Environmental issues are often ambiguous and complex (Vatn and Bromley 1994), and unlike personal issues, people differ in their exposure to relevant information. For these reasons, there are likely to be differences in how people assess the components of moral intensity for a particular issue. In addition, the components of moral intensity do not always line up. In the case of climate change, for example, lack of temporal immediacy undermines moral intensity (Weber 2006; Seabright 2010). One implication of this line of reasoning is that developing consensus about the moral intensity of an environmental issue requires public knowledge and discourse.

Protected Values and Sacred Values

The concepts of moral identity and moral intensity provide insights into what makes reactions to CV scenarios particularly moral, but they are not as helpful in explaining what type of moral reactions are prone to psychic rewards or are resistant to trade-off. A useful starting point for addressing types of moral reaction is the distinction between consequentialism (evaluates the consequences of an action to determine if it is ethical, as in utilitarianism) and deontology (focuses on the action itself or the rules from which it follows to determine if it is ethical, as in human or animal rights) that was discussed above. Consequentialist ethical reasoning would seem to be open to the kind of trade-offs that are assumed to take place in the valuation decisions in CV studies, whereas deontological ethical reasoning may lead to decision rules that limit or proscribe trade-offs. This difference appears to be inherent to the approaches. By focusing on outcomes as the ethical determinant, consequentialism must be able to weigh the different types of outcome that result from a decision to ascertain the right course of action; trade-offs seem implicit to this approach. On the other hand, by focusing on the action itself and the rules from which it follows, deontology concerns moral obligations that appear absolute; trade-offs would seem inconsistent with such moral imperatives.

However, it is possible for deontological principles to be traded-off when the outcomes at stake are significant or when the principles themselves are labile. For example, although lying may violate the deontological principle of honesty, few would question the ethics of lying in a situation in which it was the only way to save a life (an extreme case) or in which it was the only way to pull off a surprise birthday party (a mundane case). This suggests the need to develop a better understanding of the types of (and the conditions under which) deontological position that are more or less resistant to trade-offs.

The related concepts of protected values (Baron and Spranca 1997) and sacred values (Tetlock 2003) help to fill this gap in the literature. Baron and Spranca (1997) defined protected values as those that are especially resistant to trade-offs with other values, especially compensatory or economic values. They reflect strongly held deontological rules and, as such, they represent absolutes that carry moral obligation. Two interesting implications of the trade-off resistance of protected values are that people will tend to use wishful thinking to deny the need to make trade-offs and, also, they will tend to become angry when faced with violation of their protected values.

Tetlock and his colleagues (Tetlock *et al.* 2000; Tetlock 2003) have examined the related concept of sacred values, defined as: "any values that a moral community implicitly or explicitly treats as possessing infinite or transcendental significance that precludes comparisons, trade-offs, or indeed any mingling with bounded or secular values" (Tetlock *et al.* 2000: 853). They have shown that pitting sacred values against secular ones, like money, is a "taboo trade-off"; it leads to moral outrage (i.e., harsh attributions, anger, and support for retribution) and moral cleansing (i.e., symbolic acts to reaffirm the values under assault). Even though taboo trade-offs are generally resisted, they are more likely to be made when they are reframed as either tragic trade-offs (involving two sacred values) or routine trade-offs (involving two secular values).

As applied to CV studies, this work raises the question of whether a hypothetical scenario taps into a respondent's protected or sacred values. Clearly, this would depend both on the type of values that are raised in a scenario and on the set of values that are protected for a particular respondent. A practical suggestion is to include questionnaire items in CV studies that assess the extent to which the scenario relates to respondents' protected values; this information could be used to check for, or control for, possible bias in WTP estimates.

The concepts of protected values and sacred values possess interesting implications for how moral motivations may bias WTP bids. To the extent that a CV scenario taps into respondents' protected values, they are likely to experience anger or moral outrage at the WTP vehicle's pitting of their protected values against economic self-interest. This prediction clearly differs from the expectation that subjects would experience a "warm glow" from WTP contributions to valued causes. The only context in which protected values could possibly lead to a "warm glow" is if the moral cleansing of a protest bid or an extremely high bid led to a positive affect; conversely, giving in to the trade-off by making a legitimate WTP response could lead to negative feelings such as regret or guilt. (One way to test this would be to use a verbal protocol CV study, as in Schkade and Payne (1994), and assess affective reaction pre- and post-bid and to compare the latter with WTP.)

The implications for income–environment trade-offs seem straightforward. By definition, respondents whose protected values are threatened are less likely to trade-off these values against personal welfare. What is less clear, though, is how these subjects would respond to the WTP vehicle, for example, by making protest bids versus extreme bids. Moreover, research on protected values and sacred values suggests that even these subjects may give in to trade-offs under some circumstances. As mentioned above, Tetlock (2003) has shown that trade-offs between sacred values and secular values are more likely to occur if they are reframed as routine trade-offs (involving two secular values). This suggests that how the environmental good in a CV scenario is framed—for example, whether it highlights animals rights issues versus the biological or ecological aspects of the environmental good—will affect the likelihood of income–environment trade-offs. In addition, Baron and Leshner (2000) have indicated that some protected values, because they are not well formed or well thought out, are not as stable as others. They found that subjects who thought of counterexamples to their protected values became more open to trade-offs. They also found that protected values yielded to trade-offs more easily when the amount of harm was small or it was unlikely to occur. Their work implies that CV studies could benefit from distinguishing between respondents' stable and unstable protected values, and from strategies to encourage subjects to think more about the latter. It also raises the possibility of constructing scenarios with minor or improbable harms and then extrapolating the elicited values to harms that are more significant or likely. More recently, Bartels and colleagues (Bartels and Medin 2007; Bartels 2008; Iliev *et al.* 2009) have shown that protected values are more open to trade-off when attention is focused on consequences, either through the procedure used to elicit preferences or through the options presented in the choice context. This work suggests that designing CV scenarios and questions to direct subjects' attention to consequences will increase the flexibility of protected values.

More broadly, protected or sacred values point to the importance of "meaning, not money" (Iliev *et al.* 2009: 190) in environmental decisions. They help to keep people morally whole in the midst of pressures to compromise or trade-off; in relation to the prior topic, they literally protect moral identity. However, the challenge posed by protected values is integrating them with the very real need, especially in a public policy context, to determine the economic value of environmental goods and services. Recent research suggests that this challenge may be less daunting that it appears at first blush. As reviewed above, attentional focus and framing effects can make protected values more open to trade-off; under these circumstances, the preferences exhibited by protected values can even appear utilitarian (Bartels and Medin 2007; Bartels 2008; Iliev *et al.* 2009). This work suggests that people with protected values care deeply about the matter at hand, so deeply that salient utilitarian considerations cannot be excluded from the decision process. As Bartels (2008) has noted: "It seems reasonable that people who care more about not harming a resource (people with PVs) might also tend to care a great deal about the ultimate consequences realized in a domain (i.e., the good to be promoted)." One implication of this work for integrating moral principles and economic valuation is to present valuation queries in a frame that fully captures the public policy need to consider consequences.

Moral Heuristics

The concept of moral heuristics is another way to think about moral reactions to CV scenarios and their potential effect on WTP valuations. There is a well-developed literature in the decision sciences that describes the use of heuristics, or mental rules of thumb, as a means to simplify the decision process. Heuristics provide a way to make "fast and frugal" (Gigerenzer and Goldstein 1996) judgments about complex matters, given our limited information-processing capabilities. Recently, Sunstein (2005), among others (e.g., Hanselmann and Tanner 2008), has begun to extend the concept of heuristic to moral reasoning. He has argued that, just like heuristics in other realms, moral heuristics operate through a process of "attribute substitution ... Unsure of what to think or do about a target attribute (what morality requires, what the law is), people might substitute a heuristic attribute instead—asking, for example, about the view of trusted authorities" (pp. 532–533). His catalog of the use of moral heuristics include risk regulation (cost–benefit analysis, emissions trading, and betrayals), punishment (pointless punishment and probability of detection), "playing God" in the domains of reproduction and nature, and the act–omission distinction. For example, he has suggested that some of the ethical objections to emissions trading seem to rest on the moral heuristic: "People should not be permitted to engage in moral wrongdoing for a fee" (p. 537), or that many of the moral injunctions against "playing God" with nature (e.g., genetic engineering of food) are based on the moral heuristic: "Do not tamper with nature" (p. 539). His overall argument is that although moral heuristics usually work well because they "represent generalizations from a range of problems for which they are indeed well-suited," they can lead to moral mistakes "when the generalizations are wrenched out of context and treated as freestanding or universal principles, applicable to situations in which their justifications no longer operate" (p. 531).

One limitation of Sunstein's (2005) analysis is that he does not specify when people do and do not rely on moral heuristics. Assuming that people rely on them some of the time, and that they use more formal reasoning processes at other times, it is important to identify the conditions that account for the use of one over the other. Although an understanding of these conditions will not solve the question of the accuracy, in an absolute sense, of moral heuristics, it does provide insights into their "ecological rationality" (Gigerenzer 2008). Under conditions of uncertainty or complexity, moral heuristics may be as effective as analytical reasoning at solving moral problems.

I propose that moral heuristics, like heuristics in other domains, tend to be used under conditions of complexity. This argument is consistent with the notion that heuristics stem from the need to solve problems that are relatively intractable given our bounded rationality. Following Opaluch and Segerson (1989), I define complexity as uncertainty both about the possible outcomes and about their probabilities. As they observed: "if a choice situation involves many possible states of the world and there is uncertainty about both the probabilities of the different states occurring and the possible outcomes under these states ... then rather than trying to use very imperfect information to balance possible costs and benefits, a decision-maker may instead choose to rely on the use of a rule of thumb" (p. 87). Applied to CV studies, this perspective suggests that the greater the complexity of the hypothetical scenario, the more likely respondents are to rely on moral heuristics to formulate their response.

The concept of moral heuristics possesses implications, albeit speculative, for psychic rewards and trade-off resistance. Although the literature on moral heuristics is silent about the role of affect, it is clear that reliance on heuristics lessens the cognitive burden of decision making. This implies that, compared with a more analytical reasoning process, the mental ease of using heuristics may be an implicit psychic reward. In terms of income–environment trade-offs, moral heuristics as described by Sunstein (2005) appear absolute and, therefore, would be resistant to trade-off with other values. It is not clear, however, whether the judgmental process used to understand the CV scenario is the same as, or carries over to, the process used to make a WTP bid. If they involve two different decisions, an interesting research question is whether the use of moral heuristics in the first judgment (about the scenario) spills over to the process used to make the second judgment (about WTP). If the decisions are inseparable or if they use similar processes—either of which seems more likely than the assumption that an initial decision based on heuristics leads into an analytically-based WTP judgment—then reliance on moral heuristics would lead to "fast and frugal" (Gigerenzer and Goldstein 1996) WTP responses. The strength or availability of the moral heuristic may affect WTP, with salient moral conclusions leading to higher valuations.

A broader implication is that, under some circumstances, moral heuristics may lead to decisions that are as rational as those based on expected utility. As mentioned above, Sunstein (2005) has argued that although moral heuristics are generally accurate, they can lead to significant mistakes of judgment. In contrast, my view of moral heuristics as a response to complexity suggests that they may be "ecologically rational" (Gigerenzer 2008) or well adapted to such decision environments. A decision about the preservation of a species, wetland or other environmental resource faces a lot of unknowables, including the functional contribution of the environmental good (Vatn and Bromley 1994), the outcomes and their probabilities, and the loss function. Under these circumstances, a moral heuristic may function as a kind of precautionary principle, ensuring "that an allowance or margin of error be made for those uses of the environment that may result in unexpected and uncertain—though potentially large—future losses" (Pearce and Barbier 2000: 241). Interestingly, in this case the descriptive and normative approaches to environmental management seem to dovetail. Both suggest that under conditions of uncertainty and potential irreversibility, it may make sense to reject cost–benefit analysis in favor of a more general principle that safeguards welfare.

Conclusion

In this essay I have suggested several ways to think about moral motivations in CV studies: moral identity (Aquino and Reed 2002) and moral intensity (Jones 1991); protected values (Baron and Spranca 1997) or sacred values (Tetlock 2003); and moral heuristics (Sunstein 2005). Each of these provides different insights into why CV scenarios elicit moral concerns and how this may bias WTP bids, and they offer a number of avenues for future research. More generally, this analysis suggests that moral motivations may be more rational than they appear. They provide a way to enact moral identity, to protect core values, or to make safe decisions under complexity. For any or all of these reasons, it might be sensible to make such choices "without prices—and without apologies" (Vatn and Bromley 1994: 145).

The larger policy question, though, is how to bridge the divide between moral considerations and economic valuation in environmental decisions. Although much more work is needed, the preceding analysis offers a few insights. One is to recognize that, to some degree, people are capable of resolving conflicts between moral concerns and economic realities in their own decision-making process. As indicated above, people with protected values can be flexible when the need is clear. One way to do this is to design CV or other economic valuation studies in a way that fully captures the very real trade-offs implicit in the policy debate. Another insight is that the relative merits of moral claims and utility calculations depend on the decision context. As argued above, under conditions of uncertainty and potential irreversibility, it may be sensible to reject cost–benefit calculations in favor of moral principles. Similarly, Bennis *et al.* (2010) have indicated that cost–benefit analyses lead to optimal outcomes when consequences can be clearly anticipated, but that moral rules may be preferable when the context is socially complex or when it concerns rare but potentially costly events. The general implication of this insight is to adopt a contingency approach to decision standards rather than trying to determine the one best standard or trying to blend standards. Empirical work is needed to pin down the specific conditions, and specific advantages, that favor moral principles or utility calculations as a basis for environmental decisions.

References

Adamowicz, W.L. (2004) "What's it Worth? An Examination of Historical Trends and Future Directions in Environmental Valuation," *Australian Journal of Agricultural and Resource Economics*, 48 (3): 419–443.

Aquino, K. and Reed, A. (2002) "The Self-importance of Moral Identity," *Journal of Personality and Social Psychology*, 83 (6): 1423–1440.

Baron, J. and Leshner, S. (2000) "How Serious are Expressions of Protected Values?" *Journal of Experimental Psychology: Applied*, 6 (3): 183–194.

Baron, J. and Spranca, M. (1997) "Protected Values," *Organizational Behavior and Human Decision Processes*, 70 (1): 1–16.

Bartels, D.M. (2008) "Principled Moral Sentiment and the Flexibility of Moral Judgment and Decision Making," *Cognition*, 108: 381–417.

Bartels, D.M. and Medin, D.L. (2007) "Are Morally Motivated Decision Makers Insensitive to the Consequences of their Choices?" *Psychological Science*, 18: 24–28.

Bennett, R. and Blaney, R. (2002) "Social Consensus, Moral Intensity and Willingness to Pay to Address a Farm Animal Welfare Issue," *Journal of Economic Psychology*, 23: 501–520.

Bennis, W.M., Medin, D.L., and Bartels, D.M. (2010) "The Costs and Benefits of Calculation and Moral Rules," *Perspectives on Psychological Science*, 5: 187–202.

Bulte, E., Gerking, S., List, J.A., and de Zeeuw, A. (2005) "The Effect of Varying the Causes of Environmental Problems on State WTP Values: Evidence From a Field Study," *Journal of Environmental Economics and Management*, 49: 330–342.

Chilton, S.M. and Hutchinson, W.G. (2003) "A Qualitative Examination of How Respondents in a Contingent Valuation Study Rationalize their WTP Responses to an Increase in the Quantity of the Environmental Good," *Journal of Economic Psychology*, 24: 65–75.

Cooper, P., Poe, G.L., and Bateman, I.J. (2004) "The Structure of Motivation for Contingent Values: A Case Study of Lake Water Quality Improvement," *Ecological Economics*, 50: 69–82.

DesJardins, J. (2011) *An Introduction to Business Ethics*, 4th edn, New York: McGraw-Hill.

Edwards, S.F. (1986) "Ethical Preferences and the Assessment of Existence Values: Does the Neoclassical Model Fit?" *Northeastern Journal of Agricultural and Resource Economics*, 15 (2): 145–150.

Felder, F. (2007) "Ships in the Night: Climate Change, Moral Imperative, and Economic Tradeoffs,"

September 18, web log post, available at: http://blog.nj.com/njv_frank_felder/index.html.
Gigerenzer, G. (2008) "Why Heuristics Work," *Perspectives on Psychological Science*, 3 (1): 20–29.
Gigerenzer, G. and Goldstein, D.G. (1996) "Reasoning the Fast and Frugal Way: Models of Bounded Rationality," *Psychological Review*, 103: 650–669.
Gore, A. (2006) "Global Warming is an Immediate Crisis," September 18, available at: http://www.causesofglobalwarming.net/al_gore.html.
Guagnano, G.A., Dietz, T., and Stern, P.C. (1994) "Willingness to Pay for Public Goods: A Test of the Contribution Model," *Psychological Science*, 5 (6): 411–415.
Hanselmann, M. and Tanner, C. (2008) "Taboos and Conflicts in Decision Making: Sacred Values, Decision Difficulty, and Emotions," *Judgment and Decision Making*, 3 (1): 51–63.
Hansla, A., Gamble, A., Juliusson, A., and Gärling, T. (2008) "Psychological Determinants of Attitude Towards and Willingness to Pay for Green Electricity," *Energy Policy*, 36: 768–774.
Iliev, R., Sachdeva, S., Bartels, D.M., Joseph, C., Suzuki, S., and Medin, D.L. (2009) "Attending to Moral Values," in *Psychology of Learning and Motivation, vol. 50: Moral Judgment and Decision Making* (eds D.M. Bartels, C.W. Bauman, L.J. Skitka, and D.L. Medin), San Diego, CA: Academic Press; pp. 169–192.
Jones, T. (1991) "Ethical Decision Making by Individuals in Organizations: An Issue-contingent Model," *Academy of Management Review*, 16 (2): 231–248.
Kahneman, D. and Knetsch, J.L. (1992) "Valuing Public Goods: The Purchase of Moral Satisfaction," *Journal of Environmental Economics and Management*, 22: 57–70.
Kahneman, D., Ritov, I., Jacowitz, K.E., and Grant, P. (1993) "Stated Willingness to Pay for Public Goods: A Psychological Perspective," *Psychological Science*, 4 (5): 310–315.
Kerim, S. (2007) "Tackling Climate Change a Moral Obligation, General Assembly President says," September 24, UN News Centre website at: http://www.un.org/apps/news/story.asp?NewsID=23930&Cr=climate&Cr1=change.
Kotchen, M.J. and Reiling, S.D. (2000) "Environmental Attitudes, Motivations, and Contingent Valuation of Nonuse Values: A Case Study Involving Endangered Species," *Ecological Economics*, 32: 93–107.
McMahon, J.M. and Harvey, R.J. (2007) "The Effect of Moral Intensity on Ethical Judgment," *Journal of Business Ethics*, 72 (4): 335–357.
Opaluch, J.J. and Segerson, K. (1989) "Rational Roots of "Irrational" Behavior: New Theories of Economic Decision-making," *Northeastern Journal of Agricultural and Resource Economics*, 18 (2): 81–95.
Pearce, D. and Barbier, E.B. (2000) *Blueprint for a Sustainable Economy*, London: Earthscan.
Schkade, D.A. and Payne, J.W. (1994) "How People Respond to Contingent Valuation Questions: A Verbal Protocol Analysis of Willingness to Pay for an Environmental Regulation," *Journal of Environmental Economics and Management*: 26, 88–109.
Seabright, M.A. (2010) "The Role of the Affect Heuristic in Moral Reactions to Climate Change," *Journal of Global Ethics*, 6 (1): 5–15.
Spash, C.L. (2006) "Non-economic Motivation for Contingent Values: Rights and Attitudinal Beliefs in the Willingness to Pay for Environmental Improvements," *Land Economics*, 82 (4): 602–622.
Stern, P.C. (2000) "Toward a Coherent Theory of Environmentally Significant Behavior," *Journal of Social Issues*, 56 (3): 407–424.
Stevens, T.H., Echeverria, J., Glass, R.J., Hager, T., and More, T.A. (1991) "Measuring the Existence Value of Wildlife: What do CVM Estimates Really Show," *Land Economics*, 67 (4): 390–400.
Sunstein, C.R. (2005) "Moral Heuristics," *Behavioral and Brain Sciences*, 28: 531–573.
Tetlock, P.E. (2003) "Thinking the Unthinkable: Sacred Values and Taboo Cognitions," *Trends in Cognitive Sciences*, 7 (7): 320–324.
Tetlock, P.E., Kristel, O.V., Elson, S.B., Green, M.C., and Lerner, J.S. (2000) "The Psychology of the Unthinkable: Taboo Trade-offs, Forbidden Base Rates, and Heretical Counterfactuals," *Journal of Personality and Social Psychology*, 78 (5): 853–870.
Tsalikis, J., Seaton, B., and Shepherd, P. (2008) "Relative Importance Measurement of the Moral Intensity Dimensions," *Journal of Business Ethics*, 80 (3): 613–626.
Tutu, D. (2007) "Three Billion Reasons for Bush to take Action on Climate Change at G8," June 7, Huffington Post at: http://www.huffingtonpost.com/desmond-tutu/three-billion-reasons-for_b_51108.html.
Vatn, A. and Bromley, D.W. (1994) "Choices Without Prices Without Apologies," *Journal of Environmental Economics and Management*, 26: 129–148.
Weber, E.U. (2006) "Experience-based and Description-based Perceptions of Long-term Risk: Why Global Warming Does Not Scare Us (Yet)," *Climate Change*, 77: 103–120.

B. Climate Change

Does a Failure in Global Leadership Mean It's All Over?

Climate, Population, and Progress

Ruth Irwin

Modern progress is both confirmed, interrupted, and dissolved by two dynamic changes in the human condition: climate change and peak population. Climate change presents an extinction event that brings "progress" to a halt. The "progress" of exponential population growth will peak around 2050. Declining birth rate and longevity is already aging the population in "developed" countries. I argue that population degrowth is an inevitable function of modernity, in the same way that the land clearances were an inevitable function of the early stages of industrial capitalism. This is a "progress" that shifts from exponential growth in population and economics, to exponential degrowth within the next century. Instead of viewing climate change and peak population as a calamity, I propose that together they constitute conditions for renewal. Modern technological progress has been problematic for a long time. Climate change and peak population make it very clear what is at risk. Up until now, technology and its efficiencies have shaped the modern horizon of thought and efforts to exhort people to behave "ethically" have had limited impact. But climate change and peak population make it clearer what elements of industrialism are sustainable and what elements of industrialism are putting multitudes of species at risk of extinction. Population degrowth means we can no longer rely on the engine of consumerism as the justification for economics. By examining the cultural consequences of climate change and peak population we are better able to perceive how technology itself needs to be contained in a new horizon of thought.

Idealist conceptions of "progress" believe the process of change to be teleological and tend toward an ultimate end, or goal. That end is viewed as either Utopia or Dystopia depending on the optimistic or pessimistic outlook of the philosophy (for an example, see Irwin 2008 on the unfounded optimism of neoliberalism and contemporary pragmatism). Optimistically, the discourse of classical and neoliberal economics posits technological innovation as a crucial mechanism to extract profit from an otherwise flat (or perfect) market. Technological innovation introduces efficiencies to production processes or introduces new artifacts to be sold on the market—both of which could potentially address the problem of climate change. In this view, the industrial pollution emitted by technology is the danger, but we can progress from this heritage through the potential for clean-green technology to ultimately save us. Through the progressive impulse of business-as-usually conceptualized, technological innovation could save the day.

On the other hand, a dystopian view of climate change will extol the opposite scenario. Business-as-usual is about increasing profit and market share, which inevitably results in increasing amounts of consumerism to create higher turnover. Consumer goods have enormous quantities of embedded emissions and are largely responsible for climate change. Climate change confirms the dystopian idealization of "progress" as a type of Armageddon flashpoint, which finalizes the progress of technological innovation with an insurmountable climax. Unlike its eschatological model, the progress of modernity is unlikely to result in the "select" ascending to Heaven and the renewal of Heaven on Earth for future generations. Instead, the extinction period intimated by extreme climate change will be unsurvivable for the majority of species, and *homo sapiens* will be no exception. Climate change presents an "end of history" that is not merely a descent into the banality of consumerism (Fukuyama 1991), nor even, an end of *this* particular civilization (Diamond 2005); but an end of our planetary ecological niche. Thus, the discourse of progress is so determinist (whether it be calamitous or optimistic) that it makes it very difficult for people within the modern horizon of thought to appraise the future with some modicum of hope or despair without slotting neatly into the determinist framework of utopian progress or dystopian progress. There does not appear to be an option to extricate ourselves from the consequences of the progressive unfolding of industrial consumerism. It is nigh on impossible to imagine any other options than "business-as-usual."

Yet I suggest that both climate change and population offer unprecedented ways of reflecting on progress and technological innovation that neither throw the baby out with the bathwater nor remain caught in the dystopia–utopia of business-as-usual. Population changes erode the narrative of progress in a different way. Population peaks in a mere 40–100 years, after several hundred years of exponential growth—or progress. Having peaked, indications are that population will decrease, possibly as quickly and as far as it increased. This means that modernity is a bubble, which emerged from a stable population of less than half a billion people for most of the Holocene epoch to 9–10 billion and back again over a period of 400 years. Thus far, we have been living in the exponential growth period of that bubble, but in our lifetimes, the reduction of population will begin and degrowth will impact on economics, immigration, and social structures in new and challenging ways.

Population and climate change coalesce in unexpected divergences from the prevailing modern assumptions about migrants, labor and long-standing accretions of prosperity. Billowing storm clouds force millions of ecological refugees to flee south from the ice that is covering the North American continent in the closing scenes of the film *The Day After Tomorrow* (2004).[1] While it is unlikely that one severe storm will trigger a climatic tipping point, climate change and migration is changing the physical and sociopolitical landscape. There is no doubt that modern consumerism and population pressure is impacting on the planet. However, the prevailing assumption is that it is traditionally vulnerable groups (the developing counties and the poor, such as Tuvalu, Kiribati, Bangladesh) that will suffer the substantive affects of climate change. In the film, in response to the apocalyptic climate change, Mexico rolls back the barbed wire that separates the borders and welcomes the migrants in. This beautiful reversal of the gate-keeping that has protected wealthy countries from the massive numbers of poor migrants and political and ecological refugees is more than ironic. In my opinion, the film is intuitively prescient about the reversals in migration that will occur in the future.

As populations go through demographic transition and life spans continue to get longer, young people will increasingly be in short supply. During the 2000s the United Nations Population division forecast that population would peak at around 9.2 billion in 2050, and over the following century, dropping birth rates will mean that all countries, including African nations, will have falling net populations (UN Pop. 2003). These forecasts were significantly downgraded in 2011, as African nations began shifting toward demographic transition (i.e., less than replacement birth rate of 2.1 per woman), but more slowly than originally anticipated (UN Pop. 2011). However, whether peak population is 9.2 billion in 2050 or 10 billion in 2100, the *rate of increase* is slowing in every nation, and the percentage of children is decreasing likewise. It is quite likely that with time, the decrease will be at an exponential rate similar to the rate at which the population increased over the last couple of hundred years. Across the planet, immigrants and working age people will be in short supply. This could mean that unlike the draconian illegal migrant detention centers in places like Australia, toward the end of this century young migrants will be in great demand and rich nations will have policies and incentives in place to attract them.

However, these insights into the changes in demographics and climate are missing from the prevailing discourse of modern progress. Instead, the normative assumptions that inform policy making and leadership continue to rest on the assumption that stable temperature conditions of the Holocene epoch will continue to prevail and that the exponential increase in population will continue to buoy consumer confidence and economic growth. Without the insights into population peak and degrowth, the increasing pressure of sheer numbers and increased expectations of consumerism add progressively more and more strain on finite resources. The modern worldview has little more than a faith in technological innovation to address that pressure. We understand that in the immediate future, and for the next 80–100 years, climate change, deforestation, water stress, resource exhaustion, pollution, and rubbish are all threatening human communities and the ecosystems on which we rely all over the world. Existing consumer lifestyles that prevail in the developed nations and are aspirational for the undeveloped nations are at threat. Simultaneously, consumerism itself is the threat that is destroying ecological systems everywhere. Add to that mix the rapid *increase* of 1 billion people every 12–14 years over the last 60 years, and a forecast increase of another 2 billion in the next 40 years, puts the limitations of the planet's ecosystems under severe stress. The Fourth Assessment Report of the IPCC attributes climate change to the radiative forcing of consumerism and population growth:

> The effect on global emissions of the decrease in global energy intensity (–33%) during 1970 to 2004 has been smaller than the combined effect of global income growth (77%) and global population growth (69%); both drivers of increasing energy-related CO_2 emissions. (Pachauri and Riemakers 2007: 37)

The usual response to the immediate material reality is for more "progress." Technology is getting better: faster, smaller, more efficient. Technology stimulates the global economy and because of the redistribution guaranteed by Keynesian welfare, more and more people are better off. Up until now, population has continued its unrelenting growth and threatens the carrying capacity of planetary resources. It forecasts exponential consumerism, exponential economic growth, exponential pollution, underpinned by exponential population growth. The expectations are either dystopian or utopian, but there is little possibility for, as Whitehead (1929) put it, process reality rather than progressive reality.

Leadership

As far as climate change and pollution are concerned, a rapidly declining global population is a very desirable thing. On the rare occasions that it does come to their attention, this is not a view shared by economists or policy makers, as their normative assumptions about progress and growth rely on the fundamental assumption that the underlying population is exponentially increasing. Furthermore, most of the population growth still occurring is in very poor nations in west and east Africa, so the burden of vast numbers of people is being borne out of sight of the "developed West." Yet their most able and competent people are queuing up to migrate to richer nations, so offsetting and making invisible the domestic degrowth in developed nations. Thus, demographic transition has not yet had an impact on richer nations, and their leaders are almost completely unaware of it. Likewise, despite clearly articulated demands for the reduction of greenhouse gas emissions by reducing consumerism and commensurate economic "development," this is carefully excluded from the emergent discourses on climate-change mitigation and adaptation (see Irwin 2008).

Unsurprisingly, given the dilemma over "progress," there is a crisis in leadership on climate change. Since its recognition in 1992, leaders have been unable to come up with any effective global plan to reverse or halt greenhouse gas emissions. For a while there was some enthusiasm for "decoupling" economic growth from resource consumption and emissions through the "knowledge economy" (Irwin 2008), but this neoliberal optimism has faded away. The Kyoto Protocol attempted to draw a line in the sand at 1990 levels of CO_2 emissions. The Kyoto Protocol was signed by 191 countries, who committed to bringing emissions down to 20% below 1990 levels by 2012. Sadly, with the important exception of some countries in the EU, despite their legal commitments, nearly all countries are at least 20% above 1990 levels.

This is no mere policy pedantry. Scientists both within the IPCC and in the multitude of climate-change institutes around the world are increasingly strident in their assertions that if global average temperatures rise by 2°C, it becomes 50% likely to trigger irreversible tipping points in many ecosystems (Rahmstorf 2009). Whether this becomes a planetary climatic shift from a temperate period to an ice age is unknowable until its too late. As yet, leadership continues its stalemate.

As the Kyoto Protocol's period of commitment draws to a close, global conventions at Copenhagen and Cancun in 2010 and 2011 were unable to reach any agreement that even attempted to enshrine limits to greenhouse gas (GHG) emissions into law. As I write, the potential for agreement on effective global legislation at the next COP at Durban looks bleak. While it is true that some nations, provinces, regions and local councils are being proactive about climate change, in general there is a vacuum in leadership on the issue.

Leadership is currently in a bind from multiple sources: the global nature of the externalities; the short-termism of democracy; and the pressure from lobby groups such as the Koch brothers, Exxon Mobil (Oreskes and Conway 2010), and OPEC. There is normative pressure to continue the economic growth model from nearly all national interest groups, including taxpayers, small and corporate business, the media, and local government (who need development to supplement inadequate local tax for provision of services and infrastructure). Education has not played a clear hand yet.

Unsurprisingly, given the active pursuit of development for so long, there is also pressure for the opportunity to develop toward the same excessive consumerism that is considered normal by the West from China, Russia, India, Latin America, Africa and elsewhere.

Fundamentally, throughout the modern world there remains a deep-seated faith in the concept of progress, especially technological progress, consumerism, and economic growth. Commensurately, there is a deep-seated fear that there are no alternatives to progress, and that the eschatological Armageddon stories that have fuelled the modern narrative may be inevitable. After all, while we think in short-term policy frameworks of 20–30-year time spans, the outlook is always terrifying; several billion more people and substantially less raw resources. From a short-term perspective, population and climate change rear up as potential disaster with no indication of how to escape the teleological direction that flows toward increasingly difficult conditions.

Given the entrenched difficulties of the situation, it behoves us to consider how technological modernity came about, how it shapes our expectations, and what could expel us from its determinist teleology. It is necessary to consider the onset of these technological directives; what shifted human subjectivity from complex, grounded, and beholden to nature, to technologically efficient, free, and resourceful. Where are the problems, where are the benefits, and why is it not clear to everyone in what direction society needs to move? The inability to see consumerism and economic "growth" as a problem is not willful. It stems from a more profound blindness, one of utter faith and familiarity: but more so. It is to the onset of our faith in economics and technological progress we now turn.

Technological *Tempo*

Modern culture is a result of a profound shift in the nature of technology. To understand modernity and discern what is problematic and what is helpful, it is important to understand what exactly has changed from earlier ages. Modern technology has affected our self-understanding, as individuals, and as a species. Human beings have transformed the scale of our impact on our ecological niche, but as a species we are slow to respond to the scale of our own impact. In many ways, our problems are simply that we have not properly adjusted to the change that modern technology has unleashed.

The agricultural technology of the Middle Ages was bound by the natural rhythm of the seasons. When trees were mature, fruit ripened and could be harvested; when fruit ripened the bottling season began; when the calves were born, cows could be milked and cheese could be made. The rate of maturity is not always annual, but production and consumption in these times were dictated by the pace of ecology.

The beginning of the modern era signaled a shift in the nature of storage. Once rivers were dammed for hydropower, the energy produced could be used on demand (Heidegger 1977). Energy is no longer at the tempo of the snow-fed swollen creeks, but can be converted whenever communities want to consume it. The dam itself stores potential power, and it can be released at as required. The tempo shifted from ecological constraints to the pace of consumerism. Production had been seasonal, but in the modern era, with energy available at any time, transport and storage is no longer problematic. The pace of production changes from that set by ecology to the needs (or desires) of consumerism.

This technological transformation has been incredibly helpful. Communities no longer starve if the crop fails. Drought, flood, tempest are serious in an immediate sense, but in modern societies they are less likely to be compounded by longer-term starvation.

Since the long centuries of pastoral agriculture, production has been transformed. Labor has changed from seasonal intensity, when bands of workers worked long and hard for a few months a year and sporadically and easily for most of the rest of the year, to the monotonist intensity of Taylorist production lines. Taylorism often takes place in factories, where one worker becomes expert at one tiny fraction of a complex production line, endlessly reproducing the same tiny movement, the same boring but vital task, on countless numbers of articles that are later assembled into the final product. Storing these items for long periods has taken space, but is not very problematic, as with international shipping items can be transported from one part of the world to another and assembly from globally produced parts has become commonplace. Global Taylorism further frees local communities from the knowledge and constraints of their local ecological conditions.

Lately there has been another iteration of the modern pace of consumerism. With the phenomenal increase in telecommunications and information technology it is now easier than ever to estimate the demands of consumers. Large stockpiles of material goods are no longer necessary because the information flows make responding to need speedy and accurate. Coupled with information technologies, innovation means "just in time production" is more manageable. For example, publishers no longer need to have large print runs of books that are then stockpiled in warehouses until they all sell. They can program small print runs and sell texts on demand.

These shifts in technology, from the pace of local ecology to the pace of global consumer demand has radically changed the style, knowledge base, beliefs, and the focus of the people involved in modernity. Heidegger calls this transformation in knowledge and beliefs the technological *Gestell*. Within the horizon of knowledge created by modern technology *everything* is perceived as consumable. Features in the local environment are losing their resonance. A rock is no longer a landmark and an enigmatic element of landscape, but is dug up and carried away for sale in a distant gardening center. Human beings are not understood primarily as thoughtful and intelligent, or supple, fluid, graceful and elegant, flexible or funny. Human beings are just like the environment: a potential resource in the systemization of consumerism.

Human resources may add value to their own potential on the labor market by training or life-long learning. "The danger" of the technological *Gestell* is that it makes everything and everyone disposable in the global machinery of consumerism. Each individual is simply a place-holder, and can be replaced by any other suitably trained individual. Disciplined regimes of bodily skills, along with time management, make an individual's resource value higher. Talent at rational deductive logic maybe a useful tool, facilitating scientific knowledge and new modes of efficiency or regulation for the good of the progressive modern project. However, imaginative critical thinking is more problematic; on the one hand, like technological innovation, critique is vital for progressive adaptation, but it is also potentially undermining of the global machine, and so while analysis is encouraged, critique and thinking is not. The fundamental change that underlies the transformation of culture from agriculture to industrialism is technology itself.

Technological *Gestell*

In 1955, the German philosopher Heidegger, wrote an essay on the essence of technology. He traced it back to Ancient Greece but, of course, technology is far older than the Greeks. Heidegger took ideas from two of his contemporaries, Jünger and Spengler. All three had lived through both the First and Second World Wars, and had seen the devastation wrought by the industrialization of war. *Homo sapiens* had been wielding tools for thousands of years, but modern man has developed something profoundly new. Something about technology has shifted, and it has affected the environment and what it means to be human. Heidegger (1977), in his unusual, enigmatic and unique fashion proposed that the essence of technology is "nothing technological."

Modern technology challenges the environment in new ways. Once the stick, then the stone adze, and later the metal spade were the tools employed to help human labor and encourage the soil to loosen and the sown seed to grow. Of late, the machinery involved in agriculture separates human labor from the soil, and allows the illusion of mastery over ecology. Top-dressing fertilizes pasture from an airplane and literally removes the farmer from contact with the soil. Weed killing is done with toxic chemicals and "Roundup Ready" plants are genetically engineered to resist the insecticides and herbicides that poison other species. Farming now takes place in laboratories and mechanical workshops. Toil has little to do with soil. The illusion of mastery over nature prevails in the technological horizon of modernity. Modern technology pervades multiple aspects of life, so it is difficult to imagine how things would be without technological interaction. Heidegger called this all pervasive framework of thought the technological *Gestell*.

Heidegger's concept of *Gestellen* needs introduction. The root is *stellen*. It means to place, to locate; the *ge-* makes the term active—locating, positioning, framing. It is an horizon of thought. While *stelle* is the root of position, it also takes a linguistic turn: positing (naming). And it can be more violent: as imposition, wresting forth, imposing, or posing. In the case of technological *Gestellen*, the horizon of thought is framed by efficient ordering of technology. All things, including people, are inserted into the giant machinery of consumerism, so that they are either in the process of enabling consumerism, or they are potential, in storage or stockpiled for future consumerism. The role of humanity is like the "foreman" ordering the order, mastering the demands on environmental resources.

The technological *Gestell* enframes our understanding of everything, from planetary "resources" to human "resources." Technology delimits our horizon of thought. Heidegger's synopsis of the technological *Gestell* is as follows:

> Enframing means the gathering together of that setting-upon which sets upon man, i.e., challenges him forth, to reveal the real, in the mode of ordering, as standing-reserve. Enframing means that way of revealing which holds sway in the essence of modern technology which is itself nothing technological. (Heidegger 1977: 20)

Mastery over nature is, drawing from Hölderlin's poem, *Patmos*, "the danger," but embedded in the danger is the "saving power" (Heidegger 1977). Absorption in the technological horizon might be efficient, but it also lends weight to a particular form of alienation and this constitutes the conditions under which we "forget" to ask the important question: "what is being." Through the technological *Gestell*, people are relieved of their direct relation with ecology. This freedom has its dark side. The alienation from ecology is a loss. We have lost a crucial element of what our species-being is all about (Marx 1844: Manuscripts). We lost a facet of our humanity at the same moment that we lost our awareness of ecological place. And it is the feeling of loss that constitutes the saving power. With it, as we shall discover more clearly later, the essence of technology becomes visible for the first time.

In general, we are so engrossed in the late modern technological horizon that we rarely pause and ask why it might be problematic. Freedom from the immediate ecological constraints transformed human communities. We have become increasingly global in interrelated arenas: production, consumerism, communication technologies, such as the media, and in global outlook. We know as much (or as little) about drought and war in Somalia as we do about the countryside less than 100 km from our own dwelling. Given that modern communities are no longer dependent on local ecological systems, and we have greater freedom, health, and sophistication than ever before, why bother to interrogate technological "progress" as a boundary on our comprehension?

Climate change brings this boundary to our horizon of knowledge into view for the first time in its *global* aspect. Technological progress has freed us from the constraints of local ecological conditions and allowed us to "master" nature, but, at the same time, this industrial mastery produces many tons of GHG emissions and ultimately results in climate change. Global GHG emissions brings into view the tipping point past which the climate could change so dramatically that the planet could resemble the ice sheets of Neptune rather than the green hues of Earth. This is the line over which we cannot survive (Irwin 2008, 2010). With climate change, our reliance on the ecological comes back into view in a global, planetary dimension that it has never had before.

Up until 1989, when the Brundtland report signaled a new era in global discourse, the alienation of modern practices from ecology was almost invisible. Before 1989, particular, localized ecological niches could be "denatured" by deforestation, soil runoff, chemicals, toxins, dioxins, radiation, concrete and more; and though unfortunate, it did not really matter to the well-being of local communities because global trade rescued them. Climate change brings our fundamental lack of mastery over ecology back into view in new and *technological* ways.

Climate change is showing up our ecological embeddedness to conscious thought with an hitherto unknown clarity. Climate change brings the faulty reasoning of mastery over nature into harsh reality because we are finding that continuing business-as-usual has brought us to the verge of catastrophe. It brings us to the verge, and perhaps we will be unable to halt our previous normal ways of modern living and we will trip *beyond* the tipping point.

There is, however, no *beyond* the tipping point for human beings. While it is true that the Earth will continue to exist long after humanity is extinct, there will be no human subject there to register it. This is a kind of idealist solipsism writ large. As Berkeley once pronounced: "If a tree falls in a forest and no-one is around to hear it, does it make a sound?" (1710: s. 20). From within, or without, the modernist framework there is no "over the line" (Heidegger 1999: 291–232) or "beyond the tipping point" of climate change. Over the line is the nothingness of extinction (Irwin 2008, 2010).

Proximity to the line of extinction brings "the danger" into harsh relief. The danger of the line of climate change makes it possible to understand how technology is still beholden to ecology, despite its shift in pace from seasonal production to mass storage, and the globalized demands of consumerism.

Finally, the essence of technology starts to become clearer; modern technology reaches into the realm of being and shapes our understanding of all things. The essence is the technological *Gestell* itself: the horizon of thought that has celebrated progress, growth, and freedom. The essence of technology is the shaping of thought. It is the consumerist ethos that has taken over every possible interpretation of natural objects and people as a potential "resource," and virtually annihilated other, older, more subtle ways of knowing.

The proximity to the tipping point of climate change and nihilism actually throws new light on the question of technology itself. While the technological *Gestell* has dominated our thinking, we have blindly accepted the role of modern technology in storage, efficiency, and progress. But the proximity to climate change makes it clear that we need to rethink our relation to technology. The existing one is too problematic. It brings with it pollution, extinctions, ecological destruction: a plethora of clumsy, ignorant and ignoble ways of doing things. This questioning of the "essence" of technology is itself, for Heidegger, the saving power.

He has a good point. We cannot, with 7 billion people currently alive on the planet, and expected to rise to well over 9 billion in the next 40 years cope without sophisticated, and efficient, technology. But the mining of all things as resources in the machinery of consumerism does not have to dominate the way technology, ecology, and people intersect. If ecology is brought to the fore, as climate change really insists that it should, then technology changes role. It becomes more about the efficient preservation of ecological niches than about the blind extraction of anything to provide fodder for consumerism. Ecology needs to enframe the technological *Gestell*.

We are not yet there. A good example is the European Union (EU). Some countries in the EU, such as Germany, are among the only nations worldwide who have managed to substantively decrease their CO_2 emissions. Nevertheless, they still expect large-scale storage and efficient production tied to long-range transport to solve future energy generation. One of the schemes being taken very seriously by the EU is to put millions of photovoltaic cells in a Middle Eastern desert and then stretch a huge high voltage cable back across the Middle East to Europe (McKie 2007). There is no cognizance of the large amount of entropy involved in such a scheme (like a long-range heater), or the massive impact it will have on the desert ecology. It is another example of the old technological *Gestell* that is so globalized and so alienated from any particular ecological system that the costs to the environment simply do not register.

Perhaps we should not be too surprised that a shift in mindset from global technology toward planetary ecology has not taken place with lightening-speed immediacy. Adapting to change, especially expectations and thought patterns, takes willingness and reflection.

Adaptation and Population

During the era of modernity, the technological horizon altered the way individuals see themselves, the way families organize themselves, and the way the world population rapidly flourished. These changes are complex and cannot be understood as simply "good" or "evil." One example is the land clearances, which were the first phase of the transition toward modernity. In every country this is usually the cause of huge political and ecological turmoil. Economists justify land clearances and the privatization of the commons as a painful but transitionary period (see Stern 2006 for recent examples). There is little or no cognizance of the deep social and ecological costs that are then entrenched and are hard to remediate (see Seják *et al.* 2009 for financial estimates of ecological contribution to "environmental services"). Yet it should be possible that clearances could be followed by more ecological industrial activity and better planned, medium-density, green urban areas than has been the case up until now.

To consider the transition toward late modern technological culture in a more positive light, it is worth thinking about the social response to rubbish disposal. In ancient traditional societies, food and other materials were protected and transported in easily disposable clay or large leaves, rather than mass-produced, lightweight, hardy plastic or paper packaging. If people threw out their leaves or clay pots, they disintegrated back into the dirt in no time. It takes societies time to adjust to the impermeable nature of modern packaging, together with advertising public relations exercises to convince them en masse that rubbish disposal needs to be a concerted effort rather than a casual flick of the wrist. Litter is a modern narrative.

Family size, too, is adjusting to the changes that modern technology affords us. Freedom from the ecological constraints of local produce has allowed modern humanity to flourish. Global population for most of the Holocene era was estimated to have been less than half a billion people worldwide. Since the beginning of the modern period, we have gone from 1 billion to almost 7 billion in little more than 200 years. As we enter the Anthropocene epoch, global population is forecast to increase to at least 9.3 billion people (UN Pop. 2003, 2011). On the one hand, modern technology has allowed human beings to flourish, on the other hand, huge population levels combined with global consumerism is placing unsustainable strains on the

Earth's resources. Fish stocks, forests, wild animals, birds, butterflies and other insects, and reptiles are all facing extinction as their habitat is sacrificed for agriculture, mining, and industry.

Gone are the days when infant mortality was extremely high and extended families supported their own infirm or elderly members. Instead, the economic prerogatives of modernity make children expensive and birth control much easier to access.[2] Increasingly, the state welfare safety net is more reliable, especially the modern health system, which means that the infirm or the elderly are supported in the public domain as much as by the family unit. The reliability of the health system is gradually entering human consciousness. Gradually family size is reducing, so that on average, as countries go through demographic transition, the number of children per family have diminished from nine or eleven to less than two in just three generations. Thus, without the overt governance of one child per family policies, or the draconian measures advocated by Paul Ehrlich in the 1970s, modern societies all over the world are gradually decreasing their *rate* of population increase, and the UN predicts that global population will peak and then *decline* somewhere between 2050 and 2100 (UN Pop. 2003, 2011).

All countries in the world, including Somalia and other war-ravaged nations, are gradually moving toward demographic transition. Demographic transition is when the birth-rate is less than 2.1 children per couple (replacement rate). While the number of children a couple have is clearly to do with their decision making and "free will," when seen on this sort of statistical scale it is clear that it is also about generations of families adjusting—adapting—to the new discourses of health and welfare, and the changes that modern technologies, such as contraception, make possible.

It will take some time yet for these alterations to show significantly in our global demographic profile. Already in some countries longevity and low birth-rates are creating an aging population. When average birth-rate is less than replacement, the domestic population lags, and then shifts through zero to negative population growth. The decrease in domestic populations is being supplemented by immigration to maintain stable or slowly growing populations. Immigration works, but only while there are still some nations with an abundance of people. That abundance will end roughly between 2050 and 2100, and then the decline will begin in earnest. The UN Population Division graphs (2004) showing the *rate* of population growth, indicate that without supplementation from immigration population will decline almost as fast as it increased. That could be a decrease of 1 billion people every 14 years. It also means vastly less people of working age, and proportionally many more in the 60–90-year-old bracket.

Economists talk about demand in terms of numbers of potential consumers. But, as yet, they have not had to contend with a contraction in consumerism based on a contraction in population. Nevertheless, "new markets" rely on "new consumers," and globally we have simply been breeding them for two centuries. Once that stops, there will remain a lag as some countries continue to "develop," and nomadic and tribal agricultural peoples are further persuaded to become consumers. But by 2120, global consumerism will inevitably begin to contract.

The concept of "progress" has long been delegated to economic pressures tied to stimulating technological innovation: a nub of the "Invisible Hand." It turns out that "progress" has a deeper drive than profit and self-interest. Almost exactly as Malthus argued in 1798, population growth has underpinned progress, and progress has driven and is ultimately enabling population to slow down and decline.

Data indicates that after demographic transition population decline continues, possibly at an exponential rate (smaller numbers of fertile-aged couples having fewer than the replacement number of children, means exponentially fewer fertile couples in future generations). It is probable that the population will level out again, but whether that leveling occurs at its peak of 9 or 10 billion (unlikely), or even at its original stable point of less than half a billion, is unknown. In biology, when species are no longer constrained by erstwhile ecological limitations, the population will boom to a point where the by-products exceed the ecological niche, and the population dives again, often to roughly its initial equilibrium point.

Enoughness

Back in the present, nations have been looking to their leaders to advise them on moral and legal regulation that will govern a change in behavior and bring GHG emissions under control. My argument is that with the best will in the world, leadership cannot address some of the entrenched dynamics of capitalism until global communities are ready for change (Bateson 1977; Irwin 2008). Some changes will be extremely difficult to create as the infrastructure is not in place,

For several generations there have been indicators that the modern technological horizon is gradually changing the consciousness of people in modern society to "save" them, as much as place them in "danger" of forgetting the question of what makes it meaningful to be alive. Generation X played around with ideas about the freedom offered by utopian technological progress, so that full employment could be achieved if everyone worked only a 25- or 30-hour week and holiday periods could be extended for all. Sadly, the dynamics of the market's Invisible Hand "balanced" entrenched "acceptable" levels of unemployment to maintain high profits by keeping wages low. Consumerism was encouraged by faith in economic growth without any regard to the costs it meted on the environment or family finances. Neoliberalism touted minimal government regulation and increased efficiency, but put more middle management and accountability schemes in place than had ever before occurred, so workloads *increased* and holiday periods decreased. Since the Velvet Revolution in 1989, capitalism has taken over the erstwhile communist bloc, and consumerism has become the dystopian "End of History" (Fukuyama 1991). However, the technological *Gestell* can transform beyond the redundant narrative of economic "growth" and "progress."

It takes a while for modern societies to adjust to the new parameters that the freedom of mass storage and the scale of global production and transport that modern technology provide. An obsession with consumerism reminds me of the filthy rubbish heaps that used to clog up the roads and beaches of my own country before the public relations exercise on "Clean Green New Zealand" in the 1980s. The mass storage of early modernity is becoming increasingly unnecessary as just-in-time production allows the pace of consumerism to dictate the pace of production. This means that conspicuous consumption is becoming passé in the same way that litter was a relic of a more pastoral age. Going shopping as a past-time is an obsession of the noveau riche (like Esmeralda Marcos' shoes).

This shift toward flourishing and enoughness disturbs the fundamentals of the market balance directed by the aggregation of rational utility maximizing agents of the Invisible Hand. Recent research into "happiness" shows that up to a moderate income, increases in money corresponds to increases in happiness, but quickly thereafter wealth creates anxiety and time pressures, which, paradoxically, decrease happiness and satisfaction (cf. Duncan 2010). "Enoughness" makes people happy, too much is miserable.

"Enoughness" ensures happiness far better than ever-increasing levels of wealth, worthless work, and competition anxiety. Research into "enoughness" and "degrowth" (Daly 1996) has been around in various iterations for a long time. Thus far, policy makers have disregarded degrowth as an idea stemming from the "whacky fringe" (despite authors who have lead the World Bank and the Sustainability Commission). The Keynesian settlement still dominates policy in terms of economic growth for state provision of essentials such as universal education, and the Invisible Hand is thought to do the distribution of cheap goods and services to the impoverished as much as the rich. But whether corporate CEOs, politicians, and bureaucrats like it or not, degrowth is a mere 40 years away. Climate change ought to bring that horizon even closer.

Climate change is bringing resource exhaustion and the toxicity and pollution of modern technology into stark relief in an unprecedented way. People in late modern societies are still free of the local constraints on crop production because they can store food for long periods or, better, trade their way out of localized famines. But climate change ensures that populations have to be much more aware of how technological production impacts on the global atmosphere, endangering ecosystems all over the world. Straightforward alienation of urban lifestyles from rural ecology is no longer possible, and all people have to make better lifestyle decisions to improve their ecological footprint.

In conclusion, both climate change and peak population are bringing our attention to how redundant the discourse of "progress" really is. We are still in the turbulent times of believing in, and acting with short-sighted faith, an irrational and obsolescent mode of economics and technological "innovation." But increasingly, the illusion of our mastery over nature is becoming obvious, and the technological *Gestell* will have to transform to accommodate the irruptions of ecological necessity into our worldview. Forgoing the teleological quest for progressive utopia or dystopia will bring our attention back to what makes life meaningful and content.

While climate change and global population gives us plenty to be frightened about, they also present a new framework for guiding the transformation of modernity. Proximity to climate change has brought the limitations of consumerism into view. It shows us that our illusions of grandeur and mastery over local ecological niches were short-lived and brought false comfort. Climate change makes it clear that however technological modernity may be, we are still a species among other species, and the planetary ecological niche that we have as home is the root and foundation of all that we are or can ever be. Making visible the technological *Gestell* will hopefully give us the direction for a sophisticated, technologically savvy, and ecologically grounded society. As the consequences of climate change and population growth and degrowth intensify their impact, these parameters will become increasingly visible to us all.

Notes

1 The scientific inaccuracy of this film is common knowledge, and its use here (as in the original) is metaphorical.

2 Although the Bush Administration and the Vatican impeded access to birth control in western and central Africa, slowing the transition to lower birth rates there.

References

Bateson, Gregory (1979) *Mind and Nature: A Necessary Unity*, London: Wildwood House.

Berkeley, George ([1710] 1982) *A Treatise Concerning the Principles of Human Knowledge*, ed. Kenneth Winkler, (Indianapolis, IN: Hackett.

Daly, Herman (1996) *Beyond Growth: The Economics of Sustainable Development*, Boston, MA: Beacon Press.

Duncan L.G. (2010) "Should Happiness Maximization be the Goal of Government?" *Journal of Happiness Studies*, 11: 163–178.

Emmerich, R. (producer) (2004) *The Day After Tomorrow*, Canada: Fox Films.

Fukuyama, Francis (1992) *The End of History and the Last Man*, New York: Free Press.

Heidegger, M. ([1954] 1977) "The Question Concerning Technology," in *The Question Concerning Technology and Other Essays* (trans. and Introduction William Lovitt), New York: Harper & Row; pp. 3–35.

Heidegger, M. ([1955] 1999) "On the Question of Being, *Über 'Die Linie'*," in *Pathmarks* (ed. and trans. William McNeill), Cambridge: Cambridge University Press; pp. 291–322.

Irwin, R. (2008) *Heidegger, Politics and Climate Change: Risking It All*, London: Continuum.

Irwin, R. (2010) *Climate Change and Philosophy: Transformational Possibilities*, London: Continuum.

Malthus, Thomas (1798) *An Essay on the Principle of Population*, London: Johnston Press.

Marx, K. ([1844, 1932] 1959) *Economic and Philosophical Manuscripts* (trans. Martin Mulligan), Moscow: Progress Publishers, transcribed by Andy Blunden for Marx.org, available at: http://www.marxists.org/archive/marx/works/1844/manuscripts/preface.htm.

McKie, Robin (2007) "How Africa's Desert Sun can Bring Europe Power," *The Guardian*, available at: http://www.guardian.co.uk/environment/2007/dec/02/renewableenergy.solarpower.

Oreskes, Naomi and Eric Conway (2010) *Merchants of Doubt*, New York: Bloomsbury Press.

Pachauri, R.K. and Reisinger, A. (eds) (2007) *Climate Change: 2007 Synthesis Report*, Geneva: Intergovernmental Panel on Climate Change.

Rahmstorf, S. (2009) "Sea Level Rise," keynote speech at the Climate Change Congress, Copenhagen, Denmark, March 10, Potsdam Institute for Climate Impact Research.

Seják, J., Pokorný, J., Cudlín, P., Burešová, R., and Prokopová, M. (2009) "Energy–Water–Vegetation-based Environmental Accounting of Ecosystem Services and Stocks," Proceedings of the 5th EA-SDI EMAN Conference on Environmental Accounting: Sustainable Development Indicators, April 23–24, 2009, Prague, Czech Republic; pp. 39–48.

Stern, Nicholas (2006) *The Stern Review on the Economics of Climate Change*, London: HM Treasury.

United Nations Population Division (2003) "Long Range Population Projections," United Nations, Department of Economic and Social Affairs, available at: http://www.un.org/esa/population/publications/longrange/long-range_working-paper_final.pdf.

United Nations Population Division (2004) "World Population to 2300," United Nations, Department of Economic and Social Affairs, available at: http://www.un.org/esa/population/publications/longrange2/WorldPop2300final.pdf.

United Nations Population Division (2011) "Updates," United Nations, Department of Economic and Social Affairs, graphs available at: http://esa.un.org/unpd/wpp/Analytical-Figures/htm/fig_3.htm; http://esa.un.org/unpd/wpp/Analytical-Figures/htm/fig_6.htm; http://esa.un.org/unpd/wpp/Analytical-Figures/htm/fig_12.htm.

Whitehead, A.N. (1929) *Process and Reality*, London: Macmillan.

Further Reading

Altvater, Elmar (2007) "The Social and Natural Environment of Fossil Capitalism," *Socialist Register*, 43: 37–59.

Diamond, Jared (2005) *Collapse: How Societies Choose to Fail or Succeed*, New York: Viking.

Ehrlich, Paul ([1968] 1971) *The Population Bomb*, New York: Ballantine.

Falcon-Lang, Howard (2011) "Anthropocene: Have Humans Created a New Geological Age?" BBC News, Science and Environment, May 10, available at: http://www.bbc.co.uk/news/science-environment-13335683.

Heidegger, M. ([1924] 1985) *History of the Concept of Time, Prolegomena*, Bloomington, IN: Indiana University Press.

Ruddiman, W. (2007) *Plows, Plagues, and Petroleum; How Humans Took Control of Climate*, Princeton, NJ: Princeton University Press.

Steffen, Alex (2008) "What are the Sustainability Implications of Peak Population?" *Worldchanging*, available at: http://www.worldchanging.com/archives/007830.html.

United Nations Population Division (1999) "The World at 6 Billion," United Nations, Department of Economic and Social Affairs, available at: http://www.un.org/esa/population/publications/sixbillion/sixbilpart1.pdf.

United Nations Population Division (2003) "Partnership and Reproductive Behaviour in Low-fertility Countries," United Nations, Department of Economic and Social Affairs, available at: http://www.un.org/esa/population/publications/reprobehavior/partrepro.pdf.

Collective Responsibility and Climate Change

SEUMAS MILLER

In this essay I address the issue of collective moral responsibility for climate change. In the first section I outline my account of joint action, including joint epistemic action, as a necessary preliminary to elaborating my account of collective moral responsibility in the second section. In the third and final section I apply this account of collective moral responsibility to the matter of human-induced, harmful climate change.

1. Joint Action

Joint action consists of multiple individual actions performed by multiple agents and directed toward a collective end, for example, a team of workers building the Empire State building, a team of terrorists destroying the Twin Towers killing thousands, a team of climate scientists seeking the causes of harmful climate change.[1] A collective end is an individual end that each of the participating agents has, but it is an end that no one agent acting alone realizes on his or her own. So each agent acts interdependently with the other agents in the service of the same shared end: the collective end. Again, consider the collective end of a security organization, such as the FBI, whose members may be jointly working to prevent harm, notably great harms planned by criminal organizations such as terrorist groups; or consider a team of scientists working on the de-sequestration of carbon dioxide from coal burning.

Joint actions exist on a spectrum. A one end of the spectrum there are joint actions undertaken by a small number of agents performing a one-off simple action at a moment in time, for example, two lab assistants lifting some equipment onto a bench. At the other end of the spectrum there are large numbers of institutionally structured agents undertaking complex and often repetitive tasks over very long stretches of history, for example, those who built the Great Wall of China, climate scientists determining the extent of human-induced climate change.

Joint activity within institutions typically also involves a degree of competition between the very same institutional actors who are cooperating in the joint activity, for example, rivals for scarce management positions in a corporation. Moreover, in many institutional settings organizations compete with one another, for example, business organizations in market settings. Here there is joint activity at a number of levels. For one thing, each competing organization (e.g., a single corporation) comprises a "team" of individual agents who cooperate with one another and work jointly to secure the collective ends of the organization (e.g., a mining company trying to maximize market share). For another thing, each "team" (e.g., each corporation) is engaged in *joint* compliance with the regulatory framework that governs their competitive market behavior; that is, each complies with, say, the regulations of free and fair competition interdependently with the others doing so, and in the service of ensuring the ongoing existence of the market in question. This is consistent with the existence of a regulator that applies sanctions to those organizations that breach the regulations, including safety regulations that might be regarded as a costly and unnecessary impost on business; the latter compliance mechanism is an "add-on" to the fundamental underlying structure of interdependence of action in the service of collective ends that is constitutive of market mechanisms.[2]

Let us consider further the notion of a joint action and the correlative notion of a collective end. As stated above, joint actions involve multiple agents with the same end, for example, to build a house (the collective end) or map the human genome. Note the following points:

First, each agent's individual action is a (possibly small) causal contribution to the collective end, for example, building the Great Wall of China, mapping the human genome.

Second, each agent's individual action or omission is performed on condition that others perform their contributory actions/omissions; there is interdependence of action.

Third, each has the collective end only on condition others have the collective end; there is interdependence of ends.

Fourth, what the collective end is and that it is being pursued is a matter of mutual true belief among the participants (A and B mutually truly believe that p if, and only if, A believes truly that p, B believes truly that p, A believes that B believes that p, etc.[3]).

Fifth, collective ends are purely conative states; they are not affective states such as feelings or desires. Accordingly, we need to distinguish the mental states constitutive of joint actions (i.e., intentions, ends, and beliefs) from the mental states that might motivate some joint actions (e.g., feelings and desires).

Joint actions can realize collective ends that are also goods, namely, collective goods. Examples of such collective goods are a law-abiding society and an economically viable "green" technology sector. At an organizational level, a collective good might be the realization of a collective end that consists in harm minimization or prevention. Thus, a firm might have as one of its collective ends the avoidance any major industrial accidents or the prevention of any serious security breaches. Note that in my sense of the term "collective good," a collective good is simply a good that is produced by joint action directed to a collective end, the realization of which consists in the provision of that good. Such joint action includes action that consists in joint compliance with safety and security procedures that has as a collective end the collective good of prevention of harm.

Such collective goods are not necessarily reducible to an aggregate of individual benefits. Relational goods produced by joint activity, such as social harmony and mutual scientific knowledge (each knows that p and each knows that each knows that p, etc.), are cases in point.

Some collective goods are goods that are jointly pursued for their own sake; that is, they are not pursued merely as a means to some further individual or collective end. Various kinds of collective interest, such as the national interest or the interests of the mining industry, are examples of this.

Moreover, a belief in the value of collective goods can motivate action irrespective of individual self-interest, for example, a soldier giving his life in the national interest, a whistleblower blowing the whistle on a logging company's illegal destruction of old-growth forests.

It will be evident from the above that we are distinguishing between self-interested reasons (or motives) for individual and joint action, for example, so-called "sticks" and "carrots," and moral reasons (or motives) for action (including joint action), and claiming that the latter is not reducible to the former (and vice versa).

It will be further evident that we hold that moral reasons, for example, a belief that polluting the environment is wrong, a belief in the common good, can motivate in and of themselves. So individual self-interest is not the only motive for action. Moreover, even when the motive of self-interest is present, which it obviously typically is, it is not necessarily the dominant motivation.

Armed with this general characterization of joint action, collective goods, and so on, let us now turn to joint epistemic action, as opposed to joint behavioral action

2. Joint Epistemic Action

Epistemic actions are actions of acquiring knowledge. Here we can distinguish between so-called "knowledge-that" and "knowledge-how"; the former being propositional knowledge (knowledge of the truth of some proposition), the latter being practical knowledge (knowledge of how to undertake some activity or produce some artifact). The definition of propositional knowledge, in particular, is philosophically controversial, but let us assume for our purposes here that someone, A, has knowledge that p if, and only if, A has a true belief that p, and A has a justification for believing that p that does not rely on some other false belief.[4]

The methods of acquiring propositional knowledge are manifold, but for scientific knowledge they include observation, calculation, and testimony. Moreover, the acquisition of these methods is very often the acquisition of knowledge-how, for example, how to calculate, how to use a microscope, how to "read" an x-ray chart.

In the case of the engineering sciences, there is an even more obvious and intimate relationship between propositional and practical knowledge, since both are in the service of constructing or making things. Thus, in order to build an airplane engineers have to have prior practical ("how-to") knowledge, and that practical knowledge, in part, comprises propositional knowledge, for example, with respect to load-bearing capacity. Moreover, this engineering model has increasing applicability in new and emerging sciences such as nanotechnology.

What counts as sufficient evidence for the possession of knowledge varies from one kind of investigation and one kind of investigative context to another. Thus, a scientist would need his or her experimental results to be replicated by other scientists before it was confirmed as scientific knowledge. A detective investigating a series of murders, for example, the Yorkshire Ripper, will be focused not only on physical evidence, but also on motive (a mental state and opportunity). Moreover, the evidential threshold for being found guilty is beyond reasonable doubt.

Whereas the acquisition of practical knowledge is readily seen as emanating from action and, indeed, as being a species of action ("knowledge-in-action"), the acquisition of propositional knowledge is a different matter. However, coming to truly believe that p on the basis of evidence, that is, propositional knowledge acquisition, is action in at least three respects.

First, the agent, A, makes a decision to investigate some matter with a view to finding out the truth; the action resulting from this decision is epistemic action. For example, a detective intentionally gathers evidence having as an end to know who is the serial killer of prostitutes in Yorkshire, that is, who the Yorkshire Ripper is. Thus, the detective gathers physical evidence in relation to the precise cause and time of death of the Ripper's victims; the detective also interviews people who live in the vicinity of attacks, and so on. Here A has decided that A will come to have a true belief with respect to some matter—as opposed to not having any belief with respect to that matter, for example, a true belief with respect to who the Yorkshire Ripper is. A's decision is between coming to have true belief and being in state of ignorance, and, in conducting the investigation, A has decided in favor of the former. Similarly, a scientist seeking to discover the genetic structure of some organism makes a decision to come to have a true belief with respect to this matter rather than remaining in ignorance.

Second, the agent, A, intentionally makes inferences from A's pre-existing network of beliefs; these inferences to new beliefs are epistemic actions. For example, a forensic scientist might infer the time of death of a murder victim, on the basis of A's prior belief that rigor mortis sets in within 10 hours after death.

Third, in many cases A makes a judgment that p in the sense that when faced with a decision between believing that p and believing that not p, A decides in favor of p; again, A is performing an epistemic action. For example, our detective, A, intentionally makes an evidence-based judgment (mental act) that Sutcliffe is the Yorkshire Ripper (as opposed to that Sutcliffe is not the Yorkshire Ripper), and does so having as an end the truth of the matter. Here, A is deciding between believing that p and believing that not p; but A is still aiming at truth (not falsity). A is not deciding to believe what he thinks is false. Similarly, our forensic scientist makes an evidence-based judgment in relation to the cause of death of the victim having as an end the truth of the matter. Here the scientist is deciding between believing that the cause of death was x and believing that the cause of death was not x (but was, say, y).

As is the case with non-epistemic action, much epistemic action—whether it be propositional or practical epistemic action or, more likely, an integrated mix of both—is joint action, that is, joint epistemic action. Joint epistemic action is knowledge acquisition involving multiple epistemic agents seeking to realize a collective epistemic end. For example, a team of scientists seeking knowledge of how to generate solar energy efficiently is engaged in joint epistemic action.[5]

In cases of joint epistemic action, there is mutual true belief among the epistemic agents that each has the same collective epistemic end, for example, to discover how to generate solar energy efficiently. Moreover, there is typically a division of epistemic labor. Thus, in scientific cases some scientists are engaged in devising experiments, others in replicating experiments, and so on. So, as is the case with joint action more generally, joint epistemic action involves interdependence of individual action, albeit interdependence of individual epistemic action.

As we saw above, knowledge of the extent of human-induced, harmful climate change, for example, is joint epistemic action that involves a collective epistemic end, and also involves a division of epistemic labor and interdependence of epistemic action.

A collective epistemic end can be both a collective good pursued for its own sake and also the means to further ends. Knowledge of the means to generate solar energy is a case in point. Such knowledge consists of propositional and practical knowledge; knowledge of solar energy and knowledge of how to produce it. However, this knowledge has as a further (collective) end: the actual production of, say, solar energy cells. And this end has, in turn, a still further end, namely, to reduce reliance on fossil fuels.

If knowledge of how to reduce human-induced, harmful climate change is a collective end in itself, then it is not simply a means to individual ends, viz. each having as an end that he or she knows how to reduce his or her contribution to global warming. Rather, it is mutually believed that knowledge of is a collective good. However, in my view, moral beliefs can have motivational force.[6] In that case, the mutual belief that knowledge of how to reduce human-induced, harmful climate change is a collective good can have motivational force.

It follows from this that—as we saw with joint action more generally—joint epistemic action can be collectively self-motivating and does not necessarily have to rely on prior affective states such as desires.

3. Collective Moral Responsibility

Let me now outline my account of collective moral responsibility (French 2006). I note that this account is underpinned by my analysis of joint action (including joint epistemic action).

There are individual moral responsibilities, but there are also collective moral responsibilities. It will turn out that these two sets of responsibilities are importantly related; indeed, a collective moral responsibility is a species of individual moral responsibility.

Let us distinguish between natural, institutional, and moral responsibility and, in respect of responsibility, between individual and collective responsibility.

An agent, A, has natural responsibility for some action, x, if A intentionally did x for a reason and x was under A's control, for example, A dug a tunnel (action x) to enable his escape from prison.

Agent A has institutional responsibility for action x, if A has an institutional role that has as one of its tasks to x. Thus, for example, laboratory assistant, A, has the institutional responsibility to ensure that a supply of dangerous toxins are safely and securely contained; moreover, A has this responsibility even if A does not in fact do this.

What of moral responsibility? Roughly speaking, agents have moral responsibility for natural or institutional actions if those actions have moral significance. So, if A is naturally or institutionally responsible for x (or for some foreseeable outcome of x, O) and x (or O) is morally significant then, other things being equal, A is morally responsible for x (or O), and, other things being equal, can be praised or blamed for x (or O).

Note that other things might not be equal if, for example, A is a psychopath (and, therefore, incapable of acting in a morally responsible fashion) or if A does something wrong, but has a good excuse (and, therefore, ought not to be blamed).

Note also that if O involves some intervening agent, B, who directly causes O, then A may have diminished moral responsibility for O. Suppose, for example, that the unsecured dangerous toxins in the above example are stolen by B and end up causing a number of deaths. Perhaps the laboratory assistant has diminished moral responsibility for these deaths, that is, he or she does not have the same degree of responsibility as B.

Let us now consider collective moral responsibility. In essence, the account of collective moral responsibility mirrors that of individual moral responsibility, the key difference being that the actions in question are joint actions, including joint epistemic actions.

Accordingly, if agents A, B, C, etc. are naturally or institutionally responsible for a joint (including epistemic) activity x (and/or some foreseeable outcome of x, O) and x (and/or O) is morally significant then, other things being equal, A, B, C, etc. are collectively (i.e., jointly) morally responsible for x (and/or O), and, other things being equal, can be praised or blamed for x (and/or O).

The "other things being equal" clauses function here as they did in the above account of individual moral responsibility. Moreover, as was seen to be the case with individual moral responsibility, if there are additional intervening (individual or joint) actions, then those jointly responsible for the joint action in question and its outcome, may have diminished moral responsibility.

4. Climate Change

Evidently, the emission into the atmosphere of excessive quantities of greenhouse gases (GHG) (importantly, carbon, and to a lesser extent methane) produced by human activities (notably the burning of fossil fuels) are causing changes in global climactic conditions (especially global warming), which are, in turn, likely to have catastrophic consequences for human and other life forms on the planet, if the rate of emissions is not slowed and ultimately stabilized at an acceptable level. The changes in question include the melting of the ice-caps and consequent rising sea levels, variations in seasonal rainfall patterns, which impact negatively on food production, and increased levels of natural disasters, such as hurricanes, tsunamis, and the like. While there is dispute about the direct empirical evidence for global warming and what, if anything, ought to be done by way of response, there is general agreement in relation to the high and increasing levels of human-induced carbon emissions, in particular, and the reality of the "greenhouse effect" (Gardiner 2004; Vanderheiden 2008).[7] Moreover, it is indisputable that thus far (i.e., since the Industrial Revolution in the late eighteenth century) it has been the developed economies that have contributed the lion's share of human-induced carbon emissions, albeit that developing economies, notably China and India, are now major contributors.

In what follows I abstract away from the details, ignore extreme forms of climate skepticism, and simply assume that the human race is likely to suffer catastrophe at some point in the future unless it addresses the problem of human-induced climate change and does so quite soon.[8]

Let us now turn to the global issue of collective moral responsibility for harmful, climate change caused by human action.[9]

The Intergovernmental Panel on Climate Change's (IPCC) 1990 Report drew the world's attention to harmful climate change consequent upon, in particular, human-produced carbon emissions. Accordingly, since 1990 each one of millions of the Earth's human inhabitants, especially in the developed world, have not only made a minute causal contribution to current massive environmental damage and consequent large-scale harm to humans, for example, climate change causing rising sea levels and flooding of Pacific island villages, they have done so knowingly (in some sense, but see below). Can we conclude from this that the millions in question are collectively morally responsible for the harm already done and the future harm already in train? Naturally, we here rely on the above-described theoretical account of collective moral responsibility, since the meaning in ordinary language of the term, "collective moral responsibility," is more or less indeterminate and (as noted above) if one turns to the theorists one finds an array of competing theoretical accounts with diverse practical implications.

One important difference between the climate-change scenario and many other collective responsibility scenarios is that it is not the case in the climate-change scenario that each had as an end that the harm be done; in the climate-change scenario there are foreseen untoward consequences, but they are not intended or otherwise aimed at. A second important difference between the climate-change scenario and many other collective responsibility scenarios is in the number of participants (millions in the climate-change scenario versus a handful in many other scenarios) and the magnitude of the causal contribution that each makes (minute versus substantial). Naturally, these two differences are morally important; however, I am trying to identify additional moral considerations.

Let us further elaborate the climate-change scenario. Each of us unavoidably produces carbon emissions and, therefore, necessarily makes some contribution to the total quantum of carbon emissions produced by human activity; each of us has to do so in order to survive. Nevertheless, if each of us had reduced our carbon emissions to the level required for us to survive (or even somewhat above that level), that is, if each of us had forgone luxury emissions, then the harm consequent upon our 1990–2010 emissions would, in turn, have been reduced to a morally acceptable level.

Assume that the large-scale harm caused by this total quantum of luxury emissions was foreseeable. Thus, each individual (or most of them) was aware of the likelihood of the harm consequent upon this quantum of luxury emissions. Assume further that each individual, considered on his or her own, could have avoided the production of his or her contributing luxury emissions, for example, by selling his or her car and any of his or her appliances that use a large amount of electricity generated by burning coal, installing a solar energy heater in his or her roof, becoming a vegetarian, and quitting his or her job at a petrol station in favor of going on welfare. Accordingly, each is not only fully, individually, *naturally* responsible for the minute luxury emissions he or she individually produced, each is also fully, individually, *morally* responsible for those emissions since they have moral significance; they are a causal contribution to the large-scale harm. Is it morally wrong to do something that is in itself morally innocuous, but that you know will make a tiny causal contribution to a massive harm? (Naturally, there are morally relevant differences in the size of contributions made by individuals and, crucially, differences between the average (and aggregate) contributions of the members of developed nation-states and those of undeveloped and developing nation-states (Pickering *et al.* 2010).) Surely it is, at least in some cases. If so, then it is presumably a minor wrongdoing. At any rate, I am going to assume that in the climate-change scenario each of the millions is fully morally responsible for a minor wrongdoing (in the sense of knowingly, albeit unintentionally, contributing causally to harming others).

As we have seen, the millions considered in aggregate are *causally* responsible for the large-scale harm done by the carbon emissions. (And being causally responsible for harming others is typically a morally relevant consideration, including in relation to climate change, albeit it does not constitute moral responsibility in the sense elaborated above since it does not necessarily involve knowledge that the harm will be caused.)

It would be absurd to claim that each of us is fully morally responsible for the large-scale harm caused by the totality of 1990–2010 luxury carbon emissions, for example, Jones is not fully morally responsible for the loss of habitats and lives consequent upon the climate change in question. Rather, each of the millions has at most a radically diminished moral responsibility for the large-scale harm resulting from the 1990–2010 emissions.

Doubtless, the reason for the absurdity of the claim of full individual moral responsibility for the massive harm lies in part in the large numbers involved in the climate-change scenario, and the fact that each makes a tiny causal contribution to harming (for the most part) future persons. Moreover, in the climate-change scenario the action performed by each (his or her carbon emissions) are not harmful per se, but rather in aggregate have harmful effects that are in the distant future, at the end of a long and complex causal chain, and (most of) the persons in harm's way are notional in the sense that they do not yet exist. In such contexts of causal responsibility, moral responsibility is diffuse (and is a species of aggregate individual moral responsibility, as opposed to collective moral responsibility per se). Moreover, the idea of moral responsibility is likely to be somewhat inchoate in the minds of the agents in question, and likely also (relatedly) to lack a strong psychological underpinning.

So far so good, but I suggest that we have still not identified all the important moral considerations in play. What moral consideration is there, in addition to those just mentioned, by virtue of which each of us is not fully morally responsible for the harm consequent on 1990–2010 luxury carbon emissions? I suggest that a key consideration is that practically speaking—as opposed to as a matter of logic—the millions who caused harmful climate change could not have acted so as to avert the harm done by the 1990–2010 emissions (future emissions and the consequent harm are another matter—see below). Let me defend this claim.

The two main positive responses to human-induced, harmful climate change are mitigation and adaptation measures. Mitigation measures are aimed at reducing carbon emissions and consist of interventions in the causal chain at the point at which human activities cause environmental damage (e.g., by emitting excessive quantities of carbon). Adaptation measures are interventions in the causal chain at the point at which environmental damage, for example, rising sea levels resulting from global warming, causes harm to humans, for example, flooding of coastal villages. Thus, relocating to higher ground is adaptation. Presumably, in the long term mitigation must take priority, since in the long term ever-increasing carbon emissions will make the planet uninhabitable. At any rate, I take it that it is the reshaping of existing institutions, and the development of new technologies, in the service of mitigation and/or adaptation that is the principal means by which to avert the harm to present and future humans caused by environmentally damaging emissions and, specifically, a necessary means if 1990–2010 luxury emissions were to have been reduced to the level at which the consequent harm would not in turn rise above a morally acceptable level.[10]

Accordingly, only if each (or most, or a very large percentage) of the millions of the Earth's human inhabitants could have, jointly with the others (or most of the others), during the period 1990–2010, formed a collective end to avert the harm consequent upon luxury emissions, and devised and deployed the institutional and technological means to realize this end, for example, mutual knowledge of required emission reduction targets, "clean" energy organizations, compliance mechanisms, then is it the case that all (or most) of the millions are collectively morally responsible for the harm caused by 1990–2010 luxury emissions. Note the dependence of the realization of a collective behavioral end on joint epistemic action (the collective end of which is mutual knowledge of emission reduction targets).

However, I suggest that between 1990 and 2010 each (or most) of the (relevant) millions could not reasonably have been expected to have, jointly with the others, formed the requisite collective end, and designed and implemented the technological and institutional means to realize it. For one thing, and notwithstanding the 1990 IPCC Report, it is not the case that there was sufficiently widespread and adequate *mutual* knowledge—that is, each not only knows but also knows that most others know etc.—of harmful, human-produced, luxury carbon emissions among members of the relevant populations; nor was there such mutual knowledge of the necessary institutional and technological means to reduce these emissions.

For another thing, even if the members of these populations had the necessary mutual knowledge, they were not in a position themselves to implement such fundamental institutional and technological change. Here it is important to understand that while it might be feasible for each individual member of a large group to do x, it might not be feasible for all, or most, of the members of the group to do x; to suppose otherwise is to commit a version of the fallacy of composition. Thus, while it might be possible for any singe member of a community to go on welfare, it is not possible for everyone to do so; since with everyone out of work eventually there would be no welfare funds to be dispersed. Again, while it might be feasible for one or a minority of people to immediately and simultaneously switch to alternative energy sources, it is not feasible for everyone to do so immediately and simultaneously, since an entire national—indeed, international—system of energy infrastructure based on fossil fuels cannot be replaced overnight, but will take decades of well-planned and coordinated institutional redesign and technological development. I conclude that the millions are not collectively morally responsible for the harm in question, and each is certainly not fully morally responsible for that harm (including for the initial reasons given above).

It might be argued in response to this that the members of the relevant governments are collectively morally responsible for the harm in question since (within the 1990–2010 time frame) they could have acted in accordance with the collective end to avert the harm, and devised and implemented the required mitigation and adaptation measures by causing the necessary redesigning and reshaping of relevant institutions. Notwithstanding the collective action problems faced by national governments (e.g., if one nation-state substantially cuts carbon emissions and the others do not, then the first will be significantly economically disadvantaged), and the pressure to maintain the status quo applied by powerful corporations (e.g., oil companies) and community interest groups (e.g., mining communities), arguably the members of these governments are collectively morally responsible for failing to put in place policies to avert or substantially ameliorate the harm done (or about to be done) by 1990–2010 luxury carbon emissions. However, the members of the governments in questions are not morally responsible for the harm itself; a few thousand politicians did not produce a quantum of luxury carbon emissions sufficient to cause the massive harm in question. It is one thing to cause harm, it is another to fail to intervene to prevent harm being done.

We have discussed collective moral responsibility for the harm caused by the 1990–2010 luxury carbon emissions, that is, we have been concerned with retrospective collective moral responsibility. But there is an urgent need to look at things prospectively: to consider the collective moral responsibility to act to avert future harms. However, that is a topic for another occasion.

Notes

1 Seumas Miller (2001) *Social Action: A Teleological Account*, New York: Cambridge University Press; ch. 1.
2 Seumas Miller (2010) *The Moral Foundations of Social Institutions: A Philosophical Study*, New York: Cambridge University Press; pp. 50–52 and ch. 2.
3 Miller, *Social Action*, pp. 56–59.
4 See, e.g., Paul Moser (1989) *Knowledge and Evidence*, Cambridge: Cambridge University Press.
5 See Miller, *Moral Foundations of Social Institutions*; ch. 11.
6 See, e.g., Stanley Benn (1988) *A Theory of Freedom*, Cambridge: Cambridge University Press; ch. 2.
7 The "greenhouse effect" works roughly as follows: GHG simultaneously admit short-wave solar radiation while blocking some of the long-wave radiation emanating from the Earth's surface, thereby ensuring that the temperature at the Earth's surface is greater than it otherwise would be.
8 Weaker epistemic assumptions are, of course, consistent with accepting the need to act to avoid catastrophe, e.g., that catastrophe has a 50% chance of taking place if we do not act or even that we are not sure of the probability in question.
9 I will not concern myself in what follows with the common resource or "sink" issue; roughly, the issue of the injustice arising from the fact that the citizens of developed economies have exhausted the limited capacity of the Earth to absorb carbon emissions and, thereby, denied others from their "fair share" of that common resource (Gardiner 2004).
10 I realize that the latter claim, in particular, is disputable. However, given that those in the developing world were responsible for the lion's share of carbon emissions during this period, and given the dependence of most citizens on current institutions and technologies, it is surely plausible that reshaping institutions and developing new technologies would have been necessary. For example, a return to a more primitive economic and technological system for modern citizens is not a feasible option.

References

Benn, Stanley (1988) *A Theory of Freedom*, Cambridge: Cambridge University Press.

French, Peter A. (ed.) (2006) "Collective Responsibility," *Midwest Studies in Philosophy*, XXX: 1–15.

Gardiner, Stephen (2004) "Ethics and Global Climate Change," *Ethics*, 114 (3): 555–600,

Miller, Seumas (2001) *Social Action: A Teleological Account*, New York: Cambridge University Press.

Miller, Seumas (2010) *The Moral Foundations of Social Institutions: A Philosophical Study*, New York: Cambridge University Press.

Moser, Paul (1989) *Knowledge and Evidence*, Cambridge: Cambridge University Press.

Pickering, Jonathan, Vanderheiden, Steve and Miller, Seumas (2010) "Ethical Issues in the United Nations Climate Negotiations: A Preliminary Analysis of Parties' Positions," unpublished paper posted on CAPPE website at: www.cappe.edu.au.

Vanderheiden, Steve (2008) *Atmospheric Justice*, Oxford: Oxford University Press.

Further Reading

Goldman, Alvin (1999) *Knowledge in a Social World*, Oxford: Clarendon Press.

Lehrer, Keith (1987) *Knowledge*, Oxford: Oxford University Press.

Miller, Seumas (2008) "Collective Responsibility and Information and Communication Technology," in *Moral Philosophy and Information Technology* (eds J. van den Hoven and J. Weckert), New York: Cambridge University Press.

Montmarquet, James (1993) *Epistemic Virtue and Doxastic Responsibility*, Lanham, MD: Rowman & Littlefield.

Evaluating a Case Study

Applying Ethical Issues

You are finally at the last stage of the process of evaluating case studies. By this point, you have (a) chosen a practical ethical viewpoint (including the choice of an ethical theory and practical linking principles, whose point of view you will adopt), (b) listed professional, cost, and ethical issues, and (c) annotated the issues lists by examining how embedded each issue is to the essential nature of the case at hand. What remains is the ability to come to an action decision once these three steps have been completed. The final step is to discuss your conclusions.

To do this, you must enter an argumentative phase. In this phase, I suggest that you create brainstorming sheets headed by the possible courses of action open to you. Prepare an argument on each sheet to support that particular course of action utilizing the annotated charts you have already prepared. Then compare what you believe to be the pivotal issues that drive each argument. Use your chosen ethical theory to decide which issue is most compelling. Be prepared to defend your outcomes/action recommendation.

Let us return to the case of contraception in the less-developed countries. As you may recall, the case was as follows.[1] You are a regional director at the World Health Organization. One of your duties is to supervise the distribution of birth control devices to less-developed countries. The product of choice has been the intrauterine device (IUD), which has proved to be effective and inexpensive.

The problem is that in the United States, several hundred users of the IUD have contracted pelvic inflammatory infections that have been linked to use of the IUD.

As regional director, you must decide whether to continue to supply IUDs to women in less-developed countries.

ABC Corporation is a large multinational company that has a considerable inventory of IUDs that it cannot sell in the United States. The company would rather not write off its entire inventory and has consequently made a very attractive offer to sell the World Health Organization all of its existing inventory and to assist in distributing the product regionally.

As regional director, you must decide whether to accept ABC's offer to supply IUDs to women in less-developed countries.

Remember that in this case, the professional practice cost considerations, and the ethical issues were both deeply embedded, which creates an intractable conflict; there is no simple way to justify one instead of the other.

What you must do is (a) consult your worldview and see what it dictates that you do and (b) consult the ethical theory of your deepest convictions and see what it would dictate that you do. Is there a synonymy between these? If not, then engage in a dialogue between your worldview and the professional practice. Let each inform on the other. In the end, you should be able to come to some resolution.[2]

One step in this direction is to examine the arguments that support each. What are the critical premises in these arguments?[3] In any argument, there is a conclusion. If you want to contrast two arguments, you must begin by contrasting two conclusions. Conclusions are supported by premises that (logically) cause the acceptance of the conclusion. Therefore, what you must do is to create at least two arguments that entail different conclusions. To do this, create brainstorming lists on the *key issue(s)* involved in the argument. The key issue is that concept that makes the difference. This case has a number of key issues. Let us try to construct arguments that are both for and against the position.

Sample "Pro" Brainstorming Sheet for the Position

Position to be supported. Accept ABC Corporation's offer and continue to provide IUDs in less-developed countries.

Key Thoughts on the Subject

1. As a public health professional, you are enjoined to benefit the greatest number of people possible in your health policy.
2. It is a fact that in less-developed countries, millions die of starvation each year. The simple cause of starvation is too many people for the available food. When you decrease the number of people (given a level food source), more people can eat.
3. There are "blips" to any project. In this case, it is a few hundred or so cases of pelvic inflammatory infection. These casualties pale when compared to the number who will benefit from continuing to provide IUDs.
4. Utilitarian ethical theory dictates that the general good supersedes any individual's good.
5. In less-developed countries, the general good is advanced by continuing to distribute IUDs since more people (by far) benefit than are hurt.
6. ABC Corporation is willing to give a heavily discounted price on its present inventory and provide some regional assistance in the distribution of the product. This will allow the World Health Organization to reach more people than ever before and thus fulfill its mission.

Argument

1. In countries that have a limited amount of food that would feed only a certain population (n), increases in population ($n + x$), will result in x not having enough food to live: fact.
2. Many less-developed countries experience the condition mentioned in premise 1: assertion.
3. In many less-developed countries, x increase in population will result in x number of people starving to death: 1, 2.
4. Many children who are born are not planned: assertion.

5. If one subtracts the number of unplanned births from the total birth rate, the number of births decreases significantly: assertion.
6. If all children were planned, the number (more than x) of births would decrease significantly: assertion.
7. If all children were planned, less-developed countries would not experience starvation (given constant crop production): 3–6.
8. The IUD is the most effective birth control device in the less-developed countries: assertion.
9. The imperative of professional conduct in public health is to help as many people as possible: fact.
10. Public health professional standards dictate that the IUD should be provided to women in less-developed countries: 7, 8.
11. ABC Corporation has made an offer to substantially reduce the cost of its IUD inventory and to assist in regional distribution: fact.
12. ABC's offer will allow you to reach more women than you had before: fact.
13. Cost considerations bolster the professional practice standards: 9–12.
14. The IUD poses potential health risks to some women (less than 5 percent): fact.
15. The ethical imperative of Utilitarianism dictates that the right ethical decision is to advance the cause of the common good: fact.
16. Distributing IUDs helps more people in less-developed countries than it hurts: fact.
17. Utilitarianism dictates that the IUD should be provided to women in less-developed countries: 11–13.
18. The regional director must continue the distribution of IUDs to less-developed countries: 10, 13, 17.

Sample "Con" Brainstorming Sheet Against the Position

Position to be supported. Reject ABC Corporation's offer and stop selling IUDs in less-developed countries.

Key Thoughts on the Subject

1. As a public health professional, you are enjoined to benefit the greatest number of people possible in your health policy.
2. It is a fact that in less-developed countries, millions die of starvation each year. The simple cause of starvation is too many people for the available food. When you decrease the number of people (given a level food source), more people can eat.
3. There are "blips" to any project. In this case, it is a few hundred or so cases of pelvic inflammatory infection. These casualties pale when compared to the number who will benefit from continuing to provide IUDs.
4. Human life is precious. No amount of practical gain can weigh against one human life.
5. Ends do not justify the means. One may have a very good end in mind, but unless the means to that end are just, the end cannot be willed.

Argument

1. In countries that have a limited amount of food that would feed only a certain population (n), increases in population ($n + x$) will result in x not having enough food to live: fact.
2. Many less-developed countries describe the conditions mentioned in premise 1: assertion.
3. In many less-developed countries, x increase in population will result in x number of people starving to deaths: 1, 2.
4. Many children who are born are not planned: assertion.
5. If one subtracts the number of unplanned births from the total birth rate, the number of births decreases significantly: assertion.
6. If all children were planned, the number (more than x) of births would decrease significantly: assertion.
7. If all children were planned, less-developed countries would not experience starvation (given constant crop production): 3–6.
8. The IUD is the most effective birth control device in less-developed countries: assertion.
9. The imperative of professional conduct in public health is to help as many people as possible: fact.
10. Public health professional standards dictate that the IUD should be provided to women in less-developed countries: 7, 8, 9.
11. The IUD poses potential health risks to some women (less than 5 percent): fact.
12. The ethical imperative of Deontology dictates that knowingly jeopardizing the essential health of any person is absolutely impermissible no matter what the practical advantage: assertion.
13. ABC Corporation's offer is attractive from a mere cost perspective: fact.
14. It is absolutely ethically impermissible (under Deontology) to provide IUDs to women in less-developed countries when the devices have been shown to be deleterious to the health of Americans: 10, 11, 12, 13.
15. In cases of conflict, an absolute ethical imperative trumps an absolute professional standards imperative: assertion.
16. The director must reject ABC Corporation's offer and halt the distribution of IUDs to less-developed countries: 10, 14, 15.

Obviously, the crucial difference in these two arguments is the choice of an ethical theory and the way each is interpreted. Thus, whether a person takes a pro or con position is a function of the underlying value system that person holds. The way a person chooses a value system and the broader practical viewpoint is through the person's worldview and its accompanying baggage.

You must determine how to apply your practical ethical viewpoint. This requires careful attention to the theory and the linking principles you have chosen and the way they affect your evaluation of actual cases. To be an authentic seeker of truth, you must engage in this dialectical process. To do less is to diminish yourself as a person.

You are now ready to evaluate a case study.

Macro and Micro Cases[4]

Macro Case 1. You are the chairperson of an environmental impact study concerning a new dam on the Columbia River. Proponents of the dam say that they have developed a new "fish ladder" for spawning salmon that is easier than all previous designs. They describe it as beinging an "interstate highway" compared to other (older) designs. Proponents also cite the fact that the energy needs of the Pacific Northwest are ever increasing; present facilities will not meet demand. Either they must meet demand via hydroelectric plants or take the advice of the Hanford people and construct a nuclear power plant. Obviously, the latter is less attractive to people in the region. Everyone would be afraid of an accident.

On the other hand, the salmon ladders in the past have proved to be great barriers to spawning. Seventeen species of salmon are at dangerously low population levels, and this dam might tilt the balance.

You must write an executive report to the committee for or against the dam. Should it be built? What factors are important for your decision? What moral principles are relevant? Will it make a difference if your stance toward environmental ethics is anthropocentric or biocentric?

Macro Case 2. You are the county commissioner and must recommend to the county council whether to go ahead on ABC Company's plan to open a new copper mine. All the data suggest that a rich lode is relatively near the surface of the earth. Your county has been economically depressed for twenty years since the sawmill closed. This new mine promises to bring three hundred jobs to a region that has been experiencing 21 percent unemployment (which would be higher except that many people have left). The mine could revitalize the region that has been teetering on extinction.

The problem is that the lode is not located near any existing road. In fact, half of the lode is under X-4 (a mountain in a chain that surrounds your Montana valley). The company proposes to level X-4 to build an access road and to make its strip mining enterprise more affordable. It would like to share the costs of this venture equally with the state. The state has already approved the money for it, but at a town meeting on this issue, people expressed very strong opposition to the prospect of leveling a two thousand-foot mountain. Certainly, all the other mountains in the chain will be left, but is it really right to demolish a mountain? You must report to the county commissioners, who have jurisdiction over issuing permits for this procedure. Is the prospect of more jobs more important than X-4? What ethical issues are at stake? Does it make a difference if you base recommendation on anthropocentric or biocentric principles? Why or why not?

Macro Case 3. You are a senior staffer at Senator Mary Reason's office. She is asking you to write a report on whether the current Corporate Average Fuel Economy standards (CAFE) should be raised by 10% in order to decrease pollution in the United States. Your boss is on the fence on this. She sees both sides. You may lose your job if you go too far one way or the other. On the other hand, you have a law degree from a top university. If she fires you, you will probably not miss a paycheck (after you are hired by a top law firm). But you want to do this right. Write a two-page executive summary on your recommendations on pollution reduction based on empirical data and on ethical principles.

Macro Case 4. You are a senior official at the International Monetary Fund (IMF). The ABC Corporation (the world's foremost builder of dams) wants to build a dam in India that would destroy an ancient temple and statuary that cannot be moved. In addition, the artificial lake would relocate 100 000 people from an area they have lived in for a millennium (albeit constantly on the edge of starvation). But the dam would enable better irrigation and thus enable more efficient farming for 25 000 people who could live quite well on their produce. You are discussing the project with Mr Rafi, a senior vice president at ABC over tea. Part of you thinks that it's a mad tea party. Set out your discussion as a scene in a play. Be sure to cite relative embeddedness and an ethical theory.

Micro Case 1. Your name is Janet Belle. You live in a suburb of Chicago, Winetka, a wealthy suburb. You love your lawn and spend three hours a week caring for it—no lawn service for you! Your lawn is one of the few things in your life that brings you happiness. You mow, mulch, and fertilize your lawn. The problem is that the weed and feed mix you use—XYZ's Kill 'em and Grow 'em—has been cited as polluting Lake Michigan's water table. The lake has been so polluted lately that fish caught there have been deemed not fit for human consumption. Thousands of people in the northern suburbs have changed from XYZ's product on the advice of the Environmental Protection Agency. At first, you also tried other products, but none of them worked as well as XYZ. Almost everybody else has switched from XYZ, but why can't you just go on using it yourself? You can mix it in the garage so that your neighbors won't know what you're doing. After all, it works; you love your yard; and how much harm will only a few people continuing to use the forbidden brand cause? Analyze this from your point of view, that of collective responsibility, and from your grown child's point of view.

Micro Case 2. You are ready to buy a car and are attracted to the new sports utility vehicle, Space Command Navigator. This is one of the largest and most powerful of its class. No one could look down at you in this baby—you are 6 feet off the ground! It gives you a feeling of power and command. Life has not been so good for you; you are a short person who is tired of looking up to others. You are also very average and are tired of people snubbing you. Here is your chance to look down on others. However, you note that the class of sports utility vehicles (really trucks) pollute the atmosphere much more than almost every other vehicle on the market and that the amount of energy necessary to construct one of these trucks is three to four times that necessary to build a comparable car. You know it is not the most "green" car, but what the heck? This is the vehicle of your dreams. Should you go purchase it? What are the ethical issues at stake? Does it make a difference if you base your environmental theory on anthropocentric or biocentric principles? Explain.

Micro Case 3. You are a scout leader. Your troop is on a campout near the ocean. You rise very early one morning to take a walk on the beach. When you get to the beach you notice three things: (1) there are hundreds of starfish that have washed up onto the beach (a potentially fatal place to be for a starfish); (2) the tide is slowly coming in and should cover the starfish in 60 minutes (by which time most of the starfish will be dead); and (3) one of your scouts is on the beach taking the starfish one-at-a-time to the water and tossing it in. You approach the scout and say, "What do you think you're doing?" The scout replies, "Saving some starfish." "But there are hundreds of starfish on the beach and they're dying even as we speak. Let's go back, this is hopeless." But the scout kept going as he picked up another starfish and tossed it in. Then the scout replied, "It may be hopeless, but I'm sure that starfish is glad I'm here."

Find a way to analyze this case to support either the scout or the scout leader using concepts from the chapter.

Micro Case 4. You are a college student. It is an election year. You are torn between working for candidate A because she supports anti-pollution and anti-climate change legislation. These are positions about which you agree. However, there is also candidate B who believes in a smaller libertarian governmental model that the candidate says is in tune with the US Constitution. This is also a position about which you agree. You want to work for one candidate's election. How do you decide? Compose an email to your parents telling them why you are supporting one candidate over the other. Be sure to cite a moral theory in your justification.

Notes

1 I have heard that many of the structural problems with the IUD that caused pelvic inflammatory infection have not been rectified. I am not competent to comment on this; nevertheless, for this case, let us assume that these problems still obtain.

2 This dialectical interaction is described in Chapter 8 of *Basic Ethics*.

3 See my book, *Critical Inquiry*, Boulder, CO: Westview, 2010, on the details of this process.

4 For more on macro and micro cases, see the overview on p. 26.

6
Animal Rights

General Overview: This chapter examines the applied problems of animal rights and of biodiversity. The first of these problems centers on *homo sapiens'* place in the biosphere. This was discussed in the theory essays regarding deep ecology, social ecology, eco-feminism, and the anthropocentric–biocentric debate. It is a foundational question. Are humans to be understood as at the top of the *scala naturae*? Or is there some sort of species egalitarianism at work? The answer to these questions is pivotal to both sections of this chapter. Whether humans can do what is in their instrumental best interest to animals affects our treatment of them and how we think about maintaining biodiversity as we can. Both of these questions are pivotal in answering if we are to create consistent environmental policy.

Overview: The status of animals has been a source of great controversy at least since the time of Theophrastus (Aristotle's student) who declared himself to be a vegetarian on moral grounds. Certainly, humans have traditionally taken a view based on the so-called scale of nature (*scala naturae*). According to this scale, there is a linear progression of worth beginning with the soulless rocks and dirt and ascending to the plants (with their nutritive soul), to the animals (with their sensitive and/or motor soul), and ending with humans (with their rational soul). Augustine added to Aristotle's scale by setting angels and the company of heaven above humans with God on top, looking over everything. Because the scale of nature has sharp divisions and because the Judeo-Christian–Muslim traditions accept that God created humans in God's own image, it has been the assumption that this image refers to rationality and that this characteristic sets humans to be like God. Thus, because of this rationality, humans can claim to be different in kind from other living things. Proximately, they are just above the animals. Remotely, they are above plants and soulless things (like the land). This Aristotelian categorization has been with us for almost 2400 years. Combined with the religious accounts of creation, it has set the prevailing public attitude about uses of animals.

Environmental Ethics, Second Edition. Edited by Michael Boylan.

The reader must be careful, however, to sort out several different gradations of behavior toward animals. First, gratuitous cruelty, as when someone tortures an animal merely out of anger or sadism. Second, causing pain and/or death in experiments with animals to develop new medicines and other products for human use. Third, killing animals for their skins or other singular body parts. Fourth, killing animals for food. Fifth, the subjugation of animals to humans who make the animals fit into our way of life (not to interrupt our neighborhoods or daily lives) or else pay the price. Each case involves us in different ethical issues. Where do we draw the line? Do we draw the line?

Peter Singer argues that the foundation of respect is the ability to feel pain or to suffer (these are synonymous for Singer). He cites Bentham, who says: "The question is not, Can they *reason*? Nor Can they *talk*? But Can they *suffer*?"[1] Bentham puts the question in this way because he is keen on grounding conventional, societal rights on a principle of societal pleasure and pain. If pleasure and pain are the most primitive things we can say about humans and their *raison d'être*, then this is something that humans share with many animals. (Certainly, all vertebrates with central nervous systems can be said to feel system pain as a result of their biological "wiring.")

If Bentham is correct about the grounding of conventional, societal rights, and if many animals also feel pleasure and pain as humans do, then it would seem arbitrary to deny animals the rights accorded to humans. The only possible explanation would be some sort of unjustified discrimination analogous to racism or sexism. By denying these other animals rights, humans are involved in *speciesism*. We attribute all types of rights to ourselves, but deny them to animals when the standard that grounds rights is the same for each. If Singer is correct about the foundation of rights, then clearly it is time for a change. Specifics on what changes they might be are discussed in Regan's essay.

Regan makes the case for: (a) the total abolition of the use of animals in science; (b) the total dissolution of commercial animal agriculture; and (c) the total elimination of commercial and sport hunting and trapping. The reason for Regan's position is that animals should not be viewed as being resources for humans. Those who view animals as resources often use utilitarianism as the basis of their position (as per Singer's essay). Regan rejects utilitarianism for a rights-based theory designed to protect individual rights (be they human or some other animal). The ethical basis of this right comes from the notion that we are, each of us, the experiencing subject of a life—each of us is a conscious creature having an individual welfare that has importance to us whatever our usefulness to others. Both animals and humans share in the moral basis for rights (according to Regan) so that both animals and humans are equally accorded moral rights.

Mary Anne Warren (1946–2010) characterizes Regan's position as a "strong animal rights position." She disagrees with Regan that we should quickly reject the Aristotelian "reason standard" for determining moral worth. Thus, Regan's position for inherent worth as the basis for animal rights (described earlier) should be rejected. In its place, Warren argues for a "weak animal rights position" that any animal that is rational (i.e., pursues self-chosen satisfactions as a part of life) should be given the opportunity to explore those paths. Second, any creature capable of conscious pain and suffering should not be cruelly used. Third, no sentient animal should be killed without good reason.

In the fourth essay I generally support Mary Anne Warren's "weak animal rights" position. In particular, the following positions are discussed: (a) the flaws in the "strong animal rights position" and (b) a critical examination of the weak animal rights position, including (1) any creature whose natural mode of life includes the pursuit of certain satisfactions has the right not to be forced to exist without the opportunity to pursue those satisfactions; (2) any creature that is capable of pain, suffering, or frustration has the right that such experiences should not be deliberately inflicted upon it without some compelling reason; (3) no sentient being should be killed without good reason. In the practice of implementing these principles, it is understood that there needs to be an overarching tie-breaking system that will apply to all non-human organisms. However, I do disagree on some points, as well.

In the final essay, Dale Jamieson discusses the issue of domination via the institution of zoos. Jamieson argues against zoos on several fronts. First, most animals (from their intrinsic interests) would like to be free in their natural habitat. Second, zoos are extrinsically justified for how they can amuse *homo sapiens*. This puts our (relatively shallow) interests above theirs (deep intrinsic). All the various arguments for zoos (such as promoting scientific understanding or research) are shown to be invalid. In the end, "Zoos teach us a false sense of our place in the natural order. The means of confinement mark a difference between humans and other animals. They are there at our pleasure, to be used for our purposes." Thus, in the end, Jamieson adopts a biocentric argument. Under those assumptions, we should abolish zoos.

Note

1 J. Bentham (1789) *Introduction to the Principles of Morals and Legislation*, New York: Hafner; p. 34.

All Animals Are Equal

PETER SINGER

"Animal Liberation" may sound more like a parody of other liberation movements than a serious objective. The idea of "The Rights of Animals" actually was once used to parody the case for women's rights. When Mary Wollstonecraft, a forerunner of today's feminists, published her *Vindication of the Rights of Woman* in 1792, her views were widely regarded as absurd, and before long an anonymous publication appeared entitled *A Vindication of the Rights of Brutes*. The author of this satirical work (now known to have been Thomas Taylor, a distinguished Cambridge philosopher) tried to refute Mary Wollstonecraft's arguments by showing that they could be carried one stage further. If the argument for equality was sound when applied to women, why should it not be applied to dogs, cats, and horses? The reasoning seemed to hold for these "brutes" too; yet to hold that brutes had rights was manifestly absurd. Therefore the reasoning by which this conclusion had been reached must be unsound, and if unsound when applied to brutes, it must also be unsound when applied to women, since the very same arguments had been used in each case.

In order to explain the basis of the case for the equality of animals, it will be helpful to start with an examination of the case for the equality of women. Let us assume that we wish to defend the case for women's rights against the attack by Thomas Taylor. How should we reply?

One way in which we might reply is by saying that the case for equality between men and women cannot validly be extended to nonhuman animals. Women have a right to vote, for instance, because they are just as capable of making rational decisions about the future as men are; dogs, on the other hand, are incapable of understanding the significance of voting, so they cannot have the right to vote. There are many other obvious ways in which men and women resemble each other closely, while humans and animals differ greatly. So, it might be said, men and women are similar beings and should have similar rights, while humans and nonhumans are different and should not have equal rights.

The reasoning behind this reply to Taylor's analogy is correct up to a point, but it does not go far enough. There are obviously important differences between humans and other animals, and these differences must give rise to some differences in the rights that each have. Recognizing this evident fact, however, is no barrier to the case for extending the basic principle of equality to nonhuman animals. The differences that exist between men and women are equally undeniable, and the supporters of Women's Liberation are aware that these differences may give rise to different rights. Many feminists hold that women have the right to an abortion on request. It does not follow that since these same feminists are campaigning for equality between men and women they must support the right of men to have abortions too. Since a man cannot have an abortion, it is meaningless to talk of his right to have one. Since dogs can't vote, it is meaningless to talk of their right to vote. There is no reason why either Women's Liberation or Animal Liberation should get involved in such nonsense. The extension of the basic principle of equality from one group to another does not imply that we must treat both groups in exactly the same way, or grant exactly the same rights to both groups. Whether we should do so will depend on the nature of the members of the two groups. The basic principle of equality does not require equal or identical *treatment;* it requires equal consideration. Equal consideration for different beings may lead to different treatment and different rights.

So there is a different way of replying to Taylor's attempt to parody the case for women's rights, a way that does not deny the obvious differences between human beings and nonhumans but goes more deeply into the question of equality and concludes by finding nothing absurd in the idea that the basic-principle of equality applies to so-called brutes. At this point such a conclusion may appear odd; but if we examine more deeply the basis on which our opposition to discrimination on grounds of race or sex ultimately rests, we will see that we would be on shaky ground if we were to demand equality for blacks, women, and other groups of oppressed humans while denying equal consideration to nonhumans. To make this clear we need to see, first, exactly why racism and sexism are wrong. When we say that all human beings, whatever their race, creed, or sex, are equal, what is it that we are asserting? Those who wish to defend hierarchical, inegalitarian societies have often pointed out that by whatever test we choose it simply is not true that all humans are equal. Like it or not we must face the fact that humans come in different shapes and sizes; they come with different moral capacities, different intellectual abilities, different amounts of benevolent feeling and sensitivity to the needs of others, different abilities to communicate effectively, and different capacities to experience pleasure and pain. In short, if the demand for equality were based on the actual equality of all human beings, we would have to stop demanding equality.

Still, one might cling to the view that the demand for equality among human beings is based on the actual equality of the different races and sexes. Although, it may be said, humans differ as individuals, there are no differences between the races and sexes as such. From the mere fact that a person is black or a woman we cannot infer anything about that person's intellectual or moral capacities. This, it may be said, is why racism and sexism are wrong. The white racist claims that whites are superior to blacks, but this is false; although there are differences among individuals, some blacks are superior to some whites in all of the capacities and abilities that could conceivably be relevant. The opponent of sexism would say the same: a person's sex is no guide to his or her abilities, and this is why it is unjustifiable to discriminate on the basis of sex.

The existence of individual variations that cut across the lines of race or sex, however, provides us with no defense at all against a more sophisticated opponent of equality, one who proposes that, say, the interests of all those with IQ scores below 100 be given less consideration than the interests of those with ratings over 100. Perhaps those scoring below the mark would, in this society, be made the slaves of those scoring higher. Would a hierarchical society of this sort really be so much better than one based on race or sex? I think not. But if we tie the moral principle of equality to the factual equality of the different races or sexes, taken as a whole, our opposition to racism and sexism does not provide us with any basis for objecting to this kind of inegalitarianism.

There is a second important reason why we ought not to base our opposition to racism and sexism on any kind of factual equality, even the limited kind that asserts that variations in capacities and abilities are spread evenly among the different races and between the sexes: we can have no absolute guarantee that these capacities and abilities really are distributed evenly, without regard to race or sex, among human beings. So far as actual abilities are concerned there do seem to be certain measurable differences both among races and between sexes. These differences do not, of course, appear in every case, but only when averages are taken. More important still, we do not yet know how many of these differences are really due to the different genetic endowments of the different races and sexes, and how many are due to poor schools, poor housing, and other factors that are the result of past and continuing discrimination. Perhaps all of the important differences will eventually prove to be environmental rather than genetic. Anyone opposed to racism and sexism will certainly hope that this will be so, for it will make the task of ending discrimination a lot easier; nevertheless, it would be dangerous to rest the case against racism and sexism on the belief that all significant differences are environmental in origin. The opponent of, say, racism who takes this line will be unable to avoid conceding that if differences in ability did after all prove to have some genetic connection with race, racism would in some way be defensible.

Fortunately there is no need to pin the case for equality to one particular outcome of a scientific investigation. The appropriate response to those who claim to have found evidence of genetically based differences in ability among the races or between the sexes is not to stick to the belief that the genetic explanation must be wrong, whatever evidence to the contrary may turn up; instead we should make it quite clear that the claim to equality does not depend on intelligence, moral capacity, physical strength, or similar matters of fact. Equality is a moral idea, not an assertion of fact. There is no logically compelling reason for assuming that a factual difference in ability between two people justifies any difference in the amount of consideration we give to their needs and interests. *The principle of the equality of human beings is not a description of an alleged actual equality among humans: it is a prescription of how we should treat human beings*.

Jeremy Bentham, the founder of the reforming utilitarian school of moral philosophy, incorporated the essential basis of moral equality into his system of ethics by means of the formula: "Each to count for one and none for more than one." In other words, the interests of every being affected by an action are to be taken into account and given the same weight as the like interests of any other being. A later utilitarian, Henry Sidgwick, put the point in this way: "The good of any one individual is of no more importance, from the point of view (if I may say so) of the Universe, than the good of any other." More recently the leading figures in contemporary moral philosophy have shown a great deal of agreement in specifying as a fundamental presupposition of their moral theories some similar requirement that works to give everyone's interests equal consideration—although these writers generally cannot agree on how this requirement is best formulated.

It is an implication of this principle of equality that our concern for others and our readiness to consider their interest ought not to depend on what they are like or on what abilities they may possess. Precisely what our concern or consideration requires us to do may vary according to the characteristics of those affected by what we do: concern for the well-being of children growing up in America would require that we teach them to read; concern for the well-being of pigs may require no more than that we leave them with other pigs in a place where there is adequate food and room to run freely. But the basic element—the taking into account of the interests of the being, whatever those interests may be—must, according to the principle of equality, be extended to all beings, black or white, masculine or feminine, human or nonhuman.

Thomas Jefferson, who was responsible for writing the principle of the equality of men into the American Declaration of Independence, saw this point. It led him to oppose slavery even though he was unable to free himself fully from his slaveholding background. He wrote in a letter to the author of a book that emphasized the notable intellectual achievements of Negroes in order to refute the then common view that they had limited intellectual capacities:

> Be assured that no person living wishes more sincerely than I do, to see a complete refutation of the doubts I myself have entertained and expressed on the grade of understanding alloted to them by nature, and to find that they are on a par with ourselves ... but whatever be their degree of talent it is no measure of their rights. Because Sir Isaac Newton was superior to others in understanding, he was not therefore lord of the property or persons of others.

Similarly, when in the 1850s the call for women's rights was raised in the United States, a remarkable black feminist named Sojourner Truth made the same point in more robust terms at a feminist convention:

> They talk about this thing in the head; what do they call it? ["Intellect," whispered someone nearby.] That's it. What's that got to do with women's rights or Negroes' rights? If my cup won't hold but a pint and yours holds a quart, wouldn't you be mean not to let me have my little half-measure full?

It is on this basis that the case against racism and the case against sexism must both ultimately rest; and it is in accordance with this principle that the attitude that we may call "speciesism," by analogy with racism, must also be condemned. Speciesism—the word is not an attractive one, but I can think of no better term—is a prejudice or attitude of bias in favor of the interests of members of one's own species and against those of members of other species. It should be obvious that the fundamental objections to racism and sexism made by Thomas Jefferson and Sojourner Truth apply equally to speciesism. If possessing a higher degree of intelligence does not entitle one human to use another for his or her own ends, how can it entitle humans to exploit non-humans for the same purpose?

Many philosophers and other writers have proposed the principle of equal consideration of interests, in some form or other, as a basic moral principle; but not many of them have recognized that this principle applies to members of other species as well as to our own. Jeremy Bentham was one of the few who did realize this. In a forward-looking passage written at a time when black slaves had been freed by the French but in the British dominions were still being treated in the way we now treat animals, Bentham wrote:

> The day *may* come when the rest of the animal creation may acquire those rights which never could have been withholden from them but by the hand of tyranny. The French have already discovered that the blackness of the skin is no reason why a human being should be abandoned without redress to the caprice of a tormentor. It may one day come to be recognized that the number of the legs, the villosity of the skin, or the termination of the *os sacrum* are reasons equally insufficient for abandoning a sensitive being to the same fate. What else is it that should trace the insuperable line? Is it the faculty of reason, or perhaps the faculty of discourse? But a full-grown horse or dog is beyond comparison a more rational, as well as a more conversable animal, than an infant of a day or a week or even a month, old. But suppose they were otherwise, what would it avail? The question is not, Can they *reason*? nor Can they *talk*? but, Can they *suffer*?

In this passage Bentham points to the capacity for suffering as the vital characteristic that gives a being the right to equal consideration. The capacity for suffering—or more strictly, for suffering and/or enjoyment or happiness—is not just another characteristic like the capacity for language or higher mathematics. Bentham is not saying that those who try to mark "the insuperable line" that determines whether the interests of a being should be considered happen to have chosen the wrong characteristic. By saying that we must consider the interests of all beings with the capacity for suffering or enjoyment Bentham does not arbitrarily exclude from consideration any interests at all—as those who draw the line with reference to the possession of reason or language do. The capacity for suffering and enjoyment is a *prerequisite for having interests at all*, a condition that must be satisfied before we can speak of interests in a meaningful way. It would be nonsense to say that it was not in the interests of a stone to be kicked along the road by a schoolboy. A stone does not have interests because it cannot suffer. Nothing that we can do to it could possibly make any difference to its welfare. The capacity for suffering and enjoyment is, however, not only necessary, but also sufficient for us to say that a being has interests—at an absolute minimum, an interest in not suffering. A mouse, for example, does have an interest in not being kicked along the road, because it will suffer if it is.

Although Bentham speaks of "rights" in the passage I have quoted, the argument is really about equality rather than about rights. Indeed, in a different passage, Bentham famously described "natural rights" as "nonsense" and "natural and imprescriptable rights" as "nonsense upon stilts." He talked of moral rights as a shorthand way of referring to protections that people and animals morally ought to have; but the real weight of the moral argument does not rest on the assertion of the existence of the right, for this in turn has to be justified on the basis of the possibilities for suffering and happiness. In this way we can argue for equality for animals without getting embroiled in philosophical controversies about the ultimate nature of rights.

In misguided attempts to refute the arguments of this book, some philosophers have gone to much trouble developing arguments to show that animals do not have rights. They have claimed that to have rights a being must be autonomous, or must be a member of a community, or must have the ability to respect the rights of others, or must possess a sense of justice. These claims are irrelevant to the case for Animal Liberation. The language of rights is a convenient political shorthand. It is even more valuable in the era of thirty-second TV news clips than it was in Bentham's day; but in the argument for a radical change in our attitude to animals, it is in no way necessary.

If a being suffers there can be no moral justification for refusing to take that suffering into consideration. No matter what the nature of the being, the principle of equality requires that its suffering be counted equally with the like suffering—insofar as rough comparisons can be made—of any other being. If a being is not capable of suffering, or of experiencing enjoyment or happiness, there is nothing to be taken into account. So the limit of sentience (using the term as a convenient if not strictly accurate shorthand for the capacity to suffer and/or experience enjoyment) is the only defensible boundary of concern for the interests of others. To mark this boundary by some other characteristic like intelligence or rationality would be to mark it in an arbitrary manner. Why not choose some other characteristic, like skin color?

Racists violate the principle of equality by giving greater weight to the interests of members of their own race when there is a clash between their interests and the interests of those of another race. Sexists violate the principle of equality by favoring the interests of their own sex. Similarly, speciesists allow the interests of their own species to override the greater interests of members of other species. The pattern is identical in each case.

Most human beings are speciesists.... [O]rdinary human beings—not a few exceptionally cruel or heartless humans, but the overwhelming majority of humans—take an active part in, acquiesce in, and allow their taxes to pay for practices that require the sacrifice of the most important interests of members of other species in order to promote the most trivial interests of our own species.

There is, however, one general defense of the practices ... that needs to be disposed of before we discuss the practices themselves. It is a defense which, if true, would allow us to do anything at all to nonhumans for the slightest reason, or for no reason at all, without incurring any justifiable reproach. This defense claims that we are never guilty of neglecting the interests of other animals for one breathtakingly simple reason: they have no interests. Nonhuman animals have no interests, according to this view, because they are not capable of suffering. By this is not meant merely that they are not capable of suffering in all the ways that human beings are—for instance, that a calf is not capable of suffering from the knowledge that it will be killed in six months time. That modest claim is, no doubt, true; but it does not clear humans of the charge of speciesism, since it allows that animals may suffer in other ways—for instance, by being given electric shocks, or being kept in small, cramped cages. The defense I am about to discuss is the much more sweeping, although correspondingly less plausible, claim that animals are incapable of suffering in any way at all; that they are, in fact, unconscious automata, possessing neither thoughts nor feelings nor a mental life of any kind....

Do animals other than humans feel pain? How do we know? Well, how do we know if anyone, human or nonhuman, feels pain? We know that we ourselves can feel pain. We know this from the direct experience of pain that we have when, for instance, somebody presses a lighted cigarette against the back of our hand. But how do we know that anyone else feels pain? We cannot directly experience anyone else's pain, whether that "anyone" is our best friend or a stray dog. Pain is a state of consciousness, a "mental event," and as such it can never be observed. Behavior like writhing, screaming, or drawing one's hand away from the lighted cigarette is not pain itself; nor are the recordings a neurologist might make of activity within the brain observations of pain itself. Pain is something that we feel, and we can only infer that others are feeling it from various external indications.

In theory, we *could* always be mistaken when we assume that other human beings feel pain. It is conceivable that one of our close friends is really a cleverly constructed robot, controlled by a brilliant scientist so as to give all the signs of feeling pain, but really no more sensitive than any other machine. We can never know, with absolute certainty, that this is not the case. But while this might present a puzzle for philosophers, none of us has the slightest real doubt that our close friends feel pain just as we do. This is an inference, but a perfectly reasonable one, based on observations of their behavior in situations in which we would feel pain, and on the fact that we have every reason to assume that our friends are beings like us, with nervous systems like ours that can be assumed to function as ours do and to produce similar feelings in similar circumstances.

If it is justifiable to assume that other human beings feel pain as we do, is there any reason why a similar inference should be unjustifiable in the case of other animals?

Nearly all the external signs that lead us to infer pain in other humans can be seen in other species, especially the species most closely related to us—the species of mammals and birds. The behavioral signs include writhing, facial contortions, moaning, yelping or other forms of calling, attempts to avoid the source of pain, appearance of fear at the prospect of its repetition, and so on. In addition, we know that these animals have nervous systems very like ours, which respond physiologically as ours do when the animal is in circumstances in which we would feel pain: an initial rise of blood pressure, dilated pupils, perspiration, an increased pulse rate, and, if the stimulus continues, a fall in blood pressure. Although human beings have a more developed cerebral cortex than other animals, this part of the brain is concerned with thinking functions rather than with basic impulses, emotions, and feelings. These impulses, emotions, and feelings are located in the diencephalon, which is well developed in many other species of animals, especially mammals and birds.

We also know that the nervous systems of other animals were not artificially constructed—as a robot might be artificially constructed—to mimic the pain behavior of humans. The nervous systems of animals evolved as our own did, and in fact the evolutionary history of human beings and other animals, especially mammals, did not diverge until the central features of our nervous systems were already in existence. A capacity to feel pain obviously enhances a species' prospects of survival, since it causes members of the species to avoid sources of injury. It is surely unreasonable to suppose that nervous systems that are virtually identical physiologically, have a common origin and a common evolutionary function, and result in similar forms of behavior in similar circumstances should actually operate in an entirely different manner on the level of subjective feelings.

It has long been accepted as sound policy in science to search for the simplest possible explanation of whatever it is we are trying to explain. Occasionally it has been claimed that it is for this reason "unscientific" to explain the behavior of animals by theories that refer to the animal's conscious feelings, desires, and so on—the idea being that if the behavior in question can be explained without invoking consciousness or feelings, that will be the simpler theory. Yet we can now see that such explanations, when assessed with respect to the actual behavior of both human and nonhuman animals, are actually far more complex than rival explanations. For we know from our own experience that explanations of our own behavior that did not refer to consciousness and the feeling of pain would be incomplete; and it is simpler to assume that the similar behavior of animals with similar nervous systems is to be explained in the same way than to try to invent some other explanation for the behavior of nonhuman animals as well as an explanation for the divergence between humans and nonhumans in this respect.

The overwhelming majority of scientists who have addressed themselves to this question agree. Lord Brain, one of the most eminent neurologists of our time, has said:

> I personally can see no reason for conceding mind to my fellow men and denying it to animals.... I at least cannot doubt that the interests and activities of animals are correlated with awareness and feeling in the same way as my own, and which may be, for aught I know, just as vivid.

The author of a book on pain writes:

> Every particle of factual evidence supports the contention that the higher mammalian vertebrates experience pain sensations at least as acute as our own. To say that they feel less because they are lower animals is an absurdity; it can easily be shown that many of their senses are far more acute than ours—visual acuity in certain birds, hearing in most wild animals, and touch in others; these animals depend more than we do today on the sharpest possible awareness of a hostile environment. Apart from the complexity of the cerebral cortex (which does not directly perceive pain) their nervous systems are almost identical to ours and their reactions to pain remarkably similar, though lacking (so far as we know) the philosophical and moral overtones. The emotional element is all too evident, mainly in the form of fear and anger.

In Britain, three separate expert government committees on matters relating to animals have accepted the conclusion that animals feel pain. After noting the obvious behavioral evidence for this view, the members of the Committee on Cruelty to Wild Animals, set up in 1951, said:

> ... we believe that the physiological, and more particularly the anatomical, evidence fully justifies and reinforces the commonsense belief that animals feel pain.

And after discussing the evolutionary value of pain the committee's report concluded that pain is "of clear-cut biological usefulness" and this is "a third type of evidence that animals feel pain." The committee members then went on to consider forms of suffering other than mere physical pain and added that they were "satisfied that animals do suffer from acute fear and terror." Subsequent reports by British government committees on experiments on animals and on the welfare of animals under intensive farming methods agreed with this view, concluding that animals are capable of suffering both from straightforward physical injuries and from fear, anxiety, stress, and so on. Finally, within the last decade, the publication of scientific studies with titles such as *Animal Thought, Animal Thinking*, and *Animal Suffering: The Science of Animal Welfare* have made it plain that conscious awareness in nonhuman animals is now generally accepted as a serious subject for investigation.

That might well be thought enough to settle the matter; but one more objection needs to be considered. Human beings in pain, after all, have one behavioral sign that nonhuman animals do not have: a developed language. Other animals may communicate with each other, but not, it seems, in the complicated way we do. Some philosophers, including Descartes, have thought it important that while humans can tell each other about their experience of pain in great detail, other animals cannot. (Interestingly, this once neat dividing line between humans and other species has now been threatened by the discovery that chimpanzees can be taught a language.) But as Bentham pointed out long ago, the ability to use language is not relevant to the question of how a being ought to be treated—unless that ability can be linked to the capacity to suffer, so that the absence of a language casts doubt on the existence of this capacity.

This link may be attempted in two ways. First, there is a hazy line of philosophical thought, deriving perhaps from some doctrines associated with the influential philosopher

Ludwig Wittgenstein, which maintains that we cannot meaningfully attribute states of consciousness to beings without language. This position seems to me very implausible. Language may be necessary for abstract thought, at some level anyway; but states like pain are more primitive, and have nothing to do with language.

The second and more easily understood way of linking language and the existence of pain is to say that the best evidence we can have that other creatures are in pain is that they tell us that they are. This is a distinct line of argument, for it is denying not that non-language-users conceivably *could* suffer, but only that we could ever have sufficient reason to *believe* that they are suffering. Still, this line of argument fails too. As Jane Goodall has pointed out in her study of chimpanzees, *In the Shadow of Man*, when it comes to the expression of feelings and emotions language is less important than nonlinguistic modes of communication such as a cheering pat on the back, an exuberant embrace, a clasp of the hands, and so on. The basic signals we use to convey pain, fear, anger, love, joy, surprise, sexual arousal, and many other emotional states are not specific to our own species. The statement "I am in pain" may be one piece of evidence for the conclusion that the speaker is in pain, but it is not the only possible evidence, and since people sometimes tell lies, not even the best possible evidence.

Even if there were stronger grounds for refusing to attribute pain to those who do not have a language, the consequences of this refusal might lead us to reject the conclusion. Human infants and young children are unable to use language. Are we to deny that a year-old child can suffer? If not, language cannot be crucial. Of course, most parents understand the responses of their children better than they understand the responses of other animals; but this is just a fact about the relatively greater knowledge that we have of our own species and the greater contact we have with infants as compared to animals. Those who have studied the behavior of other animals and those who have animals as companions soon learn to understand their responses as well as we understand those of an infant, and sometimes better.

So to conclude: there are no good reasons, scientific or philosophical, for denying that animals feel pain. If we do not doubt that other humans feel pain we should not doubt that other animals do so too.

Animals can feel pain. As we saw earlier, there can be no moral justification for regarding the pain (or pleasure) that animals feel as less important than the same amount of pain (or pleasure) felt by humans. But what practical consequences follow from this conclusion? To prevent misunderstanding I shall spell out what I mean a little more fully.

If I give a horse a hard slap across its rump with my open hand, the horse may start, but it presumably feels little pain. Its skin is thick enough to protect it against a mere slap. If I slap a baby in the same way, however, the baby will cry and presumably feel pain, for its skin is more sensitive. So it is worse to slap a baby than a horse, if both slaps are administered with equal force. But there must be some kind of blow—I don't know exactly what it would be, but perhaps a blow with a heavy stick—that would cause the horse as much pain as we cause a baby by slapping it with our hand. That is what I mean by "the same amount of pain," and if we consider it wrong to inflict that much pain on a baby for no good reason then we must, unless we are speciesists, consider it equally wrong to inflict the same amount of pain on a horse for no good reason.

Other differences between humans and animals cause other complications. Normal adult human beings have mental capacities that will, in certain circumstances, lead them to suffer more than animals would in the same circumstances. If, for instance, we decided to perform extremely painful or lethal scientific experiments on normal adult humans, kidnapped at random from public parks for this purpose, adults who enjoy strolling in parks would become fearful that they would be kidnapped. The resultant terror would be a form of suffering additional to the pain of the experiment. The same experiments performed on nonhuman animals would cause less suffering since the animals would not have the anticipatory dread of being kidnapped and experimented upon. This does not mean, of course, that it would be *right* to perform the experiment on animals, but only that there is a reason, which is *not* speciesist, for preferring to use animals rather than normal adult human beings, if the experiment is to be done at all. It should be noted, however, that this same argument gives us a reason for preferring to use human infants—orphans perhaps—or severely retarded human beings for experiments, rather than adults, since infants and retarded humans would also have no idea of what was going to happen to them. So far as this argument is concerned nonhuman animals and infants and retarded humans are in the same category; and if we use this argument to justify experiments on nonhuman animals we have to ask ourselves whether we are also prepared to allow experiments on human infants and retarded adults; and if we make a distinction between animals and these humans, on what basis can we do it other than a bare-faced—and morally indefensible—preference for members of our own species?

There are many matters in which the superior mental powers of normal adult humans make a difference: anticipation, more detailed memory, greater knowledge of what is happening, and so on. Yet these differences do not all point to greater suffering on the part of the normal human being. Sometimes animals may suffer more because of their more limited understanding. If, for instance, we are taking prisoners in wartime we can explain to them that although they must submit to capture, search, and confinement, they will not otherwise be harmed and will be set free at the conclusion of hostilities. If we capture wild animals, however, we cannot explain that we are not threatening their lives. A wild animal cannot distinguish an attempt to overpower and confine from an attempt to kill; the one causes as much terror as the other.

It may be objected that comparisons of the sufferings of different species are impossible to make and that for this reason when the interests of animals and humans clash the principle of equality gives no guidance. It is probably true that comparisons of suffering between members of different species cannot be made precisely, but precision is not essential. Even if we were to prevent the infliction of suffering on animals only when it is quite certain that the interests of humans will not be affected to anything like the extent that animals are affected, we would be forced to make radical changes in our treatment of animals that would involve our diet, the farming methods we use, experimental procedures in many fields of science, our approach to wildlife and to hunting, trapping and the wearing of furs, and areas of entertainment like circuses, rodeos, and zoos. As a result, a vast amount of suffering would be avoided.

So far I have said a lot about inflicting suffering on animals, but nothing about killing them. This omission has been deliberate. The application of the principle of equality to the infliction of suffering is, in theory at least, fairly straightforward. Pain and suffering are in themselves bad and should be prevented or minimized, irrespective of the race, sex, or species of the being that suffers. How bad a pain is depends on how intense it is and how long it lasts, but pains of the same intensity and duration are equally bad, whether felt by humans or animals.

The wrongness of killing a being is more complicated. I have kept, and shall continue to keep, the question of killing in the background because in the present state of human tyranny over other species the more simple, straightforward principle of equal consideration of pain or pleasure is a sufficient basis for identifying and protesting against all the major abuses of animals that human beings practice. Nevertheless, it is necessary to say something about killing.

Just as most human beings are speciesists in their readiness to cause pain to animals when they would not cause a similar pain to humans for the same reason, so most human beings are speciesists in their readiness to kill other animals when they would not kill human beings. We need to proceed more cautiously here, however, because people hold widely differing views about when it is legitimate to kill humans, as the continuing debates over abortion and euthanasia attest. Nor have moral philosophers been able to agree on exactly what it is that makes it wrong to kill human beings, and under what circumstances killing a human being may be justifiable.

Let us consider first the view that it is always wrong to take an innocent human life. We may call this the "sanctity of life" view. People who take this view oppose abortion and euthanasia. They do not usually, however, oppose the killing of nonhuman animals—so perhaps it would be more accurate to describe this view as the "sanctity of *human* life" view. The belief that human life, and only human life, is sacrosanct is a form of speciesism. To see this, consider the following example.

Assume that, as sometimes happens, an infant has been born with massive and irreparable brain damage. The damage is so severe that the infant can never be any more than a "human vegetable," unable to talk, recognize other people, act independently of others, or develop a sense of self-awareness. The parents of the infant, realizing that they cannot hope for any improvement in their child's condition and being in any case unwilling to spend, or ask the state to spend, the thousands of dollars that would be needed annually for proper care of the infant, ask the doctor to kill the infant painlessly.

Should the doctor do what the parents ask? Legally, the doctor should not, and in this respect the law reflects the sanctity of life view. The life of every human being is sacred. Yet people who would say this about the infant do not object to the killing of nonhuman animals. How can they justify their different judgments? Adult chimpanzees, dogs, pigs, and members of many other species far surpass the brain-damaged infant in their ability to relate to others, act independently, be self-aware, and any other capacity that could reasonably be said to give value to life. With the most intensive care possible, some severely retarded infants can never achieve the intelligence level of a dog. Nor can we appeal to the concern of the infant's parents, since they themselves, in this imaginary example (and in some actual cases) do not want the infant kept alive. The only thing that distinguishes the infant from the animal, in the eyes of those who claim it has a "right to life," is that it is, biologically, a member of the species Homo sapiens, whereas chimpanzees, dogs, and pigs are not. But to use *this* difference as the basis for granting a right to life to the infant and not to the other animals is, of course, pure speciesism. It is exactly the kind of arbitrary difference that the most crude and overt kind of racist uses in attempting to justify racial discrimination.

This does not mean that to avoid speciesism we must hold that it is as wrong to kill a dog as it is to kill a human being in full possession of his or her faculties. The only position that is irredeemably speciesist is the one that tries to make the boundary of the right to life run exactly parallel to the boundary of our own species. Those who hold the sanctity of life view do this, because while distinguishing sharply between human beings and other animals they allow no distinctions to be made within our own species, objecting to the killing of the severely retarded and the hopelessly senile as strongly as they object to the killing of normal adults.

To avoid speciesism we must allow that beings who are similar in all relevant respects have a similar right to life—and mere membership in our own biological species cannot be a morally relevant criterion for this right. Within these limits we could still hold, for instance, that it is worse to kill a normal adult human, with a capacity for self-awareness and the ability to plan for the future and have meaningful relations with others, than it is to kill a mouse, which presumably does not share all of these characteristics; or we might appeal to the close family and other personal ties that humans have but mice do not have to the same degree; or we might think that it is the consequences for other humans, who will be put in fear for their own lives, that makes the crucial difference; or we might think it is some combination of these factors, or other factors altogether.

Whatever criteria we choose, however, we will have to admit that they do not follow precisely the boundary of our own species. We may legitimately hold that there are some features of certain beings that make their lives more valuable than those of other beings; but there will surely be some nonhuman animals whose lives, by any standards, are more valuable than the lives of some humans. A chimpanzee, dog, or pig, for instance, will have a higher degree of self-awareness and a greater capacity for meaningful relations with others than a severely retarded infant or someone in a state of advanced senility. So if we base the right to life on these characteristics we must grant these animals a right to life as good as, or better than, such retarded or senile humans.

This argument cuts both ways. It could be taken as showing that chimpanzees, dogs, and pigs, along with some other species, have a right to life and we commit a grave moral offense whenever we kill them, even when they are old and suffering and our intention is to put them out of their misery. Alternatively one could take the argument as showing that the severely retarded and hopelessly senile have no right to life and may be killed for quite trivial reasons, as we now kill animals.

Since the main concern of this book is with ethical questions having to do with animals and not with the morality of euthanasia I shall not attempt to settle this issue finally. I think it is reasonably clear, though, that while both of the positions just described avoid speciesism, neither is satisfactory. What we need is some middle position that would avoid speciesism but would not make the lives of the retarded and senile as cheap as the lives of pigs and dogs now are, or make the lives of pigs and dogs so sacrosanct that we think it wrong to put them out of hopeless misery. What we must do is bring nonhuman animals within our sphere of moral concern and cease to treat their lives as expendable for whatever trivial purposes we may have. At the same time, once we realize that the fact that a being is a member of our own species is not in itself enough to make it always wrong to kill that being, we may come to reconsider our policy of preserving human lives at all costs, even when there is no prospect of a meaningful life or of existence without terrible pain.

I conclude, then, that a rejection of speciesism does not imply that all lives are of equal worth. While self-awareness, the capacity to think ahead and have hopes and aspirations for the future, the capacity for meaningful relations with others and so on are not relevant to the question of inflicting pain—since pain is pain, whatever other capacities, beyond the capacity to feel pain, the being may have—these capacities are relevant to the question of taking life. It is not arbitrary to hold that the life of a self-aware being, capable of abstract thought, of planning for the future, of complex acts of communication, and so on, is more valuable than the life of a being without these capacities. To see the difference between the issues of inflicting pain and taking life, consider how we would choose within our own species. If we had to choose to save the life of a normal human being or an intellectually disabled human being, we would probably choose to save the life of a normal human being; but if we had to choose between preventing pain in the normal human being or the intellectually disabled one—imagine that both have received painful but superficial injuries, and we only have enough painkiller for one of them—it is not nearly so clear how we ought to choose. The same is true when we consider other species. The evil of pain is, in itself, unaffected by the other characteristics of the being who feels the pain; the value of life is affected by these other characteristics. To give just one reason for this difference, to take the life of a being who has been hoping, planning, and working for some future goal is to deprive that being of the fulfillment of all those efforts; to take the life of a being with a mental capacity below the level needed to grasp that one is a being with a future—much less make plans for the future—cannot involve this particular kind of loss.

Normally this will mean that if we have to choose between the life of a human being and the life of another animal we should choose to save the life of the human; but there may be special cases in which the reverse holds true, because the human being in question does not have the capacities of a normal human being. So this view is not speciesist, although it may appear to be at first glance. The preference, in normal cases, for saving a human life over the life of an animal when a choice *has* to be made is a preference based on the characteristics that normal humans have, and not on the mere fact that they are members of our own species. This is why when we consider members of our own species who lack the characteristics of normal humans we can no longer say that their lives are always to be preferred to those of other animals.... In general, though, the question of when it is wrong to kill (painlessly) an animal is one to which we need give no precise answer. As long as we remember that we should give the same respect to the lives of animals as we give to the lives of those humans at a similar mental level, we shall not go far wrong.

In any case, the conclusions that are argued for in this book flow from the principle of minimizing suffering alone. The idea that it is also wrong to kill animals painlessly gives some of these conclusions additional support that is welcome but strictly unnecessary. Interestingly enough, this is true even of the conclusion that we ought to become vegetarians, a conclusion that in the popular mind is generally based on some kind of absolute prohibition on killing....

That is why I have chosen to discuss these particular forms of speciesism. They are at its heart. They cause more suffering to a greater number of animals than anything else that human beings do. To stop them we must change the policies of our government, and we must change our own lives, to the extent of changing our diet. If these officially promoted and almost universally accepted forms of speciesism can be abolished, abolition of the other speciesist practices cannot be far behind.

The Radical Egalitarian Case for Animal Rights

Tom Regan

I regard myself as an advocate of animal rights—as a part of the animal rights movement. That movement, as I conceive it, is committed to a number of goals, including:

1. the total abolition of the use of animals in science
2. the total dissolution of commercial animal agriculture
3. and the total elimination of commercial and sport hunting and trapping.

There are, I know, people who profess to believe in animal rights who do not avow these goals. Factory farming they say, is wrong—violates animals' rights—but traditional animal agriculture is all right. Toxicity tests of cosmetics on animals violate their rights; but not important medical research—cancer research, for example. The clubbing of baby seals is abhorrent; but not the harvesting of adult seals. I used to think I understood this reasoning. Not any more. You don't change unjust institutions by tidying them up.

What's wrong—what's fundamentally wrong—with the way animals are treated isn't the details that vary from case to case. It's the whole system. The forlornness of the veal calf is pathetic—heart wrenching; the pulsing pain of the chimp with electrodes planted deep in her brain is repulsive; the slow, torturous death of the raccoon caught in the leg hold trap, agonizing. But what is fundamentally wrong isn't the pain, isn't the suffering, isn't the deprivation. These compound what's wrong. Sometimes—often—they make it much worse. But they are not the fundamental wrong.

The fundamental wrong is the system that allows us to view animals as our resources, here for us—to be eaten, or surgically manipulated, or put in our cross-hairs for sport or money. Once we accept this view of animals—as our resources—the rest is as predictable as it is regrettable. Why worry about their loneliness, their pain, their death? Since animals exist for us, here to benefit us in one way or another, what harms them really doesn't matter—or matters only if it starts to bother us, makes us feel a trifle uneasy

---

Tom Regan, "The Radical Egalitarian Case for Animal Rights," from *In Defence of Animals* (ed. Peter Singer), Blackwell, 1985; pp. 320–330. Reprinted with permission of John Wiley & Sons, Ltd.

when we eat our veal scampi, for example. So, yes, let us get veal calves out of solitary confinement, give them more space, a little straw, a few companions. But let us keep our veal scampi.

But a little straw, more space, and a few companions don't eliminate—don't even touch—the fundamental wrong, the wrong that attaches to our viewing and treating these animals as our resources. A veal calf killed to be eaten after living in close confinement is viewed and treated in this way: but so, too, is another who is raised (as they say) "more humanely." To right the fundamental wrong of our treatment of farm animals requires more than making rearing methods "more human"—requires something quite different—requires the *total dissolution of commercial animal agriculture*.

How we do this—whether we do this, or as in the case of animals in science, whether and how we abolish their use—these are to a large extent political questions. People must change their beliefs before they change their habits. Enough people, especially those elected to public office, must believe in change—must want it—before we will have laws that protect the rights of animals. This process of change is very complicated, very demanding, very exhausting, calling for the efforts of many hands—in education, publicity, political organization and activity, down to the licking of envelopes and stamps. As a trained and practicing philosopher the sort of contribution I can make is limited, but I like to think, important. The currency of philosophy is ideas—their meaning and rational foundation—not the nuts and bolts of the legislative process say, or the mechanics of community organization. That's what I have been exploring over the past ten years or so in my essays and talks and, more recently, in my book, *The Case for Animal Rights*.[1] I believe the major conclusions I reach in that book are true because they are supported by the weight of the *best arguments*. I believe the idea of animal rights has reason, not just emotion, on its side.

In the space I have at my disposal here I can only sketch, in the barest outlines, some of the main features of the book. Its main themes—and we should not be surprised by this—involve asking and answering deep foundational moral questions, questions about what morality is, how it should be understood, what is the best moral theory all considered. I hope I can convey something of the shape I think this theory is. The attempt to do this will be—to use a word a friendly critic once used to describe my work—cerebral. In fact I was told by this person that my work is "too cerebral." But this is misleading. My feelings about how animals sometimes are treated are just as deep and just as strong as those of my more volatile compatriots. Philosophers do—to use the jargon of the day—have a right side to their brains. If it's the left side we contribute or mainly should—that's because what talents we have reside there.

How to proceed? We begin by asking how the moral status of animals has been understood by thinkers who deny that animals have rights. Then we test the mettle of their ideas by seeing how well they stand up under the heat of fair criticism. If we start our thinking in this way we soon find that some people believe that we have no duties directly to animals—that we owe nothing to *them*—that we can do nothing that *wrongs them*. Rather, we can do wrong acts that involve animals, and so we have duties regarding them, though none to them. Such views may be called indirect duty views. By way of illustration:

Suppose your neighbor kicks your dog. Then your neighbor has done something wrong. But not to your dog. The wrong that has been done is a wrong to you. After all, it is wrong to upset people, and your neighbor's kicking your dog upsets you. So you are the one who is wronged, not your dog. Or again: by kicking your dog your neighbor damages your property. And since it is wrong to damage another person's property, your neighbor has done something wrong—to you, of course, not to your dog. Your neighbor no more wrongs your dog than your car would be wronged if the windshield were smashed. Your neighbor's duties involving your dog are indirect duties to you. More generally, all of our duties regarding animals are indirect duties to one another—to humanity.

How could someone try to justify such a view? One could say that your dog doesn't feel anything and so isn't hurt by your neighbor's kick, doesn't care about the pain since none is felt, is as unaware of anything as your windshield. Someone could say this but no rational person will since, among other considerations, such a view will commit one who holds it to the position that no human being feels pain either—that human beings also don't care about what happens to them. A second possibility is that though both humans and your dog are hurt when kicked, it is only human pain that matters. But, again, no rational person can believe this. Pain is pain wheresoever it occurs. If your neighbor's causing you pain is wrong because of the pain that is caused, we cannot rationally ignore or dismiss the moral relevance of the pain your dog feels.

Philosophers who hold indirect duty views—and many still do—have come to understand that they must avoid the two defects just noted—avoid, that is, both the view that animals don't feel anything as well as the idea that only human pain can be morally relevant. Among such thinkers the sort of view now favored is one or another form of what is called *contractarianism*.

Here, very crudely, is the root idea: morality consists of a set of rules that individuals voluntarily agree to abide by—as we do when we sign a contract (hence the name: contractarianism). Those who understand and accept the terms of the contract are covered directly—have rights created by, and recognized and protected in, the contract. And these contractors can also have protection spelled out for others who, though they lack the ability to understand morality and so cannot sign the contract themselves, are loved or cherished by those who can. Thus young children, for example, are unable to sign and lack rights. But they are protected by the contract nonetheless because of the sentimental interests of others, most notably their parents. So we have, then, duties involving these children, duties regarding them, but no duties to them. Our duties in their case are indirect duties to other human beings, usually their parents.

As for animals, since they cannot understand the contract, they obviously cannot sign; and since they cannot sign; they have no rights. Like children, however, some animals are the objects of the sentimental interest of others. You, for example, love your dog … or cat. So these animals—those enough people care about: companion animals, whales, baby seals, the American bald eagle—these animals, though they lack rights themselves, will be protected because of the sentimental interests of people. I have, then, according to contractarianism, no duty directly to your dog or any other animal, not even the duty not to cause them pain or suffering; my duty not to hurt them is a duty I have to those people who care about what happens to them. As for other animals, where no or little sentimental interest is present—farm animals, for example, or laboratory rats—what duties we have grow weaker and weaker, perhaps to the vanishing point. The pain and death they endure, though real, are not wrong if no one cares about them.

Contractarianism could be a hard view to refute when it comes to the moral status of animals if it was an adequate theoretical approach to the moral status of human beings. It is not adequate in this latter respect, however, which makes the question of its adequacy in the former—regarding animals—utterly moot. For consider: morality, according to the (crude) contractarian position before us, consists of rules people agree to abide by. What people? Well, enough to make a difference—enough, that is, so that collectively they have the power to enforce the rules that are drawn up in the contract. That is very well and good for the signatories—but not so good for anyone who is not asked to sign. And there is nothing in contractarianism of the sort we are discussing that guarantees or requires that everyone will have a chance to participate equitably in framing the rules of morality. The result is that this approach to ethics could sanction the most blatant forms of social, economic, moral, and political injustice, ranging from a repressive caste system to systematic racial or sexual discrimination. Might, on this theory, does make right. Let those who are the victims of injustice suffer as they will. It matters not so long as no one else—no contractor, or too few of them—cares about it. Such a theory takes one's moral breath away ... as if, for example, there is nothing wrong with apartheid in South Africa if too few white South Africans are upset by it. A theory with so little to recommend it at the level of the ethics of our treatment of our fellow humans cannot have anything more to recommend it when it comes to the ethics of how we treat our fellow animals.

The version of contractarianism just examined is, as I have noted, a crude variety, and in fairness to those of a contractarian persuasion it must be noted that much more refined, subtle, and ingenious varieties are possible. For example, John Rawls, in his *A Theory of Justice*, sets forth a version of contractarianism that forces the contractors to ignore the accidental features of being a human being—for example, whether one is white or black, male or female, a genius or of modest intellect. Only by ignoring such features, Rawls believes, can we insure that the principles of justice contractors would agree upon are not based on bias or prejudice. Despite the improvement a view such as Rawls's shows over the cruder forms of contractarianism, it remains deficient: it systematically denies that we have direct duties to those human beings who do not have a sense of justice—young children, for instance, and many mentally retarded humans. And yet it seems reasonably certain that, were we to torture a young child or a retarded elder, we would be doing something that wrongs them, not something that is wrong if (and only if) other humans with a sense of justice are upset. And since this is true in the case of these humans, we cannot rationally deny the same in the case of animals.

Indirect duty views, then, including the best among them, fail to command our rational assent. Whatever ethical theory we rationally should accept, therefore, it must at least recognize that we have some duties directly to animals, just as we have some duties directly to each other. The next two theories I'll sketch attempt to meet this requirement.

The first I call the *cruelty–kindness* view. Simply stated, this view says that we have a direct duty to be kind to animals and a direct duty not to be cruel to them. Despite the familiar, reassuring ring of these ideas, I do not believe this view offers an adequate theory. To make this clearer, consider kindness. A kind person acts from a certain kind of motive—compassion or concern, for example. And that is a virtue. But there is no guarantee that a kind act is a right act. If I am a generous racist, for example, I will be inclined to act kindly toward members of my own own race, favoring their interests above others. My kindness would be real and, so far as it goes, good. But I trust it is too obvious to require comment that my kind acts may not be above moral reproach—may, in fact, be positively wrong because rooted in injustice. So kindness, not withstanding its status as a virtue to be encouraged, simply will not cancel the weight of a theory of right action.

Cruelty fares no better. People or their acts are cruel if they display either a lack of sympathy for or, worse, the presence of enjoyment in, seeing another suffer. Cruelty in all its guises *is* a bad thing—*is* a tragic human failing. But just as a person's being motivated by kindness does not guarantee that they do what is right, so the absence of cruelty does not assure that they avoid doing what is wrong. Many people who perform abortions, for example, are not cruel, sadistic people. But that fact about their character and motivation does not settle the terribly difficult question about the morality of abortion. The case is no different when we examine the ethics of our treatment of animals. So, yes, let us be for kindness and against cruelty. But let us not suppose that being for the one and against the other answers questions about moral right and wrong.

Some people think the theory we are looking for is *utilitarianism*. A utilitarian accepts two moral principles. The first is a principle of *equality: everyone's interests count, and similar interests must be counted as having similar weight or importance*. White or black, male or female, American or Iranian, human or animal: everyone's pain or frustration matter and matter equally with the like pain or frustration of anyone else. The second principle a utilitarian accepts is the principle of *utility: do that act that will bring about the best balance of satisfaction over frustration for everyone affected by the outcome*.

As a utilitarian, then, here is how I am to approach the task of deciding what I morally ought to do: I must ask who will be affected if I choose to do one thing rather than another, how much each individual will be affected, and where the best results are most likely to lie—which option, in other words, is most likely to bring about the best results, the best balance of satisfaction over frustration. That option, whatever it may be, is the one I ought to choose. That is where my moral duty lies.

The great appeal of utilitarianism rests with its uncompromising *egalitarianism*: everyone's interests count and count equally with the like interests of everyone else. The kind of odious discrimination some forms of contractarianism can justify—discrimination based on race or sex, for example—seems disallowed in principle by utilitarianism, as is speciesism—systematic discrimination based on species membership.

The sort of equality we find in utilitarianism, however, is not the sort an advocate of animal or human rights should have in mind. Utilitarianism has no room for the *equal moral rights of different individuals because it has no room for their equal inherent value or worth*. What has value for the utilitarian is the satisfaction of an individual's interests, not the individual whose interests they are. A universe in which you satisfy your desire for water, food, and warmth, is, other things being equal, better than a universe in which these desires are frustrated. And the same is true in the case of an animal with similar desires. But neither you nor the animal have any value in your own right. *Only your feelings do*.

Here is an analogy to help make the philosophical point clearer: a cup contains different liquids—sometimes sweet, sometimes bitter, sometimes a mix of the two. What has value are the liquids: the sweeter the better, the bitter the worse. The cup—the container—has no value. It's what goes into it, not what they go into, that has value. For the utilitarian, you and I are like the cup; we have no value as individuals and thus no equal value. What has value is what goes into us, what we serve as receptacles for; our feelings of satisfaction have positive value, our feelings of frustration have negative value.

Serious problems arise for utilitarianism when we remind ourselves that it enjoins us to bring about the best consequences. What does this mean? It doesn't mean the best consequences for me alone, or for my family or friends, or any other person taken individually. No, what we must do is, roughly, as follows: we must add up—somehow!—the separate satisfactions and frustrations of everyone likely to be affected by our choice, the satisfactions in one column, the frustrations in the other. We must total each column for each of the opinions before us. That is what it means to say the theory is aggregative. And then we must choose that option which is most likely to bring about the best balance of totaled satisfactions over totaled frustrations. Whatever act would lead to this outcome is the one we morally ought to perform—is where our moral duty lies. And that act quite clearly might not be the same one that would bring about the best results for me personally, or my family or friends, or a lab animal. The best aggregated consequences for everyone concerned are not necessarily the best for each individual.

That utilitarianism is an aggregative theory—that different individual's satisfactions or frustrations are added, or summed, or totaled—is the key objection to this theory. My Aunt Bea is old, inactive, a cranky, sour person, though not physically ill. She prefers to go on living. She is also rather rich. I could make a fortune if I could get my hands on her money, money she intends to give me in any event, after she dies, but which she refuses to give me now. In order to avoid a huge tax bite, I plan to donate a handsome sum of my profits to a local children's hospital. Many, many children will benefit from my generosity, and much joy will be brought to their parents, relatives, and friends. If I don't get the money rather soon, all these ambitions will come to naught. The once-in-a-lifetime-opportunity to make a real killing will be gone. Why, then, not really kill my Aunt Bea? Oh, of course I *might* get caught. But I'm no fool and, besides, her doctor can be counted on to cooperate (he has an eye for the same investment and I happen to know a good deal about his shady past). The deed can be done… professionally, shall we say. There is *very* little chance of getting caught. And as for my conscience being guilt ridden, I am a resourceful sort of fellow and will take more than sufficient comfort—as I lie on the beach at Acapulco—in contemplating the joy and health I have brought to so many others.

Suppose Aunt Bea is killed and the rest of the story comes out as told. Would I have done anything wrong? Anything immoral? One would have thought that I had. But not according to utilitarianism. Since what I did brought about the best balance of totaled satisfaction over frustration for all those affected by the outcome, what I did was not wrong. Indeed, in killing Aunt Bea the physician and I did what duty required.

This same kind of argument can be repeated in all sorts of cases, illustrating time after time, how the utilitarian's position leads to results that impartial people find morally callous. It is wrong to kill my Aunt Bea in the name of bringing about the best results for others. A good end does not justify an evil means. Any adequate moral theory will have to explain why this is so. Utilitarianism fails in this respect and so cannot be the theory we seek.

What to do? Where to begin anew? The place to begin, I think, is with the utilitarian's view of the value of the individual—or, rather, lack of value. In its place suppose we consider that you and I, for example, do have value as individuals—what we'll call *inherent value*. To say we have such value is to say that we are something more than, something different from, mere receptacles. Moreover, to insure that we do not pave the way for such injustices as slavery or sexual discrimination, we must believe that all who have inherent value have it equally, regardless of their sex, race, religion, birthplace, and so on. Similarly to be discarded as irrelevant are one's talents or skills, intelligence and wealth, personality or pathology, whether one is loved and admired—or despised and loathed. The genius and the retarded child, the prince and the pauper, the brain surgeon and the fruit vendor, Mother Theresa and the most unscrupulous used car salesman—all have inherent value, all possess it *equally*, and *all have an equal right to be treated with respect*, to be treated in ways that do not reduce them to the status of things, as if they exist as resources for others. My value as an individual is independent of my usefulness to you. Yours is not dependent on your usefulness to me. For either of us to treat the other in ways that fail to show respect for the other's independent value is to act immorally—is to violate the individual's rights.

Some of the rational virtues of this view—what I call the rights view—should be evident. Unlike (crude) contractarianism, for example, the rights view *in principle* denies the moral tolerability of any and all forms of racial, sexual, or social discrimination; and unlike utilitarianism, this view *in principle* denies that we can justify good results by using evil means that violate an individual's rights—denies, for example, that it could be moral to kill my Aunt Bea to harvest beneficial consequences for others. That would be to sanction the disrespectful treatment of the individual in the name of the social good, something the rights view will not—categorically will not—ever allow.

The rights view—or so I believe—is rationally the most satisfactory moral theory. It surpasses all other theories in the degree to which it illuminates and explains the foundation of our duties to one another—the domain of human morality. On this score, it has the best reasons, the best arguments, on its side. Of course, if it were possible to show that only human beings are included within its scope, then a person like myself, who believes in animal rights, would be obliged to look elsewhere than to the rights view.

But attempts to limit its scope to humans only can be shown to be rationally defective. Animals, it is true, lack many of the abilities humans possess. They can't read, do higher mathematics, build a bookcase, or make *baba ghanoush*. Neither can many human beings, however, and yet we don't say—and shouldn't say—that they (these humans) therefore have less inherent value, less of a right to be treated with respect, than do others. It is the *similarities* between those human beings who most clearly, most noncontroversially have such value—the people reading this, for example—it is our similarities, not our differences, that matter most. And the really crucial, the basic similarity is simply this; *we are each of us the experiencing subject of a life, each of us a conscious creature having an individual welfare that has importance to us whatever our usefulness to others*. We want and prefer things; believe and feel things; recall and expect things. And all these dimensions of our life, including our pleasure and pain, our enjoyment and suffering, our satisfaction and frustration, our continued existence or our untimely death—all make a difference to the quality of our life as lived, as experienced by us as individuals. As the same is true of those animals who concern us (those who are eaten and trapped, for example), they, too, must be viewed as the experiencing subjects of a life with inherent value of their own.

There are some who resist the idea that animals have inherent value. "Only humans have such value," they profess. How might this narrow view be defended? Shall we say that only humans have the requisite intelligence, or autonomy, or reason? But there are many, many humans who will fail to meet these standards and yet who are reasonably viewed as having value above and beyond their usefulness to others. Shall we claim that only humans belong to the right species—the species *Homo sapiens*? But this is blatant speciesism. Will it be said, then, that all—and only—humans have immortal souls? Then our opponents more than have their work cut out for them. I am myself not ill-disposed to there being immortal souls. Personally, I profoundly hope I have one. But I would not want to rest my position on a controversial, ethical issue on the even more controversial question about who or what has an immortal soul. That is to dig one's hole deeper, not climb out. Rationally, it is better to resolve moral issues without making more controversial assumptions than are needed. The question of who has inherent value is such a question, one that is more rationally resolved without the introduction of the idea of immortal souls than by its use.

Well, perhaps some will say that animals have some inherent value, only *less* than we do. Once again, however, attempts to defend this view can be shown to lack rational justification. What could be the basis of our having more inherent value than animals? Will it be their lack of reason, or autonomy, or intellect? Only if we are willing to make the same judgment in the case of humans who are similarly deficient. But it is not true that such humans—the retarded child, for example, or the mentally deranged—have less inherent value than you or I. Neither, then, can we rationally sustain the view that animals like them in being the experiencing subjects of a life have less inherent value. *All who have inherent value have it equally, whether they be human animals or not.*

Inherent value, then, belongs equally to those who are the experiencing subjects of a life. Whether it belongs to others—to rocks and rivers, trees and glaciers, for example—we do not know. And may never know. But neither do we need to know, if we are to make the case for animal rights. We do not need to know how many people, for example, are eligible to vote in the next presidential election before we can know whether I am. Similarly, we do not need to know *how many* individuals have inherent value before we can know that some do. When it comes to the case for animal rights, then what we need to know is whether the animals who, in our culture are routinely eaten, hunted, and used in our laboratories, for example, are like us in being subjects of a life. And we *do* know this. We do *know* that many—literally, billions and billions—of these animals are subjects of a life in the sense explained and so have inherent value if we do. And since, in order to have the best theory of our duties to one another, we must recognize our equal inherent value, as individuals, *reason*—not sentiment, not emotion—*reason compels us to recognize the equal inherent value of these animals*. And, with this, their equal right to be treated with respect.

That, *very* roughly, is the shape and feel of the case for animal rights. Most of the details of the supporting argument are missing. They are to be found in the book I alluded to earlier. Here, the details go begging and I must in closing, limit myself to four final points.

The first is how the theory that underlies the case for animal rights shows that the animal rights movement is a part of, not antagonistic to, the human rights movement. The theory that rationally grounds the rights of animals also grounds the rights of humans. Thus are those involved in the animal rights movement partners in the struggle to secure respect for human rights—the rights of women, for example, or minorities and workers. The animal rights movement is cut from the same moral cloth as these.

Second, having set out the broad outlines of the rights view, I can now say why its *implications for farming and science*, for example, are both clear and uncompromising. In the case of using animals in science, the rights view is categorically abolitionist. *Lab animals are not our tasters; we are not their kings*. Because these animals are treated—routinely, systematically—as if their value is reducible to their usefulness to others, they are routinely systematically treated with a lack of respect, and thus their rights routinely, systematically violated. This is just as true when they are used in trivial, duplicative, unnecessary or unwise research as it is when they are used in studies that hold out real promise of human benefits. We can't justify harming or killing a human being (my Aunt Bea, for example) just for these sorts of reasons. Neither can we do so even in the case of so lowly a creature as a laboratory rat. It is not just refinement or reduction that are called for, not just larger, cleaner cages, not just more generous use of anesthetic or the elimination of multiple surgery, not just tidying up the system. It is replacement—completely. The best we can do when it comes to using animals in science is—not to use them. That is where our duty lies, according to the rights view.

As for commercial animal agriculture, the rights view takes a similar abolitionist position. The fundamental moral wrong here is not that animals are kept in stressful close confinement, or in isolation, or that they have their pain and suffering, their needs and preferences ignored or discounted. *All* these *are* wrong, of course, but they are not the fundamental wrong. They are symptoms and effects of the deeper, systematic wrong that allows these animals to be viewed and treated as lacking independent value, as resources for us—as, indeed, a renewable resource. Giving farm animals more space, more natural environments, more companions does not right the fundamental wrong, any more than giving lab animals more anesthesia or bigger, cleaner cages would right the fundamental wrong in their case. Nothing less than the total dissolution of commercial animal agriculture will do this, just as, for similar reasons I won't develop at length here, morality requires nothing less than the total elimination of commercial and sport hunting and trapping. The rights view's implications, then, as I have said, are clear—and are uncompromising.

My last two points are about philosophy—my profession. It is most obviously, no substitute for political action. The words I have written here and in other places by themselves don't change a thing. It is what we do with the thoughts the words express—our acts, our deeds—that change things. All that philosophy can do, and all I have attempted, is to offer a vision of what our deeds could aim at. And the why. But not the how.

Finally, I am reminded of my thoughtful critic, the one I mentioned earlier, who chastised me for being "too cerebral." Well, cerebral I have been: indirect duty views, utilitarianism, contractarianism—hardly the stuff deep passions are made of. I am also reminded, however, of the image another friend once set before me—the image of the ballerina as expressive of disciplined passion. Long hours of sweat and toil, of loneliness and practice, of doubt and fatigue; that is the discipline of her craft. But the passion is there, too: the fierce drive to excel, to speak through her body, to do it right, to pierce our minds. That is the image of philosophy I would leave with you; not "too cerebral," but *disciplined passion*. Of the discipline, enough has been seen. As for the passion:

There are times, and these are not infrequent, when tears come to my eyes when I see, or read, or hear of the wretched plight of animals in the hands of humans. Their pain, their suffering, their loneliness, their innocence, their death. Anger. Rage. Pity. Sorrow. Disgust. The whole creation groans under the weight of the evil we humans visit upon these mute, powerless creatures. It *is* our heart, not just our head, that calls for an end, that demands of us that we overcome, for them, the habits and forces behind their systematic oppression. All great movements, it is written, go through three stages: ridicule, discussion, adoption. It is the realization of this third stage—adoption—that demands both our passion and our discipline, our heart and our head. *The fate of animals is in our hands. God grant we are equal to the task.*

Note

1 Tom Regan, *The Case for Animal Rights* (Berkeley: University of California Press, 1983).

A Critique of Regan's Animal Rights Theory

Mary Anne Warren

Tom Regan has produced what is perhaps the definitive defense of the view that the basic moral rights of at least some non-human animals are in no way inferior to our own. In *The Case for Animal Rights*, he argues that all normal mammals over a year of age have the same basic moral rights.[1] Non-human mammals have essentially the same right not to be harmed or killed as we do. I shall call this "the strong animal rights position," although it is weaker than the claims made by some animal liberationists in that it ascribes rights to only some sentient animals.[2]

Mary Anne Warren, "A Critique of Regan's Animal Rights Theory," from *Between Species*, 2 (4) (1987): 331–333, see at: http://digitalcommons.calpoly.edu/bts. Reprinted with permission.

I will argue that Regan's case for the strong animal rights position is unpersuasive and that this position entails consequences which a reasonable person cannot accept. I do not deny that some non-human animals have moral rights; indeed, I would extend the scope of the rights claim to include all sentient animals, that is, all those capable of having experiences, including experiences of pleasure or satisfaction and pain, suffering, or frustration.[3] However, I do not think that the moral rights of most non-human animals are identical in strength to those of persons.[4] The rights of most non-human animals may be overridden in circumstances which would not justify overriding the rights of persons. There are, for instance, compelling realities which sometimes require that we kill animals for reasons which could not justify the killing of persons. I will call this view "the weak animal rights" position, even though it ascribes rights to a wider range of animals than does the strong animal rights position.

I will begin by summarizing Regan's case for the strong animal rights position and noting two problems with it. Next, I will explore some consequences of the strong animal rights position which I think are unacceptable. Finally, I will outline the case for the weak animal rights position.

Regan's Case

Regan's argument moves through three stages. First, he argues that normal, mature mammals are not only sentient but have other mental capacities as well. These include the capacities for emotion, memory, belief, desire, the use of general concepts, intentional action, a sense of the future, and some degree of self-awareness. Creatures with such capacities are said to be subjects-of-a-life. They are not only alive in the biological sense but have a psychological identity over time and an existence which can go better or worse for them. Thus, they can be harmed or benefited. These are plausible claims, and well defended. One of the strongest parts of the book is the rebuttal of philosophers, such as R.G. Frey, who object to the application of such mentalistic terms to creatures that do not use a human-style language.[5] The second and third stages of the argument are more problematic.

In the second stage, Regan argues that subjects-of-a-life have inherent value. His concept of inherent value grows out of his opposition to utilitarianism. Utilitarian moral theory, he says, treats individuals as "mere receptacles" for morally significant value, in that harm to one individual may be justified by the production of a greater net benefit to other individuals. In opposition to this, he holds that subjects-of-a-life have a value independent of both the value they may place upon their lives or experiences and the value others may place upon them.

Inherent value, Regan argues, does not come in degrees. To hold that some individuals have more inherent value than others is to adopt a "perfectionist" theory, i.e., one which assigns different moral worth to individuals according to how well they are thought to exemplify some virtue(s), such as intelligence or moral autonomy. Perfectionist theories have been used, at least since the time of Aristotle, to rationalize such injustices as slavery and male domination, as well as the unrestrained exploitation of animals. Regan argues that if we reject these injustices, then we must also reject perfectionism and conclude that all subjects-of-a-life have equal inherent value. Moral agents have no more inherent value than moral patients, i.e., subjects-of-a-life who are not morally responsible for their actions.

In the third phase of the argument, Regan uses the thesis of equal inherent value to derive strong moral rights for all subjects-of-a-life. This thesis underlies the Respect Principle, which forbids us to treat beings who have inherent value as mere receptacles, i.e., mere means to the production of the greatest overall good. This principle, in turn, underlies the Harm Principle, which says that we have a direct *prima facie* duty not to harm beings who have inherent value. Together, these principles give rise to moral rights. Rights are defined as valid claims, claims to certain goods and against certain beings, i.e., moral agents. Moral rights generate duties not only to refrain from inflicting harm upon beings with inherent value but also to come to their aid when they are threatened by other moral agents. Rights are not absolute but may be overridden in certain circumstances. Just what these circumstances are we will consider later. But first, let's look at some difficulties in the theory as thus far presented.

The Mystery of Inherent Value

Inherent value is a key concept in Regan's theory. It is the bridge between the plausible claim that all normal, mature mammals—human or otherwise—are subjects-of-a-life and the more debatable claim that they all have basic moral rights of the same strength. But it is a highly obscure concept, and its obscurity makes it ill-suited to play this crucial role.

Inherent value is defined almost entirely in negative terms. It is not dependent upon the value which either the inherently valuable individual or anyone else may place upon that individual's life or experiences. It is not (necessarily) a function of sentience or any other mental capacity, because, Regan says, some entities which are not sentient (e.g., trees, rivers, or rocks) may, nevertheless, have inherent value. It cannot attach to anything other than an individual; species, ecosystems, and the like cannot have inherent value.

These are some of the things which inherent value is not. But what is it? Unfortunately, we are not told. Inherent value appears as a mysterious non-natural property which we must take on faith. Regan says that it is a *postulate* that subjects-of-a-life have inherent value, a postulate justified by the fact that it avoids certain absurdities which he thinks follow from a purely utilitarian theory. But why is the postulate that *subjects-of-a-life* have inherent value? If the inherent value of a being is completely independent of the value that it or anyone else places upon its experiences, then why does the fact that it has certain sorts of experiences constitute evidence that it has inherent value? If the reason is that subjects-of-a-life have an existence which can go better or worse for them, then why isn't the appropriate conclusion that all sentient beings have inherent value, since they would all seem to meet that condition? Sentient but mentally unsophisticated beings may have a less extensive range of possible satisfactions and frustrations, but why should it follow that they have—or may have—no inherent value at all?

In the absence of a positive account of inherent value, it is also difficult to grasp the connection between being inherently valuable and having moral rights. Intuitively, it seems that value is one thing, and rights are another. It does not seem incoherent to say that some things (e.g., mountains, rivers, redwood trees) are inherently valuable and yet are not the sorts of things which can have moral rights. Nor does it seem incoherent to ascribe inherent value to some things which are not individuals, e.g., plant or animal species, though it may well be incoherent to ascribe moral rights to such things.

In short, the concept of inherent value seems to create at least as many problems as it solves. If inherent value is based on some natural property, then why not try to identify that property and explain its moral significance, without appealing to inherent value? And if it is not based on any natural property, then why should we believe in it? That it may enable us to avoid some of the problems faced by the utilitarian is not a sufficient reason, if it creates other problems which are just as serious.

Is There a Sharp Line?

Perhaps the most serious problems are those that arise when we try to apply the strong animal rights position to animals other than normal, mature mammals. Regan's theory requires us to divide all living things into two categories: those which have the same inherent value and the same basic moral rights that we do, and those which have no inherent value and presumably no moral rights. But wherever we try to draw the line, such a sharp division is implausible.

It would surely be arbitrary to draw such a sharp line between normal, mature mammals and all other living things. Some birds (e.g., crows, magpies, parrots, mynahs) appear to be just as mentally sophisticated as most mammals and thus are equally strong candidates for inclusion under the subject-of-a-life criterion. Regan is not in fact advocating that we draw the line here. His claim is only that normal mature mammals are clear cases, while other cases are less clear. Yet, on his theory, there must be such a sharp line *somewhere*, since there are no degrees of inherent value. But why should we believe that there is a sharp line between creatures that are subjects-of-a-life and creatures that are not? Isn't it more likely that "subjecthood" comes in degrees, that some creatures have only a little self-awareness, and only a little capacity to anticipate the future, while some have a little more, and some a good deal more?

Should we, for instance, regard fish, amphibians, and reptiles as subjects-of-a-life? A simple yes-or-no answer seems inadequate. On the one hand, some of their behavior is difficult to explain without the assumption that they have sensations, beliefs, desires, emotions, and memories; on the other hand, they do not seem to exhibit very much self-awareness or very much conscious anticipation of future events. Do they have enough mental sophistication to count as subjects-of-a-life? Exactly how much is enough?

It is still more unclear what we should say about insects, spiders, octopi, and other invertebrate animals which have brains and sensory organs but whose minds (if they have minds) are even more alien to us than those of fish or reptiles. Such creatures are probably sentient. Some people doubt that they can feel pain, since they lack certain neurological structures which are crucial to the processing of pain impulses in vertebrate animals. But this argument is inconclusive, since their nervous systems might process pain in ways different from ours. When injured, they sometimes act as if they are in pain. On evolutionary grounds, it seems unlikely that highly mobile creatures with complex sensory systems would not have developed a capacity for pain (and pleasure), since such a capacity has obvious survival value. It must, however, be admitted that we do not *know* whether spiders can feel pain (or something very like it), let alone whether they have emotions, memories, beliefs, desires, self-awareness, or a sense of the future.

Even more mysterious are the mental capacities (if any) of mobile micro-fauna. The brisk and efficient way that paramecia move about in their incessant search for food *might* indicate some kind of sentience, in spite of their lack of eyes, ears, brains, and other organs associated with sentience in more complex organisms. It is conceivable—though not very probable—that they, too, are subjects-of-a-life.

The existence of a few unclear cases need not pose a serious problem for a moral theory, but in this case, the unclear cases constitute most of those with which an adequate theory of animal rights would need to deal. The subject-of-a-life criterion can provide us with little or no moral guidance in our interactions with the vast majority of animals. That might be acceptable if it could be supplemented with additional principles which would provide such guidance. However, the radical dualism of the theory precludes supplementing it in this way. We are forced to say that either a spider has the same right to life as you and I do, or it has no right to life whatever—and that only the gods know which of these alternatives is true.

Regan's suggestion for dealing with such unclear cases is to apply the "benefit of the doubt" principle. That is, when dealing with beings that may or may not be subjects-of-a-life, we should act as if they are.[6] But if we try to apply this principle to the entire range of doubtful cases, we will find ourselves with moral obligations which we cannot possibly fulfill. In many climates, it is virtually impossible to live without swatting mosquitoes and exterminating cockroaches, and not all of us can afford to hire someone to sweep the path before we walk, in order to make sure that we do not step on ants. Thus, we are still faced with the daunting task of drawing a sharp line somewhere on the continuum of life forms—this time, a line demarcating the limits of the benefit of the doubt principle.

The weak animal rights theory provides a more plausible way of dealing with this range of cases, in that it allows the rights of animals of different kinds to vary in strength....

Why Are Animal Rights Weaker Than Human Rights?

How can we justify regarding the rights of persons as generally stronger than those of sentient beings which are not persons? There are a plethora of bad justifications, based on religious premises or false or unprovable claims about the differences between human and non-human nature. But there is one difference which has a clear moral relevance: people are at least sometimes capable of being moved to action or inaction by the force of reasoned argument. Rationality rests upon other mental capacities, notably those which Regan cites as criteria for being a subject-of-a-life. We share these capacities with many other animals. But it is not just because we are subjects-of-a-life that we are both able and morally compelled to recognize one another as beings with equal basic moral rights. It is also because we are able to "listen to reason" in order to settle our conflicts and cooperate in shared projects. This capacity, unlike the others, may require something like a human language.

Why is rationality morally relevant? It does not make us "better" than other animals or more "perfect." It does not even automatically make us more intelligent. (Bad reasoning reduces our effective intelligence rather than increasing it.) But it is morally relevant insofar as it provides greater possibilities for cooperation and for the nonviolent resolution of problems. It also makes us more dangerous than non-rational beings can ever be. Because we are potentially more dangerous and less predictable than wolves, we need an articulated system of morality to regulate our conduct. Any human morality, to be workable in the long run, must recognize the equal moral status of all persons, whether through the postulate of equal basic moral rights or in some other way. The recognition of the moral equality of other persons is the price we must each pay for their recognition of our moral equality. Without this mutual recognition of moral equality, human society can exist only in a state of chronic and bitter conflict. The war between the sexes will persist so long as there is sexism and male domination; racial conflict will never be eliminated so long as there are racist laws and practices. But, to the extent that we achieve a mutual recognition of equality, we can hope to live together, perhaps as peacefully as wolves, achieving (in part) through explicit moral principles what they do not seem to need explicit moral principles to achieve.

Why not extend this recognition of moral equality to other creatures, even though they cannot do the same for us? The answer is that we cannot. Because we cannot reason with most non-human animals, we cannot always solve the problems which they may cause without harming them—although we are always obligated to try. We cannot negotiate a treaty with the feral cats and foxes, requiring them to stop preying on endangered native species in return for suitable concessions on our part.

> If rats invade our houses ... we cannot reason with them, hoping to persuade them of the injustice they do us. We can only attempt to get rid of them.[7]

Aristotle was not wrong in claiming that the capacity to alter one's behavior on the basis of reasoned argument is relevant to the full moral status which he accorded to free men. Of course, he was wrong in his other premise, that women and slaves by nature cannot reason well enough to function as autonomous moral agents. Had that premise been true, so would his conclusion that women and slaves are not quite the moral equals of free men. In the case of most non-human animals, the corresponding premise is true. If, on the other hand, there are animals with whom we can learn to reason, then we are obligated to do this and to regard them as our moral equals.

Thus, to distinguish between the rights of persons and those of most other animals on the grounds that only people can alter their behavior on the basis of reasoned argument does not commit us to a perfectionist theory of the sort Aristotle endorsed. There is no excuse for refusing to recognize the moral equality of some people on the grounds that we don't regard them as quite as rational as we are, since it is perfectly clear that most people can reason well enough to determine how to act so as to respect the basic rights of others (if they choose to), and that is enough for moral equality.

But what about people who are clearly not rational? It is often argued that sophisticated mental capacities such as rationality cannot be essential for the possession of equal basic moral rights, since nearly everyone agrees that human infants and mentally incompetent persons have such rights, even though they may lack those sophisticated mental capacities. But this argument is inconclusive, because there are powerful practical and emotional reasons for protecting non-rational human beings, reasons which are absent in the case of most non-human animals. Infancy and mental incompetence are human conditions which all of us either have experienced or are likely to experience at some time. We also protect babies and mentally incompetent people because we care for them. We don't normally care for animals in the same way, and when we do—e.g., in the case of much-loved pets—we may regard them as having special rights by virtue of their relationship to us. We protect them not only for their sake but also for our own, lest we be hurt by harm done to them. Regan holds that such "side-effects" are irrelevant to moral rights, and perhaps they are. But in ordinary usage, there is no sharp line between moral rights and those moral protections which are not rights. The extension of strong moral protections to infants and the mentally impaired in no way proves that non-human animals have the same basic moral rights as people.

Why Speak of "Animal Rights" at All?

If, as I have argued, reality precludes our treating all animals as our moral equals, then why should we still ascribe rights to them? Everyone agrees that animals are entitled to some protection against human abuse, but why speak of animal *rights* if we are not prepared to accept most animals as our moral equals? The weak animal rights position may seem an unstable compromise between the bold claim that animals have the same basic moral rights that we do and the more common view that animals have no rights at all.

It is probably impossible to either prove or disprove the thesis that animals have moral rights by producing an analysis of the concept of a moral right and checking to see if some or all animals satisfy the conditions for having rights. The concept of a moral right is complex, and it is not clear which of its strands are essential. Paradigm rights holders, i.e., mature and mentally competent persons, are *both* rational and morally autonomous beings and sentient subjects-of-a-life. Opponents of animal rights claim that rationality and moral autonomy are essential for the possession of rights, while defenders of animal rights claim that they are not. The ordinary concept of a moral right is probably not precise enough to enable us to determine who is right on purely definitional grounds.

If logical analysis will not answer the question of whether animals have moral rights, practical considerations may, nevertheless incline us to say that they do. The most plausible alternative to the view that animals have moral rights is that, while they do not have *rights*, we are, nevertheless, obligated not to be cruel to them. Regan argues persuasively that the injunction to avoid being cruel to animals is inadequate to express our obligations towards animals, because it focuses on the mental states of those who cause animal suffering, rather than on the harm done to the animals themselves (p. 328). Cruelty is inflicting pain or suffering and either taking pleasure in that pain or suffering or being more or less indifferent to it. Thus, to express the demand for the decent treatment of animals in terms of the rejection of cruelty is to invite the too easy response that those who subject animals to suffering are not being cruel because they regret the suffering they cause but sincerely believe that what they do is justified. The injunction to avoid cruelty is also inadequate in that it does not preclude the killing of animals—for any reason, however trivial—so long as it is done relatively painlessly.

The inadequacy of the anti-cruelty view provides one practical reason for speaking of animal rights. Another practical reason is that this is an age in which nearly all significant moral claims tend to be expressed in terms of rights. Thus, the denial that animals have rights, however carefully qualified, is likely to be taken to mean that we may do whatever we like to them, provided that we do not violate any human rights. In such a context, speaking of the rights of animals may be the only way to persuade many people to take seriously protests against the abuse of animals.

Why not extend this line of argument and speak of the rights of trees, mountains, oceans, or anything else which we may wish to see protected from destruction? Some environmentalists have not hesitated to speak in this way, and, given the importance of protecting such elements of the natural world, they cannot be blamed for using this rhetorical device. But, I would argue that moral rights can meaningfully be ascribed only to entities which have some capacity for sentience. This is because moral rights are protections designed to protect rights holders from harms or to provide them with benefits which matter to *them*. Only beings capable of sentience can be harmed or benefited in ways which matter to them, for only such beings can like or dislike what happens to them or prefer some conditions to others. Thus, sentient animals, unlike mountains, rivers, or species, are at least logically possible candidates for moral rights. This fact together with the need to end current abuses of animals—e.g., in scientific research …—provides a plausible case for speaking of animal rights.

Conclusion

I have argued that Regan's case for ascribing strong moral rights to all normal, mature mammals is unpersuasive because (1) it rests upon the obscure concept of inherent value, which is defined only in negative terms, and (2) it seems to preclude any plausible answer to questions about the moral status of the vast majority of sentient animals.…

The weak animal rights theory asserts that (1) any creature whose natural mode of life includes the pursuit of certain satisfactions has the right not to be forced to exist without the opportunity to pursue those satisfactions; (2) that any creature which is capable of pain, suffering, or frustration has the right that such experiences not be deliberately inflicted upon it without some compelling reason; and (3) that no sentient being should be killed without good reason. However, moral rights are not an all-or-nothing affair. The strength of the reasons required to override the rights of a non-human organism varies, depending upon—among other things—the probability that it is sentient and (if it is clearly sentient) its probable degree of mental sophistication.…

Notes

1 Tom Regan, *The Case for Animal Rights* (Berkeley: University of California Press, 1983). All page references are to this edition.

2 For instance, Peter Singer, although he does nor like to speak of rights, includes all sentient beings under the protection of his basic utilitarian principle of

equal respect for like interests. (*Animal Liberation* [New York: Avon Books, 1975]; p. 3.)

3 The capacity for sentience like all of the mental capacities mentioned in what follows is a disposition. Dispositions do not disappear whenever they are not currently manifested. Thus, sleeping or temporarily unconscious persons or non-human animals are still sentient in the relevant sense (i.e., still capable of sentience), so long as they still have the neurological mechanisms necessary for the occurrence of experiences.

4 It is possible, perhaps probable that some non-human animals—such as cetaceans and anthropoid apes—should be regarded as persons. If so, then the weak animal rights position holds that these animals have the same basic moral rights as human persons.

5 See R.G. Frey, *Interests and Rights: The Case Against Animals* (Oxford: Oxford University Press, 1980).

6 See, for instance, p. 319, where Regan appeals to the benefit of the doubt principle when dealing with infanticide and late-term abortion.

7 Bonnie Steinbock, "Speciesism and the Idea of Equality," *Philosophy* 53 (1978): 253.

Mary Anne Warren and "Duties to Animals"[1]

MICHAEL BOYLAN

This essay will examine and defend Mary Anne Warren's weak animal rights position, particularly in the context of Tom Regan's strong animal rights position.[2] In doing so, I will rely both on a published paper of Dr Warren's,[3] and some discussions I had with her about a book that she was preparing on this subject for my series at Prentice-Hall: *Basic Ethics in Action*.

To begin, I would like to go over her reconstruction of Regan's strong animal rights argument. I have set it out as follows:

1. Normal mammals are not only sentient, but have other intellectual capacities as well (such as emotion, memory, belief, desire, use of general concepts, intentional action, a sense of the future, and self-awareness): assertion.
2. All creatures that have the capacities mentioned in No. 1 are "subjects-of-a-life": assertion.
3. Normal mammals are subjects-of-a-life: 1, 2.
4. All subjects-of-a-life are not only alive in a biological sense, but also possess psychological identity: assertion.
5. Those creatures that have psychological identity can, over time, be benefited or harmed: fact.
6. All mammals can over time be benefited and harmed: 3–5.
7. Utilitarian moral theory treats individuals as "mere receptacles" for morally significant value: assertion.
8. Utilitarianism does not allow for value independent of what others may place upon them: fact.

9. In utilitarianism harm to one individual may be justified by the production of a greater net benefit to other individuals: 7, 8.
10. Subjects-of-a-life—*contra* utilitarianism—have an inherent value independent of what others may place upon them: assertion.
11. Utilitarianism is wrong when dealing with subjects-of-a-life: 7–10.
12. Perfectionism allows for differential value to be placed upon people: fact.
13. Differential value would be a value that is acquired in degrees: fact.
14. We get inherent value all at once: assertion.
15. Perfectionism is wrong with respect to acquiring inherent value: 12–14.
16. Subjects-of-a-life have inherent value: 11, 15.
17. The *respect principle* (that forbids us to treat beings that have inherent value as mere receptacles on the path to the general good) is correct: assertion.
18. The *harm principle* says we have a direct *prima facie* duty not to harm beings who have inherent value: assertion.
19. Rights claims are made by individuals against other individuals not only to refrain from inflicting harm upon beings with inherent value, but also to come to their aid when they are threatened by other moral agents: assertion.
20. All rights claims entail *prima facie* duties incumbent upon all to respect and not to harm others that can be benefited or harmed and have inherent value: 17–19.
21. All mammals properly possess rights to forbearance of harm and protection from harms caused by others: 6, 16, 20.

Warren's key concern with this argument begins with the understanding of "inherent value." The idea of *inherent* has a long tradition in philosophy. In ancient Greek philosophy it is depicted as *kath'auto*—in Latin *per se*. It means "through itself." If something is inherently valuable, it derives its value through itself—or through an immediate examination of the definition of the term itself. Warren asserts that Regan's idea of inherent value is not adequately supported. Instead, it is a mysterious intuited posit that is set forth without argument. If this is correct, then Regan is guilty of the fallacy of asserting the conclusion (meaning that he has not offered inferential support for his point of contention).

Regan describes his conjecture about inherent value as a "postulate." This is not, therefore, a conclusion for which there is an argument, but an external value that is set in place in order to derive his conclusion.

A second concern of Warren is whether there is a connection between inherent value (however justified) and moral rights. For example, might some things, such as trees, ponds, and mountains, have inherent value (under some sort of valuation), but does this entail a moral right? Warren is skeptical.

In short, Warren thinks that the intellectual concept of inherent value so applied, is fraught with difficulty and so should not be the bulwark for a theory of animal rights.

The Sharp Line Divide

The inherent value → moral rights paradigm creates a sharp divide according to Warren. This divide separates: (a) those that have inherent value and therefore moral rights; versus (b) those that do not have inherent value and therefore do not possess moral rights. Warren calls this all-or-nothing position "dualism." She thinks that this sharp divide is necessary to Regan's argument and that it is wrong—thus providing a pivotal reason for rejecting the strong animal rights position. The reason for this is that *inherent value* is not naturally supported. We do not observe any observable properties that could see inherent value being conferred all at once. What we do observe is developmental traits that come to be as the organism moves toward maturity.

Because inherent value is a "posit" it has, instead, the status of a non-natural truth (on the scale of G.E. Moore's "good"). This would be correct, of course, only if Regan thought that what he was asserting was *true*. If his posit was an anti-realist, non-natural posit, then the proof would be constructed through some conventional political action and ascertained via some sort of public opinion poll of what people in various regions of the globe thought about what inherent value meant and how it should be applied. Warren's take on Regan here is that he is asserting non-natural realism, and I agree.

Back to Warren, she believes that *subject-hood* comes in stages. She queries the sentient capabilities of various species of animals from mammals (Regan's primary explanandum) to fish, amphibians, and reptiles, to invertebrates to protozoan fauna. She searches for some natural basis for attributing a moral right because of some particular characteristic.

In the process Warren rejects traditional *scala naturae* arguments about being "better." Instead, she wants to assert that what is missing from the strong animal rights position (as set out by Regan) is "the ability to listen to reason"[4] in order to settle conflicts and cooperate in shared projects. This capacity amounts to something like the ability to execute human language or something that is equal or more complicated.

Warren argues that the ability to set out claims for one's position that are rationally based and can respond to critical rational responses is critical to the difference between animals and humans in their interactions on Earth. The fact that animals cannot engage in such a dialogue with their own species (as far as we can know) or with *homo sapiens* means that they do not possess the essential characteristic that would confer moral rights. This means that animal rights (such as they may exist) are asymmetrical to human rights.

This is a position with which I agree (though as I will point out later my version is somewhat different in its exposition).

How Should We Regard Animals?

Warren rightly argues that since animals cannot confer with us in problem-solving they do not possess what is morally relevant about reason: the ability to enter into cooperative dialogue for the sake of peace and conflict resolution. This, then, leads to the question of just how we should regard animals, and if they have some variety of rights, how far do these rights extend?

Warren begins this discussion by wondering whether the word "right" is appropriate for animals. Since rights language is so inextricably tied to reason and reasoning, and since this stronger sense of reason is absent in animals, perhaps we should give up that sort of term when dealing with animals? Rights language with humans requires autonomous, sentient subjects-of-a-life. But on Warren's account of gradualism (as opposed to dualism), might it be the case that some sort of proportional response would be correct? What might this look like?

One feature that it would possess is a duty upon people not to be cruel to animals. Regan does not like this approach because the emphasis is upon the subject doing the harm and not upon the animal itself.

Cruelty, according to Warren, is the causing of harm and then either enjoying it or being indifferent to it.[5] The question is whether putting the burden of a non-correlative duty is strong enough to stop cruelty to animals? If the reason rests upon the possible perpetrator only, does this render such actions as sort of optional?

Warren takes these questions to heart and fashions an *environmental moral rights language* that applies to certain animals (according to their capability to engage in some of the aspects of what grounds moral theory for Warren: rational dialogue for the purposes of cooperation and for peace and conflict resolution). Obviously, primates possess these capabilities to a higher degree than do fish and amphibians. It is an open question whether invertebrates (the greatest number of species in the world) possess *any* such capacity. Certainly micro-fauna (if they are considered to be animals) must be ruled out entirely.

Uncontroversial attributions may be made to mammals and perhaps to all vertebrates. Unlike the strong animal rights position, these do not come in an "all or none" package, but in the progression presentation depending upon various cognitive capabilities.

Thus, the weak animal rights position asserts:

1. animals have rights to pursue their natural mode of life;
2. animals have rights not to be subjected to pain, suffering, or frustration without a compelling reason;
3. no sentient being shall be killed without a good reason.

Obviously by fashioning all animal rights as *prima facie* rights, Warren is in line with most positions on human rights as well.[6] But what counts as a "good reason"? Is diet sufficient? What about scientific research? From my own discussions with Mary Anne I think she would answer, "yes" and then "no" (diet counts, but she is very skeptical about scientific research). However, the treatment of animals that are bred for slaughter in order to be part of our diet can be more or less humane. The organic movement, for example, emphasizes free-range animal husbandry and living conditions that satisfy Warren's criteria.

Where I Differ from Warren

As I have said above, I am largely in agreement with Warren's weak animal rights position. However, there are two points that I would like to point out in which we differ.

First, there is the grounding of moral rights in general. Warren's position is to take a rational dialogue model as primary. Whereas I think the sort of argumentative reason she describes as important, I put everything into the context of one's striving toward what one takes to be *the good*. In order to achieve this fundamental aim an individual must be able to undergo purposive action. All goods necessary to allow purposive action are thus claimable as rights in a nested hierarchy according to their embeddedness to the foundations of the possibility of action. For me, it all begins with an autonomously formed vision of the good and then moves to the ability to get oneself there.

My account is compatible with Warren's, but they are different and, when pressed with searching questions, I could see possible divergence in some instances.

Second, Warren is wary of attributing *value* to issues of environmental ethics. Her reasons for this have been outlined above. I am less leery. My reason for this is that I take it for granted that duties to animals and to nature do not operate on the model of human moral rights. This is because animals, trees, mountains, and oceans do not have the sort of autonomous conception of the good that I hold to be fundamental. (At least, there is no way to detect whether there is one—and under one epistemological model of parsimony, if x cannot be shown to be the case, then one may properly doubt whether x is the case.) Thus, even if my dog has some sophisticated conception of the good that is never communicated in any discernible way to anyone or any other animal, then it is not unreasonable to doubt whether my dog has that level of understanding and thus does not have the sophisticated conception of the good necessary for moral rights. All this is similar to Warren. However, I believe that the more we learn about nature and its inhabitants and their environment, the more that we will acquire a valuing of that objective space such that we will seek to protect it.[7]

I do not see this second difference as creating any insurmountable roadblocks. Rather, I am taking on a more expansive point because I am interested in creating a context of protection for both animals (of all sorts—even microscopic) and for insentient plants and landscapes.

In the end I think that Mary Anne Warren's position is intriguing and one which I support. I sometimes long for the book that she would have been able to finish to more fully express her weak animal rights position.

Notes

1 This essay was first presented at the APA Pacific Division 2012, in a memorial session honoring Mary Anne Warren.

2 Tom Regan (1988) *The Case for Animal Rights*, Berkeley, CA: University of California Press.

3 This volume, pp. 300–308.

4 Ibid., p. 304.

5 Ibid., p. 306.

6 This is controversial. I am at the time of writing working on a text on human rights that seeks to address objections by Charles Beitz on this matter: Charles Beitz (2009) *The Idea of Human Rights*, Oxford: Oxford University Press. See my forthcoming book *A Theory of Natural Human Rights,* Cambridge: Cambridge University Press.

7 See Michael Boylan (2001) "Worldview and the Value–Duty Link to Environmental Ethics," in *Environmental Ethics* (ed. Michael Boylan), Upper Saddle River, NJ: Prentice-Hall; pp. 180–196; this volume pp. 95–109.

Against Zoos

DALE JAMIESON

Zoos and Their History

We can start with a rough-and-ready definition of zoos: they are public parks which display animals, primarily for the purposes of recreation or education. Although large collections of animals were maintained in antiquity, they were not zoos in this sense. Typically these ancient collections were not exhibited in public parks, or they were maintained for purposes other than recreation or education.

The Romans, for example, kept animals in order to have living fodder for the games. Their enthusiasm for the games was so great that even the first tigers brought to Rome, gifts to Caesar Augustus from an Indian ruler ended up in the arena. The emperor Trajan staged 123 consecutive days of games in order to celebrate his conquest of Dacia. Eleven thousand animals were slaughtered, including lions, tigers, elephants, rhinoceroses, hippopotami, giraffes, bulls, stags, crocodiles, and serpents. The games were popular in all parts of the empire. Nearly every city had an arena and a collection of animals to stock it. In fifth-century France there were twenty-six such arenas, and they continued to thrive until at least the eighth century.

In antiquity rulers also kept large collections of animals as a sign of their power, which they would demonstrate on occasion by destroying their entire collections. This happened as late as 1719 when Elector Augustus II of Dresden personally slaughtered his entire menagerie, which included tigers, lions, bulls, bears, and boars.

The first modern zoos were founded in Vienna, Madrid, and Paris in the eighteenth century and in London and Berlin in the nineteenth. The first American zoos were established in Philadelphia and Cincinnati in the 1870s. Today in the United States alone there are hundreds of zoos, and they are visited by millions of people every year. They range from roadside menageries run by hucksters, to elaborate zoological parks staffed by trained scientists.

The Roman games no longer exist, though bullfights and rodeos follow in their tradition. Nowadays the power of our leaders is amply demonstrated by their command of nuclear weapons. Yet we still have zoos. Why?

Dale Jamieson, "Against Zoos," in *In Defense of Animals: The Second Wave* (ed. Peter Singer), Blackwell, 2005; pp. 132–143. Reprinted with permission of John Wiley & Sons, Ltd.

Animals and Liberty

Before we consider the reasons that are usually given for the survival of zoos, we should see that there is a moral presumption against keeping wild animals in captivity. What this involves, after all, is taking animals out of their native habitats, transporting them great distances, and keeping them in alien environments in which their liberty is severely restricted. It is surely true that in being taken from the wild and confined in zoos, animals are deprived of a great many goods. For the most part they are prevented from gathering their own food, developing their own social orders, and generally behaving in ways that are natural to them. These activities all require significantly more liberty than most animals are permitted in zoos. If we are justified in keeping animals in zoos, it must be because there are some important benefits that can be obtained only by doing so.

Against this it might be said that most mammals and birds added to zoo collections in recent years are captive-bred. Since these animals have never known freedom, it might be claimed that they are denied nothing by captivity. But this argument is far from compelling. A chained puppy prevented from playing or a restrained bird not allowed to fly still have interests in engaging in these activities. Imagine this argument applied to humans. It would be absurd to suggest that those who are born into slavery have no interest in freedom since they have never experienced it. Indeed, we might think that the tragedy of captivity is all the greater for those creatures who have never known liberty.

The idea that there is a presumption against keeping wild animals in captivity is not the property of some particular moral theory; it follows from most reasonable moral theories. Either we have duties to animals or we do not. If we do have duties to animals, surely they include respecting those interests which are most important to them, so long as this does not conflict with other, more stringent duties that we may have. Since an interest in liberty is central for most animals, it follows that if everything else is equal, we should respect this interest.

Suppose, on the other hand, that we do not have duties to animals. There are two further possibilities: either we have duties to people that sometimes concern animals, or what we do to animals is utterly without moral import. The latter view is quite implausible, and I shall not consider it further. People who have held the former view, that we have duties to people that concern animals, have sometimes thought that such duties arise because we can "judge the heart of a man by his treatment of animals," as Kant (1963: 240) remarked in "Duties to Animals." It is for this reason that he condemns the man who shoots a faithful dog who has become too old to serve. If we accept Kant's premise, it is surely plausible to say that someone who, for no good reason, removes wild animals from their natural habitats and denies them liberty is someone whose heart deserves to be judged harshly. If this is so, then even if we believe that we do not have duties to animals but only duties concerning them, we may still hold that there is a presumption against keeping wild animals in captivity. If this presumption is to be overcome, it must be shown that there are important benefits that can be obtained only by keeping animals in zoos.

Arguments for Zoos

What might some of these important benefits be? Four are commonly cited: amusement, education, opportunities for scientific research, and help in preserving species.

Amusement was certainly an important reason for the establishment of the early zoos, and it remains an important function of contemporary zoos as well. Most people visit zoos in order to be entertained, and any zoo that wishes to remain financially sound must cater to this desire. Even highly regarded zoos have their share of dancing bears and trained birds of prey. But although providing amusement for people is viewed by the general public as a very important function of zoos, it is hard to see how providing such amusement could possibly justify keeping wild animals in captivity.

Most curators and administrators reject the idea that the primary purpose of zoos is to provide entertainment. Indeed, many agree that the pleasure we take in viewing wild animals is not in itself a good enough reason to keep them in captivity. Some curators see baby elephant walks, for example, as a necessary evil, or defend such amusements because of their role in educating people, especially children, about animals. It is sometimes said that people must be interested in what they are seeing if they are to be educated about it, and entertainments keep people interested, thus making education possible.

This brings us to a second reason for having zoos: their role in education. This reason has been cited as long as zoos have existed. For example, in its 1898 annual report, the New York Zoological Society resolved to take "measures to inform the public of the great decrease in animal life, to stimulate sentiment in favor of better protection, and to cooperate with other scientific bodies … [in] efforts calculated to secure the perpetual preservation of our higher vertebrates." Despite the pious platitudes that are often uttered about the educational efforts of zoos, there is little evidence that zoos are very successful in educating people about animals. Indeed, a literature review commissioned by the American Zoo and Aquarium Association (available on their website) concludes that "[l]ittle to no systematic research has been conducted on the impact of visits to zoos and aquariums on visitor conservation knowledge, awareness, affect, or behavior." The research that is available is not encouraging. Stephen Kellert has found that zoo-goers display the same prejudices about animals as the general public. He is quoted in *The New York Times* (December 21, 1993, p. B 9) as saying that "[a] majority expressed willingness to eliminate whole classes of animals altogether, including mosquitoes, cockroaches, fleas, moths, and spiders." His studies have even indicated that people know less about animals after visiting a zoo than they did before. One reason why some zoos have not done a better job in educating people is that many of them make no real effort at education. In the case of others the problem is an apathetic and unappreciative public.

Edward G. Ludwig's (1981) study of the zoo in Buffalo, New York, revealed a surprising amount of dissatisfaction on the part of young, scientifically inclined zoo employees. Much of this dissatisfaction stemmed from the almost complete indifference of the public to the zoo's educational efforts. Ludwig's study indicated that most animals are viewed only briefly as people move quickly past cages. The typical zoo-goer stops only to watch baby animals or those who are begging, feeding, or making sounds. Ludwig reported that the most common expressions used to described animals are "cute," "funny-looking," "lazy," "dirty," "weird," and "strange." More recently, Frans de Waal has noted that after spending two or three minutes watching chimpanzees, zoo-goers often say as they walk away, "Oh, I could watch them for hours!"

Of course, it is undeniable that some education occurs in some zoos. But this very fact raises other issues. What is it that we want people to learn from visiting zoos? Facts about the physiology and behavior of various animals? Attitudes towards the survival of endangered species? Compassion for the fate of all animals? To what degree does education require keeping wild animals in captivity? Couldn't most of the educational benefits of zoos be obtained through videos, lectures, and computer simulations? Indeed, couldn't most of the important educational objectives better be achieved by exhibiting empty cages with explanations of why they are empty?

A third reason for having zoos is that they support scientific research. This, too, is a benefit that was pointed out long ago. Sir Humphrey Davy, one of the founders of the Zoological Society of London, wrote in 1825: "It would become Britain to offer another, and a very different series of exhibitions to the population of her metropolis; namely, animals brought from every part of the globe to be applied either to some useful purpose, or as objects of scientific research – not of vulgar admiration!" (cited in Scherrin 1905: 16). Zoos support scientific research in at least three ways: they fund field research by scientists not affiliated with zoos; they employ other scientists as members of zoo staffs; and they make otherwise inaccessible animals available for study.

We should note first that very few zoos support any real scientific research. Fewer still have staff scientists with full-time research appointments. Among those that do, it is common for their scientists to study animals in the wild rather than those in zoo collections. Much of this research, as well as other field research that is supported by zoos, could just as well be funded in a different way – say, by a government agency. The question of whether there should be zoos does not turn on the funding for field research which zoos currently provide. The significance of the research that is actually conducted in zoos is a more important consideration.

Research that is conducted in zoos can be divided into two broad categories: studies in behavior and studies in anatomy and pathology.

Behavioral research conducted on zoo animals is controversial. Some have argued that nothing can be learned by studying animals that are kept in the unnatural conditions that obtain in most zoos. Others have argued that captive animals are more interesting research subjects than are wild animals: since captive animals are free from predation, they exhibit a wider range of physical and behavioral traits than do animals in the wild, thus permitting researchers to view the full range of their genetic possibilities. Both of these positions are surely extreme. Conditions in some zoos are natural enough to permit some interesting research possibilities. But the claim that captive animals are more interesting research subjects than those in the wild is not very plausible. Environments trigger behaviors. No doubt a predation-free environment triggers behaviors different from those of an animal's natural habitat, but there is no reason to believe that better, fuller, or more accurate data can be obtained in predation-free environments than in natural habitats.

Studies in anatomy and pathology have three main purposes: to improve zoo conditions so that captive animals will live longer, be happier, and breed more frequently; to contribute to human health by providing animal models for human ailments; and to increase our knowledge of wild animals for its own sake.

The first of these aims is surely laudable, if we concede that there should be zoos in the first place. But the fact that zoo research contributes to improving conditions in zoos is not a reason for having them. If there were no zoos, there would be no need to improve them.

The second aim, to contribute to human health by providing animal models for human ailments, appears to justify zoos to some extent, but in practice this consideration is not as important as one might think. There are very severe constraints on the experiments that may be conducted on zoo animals. In a 1982 article, Montali and Bush drew the following conclusion:

> Despite the great potential of a zoo as a resource for models, there are many limitations and, of necessity, some restrictions for use. There is little opportunity to conduct overly manipulative or invasive research procedures – probably less than would be allowed in clinical research trials involving human beings. Many of the species are difficult to work with or are difficult to breed, so that the numbers of animals available for study are limited. In fact, it is safe to say that over the past years, humans have served more as "animal models" for zoo species than is true of the reverse.

Whether for this reason or others, many of the experiments that have been conducted using zoo animals as models for humans seem redundant or trivial. For example, the article cited above reports that zoo animals provide good models for studying lead toxicity in humans, since it is common for zoo animals to develop lead poisoning from chewing paint and inhaling polluted city air. There are available for study plenty of humans who suffer from lead poisoning for the same reasons. That zoos make available some additional nonhuman subjects for this kind of research seems at best unimportant and at worst deplorable.

Finally, there is the goal of obtaining knowledge about animals for its own sake. Knowledge is certainly something which is good and, everything being equal, we should encourage people to seek it for its own sake. But everything is not equal in this case. There is a moral presumption against keeping animals in captivity. This presumption can be overcome only by demonstrating that there are important benefits that must be obtained in this way if they are to be obtained at all. It is clear that this is not the case with knowledge for its own sake. There are other channels for our intellectual curiosity, ones that do not exact such a high moral price. Although our quest for knowledge for its own sake is important, it is not important enough to overcome the moral presumption against keeping animals in captivity.

In assessing the significance of research as a reason for having zoos, it is important to remember that very few zoos do any research at all. Whatever benefits result from zoo research could just as well be obtained by having a few zoos instead of the hundreds which now exist. The most this argument could establish is that we are justified in having a few very good zoos. It does not provide a defense of the vast majority of zoos which now exist.

A fourth reason for having zoos is that they preserve species that would otherwise become extinct. As the destruction of habitat accelerates and as breeding programs become increasingly successful, this rationale for zoos gains in popularity. There is some reason for questioning the commitment of zoos to species preservation: it can be argued that they continue to remove more animals from the wild than they return. In the minds of some skeptics, captive breeding programs are more about the preservation of zoos than the preservation of endangered species. Still, without such programs, the Pere David Deer, the Mongolian Wild Horse, and the California Condor would all now be extinct.

Even the best of such programs face difficulties, however. A classic study by Katherine Ralls, Kristin Brugger, and Jonathan Ballou (1979) convincingly argues that lack of genetic diversity among captive animals is a serious problem for zoo breeding programs. In some species the infant mortality rate among inbred animals is six or seven times that among noninbred animals. In other species the infant mortality rate among inbred animals is 100 percent.

Moreover, captivity substitutes selection pressures imposed by humans for those of an animal's natural habitat. After a few years in captivity, animals can begin to diverge both behaviorally and genetically from their relatives in the wild. After a century or more it is not clear that they would be the same animals, in any meaningful sense, that we set out to preserve.

There is also a dark side to zoo breeding programmes: they create many unwanted animals. In some species (lions, tigers, and zebras, for example) a few males can service an entire herd. Extra males are unnecessary to the program and are a financial burden. Some of these animals are sold and end up in the hands of individuals and institutions which lack proper facilities. Others are shot and killed by Great White Hunters in private hunting camps. An article in *US News* (August 5, 2002) exposed the widespread dumping of "surplus" animals by some of America's leading zoos. The reporter even found two endangered gibbons in a filthy cage with no water, in a bankrupt roadside zoo just off Interstate 35 in Texas. The *San Francisco Chronicle* (February 23, 2003) reports that there are now more tigers in private hands than in the wild. There is a flourishing trade in exotic animals fed by more than 1,000 internet sites, and publications such as the *Animal Finders' Guide*, which is published eighteen times per year. A recent browse finds advertisements for coyote pups ($250), baboons ($4,000 for a pair), a declawed female black bear ($500), a 12-year-old female tiger ($500), and much more. In order to avoid the "surplus" problem, some zoos have considered proposals to "recycle" excess animals: a euphemism for killing them and feeding their bodies to other zoo animals.

The ostensible purpose of zoo breeding programs is to reintroduce animals into the wild. In this regard the California Condor is often portrayed as a major success story. From a low of 22 individuals in 1982, the population has rebounded to 219, through captive breeding. Since 1992 condors have been reintroduced, but most have not survived and only six eggs have been produced in the wild. Most eggs have failed to hatch, and only one chick has fledged. Wolf reintroductions have also had only limited success. Wolves, even when they have learned how to hunt, have often not learned to avoid people. Familiarity with humans and ignorance about their own cultures have devastated reintroduced populations of big cats, great apes, bears, rhinos, and hippos.

According to the philosopher Bryan Norton, putting a captive-bred animal in the wild is "equivalent to dropping a contemporary human being in a remote area in the 18th or 19th century and saying, 'Let's see if you can make it' "(quoted in Derr 1999). In a 1995 review, Ben Beck, Associate Director of the National Zoological Park in Washington, found that of 145 documented reintroductions involving 115 species, only 16 succeeded in producing self-sustaining wild populations, and only half of these were endangered species.

Even if breeding programs were run in the best possible way, there are limits to what can be done to save endangered species in this way. At most, several hundred species could be preserved in the world's zoos, and then at very great expense. For many of these animals the zoo is likely to be the last stop on the way to extinction. Zoo professionals like to say that they are the Noahs of the modern world and that zoos are their arks, but Noah found a place to land his animals where they could thrive and multiply. If zoos are like arks, then rare animals are like passengers on a voyage of the damned, never to find a port that will let them dock or a land in which they can live in peace. The real solution, of course, is to preserve the wild nature that created these animals and has the power to sustain them. But if it is really true that we are inevitably moving towards a world in which mountain gorillas can survive only in zoos, then we must ask whether it is really better for them to live in artificial environments of our design than not to be born at all.

Even if all these questions and difficulties are overlooked, the importance of preserving endangered species does not provide much support for the existing system of zoos. Most zoos do very little breeding or breed only species which are not endangered. Many of the major breeding programs are run in special facilities which have been established for that purpose. They are often located in remote places, far from the attention of zoo-goers. (For example, the Wildlife Conservation Society [formerly the New York Zoological Society] operates its Wildlife Survival Center on St Catherine's Island off the coast of Georgia, and the National Zoo runs its Conservation and Research Center in the Shenandoah Valley of Virginia.) If our main concern is to do what we can to preserve endangered species at any cost and in any way, then we should support such large-scale breeding centers rather than conventional zoos, most of which have neither the staff nor the facilities to run successful breeding programs.

The four reasons for having zoos which I have surveyed carry some weight. But different reasons provide support for different kinds of zoo. Preservation and perhaps research are better carried out in large-scale animal preserves, but these provide few opportunities for amusement and education. Amusement and perhaps education are better provided in urban zoos, but they offer few opportunities for research and preservation. Moreover, whatever benefits are obtained from any kind of zoo, we must confront the moral presumption against keeping wild animals in captivity. Which way do the scales tip? There are two further considerations which, in my view, tip the scales against zoos.

First, captivity does not just deny animals liberty but is often detrimental to them in other respects as well. The history of chimpanzees in the zoos of Europe and America is a good example.

Chimpanzees first entered the zoo world in about 1640 when a Dutch prince, Frederick Henry of Nassau, obtained one for his castle menagerie. The chimpanzee didn't last very long. In 1835 the London Zoo obtained its first chimpanzee; he died immediately. Another was obtained in 1845; she lived six months. All through the nineteenth and early twentieth centuries zoos obtained chimpanzees who promptly died within nine months. It wasn't until the 1930s that it was discovered that chimpanzees are extremely vulnerable to human respiratory diseases, and that special steps must be taken to protect them. But for nearly a century zoos removed them from the wild and subjected them to almost certain death. Even today there are chimpanzees and other great apes living in deplorable conditions in zoos around the world.

Chimpanzees are not the only animals to suffer in zoos. It is well known that animals such as polar bears, lions, tigers, and cheetahs fare particularly badly in zoos. A recent (2003) report in *Nature* by Ros Clubb and Georgia Mason shows that repetitive stereotypic behavior and high infant mortality rates in zoos are directly related to an animal's natural home range size. For example, polar bears, whose home range in the wild is about a million times the size of its typical zoo enclosure, spend 25 percent of their days in stereotypic pacing and suffer from a 65% infant mortality rate. These results suggest that zoos simply cannot provide the necessary conditions for a decent life for many animals. Indeed, the Detroit Zoo has announced that, for ethical reasons, it will no longer keep elephants in captivity. The San Francisco Zoo has followed suit.

Many animals suffer in zoos quite unnecessarily. In 1974 Peter Batten, former director of the San Jose Zoological Gardens, undertook an exhaustive study of two hundred American zoos. In his book *Living Trophies* he documented large numbers of neurotic, overweight animals kept in cramped, cold cells and fed unpalatable synthetic food. Many had deformed feet and appendages caused by unsuitable floor surfaces. Almost every zoo studied had excessive mortality rates, resulting from preventable factors ranging from vandalism to inadequate husbandry practices. Batten's conclusion was: "The majority of American zoos are badly run, their direction incompetent, and animal husbandry inept and in some cases non-existent" (1976: ix).

Many of these same conditions are documented in Lynn Griner's (1983) review of necropsies conducted at the San Diego Zoo over a fourteen-year period. This zoo may well be the best in the country, and its staff are clearly well trained and well intentioned. Yet this study documents widespread malnutrition among zoo animals; high mortality rates from the use of anesthetics and tranquilizers; serious injuries and deaths sustained in transport; and frequent occurrences of cannibalism, infanticide, and fighting almost certainly caused by overcrowded conditions.

The Director of the National Zoo in Washington resigned in 2004 when an independent review panel commissioned by the National Academy of Sciences found severe deficiencies at the zoo in animal care, pest control, record keeping, and management that contributed to the deaths of twenty-three animals between 1998 and 2003, including, most spectacularly, the loss of two pandas to rat poison. Despite the best efforts of its well-paid public relations firm, it is difficult to trust an institution that cannot avoid killing its most charismatic and valuable animals in such a stupid and unnecessary way.

The second consideration which tips the scales against zoos is more difficult to articulate but is, to my mind, even more important. Zoos teach us a false sense of our place in the natural order. The means of confinement mark a difference between humans and other animals. They are there at our pleasure, to be used for our purposes.

Morality and perhaps our very survival require that we learn to live as one species among many rather than as one species over many. To do this, we must forget what we learn at zoos. Because what zoos teach us is false and dangerous, both humans and other animals will be better off when they are abolished.

References

Batten, P. (1976) *Living Trophies*, New York: Thomas Y. Crowell Co.

Beck, B. (1995) "Reintroduction, Zoos, Conservation, and Animal Welfare," in B. Norton, M. Hutchins, E.F. Stevens, and T.L. Maple (eds), *Ethics on the Ark: Zoos, Animal Welfare, and Wildlife Conservation*, Washington, D.C.: Smithsonian Institution Press; pp. 155–63.

Clubb, R., and Mason, G. (2003) "Animal Welfare: Captivity Effects on Wide-Ranging Carnivores," *Nature*, October 2; 425(6957): 473–474.

Derr, M. (1999) "A Rescue Plan for Threatened Species," *New York Times*, January 19.

Griner, L. (1983) *Pathology of Zoo Animals*, San Diego: Zoological Society of San Diego.

Kant, I. (1963) *Lectures on Ethics*, trans. L. Infield, New York: Harper.

Ludwig, E.G. (1981) "People at Zoos: A Sociological Approach," *International Journal for the Study of Animal Problems* 2(6): 310–316.

Montali, R., and Bush, M. (1982) "A Search for Animal Models at Zoos," *ILAR News* 26(1), Fall: 11–16.

Ralls, K., Brugger, K., and Ballou, J. (1979) "Inbreeding and Juvenile Mortality in Small Populations of Ungulates," *Science* 206: 1101–1103.

Scherrin, H. (1905) *The Zoological Society of London*, New York: Cassell and Co., Ltd.

Evaluating a Case Study

Structuring the Essay

In previous sections, you have moved from adopting an ethical theory to weighing and assessing the merits of deeply embedded cost issues and ethical issues conflicts. The process involves (a) choosing an ethical theory (whose point of view you will adopt), (b) determining your professional practice issues and ethical issues lists, (c) annotating the issues lists by examining how embedded each issue is to the essential nature of the case at hand, (d) creating a brainstorming list that includes both key thoughts on the subject and arguments for and against the possible courses of action, (e) comparing pivotal premises in those arguments using ethical considerations as part of the decision-making matrix, (f) making a judgment on which course to take (given the conflicts expressed in d and e, and (g) presenting your ideas in an essay. The essay is your recommendation to a professional review board about what to do in a specific situation.

This section represents stage (g) in this process. If we continue with the IUD case, your essay might be something like the following.

Sample Essay

Executive Summary. Although my profession would advocate my continuing to distribute IUDs to women in less-developed countries and cost issues dictate that I accept ABC Corporation's offer, it is my opinion that to do so would be immoral. Human life is too precious to put anyone at risk for population control. If IUDs are too dangerous to be sold in the United States, then they are too dangerous for women in poor countries as well. People do not give up their right to adequate health protection just because they are poor. For this reason, I am ordering a halt to the distribution of IUDs until such a time that they can be considered safe again. Furthermore, I will step up efforts to distribute alternate forms of birth control (such as the birth control pill) with better packaging that might encourage regular use.

The Introduction

In this case study, I have chosen the point of view of the regional director. This means that I must decide whether to continue distributing IUDs in less-developed countries despite a health hazard to 5 percent of the women who use this form of birth control. I will argue against continuing the distribution based on an argument that examines: (a) the imperatives of my profession, public health; (b) cost implications (c) the imperatives of ethics; and (d) the rights of the women involved. I will contend that after examining these issues, the conclusion must be to cease IUD distribution in less-developed countries until IUDs no longer pose a significant problem to women's health.

The Body of the Essay

Develop paragraphs along the lines indicated in the introduction and executive summary.

The Conclusion

Although the dictates of the normal practice of public health and cost considerations would seem to suggest that IUD distribution continue, the ethical imperatives that human life is individually precious and that each woman has a right to safe medical attention overrule the normal practice of the profession. For these reasons, my office will suspend distribution of IUDs until they no longer pose a health risk to the general population.

Comments on the Sample

The sample provides an essay structure that contains a brief epitome and the essay itself. I often encourage my students to come in with their epitome, key issues, arguments for and against, and brainstorming sheets before writing the essay itself. This way I can get an "in-progress" view of the process of composition.

Obviously, the preceding sample represents the briefest skeleton of an essay proposing a recommendation. The length can vary as can any supporting data (charts, etc.) for your position. Your instructor may ask you to present your outcomes recommendation to the entire class. When this is the assignment, remember that the same principles of any group presentation also apply here including any visual aid that will engage your audience. It is essential to include your audience in your argument as it develops.

Whether it is a written report or a group presentation, the methodology presented here should give you a chance to logically assess and respond to problems that contain moral dimensions.

The following are some general questions that some of my students have raised about writing the essay, that is, the ethical outcomes recommendation.

What if I cannot see the other side? This is a common question from students. They see everything as black or white, true or false, but truth is never advanced by prejudice. It is important as rational humans to take every argument at its face value and to determine what it says, determine the objections to the key premises, determine the strongest form of the thesis, and assess the best arguments *for* and *against* the thesis.

What is the best way to reach my assessment of the best alternative? The basic strategy of the essay is to take the best two arguments that you have selected to support the conflicting alternatives and then to focus on that single premise that seems to be at odds with the other argument. At this point, you must ask yourself, Why would someone believe in either argument 1 or argument 2? If you do not know, you cannot offer an opinion—yet.

The rational person seeks to inform herself by getting into the skin of each party. You must understand why a thinking person might think in a particular way. If you deprecate either side, you lessen yourself because you decrease your chances to make your best judgment.

The rational individual seeks the truth. You have no need to burden your psyche with illogical beliefs. Therefore, you will go to great lengths to find the truth of the key premises that you wish to examine.

In the your final essay, you will focus on one of the argument's premises and find the following:

A. The demonstrated truth of the conclusion depends on the premises that support it.
B. If those supporting premises are false, then the conclusion is not proven.
C. Since we have assumed that the premises are all necessary to get us to the conclusion, if we refute one premise, we have refuted the conclusion.

What if I place professional practice issues or cost issues or ethical issues too highly in my assessment of the outcome? The purpose of preparing an embedded issues analysis is to force you to see that not all ethical issues are central to the problem. Some issues can be solved rather easily. If this is the case, then you should do so. When it is possible to let professional practice issues determine the outcome without sacrificing ethical standards, it is your responsibility to do so. Clearly, some ethical principles cannot be sacrificed no matter what the cost. It is *your* responsibility to determine just what these cases are and just which moral principles are "show stoppers."

Are ethical values the only values an individual should consider? Each person holds a number of personally important values that are a part of his or her world-view. These must be taken into account in real situations. Often they mean that although you cannot perform such and such an act, it is not requisite that the organization forgo doing whatever the professional practice issues dictate in that situation. For example, you may be asked to perform a task on an important religious holy day. Since your religion is important to you, you cannot work on that day, but that does not mean that you will recommend the company abandon the task that another person who does not share your value could perform.

What happens when you confuse professional practice issues and ethical issues? This happens often among managers at all levels. The problem is that one set of issues is neglected or is too quickly considered to be surface embeddedness. Stop. Go through the method again step-by-step. It may restore your perspective.

Macro and Micro Cases[1]

Macro Case 1. You are the head of curriculum development for science at Bellevue Public Schools in Bellevue, Washington. One of the issues that has come before the committee is dissecting fetal pigs in Biology 1. This skill has been taught in the course for many years, but now with simulated computer programs, students can get three-dimensional effects without having to use actual fetal pigs.

One member on the committee said that it was strange that we hold so much regard for human children and the human embryo, yet we blithely butcher hundreds of thousands of fetal pigs each year without any compunction. Another member said that pigs are different from humans because they cannot reason; reason makes all the difference. A third member said that pigs are quite intelligent, so that if that were the standard, pigs would fare well. Also, he said that the cutting-edge technology for surgeons is to use computer-assisted graphics that represent anatomy as they perform tricky, experimental operations. If it is good enough for the best surgeons of the world, certainly it is good enough for first-year high school biology students.

A fourth member of the committee said that those surgeons could use computer-assisted models only *because* they have been taught on real dissections. There is no substitute for actual hands-on experience.

The committee is deadlocked and as its head, you must cast the deciding vote. Write a report to the committee explaining why you cast your vote in favor of traditional fetal pig dissection or the new proposal for computer-simulated dissection. Be sure to cite practical issues and ethical issues (including an ethical theory and linking principle).

Macro Case 2. You are the head of the Meat Inspection Agency within the Department of Agriculture. Your job traditionally has been to ensure that meat is processed in a clean, hygienic environment. However, the head of the House Agriculture Committee has ordered you to review all meat-processing procedures for legislative reform as the result of current attitudes. One such attitude is represented by an orthodox Jewish rabbi from a powerful congressional district in Brooklyn. This rabbi has suggested to you that the procedure of bleeding pork before slaughter is barbaric. This practice dates back thousands of years when no one wanted to eat pork that was slaughtered in the same way as other animals (such as cattle). Pork is clearly seen to be disgusting because of its bloody color. Thus, the practice of bleeding pigs before slaughter was adopted. This practice, the rabbi contends, is cruel because it inflicts pain on the animal in the last minutes of its life. You have thought about this. Pork does not represent the largest portion of the meat market, but it is still significant. If you think as a politician (because of your political appointment), you will decide according to what is politically expedient. When you do so, the status quo wins. However, you want to do the right thing—but what is the right thing? You must submit a draft review in three days. You must include the rabbi's concerns in your report, but you must also come up with your own recommendations. Write a report on this issue basing your reasons on practical and ethical issues (including an ethical theory and linking principle).

Macro Case 3. You are an official for the Environmental Protection Agency (EPA) and have been assigned to review a lumbering proposal for Oregon (near Mount Hood). ABC Company wants to do two things. First, it wants to cut forest lands on this tract of virgin forest (i.e., not cut by humans since recorded time—around 1840) and to replant so that by the time the last section has been harvested, the first will be covered by adult trees at least 80 percent the height of those trees that were cut first. Second, ABC wants to build a road that will accommodate its logging trucks. This will require filling in four wetland sites. However, in accordance with current federal regulations, ABC will establish four new wetland sites and therefore be in complete compliance with the law.

During public hearings, however, many people came forward to note that the lumber proposal will severely disrupt the habitat of a tree frog is unique to this area. This tree frog is the linchpin of an ecosystem, it is the prey of at least twenty species and is the predator of forty-six species. To disrupt this ecosystem, the detractors contend, would be to kill this species of frog and severely disrupt the ecosystem.

Those in favor of the project say that species are becoming extinct all the time; that is the way of nature. Ecosystems are not in some sort of static state that must be preserved but will adapt as conditions demand—this is the way of evolution. This project will employ 1800 individuals and support more than 8000 people when all social factors are considered. Will you say to a family on welfare that it must continue to live in poverty because we are concerned about losing a species of tree frog or damaging an ecosystem?

Write a report to your superiors that is due next Tuesday. In it, note the various positions and the arguments for each. Then recommend what to do based on the appropriate facts and ethical theories.

Macro Case 4. You are the head of the South East Asian Commission for Development at the World Bank. Bangladesh has submitted a proposal for the creation of a giant overflow reservoir that will be significant in solving the recurrent problem of flooding in the delta region. In years past (more than 100), people did not live in this region because of the devastation that periodically occurred. However, things are different now; because of overpopulation and the fertile soil, people now live in this region and there is substantial death and human anguish when the flooding occurs regularly.

At first, there seems to be no problem if the agency funds a project that saves lives, increases jobs, and creates hydroelectric power for the country. However, there are problems. First, there is a lack of family planning in the region. One concern involves overpopulation. With no floods to cause deaths, more people will live to reproduce, so the combination of fewer deaths and more births will lead to overpopulation and its related problems. Second, eighty known unique species of flora and fauna will be lost as the result of the ecological disruption. Third, the increase in cheap power generated may cause a boom in industrial development by foreign companies eager to cash in on it and cheap labor. (Bangladesh is one of the poorest nations of the world.)

Write a report to your superior at the World Bank recommending a course of action. Base your recommendation on a survey of the human, ecological, and the ethical factors (mentioning specifically an ethical theory and a linking principle).

Micro Case 1. You and your best friend are at odds over the issue of eating meat. Each day, the two of you eat dinner together in the dining hall. Your friend is a vegetarian and claims that you should be, too.

"Why?" you ask.

"Because you have no right to eat another animal. It's immoral. You wouldn't eat your Uncle Harold, would you?" You always hate it when your friend brings up Uncle Harold.

"I'm not eating my uncle; besides, that has nothing to do with it. Harold is a human. This hamburger I'm eating was once a cow. Have you ever seen how small the frontal lobe of a cow is? These animals are not only not rational but are also *stupid*!"

"They may be stupid but they still feel pain. They still value their lives—"

"Just a minute there; *how* can they value their lives when they do not have an abiding sense of self from which they can base their valuing?"

"You're splitting hairs. Every animal values its life. Every animal feels pain. In virtue of these two facts, you must become a vegetarian. Besides, it's good for you."

"That's another issue, but if you are so inclined to ascribe rights to animals, what about their moral responsibilities?"

"Their responsibilities?"

"Yes. Won't you tell the lion that it is immoral to kill the cheetah or zebra?"

"That's no kind of argument. That assumes a model of reason again. You notice that I didn't defend my position in terms of reason but in terms of feeling pain and not wanting to die."

You decide to stop the conversation for the time being. In the interim, you develop a dialogue between yourself and your friend on this issue at length. You want to slant the issue to one of the two sides. (In other words, there must be a winner.) Write this dialogue, grounding it on an ethical theory and in a linking principle.

Micro Case 2. You are a federal government employee at the Transportation Department and live in Gaithersburg, Maryland, a suburb of Washington, DC. Your commute to work along the I-270 corridor takes you fifty-five minutes each way. You could also take public transit for just a little more door-to-door time. The cost to drive and park is about $0.50 less each day than the cost of public transit. If your child had an emergency during the day at school, you could get to the school in about 40 minutes by car or in around 68 minutes during nonrush hours via public transit.

There has been a big push at work to promote public transportation. One of the flyers handed out recently included the following statement: "The air quality in this region is not improving. You can become a part of the solution by riding public transit"—a catchy phrase. You appreciate the environment; you have a flower garden in your Gaithersburg townhouse. However, you wonder what good your riding the subway and hopping a bus would do. One person isn't that important. All the personal factors point to driving your single-occupancy vehicle. Still, something inside you says that the only way to continue as a people is to lower pollution so that our development does not permanently disfigure the world. You have heard the term "sustainable development," which means that some sacrifices must be made to balance the costs of development.

Write a personal journal entry citing your conflicting positions and then recommending a particular course of action. Feel free to use short- and long-term time frames. Be sure to refer to an ethical theory and any applicable linking principles.

Micro Case 3. You are a family farmer with 80 acres in southwestern Michigan. You do not make enough from farming to sustain your family, so you work as a carpenter during the winter months. You have been approached by XYZ Company (the largest seed company in the world) about buying its genetically altered seeds that are resistant to insects, are hearty in most environmental conditions, and command a premium price at market. The only thing that bothers you is that these big seed companies create a single style of seed and want to pass it off as the only one that is any good. What about the old days in which you carefully selected the seed you would use because you knew how the product would taste? There were many choices then.

In addition, your college-age daughter tells you that these big seed companies will decrease biodiversity by cornering the market on seeds and standardizing products.

Even if they cannot create a monopoly, she says, they will greatly decrease biodiversity, which is a bad thing.

You are unsure what to do. You decide to go to the agent of the local grange association for her advice. Create a dialogue between yourself and the agent that highlights issues about biodiversity and your personal worldview. Create views for yourself and the agent, and then give reasons for choosing or not choosing to take XYZ's seeds.

Note

1 For more on macro and micro cases, see the overview on p. 26.

7
Sustainability

General Overview: One practical goal among most environmentalists is to create or modify systems so that they are sustainable over time. For example, in the energy industry we presently depend to a large extent upon fossil fuels that are: (1) a limited resource and (2) pollute the air and degrade the planet. Wouldn't it be better to have energy resources that would be: (1) renewable and (2) caused no harm to the environment? This latter conception is the sustainable one—because it can keep on going without causing exterior harm.

Sustainability is sometimes viewed via comparative advantage. Option A is called *sustainable* if it is more abundant and causes less harm than Option B. At the writing of this book, hydraulic fracturing (fracking) to procure natural gas is called sustainable in this comparative sense (compared with oil).

The ethical dimensions of sustainability seemed to be both *intrinsic* (it is in principle better not to waste the Earth's resources and not to harm the environment) and *anthropocentric* (future generations of people deserve more than a degraded environment in which to live).

While many would agree "in principle" that we should seek sustainable paths for the way we live, these same people might say that "in practice" we all need to live and the model we have constructed is not sustainable in this pure sense. Going back to anthropocentricism, these individuals might argue that people are the most important entity on the planet (to us) and that their well-being should be prominent. And given that we are the most powerful and can call the shots, why should we not do what we feel is best for us? Of course, the temporal component comes in again, but we are living *now*. So *for us* would skew the answer for individuals making this sort of argument.

A. Sustainability: What It Is and How It Works

Overview: This first section examines sustainability broadly to ascertain how it would operate and how we should regard it.

Environmental Ethics, Second Edition. Edited by Michael Boylan.

A good introduction to how we should think about sustainability comes from Randall Curren's essay, sustainability is taken to be a nascent field of study. Thus, the purpose of his essay is to give a structure to the domain. This includes setting out in some detail the domain of inquiry by examining the domain, itself. "Sustainability" largely displaces the language of environmental conservation. This is because it is not just about *protecting*. Instead, sustainability seeks to describe various environmental footprints and the foreseen future consequences. This gives rise to the primary meaning of "sustainable": the totality of practices of some human collectivity is *sustainable* if, and only if, it is compatible with the long-term stability of the natural systems on which the practices fundamentally depend. This definition must be viewed in the dynamics of economic growth that must be *conducive* and not merely *compatible* with the primary meaning of sustainability. In order to do this, sustainable ethics must not diminish natural capital, nor diminish satisfying opportunities to experience nature. In order to get to these outcomes, Curren suggests strategies to realize broad institutional changes that would transform societies around the world.

In the second essay Stephen M. Gardiner takes on the central issues involved with sustainability: limited resources and harm to the planet. This is a practically oriented essay that seeks its answers via the examination of a particular moral problem: climate change. Gardiner argues that the peculiar features of the climate-change problem pose substantial obstacles to our ability to make the hard choices necessary to address it. Climate change involves the convergence of a set of global, intergenerational, and theoretical problems. This convergence justifies calling it a "perfect moral storm." One consequence of this storm is that, even if the other difficult ethical questions surrounding climate change could be answered, we might still find it difficult to act. For the storm makes us extremely vulnerable to moral corruptions. Thus, Gardiner's essay sounds a precautionary note on the way public policy might go forward by avoiding the pitfalls that might lead to weak, substanceless global accords and then trumpeting them as great achievements.

Bryan G. Norton begins his essay with a different way to conceptualize environmental problems (including sustainability). Instead of considering the battle as between the anthropocentric and biocentric positions, Norton wants to introduce a spatiotemporal scaling he calls *adaptive management*. Adaptive management is characterized by: (a) experimentalism, (b) multi-scalar modeling, and (c) place-orientation. In turn, this adaptive management is supported by a commitment to a unified method: naturalism, an empirical hypothesis, and a new approach to scaling and environmental problems. Through an example of Chesapeake Bay (on the east coast of the United States), Norton contrasts earlier environmental models (often based upon a version of pragmatism) to adaptive management. This connects (in a powerful way) to a new understanding of intergenerational duties and sustainability.

B. Sustainability and Development

Overview: Some of the issues of the practicality of sustainability as a policy strategy are set in relief when we consider development. As we have seen in the previous section, there are emerging ideas about just how sustainability should fit into a public policy role. In a general way, sustainability seeks not to make things *worse*. It has a "do no harm" aspect to its sensibility. In practice, this often means that some proposed construction project that will disturb the environment by *eliminating a wetland* (for example) must be evaluated on some scale that says: (a) this is fine, people are the most important element on Earth; (b) this is fine, but you have to re-create a wetland somewhere nearby; or (c) this is not fine—the permit for the project is rejected. How do we think about various practical options as we consider sustainability and development? Two responses are: (1) weak sustainable development that seeks to maintain things as they are for a short time horizon; and (b) strong sustainable development that seeks to maintain the integrity of the ecosystem indefinitely.

In the first essay Wilfred Beckerman argues against both strong and weak sustainable development. He argues that a strong sense of sustainable development that tries to protect the environment indefinitely for future generations is impractical and morally repugnant, for such a policy would divert important resources from other more pressing environmental concerns, such as providing clean drinking water for less-developed countries.

Beckerman terms weak sustainable development in which compensation is made for resources consumed as being nothing more than human welfare maximization (in traditional economic models). If this is correct, then sustainable development, as such, is not a worthy goal. Rather we should turn to human welfare maximization as the model of choice.

Herman E. Daly takes exception with Beckerman. Daly defends a position of strong sustainable development. He agrees that weak sustainability ought not to be our goal, but argues that strong sustainable development is no sloppier than any other economic concept, such as the definition of money in the macroeconomic realm (viz., M-1, M-2, or M-1a). Thus, Daly engages Beckerman exactly on Beckerman's own terms (i.e., an economic analysis).

A. Sustainability: What It Is and How It Works

Defining Sustainability Ethics

RANDALL CURREN

Sustainability ethics is not yet a field of study, but it may be in the process of becoming one. Across many fields of endeavor and inquiry, people are grappling with the ethical import of a trajectory of human existence that is trending ever more certainly toward catastrophe—catastrophe for humanity, catastrophe for millions of other species, catastrophe for the ecosystems on which we all depend.[1] Works exploring aspects of sustainability ethics and domains of ethics closely related to sustainability have begun to appear.[2] There are explorations in the ethics of sustainability, but these explorations have not yet coalesced into a well-defined domain of inquiry guided by a clear conception of what the domain is. The aim of this essay is to frame a conception of the domain—to offer a starting point for the focused inquiry and body of practical guidance that would constitute sustainability ethics. We must first understand what sustainability is and why it is a matter of present and far-reaching concern. On the basis of that understanding, we may then address such matters as the scope, distinctiveness, basic principles, and virtues of sustainability ethics.

What Sustainability Is and Why It Matters

Talk of sustainability has become so fashionable and freewheeling that a casual observer might mistake it for a fad or effervescence of linguistic excess that will soon subside. A well-informed observer might reasonably criticize it as ill-defined or worse. At its core, however, the language of sustainability is a way of referring to the long-term dependence of human and non-human well-being on the natural world, in the face of evidence that human activities are altering, damaging, and disrupting the natural systems on which we and other species fundamentally rely. What unsustainability implies is that humanity is collectively living in such a way as to diminish opportunities to live well in the future. Indeed, *the preservation of opportunities to live well is the normative focus of concern for sustainability*. The opportunities for members of non-human species to live well are no less eligible for consideration than those of human beings under this broad conception of sustainability. I will, however, focus on human well-being in what follows; to the extent that the well-being of other species introduces distinct questions, those questions will require separate treatment.

The language of sustainability has largely displaced the language of *environmental conservation*, though without committing itself to some of the defining aspects of the logic of conservation.[3] "Environmental conservation" has signified a responsible and efficient *use of natural resources* for human benefit, subject to public regulatory oversight and guided by a scientific understanding of resource development and environmental protection. It has long been contrasted with *environmental preservation*, or the designation of wilderness areas, habitats, or species as *protected from* human exploitation. Sustainability is concerned with human well-being much as conservation is, but the conceptualization of sustainability has recognized that the dependence of human well-being on the natural environment is richer and more complex than dependence on "natural resources," and the pathways to sustainability under discussion have not been limited to conservation strategies. Natural processes of climate and flood regulation are not "natural resources," for instance, but human well-being depends on them. We now know that these processes are being disrupted by human activities, especially the burning of fossil fuels, so a more encompassing concept than "natural resource" is needed. We also know that the impact of human activities is global in reach, cumulative in effect, and remarkably persistent. The impact of our present activities on global climate and ocean chemistry will persist over the order of 10 000 years, and the persistence of impact on biodiversity will be a couple orders of magnitude beyond that. Thinking about sustainability has thus developed in connection with new ways of conceptualizing human dependence on nature. Notable among these innovations, though undoubtedly imperfect, are ecological footprint analysis and the concept of *natural capital*, or natural assets that generate streams of *ecosystem services*.

Ecological footprint analysis "accounts for the flows of energy and matter to and from any defined economy [economic *throughput* from the environment as resources and back to the environment as wastes] and converts these into the corresponding land/water area required from nature to support these flows [i.e., to produce that flow of resources and absorb those wastes]."[4] Working from an estimate of the Earth's *biocapacity*, or capacity to generate useful materials and clear wastes, the ecological footprint (EF) of an economy can be specified as a percentage of the Earth's biocapacity, with an aggregate human footprint above 100% representing *unsustainability* or expending more than the *natural income* generated by the world's existing *natural capital*. This is analogous to outspending current income by drawing down savings. Employing an analysis of this kind, the World Wildlife Fund's *Living Planet Report 2010* placed human demands on living systems in 2008 at about 150% of what is sustainable and projected that those demands would reach 200% of what is sustainable by 2030.[5] These estimates can be understood as measures of risk—systemic risk to human well-being and, by implication, the well-being of other species—manifested in the depletion of accumulated products of ecosystem activity (such as soil, groundwater aquifers, and fossil fuels) and impairment of the natural systems that provide ecosystem services. These *supporting*, *provisioning*, and *regulating* "services" include nutrient cycling and clearing of wastes; soil formation; production of food, fuels, and freshwater; climate and flood regulation. Consistent with World Wildlife Fund projections, the 2005 Millennium Ecosystem Assessment found that 60% of the world's ecosystems and the services they provide are in decline as a result of overuse.[6]

By contrast with the conservationist idea that natural "resources" should be efficiently managed, the concept and discourse of sustainability is open to strategies of not only wise stewardship of what we use, but also preservation. An accurate accounting of the value of natural capital may often justify environmental preservation strategies that shield species, habitats, and regions from direct human use. Preservation may also be defended in connection with sustainability on the grounds that experience of the natural world is a vital aspect of human well-being. Whether this is understood in terms of contributions to physical and psychological wellness, aesthetically, spiritually, or in some other way, the value of nature from the point of view of sustainability is not limited to its value as a form of "capital."[7]

Environmental sustainability

This brief history of usage suggests that the word "sustainable" refers to living in a way that preserves natural capital, or does not reduce the capacity or accumulated products of the natural systems on which one relies. I will take this to be its *primary* meaning, understanding sustainability or *environmental sustainability* as fundamentally a quality of human *practices*, the *totality of practices* of some *human collectivity* being sustainable if, and only if, it does not diminish the natural capital on which the practices *fundamentally* depend. Long-term preservation of biocapacity is compatible with natural variations, but a failure to preserve it would imply deviation from the norms of such variation—deviation of a kind that would in time make the totality of practices (the scale and character of the practices) no longer possible. This is what is meant by the practices *fundamentally* depending on the natural capital in question: that the character and scale of the dependence leaves the human collectivity in question with no feasible substitute for the natural systems and products of those systems. The idea of a *human collectivity* enables us to speak of the sustainability of human civilization in the aggregate, and also—more easily in a world less interdependent and technologically advanced than our own—the sustainability of a specific civilization, society, or group of societies that makes exclusive use of an identifiable assemblage of ecosystems. The indeterminacy of what qualifies as "long-term" stability might need to be resolved for some purposes, but defined in this way sustainability is a coherent and important object of concern. Hence:

Primary meaning of "sustainable": the totality of practices of some human collectivity is *sustainable* if, and only if, it is compatible with the preservation of the natural capital on which the practices fundamentally depend.

Primary meaning of "unsustainable": the totality of practices of some human collectivity is *unsustainable* if, and only if, it is *not* compatible with the preservation of the natural capital on which the practices fundamentally depend.

The reference in these definitions to a *totality of practices* requires some explanation. By a *practice*, I mean a structured, norm-governed form of activity making up part of a *culture*. Practices shape *activities*. They vary widely in their complexity and the learned dispositions, abilities, and understanding they involve, but their structures and norms give current activities a kind of *momentum* or forward *trajectory*. By a *totality of practices* and its *compatibility* with the long-term stability of natural systems, I mean all the *activities* of a human collectivity during some time period, considered both with respect to their dependence and impact on natural systems *and* with respect to the *momentum* or *trajectory* of the activities entailed by their structure and norms *as practices*.

This formulation allows the definitions above to capture two senses in which the way of life of a human collectivity would qualify as unsustainable. On the one hand, a collectivity's total *current activities* might already be *environmentally overextended* by using resources faster than they can be replaced, dangerously altering or impairing the natural systems on which the activities fundamentally depend, or both. This would correspond to an ecological footprint that already exceeds 100% of what is sustainable. On the other hand, a collectivity might have a culture whose practices have a momentum or trajectory that puts its activities on an *unsustainable path* or a *path toward being environmentally overextended*. In either case, we could reasonably describe the collectivity's way of life as unsustainable and conclude that a change of practices is needed to avert calamity, notwithstanding the fact that having an environmental footprint already in excess of 100% represents greater present risk. As formulated above, then, the definition of the primary meaning of "sustainable" classifies a human collectivity as sustainable just in case it is *neither* currently environmentally overextended (in excess of 100% of a sustainable footprint) nor on a path toward being environmentally overextended, given the structure and norms of its own practices. The definition of environmental unsustainability classifies a human collectivity as unsustainable if it is *either* currently environmentally overextended or on a path toward being environmentally overextended.

Some explanation of the notion of a *path* toward being environmentally overextended may be helpful. I have said that the structure and norms of practices give current activities a kind of momentum or forward trajectory. Consider the complex constellation of practices related to preparation for an adult role in society, courtship, procreation, and retirement, and ask whether the structure and norms of these practices stimulate rising levels of material consumption. Do the competitive dynamics of struggle for social and economic advantage play themselves out through rising expenditures and consumption? Are there sociopolitical dynamics of reliance on population growth and rising future consumption? How do these manifest themselves in real estate values, investment income, debt management, and the possibility of retirement?[8] In a simple agrarian society, security in old age may be predicated on each individual having a large number of children, while a wealthy society may be capable of an adequate rate of savings for everyone's retirement, but choose to rely on a growing economy to fill a savings gap. Both approaches exhibit the structure and trajectory of an unsustainable pyramid scheme. Schemes of this kind rely on flows of resources from a continually expanding base, and they collapse when the expansion stumbles. If they are systemic in a sociopolitical system, as they are in the increasingly integrated global civilization built on capitalist markets, then the recruitment of an expanding human base may continue apace so that the limitations of the planet's natural systems become the limiting factor—the base of the pyramid that *cannot* expand. It should be noted in this connection that although economic expansion may contribute to environmental protection in some limited respects, the overall environmental impact of human activity is closely linked to the growth of the world economy.[9] The dynamics of economic growth have largely determined the path we are on:

> The human presence is now so large that all we have to do to destroy the planet's climate and ecosystems and leave a ruined planet to our children and grandchildren is to keep doing exactly what we are doing today, with no growth in the human population or the world economy. Just continue to release greenhouse gasses at current rates, just continue to impoverish ecosystems and release toxic chemicals at current rates, and the world in the latter part of this century won't be fit to live in. But … human activities are not holding at current levels—they are accelerating, dramatically. It took all of history to build the $7 trillion world economy of 1950; today economic activity grows by that amount every decade. At current rates of growth, the world economy will double in size in less than two decades.[10]

Derivatives of environmental sustainability

References to sustainability seem more problematic when what is said to be sustainable without qualification is a business, technology, mode of farming, or something of the sort. Many such things could be sustainable only on a limited scale and could have the form that they do only within a larger human context, so some caution is in order. A particular practice, technology, system, or institution may exist in a form and on a scale that is *compatible with the sustainability of a human collectivity*, and to that extent may be said to be sustainable in a *derivative* and *qualified* sense. Within the context of a particular civilization, some practices may be compatible with sustainability in the primary sense however widely and frequently they are practiced (perhaps thinking of walking to work), while the sustainability of others (such as eating meat or driving a motorized vehicle to work) may be subject to limitations of scale, frequency, or both. Only the former could be said to be sustainable without qualification, even in the derivative sense of being *compatible* with sustainability in the primary sense. Systems may be environmentally *unsustainable* in a related derivative sense if the activities they involve cannot occur on the scale and at the frequency required by the system without causing the society as a whole to be unsustainable in the primary sense. The present US transportation system is unsustainable in this sense for two reasons: the pace of fuel consumption it entails far exceeds the rate at which petroleum is being generated by the Earth; and the pace of resulting greenhouse gas emissions is incompatible with climate stability and favorable ocean chemistry. Subject to the qualifications thus noted, a venture's compatibility with sustainability is undeniably important in deciding what to do.

Similarly, it may often be normatively salient to consider what is *conducive to sustainability*, and this can be defined as another derivative of the primary concept of sustainability:

Definition of "sustainability conducive": a human trait, practice, occupation, culture, institution, system, structure, or policy is *conducive to sustainability* if, and only if, it functions, within its sphere of operation in the existing state of the world, to preserve or promote sustainability in the primary sense.[11]

What distinguishes *conduciveness* to sustainability from *compatibility* with sustainability, is that the latter pertains to activities, or what we might think of as first-order activities, while the former pertains to what shapes and regulates those activities: the structures and norms of practices; social systems and settings; and associated forms of regulatory or second-order activity, from informal modes of interpersonal instruction and guidance to institutionalized reward structures, government regulatory efforts, and the offices and occupations they entail. Virtues of character and norms of professional integrity are among the human traits and norms of practice that may qualify as conducive to sustainability.

Often what we may, with some effort, have the information to judge is that one course of action is *more compatible* with sustainability or one regulatory structure or setting is *more conducive* to sustainability than another. We may not be able to quantify all of the value of ecosystem services at stake in a decision, or project the full systemic effects (both natural and social) of a decision, but we may nevertheless be in a position to make useful comparative judgments of alternative courses of action or alternative regulatory structures.[12] There may be good reason to say that preserving a wetland is more compatible with sustainability than developing it, or good reason to say that urban settings favorable to low storm water runoff and living near work are more conducive to sustainability than ones that are not.

Sociopolitical sustainability

A fact glossed over by much of the recent discourse on sustainability is that institutions, social systems, and sociopolitical regimes may be unsustainable and subject to collapse owing to factors unrelated, or only weakly related, to any tendency to undermine the natural systems on which they rely. An institution may be compatible with sustainability in the primary environmental sense, yet be *socially* unsustainable, or it might be unsustainable in both of these respects. Unregulated free markets may belong in the category of doubly unsustainable systems. They may be unsustainable not only in the derivative environmental sense that they are not, without suitable regulation, compatible with the sustainability of any human collectivity; they may also be unsustainable in the sense that, quite apart from any environmental limitations, they exhibit a tendency to destroy themselves through acquisitions that ultimately yield oligopolistic markets.[13]

The environmental sustainability of a civilization has profound ethical importance, but matters are less clear regarding the social sustainability of particular practices, institutions, and systems. The importance of environmental sustainability gives us reason to prefer practices, institutions, and systems that are conducive to sustainability, and thus reason to prefer that ones not conducive to environmental sustainability fade away or are reformed. Moreover, the *pursuit* of environmental sustainability should be predicated on institutions and systems that are not only *conducive to* environmental sustainability and human well-being, but also *durable*. We will need them to work for a long time without placing ever larger demands on the natural systems that make life on our planet possible.

Beyond this, there is no denying that we depend on the cultures and institutions we have and that their decline and collapse often entail a world of loss and suffering. If it is not addressed, environmental unsustainability will almost certainly lead to both *ecological collapse* and *sociopolitical collapse*. *Ecological collapse* denotes a rapid decline of ecosystem capacity (such as the 90% decline in ocean fish populations since the advent of deep-sea fishing in the 1950s) or disintegration of an ecosystem. *Sociopolitical collapse* may be defined as a "rapid, significant loss of an established level of socio-complexity," manifested in rapid loss of socioeconomic stratification, occupational specialization, social order and coordination, economic activity, investment in the cultural achievements of a civilization, circulation of information, and the territorial extent of sociopolitical integration.[14] Sociopolitical collapse entails grave risk to most of what people value. When sociopolitical collapse is triggered by problems of environmental unsustainability, rapid population loss and displacement are also predictable.[15] From an ecological point of view, a growing human population may be regarded as a driver of unsustainability,[16] but from an ethical point of view, a growing human population is, among other things, a growing number of people at ever increasing risk of suffering grave harm. Stabilizing population, investing as much as possible in developing and scaling up carbon-neutral energy sources, and simplifying our way of life would reduce the risks associated with ecological and sociopolitical collapse. Simplification does not simply mean making do with less opulence. It means reversing the trend toward ever more specialized and stratified occupational roles and reversing the declining marginal return and rising costs—energy, information, compensation, and regulatory costs—associated with that trend.[17]

The Focus, Scope, and Major Divisions of Sustainability Ethics

The distinctive central concern of sustainability ethics is living in a way consistent with an acceptable future, a future in which the natural world is not altered in any way that would cause the opportunities to live well to be worse than they are today. The *preservation of opportunities to live well* is the normative focus of concern for sustainability. *Sustainability ethics* may consequently be defined as the domain of ethics and ethical inquiry pertaining to every sphere and aspect of human activity as they bear on the capacity of natural systems to provide opportunities as good as the those available now, indefinitely into the future.

Preservation of opportunity

A basic question for sustainability ethics is how we shall judge whether one set of opportunities is as good as another. Intergenerational justice requires that each generation act so as to preserve equal opportunity across generations; but we do not yet have a workable conception or measure of the quality of opportunities across geographically or culturally distant contexts, let alone over extended periods of time. Synchronic equality of opportunity within a single jurisdiction may be defined in terms of the probability of members of different social classes obtaining desired occupations or positions in society; if success in obtaining the positions that are available does not vary as a function of social class membership, then opportunity is equal across social classes.[18] Geographic and cultural distances make this understanding of equal opportunity inapplicable. Global equality of opportunity could not be meaningfully construed as, for instance, a middle-class Swiss child and a Zanzibar fisherman's child having equal chances of becoming a banker, dealer in rare books, valued member of a traditional fishing community, etc. Geography and culture make a difference not only to what is feasible, but also to what kind of occupations and positions are attractive. Similar points apply to comparisons across expanses of time, as cultures and social systems evolve and the kind of occupations and associated rewards change. What is needed is a conception of equality of opportunity over time predicated on an objective account of human well-being or what people need in order to live well. We need an account based on universals of human well-being, rather than what is considered at one time or place to be a good position through which to obtain the essentials of a good life. My own inclination is to think that human well-being has both objective and subjective aspects, and that the inquiry we require will bring moral theory into conversation with the psychology of happiness. Psychological work on what does and does not contribute to happiness—most notably the evidence that materialism is damaging to happiness—is already prominent in the literature of sustainability.[19] The moral theoretic issues at stake are foundational for sustainability ethics. This having been said, it is not so difficult to identify universal human needs and potentialities that can be satisfied only by preserving natural ecosystems. The conceptualization of equality of opportunity across generations may be challenging, but a comprehensive measure of natural capital will serve as a reasonable proxy for whether one generation is living sustainably or in a manner consistent with the preservation of opportunities to live well.

Another important preliminary regarding opportunity is that neither environmental nor sociopolitical sustainability requires synchronic domestic or global equality of opportunity as a matter of principle. This is at odds with a widespread tendency to treat sustainability as a comprehensive ideal of social justice, and to treat a well-known definition of *sustainable development* as a definition of sustainability: "development that meets the needs of the present without compromising the ability of future generations to meet their own needs."[20] Defined in this way, the concept of sustainable development entails a standard of global justice, according to which the needs of everyone in the world must be met through economic development. Yet sustainability (a quality) and sustainable development (development that has certain qualities) are not the same thing. The origins of the latter can be traced to the 1972 UN Conference on the Human Environment, where developing countries took the position that economic development to alleviate poverty should not be subordinated to environmental concerns.[21] The outcome was a doctrine of environment and development, now known as sustainable development, whereby governments agreed that development and environmental protection are mutually reinforcing. This is a problematic doctrine, inasmuch as environmental damage generally increases as economic activity increases, but it expresses the political reality that global environmental problems can only be fully solved through global treaties predicated on fair terms of cooperation. In the case of climate disruption caused overwhelmingly by the North's huge head start in economic development based on fossil fuels, it is hard to imagine any basis of cooperation that would not involve major concessions to the vulnerability and needs of the global poor. The most reasonable view of the matter is that global justice has moral importance, quite apart from sustainability, and also strategic importance in the global *pursuit* of sustainability.[22] Acknowledging this makes more sense than importing extraneous ideals of justice into the very idea of sustainability.

Scope and divisions

To say that sustainability ethics pertains to every *sphere* of human activity is to identify it as an aspect of universal *personal ethics* or common morality; an aspect of *social ethics* or the ethics of diverse practices, institutions, and the special roles associated with them, including *professional* roles; and an aspect of *political justice* or the responsibilities of citizens and governments. Treating *professional ethics* as a major subdivision of social ethics, sustainability ethics may be seen as having three major divisions: personal ethics, social ethics, and political justice. To say that sustainability ethics pertains to every *aspect* of human activity as it bears on the preservation of opportunity to live well, is to imply that many aspects of what we do make a difference to sustainability, and factors as diverse as personal character, occupational role, institutional culture, and policy context shape what we do. Personal virtues, principles of common morality, derived principles, codes of professional ethics, and ethical criticism of practices, institutions, and acts of government may all come into play.

Sustainability ethics is not, like business ethics, confined to one sphere of activity, nor centered on concern with the value of the non-human natural world, as environmental ethics is. Sustainability ethics overlaps environmental ethics to the extent that the former concerns the well-being of both humans and non-humans, and it may identify principles or responsibilities that should supplement those presently acknowledged in business ethics or other domains of professional ethics. Sustainability ethics overlaps the domain of *environmental justice,* inasmuch as sustainability *is* an issue of environmental justice, but not all issues of environmental justice are issues of sustainability. Environmental justice is concerned with fairness in the distribution of environmental burdens and benefits, but a great deal of unfairness in the distribution of environmental burdens and benefits may be consistent with sustainability. Toxic hot spots that cause illness in poor communities are reprehensible and unjust, but they may exist in locations compatible with the preservation of natural capital and prospects for living well.

Principles and Virtues of Sustainability Ethics

Principles

The extent and quality of opportunities rest on the abundance of natural capital, so actions, practices, policies, and systems that diminish the abundance of natural capital are a primary concern of sustainability ethics. The *first principle* of sustainability ethics is: *do not diminish natural capital.* Having acknowledged that opportunities to experience the natural world are important to human well-being, but not captured by the idea of natural capital, a *second principle* is required: *do not diminish satisfying opportunities to experience nature.* Sustainability pertains primarily to the *totality* of practices of human collectivities, so it is these collectivities that are most obviously answerable to these principles.

As individuals, our actions diminish natural capital and opportunities to experience nature incrementally, globally, and often without any identifiable victim, making it hard to know what would count as full compliance with these principles. It feels better to do what one can to reduce consumption and waste, but how much is enough? How much difference will the voluntary actions of individuals even make? The best answer to such questions is that changing the way we live individually, and doing so voluntarily before needed policy reforms are in place, is essential.[23] It is very unlikely that political leaders will perceive a window of political opportunity to negotiate the needed treaties and enact the needed laws without a strong show of popular support for stronger environmental protection. We need such treaties and laws because the actions of individuals and voluntary associations will not suffice without global coordination and regulatory mechanisms to set safe aggregate limits for greenhouse gasses and other burdens on the Earth's natural systems. The translation of environmentally safe overall limits into enforceable limits on what individuals and corporate entities may do is the only efficacious means by which we can collectively determine what is and what is not sufficient personal and corporate restraint. Our position now is analogous to the early age of automobiles before there were speed limits and other traffic laws. A driver could slow down to reduce the risk of a collision, but how slow is safe enough? Democratically enacted speed limits and other traffic laws are the means by which we have collectively defined acceptable risk associated with automobile accidents. A carbon tax or carbon cap and trade system is one piece of what we need now to define the limits of acceptable environmental risk.

To say this is to affirm that even as environmentally conscientious individuals seek to live in ways that are compatible with sustainability, a fundamental burden we all bear—individual, institutional, and government actors alike—is to *seek fair terms of cooperation* in living sustainably. Our unsustainable energy and transportation systems already have damaging global reach, including an estimated 150 000 deaths each year that are attributable to climate disruption,[24] so it is undeniable that we are already interacting with others around the globe in ways that damage their interests. We are doing this while hesitating to negotiate a mutually agreeable climate treaty and other environmental protection treaties, and this hesitation is itself morally objectionable. It is wrong to act in ways that impose risk and harm on others, and to refuse to face them and negotiate reasonable limits on those impositions. Facing them as equals and specifying the details of our moral relations with each other in a body of common law is a requirement of basic moral respect.[25] A *third principle* of sustainability ethics is thus: *seek fair terms of cooperation conducive to sustainability. Actors whose actions affect each other are obligated to cooperate in negotiating fair terms of cooperation in living in a manner that is collectively sustainable.* Fair terms of cooperation would undoubtedly define not only the terms of participation in achieving a sustainable human footprint, but also what will constitute *wrongful* impositions of environmental risk on identifiable populations and jurisdictions. To that extent, the terms of cooperation in achieving sustainability would also address present matters of environmental justice, such as cross-border acid rain pollution that causes damage to forests in another country.

Transparency is a condition of good-faith negotiations and an ideal foundational to democracy. The less we know about what is at stake in the choices we make, the more certain it is that, as individuals and as citizens of democracies, we will fail to succeed in our goals and in protecting what we care about. Especially when the stakes are high—as they are with respect to sustainability—we should acknowledge that it is a simple matter of prudence to ensure that our institutions promote transparency, or the efficient discovery and dissemination of truths important to our interests. The institutions in question are not limited to schools, the media, and government agencies charged with protecting the public interest. In creating private corporations, modern societies have conjured inventions of law that have no obligation to serve any public purpose, and they have wagered with being able to command machinery of oversight and regulation sufficient to ensure that the activities of corporations are consistent with the public interest. In essence, the fate of modern societies is predicated on maintaining the upper hand in an informational arms race, even as the pace of technological innovation quickens and corporate resources dedicated to private interest science, public relations, advertising, litigation, and lobbying are allowed to grow without limit. A government doing its job to protect the public interest would reassess the wisdom of this wager and consider whether modifications to corporate law are in order. Is this an institutional structure that is conducive to sustainability? The evidence of massive *obstruction of transparency* with respect to sustainability and environmental risk is one reason to think that it is not.[26] Obstruction of transparency is apparent in the success of industry front groups in misleading the public about the strength of scientific consensus regarding anthropogenic climate change. It displays profound disrespect for individual self-determination and the collective self-determination of societies, so a *fourth principle* of sustainability ethics is: *do not obstruct transparency with regard to sustainability*. The foregoing also suggests a *fifth principle*: *societies and their governments should create and sustain institutions and systems that are conducive to sustainability and transparency with respect to sustainability*.

Misleading the public about the environmental impact of products and business practices may enhance profitability, and it may also serve to induce risky reliance on vulnerable systems. Inducing such reliance subjects people to risk that they would not otherwise face. Engaging in a systematic public relations campaign to create doubt about the reality of climate change and its relationship to petroleum does this by encouraging conduct that contributes to greater environmental risk in the form of drought, floods, increasingly violent storms, ocean acidification, and broad disruption of ecosystems. Together with other public relations campaigns and advertising, it also encourages conduct that contributes to greater societal risk in the form of continued investment in a transportation system that is not only incompatible with environmental sustainability, but also vulnerable to collapse as oil reserves begin their inevitable decline.

The wrongness of inducing risky reliance on vulnerable systems may be captured in a *sixth principle*: *do not subject individuals or collectivities to detrimental reliance. Do not induce or cause anyone to be in a position of fundamental reliance on vulnerable systems or resources—systems or resources that cannot be relied on without exposure to systemic risk to their fundamental interests*. This principle identifies imposition of risk per se as a form of wrong, and it focuses on the kinds of *systemic* risk that are at stake in discussions of sustainability: risks that ecosystems will collapse or that basic societal systems will suffer sharply declining capacity before sustainable alternatives can be developed and scaled up to replace them. It addresses acts of inducement, in which people are induced to rely on something that is already unreliable or will become so as a consequence of the induced reliance, and it addresses acts that cause something that is already fundamentally relied upon to become less reliable or adequate. An example of the latter sort would be the poaching of fish in Zanzibar's territorial waters, where a quarter of the islanders survive on fish caught by traditional methods within a few meters of shore.[27] The principle may apply to the actions of specific individuals and collectively to the whole of a society or civilization. Regarding the latter, it says, in essence, that it is wrong to cause future generations to be in a position of being essentially dependent on a world that cannot be dependably relied on to provide them with an acceptable quality of life.

This *principle of detrimental reliance* captures what is most ethically troubling about the human context of the Dust Bowl in the United States of the 1930s, an environmental disaster in which homesteaders were induced to farm a region unsuitable for farming, which largely destroy the grasslands constituting North America's second largest ecosystem.[28] Named the "Great American Desert" in 1820, the high plains grasslands, later rebranded the "Great Plains," were designated by surveyors as being too dry for farming. Nevertheless, with encouragement from the railroads and prairie state senators, the Enlarged Homestead Act of 1909 promoted dry-land farming by distributing parcels of undeveloped federal lands. Then, as homesteading peaked in 1914 and the First World War began, the US government encouraged planting of more wheat in response to the exclusion of Russian wheat from global markets. For a few unusually moist years high plains wheat was profitable. Farmers expanded, taking on debt justified by a high price for wheat, and with the end of the war and falling wheat prices they expanded again to cover their debt. At each step of the way, they ploughed up the native grasses that anchored the soil and an ecosystem sustaining hundreds of species. In the drought of the 1930s that followed, the unanchored soil was gathered by winds into rolling mountains, 10 000 ft high or more, blinding and suffocating cattle, obliterating roads, and dropping thousands of tons of dust on cities hundreds of miles away. A quarter of a million people, who had been *induced* to settle and farm a region that had previously supported only a few hunting camps and thirteenth-century villages, fled, leaving behind 100 million acres in ruin.

Virtues

It is fitting to close by acknowledging that I have counted virtues of character among the traits and norms of practice that may qualify as conducive to sustainability. I have made a start toward identifying basic principles of sustainability ethics, one of which calls for cooperation in formulating a body of global sustainability-conducive laws giving specificity to our sustainability-related obligations. Having done that, I would argue—without pretending to do justice to the matter—that a serviceable way to continue would be to treat such principles and laws as provisional expressions of what is reasonable or commended by reason, and work within an Aristotelian understanding of moral virtues as preserving and giving perceptual and motivational effect to good judgment.[29] The virtues of sustainability could then be spelled out and provisionally organized under the Platonic virtues of wisdom, justice, moderation, and courage—wisdom being an intellectual virtue and the remaining three being moral virtues.

Under the heading of wisdom, we would rightly seek to enable everyone to understand matters of sustainability and human well-being, distinguish important truths from propaganda, assess risk accurately, and think creatively about how to flourish in ways consistent with sustainability. Under the heading of justice, we would be justified in nurturing the virtues of cooperative global citizenship, goodwill, and consideration associated with ideals of public reason and democracy. Under the heading of moderation, we should encourage endurance in resisting needless luxuries and inducements to measure success by conspicuous consumption, together with a steady regard for the true value of things. Finally, we must hope we all find the courage to own up to the challenges at hand and do what is right and best in the face of hazards we have only begun to contemplate.

Notes

1 See Kathleen Dean Moore and Michael P. Nelson (eds) (2010) *Moral Ground: Ethical Action for a Planet in Peril*, San Antonio: Trinity University Press; Ryne Raffaelle, Wade Robison, and Evan Selinger (eds) (2010) *Sustainability Ethics: 5 Questions*, Copenhagen: Automatic Press. Both of these volumes consist of many short essays by diverse writers, including such well-known figures as the Dalai Lama, Desmond Tutu, E.O. Wilson, and Ursula K. le Guin.

2 See, e.g., David Crocker and Toby Linden (eds) (1998) *Ethics of Consumption: The Good Life, Justice, and Global Stewardship*, Lanham, MD: Rowman & Littlefield;

Brian Barry (2003) "Sustainability and Intergenerational Justice," in *Environmental Ethics* (eds A. Light and H. Rolston III), Malden, MA: Blackwell; pp. 487–499; Lisa Newton (2003) *Ethics and Sustainability*, Upper Saddle River, NJ: Prentice-Hall; Bryan Norton (2005) *Sustainability: A Philosophy of Adaptive Ecosystem Management*, Chicago, IL: University of Chicago Press; Cass Sunstein (2007) *Worst-case Scenarios*, Cambridge, MA: Harvard University Press; Randall Curren (2009) *Education for Sustainable Development: A Philosophical Assessment*, London: PESGB; Naomi Zack (2009) *Ethics for Disaster*, Lanham, MD: Rowman & Littlefield; Peter Brown and Jeremy Schmidt (eds) (2010) *Water Ethics*, Washington, DC: Island Press; Stephen Gardner *et al.* (eds) (2010) *Climate Ethics: Essential Readings*, Oxford: Oxford University Press; Laurie Ann Mazur *et al.* (eds) (2010) *A Pivotal Moment: Population, Justice, and the Environmental Challenge*, Washington, DC: Island Press.

3 A notable manifestation of this shift was the adoption of the language of sustainability by the World Conservation Union between 1980 and 1991.

4 Mathis Wackernagel and William Rees (1996) *Our Ecological Footprint*, Gabriola Island, British Columbia: New Society; p. 3.

5 World Wildlife Fund (2010) *Living Planet Report 2010*, Gland: WWF International, available at: http://www.worldwildlife.org/sites/living-planet-report.

6 See UN Foundation (2005) *The Millennium Ecosystem Assessment (summary with links)*, Geneva: UN Foundation, available at: http://www.unfoundation.org/features/millenium_ecosystem_assessment.asp. This was a comprehensive assessment co-authored by 1350 scientists from ninety-five countries and twenty-two national academies of science.

7 See Moore and Nelson, *Moral Ground*.

8 The common wisdom regarding debt is a staple of financial news and analysis: "For the best way to reduce sovereign debt, everyone agrees, is through economic growth. With growth, there are more jobs and more tax receipts, adding to government revenues, while the debt shrinks as a percentage of a rising gross domestic product." Steven Erlanger (2011) "With Prospect of US Slowdown, Europe Fears a Worsening Debt Crisis," *The New York Times*, Monday, August 8, B3.

9 See James Speth (2008) *The Bridge at the Edge of the World*, New Haven, CT: Yale University Press; pp. 46, 55–57; J.R. McNeill (2000) *Something New Under the Sun*, New York: W.W. Norton.

10 James Speth (2010) "The Limits of Growth," in *Moral Ground: Ethical Action for a Planet in Peril* (eds K.D. Moore and M.P. Nelson), San Antonio: Trinity University Press; pp. 3–8, at pp. 3 and 6. Cf. Wackernagel and Rees, *Our Ecological Footprint*, p. 1.

11 This definition is compatible with the possibility of elements in a society qualifying as conducive to sustainability only with respect to the sustainability of a different society.

12 Such comparative judgments of the impact of decisions on ecosystem services are being made using tools for mapping and evaluating natural assets. See the Natural Capital Project homepage, at: http://www.naturalcapitalproject.org/home04.html. For comparative analyses of the sustainability–conduciveness of aspects of urban design, see Patrick Condon (2010) *Seven Rules for Sustainable Communities: Design Strategies for the Post-carbon World*, Washington, DC: Island Press.

13 The defining conditions for a free market require many independent suppliers and customers, whereas oligopolistic markets have only a few independent suppliers, like the markets in many kinds of products and services today.

14 Joseph Tainter (1988) *The Collapse of Complex Societies*, Cambridge: Cambridge University Press; p. 4.

15 See Tainter, *The Collapse of Complex Societies*; Charles Redman (1999) *Human Impact on Ancient Environments*, Tucson: University of Arizona Press; Jared Diamond (2005) *Collapse*, New York: Viking; Patricia McAnany and Norman Yoffee (eds) (2010) *Questioning Collapse: Human Resilience, Ecological Vulnerability, and the Aftermath of Empire*, Cambridge: Cambridge University Press.

16 See T. Dietz., E.A. Rosa, and R. York (2007) "Driving the Human Ecological Footprint," *Frontiers in Ecology and the Environment*, 5: 13–18; Walter Dodds (2008) *Humanity's Footprint: Momentum, Impact, and Our Global Environment*, New York: Columbia University Press.

17 On simplification and the centrality of energy, see Tainter, *The Collapse of Complex Societies*; pp. 193, 197–199, 209–216.

18 This is essentially how Rawls defines fair equality of opportunity. See John Rawls (2001) *Justice as Fairness: A Restatement*, Cambridge, MA: Harvard University Press; pp. 43–44.

19 See Tim Kasser (2002) *The High Price of Materialism*, Cambridge, MA: MIT Press; Speth, *The Bridge at the Edge of the World*.

20 World Commission on Environment and Development (1978) *Our Common Future*, Geneva: United Nations, p. 12, available at: http://www.un-documents.net/wced-ocf.htm.

21 See James Speth and Peter Haas (2006) *Global Environmental Governance*, Washington, DC: Island Press; pp. 56–61.

22 For a defense of global justice predicated on human rights and basic needs, see Gillian Brock (2009) *Global Justice: A Cosmopolitan Approach*, Oxford: Oxford University Press.

23 The argument for this that follows is presented in persuasive detail by Speth and Haas in *Global Environmental Governance*.

24 World Health Organization (2007) *Climate and Health*, Geneva: WHO Media Centre, available at: http://www.who.int/mediacentre/factsheets/fs266/en.

25 See Immanuel Kant (1991) *The Metaphysics of Morals*, trans. Mary Gregor, Cambridge: Cambridge University Press; s. 6.

26 For the evidence, see Naomi Oreskes and Erik M. Conway (2010) *Merchants of Doubt*, New York: Bloomsbury Press; Kristin Shrader-Frechette (2007) *Taking Action, Saving Lives*, New York: Oxford University Press.

27 In its application to such cases, the *principle of detrimental reliance* adds pointed specificity to the *first principle's* prohibition against diminishing natural capital, subject to qualifications associated with the *third principle* or requirement to seek fair term of cooperation. Those qualifications are met in the poaching case unless there is reason to think that the protection of territorial waters is so politically unjust as to have no moral significance.

28 The account that follows is drawn from Timothy Egan (2006) *The Worst Hard Time*, New York: Mariner Books.

29 I spell out this understanding of the virtues in Randall Curren (2000) *Aristotle on the Necessity of Public Education*, Lanham, MD: Rowman & Littlefield).

A Perfect Moral Storm

Climate Change, Intergenerational Ethics, and the Problem of Moral Corruption

STEPHEN M. GARDINER

> *'There's a quiet clamor for hypocrisy and deception; and pragmatic politicians respond with ... schemes that seem to promise something for nothing. Please, spare us the truth.'*[2]

The most authoritative scientific report on climate change begins by saying:

> 'Natural, technical, and social sciences can provide essential information and evidence needed for decisions on what constitutes 'dangerous anthropogenic interference with the climate system.' At the same time, *such decisions are value judgments* ...'[3]

Stephen Gardiner, "A Perfect Moral Storm: Climate Change, Intergenerational Ethics, and the Problem of Moral Corruption," *Environmental Values*, 15 (3) (August 2006): 397–413. Reprinted with permission.

There are good grounds for this statement. Climate change is a complex problem raising issues across and between a large number of disciplines, including the physical and life sciences, political science, economics and psychology, to name just a few. But without wishing for a moment to marginalise the contributions of these disciplines, ethics does seem to play a fundamental role.

Why so? At the most general level, the reason is that we cannot get very far in discussing why climate change is a problem without invoking ethical considerations. If we do not think that our own actions are open to moral assessment, or that various interests (our own, those of our kin and country, those of distant people, future people, animals and nature) matter, then it is hard to see why climate change (or much else) poses a problem. But once we see this, then we appear to need some account of moral responsibility, morally important interests and what to do about both. And this puts us squarely in the domain of ethics.

At a more practical level, ethical questions are fundamental to the main policy decisions that must be made, such as where to set a global ceiling for greenhouse gas emissions, and how to distribute the emissions allowed by such a ceiling. For example, where the global ceiling is set depends on how the interests of the current generation are weighed against those of future generations; and how emissions are distributed under the global gap depends in part on various beliefs about the appropriate role of energy consumption in people's lives, the importance of historical responsibility for the problem, and the current needs and future aspirations of particular societies.

The relevance of ethics to substantive climate policy thus seems clear. But this is not the topic that I wish to take up here.[4] Instead, I want to discuss a further, and to some extent more basic, way in which ethical reflection sheds light on our present predicament. This has nothing much to do with the substance of a defensible climate regime; instead, it concerns the process of making climate policy.

My thesis is this. The peculiar features of the climate change problem pose substantial obstacles to our ability to make the hard choices necessary to address it. Climate change is a perfect moral storm. One consequence of this is that, even if the difficult ethical questions could be answered, we might still find it difficult to act. For the storm makes us extremely vulnerable to moral corruption.[5]

Let us say that a perfect storm is an event constituted by an unusual convergence of independently harmful factors where this convergence is likely to result in substantial, and possibly catastrophic, negative outcomes. The term 'the perfect storm' seems to have become prominent in popular culture through Sebastian Junger's book of that name and the associated Hollywood film.[6] Junger's tale is based on the true story of the *Andrea Gail*, a fishing vessel caught at sea during a convergence of three particularly bad storms.[7] The sense of the analogy is then that climate change appears to be a perfect moral storm because it involves the convergence of a number of factors that threaten our ability to behave ethically.

As climate change is a complex phenomenon, I cannot hope to identify all of the ways in which its features cause problems for ethical behaviour. Instead, I will identify three especially salient problems – analogous to the three storms that hit the *Andreas Gail* – that converge in the climate change case. These three 'storms' arise in the global, intergenerational and theoretical dimensions, and I will argue that their interaction helps to exacerbate and obscure a lurking problem of moral corruption that may be of greater practical importance than any of them.

I. The Global Storm

The first two storms arise out of three important characteristics of the climate change problem. I label these characteristics:

- Dispersion of Causes and Effects
- Fragmentation of Agency
- Institutional Inadequacy

Since these characteristics manifest themselves in two especially salient dimensions – the spatial and the temporal – it is useful to distinguish two distinct but mutually reinforcing components of the climate change problem. I shall call the first 'the Global Storm'. This corresponds to the dominant understanding of the climate change problem; and it emerges from a predominantly spatial interpretation of the three characteristics.

Let us begin with the Dispersion of Causes and Effects. Climate change is a truly global phenomenon. Emissions of greenhouse gases from any geographical location on the Earth's surface travel to the upper atmosphere and then play a role in affecting climate globally. Hence, the impact of any particular emission of greenhouse gases is not realised solely at its source, either individual or geographical; rather impacts are dispersed to other actors and regions of the Earth. Such spatial dispersion has been widely discussed.

The second characteristic is the Fragmentation of Agency. Climate change is not caused by a single agent, but by a vast number of individuals and institutions not unified by a comprehensive structure of agency. This is important because it poses a challenge to humanity's ability to respond.

In the spatial dimension, this feature is usually understood as arising out of the shape of the current international system, as constituted by states. Then the problem is that, given that there is not only no world government but also no less centralised system of global governance (or at least no effective one), it is very difficult to coordinate an effective response to global climate change.

This general argument is generally given more bite through the invocation of a certain familiar theoretical model.[8] For the international situation is usually understood in game theoretic terms as a Prisoner's Dilemma, or what Garrett Hardin calls a 'Tragedy of the Commons'.[9] For the sake of ease of exposition, let us describe the Prisoner's Dilemma scenario in terms of a paradigm case, that of over pollution.[10] Suppose that a number of distinct agents are trying to decide whether or not to engage in a polluting activity, and that their situation is characterised by the following two claims:

(PD1) It is *collectively rational* to cooperate and restrict overall pollution: each agent prefers the outcome produced by everyone restricting their individual pollution over the outcome produced by no one doing so.

(PD2) It is *individually rational* not to restrict one's own pollution: when each agent has the power to decide whether or not she will restrict her pollution, each (rationally) prefers not to do so, whatever the others do.

Agents in such a situation find themselves in a paradoxical position. On the one hand, given (PD1), they understand that it would be better for everyone if every agent cooperated; but, on the other hand, given (PD2), they also know that they should all choose to defect. This is paradoxical because it implies that if individual agents act rationally in terms of their own interests, then they collectively undermine those interests.

A Tragedy of the Commons is essentially a Prisoner's Dilemma involving a common resource. This has become the standard analytical model for understanding regional and global environmental problems in general, and climate change is no exception. Typically, the reasoning goes as follows. Imagine climate change as an international problem and conceive of the relevant parties as individual countries, who represent the interests of their citizens in perpetuity. Then, (PD1) and (PD2) appear to hold. On the one hand, no one wants serious climate change. Hence, each country prefers the outcome produced by everyone restricting their individual emissions over the outcome produced by no one doing so, and so it is collectively rational to cooperate and restrict global emissions. But, on the other hand, each country prefers to free ride on the actions of others. Hence, when each country has the power to decide whether or not she will restrict her emissions, each prefers not to do so, whatever the others do.

From this perspective, it appears that climate change is a normal tragedy of the commons. Still, there is a sense in which this turns out to be encouraging news; for, in the real world, commons problems are often resolvable under certain circumstances, and climate change seems to fill these desiderata.[11] In particular, it is widely said that parties facing a commons problem can resolve it if they benefit from a wider context of interaction; and this appears to be the case with climate change, since countries interact with each other on a number of broader issues, such as trade and security.

This brings us to the third characteristic of the climate change problem, institutional inadequacy. There is wide agreement that the appropriate means for resolving commons problems under the favourable conditions just mentioned is for the parties to agree to change the existing incentive structure through the introduction of a system of enforceable sanctions. (Hardin calls this 'mutual coercion, mutually agreed upon'.) This transforms the decision situation by foreclosing the option of free riding, so that the collectively rational action also becomes individually rational. Theoretically, then, matters seem simple; but in practice things are different. For the need for enforceable sanctions poses a challenge at the global level because of the limits of our current, largely national, institutions and the lack of an effective system of global governance. In essence, addressing climate change appears to require global regulation of greenhouse gas emissions, where this includes establishing a reliable enforcement mechanism; but the current global system – or lack of it – makes this difficult, if not impossible.

The implication of this familiar analysis, then, is that the main thing that is needed to solve the global warming problem is an effective system of global governance (at least for this issue). And there is a sense in which this is still good news. For, in principle at least, it should be possible to motivate countries to establish such a regime, since they ought to recognise that it is in their best interests to eliminate the possibility of free riding and so make genuine cooperation the rational strategy at the individual as well as collective level.

Unfortunately, however, this is not the end of the story. For there are other features of the climate change case that make the necessary global agreement more difficult, and so exacerbate the basic Global Storm.[12] Prominent amongst these is scientific uncertainty about the precise magnitude and distribution of effects, particularly at the national level.[13] One reason for this is that the lack of trustworthy data about the costs and benefits of climate change at the national level casts doubt on the truth of (PD1). Perhaps, some nations wonder, we might be better off with climate change than without it. More importantly, some countries might wonder whether they will at least be relatively better off than other countries, and so might get away with paying less to avoid the associated costs.[14] Such factors complicate the game theoretic situation, and so make agreement more difficult.

In other contexts, the problem of scientific uncertainty might not be so serious. But a second characteristic of the climate change problem exacerbates matters in this setting. The source of climate change is located deep in the infrastructure of current human civilisations; hence, attempts to combat it may have substantial ramifications for human social life. Climate change is caused by human emissions of greenhouse gases, primarily carbon dioxide. Such emissions are brought about by the burning of fossil fuels for energy. But it is this energy that supports existing economies. Hence, given that halting climate change will require deep cuts in projected global emissions over time, we can expect that such action will have profound effects on the basic economic organisation of the developed countries and on the aspirations of the developing countries.

This has several salient implications. First, it suggests that those with vested interests in the continuation of the current system – e.g., many of those with substantial political and economic power–will resist such action. Second, unless ready substitutes are found, real mitigation can be expected to have profound impacts on how humans live and how human societies evolve. Hence, action on climate change is likely to raise serious, and perhaps uncomfortable, questions about who we are and what we want to be. Third, this suggests a *status quo* bias in the face of uncertainty. Contemplating change is often uncomfortable; contemplating basic change may be unnerving, even distressing. Since the social ramifications of action appear to be large, perspicuous and concrete, but those of inaction appear uncertain, elusive and indeterminate, it is easy to see why uncertainty might exacerbate social inertia.[15]

The third feature of the climate change problem that exacerbates the basic Global Storm is that of skewed vulnerabilities. The climate change problem interacts in some unfortunate ways with the present global power structure. For one thing, the responsibility for historical and current emissions lies predominantly with the richer, more powerful nations, and the poor nations are badly situated to hold them accountable. For another, the limited evidence on regional impacts suggests that it is the poorer nations that are most vulnerable to the worst impacts of climate change.[16] Finally, action on climate change creates a moral risk for the developed nations. It embodies a recognition that there are international norms of ethics and responsibility, and reinforces the idea that international cooperation on issues involving such norms is both possible and necessary. Hence, it may encourage attention to other moral defects of the current global system, such as global poverty, human rights violations and so on.[17]

II. The Intergenerational Storm

We can now return to the three characteristics of the climate change problem identified earlier:

- Dispersion of Causes and Effects
- Fragmentation of Agency
- Institutional Inadequacy

The Global Storm emerges from a spatial reading of these characteristics; but I would argue that another, even more serious problem arises when we see them from a temporal perspective. I shall call this 'the Intergenerational Storm'.

Consider first the Dispersion of Causes and Effects. Human-induced climate change is a severely lagged phenomenon. This is partly because some of the basic mechanisms set in motion by the greenhouse effect – such as sea level rise – take a very long time to be fully realised. But it also because by far the most important greenhouse gas emitted by human beings is carbon dioxide, and once emitted molecules of carbon dioxide can spend a surprisingly long time in the upper atmosphere.[18]

Let us dwell for a moment on this second factor. The IPCC says that the average time spent by a molecule of carbon dioxide in the upper atmosphere is in the region of 5–200 years. This estimate is long enough to create a serious lagging effect; nevertheless, it obscures the fact that a significant percentage of carbon dioxide molecules remain in the atmosphere for much longer periods of time, of the order of thousands and tens of thousands of years. For instance, in a recent paper, David Archer says:

> The carbon cycle of the biosphere will take a long time to completely neutralize and sequester anthropogenic CO_2. We show a wide range of model forecasts of this effect. For the best-guess cases ... we expect that 17–33% of the fossil fuel carbon will still reside in the atmosphere 1 kyr from now, decreasing to 10–15% at 10kyr, and 7% at 100 kyr. The mean lifetime of fossil fuel CO_2 is about 30–35 kyr.[19]

This is a fact, he says, which has not yet 'reached general public awareness'.[20] Hence, he suggests that 'a better shorthand for public discussion [than the IPCC estimate] might be that CO_2 sticks around for hundreds of years, plus 25% that sticks around for ever'.[21]

The fact that carbon dioxide is a long-lived greenhouse gas has at least three important implications. The first is that climate change is a *resilient* phenomenon. Given that currently it does not seem practical to remove large quantities of carbon dioxide from the upper atmosphere, or to moderate its climatic effects, the upward trend in atmospheric concentration is not easily reversible. Hence, a goal of stabilising and then reducing carbon dioxide concentrations requires advance planning. Second, climate change impacts are *seriously backloaded*. The climate change that the earth is currently experiencing is primarily the result of emissions from some time in the past, rather than current emissions. As an illustration, it is widely accepted that by 2000 we had already committed ourselves to a rise of at least 0.5 and perhaps more than 1°C over the then-observed rise of 0.6°C.[22] Third, backloading implies that the full, cumulative effects of our current emissions will not be realised for some time in the future. So, climate change is a *substantially deferred* phenomenon.

Temporal dispersion creates a number of problems. First, as is widely noted, the resilience of climate change implies that delays in action have serious repercussions for our ability to manage the problem. Second, backloading implies that climate change poses serious epistemic difficulties, especially for normal political actors. For one thing, backloading makes it hard to grasp the connection between causes and effects, and this may undermine the motivation to act;[23] for another, it implies that by the time we realise that things are bad, we will already be committed to much more change, so it undermines the ability to respond. Third, the deferral effect calls into question the ability of standard institutions to deal with the problem. For one thing, democratic political institutions have relatively short time horizons – the next election cycle, a politician's political career – and it is doubtful whether such institutions have the wherewithal to deal with substantially deferred impacts. Even more seriously, substantial deferral is likely to undermine the will to act. This is because there is an incentive problem: the bad effects of current emissions are likely to fall, or fall disproportionately, on future generations, whereas the benefits of emissions accrue largely to the present.[24]

These last two points already raise the spectre of institutional inadequacy. But to appreciate this problem fully, we must first say something about the temporal fragmentation of agency. There is some reason to think that this might be worse than the spatial fragmentation even considered in isolation. For there is a sense in which temporal fragmentation is more intractable than spatial fragmentation: in principle, spatially fragmented agents may actually become unified and so able really to act as a single agent; but temporally fragmented agents cannot actually become unified, and so may at best only act *as if* they were a single agent.

Interesting as such questions are, they need not detain us here. For temporal fragmentation in the context of the kind of temporal dispersion that characterises climate change is clearly much worse than the associated spatial fragmentation. For the presence of backloading and deferral together brings on a new collective action problem that adds to the tragedy of the commons caused by the Global Storm, and thereby makes matters much worse.

The problem emerges when one relaxes the assumption that countries can be relied upon adequately to represent the interests of both their present and future citizens. Suppose that this is not true. Suppose instead that countries are biased towards the interests of the current generation. Then, since the benefits of carbon dioxide emission are felt primarily by the present generation, in the form of cheap energy, whereas the costs – in the form of the risk of severe and perhaps catastrophic climate change – are substantially deferred to future generations, climate change might provide an instance of a severe intergenerational collective action problem. Moreover, this problem will be iterated. Each new generation will face the same incentive structure as soon as it gains the power to decide whether or not to act.[25]

The nature of the intergenerational problem is easiest to see if we compare it to the traditional Prisoner's Dilemma. Suppose we consider a pure version of the intergenerational problem, where the generations do not overlap.[26] (Call this the 'Pure

Intergenerational Problem' (PIP).) In that case, the problem can be (roughly) characterised as follows:[27]

(PIP1) It is *collectively rational* for most generations to cooperate: (almost) every generation prefers the outcome produced by everyone restricting pollution over the outcome produced by everyone overpolluting.

(PIP2) It is *individually rational* for all generations not to cooperate: when each generation has the power to decide whether or not it will overpollute, each generation (rationally) prefers to overpollute, whatever the others do.

Now, the PIP is worse than the Prisoner's Dilemma in two main respects. The first respect is that its two constituent claims are worse. On the one hand, (PIP1) is worse than (PD1) because the first generation is not included. This means not only that one generation is not motivated to accept the collectively rational outcome, but also that the problem becomes iterated. Since subsequent generations have no reason to comply if their predecessors do not, noncompliance by the first generation has a domino effect that undermines the collective project. On the other hand, (PIP2) is worse than (PD2) because the reason for it is deeper. Both of these claims hold because the parties lack access to mechanisms (such as enforceable sanctions) that would make defection irrational. But whereas in normal Prisoner's Dilemma-type cases, this obstacle is largely practical, and can be resolved by creating appropriate institutions, in the PIP it arises because the parties do not coexist, and so seem unable to influence each other's behaviour through the creation of appropriate coercive institutions.

This problem of interaction produces the second respect in which the PIP is worse than the Prisoner's Dilemma. This is that the PIP is more difficult to resolve, because the standard solutions to the Prisoner's Dilemma are unavailable: one cannot appeal to a wider context of mutually-beneficial interaction, nor to the usual notions of reciprocity.

The upshot of all this is that in the case of climate change, the intergenerational analysis will be less optimistic about solutions than the tragedy of the commons analysis. For it implies that current populations may not be motivated to establish a fully adequate global regime, since, given the temporal dispersion of effects – and especially backloading and deferral – such a regime is probably not in *their* interests. This is a large moral problem, especially since in my view the intergenerational problem dominates the tragedy of the commons aspect in climate change.

The PIP is bad enough considered in isolation. But in the context of climate change it is also subject to morally relevant multiplier effects. First, climate change is not a static phenomenon. In failing to act appropriately, the current generation does not simply pass an existing problem along to future people, rather it adds to it, making the problem worse. For one thing, it increases the costs of coping with climate change: failing to act now increases the magnitude of future climate change and so its effects. For another, it increases mitigation costs: failing to act now makes it more difficult to change because it allows additional investment in fossil fuel based infrastructure in developed and especially less developed countries. Hence, inaction raises transition costs, making future change harder than change now. Finally, and perhaps most importantly, the current generation does not add to the problem in a linear way. Rather,

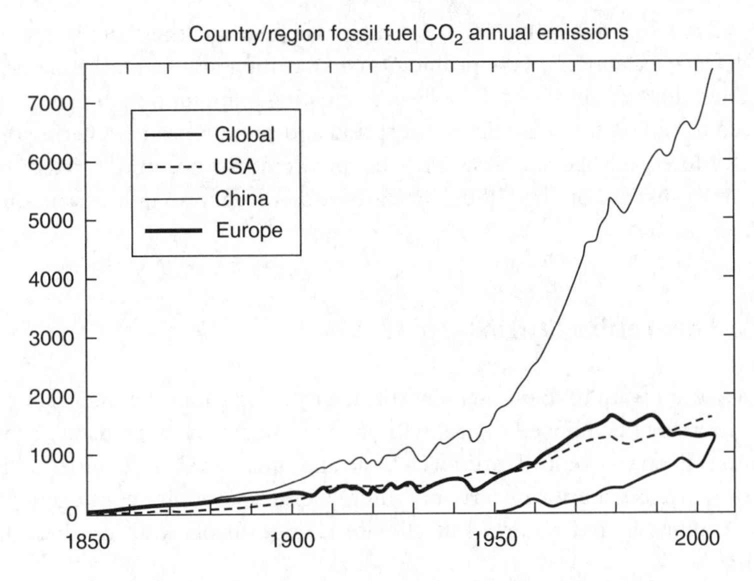

Figure 7.1 Carbon dioxide emissions from fossil fuel burning over the past 150 years

it rapidly accelerates the problem, since global emissions are increasing at a substantial rate. For total carbon dioxide emissions have more than quadrupled since 1950 (Figure 7.1). Moreover, the current growth rate is around 2 per cent per year.[28] Though 2 per cent may not seem like much, the effects of compounding make it significant, even in the near term: 'continued growth of CO_2 emissions at 2% per year would yield a 22% increase of emission rate in 10 years and a 35% increase in 15 years'.[29]

Second, insufficient action may make some generations suffer unnecessarily. Suppose that, at this point in time, climate change seriously affects the prospects of generations A, B and C. Suppose, then, that if generation A refuses to act, the effect will continue for longer, harming generations D and E. This may make generation A's inaction worse in a significant respect. In addition to failing to aid generations B and C (and probably also increasing the magnitude of harm inflicted on them), generation A now harms generations D and E, who otherwise would be spared. On some views, this might count as especially egregious, since it might be said that it violates a fundamental moral principle of 'Do No Harm'.[30]

Third, generation A's inaction may create situations where *tragic choices* must be made. One way in which a generation may act badly is if it puts in place a set of future circumstances that make it morally required for its successors (and perhaps even itself) to make other generations suffer either unnecessarily, or at least more than would otherwise be the case. For example, suppose that generation A could and should take action now in order to limit climate change such that generation D would be kept below some crucial climate threshold, but delay would mean that they would pass that threshold.[31] If passing the threshold imposes severe costs on generation D, then their situation may be so dire that they are forced to take action that will harm generation F – such as emitting even more greenhouse gases – that they would otherwise not need to consider. What I have in mind if this. Under some circumstances actions that harm innocent others may be morally permissible on grounds of self-defence, and such circumstances may arise in the climate change case.[32] Hence, the claim is that, if there is a self-defence exception on the prohibition on harming innocent others, one way in which generation A might behave badly is by creating a situation such that generation D is forced to call on the self-defence exception and so inflict extra suffering on generation F.[33] Moreover, like the basic PIP, this problem can become iterated: perhaps generation F must call on the self-defence exception too, and so inflict harm on generation H, and so on.

III. The Theoretical Storm

The final storm I want to mention is constituted by our current theoretical ineptitude. We are extremely ill-equipped to deal with many problems characteristic of the long-term future. Even our best theories face basic and often severe difficulties addressing basic issues such as scientific uncertainty, intergenerational equity, contingent persons, nonhuman animals and nature. But climate change involves all of these matters and more.[34]

Now I do not want to discuss any of these difficulties in any detail here. Instead, I want to close by gesturing at how, when they converge with each other and with the Global and Intergenerational Storms, they encourage a new and distinct problem for ethical action on climate change, the problem of moral corruption.

IV. Moral Corruption

Corruption of the kind I have in mind can be facilitated in a number of ways. Consider the following examples of possible strategies:

- Distraction
- Complacency
- Unreasonable Doubt
- Selective Attention
- Delusion
- Pandering
- False Witness
- Hypocrisy

Now, the mere listing of these strategies is probably enough to make the main point here; and I suspect that close observers of the political debate about climate change will recognise many of these mechanisms as being in play. Still, I would like to pause for a moment to draw particular attention to selective attention.

The problem is this. Since climate change involves a complex convergence of problems, it is easy to engage in *manipulative or self-deceptive* behaviour by applying one's attention selectively, to only some of the considerations that make the situation difficult. At the level of practical politics, such strategies are all too familiar. For example, many political actors emphasise considerations that appear to make inaction excusable, or even desirable (such as uncertainty or simple economic calculations with high discount rates) and action more difficult and contentious (such as the basic lifestyles issue) at the expense of those that seem to impose a clearer and more immediate burden (such as scientific consensus and the Pure Intergenerational Problem).

But selective attention strategies may also manifest themselves more generally. And this prompts a very unpleasant thought: perhaps there is a problem of corruption in the theoretical, as well as the practical, debate. For example, it is possible that the prominence of the Global Storm model is not independent of the existence of the Intergenerational Storm, but rather is encouraged by it. After all, the current generation may find it highly advantageous to focus on the Global Storm. For one thing, such a focus tends to draw attention toward various issues of global politics and scientific uncertainty that seem to problematise action, and away from issues of intergenerational ethics, which tend to demand it. Thus, an emphasis on the Global Storm at the expense of the other problems may *facilitate* a strategy of procrastination and delay. For another, since it presumes that the relevant actors are nation-states who represent the interests of their citizens in perpetuity, the Global Storm analysis has the effect of assuming away the intergenerational aspect of the climate change problem.[35] Thus, an undue emphasis on it may obscure much of what is at stake in making climate policy, and in a way that may benefit present people.[36]

In conclusion, the presence of the problem of moral corruption reveals another sense in which climate change may be a perfect moral storm. This is that its complexity may turn out to be *perfectly convenient* for us, the current generation, and indeed for each successor generation as it comes to occupy our position. For one thing, it provides each generation with the cover under which it can seem to be taking the issue seriously – by negotiating weak and largely substanceless global accords, for example, and then heralding them as great achievements[37] – when really it is simply exploiting its temporal position. For another, all of this can occur without the exploitative generation actually having to acknowledge that this is what it is doing. By avoiding overtly selfish behaviour, earlier generations can take advantage of the future without the unpleasantness of admitting it – either to others, or, perhaps more importantly, to itself.

Notes

1 This essay was originally written for presentation to an interdisciplinary workshop on *Values in Nature* at Princeton University. I thank the Center for Human Values at Princeton and the University of Washington for research support in the form of a Laurance S. Rockefeller fellowship. I also thank audiences at Iowa State University, Lewis and Clark College, the University of Washington, the Western Political Science Association and the Pacific Division of the American Philosophical Association. For comments, I am particularly grateful to Chrisoula Andreou, Kristen Hessler, Jay Odenbaugh, John Meyer, Darrel Moellendorf, Peter Singer, Harlan Wilson, Clark Wolf and an anonymous reviewer for this journal. I am especially indebted to Dale Jamieson.

2 Samuelson 2005, 41. Samuelson was talking about another intergenerational issue – social security – but his claims ring true here as well.

3 Intergovernmental Panel on Climate Change (IPCC) 2001a, p. 2; emphasis added.

4 For more on such issues, see Gardiner 2004b.

5 One might wonder why, despite the widespread agreement that climate change involves important ethical questions, there is relatively little overt discussion of them. The answer to this question is no doubt complex. But my thesis may constitute part of that answer.
6 Junger 1999.
7 This definition is my own. The term 'perfect storm' is in wide usage. However, it is difficult to find definitions of it. An online dictionary of slang offers the following: 'When three events, usually beyond one's control, converge and create a large inconvenience for an individual. Each event represents one of the storms that collided on the *Andrea Gail* in the book/movie titled the perfect storm.' Urbandictionary.com, 3/25/05.
8 The appropriateness of this model even to the spatial dimension requires some further specific, but usually undefended, background assumptions about the precise nature of the dispersion of effects and fragmentation of agency. But I shall pass over that issue here.
9 Hardin 1968. I discuss this in more detail in previous work, especially Gardiner 2001.
10 Nothing depends on the case being of this form. For a fuller characterisation, see Gardiner 2001.
11 This implies that, in the real world, commons problems do not strictly-speaking satisfy all the conditions of the prisoner's dilemma paradigm. For relevant discussion, see Shepski 2006 and Ostrom 1990.
12 There is one fortunate convergence. Several writers have emphasised that the major ethical arguments all point in the same direction: that the developed countries should bear most of the costs of the transition – including those accruing to developing countries – at least in the early stages of mitigation and adaptation. See, for example, Singer 2002 and Shue 1999.
13 Rado Dimitrov argues that we must distinguish between different kinds of uncertainty when we investigate the effects of scientific uncertainty on international regime building, and that it is uncertainties about national impacts that undermines regime formation. See Dimitrov 2003.
14 This consideration appears to play a role in US deliberation about climate change, where it is often asserted that the US faces lower marginal costs from climate change than other countries. See, for example, Mendelsohn 2001; Nitze 1994; and, by contrast, National Assessment Synthesis Team 2000.
15 Much more might be said here. I discuss some of the psychological aspects of political inertia and the role they play independently of scientific uncertainty in Gardiner unpublished.
16 This is so both because a greater proportion of their economies are in climate-sensitive sectors, and because – being poor – they are worse placed to deal with those impacts. See IPCC 2001b, 8, 16.
17 Of course, it does not help that the climate change problem arises in an unfortunate geopolitical setting. Current international relations occur against a backdrop of distraction, mistrust and severe inequalities of power. The dominant global actor and lone superpower, the United States, refuses to address climate change, and is in any case distracted by the threat of global terrorism. Moreover, the international community, including many of America's historical allies, distrust its motives, its actions and especially its uses of moral rhetoric; so there is global discord. This unfortunate state of affairs is especially problematic in relation to the developing nations, whose cooperation must be secured if the climate change problem is to be addressed. One issue is the credibility of the developed nations' commitment to solving the climate change problem. (See the next section.) Another is the North's focus on mitigation to the exclusion of adaptation issues. A third concern is the South's fear of an 'abate and switch' strategy on the part of the North. (Note that considered in isolation, these factors do not seem sufficient to explain political inertia. After all, the climate change problem originally became prominent during the 1990s, a decade with a much more promising geopolitical environment.)
18 For more on both claims, see IPCC 2001a, 16–17.
19 Archer 2005a, 5. 'kyr' means 'thousand years'.
20 Archer 2005b.
21 Archer 2005b; a similar remark occurs in Archer 2005a, 5.
22 Wigley 2005; Meehl et al. 2005; Wetherald et al., 2001.
23 This is exacerbated by the fact that the climate is an inherently chaotic system in any case, and that there is no control against which its performance might be compared.
24 The possibility of nonlinear effects, such as in abrupt climate change, complicates this point, but I do not think it undermines it. See Gardiner unpublished.
25 Elsewhere, I have argued that it is this background fact that most readily explains the weakness of the Kyoto deal. See Gardiner 2004a.

26 Generational overlap complicates the picture in some ways, but I do not think that it resolves the basic problem. See Gardiner 2003.

27 These matters are discussed in more detail in Gardiner 2003, from which the following description is drawn.

28 Hansen and Soto 2004; Hansen 2006. Graph adapted from Hansen 2006; see also Marland et al. 2005.

29 Hansen 2006, 9.

30 I owe this suggestion to Henry Shue.

31 See O'Neill and Oppenheimer 2002.

32 Traxler 2002, 107.

33 Henry Shue considers a related case in a recent paper. Shue 2005, 275–276.

34 For some discussion of the problems faced by cost–benefit analysis in particular, see Broome 1992, Spash 2002 and Gardiner (in press).

35 In particular, it conceives of the problem as one that self-interested motivation alone should be able to solve, and where failure will result in self-inflicted harm. But the intergenerational analysis makes clear that these claims are not true: current actions will largely harm (innocent) future people, and this suggests that motivations that are not generation-relative must be called upon to protect them.

36 In particular, once one identifies the Intergenerational Storm, it becomes clear that any given generation confronts two versions of the tragedy of the commons. The first version assumes that nations represent the interests of their citizens in perpetuity, and so is genuinely cross-generational; but the second assumes that nations predominantly represent the interests of their current citizens, and so is merely intragenerational. The problem is then that the collectively rational solutions to these two commons problems may be – and very likely are – different. (For example, in the case of climate change, it is probable that the intragenerational problem calls for much less mitigation of greenhouse gas emissions than the cross-generational problem.) So, we cannot take the fact that a particular generation is motivated to and engages in resolving one (the intragenerational tragedy) as evidence that they are interested in solving the other (the cross-generational version). See Gardiner 2004a.

37 Gardiner 2004a.

References

Archer, David. 2005a. 'Fate of Fossil Fuel CO_2 in Geologic Time'. *Journal of Geophysical Research*, 110: 1–6.

Archer, David. 2005b. 'How Long Will Global Warming Last?' 15 March 2005. Available at: http://www.realclimate.org/index.php/archives/2005/03/how-long-will-global-warming-last/#more-l 34.

Broome, John. 1992. *Counting the Cost of Global Warming* Isle of Harris, UK: White Horse Press.

Dimitrov, R. 2003. 'Knowledge, Power and Interests in Environmental Regime Formation'. *International Studies Quarterly* 47: 123–130.

Gardiner, Stephen M. 2001. 'The Real Tragedy of the Commons'. *Philosophy and Public Affairs* 30: 387–416.

Gardiner, Stephen M. 2003. 'The Pure Intergenerational Problem'. *Monist* 86: 481–500.

Gardiner, Stephen M. 2004a. 'The Global Warming Tragedy and the Dangerous Illusion of the Kyoto Protocol'. *Ethics and International Affairs* 18: 23–39.

Gardiner, Stephen M. 2004b. 'Ethics and Global Climate Change'. *Ethics* 114: 555–600.

Gardiner, Stephen M. In press. 'Protecting Future Generations'. In Jörg Tremmel, ed., *Handbook of Intergenerational Justice*. Cheltenham: Edgar Elgar Publishing.

Gardiner, Stephen M. Unpublished. Saved by Disaster? Abrupt Climate Change, Political Inertia, and the Possibility of an Intergenerational Arms Race. Paper presented at the workshop *Global Justice and Climate Change*, San Diego State University, April 2006.

Hansen, James. 2006. Can We Still Avoid Dangerous Human-made Climate Change? Talk presented at the New School University. February 2006.

Hansen, James and Sato, Makiko. 2004. 'Greenhouse Gas Growth Rates'. *Proceedings of the National Academy of Sciences* 101, 46: 16109–16114.

Hardin, Garrett. 1968. 'Tragedy of the Commons'. *Science* 162: 1243–1248.

Intergovernmental Panel on Climate Change (IPCC). 2001a. *Climate Change 2001: Synthesis Report*. Cambridge: Cambridge University Press. Available at: www.ipcc.ch.

Intergovernmental Panel on Climate Change (IPCC). 2001b. Summary for Policymakers. *Climate Change 2001: Impacts, Adaptation, and Vulnerability*. Cambridge: Cambridge University Press. Available at: www.ipcc.ch.

Junger, Sebastian. 1999. *A Perfect Storm: A True Story of Men Against the Sea*. Harper.

Marland, G., Boden, T. and Andreas, R.J. 2005. 'Global Co_2 Emissions from Fossil-Fuel Burning, Cement Manufacture, and Gas Flaring: 1751-2002'. Carbon Dioxide Information Analysis Center, United States Department of Energy. Available at: http://cdiac.ornl.gov/trends/emis/glo.htm.

Meehl, Gerald, Washington, Warren M., Collins, William D., Arblaster, Julie M., Hu, Aixue, Buja, Lawrence E., Strand, Warren G. and Teng, Haiyan. 2005. 'How Much More Global Warming and Sea Level Rise?' *Science* 307: 1769–1772.

Mendelsohn, Robert O. 2001. *Global Warming and the American Economy*. London: Edward Elgar.

National Assessment Synthesis Team. 2000. *Climate Change Impacts on the United States: The Potential Consequences of Climate Variability and Change*. Cambridge: Cambridge University Press, 2000. Available at www.usgcrp.gov/usgcrp/nacc/default.htm.

Nitze, W.A. 1994. 'A Failure of Presidential Leadership'. In Irving Mintzer and J. Amber Leonard, *Negotiating Climate Change: The Inside Story of the Rio Convention*. Cambridge: Cambridge University Press; 189–190.

O'Neill, Brian C. and Oppenheimer, Michael. 2002. 'Dangerous Climate Impacts and the Kyoto Protocol'. *Science* 296: 1971–1972.

Ostrom, Elinor. 1990. *Governing the Commons*. Cambridge.

Samuelson, Robert J. 2005. 'Lots of Gain And No Pain!' *Newsweek*, February 21, 41.

Shepski, Lee. 2006. Prisoner's Dilemma: the Hard Problem. Paper presented at the Pacific Division of the American Philosophical Association, March 2006.

Shue, Henry. 1999. 'Global Environment and International Inequality'. *International Affairs* 75: 531–545.

Shue, Henry. 2005. 'Responsibility of Future Generations and the Technological Transition'. In Walter Sinnott-Armstrong and Richard Howarth, eds, *Perspectives on Climate Change: Science, Economics, Politics, Ethics*. Elsevier: 265–284.

Singer, Peter. 2002. 'One Atmosphere'. In Peter Singer, *One World: The Ethics of Globalization*. New Haven, CT: Yale University Press; chapter 2.

Spash, Clive L. *Greenhouse Economics: Value and Ethics*. Routledge. 2002.

Traxler, Martino. 2002. 'Fair Chore Division for Climate Change'. *Social Theory and Practice* 28: 101–134.

Wetherald, Richard T., Stouffer, Ronald J. and Dixon, Keith W. 2001. 'Committed Warming and Its Implications for Climate Change'. *Geophysical Research Letters*, Vol. 28, No. 8, 1535–1538, at 1535, April 15.

Wigley, T.M.L. 2005. 'The Climate Change Commitment'. *Science* 307: 1766–1769.

Sustainability and Adaptation

Environmental Values and the Future

BRYAN G. NORTON

I. Introduction

Environmental ethicists have been concerned mainly with the dichotomy between humans and nonhumans, as the field has been motivated mainly by an effort to reconsider and reject "anthropocentrism" with respect to environmental *values*. Resulting debates about whether to extend "moral considerability" to various elements of nonhuman nature have been, to say the least, inconclusive; work in this genre has had little or no discernible impact on the development of sustainability theory or on public policy more generally. Here, I propose an alternative approach to re-conceptualizing our responsibilities toward nature, an approach that emphasizes the role of spatiotemporal scaling in the conceptualization of environmental problems and human responses to them. Before turning in the following sections to a description of this alternative, sometimes called "adaptive management," I begin by briefly summarizing the current situation in environmental ethics.

Most discussions in environmental ethics, which emerged as a separate subfield of ethics in the early 1970s, have turned on defining and explaining key dichotomies (Norton 2005). This trend originated in the publication of an influential essay (1967) by the historian, Lynn White, Jr., "The Historical Roots of Our Ecologic Crisis." White declared that Christianity "is the most anthropocentric religion the world has seen." White's essay prompted a series of responses by ethicists who questioned the long-standing restriction of ethics to interpersonal relations, declaring that nonhumans can have "intrinsic value" and can be "morally considerable."[1] Environmental ethicists have, accordingly, focused on the dualisms of Modernism: humans versus nonhumans, moral exclusivism, the view that all and only humans have intrinsic value, and the underlying dichotomy between body and mind. Until the early 1990s, these dichotomies dominated environmental ethics as the question of where to draw "The Line" between those beings that are morally considerable and those that are morally irrelevant dominated the field, and yet discussions of "intrinsic" value did little to improve policy or management.

The effect of emphasis on these dichotomies created an intractable conflict with anthropocentric environmental economists, blocking any integration of philosophical and economic discourse (Norton and Minteer 2002/3). Because economists insist that all values are values of human beings (consumers), they are in ontological disagreement with environmental ethicists, who wish to shift the line of moral consideration to include nonhumans and their interests.

The debate over what has intrinsic value could, of course, be brought to bear upon questions of sustainable development, as it seems reasonable for a nonanthropocentrist, who attributes intrinsic value to some nonhumans, to advocate sustainable use of "resources" for all intrinsically valuable beings. As the debates have actually evolved, however, this has not been a nexus of active discussion; having opted for nonanthropocentrism, most environmental ethicists have dismissed sustainability as an unacceptable capitulation to anthropocentrism.

By the 1990s, a few philosophers began to see that this stalemate resulted from an implicit assumption that all environmental values must be based on a single moral theory: what the legal scholar Christopher Stone called "moral monism" (Stone 1987). The debate between anthropocentrists and nonanthropocentrists, given this assumption, seemed to be a matter of establishing the exclusively "correct" theory—only one of these theories could be correct—which fueled the all-or-nothing debate and blocked any move toward a unified understanding of environmental values. Critics of the stalemate came to see that arguments for one or the other theory rest mainly on ideological commitments and *a priori* theories: no empirical evidence can be brought to bear upon whether nature has intrinsic value; and commitments to valuing objects as consumable items with a price are likewise based on *a priori* assumptions supporting economic methodology. Worse, the categorical nature of the debate has encouraged all-or-nothing answers to complex management problems, and a conceptual polarization that leads to direct oppositions and an inability to frame questions as open to compromise.

If, instead, one adopts pluralism, accepting the fact that humans value nature in many ways, and considers these values to range along a continuum from purely selfish uses to spiritual and less instrumental uses, it is unclear—and not really very important—where to "separate" one kind of value from another (Stone 1987; Norton 2005). If we attribute many kinds of value to nature and natural objects, conflicts over *why* we should protect nature are pushed into the background and the focus moves to protecting as many of the values of nature as possible, for the longest time that is foreseeable. Of course there will be arguments over priorities and immediate objectives, but if policies are devised to protect as much of nature as possible for the use and enjoyment of humans for as long into the future as possible, then it is perhaps less important whether those values preserved are counted in one theoretical framework or another.

The viewpoint advanced here is referred to as *environmental pragmatism*, which is advanced as a philosophy of environmental action that begins with on-the-ground problems, not with ideological arguments over theories regarding what kind of value nature has (Light and Katz 1996; Norton 2005). Environmental pragmatism has opened up what can be called a "third way" in the understanding of environmental values: it by-passes theoretically grounded, ideological issues and focuses on learning our way out of uncertainty in particular situations. If the "true" value of natural systems is unknown today, this is all the more reason to save them for the future, where their full and true value may be learned.

Further, pragmatism is a forward-looking philosophy, defining truth as that which will prevail, within the community of inquirers, in the long run. This feature makes it a natural complement to the theory of sustainable development, and acts as the unifying thread in the justification of preservation efforts at all scales: this forward-looking sense of responsibility and commitment to learning our way to sustainability can be thought of as pragmatism's contribution to the theory of sustainable development (Lee 1993; Norton 1999; Norton 2005).

I will here propose one approach to a new environmental philosophy, a philosophy, based in pragmatism, that encourages a learning-by-doing approach to living sustainably. This philosophy emphasizes social learning and community adaptation, and it derives its method more from the epistemology of pragmatism than from theoretical ethics.

II. Adaptive Management

This new, pragmatic approach to environmental philosophy, it turns out, is well suited to supporting an emerging and increasingly popular approach to environmental policy and action, referred to as "adaptive management." This approach involves a search for a locally anchored conception of sustainability, and sets out to use science and social learning as tools to achieve cooperation in the pursuit of sustainable management goals (Walters 1986; Lee 1993; Gunderson *et al.* 1995; Gunderson and Holling 2002; Norton 2005). In the United States, many of these ideas were first articulated by the philosophical forester, Aldo Leopold, who emphasized the importance of multiscalar adaptation in his essay, "Thinking Like A Mountain," and who advocated for scientific management throughout his career (Norton 1990).

Adaptive management has been defined by three characteristics:

1. Experimentalism: adaptive managers respond to uncertainty by undertaking reversible actions and studying outcomes to reduce uncertainty at the next decision point.
2. Multiscalar modeling: adaptive managers model environmental problems within multiscaled space–time systems.
3. Place-orientation: adaptive managers address environmental problems from a "place," which means problems are embedded in a local context of natural systems but also of political forces.

Early adaptive managers were mostly ecologists, and discussions to date have emphasized learning in response to scientific uncertainty. They have paid less attention to developing appropriate processes for *evaluating environmental change* and for setting *goals* for environmental management. Here, by undergirding adaptive management with pragmatic philosophy, I develop an approach to adaptive management that supports a rational approach to value formation and reformation. The philosophical support for adaptive management can be summarized by showing how adaptive management can be supported on three intellectual pillars.

1. A commitment to a unified method: naturalism

For pragmatists, there is only one method—the method of experience—for evaluating human assertions, including assertions with mixes of descriptive and prescriptive content. The scientific method is embraced as the epistemological test for evaluating scientific hypotheses, and also for learning what is valuable to individuals and cultures. Pragmatism eschews a sharp distinction between facts (science) and values (ethics).

2. An empirical hypothesis

The values of people who care about the environment are expressed in the ways they (a) "bound" the natural system associated with a given problem, and (b) the choices they make in focusing on physical dynamics they use to "model" those problems.

3. A new approach to scaling and environmental problems

Building on this empirical hypothesis, we proceed by identifying ways in which values, explicitly or implicitly, determine the temporal and spatial "horizons" over which impacts will be measured and processes of change monitored. What is often not noticed is the extent to which modeling choices that set boundaries and the scale of a problematic system are shaped by social values. Pragmatists, by recognizing the ways in which values shape the models we propose for analyzing environmental change, are able to address issues where values and scientific disagreements are mixed together.

III. Naturalism: The Method of Experience

While environmental ethicists have emphasized the distinction between anthropocentric and nonanthropocentric values, they have paid less attention to an equally important dichotomy, that between "facts" and "values": between descriptive and prescriptive language. Analytic philosophers have been very cautious about mixing facts and values in argumentation, a trend initiated by David Hume (2007), who promulgated "Hume's Law," which is usually taken to deny the possibility of deducing an "ought" proposition from any body of "is" propositions.

Recently, two prominent environmental ethicists have argued, following Hume, that we should forsake science and descriptive studies in support of environmental goals, and concentrate on protecting "intrinsic values" in natural systems, processes, and elements. J. Baird Callicott (2002) and Mark Sagoff (2004) have both argued that environmentalists should play down instrumental arguments for saving species and biodiversity, basing their main arguments on the "intrinsic value" of Nature. Sagoff says: "indeed environmental policy is most characterized by the opposition between instrumental values and aesthetic and moral judgments and convictions" (2004: 20). He goes on to argue that: "Environmental controversies ... turn on the discovery and acceptance of moral and aesthetic judgments as facts" (p. 39). Unfortunately, he describes no means of separating fact from fiction in assertions that this or that has intrinsic value, and explicitly claims that scientific arguments have no bearing on defending environmental values or goals.

Callicott (2002) joins Sagoff in sharply separating science from ethics, and instrumental uses from noninstrumental appreciation: "We subjects value objects in one or both of at least two ways—instrumentally or intrinsically—between which there is no middle term" (p. 16). Callicott goes on to emphasize the subjective source of these intrinsic values: "All value, in short, is of subjective provenance. And I hold that intrinsic value should be defined negatively, in contradistinction to instrumental value, as the value of something that is left over when all its instrumental value has been subtracted. ('intrinsic value' and 'noninstrumental value' are two names for one and the same thing)." Emphasizing the personal and the subjective nature of intrinsic valuings, he says: "Indeed, it is logically possible to value intrinsically anything under the sun—an old worn-out shoe, for example" (Callicott 2002: 10). Callicott and Sagoff, then, have called for a strategy of emphasizing intrinsic values over instrumental uses of nature in arguing for the protection of nature. They rely on a sharp dichotomy between descriptive and prescriptive discourse, and on sharply separating instrumental reasons for protecting nature from noninstrumental reasons. Since these non-natural qualities are, apparently, apprehended through intuition or created by emotional affects, they seem unlikely to provide intersubjectively valid reasons for environmental action.

B.A.O. Williams (1985) provides a less theory-driven view of the relation between factual and evaluative discourse. He argued persuasively that, in ordinary discourse, fact-discourse and value-discourse are inseparable; when philosophers separate them, they do so on the basis of a specialized theory, such as logical positivism. In the ordinary discourse in which citizens discuss and evaluate their environment, these discourses are inseparable; to insist on partitioning policy-discourse into fact-discourse (positivistic science) and value-discourse is to artificialize that discourse.

Pragmatists such as C.S. Peirce and John Dewey, have offered an alternative to this sharp separation of facts and values; they advocate a unified, pragmatic epistemology for environmental science and policy discourse, a discourse conducted so as to maximize social learning among participants (Dewey 1927, 1966; Lee 1993). This epistemology insists upon a single method—the method of experience—and this method applies equally to factual claims and evaluative ones. Following Dewey, assertions that something or some process is *valued* are taken as a hypothesis that that thing or process is *valuable*. Pursuing that value, and acting upon associated values, provides communities with experience that can support or undermine the claim that the thing or process is indeed valuable.

When environmental ethicists insist upon a sharp separation of facts from values, means from ends, and instrumental from noinstrumental values, this makes connections between ecological change and social values more abstract, theoretical, and tenuous. Non-naturalism construes environmental values in ways that are not easily related to measurable scientific trends. If the public and policy makers are going to support environmental actions, it will be necessary to cite values and to explain and justify environmentally motivated actions, but how could one would link "non-natural" qualities of nature with empirically measurable indicators? Enforcement of this distinction makes the integration of the discourses of environmental science and environmental value virtually impossible, and it creates a situation in which managers must look outside the adaptive process for indications of social value. They must *either* turn to economists' measurements of consumers' unconsidered preferences, *or* they can ask environmental ethicists to divine the nature of nature's non-natural qualities.

So the first pillar of the pragmatic approach is methodological naturalism. This method, while not expecting *deductions* from facts to values, relies on the open-ended, public process of challenging beliefs and values with contrary experience. From these challenges, we expect attitudes, values, and beliefs to change—but the changes cannot be justified by deductive arguments flowing one way from facts to values. The changes needed to support a new conservation consciousness are usually re-organizations and re-conceptualizations of facts, not deductions from value-neutral facts. The specific means by which assertions of value are connected will be through the development and refinement of measurable indicators that reflect values articulated by the stakeholders who represent multiple positions within the community.

IV. An Empirical Hypothesis

Two assumptions that Hume made in formulating his law should be challenged. By stating the law as a prohibition against deriving "ought" sentences from "is" sentences, Hume implied that fact-discourse and evaluative-discourse *could* be sharply separated, and that the difference *would* announce itself syntactically via the evident copula. In real-discourse, they are all mixed together in ordinary speech; to separate them artificializes normal discourse in important ways.

How, exactly, *do* values manifest themselves in scientific, descriptive literature that claims to be "value-free"? In order to answer this question, it is useful to follow Funtowicz and Ravetz (1990, 1995) in distinguishing between "curiosity-driven" (discipline-driven) science and "mission-oriented" (problem-driven) science. Authors who place their research in disciplinary journals succeed, to varying degrees, in purging evidence of values from their scientific papers. Adaptive management, however, is an active, mission-oriented science and, as Funtowicz and Ravetz argue, it often takes place in contexts where stakeholders have different perspectives and interests. In these contexts, scientific models and reports that are taken to bear on management decisions will, in effect, be "peer reviewed" not only by appropriate disciplinary scientists, but also by scientists in different fields, and by interested laypersons. This places a transparency requirement on scientific discourse: if science is to be advanced as a guide to controversial policies, then that science must be explainable—and explained—in ordinary speech that requires no scientific credentials to understand.

When attention shifts from disciplinary science to mission-oriented science, values slip back into the discourse in the process of developing models of a specific problem in a specific place. Models are necessary to apply abstract scientific terms, such as "ecosystem," to a particular place, with particular boundaries. So, if we want to find values implicit in scientific work, we should look closely at the discourse of management science at the point where models are introduced to bound and give structure to a system that is regarded as degraded or in need of "management." The values and interests of participants are coded into the mental modeling as participants in the local discourse set boundaries around systems considered to be problematic.

This hypothesis suggests that values enter public debates about what to do stealthily: they are hidden in the scales and dynamics depicted in the models used to understand the environmental problem at hand. Further, values can be expressed in choices to treat a particular variable as important to monitor. If it is accepted that values function in this way, then it is appropriate to encourage citizens, stakeholders, and interested opinions to express their values concretely by arguing for giving priority, for example, to a particular indicator in monitoring and management.

A historical example may help to illustrate what is claimed in the hypotheses. Chesapeake Bay, on the east coast of the United States, is among the most productive—and loved—bodies of water in the world. By the 1970s there were multiple danger signals that the bay was becoming polluted, and yet it was unclear what it was that was driving the widespread changes in bay functioning, especially the increasing turbidity and consequent die-back of the vast underwater grass flats that formed the base of the bay's foodweb. Until the 1970s, when the US Environmental Protection Agency (EPA) undertook a detailed scientific study, pollution issues had mostly centered around toxic and point-source pollution problems, including polluting industries and inadequate sewage treatment in a densely packed area of residences, agriculture, and industry. It was learned that, while environmental monitors were paying attention to small-scale, local variables, a large-scale variable associated with a larger-scale dynamic—one driven by the total input of nutrients into the bay from its tributaries—posed a slower moving, but more profound threat to bay health. Agricultural and residential runoff of nitrogen and phosphorous was causing algal blooms and anoxia in deep waters, resulting in increased turbidity and reducing submerged aquatic vegetation beds. The rich farmlands of Pennsylvania, the Piedmont, and the coastal plain all drain into the Chesapeake. To save the Chesapeake, it would be necessary to gain the cooperation of countless upstream users of the waters that eventually enter the bay, a monumental task, since Pennsylvania and the District of Columbia, situated upstream on tributaries, had no coastline on the bay and no direct stake in its protection.

Nevertheless, against all odds, the larger bay community—assisted by the EPA study and countless private research efforts—succeeded in transforming the public consciousness to think of the bay as an organic, connected watershed. Tom Horton, an environmental journalist and activist said it best when, at the height of this period of intense social learning, he wrote: "We are throwing out our old maps of the bay. They are outdated not because of shoaling or erosion or political boundary shifts, but because the public needs a radically new perception of North America's greatest estuary" (Horton 1987: 7–8). He pointed out that, as the problem with bay water quality expanded beyond point-source pollution, to include nonpoint sources, residents of the area had to change their mental model of the processes of pollution; and they had to address activities throughout the watershed.

What is important to learn from this analysis is that the "transformation" of the bay from an estuary into a watershed occurred in a context of mission-oriented science, and it was as much a process of transformation of public consciousness as it was a change in scientific understanding. It was a dramatic change in perspective that was driven by values: an outpouring of love and commitments not to let the bay become further degraded. In order to address the problem of bay water quality, it was necessary to create a new "model" of what was going wrong. The shift in models led to a public campaign, driven by the deep and varied values residents felt toward the bay, which was marked, for example, by the outstanding success of the Chesapeake Bay Foundation, a private foundation that advocates, educates, and supports science to guide bay management). So, we have here an example of a value-driven re-mapping of a complex natural system, how it works, and how pollution is being delivered into it. We can say that a new "cultural model" was formed (Kempton *et al.* 1995; Kempton and Falk 2000; Paolisso 2002), and Chesapeake Bay management, while not perfect, of course, has been a model of cross-state cooperation as serious steps have been taken throughout the watershed to reduce nonpoint-source as well as point-source pollution.

So, as the hypothesis under consideration would predict, residents and officials of the bay area, upon being convinced that the bay's health was threatened, and that a large part of the problem came from the larger-scale watershed system, shifted to a larger perspective on bay health, a perspective that is more aligned with a scientific understanding of the problem faced. This shift in perspective, however, is not just scientific: it expresses a deep and varied set of social values that residents and stakeholders feel toward the bay. And, when Horton describes the change in hydrological and cartographic terms, the underlying truth is that the shift to a watershed-sized model was the expression of an implicit value, a sense of caring for the health of the bay as a part of one's way of life. Through social learning, the residents of the area discovered how to "think like a watershed," and began living in a larger "place" than before.

It has been hypothesized here that social values are imputed to environmental and ecological systems implicitly in the process of developing "models"—either cultural or scientific—of the problem that needs addressing. These models, if they are similar across all participants in public deliberations, can be very helpful in developing common understandings and developing experimental actions. If they are very different, communication may be difficult, and environmental problems remain recalcitrant, dividing communities and undermining cooperative and experimental action. In many cases, communities are paralyzed because they have not experienced the kind of social learning experience that took place in the Chesapeake region, and cooperative action to address pressing and perceived problems are gridlocked. Differing values and interests –according to the hypothesis of this part—thus inform and shape the model's participants use to understand environmental problems in their areas. Diversity of perspective and differences about value are thus key aspects of difficulties in deciding what, exactly, is the problem to be addressed.

V. Scaling and Environmental Problem Formulation

Environmental disputes are so difficult, among other reasons, because it is so difficult to provide a definitive problem formulation. This feature was well explained by Rittel and Webber (1973), who distinguished "benign" and "wicked" problems. Benign problems, they said, have determinate answers, and when the answer solution is found, the problem is uncontroversially "solved." Mathematics and some areas of science exemplify benign problems. Wicked problems, on the other hand, resist unified problem formulation; there is controversy regarding what models to use and what data are important. Rittel and Webber suggest that wicked problems, because they are perceived differently by different interest groups with different values and goals, have no determinate solution because there is no agreement on the problem formulation. They can be "resolved" by finding a temporary balance among competing interests and social goals, but as the situation changes, the problem changes and becomes more open-ended. Rittel and Webber explicitly mention that wicked problems have a way of coming back in new forms; as society addresses one symptom or set of symptoms, new symptoms appear, sometimes as unintended effects of treatments of the original problem.

Most environmental problems are wicked problems; they affect multiple values, and they impact different elements of the community differently, encouraging the development of multiple models of understanding and remedy. While resistance to unified problem formulation is endemic to wicked problems, and requires iterative negotiations to find even temporary resolutions and agreements on actions, one aspect of wicked problems—the temporal open-endedness that often attends wicked problems and brings them back in more virulent form as larger and larger systems are affected—may be susceptible to clarification through modeling.

For example, general systems theory offers a basic model of humans embedded within multiple layers of dynamics, with smaller subsystems changing more rapidly than the larger systems that provide their environment. This conceptual apparatus allows us to see human decision makers as subsystems within an "environment": the ecological system in which they act, which in turn embodies more system levels. These larger, slower-changing systems provide the environment for adaptation by subsystems (including organisms and places—composed of individuals and cultures). This convention allows us to associate temporal "horizons" with changing features of landscapes as is illustrated in the famous metaphor used by Aldo Leopold, a forester and wildlife manager. Leopold set out to remove predators from the Forest Service ranges he managed in the southwestern United States. When the deer starved for lack of browse, he regretted his decision to extirpate wolves, chiding himself for not yet having learned to "think like a mountain" (Leopold 1949). He had not yet, that is, understood the role of the targeted species in the larger and slower-changing environmental system. When he came to understand that role, he accepted responsibilities for the long-term consequences of his decisions, and advocated wolf protection in wilderness areas.

Leopold's account parallels the above Chesapeake Bay case. In both cases, human activities—intended to improve the lot of human consumers of nature's bounty—threatened larger-scale dynamics. Thinking like a mountain –or a watershed—requires accepting responsibility for the impacts one's decisions will have on larger scales and subsequent generations. Accepting this responsibility is inseparable from adopting a larger ecophysical model of the system under management. At this point in time, armed with some knowledge of changing systems and how to model these, we are beginning to accept moral responsibility for actions that were once thought to be morally neutral. In both cases, accepting moral responsibility—and a sense of caring—were inseparable from adopting a changing causal model of what has happened to deer populations on Leopold's metaphoric mountain, and to submerged aquatic vegetation in the Chesapeake. Chesapeake residents, busily plying their trades and tending their lawns, discovered that the ways in which they were pursuing their economic well-being could turn the Chesapeake into an anaerobic slime pond. In both cases, the total impacts of individual actions to improve individual well-being threaten the mix of opportunities and constraints faced by subsequent generations.

Given our expanding knowledge of our impacts on the larger and normally slower-changing systems that form our environment, it seems reasonable also to accept responsibility for activities that can change the range of choices that will be open to posterity. Provided that prior generations accept responsibility for their impacts on the choice sets of subsequent generations, a "schematic definition" of sustainability can be constructed on this pluralistic multiscalar basis.

Given this multiscalar conceptualization, we see individual organisms as facing their "environment" as a mixture of opportunities and constraints; some of the chooser's choices result in survival; the chooser lives to choose again. If the chooser survives and has offspring, the offspring will also choose in the face of similar, but changing environmental conditions. Some choices lead to death with no offspring. Other choices lead to continuation and to offspring who will face similar, but possibly a changing array of possibilities and limitations. This is the basic structure of an evolution-through-selection model that interprets the environment of a chooser as a mixture of opportunities and constraints; it contextualizes the "game" of adaptation and survival and can be represented as in Figure 7.2.

Community-level success thus requires success on two levels: at least some individuals from each generation must be sufficiently adapted to the environment to survive and reproduce, *and*, for the population to survive over many generations, the collective actions

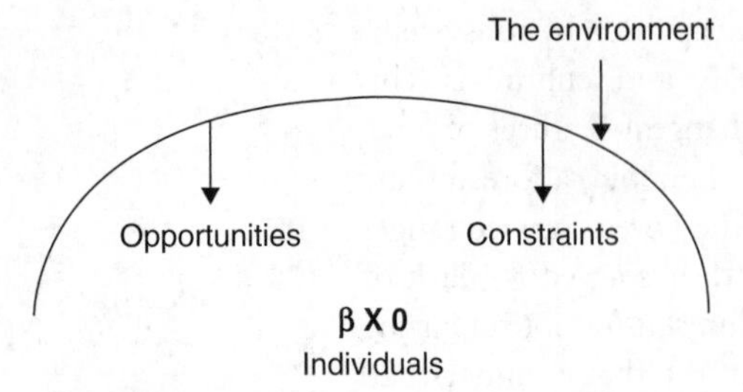

Figure 7.2 At a given time

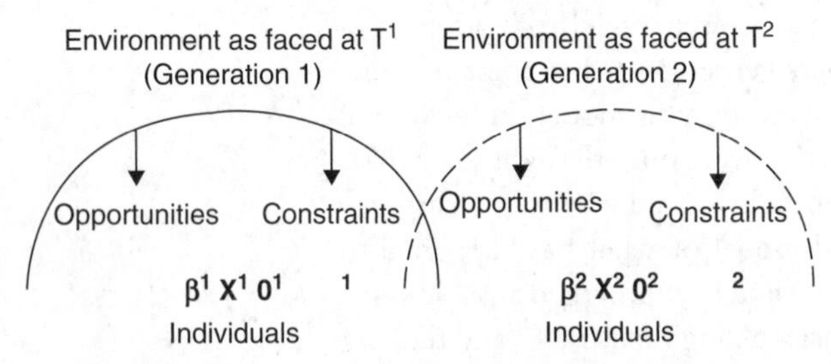

Figure 7.3 The cross-scale dynamic across time

of the population must be appropriate for (adaptive to) its environment. Since humans are necessarily social animals (because of the long period of helpless infancy of human babies), individual survival depends also on reasonable levels of stability in the "ecological background," the stage on which individuals act. This simple model, if given a temporal expression, represents the relationship between individuals who live in an earlier generation and those who live later, and the possibility that later generations might face opportunities limited by the collective choices their predecessors is represented in Figure 7.3.

From this simple framework, a schematic definition of sustainability emerges: individuals in earlier generations alter their environment, using up some resources, leaving others. If all individuals in the earlier generations overconsume, and if they do not create new opportunities, then they will have changed the environment that subsequent generations encounter, making survival more difficult. A set of behaviors is thus understood as sustainable if, and only if, its practice in generation *m* will not reduce the mixture of opportunities to constraints that will be encountered by individuals (β, X, O) in subsequent generations *n*, *o*, *p*.

Because of the place-based emphasis of adaptive management and the recognition of pervasive uncertainty, there is only so much that one can say about what is sustainable at the very general level of a universal definition. Speaking at this level of general theory, sustainability is best thought of as a cluster of variables standing for opportunities; local communities can fill in the blanks, so to speak, to form a set of criteria and goals that reflect their needs and values. While local determination must play a key role in the details, adaptive management, and its associated definitional schema, makes evident the *structure* and *internal relationships* that are essential to more specific, locally applicable definitions of sustainable policies.

Although the model has a "flat," schematic character, it could also be given a richer, normative-moral interpretation, as is hinted at by use of the terms *opportunities* and *constraints*. If we stipulate that the actors are human individuals, then the simple model provides a representation of intergenerational impacts of decisions regarding resources; our little model can thus be enriched to allow a normative interpretation or analogue. If we accept that having a range of choices is good for free human individuals, we can see the structure, in skeletal form, of the normative theory of sustainability. An action or a policy is not sustainable if it will reduce the mix of opportunities to constraints in the future.

Each generation stands in this asymmetric relationship to subsequent ones: choices made today could, in principle, reduce the range of free choices available to subsequent generations. Thus, it makes sense to recognize impacts that play out on multiple, distinct scales. If it is agreed that maintaining a constant or expanding set of choices for the future is good, and that imposing crushing constraints on future people is bad, our little model has the potential to represent, and relate to each other, the short- and long-term impacts of choices, *and* to allow either a physical, descriptive interpretation or a normative one.

This schematic definition, understood within the general model of adaptive management, captures two of our most important basic intuitions about sustainability: (1) that sustainability, incorporating a multiscalar and multi-criteria analysis, refers to a relationship between generations existing at different times—a relationship having to do with the physical existence of important opportunities; and (2) that this relationship has an important *normative* dimension, a dimension that cannot be captured by economic measures alone, but ones that involve important questions of intergenerational equity. Thus, we can tentatively put adaptive management—complete with a schematic definition of sustainability—forward as a useful and comprehensive approach to environmental science and management. Adaptive management, in this context, encompasses the experimental search for better understanding, better goals, and better decisions.

VI. Conclusion

It has been claimed that, *provided one accepts responsibility for one's impacts on the future and the set of choices (adaptations) available to future people*, a plausible definition of sustainability results. Multiscalar thinking, an emphasis on experience, and a forward-looking, pragmatic, problem-oriented attitude have been argued to be adequate to adaptive management processes, even though the goal of "sustainable development" is not yet clearly defined in general terms. By recognizing that we can learn from experience, and by developing multiple criteria associated with different scales, it is possible for a community—much as the Chesapeake community did—to learn itself into a new set of indicators, a new set of concerns, and a whole new understanding of their place and the space around that place. If environmental ethics is to contribute to pursuit of sustainable development, that contribution seems more likely to come from the pluralist, pragmatic line of analysis, functioning as a "philosophy" of adaptive management, than from sterile discussions of which elements of nature have intrinsic value and moral considerability.

Note

1 For a detailed account of the impact of White's paper on the history of environmental ethics, see Norton (2005: s. 5.3).

References

Callicott, J. Baird (2002) "The Pragmatic Power and Promise of Theoretical Environmental Ethics," *Environmental Values*, 11: 3–25.

Dewey, John (1927) *The Public and Its Problems*, Athens, OH: Swallow Press, Ohio University Press.

Dewey, John (1966) *Logic: The Theory of Inquiry*, New York: Holt, Rhinehart, Winston.

Funtowicz, Sylvio, and J.R. Ravetz (1990) *Uncertainty and Quality in Science for Policy*, Dordrecht: Kluwer Academic.

Funtowicz, Sylvio, and J.R. Ravetz (1995) "Science for a Post-normal Age," in *Perspectives on Ecological Integrity* (eds L. Westra and J. Lemons), Dordrecht: Kluwer Academic; pp. 146–161.

Gunderson, L.H. and C.S. Holling (2002) *Panarchy: Understanding Transformations in Human and Natural Systems*, Washington, DC: Island Press.

Gunderson, L.H., C.S. Holling, and S.S. Light (1995) *Barriers and Bridges to the Renewal of Ecosystems and Institutions*, New York: Columbia University Press.

Horton, Tom (1987) *Bay Country*, Baltimore, MD: Johns Hopkins University Press.

Hume, D. ([1739–1740] 2007) "A Treatise of Human Nature," in *The Clarendon Edition of the Works of David Hume*, vol. I, eds D.F. Norton and M.A. Norton, Oxford: Oxford University Press.

Kempton, Willett and J. Falk (2000) "Cultural Models of Pfisteria: Toward Cultivating More Appropriate Risk Perceptions," *Coastal Management* 28 (4): 273–285.

Kempton, Willett, J.S. Boster, and J.A. Hartley (1995) *Environmental Values in American Culture*, Cambridge, MA: MIT Press.

Lee, Kai (1993) *Compass and Gyroscope: Integrating Science and Politics for the Environment*, Washington, DC: Island Press.

Leopold, Aldo (1949) *A Sand County Almanac and Sketches Here and There*, Oxford: Oxford University Press.

Light, A. and E. Katz (1996) *Environmental Pragmatism*, London: Routledge.

Norton, B.G. (1990) "Context and Hierarchy in Aldo Leopold's Theory of Environmental Management," *Ecological Economics*, 2: 119–127.

Norton, B.G. (2005) *Sustainability: A Philosophy of Adaptive Ecosystem Management* Chicago, IL: University of Chicago Press.

Norton, Bryan (1999) "Pragmatism, Adaptive Management, and Sustainability," *Environmental Values*, 8: 451–466.

Norton, Bryan and Ben A. Minteer (2002/3) "From Environmental Ethics to Environmental Public Philosophy: Ethicists and Economists, 1973–2010," in *International Yearbook of Environmental and Resource Economics 2002/2003* (eds Tom Tietenberg and Henk Folmer), Northampton, MA: Edward Elgar; pp. 373–407.

Paolisso, M. (2002) "Blue Crabs and Controversy on the Chesapeake Bay: A Cultural Model for Understanding Watermen's Reasoning about Blue Crab Management," *Human Organization* 61 (3): 226–239.

Rittel, H.W.J. and M.M. Webber (1973) "Dilemmas in a General Theory of Planning," *Policy Sciences*, 4: 155–169.

Sagoff, Mark (2004) *Price, Principle, and the Environment*, New York: Cambridge University Press.

Stone, Christopher (1987) *Earth and Other Ethics: The Case for Moral Pluralism*, New York: Harper & Row.

Walters, C. (1986) *Adaptive Management of Renewable Resources*, New York: Macmillan).

White, Lynn (1967) "Historic Roots of our Ecological Crisis," *Science* 155: 1203–1207.

Williams, Bernard A.O. (1985) *Ethics and the Limits of Philosophy*, Cambridge, MA: Harvard University Press.

B. Sustainability and Development

'Sustainable Development'

Is It a Useful Concept?

Wilfred Beckerman

1. 'Sustainable Development': Technical Condition or Moral Injunction?

During the last few years the fashionable concept in environmental discourse has been 'sustainable development'. It has spawned a vast literature and has strengthened the arm of empire builders in many research institutes, Universities, national and international bureaucracies and statistical offices. Environmental pressure groups present the concept of sustainable development as an important new contribution to the environmental debate. It is claimed that it brings new insights into the way that concern for the environment and the interests of future generations should be taken into account in policy analysis. But in fact it only muddles the issues. As two distinguished authorities in this area, Partha Dasgupta and Karl-Göran Mäler, point out '... most writings on sustainable development start from scratch and some proceed to get things hopelessly wrong. It would be difficult to find another field of research endeavour in the social sciences that has displayed such intellectual regress.'[2]

It seems high time, therefore, for somebody to spell out why, if the Emperor of Sustainable Development has any clothes at all, they are pretty threadbare. In this essay I maintain that 'sustainable development' has been defined in such a way as to be either morally repugnant or logically redundant. It is true that, in the past, economic policy has tended to ignore environmental issues, particularly those having very long run consequences. It is right, therefore, that they should now be given proper place in the conduct of policy. But this can be done without elevating sustainability to the status of some overriding criterion of policy. After all I am sure that the reader can easily think of innumerable human activities that are highly desirable but, alas, not indefinitely sustainable!

In 1992, at Rio de Janeiro, the United Nations held a Conference on Environment and Development (UNCED), in which almost all the countries in the world participated. At this conference the countries adopted a major document of several hundred pages,

Wilfred Beckerman, "'Sustainable Development': Is It a Useful Concept?" *Environmental Values*, 3 (1994): 191–209. Reprinted with permission.

known as 'Agenda 21', which set out, amongst other things, the agreed intentions of the countries to take account of environmental objectives in their domestic policies, to monitor their own developments from the point of view of their 'sustainability' taking full account of environmental changes, and to submit regular reports on these developments to a newly established 'Commission on Sustainable Development' (CSD).[3]

Agenda 21 is full of references to 'sustainable development'. For example, Chapter 8 states that 'Governments, in cooperation, where appropriate, with international organisations, should adopt a national strategy for sustainable development ...'. It goes on to say that countries should draw up sustainable development strategies the goals of which '... should be to ensure socially responsible economic development while protecting the resources base and the environment for the benefit of future generations'. But what are socially responsible goals in this area, how far should we protect the resource base, whatever that means, and what are the legitimate interests of future generations that have to be protected?

All these, and many other, questions arise immediately one asks what exactly does 'sustainable development' mean, and what is so good about it? As many writers have pointed out, there is a danger that sustainable development is treated as a 'motherhood and apple pie' objective.[4] But, as Harvey Brooks puts it, 'For the concept of sustainability in the process of development to be operationally useful it must be more than just an expression of social values or political preferences disguised in scientific language. Ideally it should be defined so that one could specify a set of measurable criteria such that individuals and groups with widely differing values, political preferences, or assumptions about human nature could agree whether the criteria are being met in a concrete development program.'[5]

It may well be that this is asking too much of the concept of sustainable development and that it can be of some use without being fully operational. But, as it stands, the concept is basically flawed. This is because it mixes up together the technical characteristics of a particular development path with a moral injunction to pursue it. And a definition of whether any particular development path is technically sustainable does not, by itself, carry any special moral force. The definition of a straight line does not imply that there is any particular moral virtue in always walking in straight lines. But most definitions of sustainable development on the market tend to incorporate some ethical injunction without apparently any recognition of the need to demonstrate why that particular ethical injunction is better than many others that one could think up. One obvious rival injunction would be to seek the highest welfare for society over some specified time period.

The result of the fusion of technical characteristics with moral injunctions is that the distinction between positive propositions about the threat to the continuation of any development path and normative propositions concerning the optimality of any particular pattern of development is hopelessly blurred.[6] Instead, a sustainable development path should be defined simply as one that can be sustained over some specified time period, and whether or not it *ought* to be followed is another matter. It should be treated, in other words, as a purely technical concept—not that this necessarily makes it easy to define operationally.[7]

This is most clearly seen when evaluating the desirability of embarking on some specific project. Consider, for example, a simple mining project in a poor country.

Implementing the project might be the best way for the people concerned to obtain some funds to keep alive and to build up productive facilities that would enable them to survive in the future. This might include investing in some other activity—such as promoting sustainable agriculture, or investing in their education and technical training. In this case although the project will not be technically sustainable, it ought to be carried out. In the economist's jargon it will be 'optimal'. And one can also imagine the opposite scenario of specific projects that might be sustainable—such as certain forestry projects where replanting can offset the cutting—but that are not 'optimal', perhaps because they are not worthwhile from an economic point of view and would involve the community in excessive costs of cutting and transport relative to the revenues it could earn from sale of the timber.

In other words, immediately one draws the distinction between sustainability, defined as a purely technical concept, and optimality, which is a normative concept, it is obvious that many economic activities that are unsustainable may be perfectly optimal, and many that are sustainable may not even be desirable, let alone optimal. As Little and Mirrlees put it in the context of project analysis 'Sustainability has come to be used in recent years in connection with projects.... It has no merit. Whether a project is sustainable (forever?—or just a long time?) has nothing to do with whether it is desirable. If unsustainability were really regarded as a reason for rejecting a project, there would be no mining, and no industry. The world would be a very primitive place.'[8]

2. Changing Fashions in 'Sustainable Development'

One of the most famous of the definitions of sustainable development is that contained in *Our Common Future*, the 1987 report of the World Commission on the Environment and Development.[9] This report, which is known as the 'Brundtland Report', after its chairperson, Mrs Brundtland, the Prime Minister of Norway, defined sustainable development as '... development that meets the needs of the present without compromising the ability of future generations to meet their own needs'. But such a criterion is totally useless since 'needs' are a subjective concept. People at different points in time, or in different income levels, or with different cultural or national backgrounds, will differ with respect to what 'needs' they regard as important. Hence, the injunction to enable future generations to meet their needs does not provide any clear guidance as to what has to be preserved in order that future generations may do so.

Over the past few years innumerable definitions of sustainable development have been proposed.[10] But one can identify a clear trend in them. At the beginning, sustainability was interpreted as a requirement to preserve intact the environment as we find it today in all its forms. The Brundtland report, for example, stated that 'The loss of plant and animal species can greatly limit the options of future generations; so sustainable development requires the conservation of plant and animal species'.

But, one might ask, how far does the Brundtland report's injunction to conserve plant and animal species really go? Is one supposed to preserve all of them? And at what price? Is one supposed to mount a large operation, at astronomic cost, to ensure the survival of every known and unknown species on the grounds that it might give pleasure to future generations, or that it might turn out, in 100 years time, to have medicinal properties? About 98 percent of all the species that have ever existed are believed to have become extinct, but most people do not suffer any great sense of loss as a result. How many people lose sleep because it is no longer possible to see a live Dinosaur?

Clearly, such an absolutist concept of 'sustainable development' is morally repugnant. Given the acute poverty and environmental degradation in which a large part of the world's population live, one could not justify using up vast resources in an attempt to preserve from extinction, say, every one of the several million species of beetles that exist. For the cost of such a task would be partly, if not wholly, resources that could otherwise have been devoted to more urgent environmental concerns, such as increasing access to clean drinking water or sanitation in the Third World.

As it soon became obvious that the 'strong' concept of sustainable development was morally repugnant, as well as totally impracticable, many environmentalists shifted their ground. A new version of the concept was adopted, known in the literature as 'weak' sustainability. This allows for some natural resources to be run down as long as adequate compensation is provided by increases in other resources, perhaps even in the form of man-made capital.[11] But what constitutes adequate compensation? How many more schools or hospitals or houses or factories or machines are required to compensate for using up of some mineral resources or forests or clean atmosphere? The answer, it turned out, was that the acceptability of the substitution had to be judged by its contribution to sustaining human welfare.

This is clear from one of the latest definitions provided by David Pearce, who is the author of numerous works on sustainability. His definition is that "Sustainability' therefore implies something about maintaining the level of human well-being so that it might improve but at least never declines (or, not more than temporarily, anyway). Interpreted this way, sustainable development becomes equivalent to some requirement that well-being does not decline through time.'[12]

The first important feature of this definition is that it is couched in terms of maintaining 'well-being', not in terms of maintaining the level of consumption or GNP, or even in terms of maintaining intact the overall stock of natural capital, a condition that is found in many definitions of sustainable development including one to which David Pearce had earlier subscribed (though in collaboration with two other authors who clearly had a bad influence on him[13]). This implies, for example, that sustainable development could include the replacement of natural capital by man-made capital, provided the increase in the latter compensated future generations for any fall in their welfare that might have been caused by the depletion of natural capital. In other words, it allows for substitutability between different forms of natural capital and man-made capital, provided that, on balance, there is no decline in welfare.

But this amounts to selling a crucial pass in any struggle to preserve the independent usefulness of the concept of sustainability. For if the choice between preserving natural capital and adding to (or preserving) man-made capital depends on which makes the greatest contribution to welfare the concept of sustainable development becomes redundant. In the attempt to rid the original 'strong' concept of sustainable development of its most obvious weaknesses the baby has been thrown out with the bath water. For it appears now that what society should aim at is not 'sustainability', but the maximisation of welfare. In other words, it should pursue the old-fashioned economist's concept of 'optimality'.

3. Optimality and Sustainability for the Rational Individual

Suppose somebody wants to choose between two possible courses of action—e.g. which of two possible careers to pursue. Let us assume, for the sake of the argument, that the only difference between the two careers is the level of income she would earn in each and hence the level of consumption that she can enjoy, and that they are roughly the same as regards conditions of work, prestige, job satisfaction, life expectation, location and everything else. Let us also assume that her welfare at any point of time—her 'instantaneous welfare'— is correlated with her income at that point of time.[14] Suppose now that one of the careers will ensure her a steady but very modest level of income, and hence welfare, throughout her life, and the other will ensure her an income/welfare level that is higher than in the first alternative *in every single year of her life*, but that includes a decline in income/welfare in the middle of her life, say, when it may decline for a few years (possibly followed by a further rise, though this condition is not essential to the argument). Which path will she choose? Obviously she will choose the latter.[15] Her 'optimal' path is the one that maximises her welfare over her lifetime. In this simplified example, the 'present value' of her lifetime income must be higher in the latter case than in the former.

Why should she care about a temporary decline in her income/welfare if it is by choosing the path containing it that she will maximise the present value of her total welfare over the whole of her life? Insofar as the prospect of a temporary decline in income worried her she would simply invest more heavily in earlier years and use the subsequent extra income to boost her income in the years when income would otherwise decline. If this entailed too great a loss of welfare earlier—e.g. the subjective cost of the greater risk burden that such an investment policy would imply—the path containing the decline in income would be the one that maximised the present value of her welfare over her life.

Of course, in this example, the problem is simplified in two ways. First, it was assumed that the level of welfare expected in the non-sustainable path is greater in every year than it is in the sustainable path, in spite of the temporary decline in welfare in the former. Secondly, only one person is involved, so there is no need to take account of the way in which the two income paths differ with respect to their effect on the equality with which incomes are distributed among different members of the population, let alone between different generations. We shall examine the distributional considerations in the next section, when we consider welfare maximisation for society as a whole.

Meanwhile, as regards the first problem, suppose our rational individual is faced with a choice between two paths of income which intersect—i.e. one is higher than the other in some years but lower in others. In this case, to compare the 'present values' of the two income streams she would discount future incomes at whatever rate of interest she could get on her savings and investment. But, again, there seems to be no reason why the rational individual should attach special importance to a temporary decline in income during her lifetime. The time path of her income stream throughout her life will be taken care of in the discounting exercise. She will be free to borrow, or lend, in such a way as to allocate her consumption over time in such a way that it maximises the present value of her welfare.

4. Optimality for Society and the Distribution Problem

As regards the second simplification in our example, when one is concerned with optimality for society as a whole, rather than for an individual, account has to be taken of distributional considerations. This applies whether one is maximising welfare of society at any moment of time or maximising welfare over some time period. Making due allowance for distributional considerations means that when we are seeking to maximise total social welfare at any point of time we will be concerned with the manner in which the total consumption of society is distributed amongst the population at the point in time in question—e.g. how equally, or justly (which may not be the same thing) it is distributed. And if we are seeking to maximise welfare over time whilst making allowance for distributional considerations we would be concerned with the distribution of consumption over time—e.g. how equally, or justly, consumption is distributed between different generations.

Both procedures fit easily into welfare economics. Environmentalists may not be aware of the fact that it has long been conventional to include distributional considerations into the concept of economic welfare—which is a component of total welfare—that one seeks to maximise. In the opinion of the great economist A.C. Pigou, who might be regarded as the father of welfare economics, 'Any cause which increases the absolute share of real income in the hands of the poor, provided that it does not lead to a contraction in the size of the national dividend from any point of view, will, in general, increase economic welfare'.[16] Distributional considerations are even included in standard techniques of cost–benefit analysis pioneered by Ian Little and J.A. Mirrlees.[17] I myself have published estimates of growth rates of national income in different countries adjusted for changes in their internal income distributions, and others had already done so before me.[18]

Welfare can also be defined to include considerations of social justice and freedom, and so on. Of course, the more widely one draws the net of welfare to include such variables the greater the difficulty in making them all commensurate with each other. It is true that this makes it more difficult to define exactly what is meant by the 'maximisation' operation. But the same difficulty is encountered by any proposition to the effect that 'welfare' (or 'well-being') had declined in any specific time period.

How one should maximise the present value of society's welfare over time in a way that takes due account of the interests of future generations raises difficult, and relatively novel, problems of inter-generational justice that lie outside the scope of this essay.[19] In the absence of any obvious consensus view to the contrary we shall assume here that a unit of *welfare* accruing to some future generation should be given the same weight in arriving at the present value of the stream of welfare over time as an equal unit of welfare accruing to the present generation. In other words, we should not discriminate against future generations. We should not, therefore, discount *welfare* for time per se. This means that we do not advocate 'pure' time preference, which is a preference for consumption now, rather than later, purely on account of its precedence in time. There may, of course, be good reasons for doing so, such as the possibility that the human race will become extinct in a relevant time period.[20] Or one may simply wish to impose on the discounting operation some particular ethical views concerning the relative importance—or lack of it—of *welfare* accruing to different generations.[21]

But although we shall abstain from any such discounting of welfare, this does not mean that we should not discount *consumption*. That is to say we have to allow for whatever increase in productivity we may expect to take place over time as a result of investment and technological progress. For an increase in productivity would mean that any particular item of consumption will be 'cheaper' in future than it is now (allowing for inflation, of course). Hence, we would not value a unit of consumption to be delivered in ten years' time, say, at the same price as we would value it for delivery today. For instead of paying now for it to be delivered in ten years' time one could invest the money so that in ten years' time one could buy it and still have something left over. In the long run, for society as a whole, how much is left over depends on the (real) rate of growth of the economy, since that determines, roughly speaking, the (real) rate of return we could get on our money today.

We might even want to go further than that in our discounting procedure. We might want to make an additional allowance for the fact that, as consumption levels rise, the welfare that one can obtain from additional ('marginal') units of consumption will fall. This application of the law of diminishing marginal utility would be one particular way of taking account of distributional concerns. That is to say, it would allow for the fact that higher consumption will not provide *proportionately* higher welfare to rich people as to poor people. Taking account of differences in the incomes accruing to different generations in this way would be the inter-temporal counterpart of some conventional cost–benefit methods of allowing for the way that, say, any specific project at any moment of time may confer benefits on different income groups in society by attaching weights to their income levels. In applying this procedure to inter-generational comparisons of income and welfare levels one would still not be discounting 'welfare' at all. One would be simply assuming that higher levels of consumption do not bring proportionately higher levels of welfare.

Finally, in the same way that we may assume that individuals derive less welfare from additional consumption the higher is their consumption, we may also decide that society as a whole derives less welfare from the sum of the welfare of its members if this is distributed unequally among them. In our estimate of the present value of welfare over time, therefore, one could then attach lower weight to a unit of welfare accruing to society when social welfare was expected to be high than in periods when it was expected to be low. But this would be nothing to do with discounting for time per se.[22]

Thus the use of a discount rate does not necessarily mean, as most environmentalists—and some philosophers—appear to believe, that we attach less value to the *welfare* of future generations simply because it comes later in time.[23] On the contrary, rationing investment according to the discount rate helps to ensure that we invest now in projects that will give future generations more welfare than if we invested, instead, in projects—some of which may be environmental projects—that yield lower returns. In this way it maximises the welfare of future generations. It is in no way 'unfair' to them since we would discount future returns in the same way even if we expected to live for another two centuries and hence be amongst the generation that has to bear the consequences of our present decisions.[24]

5. Optimality versus Sustainability

We have argued above that (a) distributional considerations can—and invariably are—included in the economist's concept of 'welfare'; (b) this applies also to the inter-generational distribution of income and welfare; and (c) one way of doing this (though not necessarily the only way) is by appropriate choice of the discount rate used to estimate the present value of welfare that society should seek to maximise. In view of this there does not appear to be any independent role left for 'sustainability' as a separate objective of policy, independent of maximisation of the present value of welfare. For if future generations have lower incomes as a result of any particular environmental policy this will show up—other things being equal—in a lower present value of income over whatever time period our views on inter-generational justice regard as relevant. We might also want to allow for the fact that marginal units of consumption probably add more to welfare at lower levels of consumption than at higher levels.

Nor does there seem to be any special role left to play for the particular possibility that future levels of welfare may include some decline. And this is related to the second important feature of the Pearce definition of sustainability quoted above, which is that wellbeing must never decline, 'or, not more than temporarily'.[25] Apart from the qualification about a temporary decline this is in line with most recent definitions of sustainable development. It is anyway implicit in any definition of sustainability that requires that any substitution of man-made capital for natural capital can only be justified if it makes an equal contribution to welfare. As John Pezzey rightly says in his survey of the various definitions used, most of them '… understand sustainability to mean sustaining an improvement (or at least maintenance) in the quality of life, rather than just sustaining the existence of life'. He goes on to adopt a 'standard definition of sustainable development' according to which welfare per head of population must never decline (as in the latest Pearce definition mentioned above, but without the 'temporary' qualification this had included).[26]

One is always free, of course, to define welfare however one wishes. But it would be very curious to insist on defining it to *include* all sorts of environmental, distributional, social, and other considerations, but to *exclude* changes in the level of welfare (as distinct from the level itself). Indeed, it seems self-contradictory to do so. If a decline in welfare did not affect welfare, why bother about it? And if it does affect welfare, why cannot it be included in the concept of welfare that one is trying to maximise? As indicated above, one might want to adopt a concept of welfare maximisation that left no room for incommensurate objectives, such as integrity, or freedom. In that case, it would be sensible to talk about maximising welfare subject to some constraint on these other incommensurate objectives. But there seems no reason to treat *changes* in welfare levels in this way.

Furthermore, not only does it seem illogical to exclude a decline in welfare from the concept of welfare that optimal policy should seek to maximise, it is not clear why some special moral significance should be attached to *declines* in the level of welfare. It is no doubt true that a very rich man may suffer some extra loss of welfare if he has had a bad year on the stock exchange and has had to sell his yacht. He would not miss the yacht so much if he had never had it before. But we cannot be expected to be very sorry for him. After all, how did he become rich if not as a result of a lot of *increases* in income in earlier years which, if we are to be consistent, should be given an additional value, on top of their effect in bringing him to a higher level. Anyway, it may well be that he will lose less welfare from having to give up the yacht—which may have been a nuisance and entailed all sorts of responsibilities—than the joy he experienced when he first got his new toy.

On the other hand, it may be argued that this does not apply to different generations. For if some particular generation experiences a decline in its welfare one cannot assume that it was the same generation that enjoyed the previous increases. Nevertheless, if future generations experience a dip in welfare in any period, we cannot be expected to be very sorry for them *irrespective of their welfare levels*. And even if we are there seems to be no justification for switching to a development path that yields a lower present value of welfare in order to avoid the temporary decline. For that would imply inflicting on some other generation a loss of welfare greater than the one that was incurred by some particular generation *solely because of the temporary decline*. And it is far from obvious that there is any moral justification for shielding future generations from any decline in income or welfare irrespective of whatever sacrifice of welfare this might inflict on other generations.

In other words, if we are to attach a separate value to *changes* in welfare, they need not be only negative. We should also include the increases in welfare—the rise that preceded the fall. Indeed, if the hypothecated temporary decline in welfare that is to be avoided at all costs is from a higher level of welfare than the one we enjoy now, the preceding generations must have experienced more increases in welfare than declines in welfare. On balance, therefore, the future generations that enjoyed the increases in welfare should be credited with even more welfare than the simple present value exercise would have permitted. As well as being credited with more welfare for reaching higher levels, they would be credited with even more welfare because they reached the higher levels in the only possible way, namely by experiencing more increases than declines!

Thus, the exclusion of *changes* in welfare—as distinct from the level of welfare—from the concept of welfare the present value of which society should seek to maximise is open to two objections. First, it appears to be simply logically self-contraditory. At the same time, if one is consistent one should take account of positive as well as negative changes in welfare, so that it is far from obvious how the incorporation of changes in welfare in the concept of welfare that society should maximise would affect its value. One might add a third objection, namely, why should negative changes in welfare be singled out for special treatment anyway?

Of course, if the decline in living standards of future generations continued to the point that human life on this planet was no longer possible, the simple optimisation rule comes up against another tricky question. This is whether it makes sense to talk about the loss of welfare caused by the extinction of the human race. As Thomas Nagel points out, 'none of us existed before we were born (or conceived), but few regard that as a misfortune'.[27] Would the non-existence of the human race constitute a negative item in the overall total of welfare? Perhaps the welfare of such wild-life that remained might be much higher?

6. Should 'Sustainability' Be a Constraint?

The preceding discussion should make it obvious—if it were not already so—that not only should we stick to welfare maximisation, rather than sustainability, as an overriding objective of policy, but that sustainability cannot even be regarded as a logical constraint on welfare maximisation. Mimicry of the economist's use of the concept of a constraint is the latest twist in the evolution of the concept of sustainable development. It represents a further step in the retreat, under fire, by those environmentalists who have presented the 'sustainable development' concept as a great breakthrough in our thinking on the subject. First they retreat from strong sustainability to weak sustainability, and then from weak sustainability as an objective of policy to weak sustainability as just a constraint. The idea now is that welfare should be maximised but subject to the constraint that the path of development being followed be sustainable. However, this appears to represent a mis-interpretation of the concept of a 'constraint'.

Economic theory is dominated by the notion of how to make optimal choices when faced with constraints of one kind or another. For example, it is full of the analysis of how firms may seek to maximise profits *subject to constraints*, such as the prices they can charge for the goods they sell or the wages they need pay employees, and so on. Or households are treated as maximising utility *subject to constraints* in terms of their incomes and the prices of goods they buy, and so on. If, for example, the firm could relax the wage constraint and pay employees lower wages it could make higher profits. If a household could relax its income constraint by earning more, or by borrowing, it could increase welfare. In many other contexts, too, it might be analytically convenient to seek to maximise some objective, such as total economic welfare, subject to some constraint in terms of the other objectives, such as freedom, or justice.

But it is obvious that only if there is a conflict between the 'constraint' and what it is that one is trying to maximise does it make sense to use the term 'constraint'. For a constraint is something that, if relaxed, enables one to obtain more of whatever it is one is trying to maximise. Where there is no conflict, however, there is no scope for a 'constraint'.

Sustainable development could only constitute a constraint on welfare maximisation, therefore, if it conflicted with it. It is, of course, possible to define sustainable development in such a way that it does conflict with welfare maximisation over the time period in question. 'Strong sustainability', for example, would do so. For it is quite likely that the attempt to preserve all existing species and other environmental facilities would lead to a reduction in welfare as commonly defined. But, as we have seen, 'strong' sustainability has been more or less abandoned on account of its moral inacceptability. And the capital stock component of 'weak' sustainability obviously cannot conflict with welfare maximisation since the criterion of whether a substitution of man-made for natural capital is acceptable is whether it makes an adequate contribution to welfare.

For sustainability to constitute a constraint on welfare maximisation, therefore, some other source of conflict between sustainability and welfare maximisation has to be found. We have discussed at some length one that has been given much prominence, namely distributional considerations, particularly the inter-generational distribution of welfare. We have shown that whilst it is, of course, open to anybody to define welfare in such as way as to take no account of distributional considerations it would violate a long tradition in economics to the effect that income distribution was an integral part of welfare and that inter-temporal distribution can be handled through the appropriate choice of the discount rate. We have also argued the notion that declines in welfare—particularly temporary declines—should be given special consideration and constitute constraints on welfare maximisation is also open to serious objections.

The advocates of sustainable development as a constraint, therefore, face a dilemma. Either they stick to 'strong' sustainability, which is logical, but requires subscribing to a morally repugnant and totally impracticable objective, or they switch to some welfare-based concept of sustainability, in which case they are advocating a concept that appears to be redundant and unable to qualify as a logical constraint on welfare maximisation.

7. Sustainability and the Measurement of National Income

As pointed out above, most environmentalists mix up, in their own concept of sustainable development, the technical characteristics of a development path with its moral superiority. It is perhaps because of this confusion that they also mis-interpret perfectly legitimate technical definitions that some economists have proposed, such the definition of maintaining capital intact, or the conditions to be satisfied IF it is required to ensure constant levels of consumption per head, as carrying with them ethical force that their originators would not necessarily attach to them at all.

For example, a famous definition of income by the late Sir John Hicks, a Nobel Laureate in Economics, is that national income is the output of a nation's economy *after maintaining capital intact*—i.e. after allowing for the amount of capital used up in the course of producing the output in question. Obviously, if the capital that is gradually 'used up' in the course of time through wear and tear and so on is not replaced then, in the longer run, output will begin to decline and it will not be possible to maintain income levels. But this Hicksian definition of income, with its emphasis on the need to maintain capital intact in order to maintain income levels, is a purely technical definition of net income and has no moral connotation whatsoever.

More recently, other economists, notably Hartwick, Weitzman, and Solow, have shown precisely how to extend the concept of net national income and maintaining capital intact to encompass the depletion of natural capital through the extraction of minerals, and precisely how much investment is required in order to compensate for using up natural capital and to maintain constant levels of consumption per head.[28] But these technical definitions of income and of sustainable consumption paths are frequently quoted by environmentalists as if they imply some moral obligation never to consume more than income so defined and hence to always maintain capital intact and to follow a sustainable growth path as so defined. But the authors of these definitions usually had no intention of suggesting that they were also laying down the law as to what is morally imperative.

For example, in a much quoted article on 'Intergenerational Equity and Exhaustible Resources' Nobel Laureate Robert M. Solow states that he is merely exploring the consequences of a straightforward application of the famous second principle of justice associated with the political philosopher, John Rawls, to the problem of optimal capital accumulation spanning several generations.[29] He states that 'It will turn out to have both advantages and disadvantages as an ethical principle in this context' (page 30). He goes on to show that in the normal situations '... the max-min [i.e. the Rawlsian] criterion does not function very well as a principle of intergenerational equity. ... It calls ... for zero net saving with stationary technology, and for negative net saving with advancing technology.' This is hardly a ringing endorsement of the principle of never allowing consumption per head to be lower in any time period than in any other time period. But it does not prevent many environmentalists from writing that Solow has demonstrated the desirability of the principle of maintaining a constant level of consumption per head.[30] Most of them must be just quoting each other without bothering to read Solow in the original.

Thus the fact that eminent economists have helped provide a precise basis for estimating how much investment a society would need to make, under certain highly simplified conditions, in order to compensate for any reduction in the stock of natural capital and to maintain 'sustainable development' (defined as no fall in welfare levels), after taking due account of damage to the environment, does not imply that this represents some ethical injunction. This not only implies nothing at all about the optimality of sustainable growth paths, it does not even imply that making such estimates is worthwhile in practice.

Even the depreciation of man-made capital is not possible to estimate with much accuracy. For it does not correspond to any actual market transactions. The flow of goods and services entering into gross national product (GNP)—such as the food consumed, the machine tools built, the services provided to consumers, and so on—are almost all the subject of two-way market transactions involving a buyer and a seller. By contrast, the depletion of the capital stock is not, as a rule, the subject of any transactions between buyers and sellers. True, firms will show estimates of depreciation in their accounts, but, for many reasons that lie outside the scope of this paper, nobody in the trade would rely on these as being objective and accurate estimates of any conceptually valid true measure of capital consumption.[31] But at least the assets in question did go through the market at one time in their life, and in some cases it may be possible to use second-hand prices to estimate the value of capital goods that have been discarded.

By contrast most environmental assets never did pass through the market place at all. In almost all cases there are no market observations of the value to be attached to clean air or water or beautiful landscape. It is true that newly extracted supplies of minerals do pass through the market, but the known reserves are only the reserves that have been found worthwhile identifying given prices at any point of time. As I explained in detail about twenty years ago, insofar as demand may exceed supply for any length of time this will lead to a rise in price which, in turn, invariably sets in motion many feedback mechanisms to restore the balance between supply and demand. These include increases in exploration and discovery of new reserves, improvements in extraction and refinement techniques, but also economies and substitution in the use of the materials in question.[32] Also, there are obvious difficulties in using prices of minerals at any point of time as guide to the prices that they will fetch for the next few centuries, so that it is impossible to put any reasonable values on these resources.

8. Conclusions

What we have seen so far then is that:—

(i) 'sustainability' should be interpreted purely as a technical characteristic of any project, programme or development path, not as implying any moral injunction of over-riding criterion of choice;
(ii) the 'optimal' choice for society is to maximise the present value of welfare over whatever time period is regarded as relevant given one's views on inter-generational justice. This can make allowance for distributional considerations, including inter-temporal distribution, by attaching weights to the welfare accruing to different generations in any estimate of the present value of social welfare, as, for example, by appropriate choice of the discount rate;
(iii) since, anyway, most environmentalists have now dropped 'strong' sustainability and now define the 'sustainability' condition in terms of how much contribution different components of the total capital stock contribute to welfare, insofar as society seeks to maximise welfare the sustainability condition becomes redundant and cannot even be treated as a 'constraint'.

None of the above conclusions means that we are not left with serious environmental problems when attempting to decide what is an *optimal* policy. As I have always maintained the world is faced with real environmental problems. Economists have been well aware of the fact that, left to itself, the environment will not be managed in a socially optimal manner. There are too many market imperfections. The most important is probably the absence of well-defined property rights. But in many cases—particularly with global environmental issues, such as the preservation of biodiversity or the prevention of excessive production of greenhouse gases—it is not easy to see what economic incentives can be devised and implemented internationally in order to secure socially optimal co-operative action. These are serious issues, many of them requiring extensive scientific research and economic research into, for example, the economic evaluation of environmental assets, or the costs of pollution reduction, or the relative efficacy of alternative schemes to achieve socially optimal levels of environmental protection.

Serious research into these and related environmental problems is being carried out in various institutions all over the world.[33] It is unfortunate that too much time and effort is also being devoted to developing the implications of the sustainable development concept, including innumerable commissions and committees set up to report on it and innumerable research programmes designed to measure it.[34] Outside a few devloping countries heavily dependent on limited supplies of some minerals or other primary product, the measurement of some wider concept of 'sustainable GNP' is a waste of time and effort and such estimates as have been made for developed countries are virtually worthless.

Notes

1 Emeritus Fellow of Balliol College, Oxford. I wish to express my particular gratitude to John Pezzey who has helped me remedy some serious deficiencies in an earlier draft of this essay, as well as to an anonymous referee for several constructive comments. Needless to say I alone am responsible for all remaining defects.

2 Dasgupta and Mäler 1994.

3 The legal status of Agenda 21 is far from clear although it was later enshrined in a resolution of the Second Committee of the General Assembly of the UN (at its 51st meeting on the 16th December 1992). But this only urged governments and international bodies to take the action necessary to follow up the agreements reached in Rio, and there is no question of countries that do not take much notice of it being brought before the International Court of Justice! After all, most countries in the world are constantly in breach of various more binding commitments into which they have entered concerning human rights without ever being pursued in the courts or penalised in any way.

4 See, for example, Pearce Markandya and Barbier 1989, p. 1; Solow 1991; Pezzey 1992a, p.1.

5 Brooks 1992, p. 30.

6 See criticism along these lines by Dasgupta and Mäler (1990, p. 106), in which they take specific issue with a definition of SD by D. Pearce, Barbier and Markandya, which required no decline in the natural capital stock. This condition differs significantly from one proposed by the same authors but with their names in a different order, namely in Pearce, Markandya and Barbier 1989, p. 3. It is interesting that changing the order of the authors changes their views on the definition of SD.

7 Even at a technical level, whether some project or development programme is sustainable or not depends on numerous assumptions—e.g. concerning availability of inputs, of foreign loans, and so on.

8 Little and Mirrlees 1990, p. 365.

9 World Commission on Environment and Development, 1987.

10 An excellent recent survey is contained in Appendix 1 of Pezzey 1992a.

11 See Pezzey 1992a and Pezzey 1992b.

12 Pearce 1993, p. 48.

13 On page 48 of Pearce et al. 1989, this maintenance of the stock of natural capital seems to be the concept of sustainable development to which the authors subscribe, though wider concepts are also given their due.

14 We abstract here from the question of whether, at the margin, she derives as much welfare from a unit of consumption as from a unit of income devoted to investment.

15 This example does not depend at all on any assumptions about the individual's rate of time preference.

16 Pigou 1932, p. 89. The link between economic welfare and distribution is very forcibly expressed in, for example, de V. Graaff 1957, p. 92. Nowadays, of course, refinements to the theory enable one to combine changes in distribution with changes in real income in such a way as to weaken the force of Pigou's proviso concerning the importance of not reducing total real income.

17 See, in particular, Little and Mirrlees 1974.

18 See Beckerman 1978, chapter 4, 'The adjustment of growth rates for changes in income distribution'. In this study I adjusted the growth rates of nine OECD countries to take account of income distribution changes.

19 Some of the difficulties surrounding the problem of our obligations to future generations are discussed in Pasek 1992.

20 As proposed by Dasgupta and Heal 1979, p. 262.

21 One interesting attempt to relate alternative ethical views concerning inter-generational justice is in d'Arge, Schultze and Brookshire 1982.

22 See, for example, a formal exposition of this type of egalitarianism in Broome 1991, pp. 178–180.

23 See, for example, Partridge 1981. One distinguished philosopher who has made extensive criticisms along these lines is Derek Parfit, as in Parfit 1984, Appendix F.

24 We might, however, use a slightly lower discount rate to allow for the reduced risk of one's not surviving long enough to see the fruits of one's savings. I have attempted a fuller exposition of the discounting argument in Beckerman 1993.

25 And how temporary is the temporary decline in welfare that is permitted under the Pearce

definition? If one cannot specify this precisely the condition is totally non-operational. By this I do not mean to suggest that one should give a precise number of years. What is required is a specification of the precise criteria by which one can determine whether any particular 'temporary' decline in welfare is optimal. Economists define the optimum output of any commodity as that output at which the marginal social cost of producing it equals the marginal social benefit. This definition does not tell us exactly how much of each commodity should be produced in terms of kilograms or gallons or any other units. But it gives a precise and operational definition. By contrast definitions of sustainable development that include vague qualifications about the acceptability of "temporary" declines in social welfare, devoid of any criteria for deciding how temporary is temporary, are totally non-operational.

26 Pezzey 1992a, p. 11.

27 Nagel 1979, p. 3.

28 A relatively recent paper by R.M. Solow (1986) contains also the key references to contributions made by Hartwick, Weitzman, Dixit, and others.

29 Solow 1974, p. 30. More specifically, here, and elsewhere, Solow demonstrates that with growing population and technical progress, constant consumption per head may not be desirable. Elsewhere, he also explicitly states that 'there are social goals other than sustainability' (Solow 1992, p. 20).

30 See, for example, the generally excellent article by Mick Common and Charles Perrings (1992) where they write (p. 10) that 'Economists have always had to work hard to find a rationalization for the principle of constant consumption. In this instance, the rationalization was provided by Solow, who used the egalitarian arguments of Rawls (1971) to propose a "Rawlsian" maximin approach to the intertemporal distribution of consumption.'

31 Various other methods have been used to attempt to measure capital stocks and their depreciation, such as the use of fire insurance surveys. Or estimates have been made of the typical length of life of specific types of building or machinery or capital equipment and so on. But nobody would pretend that such estimates provide more than rough orders of magnitude at best.

32 I explained the theory and backed it up with the facts in my book *In Defence of Economic Growth*, chapter 8, 'Resources for Growth' (1974). For more recent data see, also, Beckerman 1992, Annex 2.

33 The Environment Directorate of the OECD, and the World Bank, frequently produce authoritative studies of economic valuation of environmental costs and benefits, including, for example, Munasinghe 1993; Pezzey 1992a; and Peskin and Lutz 1990. See also Barde and Pearce 1991, and the papers included in Part II of Costanza 1991.

34 These are among the tasks of the Convention on Biodiversity signed by over 150 countries at the 1992 UN Conference on Environment and Development at Rio de Janeiro.

References

Barde, Jean-Philippe and Pearce, David (eds) 1991. *Valuing the Environment*. London, Earthscan.

Beckerman, W. 1974. *In Defence of Economic Growth*. London, Jonathan Cape.

Beckerman, W. 1978. *Measures of Leisure, Equality and Welfare*. Paris, OECD.

Beckerman, W. 1992. *Economic Development and the Environment*, WPS 961, (August). Washington, D.C., The World Bank.

Beckerman, W. 1993. 'Environmental Policy and the Discount Rate', CSERGE Working Paper 93–12. University College London and the University of East Anglia, Norwich, Centre for Social and Economic Research on the Global Environment.

Brooks, Harvey 1992. 'Sustainability and Technology', in *Science and Sustainability*, p. 30. Vienna, International Institute for Applied Systems Analysis.

Broome, John 1991. *Weighing Goods*. Oxford, Blackwell.

Common, Mick and Perrings, Charles 1992. 'Towards an ecological economics of sustainability', *Ecological Economics* 6.

Costanza, Robert (ed.) 1991. *Ecological Economics: The Science and Management of Sustainability*. New York, Columbia University Press.

d'Arge, R.C., Schultze, W.D., and Brookshire, D.S., 1982. 'Carbon Dioxide and Intergenerational Choice', *American Economic Review* 72 (May).

Dasgupta, Partha and Heal, G.M. 1979. *Economic Theory and Exhaustible Resources*. Cambridge, Cambridge University Press.

Dasgupta, Partha and Mäler, Karl-Göran 1990. 'The Environment and Emerging Development Issues', in *Proceedings of the World Bank Annual Conference on Development Economics 1990*. Washington DC, The World Bank.

Dasgupta, Partha and Mäler, Karl-Göran 1994. 'Poverty, Institutions, and the Environmental-Resource Base', in Jere Behrman and T.N. Srinivasan. *Handbook of Development Economics*, Vol. 3. Amsterdam, North Holland (forthcoming).

de V. Graaff, Jan 1957. *Theoretical Welfare Economics*. Cambridge, Cambridge University Press.

Little, I.M.D. and Mirrlees, J.A. 1974. *Project Appraisal and Planning for Developing Countries*. London, Heinemann.

Little, I.M.D. and Mirrlees, J.A. 1990. 'Project Appraisal and Planning Twenty Years On', in *Proceedings of the World Bank Annual Conference on Development Economics, 1990*. Washington DC, The World Bank.

Munasinghe, Mohan 1993. 'Towards Sustainable Development: The Role of Environmental Economics and Valuation', World Bank Environment Paper No. 3. Washington, DC, The World Bank.

Nagel, Thomas 1979. *Mortal Questions*. Cambridge, Cambridge University Press.

Parfit, Derek 1984. *Reasons and Persons*. Oxford, Oxford University Press.

Partridge, E. (ed.) 1981. *Responsibilities to Future Generations*. New York, Prometheus Books.

Pasek, Joanna 1992. 'Obligations to Future Generations: A Philosophical Note', in *World Development*, 20 (4).

Pearce, David 1993. *Economic Values and the Natural World*. London, Earthscan.

Pearce, David, Markandya, A., and Barbier, E. 1989. *Blueprint for a Green Economy*. London, Earthscan.

Peskin, Henry and Lutz, Ernst 1990. 'A Survey of Resources and Environmental Accounting in Industrialized Countries'. Washington, DC, The World Bank (August).

Pezzey, J. 1992a *Sustainable Development Concepts: An Economic Analysis*, World Bank Environment Paper No. 2. Washington DC, The World Bank.

Pezzey, J. 1992b 'Sustainability: An Interdisciplinary Guide', *Environmental Values* 1: 321–362.

Pigou, A.C. 1932. *The Economics of Welfare*, 4th edition. London, Macmillan.

Solow, R.M. 1974. 'Intergenerational equity and exhaustible resources', *Review of Economic Studies*, Symposium.

Solow, R.M. 1986. 'On the intergenerational allocation of natural resources', *The Scandinavian Journal of Economics* 88.

Solow, R.M. 1991. 'Sustainability: An Economists's Perspective', lecture at the Woods Hole Oceanographic Institution Marine Policy Center, Maine.

Solow, R.M. 1992. 'An almost practical step toward sustainability', lecture on the occasion of the Fortieth Anniversary of Resources for the Future, Washington DC (October).

World Commission on Environment and Development 1987. *Our Common Future*. Oxford, Oxford University Press.

On Wilfred Beckerman's Critique of Sustainable Development

HERMAN E. DALY

Beckerman's discussion of sustainable development provides some useful clarifications, and a good occasion for making a few more. Since I advocate what he calls the 'sustainability as constraint' position, I will move straight to it, and begin with the dilemma in which he claims to have placed those like me:

> The advocates of sustainable development as a constraint, therefore, face a dilemma. Either they stick to 'strong' sustainability, which is logical, but requires subscribing to a morally repugnant and totally impractical objective, or they switch to some welfare-based concept of sustainability, in which case they are advocating a concept that appears to be redundant and unable to qualify as a logical constraint on welfare maximisation.
>
> (Beckerman 1994: 203)

I advocate strong sustainability, thereby receiving Beckerman's blessing in the realm of logic but provoking his righteous indignation in the realms of morality and practicality. Consequently I will focus on a reply to those charges. But first, I must congratulate him for his effective demolition of 'weak sustainability'. I hope he has more success than I have had in converting the many environmental economists who still cling to it.

Beckerman's concept of strong sustainability, however, is one made up by himself in order to serve as a straw man. In the literature, weak sustainability assumes that manmade and natural capital are basically substitutes. He got that right. Strong sustainability assumes that manmade and natural capital are basically complements. Beckerman completely missed that one. He thinks strong sustainability means that no species could ever go extinct, nor any nonrenewable resource should ever be taken from the ground, no matter how many people are starving. I have referred to that concept as 'absurdly strong sustainability' in order to dismiss it, so as to focus on the relevant issue: namely are manmade and natural capital substitutes or complements? That is really what is at issue between strong and weak sustainability. Since Beckerman got the definition right for weak sustainability his arguments against it are relevant, and as I said above, convincing. But since he got the definition of strong sustainability wrong, in spite of the obvious symmetry of the cases, his arguments against it are irrelevant.

Herman E. Daly, "On Wilfred Beckerman's Critique of Sustainable Development," *Environmental Values*, 4 (1995): 49–55. Reprinted with permission.

He indeed demonstrated that 'absurdly strong sustainability' is in fact absurd! Let me accept that, and move on to the real issue.

I did not even find the word 'complementarity' or its derivatives in the article, and that is the key to strong sustainability. If natural and manmade capital were substitutes (weak sustainability) then neither could be a limiting factor. If, however, they are complements (strong sustainability), then the one in short supply is limiting. Historically, in the 'empty world' economy, manmade capital was limiting and natural capital superabundant. We have now, due to demographic and economic growth, entered the era of the 'full world' economy, in which the roles are reversed. More and more it is remaining natural capital that now plays the role of limiting factor. The fish catch is not limited by fishing boats, but by remaining populations of fish in the sea. Economic logic says to economise on and invest in the limiting factor. For this reason we put the constraint on natural capital. Maximise current welfare subject to the constraint that natural capital be maintained intact over generations.

Let me agree with Beckerman not only in rejecting weak sustainability, but also in rejecting the attempt to define sustainable development in terms of welfare of future generations. To his reasons I would only add that the welfare of future generations is beyond our control and fundamentally none of our business. As any parent knows, you cannot bequeath welfare. You can only pass on physical requirements for welfare. Nowadays natural capital is the critical requirement. A bequest of a fishing fleet with no fish left is worthless. But even the bequest of a world full of both fish and fishing boats does not guarantee welfare. The future is always free to make itself miserable with whatever we leave to it. Our obligation therefore is not to guarantee their welfare but their capacity to produce, in the form of a minimum level of natural capital, the limiting factor. This can be operationalised in some simple rules of management. Projects should be designed (constrained) so that:

Output Rule: waste outputs are within the natural absorptive capacities of the environment. (i.e., nondepletion of the sink services of natural capital).

Input Rules: (a) For renewable inputs, harvest rates should not exceed regeneration rates (nondepletion of the source services of natural capital. (b) For nonrenewable inputs the rate of depletion should be equal to the rate at which renewable substitutes can be developed. If a renewable stock is consciously divested (i.e. exploited nonrenewably), it should be subject to the rule for nonrenewables.

Rule (b) is a 'quasi-sustainability' rule for the exploitation of nonrenewables, based on the fact that they are a capital inventory, and it has been operationalised by El Serafy.[1] The question of what qualifies as a renewable substitute is important, and relevant to strong versus weak sustainability. Weak sustainability would imply acceptance of any asset with the required rate of return. Strong sustainability requires a real rather than a merely financial substitute—e.g., a capital set-aside from petroleum depletion should be invested in new energy supplies, including improvements in energy efficiency, but not in, say, law schools, medical research, or MacDonald's Hamburger franchises.

A point sure to be contested is the assertion that manmade and natural capital are complements. Many economists insist that they are substitutes. Since this really is the key issue, and since Beckerman ignores it, it is necessary to repeat here the case for complementarity.

a. One way to make an argument is to assume the opposite and show that it is absurd. If manmade capital were a near perfect substitute for natural capital then natural capital would be a near perfect substitute for manmade capital. But if so, there would have been no reason to accumulate manmade capital in the first place, since we humans were already endowed by nature with a near perfect substitute. But historically we did accumulate manmade capital—precisely because it is complementary to natural capital.
b. Manmade capital is itself a physical transformation of natural resources which are the flow yield from the stock of natural capital. Therefore, producing more of the alleged substitute (manmade capital)—physically requires more of the very thing being substituted for (natural capital)—the defining condition of complementarity!
c. Manmade capital (along with labour) is an agent of transformation of the resource flow from raw material inputs into product outputs. The natural resource flow (and the natural capital stock that generates it) are the material cause of production; the capital stock that transforms raw material inputs into product outputs is the efficient cause of production. One cannot substitute efficient cause for material cause—as one cannot build the same wooden house with half the timber no matter how many saws and carpenters one tries to substitute. Also, to process more timber into more wooden houses, in the same time period, requires more saws, carpenters, etc. Clearly the basic relation of manmade and natural capital is one of complementarity, not substitutability. Of course one could substitute bricks for timber, but that is the substitution of one resource input for another, not the substitution of capital for resources.[2] In making a brick house one would face the analogous inability of trowels and masons to substitute for bricks.

The complementarity of manmade and natural capital is made obvious at a concrete and commonsense level by asking: what good is a saw-mill without a forest; a fishing boat without populations of fish; a refinery without petroleum deposits; an irrigated farm without an aquifer or river? We have long recognised the complementarity between public infrastructure and private capital—what good is a car or truck without roads to drive on? Following Lotka and Georgescu-Roegen we can take the concept of natural capital even further and distinguish between endosomatic (within-skin) and exosomatic (outside-skin) natural capital. We can then ask, what good is the private endosomatic capital of our lungs and respiratory system without the public exosomatic capital of green plants that take up our carbon dioxide in the short run, while in the long run replenishing the enormous atmospheric stock of oxygen and keeping the atmosphere at the proper mix of gases—i.e. the mix to which our respiratory system is adapted and therefore complementary.

If natural and manmade capital are obviously complements, how is it that economists have overwhelmingly treated them as substitutes? *First*, not all economists have—Leontier's input–output economics with its assumption of fixed factor proportions treats all factors as complements. *Second*, the formal, mathematical definitions of complementarity and substitutability are such that in the two-factor case the factors must be substitutes.[3] Since most textbooks are written on two-dimensional paper this case receives most attention. *Third*, mathematical convenience continues to dominate reality in the general reliance on Cobb–Douglas and other constant elasticity of substitution production functions in which there is near infinite substitutability of factors, in particular of capital for resources.[4] Thankfully some economists have begun to constrain this substitution by the law of conservation of mass! *Fourth*, exclusive myopic attention to the margin results in very limited and marginal possibilities for substitution obscuring overall relations of complementarity. For example, private expenditure on extra car maintenance may substitute for reduced public expenditure on roads. But this marginal element of substitution (car repairs for road repairs) should not obscure the fact that cars and roads are basically complementary forms of capital.[5] *Fifth*, there may well be substitution of capital for resources in aggregate production functions reflecting a change in product mix from resource-intensive to capital-intensive products. But this is an artefact of changing product aggregation, not factor substitution along a given product isoquant. Also, a new product may be designed that gives the same service with less resource use—e.g., light bulbs that give more lumens per watt. This is technical progress, a qualitative improvement in the state of the art, not the substitution of a quantity of capital for a quantity of resources in the production of a given quantity of a specific product.

No one denies the reality of technical progress, but to call such changes the substitution of capital for resources (or of manmade for natural capital) is a serious confusion. It seems that some economists are counting as 'capital' all improvements in knowledge, technology, managerial skills, etc.—in short, anything that would increase the efficiency with which resources are used. If this is the usage, then 'capital' and resources would by definition be substitutes in the same sense that more efficient use of a resource is a good substitute for having more of the resource. But formally to define capital as efficiency would make a mockery of the neoclassical theory of production, where efficiency is a ratio of output to input, and capital is a quantity of input.

It was necessary, I think, to go deeply into the issue of complementarity because it is the key to strong sustainability, and by omitting it Beckerman failed to deal with the most important issue in the sustainable development debate.

Turning now to other problems, Beckerman thinks that discounting is the proper way to balance present and future claims on the resource base. But a discount rate is part of the price system, and prices allocate subject to a given distribution of ownership. The key question is the given distribution of ownership between different generations, which are different people. If the resource base is thought to belong entirely to the present generation we get one set of prices, including interest (discount) rate. If the resource base is thought to be distributed in ownership over many generations we get an entirely different set of prices, including a different interest rate. Both sets of prices are efficient, given the distribution.[6] Strong sustainability as a constraint is a way of implicitly providing property rights in the resource base to future generations. It says they have ownership claims to as much natural capital as the present—i.e. the rule is to keep natural capital intact. Strong sustainability requires that manmade and natural capital each be maintained intact separately, since they are considered complements: weak sustainability requires that only the sum of the two be maintained intact, since they are presumed to be substitutes. As natural capital more and more becomes the limiting factor the importance of keeping it separately intact increases.

Beckerman recognises that sustainability of consumption is built into the Hicksian definition of income. But he downplays this respectable lineage by saying that Hicks's definition of income is a purely technical concept, containing no moral injunction against capital consumption. While this is true in terms of accounting definitions, it is also rather disingenuous to pretend that the prudential motive of avoiding inadvertent impoverishment by consuming beyond income played no role in Hicks's formulation of the concept. Hicksian income is a concept consciously designed to inform prudential (sustainable) consumption, even though it does not mandate it. Extending the definitional requirement to keep capital intact to natural capital as well as manmade capital is a small step, and one totally within the spirit of Hicks's prudential concerns. And, given that natural capital is now the limiting factor, leaving it out of consideration vitiates the very meaning of income and runs contrary to its prudential motivation.

In sum, I agree with Beckerman that weak sustainability is a muddle, and that definitions in terms of the welfare of future generations are nonoperational. However, I have shown that strong sustainability is neither morally reprehensible nor operationally impractical, and that Beckerman's view to the contrary is based on his mistaken definition of strong sustainability. With proper definition strong sustainability retains Beckerman's blessing as a logical constraint, since it really does limit present welfare maximisation and is not defined implicitly in terms of the same welfare maximisation that it is supposed to limit. Strong sustainability also provides a better way of respecting the rights of future generations than does discounting. Furthermore, it represents a logical extension of the Hicksian income concept.

For all of the above reasons I believe that sustainable development, properly clarified (as Beckerman rightly demands), is an indispensable concept. All important concepts are dialectically vague at the margins. I claim that sustainable development is at least as clear a concept as 'money'. Is money really Ml or M2, or is it M1a? Do we count Eurodollar-based loans in the US money supply? How liquid does an asset have to be before it counts as 'quasimoney', etc.? Yet the human mind is clever. We not only can handle the concept of money, but would have a hard time without it. The same, I suggest, is true for the concept of sustainable development.

Notes

1 El Serafy 1988.

2 Regarding the house example I am frequently told that insulation (capital) is a substitute for resources (energy for space heating). If the house is considered the final product, then capital (agent of production, efficient cause) cannot end up as a part (material cause) of the house, whether as wood, brick, or insulating material. The insulating material is a resource like wood or brick, not capital. If the final product is not taken as the house but the service of the house in providing warmth, then the entire house, not only insulating material, is capital. In this case more or better capital (a well-insulated house) does reduce the waste of energy. Increasing the efficiency with which a resource is used is certainly a good substitute for more of the resource. But these kinds of waste-reducing efficiency measures (recycling prompt scrap, sweeping up sawdust and using it for fuel or particle board, reducing heat loss from a house, etc.) are all rather marginal substitutions that soon reach their limit.

3 The usual definition of complementarity requires that for a given constant output a rise in the price of one factor would reduce the quantity of both factors. In the two factor case both factors means all factors, and it is impossible to keep output constant while reducing the input of all factors. But complementarity might be defined back into existence in the two factor case by avoiding the constant output condition. For example, two factors could be considered complements if an increase in one alone will not increase output, but an increase in the other will—and perfect complements if an increase in neither factor alone will increase output, but an increase in both will. It is not sufficient to treat complementarity as if it were nothing more than 'limited substitutability'. That means that we could get along with only one factor well enough, with only the other less well, but that we do not need both. Complementarily means we need both, and that the one in shortest supply is limiting.

4 N. Georgescu-Roegen deserves to be quoted at length on this point because so few people have understood it. He writes the 'Solow–Stiglitz variant' of the Cobb–Douglas function as:

$$Q = K^{a_1} R^{a_2} L^{a_3} \qquad (1)$$

'where Q is output, K is the stock of capital, R is the flow of natural resources used in production, L is the labour supply, and $a_1 + a_2 + a_3 = 1$ and of course, $a_1 > 0$. From this formula it follows that with a constant labour power, L_0, one could obtain any Q_0, if the flow of natural resources satisfies the condition

$$R^{a_2} = \frac{Q_0}{K^{a_1} L_0^{a_3}} \qquad (2)$$

This shows that R may be as small as we wish, provided K is sufficiently large. Ergo, we can obtain a constant annual product indefinitely even from a very small stock of resources $R > O$, if we decompose R into an infinite series $R = \Sigma R_i$ with $R_i \rightarrow O$, use R_i in year i, and increase the stock of capital each year as required by (2). But this *ergo* is not valid in actuality. In actuality, the increase of capital implies an additional depletion of resources. And if $K \rightarrow \infty$, then R will rapidly be exhausted by the production of capital. Solow and Stiglitz could not have come out with their conjuring trick had they borne in mind, first, that any material process consists in the transformation of some materials into others (the flow elements) by some agents (the fund elements), and second, that natural resources are the very sap of the economic process. They are not just like any other production factor. A change in capital or labour can only diminish the amount of waste in the production of a commodity: no agent can create the material on which it works. Nor can capital create the stuff out of which it is made. In some cases it may also be that the same service can be provided by a design that requires less matter or energy. But even in this direction there exists a limit, unless we believe that the ultimate fate of the economic process is an earthly Garden of Eden. The question that confronts us today is whether we are going to discover new sources of energy that can be safely used. No elasticities of some Cobb–Douglas function can help us to answer it.' (Georgescu-Roegen 1979)

5 At the margin a right glove can substitute for a left glove by turning it inside out. Socks can substitute for shoes by wearing an extra pair to compensate for thinning soles. But in spite of this marginal substitution, shoes and socks, right and left gloves, etc. are still complements. Basically the same is true for manmade and natural capital. Picture their isoquants as L-shaped, having a 90° angle. Erase the angle and draw in a tiny 90° arc connecting the two legs of the L. This seems close to reality. However, this very marginal range of substitution has been over-extrapolated to the degree that even a Nobel Laureate economist has gravely opined that, thanks to substitution, '.... the world can, in effect, get along without natural resources.' (Solow 1974)

6 See Norgaard and Howarth 1991.

References

Beckerman, Wilfred 1994. "'Sustainable Development': Is It a Useful Concept?" *Environmental Values*, 3: 191–209.

El Serafy, Salah 1988. 'The Proper Calculation of Income from Depletable Natural Resources', in Y. Ahmad, S. El Serafy, and E. Lutz (eds), *Environmental Accounting for Sustainable Development*. Washington, DC: The World Bank.

Georgescu-Roegen, N. 1979. 'Comments ...' in V. Kerry Smith (ed.) *Scarcity and Growth Reconsidered*, p. 98. Baltimore: Resources for the Future and Johns Hopkins Press.

Norgaard, R. and Howarth, R. 1991. 'Sustainability and Discounting the Future', in R. Costanza (ed.) *Ecological Economics*. New York: Columbia University Press.

Solow, Robert 1974. 'The Economics of Resources or the Resources of Economics', *AER*, May, p. 11.

Evaluating a Case Study

Cases on Sustainability

Macro Case 1. You are a high ranking official at the Environmental Protection Agency (EPA). The XYZ Company wants to construct an oil pipeline from Canada to New Orleans. They have completed all the paperwork and have done an environmental impact study that shows which ecosystems would be affected. You must make a report to the head of the EPA either recommending that the project should go ahead or be cancelled. Recently, at a training session you learned about *adaptive management*. You want to use this sort of reasoning as the basis of your report, therefore: frame the problem (with as many details as you like) in this way and write a two-page report to your boss either pro or con the project.

Micro Case 1. You are two years out of college and are about to buy your first car. You are attracted to a plug-in hybrid car that gets 75 miles a gallon, and has a maximum speed of 70 miles per hour and can seat five. Your husband has his eye on a sports utility vehicle (SUV) that gets 12 miles a gallon, can seat seven and has double the trunk capacity. Your husband points out that you both plan to start a family in a few years. You point out that you had agreed to have only one or, at most, two children. Either car could seat that family. Your husband notes that the SUV can go 120 miles per hour. You return that there is nowhere in the country that you can legally drive that fast—save at a race track. You do not want this decision to hurt your marriage, but you want to be able to frame the discussion in such a way that both your views might be heard. Write a fictional dialogue between you and your husband about using the concepts from the essays and a moral theory.

Further Reading

General Note: since many works do not fit neatly into any one category, and some of those listed may fit into several, to avoid repetition each work is listed only once.

General Works

Attfield, Robin (1983) *The Ethics of Environmental Concern*, New York: Columbia University Press.

Blackstone, William T. (ed) (1972) *Philosophy and the Environmental Crisis*, Athens, GA: University of Georgia Press.

Booth, Douglas (1993) *Valuing Nature: The Decline and Preservation of Old Growth Forests*, Lanham, MD: Rowman & Littlefield.

DesJardins, Joseph R. (1993) *Environmental Ethics*, Belmont, CA: Wadsworth.

Garrand, Greg (2012) *Ecocriticism*, 2nd edn, New York: Routledge.

Goodpaster, K.E. and K.M. Sayre (eds) (1979) *Ethics and Problems of the 21st Century*, Notre Dame, IN: Notre Dame University Press.

Hargrove, Eugene C. (1989) *Foundations of Environmental Ethics*, Upper Saddle River, NJ: Prentice Hall.

Katz, Eric (1997) *Nature as Subject*, Lanham, MD: Rowman & Littlefield.

Norton, Bryan G. (1991) *Toward Unity Among Environmentalists*, New York: Oxford University Press.

Oelschlaeger, Max (1991) *The Idea of Wilderness from Prehistory to the Present*, New Haven, CT: Yale University Press.

Rapport, David (1995) "Ecosystem Health: More than a Metaphor?" *Environmental Values*, 4 (4): 287–310.

Sarkar, Sahotra (2012) *Environmental Philosophy*, Malden, MA: John Wiley & Sons, Inc.

Sodikoff, Genese Marie (ed.) (2012) *The Anthropology of Extinction: Essays on Culture and Species Death*, Indianapolis, IN: Indiana University Press.

Sterba, James P. (ed.) (1995) *Earth Ethics*, Upper Saddle River, NJ: Prentice Hall.

Sterba, James P. (2013) *Introduction to Ethics: For Here and Now*, Boston, MA: Pearson.

Torrance, John (ed.) (1993) *The Concept of Nature*, New York: Oxford University Press.

Veer, Donald Van de and Christine Pierce (eds) (1993) *The Environmental Ethics and Policy Book*, Belmont, CA: Wadsworth.

Environmental Ethics, Second Edition. Edited by Michael Boylan.

Worldview Arguments: The Land Ethic, Deep Ecology, and Social Ecology

Bookchin, Murray (1990) "Recovering Evolution: A Reply to Eckersley and Fox," *Environmental Ethics*, 12: 253–273.

Bookchin, Murray (1990) *The Philosophy of Social Ecology: Essays on Dialectical Naturalism*, Toronto: Black Rose Books.

Bookchin, Murray (1990) *Remaking Society: Pathways to a Green Future*, Boston, MA: South End Press.

Callicott, J. Baird (ed.) (1987) *Companion to the Sand Country Almanac*, Madison, WI: University of Wisconsin Press.

Callicott, J. Baird (1989) *In Defense of the Land Ethic*, Albany, NY: SUNY Press.

Cheney, Jim (1997) "Naturalizing the Problem of Evil," *Environmental Ethics*, 19 (3): 299–314.

Clark, John (1984) *The Anarchist Moment: Reflections on Culture, Nature and Power*, Toronto: Black Rose Books.

Collins, Denis and John Barkdull (1995) "Capitalism, Environmentalism, and Mediating Structures," *Environmental Ethics*, 17 (3): 227–244.

Devall, Bill (1991) "Deep Ecology and Radical Environmentalism," *Society and Natural Resources*, 4: 247–258.

Devall, Bill and George Sessions (1985) *Deep Ecology: Living as if Nature Mattered*, Salt Lake City, UT: Peregrine Smith Books.

Diehm, Christian (2007) "Identification with Nature: What It Is and Why It Matters," *Ethics and the Environment*, 12 (2): 1–22.

Goodin, David K. (2007) "Schweitzer Reconsidered: The Applicability of Reverence for Life as Environmental Philosophy," *Environmental Ethics*, 29 (4): 403–421.

Leopold, Aldo. *A Sand County Almanac: With Essays on Conservation from Round River*. NY: Ballantine Books, 1970.

Meine, Curt (1989) *Aldo Leopold: His Life and Work*, Madison, WI: University of Wisconsin Press.

Naess, Arne (1989) *Ecology, Community and Lifestyle: Outline of an Ecosophy*, New York: Cambridge University Press.

Quilley, Stephen (2009) "The Land Ethic as an Ecological Civilizing Process: Aldo Leopold, Norbert Elias, and Environmental Philosophy," *Environmental Ethics*, 31 (2): 115–134.

Reitan, Eric H. (1996) "Deep Ecology and the Irrelevance of Morality," *Environmental Ethics*, 18 (4): 411–424.

Shaw, William (1997) "A Virtue Ethics Approach to Aldo Leopold's Land Ethic," *Environmental Ethics*, 19 (1): 53–68.

Smaje, Chris (2008) "Genesis and J. Baird Callicott: The Land Ethic Revisited," *Journal for the Study of Religion, Nature and Culture*, 2 (2): 183–198.

Starkey, Charles (2007) "The Land Ethic, Moral Development, and Ecological Rationality," *Southern Journal of Philosophy*, 45 (1): 149–175.

Tobias, Michael (ed.) (1985) *Deep Ecology*, San Diego, CA: Avant Books.

Worldview Arguments: Eco-Feminism

Biehl, Janet (1991) *Rethinking Ecofeminist Politics*, Boston, MA: South End Press.

Brownhill, Leigh (2010) "Earth Democracy and Ecosocialism: What's in a Name?" *Capitalism, Nature, Socialism*, 21 (1): 96–99.

Caldecott, Leonie and Stephanie Leland (eds) (1983) *Reclaim the Earth: Women Speak Out for Life on Earth*, London: The Women's Press.

Cook, Julie (1998) "The Philosophical Colonization of Ecofeminism," *Environmental Ethics*, 20 (3): 227–246.
Diamond, Irene and Gloria Feman Orenstein (eds) (1990) *Reweaving the World: The Emergence of Ecofeminism*, San Francisco, CA: The Sierra Club.
Gaard, Greta (ed.) (1993) *Ecofeminism: Women, Animals, Nature*, Philadelphia, PA: Temple University Press.
Harvester, Lara and Sean Blenkinsop (2010) "Environmental Education and Ecofeminist Pedagogy: Bridging the Environmental and the Social," *Canadian Journal of Environmental Education*, 15: 120–134.
Hypatia (1991) Special Issue on Ecological Feminism, 6 (Spring).
Jaggar, Alison (1988) *Feminist Politics and Human Nature*, Totowa, NJ: Rowman & Littlefield.
Kao, Grace Y. (2010) "The Universal Versus the Particular in Ecofeminist Ethics," *Journal of Religious Ethics*, 38 (4): 616–637.
Mallory, Chaone (2010) "What is Ecofeminist Political Philosophy? Gender, Nature, and the Political," *Environmental Ethics*, 32 (3): 305–322.
McIntosh, Alastair (1996) "The Emperor has no Cloths … Let us Paint our Loincloths Rainbow: A Classical and Feminist Critique of Contemporary Science Policy," *Environmental Values*, 5 (1): 3–30.
Merchant, Carolyn (1993) *Radical Ecology: The Search for a Livable World*, New York: Routledge.
Rainey, Shirley A. and Glenn S. Johnson (2009) "Grassroots Activism: An Exploration of Women of Color's Role in the Environmental Justice Movement," *Race, Gender and Class*, 16 (3): 144–173.
Warren, Karen J. and Jim Cheney (1991) "Ecological Feminism and Ecosystems Ecology," *Hypatia*, 6 (Spring): 179–197.
Westra, Laura (1993) *An Environmental Proposal for Ethics: The Principle of Integrity*, Lanham, MD: Rowman & Littlefield.

Worldview Arguments: Religion and Aesthetics

Booth, Annie L. (1998) "Learning from Others: Ecophilosophy and Traditional Native American Women's Lives," *Environmental Ethics*, 20 (1): 81–100.
Bratton, Susan Power (1992) *Six Billion and More: Human Population Regulation and Christian Ethics*, Louisville, KY: Westminster/John Knox Press.
Carlson, Allen (2010) "Contemporary Environmental Aesthetics and the Requirements of Environmentalism," *Environmental Values*, 19 (3): 289–314.
Carlson, Allen (2011) "Aesthetic Appreciation of Nature and Environmentalism," *Royal Institute of Philosophy Supplement*, 69: 137–155.
Davis, Donald Edward (1989) *Ecophilosophy: A Field Guide to the Literature*, San Pedro, CA: R. & E. Miles.
Gottlieb, Roger S. (2008) "You Gonna be Here Long? Religion and Sustainability," *Worldviews: Environment Culture Religion*, 12 (2): 163–178.
Hargrove, Eugene C. (ed.) (1986) *Religion and Environmental Crisis*, Athens, GA: University of Georgia Press.
Holbrook, Daniel (1997) "The Consequentialist Side of Environmentalist Ethics," *Environmental Values*, 6 (1): 87–96.
Lynch, Tony (1996) "Deep Ecology as an Aesthetic Movement," *Environmental Values*, 5 (2): 147–160.
McFague, Sallie (1987) *Theology for an Ecological, Nuclear Age*, Philadelphia, PA: Fortress Press.
McFayden, Ian (2008) "Our New Established Religion," *Quadrant Magazine*, 52 (9): 13–18.

O'Riordan, Tim (1997) "Valuation as Revelation and Reconciliation," *Environmental Values*, 6 (2): 169–184.
Raglon, Rebecca and Marian Scholtmeijer (1996) "Shifting Ground: Metanarratives, Epistemology, and the Stories of Nature," *Environmental Ethics*, 18 (1): 19–38.
Schalkwyk, Annalet van (2011) "Sacredness and Sustainability: Searching for a Practical Eco-Spirituality," *Religion and Theology*, 18 (1): 77–92.
Waks, Leonard J. (1996) "Environmental Claims and Citizen Rights," *Environmental Ethics*, 18 (2): 133–148.

Anthropocentric Justification

Attfield, Robin (2011) "Beyond Anthropocentrism," *Royal Institute of Philosophy Supplement*, 69: 29–46.
Baier, Annette (1982) "For the Sake of Future Generations," in *And Justice for All* (eds Tom Regan and Donald Van de Veer), Totowa, NJ: Rowman & Allanheld.
Carter, Alan (2011) "Towards a Multidimensional, Environmentalist Ethic," *Environmental Values*, 20 (3): 347–374.
DeGeorge, Richard (1980) "The Environment, Rights, and Future Generations," in *Responsibilities to Future Generations* (ed. Ernest Partridge), Buffalo, NY: Prometheus Books.
Ehrlich, Anne and Paul Ehrlich (1990) *The Population Explosion*, New York: Doubleday.
Ehrlich, Paul (1968) *The Population Bomb*, New York: Ballantine.
Golding, Martin (1972) "Obligations to Future Generations," *Monist*, 56: 85–99.
Groot, Mirjam de, Martin Drenthen, and Wouter T. de Groot (2011) "Public Visions of the Human/Nature Relationship and their Implications for Environmental Ethics," *Environmental Ethics*, 33 (1): 25–44.
Hayward, Tim (1997) "Anthropocentrism: A Misunderstood Problem," *Environmental Values*, 6 (1): 49–64.
Kavka, Gregory (1978) "The Futurity Problem," in *Obligations to Future Generations* (eds Brian Barry and R.I. Sikora), Philadelphia, PA: Temple University Press.
McShane, Katie (2007) "Anthropocentrism vs. Nonanthropocentrism: Why Should We Care?" *Environmental Values*, 16 (2): 169–185.
Mendenhall, Beth (2009) "The Environmental Crises: Why We Need Anthropocentrism," *Stance: An International Undergraduate Philosophy Journal*, 2: 35–41.
Narveson, Jan (1978) "Future People and Us." in *Obligations to Future Generations* (eds Brian Barry and R.I. Sikora), Philadelphia, PA: Temple University Press.
Parfit, Derek (1976) "On Doing the Best for our Children," in *Ethics and Population* (ed. Michael Bayles), Cambridge, MA: Schenkman.
Warren, Mary Anne (1982) "Future Generations," in *And Justice for All* (eds Tom Regan and Donald Van de Veer), Totowa, NJ: Rowman & Allanheld.

Biocentric Justification

Brennan, Andres (1988) *Thinking About Nature*, Athens, GA: University of Georgia Press.
Durland, Karánn (20080 "The Prospects for a Viable Biocentric Egalitarianism," *Environmental Ethics*, 30 (4): 401–416.
Elliot, Robert and Arran Gare (eds) (1983) *Environmental Philosophy*, University Park, PA: University of Pennsylvania Press.

Lanza, Robert (2007) "A New Theory of the Universe: Biocentrism Builds on Quantum Physics by Putting Life into the Equation," *American Scholar*, 76 (2): 18–33.
Minteer, Ben A. (2008) "Biocentric Farming? Liberty Hyde Bailey and Environmental Ethics," *Environmental Ethics*, 30 (4): 341–359.
Regan, Tom (1982) *All that Dwell Therein*, Berkeley, CA: University of California Press.
Rolston, Holmes III (1988) *Environmental Ethics*, Philadelphia, PA: Temple University Press.
Scoville, Judith N. (1995) "Value Theory and Ecology in Environmental Ethics: A Comparison of Rolston and Neibuhr," *Environmental Ethics*, 17 (2): 115–134.
Sterba, James P. (2011) "Biocentrism Defended," *Ethics, Policy and Environment*, 14 (2): 167–169.
Stone, Christopher (1987) *Earth and other Ethics*, New York: Harper & Row.
Swanton, Christine (2010) "Heideggerian Environmental Virtue Ethics," *Journal of Agricultural and Environmental Ethics*, 23 (1/2): 145–166.

Pollution and Climate Change

Buren, John van (1995) "Rights Against Polluters," *Environmental Ethics*, 17 (3): 259–276.
Driessen, Paul (2009) "The Real Climate Change Morality Crisis: Climate Change Initiatives Perpetuate Poverty, Disease and Premature Death," *Energy and Environment*, 20 (5): 763–777.
Fitzpatrick, William J. (2007) "Climate Change and the Rights of Future Generations: Social Justice Beyond Mutual Advantage," *Environmental Ethics*, 29 (4): 369–388.
García Novo, Francisco (2012) "Moral Drought: The Ethics of Water Use," *Water Policy*, 14: 65–72.
Hourdequin, Marion (2010) "Climate, Collective Action and Individual Ethical Obligations," *Environmental Values*, 19 (4): 443–464.
Joronen, Sanna Oksanen and Timo Markku Vuorisalo (2011) "Towards Weather Ethics: From Chance to Choice with Weather Modification," *Ethics, Policy and Environment*, 14 (1): 55–67.
Jyoti, Amar (2010) "Environmental Ethics: Initiatives for the Removal of Environmental Problems," *International Journal of Education and Allied Sciences* 2 (2): 93–100.
O'Hara, Dennis Patrick and Alan Abelsohn (2011) "Ethical Response to Climate Change," *Ethics and the Environment*, 16 (1): 25–50.
Rajadurai, Sivanandi and Prasanti Raveendran (2011) "Environmental Accountability for a Sustainable Earth," *Indian Journal of Science and Technology*, 4 (3): 355–360.
Resnik, David B. and Gerard Roman (2007) "Health, Justice, and the Environment," *Bioethics*, 21 (4): 230–241.
Shrader-Frechette, Kristin S. (1993) *Burying Uncertainty: Risk and the Case Against Geological Disposal of Nuclear Water*, Berkeley, CA: University of California Press.
Simon, Ted (2011) "Just Who is at Risk? The Ethics of Environmental Regulation," *Human and Experimental Toxicology*, 30 (8): 795–819.

Animal Rights and Biodiversity

Aaltola, Elisa (2008) "Personhood and Animals," *Environmental Ethics*, 30 (2): 175–193.
Carter, Alan (2010) "Biodiversity and all that Jazz," *Philosophy and Phenomenological Research*, 80 (1): 58–75.

Chan, Kai M.A. *et al.* (2007) "When Agendas Collide: Human Welfare and Biological Conservation," *Conservation Biology*, 21 (1): 59–68.
Chartier, Gary (2010) "Natural Law and Animal Rights," *Canadian Journal of Law and Jurisprudence: An International Journal of Legal Thought*, 23(1): 33–46.
DeGrazia, David (1996) *Taking Animals Seriously*, New York: Cambridge University Press.
Dogan, Aysel (2001) "A Defense of Animal Rights," *Journal of Agricultural and Environmental Ethics*, 24 (5): 473–491.
Hargrove, Eugene C. (ed.) (1993) *The Animals Rights/Environmental Ethics Debate: The Environmental Perspective*, Albany, NY: SUNY Press.
Ojala, Maria and Rolf Lidskog (2011) "What Lies Beneath the Surface? A Case Study of Citizens' Moral Reasoning with Regard to Biodiversity," *Environmental Values*, 20 (2): 217–237.
Oliver, Kelly (2008) "What is Wrong with (Animal) Rights?" *Journal of Speculative Philosophy: A Quarterly Journal of History, Criticism, and Imagination*, 22 (3): 214–224.
Reardon, Mark (2011) "Animal Ethics: Animal Welfare Or Animal Illfare?" *Ethical Perspectives: Journal of the European Ethics Network*, 18 (2): 269–285.
Regan, Tom (1983) *The Case for Animal Rights*, Berkeley, CA: University of California Press.
Regan, Tom and Peter Singer (eds) (1989) *Animal Rights and Human Obligations*, Upper Saddle River, NJ: Prentice Hall.
Ryan, John C. (1992) "Conserving Biological Diversity," *State of the World 1992*, New York: Worldwatch.
Singer, Peter (1992) *Animal Liberation: A New Ethics for Our Treatment of Animals*, New York: Avon Books.
Vieira, A.V. (2009) "Biodiversity and Nature Conservation: Some Common Arguments and Alternative Views," *Interdisciplinary Science Reviews*, 34 (4): 345–349.
Wilhere, George F. (2008) "The How-Much-is-Enough Myth," *Conservation Biology*, 22 (3): 514–517.

Sustainability

Afshar, Haleh (ed.) (1991) *Women, Development and Survival in the Third World*, London: Longman.
Attfield, Robin and Barry Wilkins (eds) (1992) *International Justice and the Third World*, London: Routledge.
Ayestarán, Ignacio (2010) "Knowledge, Responsibility and Ethics of Sustainability in View of the Global Change," *Ramon Llull Journal of Applied Ethics*, 1: 183–198.
Bryson, Ken A. (2008) "Negotiating Environmental Rights," *Ethics, Place and Environment*, 11 (3): 351–366.
Hardin, Garrett (1993) *Living Within Limits: Ecology, Economics and Population Taboos*, New York: Oxford University Press.
Jackson, Wes (1980) *New Roots for Agriculture*, Omaha, NE: University of Nebraska Press.
Lemonick, Michael D. (2009) "Top 10 Myths about Sustainability," *Scientific American Special Edition*, 19 (1): 40–45.
Pawłowski, Artur (2008) "How Many Dimensions does Sustainable Development Have?" *Sustainable Development*, 16 (2): 81–90.
Rolston III, Holmes (2007) "Critical Issues in Future Environmental Ethics," *Ethics and the Environment*, 12 (2): 139–142.
Sen, Gita, and Caren Growen (1987) *Development Crises, and Alternative Visions*, New York: Monthly Review Press.
Smith, Tanzi (2011) "Using Critical Systems Thinking to Foster an Integrated Approach to Sustainability: A Proposal for Development Practitioners," *Environment, Development and Sustainability*, 13 (1): 1–17.

Soule, Judith and Jon Piper (1992) *Farming in Nature's Image: An Ecological Approach in Agriculture*, Washington, DC: Island Press.

Stone, Christopher (1974) *Should Trees Have Standing? Toward Legal Rights for Natural Objects*, Los Altos, CA: William Kaufmann.

Tyburski, Wł. (2008) "Origin and Development of Ecological Philosophy and Environmental Ethics and their Impact on the Idea of Sustainable Development," *Sustainable Development*, 16 (2): 100–108.

Vucetich, John A. and Michael P. Nelson (2010) "Sustainability: Virtuous or Vulgar?" *Bioscience*, 60 (7): 539–544.

Wilson, E.O. (1988) "Threats to Biodiversity," in *Biodiversity* (eds E.O. Wilson and Frances Peter), Washington, DC: National Academy Press.